I0874528

Comparative Legal Cultures

The International Library of Essays in Law and Legal Theory
Series Editor: Tom D. Campbell

Schools

Natural Law, Vols I & II *John Finnis*
Justice *Thomas Morawetz*
Law and Economics, Vols I & II *Jules Coleman and Jeffrey Lange*
Critical Legal Studies *James Boyle*
Marxian Legal Theory *Csaba Varga*
Legal Reasoning, Vols I & II *Aulis Aarnio and Neil MacCormick*
Legal Positivism *Mario Jori*
American Legal Theory *Robert Summers*
Law and Language *Fred Schauer*
Sociological Theories of Law *Kahei Rokumoto*
Rights *Carlos Nino*
Law and Psychology *Martin Levine*
Feminist Legal Theory *Frances Olsen*

Areas

Criminal Law *Thomas Morawetz*
Tort Law *Ernest Weinrib*
Contract Law, Vols I & II *Larry Alexander*
Anti-Discrimination Law *Christopher McCrudden*
Consumer Law *Iain Ramsay*
International Law *Martti Koskenniemi*
Property Law *Elizabeth Mensch and Alan Freeman*
Constitutional Law *Mark Tushnet*
Procedure *Denis Galligan*
Evidence and Proof *William Twining and Alex Stein*
Administrative Law *Denis Galligan*
Child Law *Harry Krause*
Family Law, Vols I & II *Harry Krause*
Welfare Law *Peter Robson*
Medicine and the Law *Bernard Dickens*
Commercial Law *Ross Cranston*
Communications Law *David Goldberg*
Environmental Law *Michael Blumm*
Conflict of Laws *Richard Fentiman*
Law and Religion *Wojciech Sadurski*
Human Rights Law *Philip Alston*
European Community Law *Francis Snyder*

Legal Cultures

Comparative Legal Cultures *Csaba Varga*
Law and Anthropology *Peter Sack*
Hindu Law and Legal Theory *Ved Nanda*
Islamic Law and Legal Theory *Ian Edge*
Chinese Law and Legal Theory *Michael Palmer*
Socialist Law and Legal Theory *W. Butler*
Japanese Law and Legal Theory *Kiochiro Fujikura*
Law and Development *Anthony Carty*
Jewish Law and Legal Theory *Martin Golding*
Legal Education *Martin Levine*

Future Volumes

Labour Law, Common Law and Legal Theory, Civil Law and Legal Theory, Law and Society, African Law and Legal Theory, Legal Ethics and Cumulative index.

Comparative Legal Cultures

Edited by

Csaba Varga

Senior Fellow, Hungarian Academy of Sciences

NEW YORK UNIVERSITY PRESS
REFERENCE COLLECTION

© Csaba Varga 1992. For copyright of individual articles please refer to the Acknowledgements.
All rights reserved.

First published in the U.S.A. in 1992 by
NEW YORK UNIVERSITY PRESS
Washington Square
New York NY 10003

Library of Congress Cataloging-in-Publication Data
Comparative legal cultures / edited by Csaba Varga.
p. cm. — (The International library of essays in law and legal theory)
"New York University Press reference collection."
Includes index.
ISBN 0-8147-8765-7
1. Comparative law. 2. Jurisprudence. I. Varga, Csaba. 1941– . II. Series.
k561.C658 1992
340.2—dc20
[342] 91-26752
CIP

Contents

Acknowledgements ix
Series Preface xiii
Introduction xv

PART I WESTERN LEGAL CULTURE: ROOTS AND ALTERNATIVES

1 J.C. Smith (1968), 'The Unique Nature of the Concepts of Western Law', *The Canadian Bar Review / La Revue du Barreau Canadien*, **46**, No. 2, pp. 191–225. 3
2 Donald R. Kelley (1979), 'Gaius Noster: Substructures of Western Social Thought', *The American Historical Review*, **84**, pp. 619–48. 39
3 Albert Kiralfy (1985), 'Law and Right in English Legal History', *The Journal of Legal History*, **6**, No. 1, pp. 49–61. 69
4 A.G. Chloros (1978), 'Common Law, Civil Law and Socialist Law: Three Leading Systems of the World, Three Kinds of Legal Thought', *The Cambrian Law Review*, pp. 11–26. 83

PART II COMMON LAW AND CIVIL LAW: ENCOUNTERS

5 Hessel E. Yntema (1967), 'Equity in the Civil Law and the Common Law', *The American Journal of Comparative Law*, **15**, Nos. 1 and 2, pp. 60–86. 101
6 Vera Bolgar (1953), 'Why No Trusts in the Civil Law?', *The American Journal of Comparative Law*, **2**, No. 2, pp. 204–19. 129
7 Shael Herman (1981), 'Quot judices tot sententiae: A Study of the English Reaction to Continental Interpretive Techniques', *Legal Studies*, **1**, pp. 165–89. 145

PART III VARIATIONS FOR CULTURES OF LAW

8 Max Gluckman (1964), 'Natural Justice in Africa', *Natural Law Forum*, **9**, pp. 25–44. 173
9 Stanley Diamond (1971), 'The Rule of Law versus the Order of Custom', *Social Research*, **38**, pp. 42–72 193
10 Luke T. Lee and Whalen W. Lai (1978), 'The Chinese Conceptions of Law: Confucian, Legalist, and Buddhist', *The Hastings Law Journal*, **29**, pp. 1307–29. 225

11 Dai-Kwon Choi (1980), 'Western Law in a Traditional Society Korea', *The Korean Journal of Comparative Law*, **8**, pp. 177–202. 249

12 Chin Kim and Craig M. Lawson (1979), 'The Law of the Subtle Mind: The Traditional Japanese Conception of Law', *International and Comparative Law Quarterly*, **28**, No. 3, pp. 491–513. 275

13 Martin Shapiro (1980), 'Islam and Appeal', *California Law Review*, **68**, pp. 350–81. 299

PART IV COMPARATIVE LEGAL METHODS

14 Peter Stein (1979), 'Logic and Experience in Roman and Common Law', *Boston University Law Review*, **59**, No. 3, pp. 433–51. 333

15 A.M. Honoré (1973), 'Legal Reasoning in Rome and Today', *Cambrian Law Review*, pp. 58–67. 353

16 Chaim Perelman (1981), 'Legal Ontology and Legal Reasoning', *Israel Law Review*, **16**, No. 3, pp. 356–67. 363

17 Bernard Rudden (1974), 'Courts and Codes in England, France and Soviet Russia', *Tulane Law Review*, **48**, No. 4, pp. 1010–28. 375

18 Takeyoshi Kawashima (1979), 'Japanese Way of Legal Thinking', *International Journal of Law Libraries*, **7**, No. 2, pp. 127–31. 395

19 Wael B. Hallaq (1985–86), 'Legal Reasoning in Islamic Law and the Common Law: Logic and Method', *Cleveland State Law Review*, **34**, pp. 79–96. 401

20 Lawrence Rosen (1980–81), 'Equity and Discretion in a Modern Islamic Legal System', *Law & Society Review*, **15**, No. 2, pp. 217–45. 419

PART V LEGAL CULTURES IN CO-EXISTENCE AND CONFLICT

21 G.C.J.J. Van den Bergh (1969), 'Legal Pluralism in Roman Law', *The Irish Jurist*, **4**, pp. 338–50. 451

22 Upendra Baxi (1979), 'People's Law, Development, Justice', *Verfassung und Recht in Übersee*, **12**, No. 2, pp. 97–114. 465

23 Robert B. Seidman (October 1966), 'Mens Rea and the Reasonable African: The Pre-Scientific World-View and Mistake of Fact', *The International and Comparative Law Quarterly*, **15**, Part 4, pp. 1135–64. 483

PART VI DEGENERATION OF LEGAL CULTURES

24 Csaba Varga (1982), 'Lenin and the Revolutionary Law-Making', *International Review of Contemporary Law*, No. 1, pp. 47–59. 515

25 W.J. Wagner (1966), 'The Russian Judiciary Act of 1922 and Some Comments on the Administration of Justice in the Soviet Union', *Indiana Law Journal*, **41**, No. 3, pp. 420–53. 529

26 Norman S. Marsh (October 1946), 'Some Aspects of the German Legal System under National Socialism', *The Law Quarterly Review*, **62**, pp. 366–74. 563

27 Keith S. Rosenn (1971), 'The Jeito: Brazil's Institutional Bypass of the Formal Legal System and its Developmental Implications', *The American Journal of Comparative Law*, **19**, pp. 514–49. 573

Name Index 609

Acknowledgements

The editor and publishers wish to thank the following for permission to use copyright material.

The American Journal of Comparative Law for essays: Vera Bolgar (1953), 'Why No Trusts in the Civil Law?', *The American Journal of Comparative Law*, **2**, No. 2, pp. 204–19; Keith S. Rosenn (1971), 'The Jeito: Brazil's Institutional Bypass of the Formal Legal System and its Developmental Implications', *The American Journal of Comparative Law*, **19**, pp. 514–49, and Hessel E. Yntema (1967), 'Equity in the Civil Law and the Common Law', *The American Journal of Comparative Law*, **15**, Nos. 1 and 2, pp. 60–86.

American Journal of Jurisprudence for the essay: Max Gluckman (1964), 'Natural Justice in Africa', *Natural Law Forum*, **9**, pp. 25–44.

Boston University Law Review for the essay: Peter Stein (1979), 'Logic and Experience in Roman and Common Law', *Boston University Law Review*, **Vol. 59**, No. 3, pp. 433–51.

The British Institute of International and Comparative Law for essays: Chin Kim and Craig M. Lawson (1979), 'The Law of the Subtle Mind: The Traditional Japanese Conception of Law', *International and Comparative Law Quarterly*, **28**, No. 3, pp. 491–513. This article is reproduced from (1979) 3, International and Comparative Law Quarterly. 491–513 with permission from the publishers the British Institute of International and Comparative Law, and Robert B. Seidman (1966), 'Mens Rea and the Reasonable African: The Pre–Scientific World–View and Mistake of Fact', *The International and Comparative Law Quarterly*, **15**, Part 4, pp. 1135–64. This article is reproduced from (1966) **15**, International and Comparative Law Quarterly, 1135–64 with permission from the publishers the British Institute of International and Comparative Law.

Canadian Bar Foundation and J.C. Smith (1968) for the essay: 'The Unique Nature of the Concepts of Western Law', *The Canadian Bar Review / La Revue du Barreau Canadien*, **46**, No. 2, pp. 191–225. Copyright © Canadian Bar Review and J.C. Smith.

Frank Cass & Co. Ltd for the essay: Albert Kiralfy (1985), 'Law and Right in English Legal History', *The Journal of Legal History*, **Vol. 6**, No. 1, pp. 49–61.

Stanley Diamond (1971), 'The Rule of Law versus the Order of Custom', *Social Research*, **38**, pp. 42–72. Copyright © Stanley Diamond.

Wael B. Hallaq (1985–86), 'Legal Reasoning in Islamic Law and the Common Law: Logic and Method', *Cleveland State Law Review*, **34**, pp. 79–96. Copyright © Wael B. Hallaq.

Hastings College of the Law for the essay: Luke T. Lee and Whalen W. Lai (1978), 'The Chinese Conceptions of Law: Confucian, Legalist and Buddhist', *The Hastings Law Journal*, **29**, pp. 1307–29. Copyright © 1978 Hastings College of the Law, reprinted from **29** Hastings Law Journal 1307–29 with permission.

William S. Hein & Co. Inc. for the essay: A.G. Chloros (1978), 'Common Law, Civil Law and Socialist Law: Three Leading Systems of the World, Three Kinds of Legal Thought', *The Cambrian Law Review*, pp. 11–26.

Shael Herman (1981) 'Quot judices tot sententiae: A Study of the English Reaction to Continental Interpretive Techniques', *Legal Studies*, **1**, pp. 165–89. This article first appeared in (1981) **1** Legal Studies 165–89 and is reproduced with the permission of the Society of Public Teachers of Law, UK. Copyright © Shael Herman.

A.M. Honoré (1973) 'Legal Reasoning in Rome and Today', *Cambrian Law Review*, pp. 58–67. Copyright © A.M. Honoré.

The Irish Jurist for the essay: G.C.J.J. Van den Bergh (1969), 'Legal Pluralism in Roman Law', *The Irish Jurist*, **4**, pp. 338–50.

Israel Law Review for the essay: Chaim Perelman (1981), 'Legal Ontology and Legal Reasoning', *Israel Law Review*, **16**, No. 3, pp. 356–67.

Donald R. Kelley (1979), 'Gaius Noster: Substructures of Western Social Thought', *The American Historical Review*, **84**, pp. 619–48. Copyright © Donald R. Kelley.

Law and Society Association for the essay: Lawrence Rosen (1980–81), 'Equity and Discretion in a Modern Islamic Legal System', *Law & Society Review*, **15**, No. 2, pp. 217–45. Reprinted by permission of the Law & Society Association.

Fred B. Rothman & Company and the Trustees of Indiana University for the essay: W.J. Wagner (1966), 'The Russian Judiciary Act of 1922 and Some Comments on the Administration of Justice in the Soviet Union', *Indiana Law Journal*, **41**, No. 3, pp. 420–53.

Sweet & Maxwell Limited for the essay: Norman S. Marsh (1946), 'Some Aspects of the German Legal System under National Socialism', *The Law Quarterly Review*, **62**, pp. 366–74.

Tulane Law Review Association for the essay: Bernard Rudden (1974), 'Courts and Codes in England, France and Soviet Russia', *Tulane Law Review*, **48**, No. 4, pp. 1010–28.

University of California Press Journals for the essay: Martin Shapiro (1980), 'Islam and Appeal', *California Law Review*, **68**, pp. 350–81. Copyright © 1980 by California Law Review, Inc. Reprinted from California Law Review **Vol. 68**, No. 2, (1980), pp. 350–81, by permission.

Verfassung und Recht in Übersee for the essay: Upendra Baxi (1979), 'People's Law, Development, Justice', *Verfassung und Recht in Übersee*, **12**, No. 2, pp. 97–114.

Every effort has been made to trace all the copyright holders, but if any have been inadvertently overlooked the publishers will be pleased to make the necessary arrangement at the first opportunity.

Series Preface

The International Library of Law and Legal Theory is designed to provide important research materials in an accessible form. Each volume contains essays of central theoretical importance in its subject area. The series as a whole makes available an extensive range of valuable material which will be of considerable interest to those involved in the research, teaching and study of law.

The series has been divided into three sections. The Schools section is intended to represent the main distinctive approaches and topics of special concern to groups of scholars. The Areas section takes in the main branches of law with an emphasis on essays which present analytical and theoretical insights of broad application. The section on Legal Cultures makes available the distinctive legal theories of different level traditions and takes up topics of general comparative and developmental concern.

I have been delighted and impressed by the way in which the editors of the individual volumes have set about the difficult task of selecting, ordering and presenting essays from the immense quantity of academic legal writing published in journals throughout the world. Editors were asked to pick out those essays from law, philosophy and social science journals which they consider to be fundamental for the understanding of law, as seen from the perspective of a particular approach or sphere of legal interest. This is not an easy task and many difficult decisions have had to be made in order to ensure that a representative sample of the best journal essays available takes account of the scope of each topic or school.

I should like to express my thanks to all the volume editors for their willing participation and scholarly judgement. The interest and enthusiasm which the project has generated is well illustrated by the fact that an original projection of 12 volumes drawn up in 1989 has now become a list of some 60 volumes. I must also acknowledge the vision, persistence and constant cheerfulness of John Irwin and the marvellous work done by Mrs Margaret O'Reilly and Mrs Sonia Bridgman.

TOM D. CAMPBELL
Series Editor
The Faculty of Law
The Australian National University

Introduction

Individual legal cultures may deserve theoretical interest in and by themselves. Their comparison, however, transcends by far, and not surprisingly, this level of interest. This is primarily because comparative legal cultures offer the means to us by which our own *culture* can be reflected with the pattern(s) of another. As it is known, getting patterns (we are socialized in) reflected with other ones (we are less familiar with) is the way whereby any comparative approach can contribute to achieve it, that the natural human inclination which drives us to visualize everything largely absolutized and universalized, albeit it can at most be nothing but relative and particular, can eventually be moderated or somewhat counterbalanced.

In this way, the study of comparative legal cultures can be instrumental in making anyone confronted with the truth of how both the legal set-up, rooted deeply in a nation's history, and the various games it offers, are not to be regarded simply as the fruits of human wisdom or the unrivalled embodiment of eternal values, but as something more worldly and human, which is neither naturally given nor unsurpassable, even if for the time being no competitor can be seen on the scene.

In their individuality, legal cultures are the temporary outcome of interactions, conceptualizable in terms of the challenge/response paradigm. This means that the factors in play in it, their interaction and also the outcome of this can be seen as the outgrowth of a world by chance. At least, if taken by their different sorts of grouping, individual legal cultures do reveal how much commonness can in fact be found amongst apparently independent systems of legal arrangement. As a matter of fact, the basis for grouping them may be manifold and complex indeed. Their classification can be grounded by considerations in regard of their historical development and roots, foundational ideals and underlying ideology, and furthermore, the store of means and techniques they operate, the skills the use of which they assume when they are at work, as well as the political role they play in the long run and the sociological function they perform on the final account. Different sorts of typology, no matter how much they all are, on point of principle, ideal in the final analysis, can be motivated only providing that the features we have in mind are ones in common.

Accordingly, comparative research can show the extent to which legal development is determined by a random set of circumstances asserting their influence at any event at any given time, both in the short and in the long run.

Such a possible use does not stand by itself, however. Comparative investigations also provide insights into understanding the extent to which, due to the overall tendency of its operation and the single responses it has, the final outcome of the working of the legal machinery will fit in, or become adapted to, the general direction that the total motion of the prevailing social totality actually takes.

Since, if mystery can be assumed to be concealed by the life of the law, it is certainly to be found nowhere else than in the answer to the following question. How can we reach a response in real practice, a response which will feature to be the response by and of the law itself (at least according to the law's formally closed system of a pre-codified set of formal requirements) and, at the same time, which will also sensibly respond to the socially felt needs that lurk behind the facade of any legal establishment, by urging to get a genuine solution? It will be seen later on that notwithstanding the huge variety of tentative answers to this question, they are all uniform in so far as they all rotate round (if not zigzag helplessly in-between) the duality issuing from the diverging aspects and conflicting criteria that are offered by what is called 'homogeneously legal', on the one hand, and 'heterogeneously social', on the other, both of them representing aspects and criteria inherent in the contexture of the question.

With the same stroke, a comparative look at legal cultures may also help us unfold to an otherwise unthinkable depth those latent tendencies and potentialities which are inherent in the choice we do constantly make from within the store of available means, i.e. legal techniques and terminologies. For, clearly enough, we can hypostatize neither equivalency nor any simply mechanic, causal relationship between the choice of instrumentality we have made and the final outcome it will result in. To be sure, what gets at all times wedged necessarily in-between is nothing else but human practice. By speaking about praxis, I have in mind the creative output originated by each and every actor involved in the game. For, though to a varying degree, professionals and common people alike are genuine partners in the social game which is undertaken under the name of 'law'. They all have their own contribution to this huge, all-society levelled enterprise, by continuously shaping and reshaping it through their activity.

It is of crucial importance to understand here that it is not exclusively the use of instruments, like hammer, spade or sickle, i.e. parts of our physical culture, that has a personal touch of its own on the world which is going to be made up through their usage. For there are also definitions and determinations specific to social existence.

As it is largely realized by now, human institutions, constituents of our social culture, are themselves the product of speech acts we constantly perform in everyday communication situations. The act of speaking in a communication situation is itself a species of institutionalized manifestation. It springs from the fact that we can treat any well-defined circle of physically observable properties (or their intellectual representation) as a sign, by ascribing any conventionalized meaning to it.

And what else could law be conceived of to be if not a type of human institution, conventionalized from the mass of elementary situations, themselves being made up of a mass of conventions in communication?

The point is, that the choice we are making in respect of legal techniques and terminologies is not accomplished by the selection made. Selecting one technique and/or terminology is hardly more than the first step taken, which keeps on to be followed by various acts of application, each of them having the same constitutive effect on point of principle. For every component involved remains within the boundaries of linguistic conventions as a function of them. And as to the acts of application, they reconventionalize them while they are referring to them as conventions. The outcome of reconventionalization will be their own variant, standing for the continuation, concretization or actualization (in short, adaptation), of those conventions.

This is to say that, theoretically speaking, following rules (or tradition) is itself an act which, if not put in a vacuum or left in a frameless wilderness, can itself only and exclusively be interpreted within the framework of the continuation of rules (or tradition). To put it differently:

each sign claimed to have an intentionally added and conventionalized meaning is in fact a storehouse of almost unlimited sets of equally conceivable meanings. In this very sense, the sign is like a knot made at the corner of my pocket-handkerchief to serve as a reminder that I have to do something. As a matter of fact, the knot may be used as a reminder of what it was thought to remind when the knot was made. But the use is the same, moreover, the sign itself will also remain the same if, in times to come, the changed conditions will modify the contexture so that the same knot will be intended to serve, and will actually serve, as something else.

To be sure, the criterion of continuance and discontinuance is not to be found in the sign, its use, or the intention behind the use itself. For the only factor that can make a difference by distinguishing what are the never-ceasing shifts of emphasis in ordinary use from what already is a chaos, is nothing else but the continuity of social practice, asserting itself through self-organizing self-reproduction. For it is social practice regulated by continued feedback and nothing else that will finally reduce the myriad of the sets of equally conceivable theoretical possibilities to one (and no more than one) stand that can be reached as the result of interpretation. There is no need to say that the stand eventually taken will be the one that wins acceptance from the community for being most in line with the reasonable and justifiable observance of rules and tradition already established.

All this amounts to proposing that no legal culture can be equated with, or limited to, the total sum of the meanings we have actualized within the boundaries of it. Techniques and technologies provided for by the law and conceptualized in its terminology have a vast range of theoretically equal possible uses, which defies any serious attempt at their delimitation. These possible uses form an ideal potentiality that may not actually have been thought about before, or tested or made use of in real practice. Properly speaking, they keep on remaining nothing but merely latent potentialities of something which is not defined, moreover which cannot be defined, either, unless and until they are made explicit by being tested (and thereby externalized), i.e. established in the genuine sense of the word, in ideal limiting situations. This is the case when, for instance, we analyse the message of what a principle may tell us through contrasting what we are already agreed upon it says with hypotheses of what it may say in borderline cases, until we reach a point which is defined as the one of reflective equilibrium.

To put it differently, each and every system of legal stipulations and arrangement is hardly more than a potentiality which can only be considered a genuine fact of social reality in nothing but its form of concrete actualization, made by the historically given, individual act of application.

Considering all the various uses and fruits of the study of comparative legal cultures outlined above, I have to add a last item to the list. Notably, comparative approach can be a primal means of revealing the total connections that are in work in the formation, as well as in the functioning, of the complex, multi-factorial entity that the law represents. Such an investigation may also be expected to exemplify the ways in, and the extent to which the various components of any legal set-up (such as the conceptual frame, the thought patterns, the style of reasoning and arguing, the foundational ideals and ideology, possibly all being a function of coincidental factors and by chance historical determination) are in a position to shape the forms of social existence both in parts and in their totality.

There is a well-known passage formulated in the Introduction to the *Critique of Political*

Economy, in which Marx draws a parallel, quite figuratively, between the anatomy of men and the ape, proposing that the key for understanding the latter is offered by the former.[1]

Within an evolutionist outlook (which Marx certainly sympathized with in person), men perfect the developmental perspective which is only latent in the anatomy of the ape.[2] In consequence, the question of what are the open latent potentialities inherent in the path of development for the ape can only be answered retrospectively, as assessed from the perfected state it in fact achieved. To put it differently, it is only and exclusively the perfected state that offers criteria for defining what the meaning (both primitive and current, if such a differentiation makes any sense at all) of the developmental perspective of the ape was.

But I may opt for another perspective as well. By leaving aside, and preferably also abandoning, the concepts of the teleology in and laws of history, as well as such terms as necessity, meaning, or reason, all related to history (presuppositions which the evolutionist outlook is based upon), the same metaphorical expression taken from Marx can be argued for in a way which leads to the opposite direction. For it can be construed as to cast a light upon the specific characters of both men and the ape, on the one hand, and the almost infinite variety of the contextures and configurations made equally possible by those characters of men and of the ape as their latent potentiality, on the other. Clearly, within such a perspective, it is not only the idea of evolution that is lost but, in company of it, also the staking out of the direction of wherefrom and whereto has vanished. Then, claiming as Marx did that something holds a key for something else means actually nothing else and nothing more pretentious than that stand and, in consequence, that standard are taken for key, which have been considered for the last time. Or, my last choice is necessarily the one that matters and will determine the issue.[3]

For if I may credit the perhaps most elaborated theory of our time on the motive powers and factors that are at work behind the majestic facade of what is called legal evolution,[4] I shall certainly be deprived of the kind of compass with fixed directions I am so accustomed to having and which both evolutionism and theological thinking have taught me to believe in. Undoubtedly, if I trust the continued reproduction of social practice as offering the sole ground upon which we can both build and erect the yardstick whereby we can measure what we have built, I cannot even be sure any longer which of the anatomies belongs to whom, that is, which major part (i.e. area or phase) or particle (i.e. element) of legal development stands 'for men' and which 'for the ape'.

The only thing I will then take for granted is that each and every component and aspect of the process can at the most be considered relative. The relative totality (what all kinds of legal culture represents) is hardly more than that of what factors (that happen to be present there and then) which come into play (in a match that happens to take place there and then) are to be brought into existence at any time. Or it means that imitation – i.e. the repeated transplantation and adaptation of once invented patterns, taken from the part of the common heritage of mankind which has been made available to those concerned by its appropriation through cognition – is the real ultimate player of the evolving-of-the-law game. Consequently, following the manner set by Molière's character, stating with obliging flatness that '*je prend mon bien où je trouve*', the only thing that matters is not 'What is it made from?' but, instead, 'What is it made out of?'. To sum up (by paraphrasing Marx again), priority in time, i.e. the determination of which anatomy is of the man and which one is of the ape, is good at best for identifying the factors that must have been in play to produce the result in the formation of the legal construction in question.

The investigations I introduce the reader to in outline in this volume are not meant to report on the findings of the research 'law and society' movement launched some years ago.[5] This latter has the strictly sociological ambition to quantify the significant differences that can be observed in the way in which, and the efficacity with which, the different systems of legal set-up function, on the one hand, and to explore the kind of correspondence that can be drawn between various legal systems and the social systems which constitute the real substratum of them, on the other.

Properly speaking, the considerations and the tentative answers presented to the reader in this volume are not meant to report on any finding at all. For the papers themselves which have been collected here are by far not representing a definite discipline with more or less established subject and methodology. In most cases, they are essays from various areas and circles, written in varying styles by diverse authors, gathered together only by the recognition that, in spite of all this, they have something in common, namely the interest in having a global view of law in the light of the comparison of differing legal cultures.

To be more specific, comparative legal cultures sketchily exhibited by the present collection are understood as representing single items of an ideal inventory of human inventiveness, related to a particular field. They are conceived of as single configurations of individual variants, taken from the unthinkably large, though in principle nevertheless by far not limitless, stock of the possible elements we anticipate as ideally existing. As is well-known, it is of the kind and belongs to the tradition Gottfried Wilhelm Leibniz once dreamed about on a conceptual level when he created, one, a universal language, two, a *Calculus rationator* for defining the complete set of logical connections to be expressed by this language, three, a *Characteristica universalis* for establishing the logical chain of the complete set of thinkable concepts, as well as, four, an encyclopaedia for the exposition of these concepts in the axiomatic order of pure geometry.[6] Put into another context, the same idea was taken over by Lévy-Strauss with a view to arche-ethnology in the sorrowful tropics he wrote about.[7]

Comparative legal cultures are examined by a field of scholarship, which is situated at the line bordering comparative law and historical jurisprudence.

As to the proper field of comparative legal cultures, it is comparative in so far as it is interested in the commonness quite as much as in the specific features, characteristic of any group of individual legal cultures. Notwithstanding, it transcends the horizon of comparative law by going beyond the perspectives of both the positive law and its formal functioning. It has the aim set to arrive at generalizations, both of a descriptive and an evaluative nature, on the level of the legal culture as a whole. In this sense, by comparative legal cultures we hold an interest in the characterization of individual legal cultures on the level of their genus rather than their species.

At the same time, the field in question is historical in so far as it contemplates both the chain of events that may have led, and the circumstances that may have contributed, to the formation of the given culture, and predestinated the ethos which may have channelized those events into the path they have eventually taken and by which the culture concerned will also define itself. The field I am speaking about is aimed at exploring what this ethos is composed of and how it fulfils in organizing all sorts of motions which are taking place in the respective culture, into one cultural unity. This is to say that the interest specific of it is primarily of an inter-cultural character, not aspiring to fall in any kind of philosophical universalization.

In the arrangement of the present volume, my intention has been to show the variety that can be found in the realm of the cultures of law in view of their differing ethos, legal 'world concept', juristic techniques and skill (in short, the individual genius which is characteristic exclusively to the system in question). This is done by the presentation, at sufficient depth, of papers selected as case studies. We start with 'Roots and Alternatives of the so-called Western Legal Culture' (which the majority of readers should be familiar with), followed by the 'Encounters of the Cultures of Common Law and Civil Law' (a field by which even some hidden features and latent potentialities of the cultures concerned can be revealed), and ending by 'Variations for Cultures of Law' (giving a general overview of one or two aspects of primitive law, ancient law, Chinese, Korean and Japanese law, as well as Muslim law, that are conceived of as direct challenges to western law within an inter-cultural perspective).

One of the main points to realize through the study of this volume is to understand the paradigmatic role the so-called legal method has always played in shaping the individual features of a legal culture. Hence, juristic ways of arguing and reasoning within the framework of the law, the place and significance attributed to courts, codes, logic and experience, as well as discretion and equity, in the operation of this law are all seen not as something outwardly and posteriorly added to the law but as a core element of it, which, by way of its ideological shaping, can, in the final analysis, also be constitutive of its ontology. This is why 'comparative legal methods' are surveyed from instances in Rome and Talmudic jurisprudence, via common and civil law, being supplemented by Soviet Russia, in order to arrive at eastern patterns, exemplified by the Islamic jurisprudence and Japan. Or, in the present context, judicial process is interpreted as the medium through which that what is meant practically by the law in any given culture gets actualized.

In the next section when 'Legal Cultures in Co-existence and Conflict' is studied, there is something more that is at stake. Independently of whether we have a look at legal pluralism in Rome, the failure of modernization because of the persistent survival of traditional patterns in India, or the reprobation of folkways in curing by British-patterned judiciary in Africa, the case is one of interaction amongst differing cultures and, of course, of the conflict ensuing from the former.

Finally, 'Degeneration of Legal Cultures' is the last terrain I propose in this context to contemplate upon, on which hidden features and/or latent potentialities of any given legal culture can be made strikingly visible, either by exposing it to conflicting influences or through contrasting it with one of its own developmental perspectives. The instances taken from Leninist Russia, Nazi Germany, as well as one of the most powerful Latin American countries, Brazil (at a climax of the tendencies of national legal development, leading to exceptional stresses and crises), are witnesses of genuine perspectives indeed, even if of perverted ones. They show how legal cultures can react to extraordinary challenges when torn between the force of antagonistic appeals and pushes. Ironically enough, but with no premeditation, the instances of degeneration are all taken from the realm of civil law, having passed through the mill in this century.

Of course, a selection usually excels more with what it has had to omit than with what it finally includes. So it is in respect of the almost boundless topic of comparative legal cultures.

Unfortunately, some of the best papers available in the literature have been from the very start inhibited from being gathered in this volume, mainly because they have already been selected for reprint in separate, authorial collections.[8]

It is hardly necessary to say that there is also a number of other fine papers, worth reading, which, for one reason or another (for example, easy availability in well-known series, considerations as to the representation by, and the limits set for, this volume), could not be reprinted here.

With regard to the cultures of western law, essays in a general comparative characterization of their development, similarities and differences, come first to mind.[9] A particular topic of such a series of essays is the question of why and how any one of the known institutions can have developed in one of these cultures, and why it was not given a birth and how it was substituted in any other cultures.[10] There are papers to be recommended to any serious student of the subject which cast a light on the foreseeable developmental perspectives of these cultures,[11] or which, by surveying a given specific area or aspect of one of these cultures, help the reader to see what limit cases are also comprehended within the range of their potentialities.[12] Equally interesting is the subject-matter of papers which treat one or other aspect of the historical development of these cultures in the light of the subsequent implementation of some of the above-mentioned latent potentialities.[13]

The comparison of non-western cultures of law either among them[14] or with the western ones[15] opens up new perspectives to the study. Some case studies on the individual features of far-away legal cultures may also deserve interest as a basis for further comparison.[16]

The field of research expressively designated as comparative judicial style introduces to the operation modes of the actual working of any living culture of law. Comparative legal cultures can, by concentrating disciplinary attention to unfolding that what comes out of the developmental potentialities of a legal culture in responding to the challenge historically done, show the internal workings covered by the facade operation of (or with) the law, in search of becoming legally organized. In supplement to great classical topics such as legal reasoning, it can also substantially contribute to the theoretical understanding of the nature of law. In addition to outstanding papers with a general comparative approach to topical issues,[17] the analysis of both western[18] and non-western[19] patterns seems to be rather promising. And last but not least, the degeneration of legal cultures has also inspired literary investigations worth reading.[20]

Notes

1 'The anatomy of men holds a key to the anatomy of the ape.' Marx, K. (1857), *Grundrisse der Kritik der politischen Ökonomie*; see Kamenka, E. (1983), *The Portable Karl Marx*, p. 390, New York: The Viking Press.

2 'Indications of higher possibilities in the lower animal orders can, however, only be understood where the higher development is already known. Bourgeois economy thus supplies the key to the economy of the ancient world, etc.' *idem*.

3 It is another question to know whether this stand is to be understood in a neutral sense (meaning that it is the last word pronounced that is constitutive of the theoretical perspective), or in the sense of arbitrariness (as it is the case when I have a *mihi placet* expression of will), or whether it is to be regarded as the worldly embodiment of some eternal logos (standing for one or another kind of formulation of the assumption of either evolutionism or, to the contrary, the theological view of history). Moreover, I have to note that it is ironical to realise how easily either of these

understandings can slide through, by swinging into, their opposite (for instance, how easily was Marx's claiming to speak for the laws of history switched abruptly over to speaking about his own personal predilections for history).

4 I do refer here to several of the recent books and papers by Alan Watson, mainly to his (1974), *Legal Transplants: An Approach to Comparative Law*, Edinburgh: Scottish Academic Press and Charlottesville, Virginia: University Press of Virginia and (1985), *The Evolution of Law*, Baltimore: Johns Hopkins University Press and Oxford: Basil Blackwell.

5 This is a special research project chaired by Adam Podgórecki within the frame of the Research Committee on the sociology of law under the aegis of the International Sociological Association. Compare, for example, in representation of the aim set of the project, *Legal Systems and Social Systems*, (eds) Podgórecki, A., Whelar, C.J., Khosta, D. (London: Croom Helm no year).

6 Compare, for example, Varga, C. (1987), 'Leibniz und die Frage der rechtlichen Systembildung' in Mollnau, K.A. (ed.), *Materialismus und Idealismus im Rechtsdenken: Geschichte und Gegenwart*, Stuttgart: Franz Steiner Verlag, para. 2 (Archiv für Rechts-und Sozialphilosophie, Beiheft, 31).

7 Lévy-Strauss, C. (1955), *Tristes tropiques*, Paris: Librairie Plon.

8 Compare, for example, Stein, P. (1988), *The Character and Influence of the Roman Civil Law*, Historical Essays, London and Ronceverte: The Hambledon Press; and Watson, A. (1991), *Legal Origins and Legal Change*, London and Ronceverte: The Hambledon Press.

9 Compare, for example, Gomard, B. (1961), 'Civil Law, Common Law and Scandinavian Law', *Scandinavian Studies in Law*, 29–38; Price, T.W. (1965/66), 'Civil Law and Common Law: Two Ways of Thinking', *Acta Juridica*, 47–51; Smith, T.B. (1966), 'The Preservation of the Civilian Tradition in "Mixed Jurisdiction"', *Revista Juridica de la Universidad de Puerto Rico*, **35**, 263–88; Dainow, J. (1966/67), 'The Civil Law and the Common Law: Some Points of Comparison', *The American Journal of Comparative Law*, **15**, 419–35; Sundberg, J.W.F. (1969), 'Civil Law, Common Law and the Scandinavians', *Scandinavian Studies in Law*, **13**, 179–205; Merryman, J.H. (1981), 'On the Convergence (and Divergence) of the Civil Law and the Common Law', *Stanford Journal of International Law*, **17**, 357–88; Mocca, L. (1981), 'English Law Attitudes to the "Civil Law"', *Journal of Legal History*, **2**, 157–68; Gorla, G. and Mocca, L. (1981), 'A "Revisiting" of the Comparison between "Continental Law" and "English Law" (16th–19th Century)', *Journal of Legal History*, **2**, 143–56 and (1982) *Comparative Juridical Review*, **19**, 107–21; Lawson, C.M. (1982), 'The Family Affinities of Common-law and Civil-law Legal Systems', *Hastings International & Comparative Law Review*, **6**, 85–131.

10 Compare, for example, Ryan, K.W. (1961), 'The Reception of the Trust', *International and Comparative Legal Quarterly*, **10**, 265–83; Razi, G.M. (1963), 'Reflections on Equity in the Civil Law System', *American University Law Review*, **13**, 24–44; Rodriguez Ramos, M. (1970), '"Equity" in the Civil Law: A Comparative Essay', *Tulane Law Review*, **44**, 720–39; Arroyo Martinez, I. (1982), 'Trust and the Civil Law', *Louisiana Law Review*, **42**, 1709–20; Englard, I. (1985), 'The Example of Medicine in Law and Equity – On a Methodological Analogy in Classical and Jewish Thought', *Oxford Journal of Legal Studies*, **5**, 2, 238–47.

11 Compare, for example, Zepos, P.J. (1974), 'The Legacy of Civil Law', *Louisiana Law Review*, **34**, 895–906; Couto-Rua, J.C. (1977), 'The Future of the Civil Law', *Louisiana Law Review*, **37**, 645–79; Watson, A. (1984), 'The Future of the Common Law Tradition', *Dalhousie Law Review*, 67–86, (Centennial Lectures, 1983).

12 Compare, for example, Kastrati, Q. (1955), 'Some Sources of Unwritten Law in Albania', *Man*, **55**, 124–7; Walker, D.M. (1955), 'Some Characteristics of Scots Law', *The Modern Law Review*, **18**, 321–7; Reginald, P. (1960), 'A Preface to Byzantine Law', *Revista Juridica de la Universidad de Puerto Rico*, **29**, 133–41; Angelo, A.H. (1970), 'Andorra: Introduction to a Customary Legal System', *American Journal of Legal History*, **14**, 95–111; Keeton, G.W. (1972/73), 'The Canon Law and its Influence', *Loyola Review*, **19**, 1–24; Jenkins, D. (1981), 'The Medieval Welsh Idea of Law', *Tijdschrift voor Rechtsgeschiedenis*, **46**, 323–48; McLeod, N. (1982), 'The Concept of Law in Ancient Irish Jurisprudence', *The Irish Jurist*, **17**, 356–67.

13 Compare, for example, Chroust, A.H. (1946), 'The Function of Law and Justice in the Ancient World and the Middle Ages', *Journal of the History of Ideas*, **7**, 298–320; Kunkel, W. (1953), 'Legal Thought in Greece and Rome', *Juridical Review*, **65**, 1–16; Zajtay, I. (1971), 'The

Importance of the Evolution of Hungarian Law in Regard to the Theory of Sources', *Comparative and International Law Journal of South Africa*, **4**, 72–84; Colman, R.V. (1974), 'Reason and Unreason in Early Medieval Law', *Journal of Interdisciplinary History*, **4**, 571–92; Berman, H.J. (1978), 'The Background of the Western Legal Tradition in the Folklaw of the Peoples of Europe', *University of Chicago Law Review*, **45**, 553–97; Stein, P. (1986), 'The Tasks of Historical Jurisprudence', in N. MacCormick, P. Birks (eds), *The Legal Mind* Essays for Tony Honoré, pp. 293–305, Oxford: Clarendon Press; Watson, A. (1990), 'Roman Law and English Law: Two Patterns of Legal Development', *Loyola Law Review*, **36**, 247–68 (The Brendan Brown Lecture).

14 Compare, for example, Anderson, J.N.D. (1960), 'Significance of Islamic Law in the World Today', *The American Journal of Comparative Law*, **9**, 187–98; Bads, G.M. (1978), 'Islamic Law: Its Relation to Other Legal Systems', *The American Journal of Comparative Law*, **26**, 187–98; Sharma, A. (1981), 'Upmána as a Means of Valid Knowledge in Hindu Epistemology and Quiyas as a Source of Islamic Law', *Journal of the Indian Legal Institute*, **23**, 255–7; Wegner, J.R. (1982), 'Islamic and Talmudic Jurisprudence: The Four Roots of Islamic Law and their Talmudic Counterparts', *The American Journal of Legal History*, **26**, 25–71.

15 Compare, for example, Needham, J. (1951), 'Human Laws and Law of Nature in China and the West', *Journal of the History of Ideas*, **12**, 3–32 and (1951), 194–230; Rao, V.N.S. (1958), 'Hindu Jurisprudence and the Western Legal Mind', *Lawyer* (India), **4**, 19–25; Moore, C.A. and Morris, A.V. (eds) (1968), *The Status of the Individual in East and West*, Honolulu: University of Hawaii Press; Chow, D.T.W. (1975), 'Theories Concerning the Rule of Law in China and the West', *China Forum*, **2**, 2, 1–75; Hyun, S.J. (1975), 'The Traditional Laws of Korea and the Modern Laws of the West', *Korea Journal*, **15**, 10, 11–17; Fujikura, K. (1983), 'A Comparative View of Legal Culture in Japan and the United States', *Law in Japan* (an annual), **16**, 129–34; Yasaki, M., Troller, A. and Llompart, J. (eds) (1985), *Japanisches und europäisches Rechtsdenken* (Versuch einer Synthese philosophischer Grundlagen), Berlin: Duncker & Humblot, (Rechtstheorie, **16**, 2–3) with only two papers in English, on the idea of contract; May, R. (1985), *Law & Society East and West: Dharma, Life, and Nomos*, their Contribution to Thought and to Life, Wiesbaden: Franz Steiner Verlag, (Beiträge zur Südasienforschung: Südasien-Institut, Universität Heidelberg, Band 105); MacCormack, G.D. (1986), 'Law and Punishment: the Western and the Traditional Chinese "Legal Mind"' in N. MacCormick and P. Birks (eds), *The Legal Mind* Essays: for Tony Honoré, pp. 234–51, Oxford: Clarendon Press; Parker, R.B. (1987), 'Law and Language in Japan and in the United States', *Osaka University Law Review*, (34), 47–71; Smith, J.C. (1987), 'Ajase and Oedipus: Ideas of the Self in Japanese and Western Legal Consciousness', *Osaka University Law Review*, (34), 1–36.

16 Compare, for example, Sirat, A.S. (1968), 'The Modern Legal System of Afghanistan', *The American Journal of Comparative Law*, **16**, 563–9; Porat-Martin, H. (1977), 'Israeli Rabbinical Courts – Aspects of a More "Responsive" Legal System', *Diné Israel*, **8**, 49–76; Elias de Tejada, F. (1979), 'The Future of Bantu Law', *Law and Future of Society*, ARSP Beiheft NF, (11), 303–16; Sack, P. (1988), 'Melanesian Jurisprudence', *Archiv für Rechts- und Sozialphilosophie*, **II**, 91–101.

17 Compare, for example, Vinogradoff, P. (1928, 1964), 'Freie Rechtsprechung und die athenische Demokratie' in his *The Collected Papers*, pp. 15–23, Oxford: Clarendon Press, reprinted by London: Wildy; Chloros, A.G. (1956), 'Certainty and the Function of Precedent in Comparative Law', *Revue Hellénique de Droit International*, **9**, 66–79; Schiller, A.A. (1967), 'The Nature and Significance of Jurists' Law', *Boston University Law Review*, **47**, 20–39; Lawson, F.H. (1977), 'Comparative Judicial Style', *The American Journal of Comparative Law*, **25**, 364–71.

18 Compare, for example, as to a properly comparative approach: Silving, H. (1966), '"Stare decisis" in the Civil and the Common Law', *Revista Juridica de la Universidad de Puerto Rico*, **35**, 196–242; Goutal, J.L. (1976), 'Characteristics of Judicial Style in France, Britain and the USA', *The American Journal of Comparative Law*, **24**, 43–72. As a quasi-comparative description, compare: Merryman, J.H. (1965) (1966), 'The Italian Style' 'I: Doctrine'; 'II: Law'; 'III: Interpretation', *Stanford Law Review*, **18**, 39–65, 396–437, 583–611; Gorla, G. (1970), 'Civilian Judicial Decisions – An Historical Account of Italian Style', *Tulane Law Review*, **44**, 740–9;

Zweigert, K. and Puttfarken, H.-J. (1970), 'Statutory Interpretation – Civilian Style', *Tulane Law Review*, **44**, 704–19.

19 Compare, for example, Coulson, N.J. (1959), 'Muslim Custom and Case-law' New Series, *Die Welt des Islams / The World of Islam*, **6**, 13–24; Ishida, T. (1979), 'Case Law in Japan', *International Journal of Law Libraries*, **7**, 133–54; Makdisi, J. (1985), 'Legal Logic and Equity in Islamic Law', *The American Journal of Comparative Law*, **32**, 63–92.

20 Compare, for example, Loevenstein, K. (1936), 'Dictatorship and the German Constitution: 1933–1937', *The University of Chicago Law Review*, **4**, 537–74; Kirchheimer, O. (1969), 'The Legal Order of National Socialism' in F.S. Burin and K.L. Shell (eds), *Politics, Law and Social Change*, pp. 88–109, New York: Columbia; Loeber, D.A. (1970), 'Legal Rules "For Internal Use Only": A Comparative Analysis of the Practice of Withholding Government Decrees from Publication in Eastern Europe and in Western Countries', *International and Comparative Law Quarterly*, **19**, 70–98; Willig, K.C.H. (1976), 'The Bar in the Third Reich', *American Journal of Legal History*, **20**, 1–14; Salas, L. (1983), 'The Emergence and Decline of the Cuban Popular Tribunals', *Law & Society Review*, **17**, 587–612.

Part I
Western Legal Culture: Roots and Alternatives

[1]

THE CANADIAN BAR REVIEW

LA REVUE DU BARREAU CANADIEN

VOL. XLVI MAY 1968 MAI NO. 2

THE UNIQUE NATURE OF THE CONCEPTS OF WESTERN LAW

J. C. SMITH*
Vancouver

Introduction

The nature of language, although always a major concern of the philosopher, has, in recent years, become a question which permeates almost every philosophical issue. This is particularly true in England where for the past twenty-five years, the relationship between language and philosophical problems has become almost the exclusive concern of English philosophers. Such focus of attention is not, however, new to legal philosophy. Bentham, the first philosopher of the common law, was especially concerned with the nature of language and in particular, legal language.[1] This topic has since been and still remains one of the major issues of jurisprudence.

Many of the concepts of the language of law are abstract, directly referring to nothing in sensed experience. While houses and land can be seen and felt, fee simples have no existence in the empirical world. Although a deed is tangible, the rights which it represents are non-material. The event of two people making an agreement can be personally experienced or witnessed, and the

*J. C. Smith, of the Faculty of Law, University of British Columbia, Vancouver.

[1] Bentham, The Limits of Jurisprudence Defined (1945), pp. 57-87; Ogden, Bentham's Theory of Fictions (1932).

agreement itself can be recorded on a piece of paper. The contractual rights which are said to arise out of these facts, however, cannot be located anywhere in the world of fact. They are abstractions, ideas, things of the mind. These non-material "things" are grammatically treated in the same way as are real things. We speak of persons "possessing" a right in the same way as we speak of them possessing a car or a house. We speak of estates existing, being created, transferred and so on just as if we were talking about tangible objects. Such legal concepts as rights, duties, executory interests, contracts, trusts, estates, powers, corporations, and so on which are grammatically used as the subjects and objects of sentences in the same way as are the names of physical things, will be referred to as "legal constructs".

Since most of the fundamental legal concepts are constructs, and because of their grammatical importance, the nature of these concepts have been the focal point of the concern of the legal philosophers with language. As a means of clarifying the meaning of legal language, many legal philosophers have recommended that legal constructs be reduced to terms of factual experience. Such attempts have generally failed in that they do not provide a meaning for legal obligation, and are not sufficiently precise to be the basis for legal doctrine. Thus, a definition of an estate in land as a prediction as to what a court would do under given circumstances, would not be an adequate basis for differentiating between the various kinds of estates. By their very nature as constructs there is nothing in sensed experience to which they directly refer nor which will exhaust their entire meaning.

The clarification of the relation of language to the problems of jurisprudence is as essential in legal philosophy as it is in philosophy in general. A prerequisite to such a clarification is a proper understanding of the nature of the legal construct. As such concepts are extremely complex, this is not an easy task. The objective of this article is to shed some light on this problem through the comparative method. This method is particularly useful when one is dealing with fundamental extensively used concepts such as the more important legal constructs, because such concepts tend to be taken for granted as being necessary and universal. Even as the unique properties of the air we breathe can be forceably brought to our attention by its sudden absence: similarly the unique properties of legal constructs can be highlighted by comparing modern with primitive and ancient law. As stated by Professor Lawson, "Even the most complete and most logical system of law is not perfectly intelligible until it is viewed in relation to other legal systems".[2] Ancient and primitive law rather than the civil law are taken as the point of comparison because they do not contain legal constructs, while the civil law does. Such a comparison will show not only the uniqueness of the concepts of the common law, but also its essential unity with the civil law. It is because of this unity we can collectively speak of "Western law".

A comparison of the concepts of primitive and ancient with those of modern Western law also serves a secondary purpose. Many treatises dealing with ancient and primitive law are in part misleading in that the various commercial transactions and legal concepts of such systems are equated with the technical, abstract concepts of modern law. Thus the anthropologists A. E. Hoebel and L. Pospisil describe the legal concepts of primitive society in the sophisticated, theoretical Hohfeldian terms of rights, privileges, powers, immunities, and so on; and Robert H. Lowie finds the equivalent of modern incorporeal property rights in the magical formulae, dances and songs of primitive cultures.[3] To assume that because the members of a society make claims and counter-claims to property, they think in the technical, modern, Western, sense of rights and duties or ownership is to fail to realize the unique nature of those concepts, and results in a false impression of primitive law.[4]

Not only are constructs absent from the legal systems of primitive and ancient cultures, but there is no way by which the concepts of modern law can be adequately expressed in their language systems. Language it must be noted is not merely a medium for the transmission of ideas, nor just a channel through which thoughts or messages may be passed through symbolic processes. The particular language system which any person uses is an important factor in the formation of the ideas which he communicates.

---

[2] Lawson, The Field of Comparative Law (1949), 61 Jurid. Rev. 16, at p. 17.

[3] Hoebel, The Law of Primitive Man (1954), pp. 46-63; Pospisil, Kapauku Papuans and their Law, Yale University Publications in Anthropology, no. 54 (1958); Lowie, Selected Papers in Anthropology (1960), p. 225. Professor Hoebel, at p. 19 of his The Law of Primitive Man points out the danger of distorting the concepts of primitive law by the use of the vocabulary of modern law. He concludes, however, that it is sufficient to avoid this danger if we "neither blindly nor willfully force upon primitive data that are only relatively comparable the specific content of meaning associated with our terminology".

[4] Malinowski, Argonauts of the Western Pacific (1961), p. 116; Sawer, Law in Society (1965), pp. 43-47; Lloyd, Yoruba Land Law (1962), pp. 66-67; Diamond, Primitive Law (2nd ed., 1950), pp. 260-262, 391-392; Seagle, The History of Law (1946), pp. 50-57.

Our concept of what the world is, is related to the language by which we symbolize our experience of that world because our experience is organized and interpreted in the terms of our language structure. In the words of Edward Sapir, one of the earlier proponents of the above hypothesis:

> Language is a guide to "social reality". Though language is not ordinarily thought of as of essential interest to the students of social science, it powerfully conditions all our thinking about social problems and processes. Human beings do not live in the objective world alone, nor alone in the world of social activity as ordinarily understood, but are very much at the mercy of the particular language which has become the medium of expression for their society. It is quite an illusion to imagine that one adjusts to reality essentially without the use of language and that language is merely an incidental means of solving specific problems of communication or reflection. The fact of the matter is that the "real world" is to a large extent unconsciously built up on the language habits of the group. No two languages are ever sufficiently similar to be considered as representing the same social reality. The worlds in which different societies live are distinct worlds, not merely the same world with different labels attached.[5]

Although not all anthropologists accept what has become known as the Whorfian thesis, comparisons of various language systems demonstrate a close interrelationship between language and culture.[6] The importance of this relationship also was realized by certain philosophers such as Wittgenstein, Whitehead, and Russell, who have pointed out the particular ways in which our subject-predicate Indo-European languages effect our concepts of reality.[7] The implication of this relationship on legal theory has been pointed out by Professor F. S. C. Northrop, who has shown that there is a direct correlation between the kind of legal system and the conceptual structure through which a society sees and symbolizes the world.[8]

By "conceptual structure" is meant not only the sets of concepts which a people use to interpret and classify the raw facts of experience, and the language system in terms of which these

[5] Sapir, The Status of Linguistics as a Science in Mandelbaum (ed.), Selected Writings of Edward Sapir (1949), p. 160, at p. 162.

[6] Mandelbaum, *op. cit.*, *ibid.*; Whorf, Language, Thought, and Reality (1956); Hoijer (ed.), Language in Culture (1954); Henle (ed.), Language, Thought, and Culture (1958); Hymes (ed.), Language in Culture and Society (1964); Spier, Hallowell, and Newman (eds), Language, Culture, and Personality (1941); Northrop and Livingston (eds), Cross Cultural Understanding (1964).

[7] Northrop, Man, Nature and God (1962), pp. 159-176, and 238-245.

[8] Northrop, The Comparative Philosophy of Comparative Law (1960), 45 Cornell L.Q. 617 and The Complexity of Legal and Ethical Experience (1959), pp. 173-182.

concepts are thought and communicated, but also the epistemological theory as to how these concepts and terms get their meaning. Since the thought process is partially a symbolic process, (that is to say it is carried out through the use of symbols) the very conceiving of a particular concept involves the use of language. The concept, however, is not identical with the words since the same concept may be expressed by different symbols in different languages. It is difficult for a person to entertain concepts which have no corresponding symbol in his particular language. Equally what we think about our world affects our language in that a language reflects the particular epistemological theory or theories of a culture. Our Indo-European subject-predicate language system reflects an epistemological theory that all knowledge comes from the senses and that our sensed experience is objective or in other words is the same for all knowers.[9] This theory is usually referred to as naive realism. In a sentence such as, "The dress is pink", the quality of pinkness is predicated of the object dress by the syntactical structure of our language. In everyday common sense thinking, even the more philosophically sophisticated assume that the colour exists in the object and is identical for all knowers, although scientifically they realize that the pinkness is a subjective experience within the "mind" rather than a part of the "real" object.[10] A language system with a radically different syntactical structure will probably reflect a different epistemological theory.

The Burmese language, for instance, is related to an epistemological theory which assumes, as does naive realism, that all knowledge comes from the senses, but holds that such knowledge is relative to the particular experiencer.[11] Sensed datum, thus, will not be identical for different people, or for the same person at different moments. Such a theory is usually called radical empiricism. Equally, our language affects what we think about our world in that we interpret, categorize, and communicate our experience in terms of the symbols and syntax of our particular language. It is because of this interrelatedness between the sets of concepts, the language system, and the epistemological theory or theories of any people that we can lump them together conveniently as the conceptual structure.

Only concepts with which the members of a culture are familiar

---

[9] Northrop, *op. cit.*, footnote 7.

[10] Hospers, An Introduction to Philosophical Analysis (1953), pp. 380-383.

[11] Khin Maung Win, The Burmese Language: An Epistemological Approach, in Northrop and Livingston, *op. cit.*, footnote 6, p. 223.

can be expressed in the language of that culture. While the Eskimo, for instance, has fourteen different words for snow, depending upon its condition, he has no word for government. The closest that one can come to this concept in the Eskimo language is, "those who help others".[12] The linguist Professor S. A. Wurm points out in his article, "Aboriginal Languages and the Law", that "aborigine languages cannot as a rule be used to express the juristic ideas and principles involved in the operation of a white man's court of law, seeing that many of these ideas and principles are completely outside the aborigine's conceptual world, and no symbols can be available in any language for notions not forming part of the conceptual system, *i.e.*, the culture of its speakers".[13] If this be true, it follows that the language of modern law cannot be used to accurately describe the legal concepts of a culture whose conceptual system is radically different. As stated by Professor Sawer: "When discovery is made that some primitive people applied in their own speech and thinking notions closely similar to those of modern analytical jurisprudence, or some of them, and not until then, it will become appropriate to use the modern terms when describing the primitive usage."[14]

Any attempt, therefore, to analyse non-Western legal systems in terms of the categories of modern Western law will result in distortion. Professor Paul Bohannan, in his study *Justice and Judgment Among the Tiv* warns:[14A]

> I consider it to be the cardinal error of ethnographic and social analysis: the grossly ethnocentric practice of raising folk systems like "the law", designed for social action in one's own society, to the status of an analytical system, and then trying to organize the raw social data from other societies into its categories. I have also tried to avoid the equivalent error of raising the folk systems of the Romans or the Trobriand Islanders to the level of such a filing system for data which may not fit them. Such a doctrine is probably a counsel of perfection, impossible of attainment. But impossibility of attainment does not make it less desirable.

Professor Max Gluckman, on the other hand, while agreeing with Professor Bohannan that a primitive system must first be analysed in its own terms, takes issue with him on whether a model

[12] This information was received from Dean A. W. R. Carrothers of the University of Western Ontario Law School who was chairman of the Advisory Commission on the Development of Government in the Northwest Territories.

[13] Wurm, Aboriginal Languages and the Law (1963), 6 U.W. Austl. L. Rev. 1, at p. 10.

[14] Sawer, *op. cit.*, foonote 4, p. 46.

[14A] (1957), p. 69, see also pp. 101, 104-105, 111, 120, 210, 212-214.

drawn from Western law can then be used for comparative purposes. He states:[14B]

> I have tried to show . . . that what Bohannan sees as the folk system of the Tiv is widely distributed in tribal law; and Holmes, Maitland, Seagle, and many other jurists have made the point about early European law. Clearly we must not force tribal law into a Procrustean bed of Western jurisprudential concepts, but we may with care use those refined concepts for comparison and analysis. The alternative is to invent a new terminology.

Gluckman's examples, as they are mainly drawn from primitive systems and Western law prior to its tranformation through contact with classical Roman law, do not sustain his thesis that the categories of modern Western law can be used for purposes of cross-cultural comparison as between the status systems of primitive and archaic law and the construct systems of Western law.

A further problem arises in regard to some of the treatises dealing with the law of primitive cultures which have been subject to many years of colonial rule. In such societies the concepts of modern Western law often become mixed with the legal concepts of the indigenous societies and a gradual shift takes place such that the primitive concept gradually is replaced by a corresponding Western concept while the terminology remains unchanged, or a modern term is used in place of an ancient term while the concept remains unchanged. In some cases both the concept and the terminology of the colonizing culture may be adopted. Thus it is extremely difficult to isolate the pure primitive legal concepts before cultural contamination has taken place. Many authorities in treating the law of such a culture make no attempt to isolate pre-colonial concepts, but instead describe the legal system and concepts of the people at the time the study is made. Recent studies of African law in particular must be used with caution in ascertaining the nature of primitive law.

The fact that primitive and ancient cultures do not have the same kind of legal concepts as modern law does not necessarily mean that they do not have "law", or a fully developed legal system. Neither does it necessarily mean that their law is simple rather than complex. It does not mean that the various primitive and ancient legal systems are basically similar. It does mean, however, that the law of ancient and primitive cultures is quite different from Western law. Only through a comparison can the nature of this difference be shown.

[14B] Gluckman, The Ideas in Barotse Jurisprudence (1965), p. 265, see also pp. 251-272.

In Part I of this article, a comparison will be drawn between the modern law of property and contract and the closest counterpart in primitive and archaic law. This comparison will show that legal constructs are unique to classical Roman and modern civil and common law. The legal concepts of primitive and archaic law get their meaning from sensed experience and are factual rather than theoretical or abstract. This comparison will support the thesis that the strength and superiority of modern law as compared with primitive and archaic law, is derived from the presence of constructs. Western law because of this factor has spread throughout all the world and been adopted in various degrees and forms by a vast majority of the earth's population, including such nations as Turkey and Japan, who have replaced traditional legal systems, centuries old, with either the common or the civil law.

In Part II it will be shown that legal constructs first appeared in Roman law, and it was this appearance which was probably the most important factor in the development of classical Roman law. The thesis first advanced by Professor F. S. C. Northrop that legal constructs developed as a result of an important change in the conceptual structure of the Romans, and that the source of this change was the development of constructs in Greek mathematical physical philosophy, will be briefly outlined and defended. The comparative method then will again be used to clarify the nature of legal constructs by comparing them with the constructs of mathematical physics.

In Part III it will be shown that the important constructs of Roman law were adopted by the common law, making possible its transformation from an archaic to a modern legal system. In the conclusion, suggestions will be made, based on the characteristics of legal constructs highlighted by the above mentioned comparisons, as to techniques of analysis which should prove useful in further clarifying their nature.

I

The most noticeable difference in comparing the concepts of these two types of law is that, unlike modern law, primitive and archaic law contain few abstract or theoretical concepts.[15] Most concepts in such legal systems derive their meaning directly from, or in terms of sensed experience. This difference can be illustrated by comparing the modern law concepts of contract and property with

[15] Ferson, Rights and Powers: 'What are They? (1959), 12 Vand. L. Rev. 313, at p. 316.

their closest counterparts in archaic law. While every society has a concept or concepts relating to property and commercial transactions carried out upon the basis of mutual consensus, the concepts of "ownership" and "contract" in the sense of abstract bundles of jural relations exist only in classical Roman and modern law.

In modern law the term "property" has two meanings, the land or chattels, and the imageless, theoretical legal relations through which human behaviour is controlled in regard to them.[16] The concept of "ownership" as a bundle of legal relations *in rem* by which people's conduct is regulated in regard to resources is unknown in both archaic and primitive law. In primitive legal systems an individual's personal property such as wearing apparel, ornaments, tools, weapons, and horses, were his not because of any legal conception of ownership, but because of the directly sensed physical connexion between the individual and his personal goods. A number of writers have suggested that this type of property was conceived as being a part of the individual, or a manifestation or extension of his personality.[17]

Equally the concept of property in archaic law was that of physical possession.[18] The early Roman or Greek family was inseparably connected to their land through their religion.[19] The family occupied it, and it was the location of the family hearth and sacred fire which was not to be moved. The souls of their dead who were buried there possessed the fields. Thus the soil and the home belonged to the family in the sense of those dead, the living, and those yet to be born. The slaves, flocks, and herds were not owned by the family but were part of the family in a similar way as were the children.[20] The element which held the various parts together and welded them into a single unit was the relationship of the patriarchal family head to the members.[21] His power was practically without limit and was exercised over persons, slaves, flocks, and herds alike.

---

[16] Hohfeld, Fundamental Legal Conceptions (1923), p. 28.

[17] Beaglehole, Property: A Study in Social Psychology (1932), p. 134; Seagle, *op. cit.*, footnote 4, p. 51; Hobhouse, Development of the Idea of Property, in Kocourek and Wigmore (compilers), Primitive and Ancient Legal Institutions (1915), vol. 2, pp. 372-380; Hartland, Primitive Law (1924), p. 88; Westrup, Introduction to Early Roman Law, vol. II, Joint Family and Family Property (1934), pp. 160-172; Jones, Law and Legal Theory of the Greeks (1956), p. 202.

[18] Westrup, *op. cit.*, *ibid.*

[19] Fustel de Coulanges, The Ancient City (1956), pp. 60-72.

[20] Noyes, The Institution of Property (1914), p. 281; Morey, Outlines of Roman Law (1884), p. 281.

[21] Main, Ancient Law (1959), p. 263; Noyes, *op. cit.*, *ibid.*, pp. 55-56.

The primitive and archaic concepts of property are generally found to have two constituents, the empirically known physical relationship of possession, and an introspected feeling that somethings belongs to oneself, which springs from such factors as actual possession, the religion, and the family. This relationship and feeling would be often expressed by the equivalent of the English phrase, "this is mine".[22] The languages of such societies do not contain a word which corresponds to "ownership" or the "dominium" of classical Roman law.[23] The words which connote property usually mean the equivalent of physical possession or the taking of possession.[24]

When property was wrongfully taken from the possession of a person or family who considered it their own, the physical relationship of possession would be broken and that relationship would then exist towards the wrongful taker. Before the development of classical Roman law, no question of ownership could arise for a tribunal to decide as the corresponding concept to ownership was possession. The removal of possession from the prior possessor destroyed his relationship. When each of two people claimed that a certain object belonged to them, the question for the tribunal to decide was not who had the proprietary rights, but instead who had the older or the prior possession. Although the fact of the previous possession and the wrongful removal gave the original possessor an action in law, this action did not connote ownership.

The concept of property of the early common law was similar to that of archaic law.[25] In disputes regarding property, the issue was never "who owned the property?"—theoretical constructs being foreign to the people's conceptual structure—but rather "has a wrong been committed to possession". For instance, if a dispute arose in regard to a cow, the claimant would grasp the animal in dispute by the ear and swear that the animal had been stolen from him.[26] The possessor then had to show that either he had possessed

---

[22] Westrup, *op. cit.*, footnote 17, p. 160; Noyes, *op. cit.*, footnote 20, p. 78; Lloyd, *op. cit.*, footnote 4, p. 67; Jones, *op. cit.*, footnote 17, p. 203.

[23] Westrup, *op. cit.*, footnote 17, pp. 160-161; Lloyd, *op. cit.*, *ibid.*, p. 67; Diamond, *op. cit.*, footnote 4, pp. 260-261; Jones, *op. cit.*, *ibid.*, p. 298.

[24] Diamond, *op. cit.*, *ibid.*, p. 261; Smith, The Theoretical Constructs of Western Contractual Law, in Northrop and Livingston, *op. cit.*, footnote 6, pp. 255-256.

[25] Pollock and Maitland, History of English Law, vol. 1 (1952), p. 57; Laughlin, The Anglo-Saxon Legal Procedure, in Essays in Anglo-Saxon Law (1876), p. 183 at p. 212.

[26] Pollock and Maitland, *op. cit.*, *ibid.*, vol. 2, p. 157.

the animal since birth or had purchased it from a third party. If the latter was true then the third party would be accused of theft and would become the defendant.[27] A nearly identical procedure existed in such diverse cultures as the Babylonion, Greek, Continental Saxon, and Welsh.[28]

The first recorded appearance of the word "owner" in our language is 1340, and the first instance of the appearance of ownership is 1583.[29] Neither *owner* nor *ownership* became common legal terminology until the seventeenth century. The word "possession" was not introduced into legal terminology until Littleton borrowed it from Roman law in order to distinguish possession of chattels from possession of land. There was only one word used to describe an individual's relationship to his property and that was the word "seisin" which meant simply physical possession and was used equally of chattels as of land. The person of this period who was seised of land had the land itself and did not conceive of himself as holding abstract legal rights as against other people, which allowed him to enjoy his land. When he was disseised he had nothing but his legal remedies. Thus, if John came upon Blackacre and disseised Richard, John, since he was the person seised, could:

1. convey the estate to anyone else;
2. his heir would succeed to the property;
3. his widow was entitled to dower;
4. if Richard died without heirs, the land would not escheat to the lord;
5. John and not Richard owned the feudal dues to the lord.

Richard, on the other hand:

1. had nothing to alienate. He could not convey the land;
2. his wife was not entitled to dower;
3. he could not after five days from his disseisin retake possession of the land by force.

Although Richard could bring an action to recover the land, he could not convey or assign this remedy, as it was based on the di-

[27] Selden Society, vol. 60 (1941), Select Cases of Procedure Without Writ Under Henry III, Curia Regis Roll, no. 131.

[28] The Code of Hammurabi, sections 9-13 in Smith, The Origin and History of Hebrew Law (1960), pp. 184-185; Driver and Miles, The Babylonian Laws (1952), pp. 95-105; Plato, Laws, 11; Laughlin, *op. cit.*, footnote 25, p. 206; The Laws of Howel Dda, Book III, chap. ii, sections 31-38, in Kocourek and Wigmore, Sources of Ancient and Primitive Law (1915), pp. 542-543.

[29] Pollock and Maitland, *op. cit.*, footnote 25, p. 153; Diamond, *op. cit.*, footnote 4, p. 261.

rectly sensed relationship of possession which only Richard had had with the land.[30]

As the concept of ownership gradually developed in English law, the meaning of the word *seisin* began to shift to something between possession and ownership. The fact that it originally meant possession, however, may be further illustrated by a case from the *Book of Assizes*, where the plaintiff's bill was adjudged bad for pleading that the defendant had stolen and killed his horse, since as soon as the horse was removed from the plaintiff's possession, it was no longer his horse, but that of the possessor.[31] In the words of the defendant, ". . . since you have confessed the property to be in us at the time of the killing, and so your bill is repugnant; for by the tortious taking, the property was devested out of you and vested in us, and therefore we could not kill our own horse *contra pacem*".[32]

The empirical concept of property of the early English common law can also be illustrated by the methods of conveying land. Since the relationship between people and their property was the physical relationship of possession rather than the legal rights between individuals, the only way an object could be conveyed was to transfer possession.[33] This process was termed livery of seisin; that is, delivery of possession. The two parties would come upon the land, each with his witnesses, and the one would hand the other a twig or piece of turf which would symbolize the land passing from the possession of the one person to the other. Then the feoffor, as the grantor was called, would vacate the land, taking his goods with him, and the feoffee would take possession. Other methods of conveying land such as the use of the fine, common recovery, or lease and release, equally revolved around a delivery of possession, without which there could be no conveyance.

Like ownership, the concept of contract was unknown in primitive and ancient cultures untouched by classical Roman law. The term contract is commonly used in three different ways by both laymen and lawyers.[34] It is used to refer to the factual operative

---

[30] The Collected Papers of F. W. Maitland (1911), vol. 1, pp. 329-384, 407-457; Pollock and Maitland, *op. cit., ibid.*, pp. 1-183; Holdsworth, A History of English Law (5th ed., 1942), vol. 3, pp. 88-101, 351-360.

[31] Ames, The Disseisin of Chattels (1889-90), 3 Harv. L. Rev. 23, at p. 24.

[32] *Ibid.*

[33] Gulliver, Future Interests (1959), p. 37.

[34] Corbin, Offer and Acceptance and Some of the Resulting Legal Relations, in Association of American Law Schools, Selected Readings on the Law of Contracts (1931), p. 170; *Hotchkiss* v. *National City Bank* (1910), 200 Fed. 287, at p. 293.

acts of agreement, to a piece of paper on which the agreement is recorded, and to the imageless, theoretical relations to which the act of agreement gives rise. It is the latter which is not to be found in primitive and archaic law. According to Seagle, "But no one has been able to find even in any archaic legal system, whether Ashanti, Babylonian, Hebrew, early Roman, or Germanic, an example of the enforcement of transactions which were purely executory on both sides—that is, when parties had merely exchanged promises with each other and no transfer of possession or partial performance had yet taken place".[35] In his book, *Primitive Law*, Diamond points out that this, "artificial, technical and theoretical conception" was unknown in primitive legal systems.[36] Even in early Roman law, "not only the word 'contractus' but also the idea or concept of contract was unknown", writes Professor Collinet.[37] He further states that, "In the beginning of every civilization there was no contract", and that "the agreement of two or more persons never gave rise to an obligation . . .".[38]

This does not mean that primitive and archaic societies were without commercial transactions. These consisted, however, principally of exchanges of land, commodities, or money. Barter and sale, it must be noted, did not give rise to contractual relations but to new relationships of physical possession. Immediately the transaction was completed, the parties had no further relationship to each other.[39] Professor J. W. Jones, for instance, in describing Greek law states:[40]

> Despite the obscurity of the not very abundant material which has come down to us, there is good ground for supposing that Greek law, like early Roman and English law, considered sale as essentially an exchange of land or goods for money, a cash transaction giving no right to enforce payment on the one side or delivery on the other. It was a two-sided affair; but there could be no question of any outstanding obligations arising from the simple fact of agreement. In law the sale was complete or it was nothing, and it was not complete until the price had been paid: "Paying down the forty minae, I made the purchase", says a buyer. While Roman and English law eventually came to recognize the binding force of mutual promises, Greek law clung through its history to the conception of sale as a purely ready-money business.

---

[35] Seagle, *op. cit.*, footnote 4, p. 256.
[36] Diamond, *op. cit.*, footnote 4, p. 392.
[37] Collinet, The Evolution of Contract as Illustrating the General Evolution of Roman Law (1932), 48 L.Q. Rev. 488.
[38] *Ibid.*
[39] Jolowicz, Historical Introduction to Roman Law (2nd ed., 1952), p. 164; Corbin, *op. cit.*, footnote 34, p. 172.
[40] Jones, *op. cit.*, footnote 17, p. 228.

Stability of expectation in regard to patterns of trade were maintained by personal relationships, custom or by a ritualization of trading patterns such as the economic institution of the Kula described by Malinowski in *Argonauts of the Western Pacific.*[41]

The closest these systems approached the concept of contract was an incomplete conveyance where one party gave goods but did not immediately receive value in return. Such a transaction, however, did not set up a legal relation between creditor and debtor, but a common practice was for the debtor to give a hostage or his own body to insure that he completed the transaction.[42] There was no concept of a legal obligation but a failure to pay was considered a wrongful detention of the creditor's property, and a failure to repay a loan, a wrongful detention of the creditor's money. Thus the Laws of Manu provide "A creditor who himself recovers his property from his debtor must not be blamed by the King for retaking what is his own".[43] In the early common law, for instance, the action brought for a wrongful refusal to surrender a chattel to which the plaintiff was entitled was detinue, while the action for money owed was the closely related action of debt wherein the plaintiff would plead that the defendant, "has detained his money until the present time, wrongfully and to his damages, etc.".[44]

In a number of societies legal remedies were available when some one broke his oath or pledge.[45] The reason was not, however, because giving one's oath gave rise to a legal duty to perform one's agreement. Such a concept is to be found only in classical Roman and related legal systems. A remedy was available because to break one's pledge to another was to commit a wrong to him.[46] There is no distinction made in primitive and archaic law between the wrongs of injuring another or his property, or failing to keep one's pledge or oath. The division between property, contract, and tort

---

[41] Malinowski, *op. cit.*, footnote 4. See also Herslovits, Economic Life of Primitive Peoples (1940), pp. 155-212.

[42] Jolowicz, *op. cit.*, footnote 39, pp. 162-165; Seagle, *op. cit.*, footnote 4, pp. 256-257.

[43] Section 50 of the Laws of Manu, in Kocourek and Wigmore, *op. cit.*, footnote 28, p. 473.

[44] Selden Society, vol. 80 (1963), Novae Narrationes, B 209; See also Paton, Jurisprudence (2nd ed., 1951), p. 38.

[45] Sections 215-221 of the Laws of Manu, in Kocourek and Wigmore, *op. cit.*, footnote 28, p. 486; Title L. of the Lex Salica, in Kocourek and Wigmore, *op. cit.*, footnote 28, p. 507; Section 1 of the Laws of Alfred, in Attenborough, The Laws of the Earliest English Kings (1922), p. 63.

[46] Seagle, *op. cit.*, footnote 4, p. 255.

did not exist in such legal systems. Instead, their law was a law of wrongs rather than rights.[47]

Rather than attempting to fit primitive law, "into European categories like tort, contract, property rights, etc., thus hiding the most important thing about them . . .",[47A] a number of authorities on archaic and primitive law find the concept of "debt" useful to describe the legal situation arising when a wrong has been committed.[47B] The advantage of this concept over the categories of Western law is that it preserves the unified approach to wrongs, whatever their source, which was taken in archaic and primitive law. Seagle writes in regard to archaic law:[47C]

> . . . archaic law knows not so much a law of contracts as a law of debt. Indeed, its creative power seems to be exhausted in devising machinery for recording or enforcing a debt irrespective of its cause of origin. The Babylonian law recognized the *i'iltum* or obligation note which could be employed to incorporate any cause of debt. Mediaeval English law developed a general action of debt.

Professor Bohannan states concerning the law of the Tiv:[47D]

> It would be possible to consider *jir* which concerns "releasing livestock" as cases of breach of contract. Little purpose would be served by so doing, for Tiv do not have a concept "contract", and if we do so classify them, there is very grave danger of forgetting that we have applied the notion "contract" from our own culture.

Thus we see that the concepts of primitive and archaic law, in marked contrast to classical Roman and modern law, get their meaning directly in terms of sensed experience. The conceptions applied to the property and commercial relationship of these societies are factual rather than abstract. Their legal codes all follow a basic pattern of specifying patterns of behaviour to be or not to be performed, and a penalty for failure to comply. Whether we refer to the Code of Hammurabi prescribing that, "If any one breaks a man's bone, one shall break his bone", or the Laws of Manu specifying that, "With whatever limb a man of a low caste does hurt to a man of the three highest castes, even shall that limb be cut off", the same pattern will be found.[48]

---

[47] Jolowicz, *op. cit.*, footnote 39, p. 162.

[47A] Bohannan, *op. cit.*, footnote 14A, p. 102.

[47B] *Ibid.*, pp. 103-112; Gluckman, *op. cit.*, footnote 14B, pp. 242-272. Seagle, *op. cit.*, footnote 4, pp. 256-265.

[47C] Seagle, *op. cit.*, *ibid.*, p. 260.

[47D] Bohannan, *op. cit.*, footnote 14A, p. 104.

[48] Section 197 of the Code of Hammurabi, in Kocourek and Wigmore, *op. cit.*, footnote 28, p. 428; Section 279 of the Laws of Manu, in Kocourek and Wigmore, *op. cit.*, footnote 28, p. 491.

The lack of theoretical concepts in, or what some writers have termed the "materialism" of archaic and primitive law, is merely a reflection of the naive realism of primitive and archaic peoples as reflected in their languages.[49] Although the conceptual structures of such societies differ greatly from one to another, they appear to have at least one factor in common, and that is the inability to organize experience in terms of highly abstract concepts and categories having logically rather than empirically known properties.[50] This is not because of any inherent deficiency in the mind of primitive man but because he interprets new experience in terms of his own inherited conceptual structure which provides a different kind of logic and set of principles for organizing experience than the theoretical constructs of Western mathematics and science.[51]

Primitive and archaic law is a law of empirically known, psychologically sensed wrongs rather than theoretically conceived rights and duties having no existence in the material world of the senses. These legal systems were therefore static and past oriented, since they dealt basically with wrongs and compensation, that is, the restitution as far as possible of a previously existing situation which had been wrongfully disturbed. Classical Roman and modern law, on the other hand, is future oriented and a law of movement concerned with the creation, transfer, and extinction of legal relations and prediction of this future movement. Through the use of these constructs it is possible to control future human behaviour in regard to physical resources, to a degree not possible by using only concepts having a referent in sensed experience.

The most basic construct, the right, for instance, is not a thing nor can it be empirically known in the same way as an object

---

[49] Gulliver, *op. cit.*, footnote 33, pp. 36-37, 195-196; Maitland, *op. cit.*, footnote 30, pp. 372-373; Boas, The Mind of Primitive Man (1938), pp. 207-225; Levy-Bruhl, Primitive Mentality (1923); and How Natives Think (1926); Lienhardt, Modes of Thought in Primitive Society, [1953] Blackfriars, pp. 269-278; Kluckhohn, The Philosophy of the Navaho Indians in Northrop, Ideological Differences and World Order (1949), p. 356, at p. 368; Collinet, *op. cit.*, footnote 37, p. 489. The concepts of spirits and mystical or magical forces, although immaterial in the sense of being imaginary, are material concepts in the sense that they are believed to exist in fact, and are known directly or through the senses.

[50] *Ibid.* Paul Radin in his book Primitive Man as Philosopher (1957), pp. xxi-xl, is somewhat critical of Levy-Bruhl in that he appears to assume that Levy-Bruhl's thesis is that primitive languages are incapable of expressing philosophical ideas. The thesis of Levy-Bruhl, however, is not so much that primitive cultures lack philosophies as it is that the abstract, theoretical concepts of Western philosophy with its particular logic, mathematics, and science cannot be expressed in these languages.

[51] Boas, *op. cit.*, footnote 49, p. 220.

such as a tree. Most constructs of modern law such as estates, trusts, or contracts, and so on are collections or bundles of rights or jural relations. These concepts are empty forms, the parts of which are variables into which people and patterns of behaviour are put in order to accomplish certain purposes. Take, for instance, the situation where John wishes to have his fence painted by Richard but does not wish to pay until the job is completed, and Richard is willing to paint the fence but wishes to be certain of being able to collect. By use of the concept of the contract, filling in the variables with themselves and the patterns of behaviour of painting a fence and paying money, they are able to gain some control of each other's actions.

Let us take the more complex situation where a client comes to his lawyer and asks him to draft his will. There are a number of legal constructs which the lawyer may use in passing the property from a testator to the beneficiaries. The ones selected will depend upon what the testator wishes to accomplish. The client tells the lawyer that he wishes to leave his property to his wife but he is concerned that she will not be able to manage it properly. Further he wants to ensure that some property will be left for his adult children after his wife's death, but he does not want his infant son John to have anything unless and until he reaches the age of twenty-one. The draftsman then uses the construct of the trust which enables the giving of the legal relations relating to control of the property to a trust company and the relations relating to beneficial enjoyment to his wife. To ensure that there will be some property left for the children upon the death of the wife, he uses the construct of the estate by which the legal relations of ownership can be divided on the plane of time to give the wife a life estate with power to encroach on the capital. The adult children will then be given a vested remainder except for son John who will be given a contingent remainder upon the condition that he reaches twenty-one. What the legal draftsman has done is to have made a selection of certain empty legal forms developed by the law of property, in order to accomplish certain ends, and then to have filled in the variables of these forms with the appropriate persons and patterns of conduct. Such constructs of the English common law of real property are a part of almost a calculus where the lawyer is "moving in a world of pure ideas from which everything physical or material is entirely excluded".[52]

[52] Lawson, The Rational Strength of English Law (1951), p. 79 and The Law of Property (1958), pp. 15-16, 60-62.

The advantages of dealing indirectly with people and resources through the use of such concepts are many. By their use a wider sharing and distribution of a particular resource is possible. In relation to a piece of land, Blackacre for instance, the legal system creates a bundle of jural relations which all together are termed "ownership". Thus if A owns Blackacre, that is, he is the holder of the rights and powers of the jural relations, he can divide these various relations into their separate parts. He can give the right to possession by lease to B, the right to remove minerals to C, an easement to D, and so forth. He can also divide these jural relations along the plane of time into estates. He can give a life estate to B, and on his death a life estate to C, and on C's death a vested remainder to D, subject to be divested by a shifting executory interest given to E. He can also further divide his jural relations into legal relations and equitable relations, thus creating a trust. He can as well use two or all three of these methods of divisions at the same time. Thus he may give to B the right to remove minerals from the land, in trust for C for life and on his death to D.

The legal construct of the corporation enables the accumulation of large amounts of capital, physical resources, and skills, and consequently production on a scale seldom possible by other means of carrying on business enterprises. Through the use of shares (also a legal construct) ownership of such accumulations of wealth can be spread over a large number of people. It further enables the development of a skilled manager class, separate from those enjoying the benefits of ownership.

The use of such concepts allows a much greater flexibility. Ease of transfer of property is facilitated. Whereas now property can be transferred by mere agreement or deed, in legal systems where the property concept was that of physical possession property could be conveyed only by the actual transfer of that possession. A vast number of factual situations can be dealt with by the use of a minimum number of concepts. Such constructs, being theoretical, can be formulated to fit practically any human need. Their properties can be defined with much more precision than can the concepts of the world of fact. The increasing complexity of modern society, requiring a high degree of stability of expectations in regard to individual behaviour, could be possible only through such highly technical jural constructs.

II

It is generally recognized that the creation of Roman classical law was a unique achievement and one of the most important contributions of Rome to the world. Roman law, compared to all other systems of its time, according to Pringsheim, "rises like a mountain above the common level of the others".[53] It is also widely recognized that the unique factor in the development of Roman law was the presence for the first time in any legal system of legal constructs. This factor has been described in many different ways by different authorities in this field. According to Pringsheim, ". . . simplicity is the striking feature of classical law. It was reached by abstraction".[54] Professor Lawson states, "The Romans taught the world—including even the world of the common law—the possibility of forming a legal framework for society, composed of the smallest possible number of elements".[55] Wolff describes the same characteristics when he speaks of "that great, scientific treatment of the law which enabled Roman law, in a manner unique in ancient times, to combine consistency, theoretical refinement, and a high degree of practical elasticity . . .".[56] Schulz writes, "Often the jurists' statements almost give the impression of a mathematical treatise . . .".[57] Savigny, in similar terms declared that:[58]

> The conceptions and rules of their science do not seem to them to be products of their own creation—they are real beings, with whose existense and genealogy they have become acquainted through long and intimate association. That is why their whole procedure is tinged with an assurance not found elsewhere, except in mathematics, and it is no exaggeration to say that they make calculations with their conceptions.

From these writers we learn that the factor which makes classical Roman law unique is the economy of terms and principles whereby a large body of phenomena can be dealt with by use of a minimum of concepts. This is possible because Roman law contains concepts which are theoretical, having imageless logical rather than imageful naive realistic properties. The development of such concepts enabling the transformation of a typical archaic legal system into a legal science must correspond to an almost revolutionary change in the conceptual structure of the Roman lawyers. There can be little question that such a change took place and resulted from the impact of Greek philosophy.[59]

---

[53] Pringsheim, The Unique Character of Classical Roman Law (1944). 34 Journal of Roman Studies 60. [54] *Ibid.*

[55] Lawson, A Common Lawyer Looks at the Civil Law (1955), p. 67.

[56] Wolff, Roman Law (1951), p. 91.

[57] Schulz, Principles of Roman Law (1936), p. 35.

[58] Quoted in *op. cit., ibid.*, p. 36.

[59] Northrop, The Comparative Philosophy of Comparative Law, *op. cit.*, footnote 8, pp. 643-657; Schultz, History of Roman Law (1946), pp. 60-98.

In order to understand the relationship between Roman law and Greek philosophy we must first ascertain in what ways the philosophy of Greece was different from that of other cultures. The unique aspects of Greek philosophy were its mathematics, logic and science. Just as all archaic law can be taken as a single unit when contrasted with the magnitude of Roman classical law, so can all archaic mathematics and science, including Babylonian, Egyptian and Chinese, be contrasted with the magnitude of the mathematics and science of Greece.[60] Pre-Greek mathematics consisted of "a collection of empirical conclusions".[61] The great genius of the Greeks was to convert mathematics "from an empirical science into a deductive system of thought . . .".[62] They "eliminated the physical substance from mathematical concepts and left mere husks".[63] This is equivalent to saying that they eliminated the naive realistic conception of scientific objects as directly sensed material substances.

Another great contribution of the Greeks was that "They realized that mathematical constructs could be used symbolically for a rational description of both celestial and terrestial phenomena", thus establishing the science of mathematical physics.[64] Through the creation of a limited number of logical constructs they were able to deal with a maximum amount of empirical phenomena.[65] The development of Greek mathematics and science corresponded with a basic change in their conceptual structure. The Greek philosophers discovered that naive realism is a false epistemological theory in that sensed experience is subjective and illusory, as empirically known properties exist only in the mind and are not qualities of the object. They therefore concluded that reality existed in the world of ideas, particularly mathematics, the concepts of which can be the same for everyone.[66] Professor Northrop uses the term logical realism for the epistemological theory basic to Greek philosophy, that some knowledge can be created by the intellect and can be the same for everyone.[67]

[60] Kline, Mathematics in Western Culture (1954), pp. 24-39; Sambursky, Structural and Dynamic Elements in the Greek Conception of Physical Reality, in Northrop and Livingston, *op. cit.*, footnote 6, p. 237; Harris, Science, Mind and Method (1960), vol. 1; Hutten, The Origins of Science (1962), pp. 14-20, 126-127; Einstein, The World As I See It (1934), p. 31.

[61] Kline, *op. cit.*, *ibid.*, p. 24. [62] *Ibid.*, p. 30. [63] *Ibid.*, p. 31.

[64] Sambursky, *op. cit.*, footnote 60, p. 243.

[65] Sambursky, The Physical World of the Greeks (1962), p. 21.

[66] Sambursky, *op. cit.*, footnote 60, pp. 237-253; Hull, History and Philosophy of Science (1959), pp. 21-22.

[67] Northrop, Philosophical Anthropology and Practical Politics (1960), pp. 31-32.

One of the principal channels through which the influence of Greek philosophy reached the Roman lawyers was Stoicism.[68] Classical Roman law was the creation of a small group of jurisconsults, a good many of whom were Stoics. The most influential of this group was probably Q. Mucius Scaevola, who wrote a classic treatise of the law, remaining today only in a few scattered fragments.[69] It has generally been assumed that the creation of classical Roman law was the result of the introduction of the dialectical method of organizing a body of knowledge into a scientific system by dividing it into general and species and then ascertaining the principles "governing the kinds and explaining the individual cases".[70] Although the Stoics used the dialectical method, this explanation alone cannot account for the unique aspects of Roman legal science. The Stoics recognized three kinds of concepts; empirical concepts, notions or systematized empirical concepts, and universal notions which are notions not derived from experience.[71] The notion concepts would furnish the conceptual framework for the organization of empirical concepts into classes. For this a class logic is sufficient. Legal constructs, however, belong to the third Stoic category of universal notions, which require a propositional logic in order to organize an area of knowledge into a science.

Professor F. S. C. Northrop has clarified the close relationship between Stoic philosophy and Roman law.[72] In particular he has pointed out that the adoption of the concept of the variable is essential not only to Greek, but to all modern mathematics and physics, and has been one of the most important points of contact between Greek science and Roman law. The concepts of these sciences according to Professor Northrop derive their realistic meaning (that is the meaning which is the same for everyone), "Syntactically by way of the imageless logically formulated relations in which they function as entity variables or terms".[73] From this it follows that logical relations are analytic and tautological, "since the entity term or variables mean only what the relational

[68] Maine, *op. cit.*, footnote 21, pp. 45-46; Arnold, Roman Stoicism (1958), p. 384.

[69] Schulz, Roman Legal Science (1946), p. 41.

[70] *Ibid.*, p. 62.

[71] Christensen, An Essay on the Unity of Stoic Philosophy (1962), p. 57.

[72] Northrop, The Comparative Philosophy of Comparative Law, *op. cit.*, footnote 8 and The Complexity of Legal and Ethical Experience, *op. cit.*, footnote 8, pp. 216-229.

[73] Northrop, The Epistemology of Legal Judgments (1964), 58 Northwestern U.L. Rev. 732, at p. 745.

syntax formally specifies them to mean".[74] Many legal constructs get their meaning in a similar manner. Much of the confusion in jurisprudence surrounding the concept of the legal person can be dispelled, once it is realized that a legal person is a variable which gets its meaning from the sets of legal relations in which it is found.[75] The difference between different kinds of legal persons is based upon the legal relations in which they are an "x" or variable. Thus a corporation as a legal person has the meaning given it by the sets of legal relations specified by the rules of company law. A trustee is the legal person or "x" in the set of legal relations we call a trust.

Although the constructs of law differ in a number of ways from those of mathematics and physics, they have certain basic characteristics in common. They are both relational concepts. These relations are theoretical and hypothetical rather than material or empirical. This means that they can only be grasped "by speculative means". The entities of both kinds of relations are variables which get at least part of their meaning from the relations in which they are found. The variables of both kinds of constructs are either particularly or universally quantified. A particularly quantified variable is one where the relation holds for only some values of the variable, while a universally quantified variable is one where the particular relation holds for any value of the variable.[76] Those legal relations which have at least one variable universally quantified, are rights or duties *in rem*. Those having all particularly quantified variables are *in personam*.[77] In both cases the concepts cannot be deduced nor extracted from experience but are "free inventions of the human intellect".[78] The statement of Einstein that, "Experience may suggest appropriate mathematical concepts, but they most certainly cannot be deduced from it", applies equally to legal constructs.[79] Neither does either kind of construct directly give us any factual information. Again as stated by Einstein: "Pure logical thinking cannot yield us any knowledge of the empirical world; all knowledge of reality starts from experience and ends in it. Propositions arrived at by purely logical means are completely

[74] *Ibid.*

[75] Derham, Theories of Legal Personality, in Webb, Legal Personality and Political Pluralism (1958), p. 1, at p. 5; Lawson, The Creative Use of Legal Concepts (1957), 32 N.Y.U.L. Rev. 909, at p. 915.

[76] Langer, An Introduction to Symbolic Logic (2nd ed., 1953), pp. 93-97.

[77] Smith, *op. cit.*, footnote 24, pp. 274-275.

[78] Einstein, *op. cit.*, footnote 60, p. 33.

[79] *Ibid.*, p. 36.

empty as regards reality".[80] In the case of both science and law, theoretical constructs are used to deal with vast quantities of empirical phenomenon with a limited amount of concepts and principles.

One essential difference, however, between these two types of relations is that of the relationship between the variables and sensed experience. The validity of any mathematical construct depends on its conformity to nature when its variables are given specific content. There is generally little freedom of choice as to which set of mathematical relations may be epistemically correlated with particular empirical phenomenon. The validity of any legal construct in relation to the world of facts depends on its utility. Legal constructs can be created without any regard for conformity to the physical world. There is often a choice as to which construct is correlated with a particular set of facts. A judge may be free to classify a particular commercial transaction relating to real estate as either a lease or a license. A group of business men may freely decide whether to organize their commercial enterprise as a corporation or a partnership. The correctness of the choice depends upon how well the goals and policies of the community and the individuals concerned are achieved. In science, logical constructs are sought which conform with nature. In law, nature, through the legal process, is made to conform to the patterns specified in the content of the constructs. Einstein defined science as, "an attempt to make the chaotic diversity of our sense impressions correspond to a logically uniform system of thought".[81] Law might be conceived as an attempt to systematize the chaotic diversity of our social behaviour.

Whether the introduction of constructs into Roman law was intentional or unconscious is a matter of conjecture. It is the thesis of Professor F. S. C. Northrop that this was a conscious process. That Stoic ethics and physics were accepted by the majority of the educated people of the ancient world of this period is a matter of historical fact.[82] As the ancient world did not draw between science and conduct the sharp distinction introduced through Christianity and as the Stoics claimed to derive their ethics from their physics,[83] it is unreasonable to believe that the Stoic lawyers who created classical Roman law did not, to some extent, relate

[80] *Ibid.*, p. 32.
[81] Hutten, The Language of Modern Physics (1956), p. 29.
[82] Barker, From Alexander to Constantine (1956), p. 20.
[83] Hutten, *op. cit.*, footnote 60, p. 33.

their ethics and physics to their legal theory.[84] The development of a vast commercial empire encompassing a wide variety of cultures and legal systems created a need for a new jurisprudence. The highly educated and dedicated jurisconsults furnished a competent body of legal scholars who could carry out such a task, and Stoic mathematics, physics, and logic furnished an ideal conceptual structure whereby a vast diversity of situations could be dealt with by use of a minimum number of concepts.[85]

It must be noted in passing that while Roman law developed into a science filled with theoretical constructs, Greek law remained a relatively primitive system never fully developing the concept of ownership or *dominium* nor a law of contract in the sense that executory promises would be enforced. It is not difficult to account for this difference, however.[86] Classical Roman law was developed by a group of wealthy learned legal experts who practised law as a public service rather than for a fee.[87] The Greeks, on the other hand, distrusted the legal expert. Legal questions were argued in common sense terms often by the litigants themselves and were decided by large juries of citizens rather than legally trained judges. Consequently there developed not a true legal profession but instead a profession of orators trained in forensic rhetoric rather than law, who appealed to the emotions and sympathies of the jurors and avoided scientific terminology or technical analysis.[88]

III

The development of legal constructs in the English common law was primarily due to the influence of Roman law.[89] During the twelfth and thirteenth centuries an important revival of Roman law took place in Northern Italy which was marked by the found-

---

[84] Christensen, *op. cit.*, footnote 71, p. 62.

[85] Sambursky, The Physics of the Stoics (1959); Mates, Stoic Logic (1961).

[86] Jones, *op. cit.*, footnote 17, pp. 151, 217.

[87] Schulz, *op. cit.*, footnote 69, pp. 40-59; Wolff, *op. cit.*, footnote 56, p. 96.

[88] Calhoun, Introduction to Greek Legal Science (1944), p. 47; Bonner, Lawyers and Litigants in Ancient Athens (1927), pp. v, 1; Vinogradoff, Historical Jurisprudence, vol. 2 (1922), pp. 11-12; Jones, *op. cit.*, footnote 17, p. 293.

[89] See generally: Sherman, Roman Law in the Modern World (1937), vol. 1; Vinogradoff, Roman Law in Medieval Europe (3rd ed., 1961), pp. 97-118; Scrutton, The Influence of the Roman Law on the Law of England (1885); Holdsworth, A History of English Law (4th ed., 1936), vol. 2, pp. 133-149, 176-178, 202-206; Pollock and Maitland, *op. cit.*, footnote 25; Spence, The Equitable Jurisdiction of the Courts of Chancery, vols I (1846), and II (1849).

ing of a number of universities, the first and most important at Bologna. Pollock and Maitland, in describing this period state:[90]

> From every corner of Western Europe students flocked to Italy. It was as if a new gospel had been revealed. Before the end of the century complaints were loud that theology was neglected, that the liberal arts were despised, that Seius and Titius had driven Aristotle and Plato from the schools, that men would learn law and nothing but law.

William the Conqueror brought Lanfranc, who had been a famous lawyer and taught law at the law school of Pavia, to England and made him Archbishop of Canterbury, in which position there is little doubt that he exercised a definite influence upon English law. From the school of Bologna, the Lombard jurist Vacarius was brought by Archbishop Theobald and his clerk, Thomas Becket, who had himself studied law there. Vacarius was appointed professor at Oxford and was "the first teacher and the real founder of the study both of the civil and of the canon law", in England.[91] In the thirteenth century Roman law was introduced into Cambridge, and both Cambridge and Oxford taught only Roman law down to the seventeenth century. This subject next to theology was the most important study at these two universities. At the same time that the civil law was entering England through such men as Vacarius, Roman law also was brought to England through the medium of Canon law.[92] Mention need only be made of some of the important chancellors and advisors such as Guala Bicchieri, Ricardus Anglicus, William of Drogheda, who taught Roman law at Oxford, Henry of Susa, and Franciscus Accursii, all of whom were ecclesiastics, to show that the effects of Canon law were not limited to ecclesiastical matters.

In regard to the strict common law itself in contrast to Equity, Admiralty and the Ecclesiastical Courts, there can be no question but that the most important channel of Roman law was through Bracton. Bracton's most important work was his *Tractus De Legibus Et Consuetudinibus Anglicanis*, which was a *summa* similar to those of the Bolognese. Like Justinian's *Institutes*, the work is divided into three parts, the law of persons, the law of things, and the law of actions and obligations; although eight times longer than the *Institutes*, the work was still uncompleted. This book was the first scientific exposition of English law and no

[90] Pollock and Maitland, *op. cit.*, footnote 25, p. 111.

[91] Holdsworth, *op. cit.*, footnote 89, p. 147.

[92] See generally: Pollock and Maitland, *op. cit.*, footnote 25, pp. 11-135; Holdsworth, *op. cit.*, *ibid.*, pp. 137-142; Sherman, *op. cit.*, footnote 89, pp. 217-222.

English jurist again attempted such a mammoth task until Sir Edward Coke. As to the amount of Roman law in Bracton's momentous work, the authorities are in conflict.[93] Opinions have ranged from that of Sir Henry Maine who considered the borrowing to be extensive, to that of Professor Maitland who suggests that the Roman influence was not very great. The better view appears to be that Bracton used "Roman terms, Roman maxims, and Roman doctrines to construct upon native foundations a reasonable system . . .".[94] To rephrase, what Bracton did was to introduce the legal constructs of Roman law into the common law, and reinterpret it in these new terms.

The principal source of Bracton's Roman law was the *Summa Institutionum* of Azo, one of the greatest teachers produced by the University of Bologna.[95] Güterbock states, "Throughout nearly the whole of Bracton's book, we can distinctly trace the scientific influence of Azo's views and doctrines, especially in the definitions and divisions of legal notions and conceptions, which are generally clothed in Azo's words".[96] Bracton, however, did not rely upon Azo alone, but also went directly to Justinian's *Institutes*. For the next hundred years the English lawyers "were steeped in Bracton", but during the fourteenth and fifteenth centuries his influence began to wane, only to revive again to achieve its greatest influence during the sixteenth and seventeenth centuries.[97]

The influence of Roman law during the twelfth to the fourteenth centuries is summarized by Professor Sherman as follows:[98]

> From the coming of Vacarius to Oxford in the middle of the 12th century to the end of the reign of Edward I over 150 years later, the influence of Roman law on the formation of English law was go great that this whole period should be styled the "Roman epoch of English legal history". During this period, and even as late as the reign of Edward II in the first quarter of the 14th century, Roman law authorities "were habitually cited in the Common Law courts, and relied upon

---

[93] For this problem, see generally: Güterbock, Bracton and his Relation to the Roman Law (1866); Maitland (ed.), Select Passages from the Works of Bracton and Azo, Selden Society, vol. 8 (1895); Richardson, Bracton (1965); Plucknett, Early English Legal Literature (1958), pp. 42-79; Kantorowicz, Bractonian Problems (1941); Vinogradoff, *op. cit.*, footnote 89, pp. 101-118; Woodbine, The Roman Element in Bracton's De Adquirendo Rerum Dominio (1921-22), 31 Yale L.J. 827; Holdsworth, *op. cit.*, footnote 89, pp. 267-286; Maine, *op. cit.*, footnote 21, pp. 67-68.

[94] Holdsworth, *op. cit.*, footnote 89, p. 286.

[95] Maitland, *op. cit.*, footnote 21.

[96] Güterbock, *op. cit.*, footnote 93, p. 52.

[97] Holdsworth, *op. cit.*, footnote 89, p. 288.

[98] Sherman, *op. cit.*, footnote 89, p. 360.

> by legal writers, not as illustrative and secondary testimonies as at present, but as primary and as practically conclusive".

All through this period there was, however, a prejudice against Roman public law because of its absolutism. This, along with opposition towards the pretensions of the Popes and Holy Roman Emperors, eventually resulted in the development of a hostility towards Roman private law. Up to the reign of Edward I, the king's judges were mostly ecclesiastics well trained in canon and Roman law, but after his reign the ecclesiastics lost control over the common law courts and only laymen were appointed to the bench. It was also in this period that the English legal profession took a definite shape. Legal education of the common law lawyer was centered in the Inns of Court and not at Oxford or Cambridge, and thus both judges and the legal profession lost direct contact with Roman law. The common law, however, although containing much Roman law, cut off from direct borrowing, became rigid and insufficient to meet the needs of the English nation, thus necessitating the development of Equity and the jurisdiction of the Chancellor. In the form of Equity, Roman law again became an important factor in the development of the English legal system. From the time of the Norman Conquest to the reign of Henry VIII, the Chancellors were invariably high church dignatories, all trained in the civil and Canon law, who borrowed freely from Roman law in developing the principles known as "equity". Professor Sherman even goes as far as describing the conflict between the common law and equity as "a contest between feudal customary law of Germanic origin and the Roman law—the latter, however, disguised under the name of Equity".[99] During the sixteenth century a second revival of Roman law took place in England, fostered by Henry VIII who endowed a Regius professorship of civil law at both Oxford and Cambridge, and brought the renowned jurist and teacher Vives to Oxford. At this time, Courts of Equity, Admiralty, the Military Courts, the University Courts and the Ecclesiastical Courts were all basically relying on Roman law. The practitioners before these tribunals organized themselves into "The Doctor's Commons", an organization which lasted until 1858. When the conflict between equity and the common law finally came to a head during the reign of James I, it was equity which prevailed and became the supreme branch of the law. Thus we see that throughout the entire history of the development of the English legal system there was a con-

[99] *Ibid.*, p. 363.

tinual borrowing from Roman law, sometimes directly and sometimes indirectly. The reason that the common law was able to withstand the onslaught of Roman law was probably because it had adopted the technique of using constructs, thus enabling it to deal with the increasing complexity of society.

Although Bracton probably fully realized that the legal constructs which had been introduced into English law through Roman law, Continental feudalism and Canon law, were not things but jural relations, their non-empirical nature appears to have been only gradually understood by the legal profession as a whole. Some of the most important of these incorporeal rights were the feudal services owed by the tenant to his lord. The lord was not conceived as the owner of these rights but was considered to be seised of the actual land, but seised in service rather than in demesne. If the tenant refused to perform his services, the lord did not bring an action for breach of contract, or debt, but an action of novel disseisin, the writ of which was the same as one brought for ejectment from land.[100] If lord A is entitled to the services of his tenant M, and lord X succeeds in obtaining these services from M, lord A will, to protect his rights, bring a proprietary action by writ of right against lord X. According to Pollock and Maitland:[101]

> We may find A demanding from X a manor, just as though it were a physical object like a field, and yet there may well be freehold tenants of this manor, and neither A nor X is asserting any right to disturb them; the suit passes over their heads. What is more, A will say that some ancestor of his was seised in demesne of this manor. He will not thereby mean that at the time of which he speaks there were no freeholders, and that his ancestor held every parcel of the land in demesne; he will mean that of this composite thing, the manor taken as a whole, his ancestor had an immediate seisin; he held the whole manor in demesne, though of some parcels of the land which are within the precincts of the manor he was seised in service. The country of palatine of Chester, nay for the matter of that, the kingdom of Scotland, can be demanded in a proprietary action, just as Blackacre can be demanded.

Another common incorporeal right of this period was the advowson which was "the right to present a clerk to the bishop for institution as parson of some vacant church".[102] The right was originally protected by a writ of right similar to that for recovering land. Later, the assise of darrein presentment was developed

[100] Pollock and Maitland, *op. cit.*, footnote 25, vol. 2, p. 126.
[101] *Ibid.*, pp. 127-128. [102] *Ibid.*, p. 136.

as a parallel to the assise of novel disseisin. If A was seised of an advowson and granted it to B, and the Church fell vacant, B would be entitled to present. If B, before a vacancy, granted the right to C, and then the parson died, neither B nor C could present the clerk but only A. C could not present because B, never having actually presented was not seised or in other words did not have possession of the advowson. Therefore he had nothing to give to C. On the other hand B could not present himself as whatever right he had, he had given it away. Only A was seised of the advowson so only he could present.[103]

The Roman theoretical concept of property developed in equity at a much earlier period than it did within the common law. This is evident from the conception of the "use" which divides the enjoyment of ownership from the legal title, and from the fact that seisin played a much smaller part in property law as administered by the Court of Chancery, as is illustrated by the fact that equitable interests could be conveyed merely by deed without any delivery or livery of seisin, and future interests were valid whether or not there were gaps in the seisin. Gradually, because of the influence of Bracton and equity, the concept of ownership of the common law lawyer changed from that of a sensed physical relationship between the owner and the thing owned, to right and duty relations between the owner and other people in the legal system. As this transition took place, the term "seisin" still was employed so that this term, depending upon the period when it was used, meant different things. By the time of the seventeenth century, when it was replaced by "ownership", it had become to mean something nearly like the conception of ownership rather than the sensed physical relation of possession. Therefore one must not expect to find a consistent meaning for this word in English property law.

On the basis of the above historical background we can usefully divide the evolution of the common law into three broad periods, the archaic or empirical, the transitional, and the conceptual period. English law during the archaic period is the Germanic customary law of the Anglo-Saxons. There were few if any constructs since their legal concepts were empirical by nature. The transitional period begins with the introduction of constructs from Roman law, and lasts until the time when jural relations were no longer confused with the actual things to which they relate.

[103] Maitland, *op. cit.*, footnote 30, p. 380.

The development of English law during this period was greatly affected by three classical treatises. The first was Bracton's *Tractus De Legibus Et Consuetudinibus Anglicanis*, which as indicated above, was one of the primary sources through which constructs were introduced into English law. The second was *Littleton's Tenures* which appeared sometime during the latter part of the fifteenth century and might be said to mark the middle of the transitional period. This classic, although a small treatise, was written by Sir Thomas Littleton, Judge of the Common Pleas, as a text to aid his son in his legal studies. The importance of this work lies in the fact that Littleton took the semi-feudal law of real property and organized it into a systematic conceptual framework, thus laying the foundation for the intricate theoretical structure into which the English law of real property later developed.

The third of these important works, Sir Edward Coke's *The First Institute of the Laws of England* commonly known as *Coke Upon Littleton*, appeared towards the end of the transitional period. Coke used each section of *Littleton* as a basis for commentary which not only brought Littleton's work up to date but distilled into a single treatise the tremendous mass of legal material which had accumulated up to this time. Throughout this work, Coke relied heavily on Bracton, not only as a historical source, but to modernize the existing law, thus completing the last step of the integration into the English system of the concepts introduced by Bracton. Coke's writings played an important role in the modification of the law of real property to fit the newly emerging social order which was replacing feudalism.

The conceptual period was one of great growth for the common law, particularly in the field of real property. Through the adoption of various techniques of dividing the legal relations constituting ownership of real property, groups of constructs such as estates, trusts, and easements and so on were developed which were superior in regards both utility and logical structure to those of either classical Roman or the civil law.[104] English property law gradually was transformed into almost a science which was so mathematical in its precision that it has often been compared to calculus.[105]

The similarities between the common law of this period and classical Roman law have often been noted. Both systems were

---

[104] Lawson, *op. cit.*, footnote 52, pp. 89-91; Buckland and McNair, Roman Law and Common Law (2nd ed., 1952), p. 21.

[105] See *ops cit.*, footnote 52.

created by practical lawyers who resisted the legislative creation of law except where absolutely necessary. Both systems equally resisted codification in order to prevent the law from becoming rigid and obsolete. (Codification however did enter Roman law in the post-classical or Byzantine period, as the result of Greek influence.) Although the law of both systems was filled with constructs, they kept some relationship to the practical needs of society through being built up in terms of specific concrete cases or situations. These similarities, due in part to the adoption by the common law of the constructual techniques of Roman law, also result from the development in each system of a similar type of jurist. The Stoic lawyers or jurisconsults who created classical Roman law were members of the aristocracy, often holding high governmental offices, who devoted themselves to the study and practice of law as a public service.[106] They seldom argued in court, but engaged instead in giving judicial opinion in regards to specific cases, in drafting documents such as wills, contracts and formula, in advising public officials concerning the law, and in drafting edicts.

English real property law also in a great part was built up by a small group of scholastic lawyers, principally Roman Catholics, who, because of their religion, were unable to practise before the bar and therefore became pure conveyancers, spending most of their time preparing complicated property settlements where, by the use of theoretical constructs, the creation and movement of legal relations could be predicted and controlled far into the future.[107] Contrary to the usual practice of the common law, the writings of these men have often been cited by the courts as authoritative statements of the law.[108]

Conclusion

A comparison of primitive and archaic with classical Roman and modern Western law shows that the latter has constructs and the former does not. It shows further that the concepts of the former are empirical in nature while many of the concepts in the latter do not get their entire meaning in terms of sensed experience. The

[106] See *ops cit.*, footnote 87.

[107] Pollock, Holdsworth's History of English Law by W. S. Holdsworth, vols 7 and 8, [1926] J. of S.P.T.L. 37, at p. 38; Lawson, *op. cit.*, footnote 55, p. 69; Holdsworth, History of the English Law (2nd ed., 1937), vol. 7, pp. 384-387.

[108] For a list of cases showing the importance placed on the view of conveyancers by the courts see Norton, A Treatise on Deeds (2nd ed., 1928), p. 77.

implications which can be drawn from this comparison are two-fold. Firstly, primitive and archaic law is distorted when interpreted and reported in terms of the technical constructs of modern Western law, and secondly, attempts to clarify the meaning of the legal constructs of modern Western law by reducing them to empirical terms only, will, in turn, distort their nature. Professor F. S. C. Northrop has presented highly persuasive arguments for the thesis that legal constructs developed in Roman law, partially as the result of the contact of the Stoic Roman lawyers with the constructs of Greek mathematical science.[109] A comparison of these two kinds of constructs shows certain fundamental similarities. The techniques of establishing the meaning of the constructs of science, therefore, because of these similarities, should prove of some value for the analysis of the meaning of legal constructs.

The following concepts in particular are important in this regard: the variable, the propositional function, the incomplete symbol, the functional definition, epistemic correlation, the operational definition, and the distinction between analytic and semantic sentences.

A propositional function is any expression having the form of a proposition but the values or entities of which are variables which must be filled with specific content in order to give a proposition.[110] All scientific formula are propositional functions. Legal constructs such as fee-simples, easements, contracts, and so on, are collections or "bundles" of right-duty relations. Each right-duty relation is in effect, a propositional function. It is equivalent to the expression, "Y is legally obligated to X to perform pattern of behaviour Z". We do not get a complete proposition until the variables X and Y are filled with the content of specific persons and Z with a particular pattern of behaviour. By filling in the variables in this manner we can get a complete proposition such as "Henry Green is legally obligated to paint John Smith's fence".

Russell has defined incomplete symbols as those which, "have no significance in isolation, but only contribute to the significance of whole sentences".[111] A complete symbol, on the other hand, is one which has significance when standing by itself. Complete symbols generally "point" or stand for. Thus the word tree is a com-

---

[109] See *ops cit.*, footnote 72.

[110] Whitehead and Russell, Principia Mathematica (1962), pp. 38-41; Russell, The Principles of Mathematics (1903), pp. 82-88; Langer, *op. cit.*, footnote 76, pp. 90-97; Basson and Smiley, Propositional Functions (1960), 34 The Aristotelian Society 25.

[111] Russell, Portraits from Memory (1956), p. 43; Whitehead and Russell, *op. cit.*, *ibid.*, p. 66.

plete symbol in that it stands for a particular kind of plant known empirically. Incomplete symbols have no referent in sensed experience. Professor Northrop in America and H. L. A. Hart in England, have both demonstrated that legal constructs do not stand for a thing or event in sensed experience, but are incomplete symbols which gain significance when placed in a verbal contextual framework.[112]

Functional definition is a means whereby a variable can be given meaning by defining it in terms of the logical properties of the relations in which it functions as an entity.[113] Thus, a legal person may be defined as the entity variable in legal relations.[114] Constructs such as trustees, corporations, mortgagors and so on are all definable in terms of the bundle of legal relations in which they are an entity.

The fact that such terms as right, duty, contract, corporation, and so on do not refer directly to any object known through sensed experience does not mean that such concepts are unrelated to empirical phenomena. The relationship between the theoretical aspect of scientific knowledge and the facts of sensed experience are what Professor Northrop has called "epistemic correlations", and Professor Margenau has called "rules of correspondence".[115] According to Professor Northrop, "an epistemic correlation joins a thing known in the one way to what is in some sense that same thing known in a different way".[116] Thus an epistemic correlation joins a thing known theoretically, "to what is in some sense that same thing", as known empirically. The relationship, for example, between a fee simple and a particular piece of land would be that of epistemic correlation. Both the bundle of legal relations known as a fee simple and the land itself are referred to as property, but each is property as known in a different manner. The so-called "rules" of law which are derived from the cases are rules of epistemic correlation. The legal principle that certain types of mutual exchanges of promises gives rise to contractual obligation is an example of a rule of epistemic correlation or a rule of correspon-

---

[112] Northrop, The Complexity of Legal and Ethical Experience, *op. cit.*, footnote 8, pp. 21-23; Hart, Definition and Theory in Jurisprudence (1953).

[113] Northrop, *op. cit.*, footnote 7, pp. 77-82 and The Comparative Philosophy of Comparative Law, *op. cit.*, footnote 8, pp. 649-652; Russell, *op. cit.*, footnote 110, pp. 26-32.

[114] See *ops cit.*, footnote 75.

[115] Northrop, The Logic of the Sciences and the Humanities (1959), pp. 119-132; Margenau, The Nature of Physical Reality (1950), pp. 60-68.

[116] Northrop, *op. cit.*, *ibid.*, p. 119.

dence in that it specifies that this particular kind of fact situation will be conceptually related to the legal construct "contract".

In science, the validity of any mathematical construct in relation to empirical phenomena is tested by the operations of experimentation. Consequently it is possible to define the concepts of science in terms of the operations by which they are verified.[117] As long as one realizes that such definitions give only a part of the meaning of a scientific concept, then they may be useful. Definitions of legal constructs in terms of the operations of courts are a type of operational definition. The American Legal Realists, in particular, have been advocates of this method of definition.[118] As in science, such definitions are useful if one does not make the mistake of assuming that they exhaust the entire meaning of legal constructs. Through the use of operational definitions, a proper balance may be maintained between legal doctrine and the functions of the courts or what Professors McDougal and Lasswell term "perspectives and operations".[119] As well, such definitions make statements such as, "There *exists* a legal system", or "John Doe *has* a right" and so on, meaningful.

Declarative sentences are used in but two ways, either to refer to symbols, or to experience.[120] Sentences which express a relationship between symbols are termed analytic, and sentences which refer to experience are semantic.[121] A theory of physics consists of at least two parts, a formal calculus and its interpretation in terms of experience.[122] The propositions of the calculus are analytic in that they express relationships between the symbols; the propositions of the empirical interpretation are semantic in that they are declarative of the world of sensed experience.[123] Propositions in most areas of the law can be divided into two kinds. Those which express the legal doctrine, and those relating the doctrine to the world of fact. The legal doctrine is usually composed of a number of primitive constructs and concepts in terms of which more complex constructs and concepts are given meaning. Such

---

[117] Bridgman, The Logic of Modern Physics (1927), p. 5; and Reflections of a Physicist (1950), p. 15; Pap, Philosophy of Science (1962), pp. 39-57.

[118] For instance, see Cohen, The Legal Conscience (1960), pp. 33-94.

[119] Professors Lasswell and McDougal in unpublished material prepared for their course, Law, Science, and Policy, at the Yale Law School, point out that law may be defined in terms of perspectives or operations or both, and recommend that a balance of emphasis on both be maintained.

[120] Hutten, *op. cit.*, footnote 80, p. 37.

[121] *Ibid.*, pp. 36-37. [122] *Ibid.*, p. 36. [123] *Ibid.*, pp. 36-50.

relationships will be expressed by analytic sentences.[124] Semantic sentences are used to relate constructs to the world of fact. Thus, for example, the statement, "The word 'interest' is used in this Restatement both generically to include varying aggregates of rights, privileges, powers and immunities and distributively to mean any one of them", is analytic.[125] The statement, "So if a zoning ordinance were passed, the totality of interests would be affected, to the extent of the ordinance, for persons owning land within the district to which the ordinance applied", is semantic.[126]

For an adequate theory of the meaning of legal constructs, analysis should be carried out at at least three levels.[127] Adopting the terminology of Charles Morris' semiotics, these are the syntactic, semantic, and pragmatic.[128] At the syntactic level the relationship between the various key signs or words would be established and clarified. This would involve the study of legal propositions as analytic sentences or sentences having an analytic usage. At this level constructs would be studied as propositional functions and incomplete symbols, and the method of functional definition would be used to give legal entities meaning. Clarification of the relationships between these signs and the empirically known world of fact would be the goal of analysis at the semantic level. Legal propositions would be studied as semantic sentences or sentences having a semantic usage. Constructs would be given operational definitions. Analysis of the epistemic correlations or rules of correspondence would relate the syntactic with the semantic level. At the pragmatic level of analysis the relationship of signs to human behaviour would be clarified. This would include a study of the processes by which legal symbols are used to control human behaviour, and evaluation of the effectiveness of their use in implementing community policy and individual goals. This kind of analysis has been the major concern of the policy oriented jurisprudence of Professors Lasswell and McDougal. Traditional theories of jurisprudence have generally concentrated analysis at either the syntactic or semantic level. An adequate jurisprudential theory, however, must contain within it an adequate theory of the language of law. An adequate theory of legal language must, as a minimum, provide a framework for analysis at these three levels.

---

124 Lasswell and McDougal, Legal Education and Public Policy: Professional Training in the Public Interest, in McDougal and Associates, Studies in World Public Order (1960), p. 42, at pp. 121-123.

125 Restatement, Property (1936), s. 5.

126 *Ibid.*, s. 5, comment, p. 11.

127 See *op. cit.*, footnote 124.

128 Morris, Signs, Language and Behaviour (1946).

[2]

Gaius Noster: Substructures of Western Social Thought

DONALD R. KELLEY

"tu regere imperio populos, Romane, memento . . ."[1]

GAIUS, THE MOST INFLUENTIAL OF CLASSICAL JURISTS, is apparently a modern discovery. The dramatic story of his resurrection has often been told. In 1816 the historian Barthold Georg Niebuhr came across a manuscript in Verona, a text from Saint Jerome written over a much earlier work. He reported this palimpsest (at some points *ter scriptus*, a double palimpsest) to his friend Friedrich Karl von Savigny, the greatest legal scholar of the age and the emerging leader of the so-called Historical School of Law. Savigny immediately recognized it as the work of the second-century jurist Gaius, otherwise preserved only in fragmentary form in that great sixth-century anthology, the *Digest* of Justinian. "Let us hope that we can decipher more of Gaius in these pages," he wrote to Niebuhr. (So it fortunately turned out, for over eleven-twelfths of the *Institutes of Civil Law* were recovered with the help of this manuscript.) "This will surely give new life to our jurist," Savigny predicted.[2] This book, the only nearly complete pre-Justinianian text, has indeed had a profound impact upon Roman legal history and scholarship since its publication in 1820.

Yet in a deeper sense Gaius had never really been lost to view. Despite the elementary and defective form in which his work was transmitted, the structure of his *Institutes* can be traced in the thought of many generations not only of jurists but also of historians and of political and social philosophers. Whether consisting of notes by Gaius himself or by a student (the same sort of debate that has raged around the works of Aristotle), the book became more influential than those of more authoritative jurists like Ulpian and Pomponius (who, unlike Gaius, possessed the right to interpret the law, the *jus respondendi*). Distilling, simplifying, and organizing the resources of ancient legal

As so often before, I must express gratitude to friends and colleagues at the Institute for Advanced Study for sympathetic stimulation and, for material support, to the National Endowment for the Humanities.

[1] Vergil, *Aeneid*, 6. 851. Also see note 85, below.

[2] Savigny to Niebuhr, December 5, 1816, in A. Stoll, *Karl Friedrich von Savigny*, 2 (Berlin, 1929): no. 321. Also see Savigny to Eduard Schrader, July 16, 1817, in *ibid.*, no. 33: "Das muss ein neues Leben unter unseren Juristen geben!"

wisdom, Gaius became the mentor not only of Rome but also of Byzantium and Europe. He was "the true architect of Justinian's collection," his most recent commentator has told us;[3] he was the model for many later constructions as well, including national codes like the *Siete Partidas* and the *Code Napoléon*, legal treatises like Antoine Loisel's *Institutes of Customary Law*, Savigny's own *System of Modern Roman Law*, and a variety of more tangential philosophical ventures. Gaius' pedagogical role has been almost as various and substantial as that of Aristotle. To Justinian he was "Noster Gaius," and so he has remained for centuries to many others, including Savigny. He was, so to say, "our teacher."

"Gaianism" is not a conventional term, but in view of his role perhaps it should be. Many lesser authors—jurists as well as philosophers—have engendered eponymous "isms" with inferior claims, while Gaius formulated (if he did not create) one of the most distinctive and enduring systems of thought in Western history. It is not too much to say that Gaius established a dominant archetype of social thought, a more practical and human paradigm to rival the metaphysical structure of Aristotelianism.[4] Though by intent a method of teaching law, his book suggested an epistemology, a potentially "scientific" method and various guiding principles for the systematic study of society and culture. His work exhibits, it seems to me, the fundamental kinship between the old science of jurisprudence (*legitima*, *legalis*, or *civilis scientia*, as jurists liked to call it) and the modern science of society.

In recent times, however, the Gaian tradition has been virtually unappreciated, and most likely unperceived, by historians of philosophy and of culture in general. What is the reason for this? Why has such neglect fallen on Gaius' *Institutes* and not, for instance, on Cicero's relatively vacuous *De Legibus*? One answer is surely that the study of law, even in Savigny's time, has diverged from history, literature, philosophy, and other fields with which it formerly had so many vital connections. A more important answer, perhaps, is that the significance of Gaianism—even for those disciplines apparently closest to jurisprudence, such as political and social philosophy—cannot be perceived merely from the literal and legalistic surface of the text. To appreciate this significance we must try to grasp the underlying meaning of the text by deciphering another—a historical and conceptual sort of—palimpsest. Not in any sense, however, should this approach be tried through speculative interpretation or what textual critics used to call "divination." Rather, we should proceed by trying to assess some of the implications that have in fact been

[3] A. M. Honoré, *Gaius* (Oxford, 1962), 128. In general, see H. Wagner, *Studien zur allgemeinen Rechtslehre des Gaius* (Zutphen, 1978); and Pauly-Wissowa. RE 21, pt. 1 (1951): 286. The secondary (and tertiary) literature on Gaius and his text is enormous. The text, for example, is the subject of a periodical, *Gaius Studien*, begun in 1968, edited by R. G. Böhm, and published out of Freiburg. Here, as elsewhere, I will not attempt to provide bibliographical references on law and legal history, except as they bear upon relevant questions of social thought and, even then, only selectively in terms of the argument.

[4] For the standard study, see F. X. Affolter, *Das römische Institutionen-System* (Berlin, 1897). Also see Helmut Coing, *Juristische Methodenlehre* (Berlin, 1972); and H. Jolowicz, *Roman Foundations of Modern Law* (Oxford, 1957), 61–81. For the most recent survey with an excellent bibliography, see G. Fassò, *Storia della filosofia del diritto*, 3 vols. (Bologna, 1966–70).

drawn out, some of the transformations that historically have been attempted: the aim is not to read between the lines of Gaius but, instead, to survey the career of Gaianism. The subject of these remarks is not *ille* but *noster* Gaius.

Of the jurisconsult Gaius little is known, not even his full name, and his doctrinal background is not clear. When he began to teach and to assemble his book, there were already two schools of legal thought in Rome. One was the conservative and republican "Proclian," the other the imperial-minded "Sabinian." It may or may not be significant that Gaius belonged to the latter, more innovative group. Whatever its provenance, the power of Gaianism derives in general from three distinguishing features. The first is his basically historical approach, displayed most prominently in the fragment heading the famous second title of the *Digest*: "On the Origin of Law."[5] His historical orientation is, however, most concretely evident in the substance of the *Institutes*, which constitutes a kind of ordered cornucopia of Roman legal wisdom. The second is his dialectical method, which generated essential distinctions, divisions, and methods of interpretation. The last, and the most important, is the celebrated tripartite arrangement of social categories, a sequence of rubrics that entail not only moral priorities and a means of ordering reality but also a characteristic mode of perceiving and construing the world. What Gaianism suggests is not quite a doctrine (on the analogy, say, of Calvinism) but rather a methodological system (on the analogy of sixteenth-century "Ramism," which accommodated Calvinism, yet was distinct from it), a framework for a *Weltanschauung* encompassing natural as well as social experience.

Although never satisfactorily explained, the Gaian triad, set forth under the rubric *De juris divisione*, has fascinated scholars for centuries. Down to the present day it has enjoyed, if not self-evident rationality, at least extraordinary authority in some circles.[6] According to this anthropocentric, secular trinity, judicial and pedagogical cognizance had to be taken first of persons (*de personis*), second of things (*de rebus*), and last of actions (*de actionibus*): (1) "personality"—the *sine qua non*, so to speak—including degree of "liberty," kinship, citizenship, and other social relations;[7] (2) the "real" world, though for Gaius *res* could be intangible (*incorporales*) as well as tangible; and (3) the relations between and among subjects and objects—that is, "actions in a general sense, themselves divided reflexively into "personal" and "real" types. This presumably exhaustive classification represents, in effect, one enduring expression of the metaphysical foundations of social thought.

[5] *Digest*, 1. 2. 1: "*Gaius libro primo ad legem duodecim tabularum:* Facturus legum vetustarum interpretationem necessario prius ab urbis initiis repetendum existimavi. . . ."

[6] *Digest*, 1. 5. 3; and Gaius, *Institutiones*, 1. 8, in J. Baviera, ed., *Fontes Iuris Romani Antejustiniani* (Florence, 1940): "Omne autem ius quo utimur vel ad personas pertinet vel ad res vel ad actiones."

[7] In general, see Fritz Schulz, *Principles of Roman Law* (Oxford, 1936), 42, 140–63. And, in particular, see P. Duff, *Personality in Roman Private Law* (Cambridge, 1938); Paolo Zatti, *Persona giuridica e soggettività* (Padua, 1975); and Carlo Maiorca, *La Cosa in senso giuridico* (Turin, 1937). Also see Adolf Berger's standard *Encyclopaedic Dictionary of Roman Law* (Philadelphia, 1953).

This distinctive form makes it possible to isolate a Gaian tradition, even though Gaius himself had no claim to originality or profundity. For underneath the Gaian text there are still older formulations. In fact, Gaius was not the first systematizer of Roman legal science. This honor seems to belong to Quintus Mucius Scaevola, a first-century B.C. jurist who, according to Fritz Schulz, created "the first dialectical system of law in the grand manner." The Mucian scheme was quadripartite, resting upon the divisions of inheritance law, persons, things, and obligations; but it bore obvious affinities to that of Gaius. As late as the second century Scaevola's work was the subject of commentaries by Pomponius and by Gaius himself. Thereafter, it disappeared and was unknown to Justinian's editors. "Well may we complain of a fate which has preserved so utterly worthless a work as Cicero's *De Legibus*," Schulz has written with characteristic assertiveness, "but which has allowed the book which laid the foundations of not merely of Roman, but of European, jurisprudence to perish."[8] Paleographical fortune more than intellectual merit, then, leads us to celebrate a Gaian instead of a Mucian tradition, derivative and perhaps even degenerate as it might be in terms of Roman legal history.

What more fundamentally qualifies Gaian claims, of course, is the manifold indebtedness of Roman legal science in general to Greek philosophy and, more particularly, to Greek rhetoric. No one places much stock in the story (told by Pomponius and included in the *Digest*—paired, incidentally, with Gaius' celebration of history) about the visit of the *Decemviri* to Athens before the establishment of the law of the Twelve Tables, but the tale does nicely symbolize the cultural contribution of Greek thought. Although the channels of transmission are obscure, Platonic ideals, Aristotelian categories, sophistic *topoi*, and especially dialectical method constitute the original level, unfortunately illegible in detail, of the Gaian palimpsest. It was Greek conceptualization, especially the theory of interpretation so central to jurisprudence, that transformed the practice and teaching of Roman law into a Hellenistic "science" in the classical (as well as medieval and, before the present century, modern) sense of the term.[9]

More specific Greek influence can be detected at certain crucial points. Among the most important are the practice of making divisions (*divisio*, *differentia*, or, especially among medieval commentators, *distinctio*, corresponding to the Aristotelian διαίρεσις), the setting down of initial definitions (*definitio* or *regula*, corresponding to ὅροι or κανόνες), and a number of rhetorical topics, such as the contrast between the letter and the spirit, or meaning, of a statement (*verba* and *voluntas* or *ratio*). Indeed, many of the basic terms of civil law are simply translations from Greek terminology, such as the distinction between natural and civil law (*jus naturale* and *civile*, corresponding to

[8] Schulz, *History of Roman Legal Science* (Oxford, 1953), 94. Also see G. Scherillo, 'Il civilistico pre-Gaiano," in *Studi in onore di Vicenzo Arangio-Ruiz*, 3 (Naples, 1953): 445–67. On "abstraction," see Schulz, *Principles of Roman Law*, 53–65.

[9] Schulz, *History of Roman Legal Science*, 62–69. In general, see the monumental work of Erich Wolf, *Griechisches Rechtsdenken*, 6 vols. (Frankfurt, 1950–).

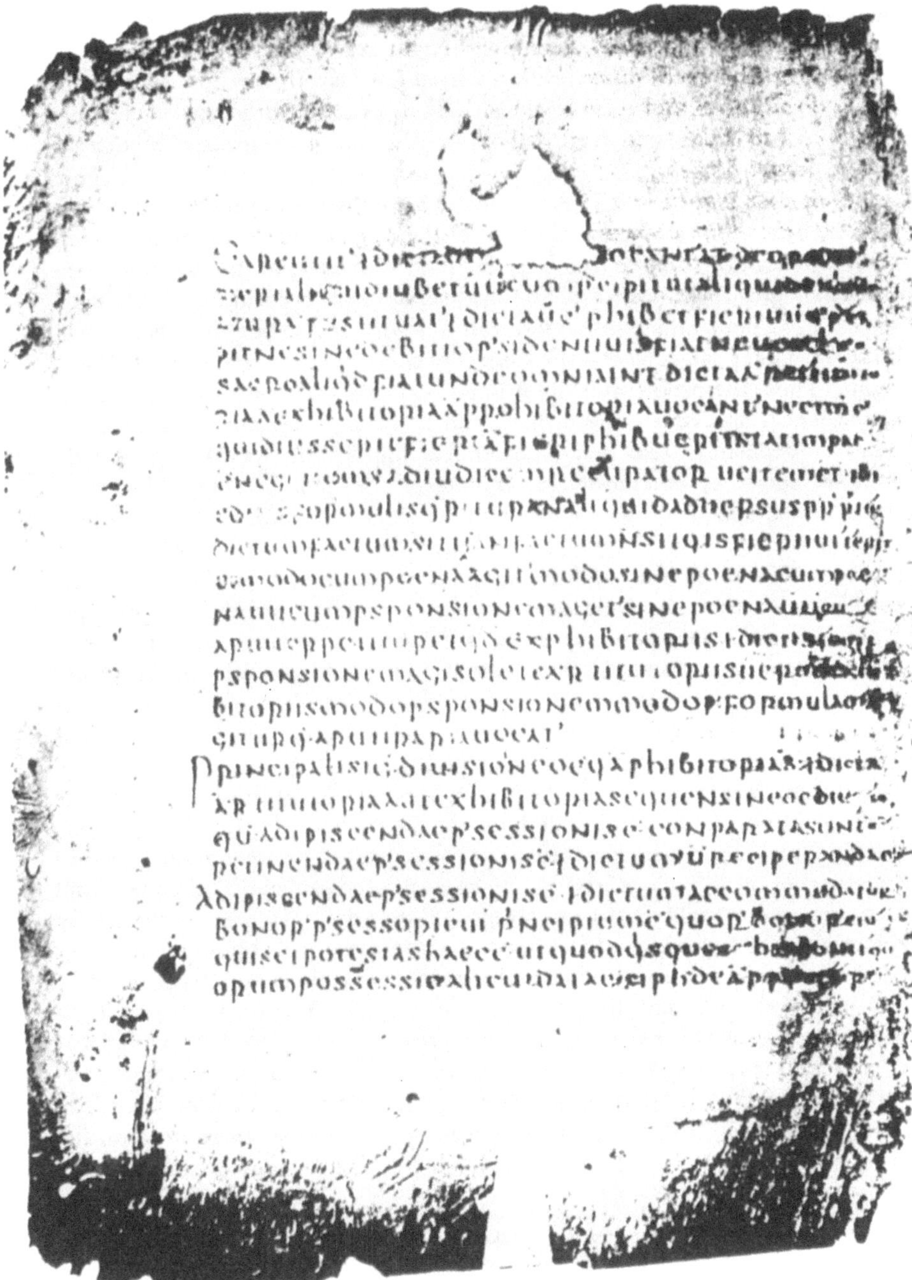

Gaius, *Institutionum*, 4. 139-44, f. singulare.

φύσει δίκαιον and *θέσει* or *νόμῳ δίκαιον*), between the law of nations and civil law (*jus gentium* and *civile*, corresponding to *κοινὸν δίκαιον* and *πολιτικόν δίκαιον*), and between written and unwritten law (*jus scriptum* and *non scriptum*, *νόμος γεγραμμένος* and *νόμος ἄγραφος*). So it was, too, with the idea of equity (*aequitas*, *ἐπιείκεια*) and the method of disputation (*disputatio in utramque partem*, *δισσοὶ λόγοι*).[10]

If Gaianism made use of Greek forms, it gave them a Latin dress and style. Indeed, behind the pedagogical intent of the *Institutes* there are philosophical implications that seem distinctively Roman. Consider, in the first place, the epistemological significance of the anthropocentric ordering of social categories. For Gaius understanding began not with cosmology, in other words, but with the human subject—the subject of consciousness, that is, as well as of rights. Thus, the problem of the human condition (*De condicione hominum* for Gaius, encompassed by the civilian rubric *De statu hominis*[11]) provided the point of departure, and the philosophical implication was a sort of rudimentary sociology of knowledge. Having established the subject, horizons could be expanded to include other individuals and natural objects, potentially possessions; and, finally, the social field could be completed with consideration of actions and interactions of various sorts. Secondly, and correlative to this, the Gaian system was aimed not merely at causal explanation—value-free science, so to speak—but also at human problems and the rendering of practical judgments. On these grounds jurisprudence was useful as well as theoretical, concerned with the life active as well as the life contemplative, and enabled jurists to argue for the superiority of their "science" and to identify it with "true philosophy."[12]

In a fundamental way, then, Gaianism was set apart from the naturalistic tradition of Greek philosophy. Perhaps the best way to clarify this is to recall the fundamental polarity that arose in Greek thought between nature (*φύσις*) and convention, or law (*νόμος*).[13] "By convention exist color and taste," said Democritus; "in reality there are atoms and the void." As later elaborated by rhetoricians, Roman as well as Greek, the opposition was by implication between the world of human will and behavior (of symbols and "civilization") and that of extra-human (objective or transcendent) reality. In the tradition of Roman law, of course, both concepts have their place: the first as a rational norm identified with natural law (*jus naturale*), the second as the human substance of civil law and that extra-Roman growth formulated as the law of nations (*jus gentium*). But the procedure was quite different. In contrast to the naturalistic or mathematical (especially Euclidean) strategy of starting with

[10] See H. Hübner, "Subjektivismus in der Entwicklung des Privatrechts," in *Festschrift für Max Kaser* (Munich, 1976), 5–42; and Giovanni Pugliese, " 'Res corporales,' 'res incorporales,' e il problema del diritto soggetivo," in *Studi in onore di Vicenzo Arangio-Ruiz*, 223–60. Also see the works cited in note 7, above.

[11] *Digest*, 1. 5; and Gaius, *Institutiones*, 1. 3.

[12] For this related subject, see my "Vera Philosophia: The Philosophical Significance of Renaissance Jurisprudence," *Journal of the History of Philosophy*, 14 (1976): 267–79, and the references cited therein.

[13] F. Heinemann, *Nomos und Physis* (Basel, 1945); and Wolf, *Griechisches Rechtsdenken*, *passim*. Also see C. A. Maschi, *La Coscienza naturalistica del diritto et degli istituti giuridici romani* (Milan, 1937); and F. Lanfranchi, *Il Diritto nei retori romani* (Milan, 1938).

general principles and reasoning from them, Gaianism gave prominence and priority to the human aspect, to what from the twelfth century onward would be termed "positive law,"[14] and then advanced, empirically in a sense, to higher degrees of rationality and universality.

What about the structural significance of Gaianism? Does the secular trinity of persons-things-actions reflect some religious or procedural convention? Does it have some logical or linguistic base? Or is it merely, as one modern expert has suggested, one more manifestation of a general Roman fixation on "trichotomy"?[15] Whatever the prehistorical source, the arrangement was repeated and elaborated in countless ways for many centuries down to the present day. It antedated, and became hardly less ingrained than, the Christian trinity; and, because of its function in liberal as well as legal education, it may have played a larger role in the history of thought than has generally been recognized. Almost seventeen centuries after Gaius the young Karl Marx complained about the trichotomizing (*trichotomisch*) method forced on him by Savigny and other of his teachers—but not before Marx composed a three-hundred-page treatise of private law based on the Gaian scheme.[16] And, though he abandoned both this scheme and the "idealism" associated with it, Marx went on, under Hegel's influence, to adopt another not dissimilar trichotomy likewise based on a dialectic of subject-object. In other ways, too, ghosts from the Roman past haunted Marx's mature works, but of course this discussion goes beyond the confines of the direct tradition of Gaianism.

After Gaius' death (a.d. 178 or later) his authority grew in legal as well as pedagogical terms, especially from 426 onward, when the law of citations named him as one of five jurists to be followed in the courts.[17] The worldwide appeal of his *Institutes* is suggested by various survivals outside Italy, such as the excerpts made for the *Breviarium* of Alaric and the sixth-century commentary made for the law school of Autun. At about the same time, Justinian remarked that Gaius' work was the only elementary textbook assigned to law students in the Byzantine schools, though by 533 it was already obsolete in some respects.[18] In fact, Justinian, or rather his editor Tribonian, preserved Gaius for posterity, until the nineteenth century at any rate, not only by citing him often (531 times to be exact) in the *Digest* but also by making his book the model for Justinian's own *Institutes*. In his preface the emperor revealed his philosophic intention of "bringing into bright harmony" (*in luculentam ereximus*

[14] Steven Kuttner has shown that "positive law" (*jus positivum*) comes from a misreading of "posited law" (*jus positum*); Kuttner, "Sur les origines du terme 'droit positif,' " *Revue historique du droit français et étranger*, 15 (1936): 728–30.

[15] H. Goudy, *Trichotomy in Roman Law* (Oxford, 1910); and Karl Friedrich von Savigny, *System des heutigen römischen Rechts*, 1 (Berlin, 1940): 322–26.

[16] Marx to Heinrich Marx, November 10–11, 1837, in *Marx-Engels Gesamtausgabe*, 1, pt. 1 (Berlin, 1927): 213–31; and see note 87, below.

[17] *Codex Theodosianus*, 1. 4. 3.

[18] "Deo auctore," Constitution prefacing the *Digest*

consonantiam) the confused mass of ancient jurisprudence and legislation, and, indeed, just at this point he made the famous proprietary claim that his manual was largely based on the work of "our Gaius" (*praecipue ex commentariis Gaii nostri. . .*).[19] Through this Byzantine vehicle and, secondarily, through the *Digest* the form and substance of Gaianism was transmitted to modern European culture.

The *Institutes* of Justinian began with the same premise as the *Institutes* of Gaius: "All of our law is related either to persons or to things or to actions." Justinian then explained the reason for that order—"it is of little purpose to know the law if we do not know the persons for whom the law was made."[20] Accordingly, Book I is a topical discussion of the title, "De personis," including analyses of the levels and limitations of personal liberty, especially in terms of paternal and marital power (the *patria potestas* of the father and the *potestas de manu* of husband and wife). Books II and III continued "De rebus" and were devoted to particular problems of possession and property, exchange and inheritance, except for those things designated as public, common to all, or unpossessable because of their ecclesiastical character (*res sacrae*). Finally, Book IV treated "De actionibus"—logically and interlockingly divided into personal and real things—and concluded with judicial procedure and criminal actions.

This Byzantine effort at remodeling differs in two fundamental respects from the Gaian original. One difference is the considerable emphasis placed upon public law, illustrated above all in the notorious, post-Gaian text from Ulpian, "What pleases the prince has the force of law" (*Quod principi placuit legis habet vigorem*).[21] This emphasis, of course, arose from Justinian's determination to exalt, if not to deify, his imperial authority above all previously recognized sources of law, including juristic responses (*responsa prudentum*); but it did not directly affect the social categories encompassed by private law. The other difference is that Justinian, drawing on later classical jurisprudence and rhetorical hyperbole, made larger philosophical claims for the science of law, even claiming for it the status of true wisdom (*divinarum ac humanarum notitia*, the equivalent of the Ciceronian formulation of *sapientia*). But his hyperbole only served to enhance the attractions of Gaianism.[22] There is no denying that from this point most of the words of the Roman legal canon are those of Justinian (or rather his paraphrase of many generations of jurists), but in many respects the assumptions and conceptual base continue to be those of "our Gaius." In any case, in this somewhat disguised form Gaianism was passed on to the West and preserved for the next phase of its posthumous career.

[19] "Imperatoriam maiestatem," Constitution prefacing the *Institutes*. And, in general, see L. Wenger, *Die Quellen des römischen Rechts* (Vienna, 1953), 600–37.

[20] *Institutes*, I. 2. 12. Also see Gaius, *Institutiones*, I. 8.

[21] *Institutes*, 7. 21. 6.

[22] *Digest*, I. I. I. The system of the *Digest*—and, indeed, that of the *Code*—has its own character and history; but it is closely related to, and in some ways dependent on, that of the *Institutes*, and it was much more severely criticized in later centuries. Because of its pedagogical and "methodical" purpose and because of its broader impact, the *Institutes* has been chosen for examination here.

The third level of the Gaian palimpsest, historically *ter scriptus*, began during the twelfth-century revival of Roman law and the establishment of professional faculties of law at the University of Bologna and elsewhere.[23] At this stage the problem of deciphering becomes increasingly complicated by the intrusion of other intellectual forces, including canon and feudal law and Aristotelian philosophy in its scholastic form. Henceforth, the Gaian tradition was enmeshed in glosses, commentaries, questions, opinions, and—though strictly forbidden by Justinian himself—more or less distorting "interpretations."[24] As Gaius' work was lost, so Gaianism became increasingly difficult to perceive.

Nevertheless, the basic principles were preserved, and certainly no alternatives were suggested. The most authoritative of glosses, that by Accursius, remains mostly grammatical corrections, small quibbles, and large justifications. About the first Gaian text in the *Digest*—the law "omnes populi" declaring that "all people are ruled by civil law or the law of nations"—Accursius wondered, "But what of those who are not so ruled?" The answer was not difficult: "I respond that these are uncivilized men."[25] This simplified version of the *disputatio in utramque partem* Accursius also applied to the broader question whether Gaius' threefold division might be false (*hoc videtur esse falsum*), and again he resolved the difficulty, in this case by arguing for a more than merely literal view of "things" and "actions." There was also a tendency, illustrated by Petrus de Bellapertica, to replace "action" by the more sophisticated concept of "obligation," which arose from an agreement (*obligatio nascens ex contractu*) and was guaranteed by natural law.[26] But despite such rationalizing tendencies the Gaian system was not seriously questioned.

Following the Glossators from the late thirteenth century, the still more philosophically minded Commentators began to diverge more basically from Gaian principles. Concerning the same law "Omnes populi," for example, Baldus had a different answer to the problem whether "all people" were indeed ruled as Gaius had asserted. "I respond that not all are," said Baldus, "for many cities have their own statutes by which they are ruled."[27] Although technically the emperor was still the only source of law, the right of people to make their own law (*jus proprium* or *jus proprissimum*) could be justified in legal

[23] For general orientation on the Roman legal tradition, see Paul Koschaker, *Europa und das römische Recht* (3d ed., Berlin, 1958). And, for bibliography, see Franz Wieacker, *Privatrechtsgeschichte der Neuzeit* (2d ed., Göttingen, 1967); and Walter Ullmann, *Law and Politics in the Middle Ages* (Ithaca, N.Y., 1975). On particular themes, see E. Cortese, *La Norma giuridica*, 2 vols. (Milan, 1962–64); and my "Clio and the Lawyers: Forms of Historical Consciousness in Medieval Jurisprudence," *Medievalia et Humanistica*, new. ser., 5 (1974): 25–29.

[24] M. Fuhrman, "Interpretatio," in *Sympotica Franz Wieacker* (Göttingen, 1970), 80–110; F. Pringelsheim, "Justinian's Prohibition of Commentaries to the Digest," in his *Gesammelte Abhandlungen*, 2 (Heidelberg, 1961): 86–106; and V. Piano Mortari, "Il Problema dell'interpretatio nei commentatori," *Annali di storia del diritto*, 2 (1958): 29–109.

[25] Accursius, *Ad Digestum*, 1. 5. 1, which is the equivalent of Gaius, *Institutiones*, 1. 8.

[26] Petrus de Bellapertica, *In libros Institutionum commentarii* (Lyon, 1536), 111. And, in general, see C. Karsten, *Die Lehre von Verträge bei den italienischen Juristen des Mittelalters* (Rostock, 1882).

[27] Baldus, *Super Digesto veteri* (Venice, 1535), f. 26. In general, see *L'Opera di Baldo, per cura dell'Università di Perugia nel V centenario della morte del grande giureconsulto* (Perugia, 1901); and, in particular, see J. Tarducci's essay in *ibid.*, 409–66; Norbert Horn, *Aequitas in den Lehren des Baldus* (Cologne, 1968); and, for the classic work, C. N. S. Woolf, *Bartolus of Sassoferrato* (Cambridge, 1913).

terms, Baldus argued; for did not the imperial rule against a people making "illicit statutes" imply that they could make *licit* ones? In this way Baldus, following his master Bartolus and other Italian jurists, built up the case for the legitimacy of city-states and other political units that were independent of imperial jurisdiction and so, presumably, of Roman forms. For some jurists, of course, there was an answer to this problem, too: such post-Roman statutes and customs should be included in the *jus gentium*.

Gaius' famous statement about the legal "condition of men" likewise received expanding interpretation—and "interpretations," as Accursius reminded his students, implied correction. In the first place the topic "De statu hominum" was an invitation to some jurists to philosophize about the human condition in general, about the natural as well as the social state of that "most worthy of creatures" (*dignissima creaturarum*), as Alberigo de Rosate called man. But the main theme was the historical change that had occurred since the time of Gaius, the difference between the ancient and the "modern state of men" (*status modernus hominum*). "In modern times" (*secundum moderna tempora*), observed Alberigo, "there are various states of men that are not treated under the title" of Gaius. "And, because the state of men is in constant motion and never at rest," he proposed to bring the discussion up to date by treating a variety of more recent questions, including those of the Jews and Saracens and different sorts of Christians (real and supposed)—laymen and clerics.[28] In fact, the general problem that absorbed most of the energies of European jurists was how to accommodate their own experience and institutions, feudal as well as ecclesiastical, to Roman forms and rules or, in other words, how to transform, as Justinian had transformed, the *jus antiquum* into a *usus modernus*. In this effort jurists increasingly turned to extra-Roman experience, but they did so in orthodox terms of custom (*consuetudo*) and the *jus gentium*, based (as Gaius had said) on "natural reason."

Another major force that acted to transform Gaianism was the intrusion, or rather re-intrusion, of Aristotelian philosophy. Attempts to find or to impose logical species, especially the use of the famous "four causes," again illustrates the infiltration of naturalism and metaphysics into jurisprudence and social thought. Accursius had accepted Gaius' demand for the study of the "origin of law," though he interpreted "necessary" as "useful" and justified it simply on grounds of logic and propriety—that it provided a way of introducing basic elements (*principia*) and that it agreed with the method of a lawyer (*advocatus*), which was to start with his exordium. For commentators like Baldus, however, concern for origins and sources was translated into the system of Aristotle's efficient, material, formal, and final causes; and, indeed, this procedure was associated with the growing claims of scholastic jurisprudence to be a rational "science" because it was universal and treated its material in terms of cause and effect (*per causas*).[29] The long-range implica-

[28] Alberigo, *In primam FF* [Digesti] *Veter. part.* (Venice, 1585), f. 44v.

[29] See R. Weigand, *Die Naturrechtslehre der Legisten und Dekretisten von Irnerius bis Accursius und von Gratian bis Johannes Teutonicus* (Munich, 1967); and my "Vera Philosophia: The Philosophical Significance of Renaissance Jurisprudence," 274.

tions of these tendencies were momentous; they continued to inform professional jurisprudence down to Savigny's time and after. Yet Gaianism was modified rather than replaced; another level was added to the multilayered Gaian text.

SERIOUS CRITICISM AND TRANSFORMATION of the Gaian paradigm began in the sixteenth century. The first condition of this mutation was the rise of humanistic jurisprudence, beginning in fifteenth-century literary circles and then infiltrating the academic and professional study of law.[30] From the second quarter of the century deepening historical perspectives and expanding geographical horizons encouraged by humanism led certain jurists to begin the task of "reforming" the Roman system of jurisprudence fixed by Gaius, codified by Justinian, and canonized by the medieval Glossators. The "reformers" wanted to fulfill the famous Ciceronian ideal of "reducing law to an art" (*jus in artem redigendo*)—or, better, Justinian's ideal of elevating it to a science, a concept that was vital and a prime rubric of Romanist jurisprudence. Pursued by elaborate violations of Justinian's strictures against "interpretation," the task was justified in the name of that abstract reason contained in the law (*recta ratio*; *ratio juris*) as well as a novel concern for "method," which was a dominant force in the intellectual life of the sixteenth century. The men involved in this enterprise were the founders of that modern school of jurisprudence that Savigny designated "the systematists" (*die Systematiker*) and that represents a latter-day Gaianism—the last, or perhaps next-to-last, layer of the Gaian palimpsest.[31]

Underlying this tradition was another movement for "reform" associated with humanism, namely the attempt to improve and to re-order dialectic by bringing it into contact with, or even submerging it in, rhetoric.[32] This aim of various pedagogical reformers, including Rudolf Agricola and Petrus Ramus, was carried over by like-minded jurists into their own field of study, which, of course, had other longer-standing ties with rhetoric in technical ways. In 1520, building on Agricola's work, Claudius Cantiuncula published his *Topica legalia* in an effort to find a better arrangement for the major "commonplaces"

[30] On the historical implications of "legal humanism," see D. Maffei, *Gli Inizi dell'umanesimo giuridico* (Milan, 1956); and my *Foundations of Modern Historical Scholarship* (New York, 1970). For the philosophical implications, see Hans Troje, *Graeca Leguntur* (Cologne, 1971), which is useful for orientation, new insights, and bibliography if not for all of its judgments.

[31] Savigny, *Das Recht des Besitzes* (7th ed., Vienna, 1865), 10. For the classic and still indispensable work on this tradition, see R. Stintzing and E. Landsberg, *Geschichte der deutschen Rechtswissenschaft*, 4 vols. (Munich, 1880–1910).

[32] See, in general, Neal Gilbert, *Renaissance Concepts of Method* (New York, 1956); and Walter Ong, *Ramus, Method, and the Decay of Dialogue* (Cambridge, 1958). On law in particular, there has been an upsurge of work lately; see, for example, Hans Troje, "Wissenschaft und System in der Jurisprudenz des 16. Jahrhunderts," in J. Blühdorn and J. Ritter, eds., *Philosophie und Rechtswissenschaft* (Frankfurt, 1969), 63–88; Aldo Mazzacane, *Scienza, logica, e ideologia nella giurisprudenza tedesca del sec. XVI* (Milan, 1971); F. Carpintero, " 'Mos italicus,' 'mos gallicus,' y el humanismo racionalista," *Ius Commune*, 6 (1977): 108–71; C. Vasoli, "La Dialettica umanistica e la metodologia giuridica nel secolo XVI," in *La Formazione storica del diritto moderna in Europa*, 1 (Florence, 1977): 237–79; and A. Giuliani, "The Influence of Rhetoric on the Law of Evidence and Pleading," *Juridical Review* (1962), 216–51.

of law (*locorum divisio*).[33] This work was pursued further in the *Methodica dialecticis ratio* by Johann Apel, who illustrated his topical reform with a series of diagrams showing the logic of social, especially as contrasted to natural, structure and process. Among German jurists like Johann Frey and Nicolaus Vigelius the influence of Ramus was particularly strong, partly because they hoped with his help to restore jurisprudence to a more central position in general learning and, through its association with oratory, to enhance its social utility. As Frey suggested in his schematic prescription for an "idea of the good and complete jurisconsult," the finished product, a paradigm of practical and theoretical knowledge, would be the "political man" (*homo politicus*).[34] But most of all, raising their sights from pedagogy to philosophy, these jurists wanted to fashion the Roman legal tradition into an orderly system; for "order," wrote Christopher Ehem, another of these legal reformers, "is the soul of things themselves" (*ordinem esse animam ipsarum rerum*).[35]

Although not generally appreciated or even admitted, the movements to reform dialectic and jurisprudence continued to have recourse to old traditions of naturalism and scholasticism, despite a lot of careless anti-Aristotelian rhetoric. Johann Oldendorp, in another treatise on "legal topics," used Aristotelian categories to organize his *materia* and *exempla* and the idea of the four causes to interpret "actions" in particular.[36] Even more systematically, Vigelius, who indeed set out to reorganize in such dialectical terms the whole *Institutes* of Justinian (*resolutio Institutionum Imp. Justiniani*), relied upon Aristotle.[37] Similar attitudes are evident in contemporary theories of "interpretation," which, despite Justinian's prohibition, had become a recognized part of law.[38] The "order" sought by critical methodologists like Jean Coras and Pietro Gammaro was a natural order, which they contrasted sharply with civil law. The latter was founded "not on nature," as Coras observed, "but only on opinion and the authority of legislators."[39] This social authority might suffice for law as an "art," but a science needed to judge "through causes"—precisely what the new theories of interpretation proposed to accomplish. A rational method, or methodical rationale (*methodica ratio*), as

[33] Cantiuncula listed twenty-five places or means of making distinctions; see his *Topica legalis*, printed with Johann Apel, *Methodica dialecticis ratio ad iurisprudentiam* (Basel, 1545).

[34] Nicholas Reusner, ed., ΧΕΙΡΑΓΩΓΙΑ *sive Cynosura iuris*, 2 (Speier, 1588), no 32: Freigius, "Idea boni et perfecti iuris consulti" (fold-out diagram in the appendix). Also see Mazzacane, *Scienza, logica, e ideologia*.

[35] Ehem, *De principis iuris libri septem* (Basel, 1556), 1.

[36] Oldendorp, *Actionum forensium progymnasmata in septem classes distincta* (Lyon, 1566), f. 3v. Also see his *Topica legalis* (Lyon, 1555). On Johann Oldendorp, see E. Wolf, *Grosse Rechtsdenker der deutschen Geistesgeschichte* (2d ed., Tübingen, 1951), 134–75; and Guido Kisch, *Erasmus und die Jurisprudenz seiner Zeit* (Basel, 1960), 227–59, *Claudius Cantiuncula* (Basel, 1970), 57–71 ("Methodenlehre"); and *Melanchthons Rechts- und Soziallehre* (Basel, 1967). For a topical analysis of Bartolus, see A. Brederode, *Loci communes . . . novi et uberrimi in Bartoli . . . opera omnia* (Basel, 1589).

[37] Vigelius, *Dialectici iuris civilis libri III* (Basel, 1620). Also see his *Methodus universi iuris civilis absolutissima* (Lyon, 1591).

[38] See V. Piano Mortari, *Ricerca sulla teoria dell'interpretazione del diritto nel sec. XVI* (Milan, 1956). Also see H. Schürpf, "Ratio interpretandi," in Stintzing and Landsberg, *Geschichte der deutschen Rechtswissenschaft*, 1: 1071.

[39] Coras, *De iure civile in artem redigendo*, in *Tractatus universi iuris*, 1 (Venice, 1584): 59; and Gammaro, *De extensionibus*, in *ibid.*, 18: 247. On Coras, see A. Fell, "The Classical Four Causes in the Renaissance Art of Law" (Ph. D. dissertation, Columbia University, 1974).

Oldendorp put it, "requires that the interpreter of law have recourse to the law of nature."[40]

Yet this widespread search for system—"methodus," "schemata," "ratio," and "partitiones" are among the operative terms—by no means implied abandoning the human and positive aspects of jurisprudence. The jurist had to judge fact as well as law; he had to find authorities as well as devise arguments. The dual aim of jurisprudence, according to Conrad Lagus, was to answer both the historical and the philosophical questions: Philosophy, he explained, was no doubt "the first part of law, that is, the truth and reason of law insofar as the human mind can attain them"; but no less essential was "the second part" (that is, history), "the bare narration of facts . . . to show the forms of law observed by Roman legislation in particular cases."[41] Precisely in this sense of "history" could law be analyzed in terms of persons, things, and actions. In the preface to his standard anthology of legal treatises on method, Nicolas Reusner provided the aphorism that best expresses the enduring importance of the Gaian scheme: "Bonus Institutionalista," he stated, "bonus Jurista."[42]

The continuing and cumulative critique of the Roman canon was an international enterprise; but the major efforts of revision were begun in France, especially by disciples of Andrea Alciato at the University of Bourges. Alciato was the founder of humanistic jurisprudence, of the *mos gallicus* as it was later called, although he personally lacked any particular systematic interests. The most notable of his followers—François Connan, Eguinaire Baron, François le Douaren, and Hugues Doneau—were deeply indebted to the humanist movement; but each made a practice of also introducing modern materials and ideas, not only feudal law, which was regularly taught at Bourges, but a variety of historical issues, such as the influence of Celtic and Frankish institutions. Each of them also contributed massively to the criticism of the Roman legal canon, and none hesitated to break with Roman forms in their attempts to realize the ideal of law as "true philosophy."

Connan's master work, published posthumously in 1557, was called *Commentaries on Civil Law*; but its general purpose was actually to shift emphasis away from civil law and to discuss instead such topics as obligation and property in terms of the law of nations, as Gaius had defined it. For Connan the *jus gentium* was equivalent to the "form of a people" (*forma populi*), and it was, logically if not chronologically, "prior to civil law." As a consequence, he tended to examine conventional topics of civil law in the context not only of natural law, identified with the "first law of nations" (*ius hoc gentium primum*), but also of European, often comparative, history. He also gave large and continuing roles to custom in the progress of legal institutions and to jurists in rationalizing these customs. "Custom interprets law," he wrote, and "judgments confirm custom" (*consuetudo legum interpretatur; res judicatae consuetudinem*

[40] Oldendorp, *Iuris naturalis gentium et civilis* εἰσαγωγή (Antwerp, 1539), sig. Aiii.

[41] Lagus, *Methodus iuris utriusque traditio* (Lyon, 1566), 3.

[42] Reusner, ΧΕΙΡΑΓΩΓΙΑ *sive Cynosura iuris*, 1: 13.

confirmat).[43] Law was, of course, grounded in nature, but the first laws (*priscae leges*) were barbaric; there was no original "golden age" (*aetas aurea*), only "the rule of lusts, factions, evils, seditions, plunderings, war, and an absence of equity and justice."[44] The perfection of law only developed over the course of time, with the ratiocinations of jurists and especially with the efforts to establish a rational system of law. Connan had reservations about the triadic system of Gaius and argued that the rubric of actions was unnecessary since it could be divided between persons and things. On a more general level, however, Connan carried on the spirit of the Gaian tradition.

So, in even more modernizing and vernacularizing terms, did Eguinaire Baron, the eldest and in some ways the most original of these four French pioneers. In addition to a manifesto of the new jurisprudence, Baron produced a series of commentaries on all parts of civil law according to a unique and self-consciously comparative method that he termed *commentaria bipertita*, by which he "accommodated civil law to French customs and legislation" (*accommodata hujus tituli ad mores Galliarum et leges regias*).[45] He "accommodated" both the *Institutes* of Gaius and the *Digest* of Justinian, in part simply by translation. He explained, for example, that "among the French the *plebs* is the Third Estate" and went on to point out parallels and contrasts in the respective social and legal systems. He agreed with Gaius that all law concerned persons, things, or actions, but his experience prompted him to expand "the condition of man" beyond the distinction of free and unfree. Women were "persons" too, and, like Connan, he was aware of their peculiar position (*quia status foeminarum deterior in multis causis*). There were also the problems of foreigners and naturalization (*aulbains, ou etrangers, et lettres de naturalité*); and, in fact, Baron composed a monograph on succession among foreigners.[46] Other difficulties, such as the antiquated Roman paternal power (*patria potestas*), likewise led him to depart from Roman convention, though without rejecting the entire Roman framework of jurisprudence. The work of Baron, a marvelous and many-sided illustration of the cultural shock that antiquity could inflict on sensitive and learned moderns, certainly deserves closer study.

Better known and probably more influential is the work of Baron's colleague and rival Le Douaren. Although these two "Alciateans" had a variety of disputes, personal and religious as well as professional and political, they fundamentally agreed about "method"; and Baron subscribed to his younger colleague's formulation that emphasized the systematic-pedagogical (*ars docendi*) as well as the humanistic-philological (*sermonis proprietas*) aspects of the

[43] Connan, *Commentariorum iuris civilis libri X* (Paris, 1557), f. 43. For analyses, see C. Bergfeld, *Franciscus Connanus* (Graz, 1968); and V. Piano Mortari, "La sistematica come ideale umanistico dell'opera di Francisco Connano," in *La Storia del diritto nel quadro delle scienze storiche* (Florence, 1966), 521–31. The same formula appears in Lagus' *Methodus iuris utriusque traditio*, 42, from the *Digest*, 1. 3. 37.

[44] Connan, *Commentariorum iuris civilis libri X*, ff. 32v, 16.

[45] Baron, *Opera omnia*, ed. F. Baudouin (Paris, 1562), *Commentarii*, *passim*, and *Institutionum civilium ab Iustiniano Caesare editarum libri IIII* (Poitou, 1550). On Baron there is no useful study of any sort.

[46] Baron, *Opera omnia*, 1: 52, 78 ("De statu hominum"), 92.

new jurisprudence.[47] For Le Douaren legal education ought to begin with the *Institutes* and, despite the humanist prejudice against scholasticism, ought to include the works of Bartolus, Baldus, and the best of the philosophical commentators. Like his friend Connan, Le Douaren was devoted to the ideal of "true philosophy," and he declared that "there is nothing either divine or human that the jurisconsult does not treat and that is not relevant to civil science." He wrote extensively on both canon law and, under the civilian heading of "custom," feudal law; and he denied that Roman law had in any sense been "received" into France. Nevertheless, civil law continued to provide the terms and framework of his legal philosophy. In his discussion of the problems of legal system, he leaned perhaps more toward the naturalistic interpretation, making an analogy to mathematics in particular, since he believed that "the elements of law, the grounds of its maxims and basic issues are as points, lines, surfaces, etc., are to geometry."[48] Such was the basis of Le Douaren's various "methodical" discussions (*methodica enarratio*, *methodica partitio*, and *tractatio*, as he characterized his interpretations of the Roman canon).

Of all of the work of the great "systematists," that of Hugues Doneau, disciple and successor of Le Douaren at Bourges, is probably the most comprehensive and influential. For Savigny, Doneau's *Commentaries on Civil Law* marked the introduction of the French school into Germany, and for Savigny's disciple R. Stintzing, the great authority in the field, Doneau was "the creator of modern jurisprudence."[49] At Bourges and later at the Universities of Altdorf and Heidelberg, Doneau carried on the work of transforming Romano-Byzantine law into a universal system in accordance with the ideal of law as "true philosophy," as an expression of "right reason."[50] Like many other contemporary "anti-Tribonianists," Doneau was much disturbed by the state of the *Code* and especially of the *Digest* of Justinian, although it was the form, or rather the formlessness, instead of the substance (the post-classical interpolations, or "Tribonianisms") that he wanted to correct. The *Institutes*, on the other hand, he continued to admire, especially the tripartite classification; and, in fact, much of his work of "reformation" consisted of trying to gather together and to arrange the scattered and sometimes contradictory material on persons, things, and actions into an intelligible and symmetrical system. For Doneau each of these headings had three subheadings: (1) divine and human, with the latter divided into public and private; (2) obligations, which followed the discussion of rights and which were grouped under "things"; and (3) forms of procedure to obtain rights, which appeared under "actions." Doneau's work, like that of his elder colleagues, shows the strong imprint of formal philosophy, including the four

[47] Le Douaren, *Opera omnia*, 1: 1. For an analysis, see W. Vogt, *Franciscus Duarenus* (Stuttgart, 1971).

[48] Le Douaren, *Opera omnia*, 1: 1. Also see Coras, *Opera omnia*, 1 (Wittemberg, 1603): 1.

[49] Stintzing, *Hugo Donellus in Altdorf* (Erlangen, 1869), 42.

[50] Doneau, *Opera omnia*, 1 (Rome, 1828): 133. On Doneau, see the old appreciation and analysis by A. Eyssell, *Doneau* (Dijon, 1860); on Doneau's significance for French systematizing and codifying efforts, see A.-J. Arnaud, *Les Origines doctrinales du Code civil français* (Paris, 1969), 121.

Aristotelian causes, and at least a touch of Ramist, or Ramoid, method; but in general the *Commentaries* remains within the Gaian tradition.

In the generation after Doneau the rising tide of "vernacular humanism" brought this tradition into contact with the tangled question of customary law. In France two close colleagues who studied at Bourges, Étienne Pasquier and Antoine Loisel, took Justinian's *Institutes* as the model and guide for their efforts to bring some system to vernacular law. Pasquier found parallels to the Gaian model in other "institutes"—Quintilian's "oratorical," Lactantius's "divine," and Ramus's "dialectical" (to which we might add Calvin's "institutes" of religion)—and began his work with a short history of Roman systematizing from the time of Scaevola.[51] Pasquier argued that law was more closely allied to rhetoric than to philosophy and that, because of the jurist's reliance on memory and human judgment, his art was called *juris prudentia* instead of *juris scientia*. Like his Latinate colleagues, Pasquier operated in the domain of the *jus gentium*, which he equated simply with "human law" (*droit humain*). His *Interpretation of the Institutes of Justinian* (unpublished until the nineteenth century) started out as a translation but ended up as a comparative study of Roman and French legal institutions, following the Gaian pattern very much in the style of Baron's work. Pasquier, however, was generally hostile to civil law, deplored its tyrannical and rigid tendencies, and was at pains to point out contrasts with French customs. With respect to the first division, for example, all French "persons" were free (*libres et franches*) except in a few antiquated provincial *coutumiers*. In most ways Loisel agreed with and, indeed, consulted Pasquier on these matters, and was more insistent on the differing status of French "persons," arguing that the primary division was between *noble* and *roturier* (itself divided into *bourgeois* and *vilain*), since all men were or could become free by baptism. Loisel's *Customary Institutes*, again following the Gaian pattern but composed of native proverbs, literary expressions of folk wisdom, and maxims of customary law, moved even further from Romanism toward some sort of national system.[52]

There were other efforts at system-building in the sixteenth century, but these works, like the celebrated *Republic* of Jean Bodin, tended to be concerned with political rather than social or legal thought. One instructive exception, abused when not neglected, is the curious construction fashioned by Bodin's rival, Pierre Grégoire of Toulouse. For Grégoire "method" was an "imitation of nature," and in his own grandiose *Republic* he tried to assemble a man-centered cosmology to emulate the natural cosmos.[53] Grégoire, like Bodin, denied the universality of the Roman tradition and, specifically, French subjection to it; but on the fundamental point, the nature of the commonwealth, he had a very different emphasis. The center of his political cosmos was occupied not

[51] Pasquier, *L'Interprètation des Institutes de Justinian, avec la conference de chaque paragraphe aux ordonnances royaux, arrestz de Parlement et coustumes gènèrales de la France*, ed. M. le duc Pasquier (Paris, 1847), 9, 45.

[52] Loisel, *Institutes coustumiers*, ed. M. Reulos (Paris, 1935).

[53] Grégoire, *De republica libri sex et viginti* (Frankfurt, 1609), 10: 54, 13: 12, 21. And see the discussion by C. Collot, *L'École doctrinale de droit public de Pont-à-Mousson* (Paris, 1965).

by the prince—as it was for Bodin and for that "most pernicious man, Machiavelli"—but by that Roman form of wisdom called law. This emphasis is even clearer in Grégoire's other systematic effort, his *Syntagma juris universi*, a book treating "all law, divine, human, and natural," according to a "new method."[54] The novelty of this method, however, fades on examination, not only because it relies on traditional views of hierarchy but also because its principal categories turn out to be variations on the old Gaian theme. The first volume (books 1-6) covers a wide range of things—natural, divine, and human (including "communal" and "feudal")—and then (books 7-19) persons and the various conditions thereof. The second volume concludes with an elaborate consideration of human "actions," criminal as well as legitimate, collective as well as individual, public as well as private. Reversing the position of the first two categories was done for the orthodox reason that in Creation things had in fact preceded persons. In general, Grégoire's work illustrates a crucial turning point in the career of Gaianism—the shift from a normative legal doctrine to a descriptive interpretation of society and culture.

Other endeavors, apart from the tinkering with the Roman system, were operating to transform modern views of jurisprudence. One was the gigantic contemporary enterprise in the field of classical and historical scholarship, although this effort may have served to confuse as well as to broaden perspectives on the old legal tradition. Jacques Cujas was the symbol and leading spirit of this critical assault on the textual aspect of this tradition. Also positive and empirical in a certain sense was the growing appreciation even among academic jurists of the value of modern judicial experience. Cujas's student, Pierre Ayrault, for example, turned from theory to practice (*usus*) as the best means of access to legal wisdom. For him the true source of law lay in particular judgments (*res judicatae* is the civilian rubric). These Ayrault regarded as the first or only or "supreme" part of the law; and he compiled a modern digest (*pandectae*) of such judgments that followed, of course, the conventional order. "Look to the practitioners," he advised, "for those things that pertain to their art."[55] Finally, there were the long-standing ideological objections to Romanism, especially national jealousy of imperial-papal intrusions and claims to universalism. In France the standard formula was "that the civil laws of the Romans may not be alleged in the courts of France or in any inferior courts on the basis of their authority but only on the basis of their rationality" (*pro ratione*).[56] In this way, though in few others, nationalism can be said to have reinforced rationalism. In all of these ways the intimidating position of the Roman canon and of Gaianism in a general sense was increasingly undermined, or at least relocated, in a more pluralistic and rational conception of human history and society.

[54] Grégoire, *Syntagma iuris universi* (Cologne, 1623). Also see his *De iuris arte, methodo, et praeceptis* (Lyon, 1580).

[55] Ayrault, *Rerum ab omni antiquitate iudiciarum Pandectae*, 1 (Geneva, 1677): 84. On *Digest*, 42. 1 ("Res judicatae"), also see Ulrich Zasius, *Opera omnia*, 3 (Lyon, 1550): col. 360. There is no modern study on Ayrault.

[56] Charles de Grassaille, *Regalium Franciae libri duo* (Paris, 1545), 45.

AT THIS POINT THE GAIAN PALIMPSEST seems to be exhausted: between the historical and empirical assaults on the one hand and the efforts of rationalization on the other, academic jurisprudence could hardly retain its conventional form; it moved, in a sense, from the letter to the spirit of Roman jurisprudence. In general, the seventeenth century was suffused not only with *l'esprit de système* but also with *l'esprit de géometrie*, and these combined with the enthusiasm for the "new science" of Galileo and Descartes to ensure that legal scholarship would be intimidated if not dominated by what has inelegantly been termed "jusnaturalism." For the next two centuries, so it seemed to many observers at that time and since, legal and social as well as political philosophy was captive to this modern idea—"antique-modern," as Otto Gierke preferred to call it—of natural law.[57] This cast of mind is a deflection from Gaianism. The resurgence and prominence of the idea of "nature" was used in the explanation and legitimation of human categories, social as well as legal (that is, descriptive as well as normative). Indeed, the "state of nature" tended to take over the function both of the moral basis of social behavior and of the historical interpretation of civilization. Thus, the significance of "convention," so essential to Gaius and other Romanists, was subordinated or distorted. Moreover, the principle of authority—and with it the force of custom, prescription, tradition, and even "interpretation" in a usual sense—tended to be overshadowed by the claims of universal reason. The result was that the "law" seemed in many ways to be dehumanized: man himself—his will, his history, his cultural individuality as well as his irrationality and perhaps sinfulness—was increasingly lost to view.

Gottfried Wilhelm Leibniz, who published his own "new method" of jurisprudence in 1667, provides the most extreme example of legal rationalism (*jurisprudentia rationalis*). Although thoroughly grounded in legal scholarship and attached to the "reformed" dialectic associated with Ramus, Leibniz turned to mathematics, specifically to Euclid, for his model of rationality. He rejected the threefold division of Gaius because, as so many others had pointed out, "actions derive from both persons and things." Most fundamental to his objection was the apparently random empiricism of conventional jurisprudence. "Its method," he remarked, "was taken from the inmost parts not of law but of fact" (*haec Methodus non ex Juris sed Facti visceribus sumpta*), "for persons and things are terms of fact, as power, obligation, and the like are terms of law."[58] The confusion and irrationality inherent in such an approach was too absurd for a modern conception of law: "Who would not laugh at such a new Euclid?" For Leibniz, however, jurisprudence, along with other humanistic studies, was subordinated to metaphysics, ultimately

[57] Still fundamental, in addition to Stintzing and Landsberg, *Geschichte der deutschen Rechtswissenshaft*, is Otto Gierke, *Das deutsche Genossenschaftsrecht*, the relevant part of which has been translated by Ernest Barker as *Natural Law and the Theory of Society, 1500–1800* (Boston, 1957); but, in general, the subject of natural law is too peripheral and too voluminous to allow bibliographical comment here.

[58] Leibniz, *Nova methodus discendae docendaeque iurisprudentiae* (Frankfurt, 1667), in *Sämtliche Schriften und Briefe*, 6, pt. 1 (Berlin, 1971): 298. On Leibniz in general, see K. Dickerhof, *Leibniz' Bedeutung für die Gesetzgebung seiner Zeit* (Freiburg, 1941), and F. Sturm, *Das römische Recht in der Sicht von Gottfried Wilhelm Leibniz* (Göttingen, 1968).

to mathematics; and his position represents a pole rather than a school of thought in the range of legal and social doctrines.

The major figure in the re-emergence of natural law was Hugo Grotius, though he, too, was steeped in humanistic and legal erudition. His main legal works were devoted to that anarchic arena of international relations, which itself seemed to represent a pre- or extra-legal "state of nature." Like Leibniz a generation later, Grotius had a basic contempt for unclassifiable particulars. "For the principles of the law of nature," he wrote in the prolegomena to the *Law of War and Peace*, "since they are always the same, can easily be brought into a systematic form; but the elements of positive law, since they often undergo change and are different in different places, are outside the domain of systematic treatment, just as other notions of particular things are."[59] In a youthful work on prizes and booty he took the same view and, reasoning from a set of general rules and law, affected an even more deliberately mathematical plan.

Yet this renewed emphasis on nature and reason is by no means the whole story of social and legal thought in the age of reason. The *ius naturale* was, after all, an essential part of the Roman legal tradition; and, as Richard Zouche reminded his seventeenth-century contemporaries, Gaius himself had explained that the basis of the law of nations was that "natural reason among men" (*naturalis ratio inter omnes homines*).[60] Indeed, the continuing association of the *jus gentium* and the *jus naturale* permitted the legal tradition to maintain its human groundings. Grotius, for example, was not only a jusnaturalist and "father of international law" but also, as Giambattista Vico later called him, the "jurisconsult of the human race."[61] Like Vico, Grotius neither forgot history nor despised tradition. He persisted in citing ancient "authorities," including not only the Bible, jurists, and scholastic philosophers but also literary and especially historical writers, who provided judgments as well as illustrations. Grotius's intentions were, perhaps, less rationalizing than universalizing; for his primary field of operations was indeed "positive law," specifically the kind of "voluntary human law" (*jus humanum voluntarium*) defined as the law of nations (*jus gentium*, exclusive of the *jus civile* as posited by Gaius). Universal law, according to Grotius, arises not only from nature and from divine ordinance but also from custom or tacit consent—that is, from human will. "And the Law of Nations is proved in the same manner as the unwritten Civil Law," he wrote, "namely, by long usage and the testimony of its professors; for this law, as Dio Chrysostom says, is 'the invention of time and experience,' and here the great historians are of the greatest service to

[59] Grotius, *De iure belli ac pacis libri tres*, trans. W. Knight (London, 1922), prolegomena, 22, and *De iure praedae commentarius*, trans. G. Williams and Q. Zeydel (Oxford, 1950), 7.

[60] Zouche, *Iuris et iudicii fecialis* (1650), ed. T. Holland (Washington, 1911), 1. Also see J. W. Textor, *Synopsis iuris gentium*, ed. L. von Bar (Washington, 1916), 2.

[61] See Dario Faucci, "Vico and Grotius: Jurisconsults of Mankind," in G. Tagliacozzo and H. White, eds., *Giambattista Vico: An International Symposium* (Baltimore, 1969), 61–76; L. Rosa, "Grozio fra il giusnaturalismo scolastico e il giusnaturalismo moderno," in *Miscellanea Adriano Gazzana*, 2 (Milan, 1960); Wolf, *Grosse Rechtsdenker der deutschen Geistesgeschicte*; and Fassò, *Storia della filosofia del diritto*.

use."[62] In these ways Grotius managed to retain at least indirect contact with the old Roman tradition.

In France at the very height of the enthusiasm for Cartesianism and that "geometric spirit" sensed and to some degree resisted by Blaise Pascal, the persistence of Gaianism is apparent in a sublimated form. The clearest example, as well as the greatest monument of jurisprudence before Robert Pothier, is the work of Pascal's friend, Jean Domat, whose great system began to appear in 1695. Although Domat's *Civil Laws* . . . were arranged . . . *in Their Natural Order* (an excellent illustration of the craving to reduce convention or history to nature), they remained, in effect, a rationalizing commentary on Roman experience. And, though he affected to seek out fundamental (natural, perhaps prehistorical) principles, Domat found their human expression in the usual texts of civil law. He gave precedence to the natural over the civil state, but he continued to conceptualize within the Roman paradigm, keeping the rubrics of persons, things, and actions. Convention and not nature, for example, led him to define persons in terms of "liberty" (or the lack thereof), citizenship (or the exclusion therefrom, as in foreign or exiled status), and fatherhood (or subjection thereto).[63] The general impression is of rationality, or the rhetoric of rationalism, imposed on the old Roman categories. Even Domat's ultimate goal, famously defined as the "spirit of the laws," was a more rationalized version of the old juristic aim of getting at the true meaning.

Montesquieu's *L'Esprit des lois* of 1748 is, of course, the work that made this phrase and concept universally famous, although the connection with the earlier legal tradition was effectively obscured by the author himself, whose claims to originality have never been disputed and seldom even examined. "My ideas are new," wrote Montesquieu, "and therefore I have been obliged to find new words, or give new acceptations to old terms, in order to convey my meaning."[64] To point out the relation of Montesquieu's system to the old Roman tradition, which he had surveyed historically in his *Grandeur and Decadence of the Romans* (1734), is not to deny its novelty or conceptual force. His basic concern was not with antecedent "laws of nature" but rather with the old law of nations and civil laws; and, if he construed his subject in an extraordinarily wide-ranging fashion, he followed the lead of Baron, Bodin, and others in adopting a comparative approach, in taking universal history and the law of (all) nations as his field, and in emphasizing climate, geography, and cultural tradition. In more specific ways, too, he retained contact with Roman forms as well as with the texts and modern scholarship of civil law, and the book has with some justice been regarded as a "new *De Legibus*." As Le Douaren and others who commented consecutively on the *Corpus juris*

[62] Grotius, *De iure belli ac pacis*, xiv.

[63] Domat, *Les Loix civiles dans leur ordre naturel*, 1 (Paris, 1835). On Domat, see R. F. Voeltzel, *Jean Domat (1625–1696)* (Paris, 1936), 107; and, most recently, G. Tarello, ed., *Materiali per una storia della cultura giuridica*, 2 (Florence, 1972): 127–57.

[64] Montesquieu, *L'Esprit des lois* (Paris, 1748), preface. On the problem of the work's structure, see Franz Neumann's introduction to the English translation, *The Spirit of the Laws*, trans. T. Nugent (New York, 1949), and, more recently, Mark Waddicor, *Montesquieu and the Philosophy of Natural Law* (The Hague, 1970); S. Goyard-Fabre, *Philosophie du droit de Montesquieu* (Paris, 1973); and Tarello, *Materiali per una storia*, vol. 1.

began with a definition of the law, its species, and its sources (*quid jus, de divisione juris*, and *unde jus*), so Montesquieu began with general definitions, continued with the species of constitutions (corresponding to democratic, aristocratic, and monarchical sources of law) and then likewise proceeded to the law of persons (liberty and servitude) and of things (commerce), family, and succession. Montesquieu also ended up with a discussion of feudal law (corresponding to the *Libri feudorum*, which modern jurists had accepted as a continuation of "Roman law"). Although Montesquieu's book may have been "without a mother" (*prolem sine matrem creatam* was its motto), it did have a kind of conceptual godfather: the "spiritual consanguinity" of the basic Roman paradigm. *The Spirit of the Laws* can be read as a set of variations, however remote and figurative, on Gaian and Justinianian themes.

As Cartesianism did not entirely efface the old Roman canon in France, *Naturrecht* did not exclude the study of positive law or even end the tradition of Gaianism in Germany. Most representative of jusnaturalism in Germany was the encyclopedic work of Johann Gottlieb Heineccius, though he belonged as well to the continuing enterprise of humanistic scholarship and looked back in particular to Le Douaren. Like Le Douaren, Heineccius worked along both philological and philosophical lines. His historical surveys of civil and Germanic law and his various investigations into crucial topics of modern critical jurisprudence—including Justinian's prohibition against "interpretation," the ignorance of Greek (that is, the "specious dictum," *Graecum est, non potest legi*), the "anti-Tribonianist sect," and biographical sketches of Cujas and other jurists—exemplify his philological analysis.[65] The second line of endeavor consists of a series of commentaries—"Elements," he called them in Euclidean style—not only of philosophy in general but also of natural law, the law of nations, and especially civil law, from the Twelve Tables down to his own day. The Gaian tradition is represented by his *Syntagma* of 1718, a systematic treatise "according to the order of the *Institutes*," but also making use of Oldendorp and other modern scholars.[66] In general, his first concern was with the human condition (*de statu hominis*), and he expressly repudiated Thomas Hobbes's naturalistic tendency to derive all law from contractual agreement. For Heineccius the mainstream of wisdom, though it certainly originated in Greek philosophy, was that "knowledge of things divine and human" (the title of another of his dissertations) identified with jurisprudence.[67] In a number of ways Heineccius—like Grotius, Domat, and others—provides a link between enthusiasm for natural law and older traditions of positive scholarship—and also, not accidentally, between the old jurisprudence and newer views of how to go about studying society.

The importance of the Roman experience in the thought of the Enlightenment is most conspicuous in the historical works of Montesquieu and Edward

[65] Heineccius, *Opera omnia*, 4 vols. (Geneva, 1744), 3: 17, 21, 171, 203. On Heineccius, see Stintzing and Landsberg, *Geschichte der deutschen Rechtswissenschaft*, 3: 179–97.

[66] Heineccius, *Antiquitatem Romanarum iurisprudentiam illustrantium syntagma secundum ordinem Institutionum Justiniani digestum*, in *Opera omnia*, 4. Also see *Opera omnia*, 1: 191.

[67] Heineccius, "De iurisprudentia divinarum humanarumque rerum notitia," in *Opera omnia*, 3: 374–89.

Gibbon, but it was not only decadence and decline that fascinated scholars. The positive force of Gaianism persisted in a variety of ways and so did the grand tradition of Renaissance scholarship that had accumulated around Roman law. François de Boutaric, like Loisel more than a century earlier, offered a comparative analysis of French customary law within the framework of Justinian's *Institutes*.[68] And Damiano Romano, in the fashion of Bodin almost two centuries earlier, offered a treatise "on the true law of nature and of nations" that was organized according to universal history and drew upon the scholarly work of François Hotman, Cujas, Doneau, Le Douaren, and many other, especially Protestant, jurists of the sixteenth and seventeenth centuries.[69] Other examples of adherence to older scholarly traditions can be found among jurists who ostensibly belonged to the natural school but who were repelled by the naturalistic excesses of Hobbes, Samuel von Pufendorf, Christian Thomasius, and Wolf. This repugnance was especially clear in the continuing efforts to improve international law, the roots of which went back directly to Gaius via Grotius. Gaian notions also continued to inform encyclopedic enterprises; for instance, Joachim Daries' *Institutions of Universal Jurisprudence*, somewhat like Grégoire de Toulouse's *Republic*, proposed to describe the nature of man, society, and public and private law in a "systematic," "methodical," and "scientific" fashion, yet again following the old Roman forms.[70]

But the clearest expression of Gaian influence during the age of Enlightenment was surely the effort to codify positive law, which came to maturity during the next century and, indeed, became a central political issue in Savigny's time. Once again the center of attention was France, where the codification movement had arisen in the sixteenth century in connection with the work of Charles Dumoulin and other "systematic" jurists already discussed. What was required for such an enterprise to succeed, according to A. -J. Arnaud, a recent historian of the movement, was the "juridical rationalism" and "modern philosophy" of the age of Descartes, especially the work of Domat and his eighteenth-century successors, including Montesquieu but even more Pothier and Henri Daguesseau, who were more directly significant for the Napoleonic Code.[71] Yet, as Arnaud himself has shown, the "order" achieved by modern philosophy retained much of its Roman composition, especially the tripartite Gaian scheme, which carried over into the French civil code. The "philosophic" ideal of the rationalizing jurists, of course, was itself a central feature of the Roman legacy. Antoine Terrasson was, perhaps, "the first historian of law really concerned with the philosophy of law"; but

[68] De Boutaric, *Les Institutes de Justinien conférès avec le droit français* (Toulouse, 1738). In general, see Klaus Luig, "Institutionen-Lehrbücher des nationalen Rechts im 17. und 18. Jahrhunderts," *Ius Commune*, 3 (1970): 64–97.

[69] Romano, *Del vero diritto della natura e delle genti* (Naples, 1757).

[70] Daries, *Institutiones iurisprudentiae universalis in quibus omnia iuris naturae socialis et gentium capta in usum auditorii sui methodica scientifica explanantur* (3d ed., Jena, 1748).

[71] Arnaud, *Les origines doctrinales du Code civil français*, 27, *passim*; and Ph. Sagnac, *La Législation civile de la revolution française* (Paris, 1898), 51.

Terrasson's history is specifically of Roman law as an embodiment of this philosophy. And, when he wrote, "Philosophy is the true source of jurisprudence," he was thinking of Ulpian, not of Descartes or Leibniz.[72] In any case, what was really required to achieve a code in France was not a conceptual effort; it was a revolution.

PARALLELING THESE RATIONALIZING TENDENCIES in the eighteenth century were various and increasingly obvious survivals of older humanistic traditions. Indeed, this resurgence of historical and literary erudition divided the Enlightenment from the earlier "age of reason." Despite attacks by naturalizing philosophers on "authority" (and, by inference, on history), positive legal and literary scholarship continued to flourish among a variety of unfashionable *érudits*, who refused to allow the new philosophy to cast everything in doubt. Neither Descartes's skepticism nor Galileo's scorn for historians ("memory experts") could stem the flow of antiquarian social, legal, and institutional history. In Germany Hermann Conring, Heineccius, and Leibniz (!), in the Netherlands Perizonius and Grotius, in France Jacques Godefroy, Terrasson, and Montesquieu, in Italy Giovanni Gravina and Ludovico Muratori, and even in England John Selden and Henry Spelman carried on the great enterprise begun by earlier humanists.[73] Without them, it is too seldom recalled, the work not only of Gibbon and other historians of the Enlightenment but also of Niebuhr and Savigny, however original and ground-breaking, would have been impossible. Indeed, Savigny's famous manifesto of the Historical School, "The Vocation of Our Age for Legislation and Jurisprudence" (1814), may be regarded as a celebration of the monumental efforts of this (philosophically) tenuous tradition of scholarship as well as an assault on naturalism and its attendant fallacies.[74] Under cover of these tendencies, Gaianism could maintain a certain precarious existence even outside of narrow professional circles.

In fact, resistance to a physical, or metaphysical, approach to the study of humanity long antedated the rise of the nineteenth-century historical schools. The first great nemesis of radical naturalism was Giambattista Vico, who was at the same time a leading champion of Roman jurisprudence. Vico waged his campaign not only against the current Cartesian form of naturalism but also against its earlier philosophical manifestations. For him a true "science" of humanity had to accommodate not only nature but also convention, not only reason but also authority (and unreason), not only determinism (*necessitas naturae*) but also the free and creative wills of men. As Le Douaren, Lagus,

[72] Terrasson, *Histoire de la jurisprudence romaine* (Paris, 1750), 101.

[73] In addition to Stintzing and Landsberg, *Geschichte der deutschen Rechtswissenschaft*, volume three, there are various specialized studies. For two notable ones, see C. Chisalberti, *Gian Vincenzo Gravina, giurista e storico* (Milan, 1962); and K. Kossert, *Hermann Conrings rechtsgeschichtliches Verdienst* (Cologne, 1939).

[74] See, for example, Savigny, *Das Recht des Besitzes*. For other works by and about Savigny, see notes 80–81, below.

Grotius, and many others had said, human science had to combine historical-philological with philosophical investigations. And according to Vico the model for such a science was neither Greek philosophy nor rhetoric, which had unfortunately remained conceptually separate, but instead that characteristic Roman kind of "wisdom" (*sapientia*) that was jurisprudence—or, rather, the modern expression of this "civil doctrine" born of humanism and best expressed by Grotius.[75] In the context of Vico's epistemology, itself derived from or, at least, analogous to civil law, the "new jurisprudence" combined the study of the cultural products of human will, the "certain," with the study of the products of God's will, or nature, which was the "true." It had to combine, in other words, an understanding of "authority," or history, with a search for "reason," or the divine ideal, in just the same way that philosophical jurists proceeded. Such was the argument of Vico's treatise, *Universal Law*, which was indeed the first version of the *New Science*—the bottom level of an intellectual palimpsest hardly less complex than Gaius' own.

Vico was one of the great transformers as well as champions of jurisprudence. His method—indeed, his obsession—to reformulate everything into historical terms meant he could not directly take over the static Gaian triad. Yet Vico himself was notoriously a trichotomizer; and his own neotrinitarian structures displayed certain analogies with those of Gaius. On the level of epistemology, or psychology, the Vichian classes were *nosse*, *velle*, and *posse*; and they might be rendered respectively as self-consciousness (perhaps self-possession or self-control), vitality (or the urge to live and to relate to others), and activity (or desire to act and to achieve). In the course of the historical process these three basic faculties of human nature were transformed into what can be considered as social, beyond a mere individual, consciousness (*mens*), rationality (*ratio*), and awareness of divinity (*Deus*). In the sphere of civil society, another homologous triad, the institutional categories, again were produced by historical development: *dominium*, which can be understood as control of things, the basis of civil possession, or property; *libertas*, in social terms the legal order, the rule of law; and *tutela*, active control over and direction of society on behalf of its values and goals—that is, government.[76]

It will not do to make too close an identification between the Vichian and the Gaian systems. For one thing Vico was inordinately proud of the "geometric" design of his "new science," and increasingly the Romanoid structure was lost in the successive and increasingly sublimated versions of the system. But both the *Universal Law* and the *New Science* contained a common denominator: both systems retained, on the one hand, a primary category of personality (that is, the subject of rights and obligations) and, on the other, a secondary category of natural reality (that is, objective "otherness," which represented the field for acquisition—both natural and civil possession). In

[75] For a fuller treatment of the place of rhetoric, see my "Vico's Road: From Philology to Jurisprudence and Back," in G. Tagliacozzo and D. Verene, eds., *Giambattista Vico's Science of Humanity* (Baltimore, 1976), 15–29.

[76] Vico, *De universi juris uno principio et fine uno*, ed. F. Nicolini (Bari, 1936).

both systems actions were defined in terms of these two classes. These remarks hardly begin to reveal Vico's relations to the legal tradition, not only to the ancient sources but to the scholarship of Domat, Grotius, the French "systematists," and other commentators of the preceding two centuries; they may, however, serve to suggest some of his importance as a link between jurisprudence and a modern philosophy of society and culture—another way in which a traditional legal science could become the point of departure for a modern social science.

In various ways Vico anticipated, even if he had no direct impact on, the new view of jurisprudence that began to appear in the late eighteenth century—the Historical School of Law, which became more fully defined, and in some ways even dominant, in the wake of the Napoleonic wars. The point of departure of this school was a historically minded—whether conservative, nationalistic, or "romantic"—rejection of theories of natural law or, at least, a reformulation of them. Its home territory was, of course, Germany, where the wars of liberation were directed not only against Napoleonic domination but also against Bonapartist and Jacobin ideology.[77] To simplify a very complex matter, the assault on rationalism and jusnaturalism (and, related to this attack, the emergence of the Historical School) took its strength from three interrelated traditions. First, the continuing efforts of antiquarian research into the national as well as the classical past followed the work of Heineccius and earlier historians and ultimately stemmed from the philological achievements of Renaissance humanism. Second, again related to sixteenth-century concerns with practical matters, "cameralistic science" (whatever its politics and goals) acted as a solvent upon grand theories of natural law, whether older rationalist schemes or newer idealistic constructs, such as that of Kant. Third, most immediate and most emotional was opposition to that concrete embodiment (or, at least, symbol) of oppressive and arbitrary systems, the Napoleonic Code (and, to some extent, its earlier Prussian and Austrian counterparts). These were the grounds on which the *Historische Rechtsschule* was established in the early nineteenth century.

The man most often regarded as the founder of this school—*Altervater*, Marx called him, and *Naturmensch*—was Gustav Hugo, whose attitudes stemmed quite directly from the tradition of classical humanism. Among other works, he published a new edition of the famous fragments of Ulpian (first published by Cujas and referred to by both Montesquieu and Vico) and a translation of Gibbon's forty-fourth chapter surveying the history of Roman law, likewise based on humanist scholarship; he also wrote voluminously on and taught legal history. He began publishing his systematic and historical works in 1789, taking as his special target "dogmatic" jusnaturalism and setting in its place his own realistic sort of natural law.[78] His system was founded on a "juristic

[77] Like Gaius himself, the *Historische Rechtsschule* has spawned a literature too voluminous to mention and a long concatenation of journals starting with those of Savigny and Hugo and ending with the *Zeitschrift der Savigny-Stiftung für Rechtsgeschichte*. See, for example, Georges Gurvitch, *L'Idée du droit social* (Paris, 1932).

[78] Hugo, *Lehrbuch des Naturrechts als eine Philosophie des positiven Rechts*, which was part of his *Lehrbuch eines civilistisches Cursus*, which began to appear in 1789.

anthropology," in which he considered the animal characteristics of persons (*der Mensch als Tier*) and went on to consider law as "natural" in the sense not of rationality but of a *de facto* growth. In one sense, Hugo recapitulated the method of Gaius, who likewise accepted without question the "reality" of past Roman experience, thereby giving "authority" to history, and then rationalized it through dialectical argument. Not surprisingly, Hugo was, like Gaius, open to charges of being arbitrary and authoritarian; and, as conventional Romanism came under fire from rationalists like Leibniz, so the Historical School was attacked by idealists—especially Hegelians, the most famous of whom was the young Marx. Although he recognized that Hugo represented a "reaction against the frivolous spirit of the eighteenth century," Marx objected to the irrationality of the alternative. About Hugo's historical method Marx observed, "Everything serves him as an authority, every authority serves him as an argument"; and about the true principles of justice he concluded that Hugo "desecrates them in the eyes of reason in order afterwards to make them honorable in the eyes of history."[79] So Hugo seemed even to justify slavery; and, in general, Marx reduced Hugo's philosophy of law to the proposition that "the sole juridical feature of man is his animal nature."

Savigny, Marx's teacher, who first joined and then superseded Hugo in the leadership of the Historical School, regarded this attack, of which he was only an indirect target, as unfair and obtuse. Throughout his life Savigny rejected the charge that his view supported the "tyranny of the past" (*Herrschaft der Vergangenheit*), and he argued that the basis of his thought was not authority but realistic human perspective. His views were expressed first in his youthful yet magisterial treatise on possession, *Das Recht des Besitzes* (1803).[80] Here Savigny decisively contributed to a discussion that had been going on for centuries, a discussion that had indeed begun with Gaius and that included other jurists, especially Le Douaren, Doneau, and Pothier. The controlling assumption of this book was that practical questions of law had to be settled in terms of Roman law understood not only systematically but also historically—that is, in terms of a process that included not only ancient forms but also medieval interpretations and modern (*heutige*) transformations. Savigny later followed this method in his treatise on the law of obligations and, above all, in his *System of Modern Roman Law*; presumably, he also maintained the same stance in his teaching and in his career as minister of justice for the reform of Prussian law. Savigny was involved, of course, in other contemporary controversies, most notably that between the "idealists" (especially the Hegelians) and the "realists," with whom he was identified; but the extent to which his ideas can be understood in terms of the longer legal tradition as well as the more immediate context of German philosophy is surprising.

[79] Marx, "Das philosophische Manifesto der historischen Rechtsschule," in *Marx-Engels Gesamtausgabe*, 1, pt. 1 (Berlin, 1927): 251–59. Also see H. Jaeger, "Marx et Savigny," *Archives de Philosophie du droit*, 12 (1967): 65–89; and J. Blühdorn, "Naturrechtskritik und 'Philosophie des positiven Rechts,' " *Tijdschrift voor Rechtsgeschiedenis*, 45 (1974): 3–17.

[80] Savigny, *Das Recht des Besitzes*, 124, and A. Rudorff's addition, 543–62. Also see Vogt, *Franciscus Duarenus*, 89–108.

From the first, Savigny, like Gaius, had systematic ambitions; and his age, like that of Gaius, was similarly divided, both ideologically and pedagogically, over jurisprudence. The basic question of the suitability of a modern code of laws for German society was the issue on which Savigny and the Historical School rose to prominence.[81] Savigny ridiculed the "positivist" notion advanced by A. F. J. Thibaut of constructing an abstract and academic code as simplistic and outmoded naturalism already discredited historically by the evident failures of the Napoleonic, Prussian, and Austrian codes of the previous half-century. Arguing that law, like language, was the product of a long and gradual development, Savigny concluded that the answer lay in the tradition of Roman law, which had been officially "common law" for three centuries and, in fact, for longer than that. As a result, he came to replace Hugo as the leader of the Historical School, especially after the publication of his manifesto of 1814 and the founding of his journal, *Zeitschrift fur geschichtliche Rechtswissenschaft*, in the following year. The premise of this journal, that a true "science" must be the product of centuries of development, was another illustration of the affinity between Savigny and Gaius. Thus, it is appropriate that in the next year came the miraculous discovery of that most ancient relic and deepest root of Roman legal science—Gaius' *Institutes*.

IRONICALLY, GAIUS APPEARED TOO LATE to be of practical value for the science of jurisprudence; it was too late in the evening for the Roman owl to take flight. The principal significance of the discovery lay in the field of historical scholarship and Roman antiquities. Even more ironically—tragically, in fact, for Savigny—the Historical School was itself more important in the long run for academic—scholarly and philosophical—than for professional achievements. In a sense this culmination of a long process of "historicizing" (*Historizierung*, as a recent historian of eighteenth-century universities calls it[82]) underlies the great works of Theodor Mommsen, Rudolf von Jhering, and others of the next century. In fact, Savigny's reputation today rests largely on his massive *History of Roman Law in the Middle Ages*, even though it was intended originally to be a preliminary study of the sources of law and, thus, ancillary to its author's professional aims and ambitions. Nevertheless, Savigny's *System of Modern Roman Law* was the principal monument of the Historical School; and in many ways it proposed, in modern terms, to carry out the same sort of task, philosophical as well as pedagogical, that Gaius had set for himself. In a sense, it was a move back toward Gaianism.

Savigny's neglected masterwork represents not only the culmination of the Historical School but also a kind of historically oriented *summa* of the legal

[81] Savigny, *Vom Beruf unserer Zeit für Gesetzgebung und Rechtswissenschaft* (Heidelberg, 1814), published with Thibaut's article and other material in J. Stern, *Thibaut und Savigny* (Darmstadt, 1959). On the problem of codification, see J. Vanderlinden, *La Concept du code en Europe occidentale du XXIIIe au XIXe siècle* (Brussels, 1967); G. Tarello, *Le Ideologie della codificazione nel secolo XVIII* (Genoa, 1971); W. Ebel, *Geschichte der Gesetzgebung in Deutschland* (2d ed., Göttingen, 1958); S. Gagnér, *Studien zur Ideengeschichte der Gesetzgebung* (Stockholm, 1960); and Koschaker, *Europa und das römische Recht*.

[82] Notker Hammerstein, *Jus und Historie* (Göttingen, 1972), 216.

tradition going back to the classical period of jurisprudence—most specifically to Gaius himself, who figures prominently in as well as provides the prototype for this treatise. Like Gaius, Savigny proposed to give shape to a vastly "rich heritage" through critical and selective judgment.[83] He rejected the current fallacy of both historical and legal scholarship, which assumed that a systematic treatment could merely be a collection of monographs (though that treatment, indeed, drew upon such works, including Savigny's own on possession and obligation). "Scientific" jurisprudence was the creation not of amateur philosophers like Cicero (or even Montesquieu, despite his training) but only of men of professional authority (*auctoritas prudentium*) like Gaius and Savigny himself. To Savigny's system in general Gaius had made at least three contributions. One was the transmission of particular formulas derived from more ancient Roman legal wisdom. Another was the distinction between the two basic kinds of law—that is, civil law and the law of nations, which was properly identified with natural law (as Savigny thought, in contradiction to those who recognized it as a third type) since it was based on "natural reason." And, almost unavoidably, the third was the notorious Gaian triad. Although Savigny had critical remarks to make about the triad, he did incorporate it into his own structure. What is more, he went on to point out a number of analogous trichotomies of Roman law that history, if not nature, had endorsed.

At the center of Savigny's (as of Gaius') cosmos was, of course, the individual "person," the first member of the Gaian trinity, which perhaps not originally but eventually opened up the whole question of the "status" and "condition" of man in a philosophical as well as a legal sense. In this connection he referred to Doneau, one of the most important of his systematizing predecessors, who elaborated on the concept of personhood by distinguishing aspects not only of life and security but also of liberty and belief (*existimatio*), all of which stemmed from an "original" rather than an "acquired" right. As Savigny described the basic *conditio hominum*, "Man stands in the midst of the outer world, and the most important element, to him in this surrounding of his, is the contact with those who are like him, by their nature and destination." From the individual Savigny moved to the social sphere, where as he put it, "in the richness of living reality all jural relations form a systematic whole." On the level of this web of jural relations (*Rechtsverhältnisse*), the counterpart of the individual was the "people" (*Volk*—that is, the Roman *gens*), and the law thereof was an expression of the old law of nations (*jus gentium*, rendered as *Volksrecht*).[84] Then, in Gaian fashion, he took up the law of things, actions, and their various derivatives and interactions. Romantic and organistic imagery aside, Savigny's strategy was quite in keeping with the Romanist tradition, which he was, in his "historicist" way, espousing.

[83] Savigny, *System des heutigen römischen Rechts*, ix, 413, 393, 38. And, for a very important article, see Aldo Mazzacane, "Savigny et la storiografia giuridica tra storia e sistema," in *Scritti in onore di Salvatore Publiatti*, 4 (Milan, 1978): 515–29.

[84] Savigny, *System des heutigen römischen Rechts*, 357, 331, xix, 17.

Savigny's influence, though restricted in the long run to the intellectual sphere (his struggle against modern jusnaturalism was defeated with the adoption of the German civil code in 1900), was profound and in many ways pervasive, illustrating again the humanist commonplace that Rome, although it had collapsed as a political structure, continued its dominance through linguistic, literary, and especially legal channels. Gibbon opened his forty-fourth chapter with the observation that "the public reason of the Romans has been silently or studiously transfused into the domestic institutions of Europe . . . ," but even deeper and more enduring has been the effect upon legal, historical, and social thought. Before Savigny this Roman influence was most conspicuously evident in the work of Montesquieu and Vico, who had also striven to recapture the essence of the tradition and give it modern form; after him, it was evident in the work of many others, not only disciples but also critics like Rudolf von Jhering, whose magisterial *Spirit of Roman Law* was devoted to the same purpose. To illustrate this purpose, both Vico and Jhering quoted the famous lines of Vergil,

> Remember, O Romans, you keep universal rule over nations
> In these ways: by maintaining peace through law,
> By doing justice to the lowly, by bringing down the haughty. . . .[85]

This prophecy might be taken as the epitaph of Savigny and his school—not only in their efforts to reform and to regulate society but also in their impact on modern social thought in general.

THE ACHIEVEMENT OF THE HISTORICAL SCHOOL had repercussions far beyond the legal scholarship of Savigny, Johann Eichhorn, and their disciples and the parallel historical writings of Barthold Georg Niebuhr and of Leopold von Ranke and his academic offspring. Based upon a total and "organic" view of culture, this approach involved many other areas of cultural study, most notably language, religion, and political economy. Out of the inter-disciplinary matrix created by these complementary and overlapping "historical schools" emerged one phase of a new discipline called sociology. One of the first historians (and in this country a founder) of that discipline pointed to the Historical School of Law, especially to the Savigny-Thibaut controversy, as seminal for the growth of sociology.[86] A more concrete illustration of this connection is Marx, whose social thought arose in the context of his legal education and, specifically, in the quarrel between the Hegelians and the Historical School; and a number of his ideas, including class structure and "alienation," were directly linked with the civilian tradition.[87] Other particular instances could be added—including, perhaps, the systematic work of Max Weber and, certainly, his sociology of law.

[85] Vico, *Diritto universale*, 214; and Rudolf von Jhering, *Der Geist des römischen Rechts auf den Stufen seiner Entwicklung*, 1 (Berlin, 1852): 306.

[86] Albion Small, *Origins of Sociology* (Chicago, 1924), 37–62.

[87] See my article, "The Metaphysics of Law: An Essay on the Very Young Marx," *AHR*, 83 (1978): 350–67, which is a continuation of the present discussion.

A central remaining question is the significance of the old Roman and Gaian paradigm for modern social thought, especially in its systematic sociological forms. Although to provide an answer moves the discussion from the historical dimension to transhistorical speculation, the question at least provides a logical *terminus ad quem* for this discussion of the afterlife of Roman forms and of Gaianism in particular. To conclude with a retrospective glance at this tradition, it seems clear that the first, and perhaps the most fundamental, continuing influence was pedagogical. Civil law was a major vehicle of secular higher education in European universities from the thirteenth to the nineteenth century (as it had been in Gaius' time), and the *Institutes* (first in a Gaian, then in a Justinianian, and finally in a national form for various European states) constituted one of the basic textbooks of Western civilization, arguably the single most influential introduction to social thought. Certainly, the overwhelming majority of social thinkers prior to Savigny were juridically trained. Secondly, Roman civil law was an almost inexhaustible source of assumptions, insights, terminology, methods, formulas, and concepts for systematic thinking about social structure and process; and even for those who, like Marx, reacted against it, the importance of civil law in negative ways was considerable. Finally, through its ideals, systematic form, and practical intentions, Roman jurisprudence furnished a "scientific" and "philosophical" model for the understanding of human society. The specific relationships between the old legal tradition and the new fields of human study, including economics, sociology, and anthropology, for the most part still await investigation.

In assessing the significance of civil law in Western social thought, let us, in conclusion, return to the original epistemological basis of the Gaian tradition. The ancient dualism of nature and convention implied a distinction between the natural and the social or historical condition of man; and Gaius' subjective and "personal" starting point gave priority to the latter, in contrast both to the intimidating political philosophy of Aristotelianism and to modern naturalism. Jurisprudence could not extricate itself from the conventional, however much it reached toward the natural: as "true philosophy," it was incorrigibly man-centered, value-laden, and action-oriented. It had to view the human condition not as a natural process or a logical construct but as a human epic or drama that focused on the conflict of wills and the means of resolving them within the overall communal pattern. Ultimately, perhaps, the natural and the conventional—reason and custom, the "spirit of law," and the reality of society—might be reconcilable; but men cannot judge, act, and live "ultimately," though they can talk about doing so. Of this human yet global approach to "science," the symbol and in some contingent (and "conventional") sense the starting point is "our Gaius."

[3]

*Law and Right in English Legal History**

ALBERT KIRALFY

Introduction

The attitude of the English lawyer towards his law as an institution independent of the machinery of its creation is ambiguous. The fundamental principles of English law are indigenous, but transplanted from the European continent in the eleventh century, and not of great antiquity. They have since developed on the basis of custom, practice, and ideas of what is right and reasonable. Hence, one would expect the English lawyer to be drawn to ideas of natural law and morals, and be a supporter of the historical and metaphysical schools of jurisprudence.

However, the opposite appears, at least superficially, to be the case where law is studied in England in abstract terms. All the emphasis is laid on authority and legality, on positive approaches. Perhaps the reason for this paradox lies mainly in the particular form assumed by the great turning point in English history – the constitutional crisis of the seventeenth century. The issue then was whether King or people should enjoy political power, especially legislative power. The assumption was made that if the people became sovereign they would know how to make good laws, and no agency has evolved to restrict the powers of Parliament over English law, nor has there been any room for any body of principles which would impose limitations on legislative sovereignty.

In this process, however, it is suggested that language has some part to play, and that this linguistic usage was largely accidental and not merely a reflection of the same forces helping to create Parliamentary institutions.[1] As a result of her history, several linguistic traditions seem to have conspired in England to bring about this result.

The English language has only one word for law, whereas most languages have several, and the word which English has retained is one which stresses the authority, or legality, of rules, rather than their inherent validity or justice. It is possible to refer to 'law' without the article, as being law in general, and 'a law' as being specific legislation

* Reprinted by permission of Leo S. Olschki, Publisher, from *La Formazione Storica del Diritto Moderno in Europa, Atti del Terzo Congresso Internazionale della Società Italiana di Storia del Diritto*, Vol. III (1977).

passed at a particular time, though the connotation of authority applies in both cases.

The problem has not been generally examined, though Sir John Salmond, a leading common law jurist, pointed out in his text-book on jurisprudence that English was peculiar in having only one word for law. He criticised English jurists for concentrating, in their theories of law, on the definition of a law as an enactment (like *lex, loi* or *Gesetz*) rather than on law in general (*jus, droit, Recht*). Salmond was consistent throughout his work in stressing the importance of right and justice in the content of law. He was also more ready than most English lawyers to admit that there had been considerable influence on our law from continental Europe. But he did not enquire further into the history of the problem of the two meanings of law and the linguistic background of our legal usage.[2] In recent times, in the United States, David Melinkoff has written an interesting work on the language of the law, which refers to several points in the history of the word law, but his work is comprehensive and does not concentrate on this issue.[3]

While the English law was developing, its main vocabulary was Anglo-Saxon, a language closely related to other Teutonic languages, including German and Danish. As a result of the Norman Conquest in 1066, Norman-French became substituted for Anglo-Saxon as the language of the law, and this dialect had much in common with modern French and with the Romance languages generally. The official language of records and Statutes after 1066 was Latin, a Latin similar to that used elsewhere in Europe at the time. Statutes came to be drafted later in French, and oral legal language became English in the fourteenth century. Having made their contributions, French died out by the sixteenth century, and Latin ceased to be used for the records in the eighteenth.

Since English was to replace French and Latin, the antecedents of legal English ought perhaps first to be considered.

Old English Legal Usage

The ancient Germanic word for law, *ae, aewe*, is found in use in the earliest recorded Anglo-Saxon laws, soon after the conversion to Christianity. Examples may be found in the Laws of Hlothhere & Eadric of Kent, dated approximately between 673 and 675 A.D. In the laws of Ine of Wessex, a just law is described as '*ryht aew*', approximate date between 688 and 694 A.D.[4] The word *ae* is related to the modern German *ehe*, to the Latin *aevum*, and the Greek *aion*. The latter words survive meaning ages, while the German *ehe* means marriage, though in the *aewe* form it is also the basis of the modern *je* and *ewig*, meaning ever.

The word *dom* related to the modern doom and damn, was another ancient word for law, stressing a decision, like the word deem, meaning to judge or think fit, which is only now beginning to be discarded from everyday use. In many of the Anglo-Saxon laws, *dom* means a particular ruling in a particular case, but it also sometimes means a legal principle,[5] in the late tenth century. In the earlier laws it refers to legislation, and this is not surprising, since the separation of the legislative and judicial powers was unusual.[6] In the Laws of Ine (c. 690) and of Edward (c. 900), just laws are described as '*ryhte domas*', and the same usage occurs widely in the laws of Edgar and Canute (late tenth and early eleventh century). Collections of laws were also called books of dooms, between the seventh and tenth century,[7] while breach of law is sometimes called '*undom*'.[8]

The word *geraednes, asetnys*, meant a specific statute, like the German *Gesetz*. *Asette* is used to mean legislate, in the seventh century Laws of Aethelbert, and of Hlothhere and Eadric, while *geraednisse* are referred to much later in 1,6, & 8 Aethelred, in the tenth to eleventh centuries.

The word *riht* was used as an adjective to mean what is right, correct and just, and as a noun, to mean truth and justice. It is not clear whether its use as a noun is post-Christian only, but such use as a noun is so widespread among the Teutonic peoples that it seems likely to be quite ancient. Proof is difficult, since all surviving Anglo-Saxon law was written and therefore dates from after the conversion. Legal examples of the word's use as a noun include, about 680 A.D., '*An eald riht*' in the Laws of Hlothhere and Eadric of Kent, 12, and '*An ald riht*' in the Laws of Wihtred of Kent, 5, also in the seventh century. '*Mid ryhte*' is used in Aethelstan 1,5. By the time of King Aethelstan, that is, 925–940 A.D., '*folcriht*' is used to refer to the general law.[9] The word is also frequently used in the tenth century Laws of Edgar, and Aethelred, and in the early eleventh century Laws of Canute. That '*riht*' had come to mean law, and not simply rightness, seems borne out by a tenth century passage where the people are told to petition the King for equitable relief if *riht* is too rigorous.[10]

The Danish Invasion

The Vikings invaded England on a number of occasions, and established many settlements in the North-Eastern half of the country. These Danes and Norwegians had ethical words similar to *riht* (e.g. *raettr*), but their usual word for law was the imperative word *log*, which denoted enacted law rather than customary rules or just principles.[11] This word seems to have had some remote common root with the Latin *lex*, which will be discussed later. It is this Danish word which became a loan word in English and replaced the Old English *dom, aewe*, and *riht*, possibly because it was forceful and unambiguous. The Danish word *wrong* also replaced the Old English *woe*, but this word is more moralistic than *law*.

Since the Anglo-Saxons otherwise preserved their own language for most purposes, the introduction of the word *law* is curious. Its supposed earliest use, in a version of a Law of 930,[12] may well have been an interpolation at a later date. The word is used in the so-called Treaty of Edward and Guthrum, as of 920, but that document is now believed to date from the early eleventh century. The earliest clear instance of its use is probably in a Law of Edgar in the tenth century where the Danes are referred to, quite properly, as having '*lage*' and the Saxons as having '*dooms*'. By the time of the Laws of the Saxon Aethelred, 978–1016, and the Dane Canute, 1016–1035, who both ruled both races, both Saxons and Danes are described as having *laws*.[13] Professor Whitelock considers that the moving spirit for the adoption of *lagu* to replace *riht* and *dom* may have been Wulfstan, a Saxon who was Bishop of London 996–1002, and Archbishop of York 1002–1023, when he died. He also had connections in the Eastern part of England where the Danes were settled.

King Canute, the Dane, in 1020, ordered continued observance of Edgar's laws (*Eadgares lage* in Old English). He was succeeded by the Saxon, Edward the Confessor. When William the Conqueror and his Normans entered England in 1066, his Old English charter to the city of London confirmed Edward's laws as follows: '*Ic wylle that yet beon allra theira lage weorthe the yt waeren on Eadwardes daege Kynges*'. The Latin charter of Henry I in 1100 promised to restore, not *legem*, but '*lagam Edwardi regis*' – compare the so-called Laws of Henry I, lxvi, 6, referring to the *laga* of the English.[14]

With the adoption of the Danish word, the Old English *riht* was reduced to an adjective again, and used to describe laws; in the tenth century, for example, we find '*rihte laga*'.[15]

As a pure conjecture, it may be that the co-existence of two races of a similar civilisation but having two different legal systems made it impossible to describe positive law as *riht*, since what was right would presumably be invariable and uniform. Such an objection would not, of course, apply to common legislation at the highest level, but even here the Kings often enacted different rules for one race from those they enacted for the other.

German Usage

It may throw into relief the effects of the replacement of *riht* by *lagu* in England, if we compare the development which took place in Germany. Old words like *ewa* were replaced, after the conversion to Christianity, by *reht*, about the year 1000. This word of course already had an adjectival meaning as 'right' or 'true'. Professor Gerhard Koebler considers that it was the revival of classical study in the early Renaissance and the influence of the Latin *jus* that caused *reht* to be used as a noun, *jus* being what was *justum*.

As in other European countries, mediaeval laws tended to be known either as statutes (*Gesetze*) or customs (*Gewohnheiten*). *Reht*, on the other hand, is found in some texts, as for example the Nuremburg Police Ordinance of 1300, 34, where it is provided that regulations must not violate unwritten or written law, '*Das Gesetzte sol der Stat an iren alten Rehten und Gesetzen niht schaden*'.

That *reht* meant law, and not justice, may appear from a phrase used in 1549, and cited by Grimm, harsh law is bad law – '*Scharf recht ein boes recht*'.[16] The word was also used to describe broad bodies of law, such as Roman law or Canon law, and these were known as '*Die beiden Rechte*'.[17]

The survival of the idea that law and right were the same, with right also being used to refer to individual rights created by law, must have given law an assumed element of inherent rightness. Consequently, German legal philosophers have concentrated on *Recht* rather than *Gesetz* as the proper subject for study,[18] and the authority of law ultimately rested on its reasonableness and not on its authorship.[19] This has had the consequence in turn that in modern times, German jurists like Radbruch have questioned the validity of unjust laws, rather as did the natural lawyers in former times. Professor Hart in England considered that the German approach was deeper than the merely linguistic,[20] but it must be pointed out that German is by no means unusual in its linguistic identification of law and right – in fact it is English which is the exceptional language in this context.

In Scandinavia itself, law did not ultimately completely replace right. In the mediaeval period, in Sweden, for example, *raett* remained in general use to mean rightness and justice, as applied to law, though distinct from positive law. For example, Upplandslagen, the Provincial law, states that it is the object of law to do right – the preamble may be modernised as '*Lag skall vara stiftad till at skillnad mellan raett och oraett*'. By the sixteenth century, *raett* had begun to recover the sense of strict law; for example, Olaus Petri in Sweden translated '*Summum jus summa injuria*' as '*Hoegsta raett aer stoersta oraett*'. *Raett* came to mean the general body of law, including unwritten law, like the German *Recht*, while *lag* is generally confined to legislation. Hence the relationship between *raett* and *lag* is now rather like that between the original Roman *jus* and *lex*.

Modern philosophers tell us that philosophy is largely a matter of words rather than ideas in themselves; however that may be, the fact that the words for law and right are found to be the same in so many languages is certainly significant. However, if this is purely a Christian development, it would lose some of its philosophic force, since it could be accounted for by a single Judaeo-Christian tradition. We do not find rightness stressed, for instance, in Greek tragedy and mythology, where almost all our abstract notions may be found first created and developed.

The Late Latin Usage

To return to English developments, Latin became the official language of English records in 1066, and remained so for many centuries. Hence it is vital to see how the clerks rendered the legal English vocabulary. Of course, Latin was no longer the original classical language, and some major changes had taken place in regard to the words for law.

I shall have little to say about the word *jus*, since it was little used in the Middle Ages, except to describe Roman law or to refer to individual rights created by law. Its original sense, of a body of principles or customs, had been lost in the Dark Ages, and the developing Romance languages, as we shall see, made little use of it, although they preserved derivatives like just and justice.

The word *lex* had already had a very chequered history by the Middle Ages. Originally, a *lex* was a specific enactment of the popular assembly, like the *Lex Aquilia*. With the accession of the Emperor Augustus, such assemblies were seldom convened, and imperial statutes were described as constitutions, or by reference to the particular form that they assumed. Hence, as early as the time of Gaius, *leges* no longer connote particular statutes, but a whole body of written law, so that a people may be described as ruled by laws and customs.[21] Gaius still refers broadly to the '*jus civile proprium Romanorum*', but to the laws and customs of the aliens as '*Leges et mores peregrinorum*'.[22] It may be that the aliens still passed laws in popular assemblies, but it is more likely that Roman lawyers were not very interested in nomenclature, just as they are said not to have been interested in theories of sources or classification. The Proemium to Justinian's Institutes uses *lex* to refer to law in general, and all nations in the Roman Empire are referred to as governed by *leges* made by the Romans. *Lex* is defined as written law (*ius scriptum*) and the *Corpus Juris* itself as *leges*, presumably because it was a written collection of rules. Unwritten law is by now regarded as antique, and as a mere imitation of written law, though historically this is quite inaccurate.[23]

The division of law into *leges* and *mores* is repeated in the West by St. Isidore of Seville, in 636 A.D.,[24] and this work seems to have been known to the compilers of some of the Barbarian Codes. These Codes were known as *leges* – the *Lex Longobardorum*, the *lex Saxonum*, etc., – presumably because they were reduced to writing, since they contained Roman rules and were not actually legislation. In the laws of the Bavarians,[25] there is an interesting instruction, that the court is to have a judge with a law book (*librium legis*) who is to give a right judgement (*rectum iudicium*).

A notable feature of early mediaeval law was the idea of personal status, or the 'personal' statute, according to which every man carried his city or tribal law with him, whereas the 'real' statute required local law to be applied. Pepin in Italy, Louis the Pious in France, and the Lombards, laid down that a man should be governed by his own law, be he Roman, Frank, or Goth.[26]

Law and custom (*lex et consuetudo*) became a trite phrase in mediaeval Europe – *vetus formula*.[27] Thus, actual legislation was known, in France until the eighteenth century, as *Ordonnances* rather than *lois*; and English statutes were referred to as *statuta*, not *leges*. The so-called *Leges Edwardi, Leges Wilelmi*, and *Leges Henrici*, however, were compilations of rules, not statutes. English common law is generally rendered in Latin as *lex communis*, though occasionally at first *jus commune* is encountered. In 1215, Magna Carta refers to English law as the '*lex regni*'.[28] Both the great English legal institutional writers of the twelfth and thirteenth centuries, Glanvill and Bracton, open their works by apologising for calling the English law *lex*, since, as they point out, it is really unwritten law: '*Leges namque Anglicanas, licet non scriptas, leges appellari non videtur absurdum*'.[29] In 1266, the Statute of Kenilworth referred to *leges ac regni consuetudines*.

In Norman-French, the law is generally called '*La Commune ley*', for example in 1300 in the *Articuli super Cartas*, '*Ou remedie ne fust avant par la commune ley*'. The Year Book Reports, between the thirteenth and the sixteenth centuries, use '*La Ley*' to refer to law in general, and in the same way in mediaeval France, '*La loi*' often meant the law in general. The Chanson de Roland refers to '*La lei de sa terre*', and Froissart to '*Toute la ley*'.[30]

The idea that *lex* means a law enacted by a ruler, whereas *jus* meant a superior moral system of law, is relatively late, and was no doubt influenced by the mediaeval controversy of Pope and Emperor, and the ideas of natural and positive law. In 1576, Jean Bodin contrasts the rightness of *jus* with the power behind *lex*.[31] '*Sed plurimum distat lex a jure; jus enim sine jussu ad id quod aequum bonum est, lex autem ad imperantis majestatem pertinet. Est enim lex nihil aliud quam summae potestatis jussum*'.

The late Latin word *directum* replaced the classical Latin *jus* as a word to describe a whole legal system. Whereas *jus* connoted an assertion of the will, the vindication of rights or a correction of some lapse, the word *rectus* in Latin signified something that was true or right. The word *rectus* is related to the Greek *orthos*, and almost certainly also to the Teutonic words like *riht* and *recht*, already discussed. Curiously enough, *rectus* itself did not acquire the meaning of law in late Latin, or the Romance languages derived from it, though *rectum* and *directum* were both used to mean individual legal rights – but the latter replaced the former in the vernacular. The model for a replacement for *jus*, however, appears to have been *directum* alone.

Experts appear generally agreed that Christianity probably inspired the idea of something objectively right and just, that is, following the right direction.[32] While, as we have seen, the written laws of the German invaders of the Western Roman Empire were called *leges*, the Christian idea of the law of God was expressed as *directum* by the seventh century. It has been suggested, indeed, that because all Romance languages use derivatives of *directum* to express right law, the use of the word for this proposal must ante-date the fall of the Western Empire; in other words, must be as old as the fourth century.[33]

Whence the 'di-' of *directum*? Why the divergence from Teutonic tongues which lack the 'Di-'? The Greeks used a word '*diortho*' to mean put right, and this may have reinforced the idea of direction, divine or otherwise, as did the Latin *dirigere*. Professor Gallo himself believes the true root was the idea of a road or way to be followed by Christians, as this metaphor is common in both Old and New Testaments, particularly in the Psalms, whose translators rendered 'road' as 'law'.[34] *Directum* could conflict with the innate moral sense, as God's ways are often mysterious.[35] It appears to be a coincidence that the Hebrew for road was '*derek*'.

Similarly, though there is a Hungarian word '*derek*' which now means straight or honest, it does not seem to be linked to the Latin *directum*. It is believed by Hungarian philologists to be a Slavonic loan word meaning 'main' or 'middle', and is also used to mean 'waist' in modern Hungarian. The modern usage meaning honest or honourable is considered to be a later, figurative usage.[36] However, the root *drek* does not appear to be used in modern Slavonic languages to mean the middle, which is usually, '*pol-*' or '*sred-*'. It may be a word *drek* meaning a Tree-Trunk (cf. Latin *Truncus*).

By the time of Charlemagne, *directum* in its Gallicised form is used to mean law. For example, in a Latin text of 802, '*per drictum et per legem; sicut per drictum debet*'.[37] The Strasbourg Oaths of 842 are similar, the word being also used to mean a subjective right and legal process in general. By the late eleventh century, the Chanson de Roland refers to the French form, '*Dieus faict entre nous le dreit*'. An interesting example of the idea of *directum* as a means of mediating disputes appears in the thirteenth century Ancien Coutumier of Normandy.[38]

> *Celuy a fait droict qui loyalment a jugé ou finé une querelle. L'on appelle droict des loix et les coustumes de Normandie pur ce que par eux est souvent le plet finé.*

The narrower sense of *droit* as a French word for strict law seems to have developed later, when, as a result of the preparation of legal commentaries on the French customs, a body of principles emerged from them.[39] Thus, Professor René David cites Bourjon, about 1720, as using the phrase '*Le droit commun de la France*'.[40]

We have seen that in England, *ley* was the usual word after the Conquest. However the word *droit* or *dreit* is used in some contexts to mean law, and not merely an individual right. Thus, in 1258, the Provisions of Oxford refer to the powers of Judges to correct wrongs '*Solum lei et dreit de la tere*'. A curious work written in the late thirteenth century and known as the 'Mirror of Justices', contains many useful examples of usage, which are lost in the English translation. Thus, the anonymous author criticises statutory provision of treble damages because, in his opinion, no-one should recover more than he has lost, '*droit ne donne a nul plus que sa demande*'.[41] The book refers to written law, '*lei escrite*', and to laws and customs, '*les leis et les usages*', but also stresses the injustice of some rules, '*Nest mye droit qe le soit puni*',[42] '*droit défend*',[43] '*countre dreit*'.[44] There is a nice old-fashioned ring about his phrase for good statutes, '*Des droites leis*'.[45]

From the beginning of the fourteenth century, the reliance on this idea of right as standard by which to judge customs and statutes gave way to appeals to reason. Of course, the French form '*Raison*' has different nuances from the modern English, connoting truth and rightness as well as justice. The reasonable man, who plays such a prominent part in modern English law, now takes the place of the right law of earlier times. The force of reason appears in many instances in the Year Books. In a famous instance in 1344, Judge Hilary said that the Judges could make law as they wished, but Judge Stonore retorted that law was rightness, '*Ley est resoun*'.[46] In 1535, in almost the last Year Book, a barrister called Montague argued that trusts existed at common law because law was reason, '*Car le comen ley nest auter forsque comen reason, et comen reason voet que un home poit mettre son trust in un auter*'.[47]

With the decline in spoken law-French by the fourteenth century, and in written law-French by the sixteenth, English was left with no specific word which meant law and right in the same concept, only the one imperative word '*law*'.

Modern English Legal Usage: Right

English law has generally restricted the word *right* to individual rights based on law. For example, the greatest mediaeval writ was the Writ of Right (*breve de recto*) which was used to recover land to which the plaintiff claimed title.[48]

The word is only occasionally used as a noun; for example, from the time of Edward II until the Crown Proceedings Act 1947, no ordinary legal action lay in the Courts to recover property taken by the Crown illegally. Instead, a Petition of Right was used, in which the King was petitioned to cause right to be done, '*Fasse droit et raison*'. If granted, the petition was endorsed that right be done, '*Que droit soit fait comme est désiré*'. This procedure is the more significant because the very important constitutional document presented by Parliament to Charles I, in 1628, took the form of a Petition of Right, and this demanded a redress of grievances, and a restoration of civil liberties of various kinds. The 1628 Petition complained in the main of violations of enacted law, by the King, under colour of his prerogative. King Charles I endorsed this Petition first with the words 'The King willeth that right be done according to the laws and customs of the realm, and that the statutes be put in due execution, that his subjects may have no cause to complain of any wrong or oppressions contrary to their just rights and liberties . . .' This is linguistically interesting, as containing almost all the words under discussion here. It was, however, not the customary phrase, and tantamount to a royal refusal to pass the Petition. The Commons succeeded ultimately in insisting that the Petition be answered with the customary '*Soit droit fait comme est désiré*'. Even greater constitutional importance attaches to the Bill of Rights in 1689, asserting various rights and liberties of the people.

An interesting modern echo of this old procedure has been provided.[49] Mr Henry Franklin, a holder of Rhodesian stock on which he had received no interest since the illegal unilateral declaration of independence in 1965, wished to enforce his right against Rhodesian funds frozen in the U.K. The 1947 Crown Proceedings Act repealed the Petitions of Right Act 1860, which in turn had reformed the procedure to be followed in such cases. However, whilst the 1947 Act applied to England and Scotland, it did not apply to claims against the Crown in respect of the (former) colonies, and accordingly the High Court held that the repeal of the 1860 Act did not abolish the possibility of proceeding by Petition of Right when claims were made against the Crown outside the 1947 Act, and that Petitions of Right could still lie in such cases at common law. A Petition of Right based largely on models in the 1860 Act was drawn up, signed by the Home Secretary, and by the Queen personally, and endorsed 'Let right be done'. The Queen referred it to the Court for decision, where it was successful, though its practical effect has been less so. The learned Judge, in arriving at his decision, considered that the Petition of Right went back to Anglo-Saxon times. This was formerly the scholarly view, but it is difficult to prove to modern satisfaction that it is quite that old. Ninth and tenth century laws[50] refer to eventual appeals to the King for failure of justice elsewhere, but this seems to be a matter of general appellate power, and not to refer to claims against the Crown alone.

As well as the notion of an overriding and ultimate jurisdiction, the idea of right also survived in the guise of fundamental law, a concept no doubt produced by an attempt to put into English the ideas underlying such words as '*droit*' in Norman French. Fundamental law, however, was a less ambiguous term than 'right', which could also have meant, and indeed normally did mean, an individual right. The doctrine is explained by a leading modern scholar as follows:[51]

> In mediaeval and Tudor England, Parliament and ... every other authority, however exalted, from the King downwards, was conceived of as being under the obligation to respect certain general principles, of reason or nature, moral principles, or the will of God. ... To the mediaeval thinker, as the whole of creation was subject to God's will, the State and law were essentially organs of right and justice, and justice was an absolute quality, not something relative merely to the law enforced in a particular place.

Another modern authority has written that[52] law was 'Designed for the enforcement of what no one doubted to be already law' (right, *jus*). In the 17th century, Sir Edward Coke, that greatest of English lawyers, strove to give this idea binding force, in the famous *Bonham's case*,[53] when he claimed that a statute could be void if 'against common right or reason'.

But this approach was not fruitful. The contest ceased to be one between fundamental right and sheer might, but became rather one between King and Parliament, neither of them now regarded as judicial organs. The Courts ceased to exercise any real control over legislation in England, and the victory of Parliament in 1688 made it much more of an absolute ruler than the Kings had ever been. Judges had been discredited by their subservience to the Monarchy, and there was no support for a third force which could sit in judgement on legislature and executive. The will of the people was now the test. Lord Halifax indicated this when he said:[54] 'Parliament may judge against right – their power is good, though their act is ill'.

I have said little about justice in this paper, as justice is a wider concept than law. Of course, the aim of law is avowed to be the pursuit of justice, but its scope in everyday law is rather restricted and spasmodic.[55] There is an interesting use of the Latin *Rectum* to mean right or law, in the 29th chapter of Magna Carta, where right is contrasted with justice in the solemn undertaking given by King John in 1215, 'To none shall we sell, to none deny, to none delay right or justice'; (*nulli vendemus, nulli negabimus aut differemus justitiam vel rectum*).

In the 17th century, Sir Edward Coke wrote that in this passage, right meant law and was identical with the Latin *jus*.[56] He claimed that the word *rectum* was used 'Because it is the right line whereby justice distributative is guided and directed' – an interpretation for which he gives no authority, but which is in line with the Christian tradition already referred to. He also contrasts law with tort, as right with wrong, and states that *injuria est contra jus*, but this usage of *jus* was uncommon. Coke concludes his summary by saying that *rectum* may be the subjective right, and offering the highly original contribution that some lawyers believed that this provision in Magna Carta referred to the Writ of Right only!

Where English equity, as distinct from common law, was concerned, orthodox Thomist views of the law of God seem to have been applied. Thus, Christopher St. Germain in 1523 in his Dialogue of a Doctor and Student[57] states: 'When the law eternal or the will of God is known to his creatures reasonable by the light of natural understanding or by the light of natural reason, that is called the law of reason'. Even today, reason and conscience as concepts have predominated in this field.

A late attempt in the eighteenth century by Lord Mansfield to apply the rule of reason to strict common law failed disastrously. In the leading case of *Rann v Hughes*[58] counsel relied on reason as an argument for enforcing a contract without consideration. The Lord Chief Baron Skinner admitted that 'It is undoubtedly true that every man is by the law of nature bound to fulfill his engagements', but he denied that this was the common law of England.

Thus, we have seen, the British people came to put their faith in political machinery rather than in philosophical ideas, in procedures rather than principles, and in Parliament rather than jurists. It is easy to see which way a majority has voted, but it is difficult to see where abstract right lies, and how it is to be tested. Indeed, one may say that the idea that there is one right solution to a problem is oversimplified, for people may be deeply divided as to what is right. The 'natural law' approach, once divided from religious orthodoxy, is impractical. On the other hand, we may have suffered from the absence of belief that laws may be good or bad, and from the assumption that the majority will always act properly. The courts, with their concept of reasonableness, have kept much closer to natural law ideals, but the pragmatic British people, as a result of their history, have limited the scope of the judges and their dangerous abstract notions.

NOTES

1. I wish to acknowledge the kind co-operation of many learned colleagues in Europe, who answered numerous queries during the compilation of this paper.
2. Sir J. Salmond, *Jurisprudence*, e.g. 11th ed. p.37.
3. D. Melinkoff, *The Language of the Law*, 1963.
4. F.L. Attenborough, *The Laws of the Earliest English Kings*, Cambridge 1922; A.J. Robertson, *The Laws of the Kings of England, Edmund to Henry I*, Cambridge 1925.
5. E.g., 3 Edgar 2, 1 (a).
6. Cf. Laws of Aethelbert, early 7th century; Laws of Hlothhere and Eadric, late 7th century; Laws of Wihtred, late 7th century.
7. Laws of Wihtred, 5, late 7th century; 1 Edward, about 900; 2 Aethelstan 5, about 930.
8. 2 Canute 15 (a), A.D. 1016–1035.
9. 6 Aethelstan 8, 1, A.D. 925–940.

10. 3 Edgar 2 (1), A.D. 959–975.
11. Prof. Klaus von See, *Altnordische Rechtswoerter*, 1964, pp. 174, 179, 181.
12. 1 Aethelstan 2, *On Godes lage*; see Prof. D. Whitelock, 56 *English Historical Review* (1941), p. 1.
13. 4 Edgar 2 & 12; *On Engla lage, on Dene lage*.
14. Duck, *The Civil Law in England*, 1679. 1724 translation xv–xvi stated that the Normans preferred Danish legal elements, because of their common Scandinavian origins.
15. 5 Aethelred 1, 6; see also 6 Aethelred 8, 49 & 50; and 2 Canute 1, 15, cf. 75, 76.
16. J. & W. Grimm, *Deutsches Wörterbuch*, 1854–1960, vol. 8 (1893), p. 376.
17. Grimm, *op. cit.*, vol. 8, 377, 404.
18. E.g. Hegel, *Philosophie des Rechts*; Stammler, *Das richtige Recht*.
19. Cf. Friedrich, *Philosophy of Law in its Historical Perspective*, English translation, pp. 136, 205.
20. H. L. A. Hart, *Harvard Law Review*, 71 (1958), p. 593.
21. I, 1.
22. I, 92.
23. Institutes, I.2.9.
24. Origines, Bk V, III.
25. Tit. 2, Ch. 15 para 2, cited Ducange, *Glossarium Mediae et Infimae Latinitatis*, Paris 1938, vol. 5, p. 77.
26. Ducange, *op. cit.*, vol. 5, p. 78.
27. Ducange, *loc. cit.*
28. Ch. 45.
29. Cf. Pollock & Maitland, *History of English Law*,. 2nd ed., Vol. 1, p. 175.
30. *Grand Larousse Encyclopédique*, vol. 6, p. 817.
31. *De Republica*, 1576, p. 162.
32. See e.g., W. C. Sforza, 'Diritto', in *Enciclopedia del diritto*, XII (1964).
33. A. Garcia-Gallo, 'Ius y Derecho', *Annuario de Historia del Derecho Español*, 1960, p. 12.
34. *Op. cit.*, p. 23.
35. *Op. cit.*, pp. 27–8.
36. I. Szamota, *Magyar oklevél-szótár* 1902–1906; see also G. Barczi, *Magyar Szófejtö Szótár*, 1941.
37. Ducange, *op. cit.*, vol. 3 p. 125.
38. Cited Godefroy, *Dictionnaire de l'ancienne Langue Française*, 1880–1902, vol. 2. (1883), p. 772.
39. Arminjon, Nolden, Wolff, *Traité de droit comparé*, 1950, vol. 1, p. 124, 'Ils s'efforcent de dégager de la comparaison des lois locales un droit coutumier commun'.
40. David, *Le droit français*, 1960, vol. 1, p. 10, referring also to Meynial, *Rev. Gen. de Droit* (1903), 326ff.
41. Selden Society, Vol. 7 (1893), p. 197.
42. *Op. cit.*, p. 182.
43. *Op. cit.*, p. 73.
44. *Op. cit.*, p. 169.
45. *Op. cit.*, p. 200.
46. Y.B. 18 & 19 Edward III (R.S.), p. 379.
47. Y.B. 27 Henry VIII Easter pl. 22, f. 10.
48. For an example see 77 Selden Society, p. 314.
49. Reported in the London *Times* 19 April 1973.
50. 3 Edgar 2; 2 Canute 17.
51. J. W. Gough, *Fundamental Law in English Constitutional History*, 1955, p. 22.
52. K. W. Pickthorne, *Early Tudor Government*, I, 135.
53. Co. Rep., 117b at 118b.
54. Cited Gough, *op. cit.*, p. 171; *Life and Letters of George Saville, Marquis of Halifax*, ed. H. C. Foxcroft (1898) ii, p. 490 et seq. *Political Thoughts and Reflections*.
55. For a full study of this problem, see F. E. Dowrick, *Justice according to the English Common Lawyers*, 1961.
56. 2 Co. Inst. p. 56.
57. Book I ch. I.
58. 1778, 7 Term Rep. 250.

[4]

COMMON LAW, CIVIL LAW AND SOCIALIST LAW: THREE LEADING SYSTEMS OF THE WORLD, THREE KINDS OF LEGAL THOUGHT

A. G. CHLOROS*

I Introduction

It is commonplace to state that legal systems cannot be reduced to abstract structures. Indeed, those Analytical jurists who have attempted to describe the inner logic of legal systems, in order to discover their common features, have generally been held to have failed because they have tended to concentrate their analysis upon concepts, while neglecting to take into account the background upon which legal systems operate. For a legal system has not only an inner logic, but a history, a sociology, a psychology and, indeed, a philosophy. In this respect, even the strictest analysis contains the seeds of defeat. For instance,

John Austin, who was interested in law "strictly so called",[1] linked his definition of law to the idea of a sanction. He defined sanction as some sort of evil,[2] thus introducing what the Austrian jurist, Hans Kelsen, later called an inadmissible psychological element.[3] But Kelsen, in his turn, could not see that the *Grundnorm*, that is, the basic constitutional norm of a legal system, depended upon sociological considerations. He came to the strange conclusion that legal norms exist before sociological jurisprudence,[4] whereas, as Professor J. Stone has amply demonstrated, "the truth seems to be exactly the reverse."[5] In other words, the alleged purity of the subsidiary norms of his legal structure is based upon a flimsy foundation. Equally, Wesley Newcomb Holfeld, after establishing the lowest common denominator of his legal system, went on to claim that, in this way, the observer could "discern common principles of justice and policy."[6] But in this respect, Holfeld overlooked David Hume's aphorism that there are no inevitable truths in the realm of human behaviour and that we cannot derive value judgments from empirical observation.[7]

All these attempts to provide an exclusively analytical view of the law have shown that analysis is an inadequate instrument of discovering the nature of a complex legal phenomenon, such as law. Indeed, law is a discipline that has such a variety of aspects that it is not surprising that the questions which were first asked by a Greek philosopher, Plato, over two thousand years ago—namely, "What is law?" and "What is justice?" —should still elude a complete and objective answer. In a different way, those who tried, in later centuries, from Hegel onwards through Sir Henry Maine to Max Weber and Marx, to define society and, therefore, law in terms of large movements of history, or as a sequence of quasi-automatic historical stages, have also failed to capture the flavour of a legal system, the analysis of which must take into account the irrational element of human society. For law regulates society and society is too complex and sophisticated to be understood as an inevitable and pre-conceived succession of scenarios.

It is as well, therefore, to set a modest objective to the comparison of

*Professor of Comparative Law, London University.

these leading legal systems which have been chosen for discussion and state, at the outset, that a full description can, at best, only be a personal point of view. Probably, the most profitable approach is to attempt simply to draw some impressionist strokes upon the canvas of the legal systems of the world. All this in the hope that, if the full picture of the three legal systems still eludes us, at least lawyers may recognise different trends and some distinctive features of each legal system.

However, this is not intended as a philosophical exercise. Philosophy is, after all, a very personal attempt to discover the truth, but also a practical demonstration that the existence of different forms of regulation of society—which is what legal systems attempt to do—may reveal trends and lead to generalisations. These can then be left to individual jurists for evaluation. Thus, any broad strokes that this essay may draw, or any generalisations made, have no exclusive claim to the truth. They represent a personal point of view. At most, they may lay a claim that the specific legal regulation, or legal practice in each system described, reflects trends which are worthy of note and may be the object of choice. Beyond this modest aim, no greater scientific objective is aimed at.

II The Common Law

It would probably be fair to say that the most distinctive features of the Common law are to be found in its technique and its philosophy. Unlike Civil law or Socialist law, Common law has an uninterrupted history of nine centuries up to the present time. At least, in the form that it applies in England, nothing has come to disturb a steady process of evolution, no doubt, to the full approval of Edmund Burke.

A. The technique

The technique of this evolution has not been through the enunciation of principle, but through a continuing flow of cases and statutes. But, of the two, it is the cases that have determined its life. Statutes have been and, in the field of lawyers' law, still are an exception. It was in the period between the two early English historians, Glanville and Bracton, that the subsequent course of the Common law was clearly determined. For, at the end of the twelfth century, Glanville wrote as a Roman lawyer and only cites two cases in his book. Bracton, on the other hand, almost one hundred years later cites five hundred cases quoting, as Sir Paul Vinogradoff showed in the early twenties, from a notebook containing over two thousand cases.[8]

Why did England reject Roman law which, after all, represented the wisdom of centuries and was a foundation of Western civilisation? The answer is a complex one, but it may be surmised that case-law represented the modern man's realisation of his own limitations. He could not get himself to describe things for all time, or to be bold enough to conceive the idea of universal justice. This could be left to God and man's efforts must necessarily have a more modest aim. At least, that was the reaction of the English lawyer. This had already been noted in the sixteenth century by Christopher St. Germain in his book *Doctor and Student*. There it is explained that where the canonist or civilian would speak of the Law of Nature, the Common lawyer speaks of reason.[9] Thus, the English judge could only claim to do justice between man and man and this with the primary purpose of keeping the peace of the realm. For the rest, there was no need for law; for law means regulation and compulsion and these were concepts from which the Englishman's mind instinctively recoils. Besides, it was in resolving disputes rather than in laying down principles, that the English judge could see justice done. Even when, in the Middle Ages, the Common law had become too rigid, the golden age of Equity, which varied, as it was said, with the length of the Chancellor's foot, was relatively brief. In our century Equity became, in effect, just as strict a system of precedents as the Common law was, and the discretionary power of the judges remained only as a faint echo of the ecclesiastical reasons behind its birth.

In this way the success of the English legal system could be verified or tested at every moment with every new case. Those who dispensed it, the judges and the lawyers, felt themselves responsible for the quality of the system, and they were sufficiently few to maintain a standard of independence, technical competence and excellence which could not easily be surpassed. To this we must add the fact that the judges, through allying themselves with Parliament in its struggle with the King, acquired an entrenched position which had a Constitutional rather than an administrative character. This is still the case in England, as can be seen by the fact that the judges are members of the legislature. They are subject to no administrative constraints and possess police powers in the form of punishment which they can mete out for contempt of Court. As to the quality of the law, it was a German scholar, Paul Koschaker who, in his book *Europ und das Römische Recht*,[10] wrote that the most effective kind of law is made when law-making is in the hands of a small group of eminent lawyers, who are able to exercise independent judgment. This is what happened in English law. It must also be recalled that the golden age of Roman law was the classical period, which was dominated by a small group of great jurists from Papinian to Modestinus.

It is interesting that when the Common law was transplanted to the United States, the same traditions were maintained, quite apart from the common origin of legal concepts and the common approach to legal problems. This is so even though in the United States the need for a federal structure diverted the traditional pragmatic approach of the Common law towards a declaration of principles. Such are, for instance, the statements contained in the U.S. Constitution.[11] But, even so, it should be noted that it was an English philosopher's thought—John Locke's—that was the foundation of the Constitution.[12] Since then, the United States held the judicial function in great esteem and its legal history is full of names of distinguished judges, mostly but not necessarily, having served on the U.S. Supreme Court, from Marshall and Story to Warren and Black. The Common law practice is highlighted in an array of Supreme Court decisions of great Constitutional importance, but also in the specific solution approach by codifications such as the Uniform Commercial Code. Last but not least, no student of the Common law can afford to ignore the profound study and analysis of the judicial process made by American pragmatism by jurists such as Oliver Wendel Holmes, Cardozo or Judge Frank.[13]

B The Philosophy

If there is realism but also consistency in the technique of the Common law, what is the philosophy that it reveals? Here one must be careful, for the interpretation of a system, the philosophy which it reveals, may only exist in the eyes of the beholder. However, it can be argued that the philosophy of the Common law, the scale of values which it attempts to express, is one in favour of rights rather than of duties, of emancipation rather than of control, of responsibility rather than paternalism. For the Common law was profoundly influenced by the tug-of-war between the English King and Parliament. Famous is the retort of Chief Justice Coke that: "The King in his own person cannot adjudge any case, either criminal or betwixt party and party; but it ought to be determined and adjudged in some Court of Justice according to the law and custom of England." Coke went on to affirm Bracton's phrase "*quod Rex non debet esse sub homine sed sub Deo et Lege*."[14] Evidence of this is not only the Magna Charta and the Bill of Rights, but also the stress which ordinary English case-law and statute place upon the right of the individual to dispose of himself and of his property to the exclusion of every other interest.

In this connexion, a few examples will suffice. But let it be noted that the examples that follow are chosen because they are in contrast with the traditions of some of the most important Civil law systems. Thus, in the field of property the Common law is endowed with a most sophisticated system of rights, which gives to the citizens a tremendous degree of choice. Freehold land exists side by side with leasehold land and, through the institution of the Trust, there is hardly any legitimate wish of the citizen which cannot be satisfied. Common lawyers are familiar with other features of the Common law of property, to the extent that it bears upon the law of succession. Thus, civilians may wonder at the freedom and ease with which successors may be appointed after the death of a testator through the exercise, by a third party, of a power of appointment. In the field of succession proper, if the Common law has erred it has been on the side of rights, by permitting the testator to dispose of his property without the control of his family and, if he so wishes, to the disadvantage of his family. In the law of Contract, remarkable is the absence of general clauses that could upset an agreement between the parties. It is this aspect, combined with what one may almost describe as a doctrinaire attachment of the Common law to precedents of definition of words and phrases, as well as to the grammatical interpretation of statutes, that has made the Common law a most efficient instrument of commercial exchange, frequently resorted to even by those who have no connection with England. In the field of Tort, there is still a reluctance to impinge on the rights of the individual for the sake of social realities. The principle of fault still predominates, and the principle of strict liability is severely limited. Last but not least, in Family law the insistence upon individual rights is expressed in the dislike for joint family property regimes, in the absence of an obligation to appoint a guardian of an infant unless there is property involved, and in the early recognition of the right of the young to leave home, set at the age of 16.

No one will, of course, pretend that this philosophy is always to be preferred to any other, or that the Common law, in pursuing its individualistic philosophy, is never led to exceed the limits which reason and justice may demand. But this is a different issue and here it is not my function to judge, but to describe the technique and the philosophy of the Common law. Nevertheless, even the strongest critics of the Common law will recognise that individualism and liberty, which are two of the most characteristic aspects of the Common law, are surely values which are part of our Western civilisation, values which, in the complex technological society in which we live, we can ill afford to do without.

III The Civil Law

In contrast to the Common law, the Civil law has a different technique and a different philosophy. The Civil law is, of course, a much older system than the Common law and has a distinguished and learned tradition which the latter lacks. That tradition goes back to the Renaissance and the discovery of the text of the Digest in Northern Italy. As Ernest Renan has pointed out, Roman law together with Greek philosophy and Christianity are the three pillars of European civilisation. What is the technique of the Civil law and what is the philosophy that it reveals?

A. *The technique*

It is, perhaps, appropriate here to make it clear that we cannot speak of a single technique of the Civil law. In its earlier form of Roman law, its technique was very pragmatic and bore many characteristics of the Common law. In the beginning there was a Code, the XII Tables. But these were not like a modern Continental codification. They were rather a collection of basic rules which constituted the strict *ius civile*. It can be claimed, no doubt with considerable justification, that the history of Roman law from the XII Tables to Justinian, is the history of the changes which the praetor, that is, the Roman judge, brought upon the *ius civile*. This was done over a period of a thousand years. What is of interest is that Roman law, just like the Common law, developed through procedure. Just as an English judge would grant a writ, so would a Civilian judge grant an *actio utilis*.[15] The Roman lawyers were, indeed, so dominated by procedure that a single transaction—sale—could be seen as two, protected by two separate actions. Thus, sale was known as *emptio-venditio* and there was one action for the vendor and another for the seller. Characteristic is the story of how the services of the law became widely available in Rome. It will be recalled that in 304 B.C. Gnaeus Flavius stole the roll with the secret forms of action, kept by the pontiffs at the Temple.

However, modern Civil law is not exactly the same as Roman law. Long before the discovery of the Roman texts in Northern Italy, Roman law was no longer a living law in Europe. The Glossators first and, later, the Commentators were able to compare local law, which was the law of the Lombards, with Roman law, to the disadvantage of the former. But, as Roman law was not practised and was, moreover, in the hands of scholars, it took a scientific turn. It became a body of general rules detached from procedure, which had lost its importance. Thus, principles began to emerge. Roman procedure actually lost its importance because, in the fragmented map of Europe of the period, each small country or City-state had developed its own special rules. Procedure had become a matter of public law. Thus, Gaius's and, later, Justinian's tripartite division of private law into persons, things and actions, lost its last part, that is 'actions'. This situation continued well into the nineteenth century, as is seen by the division of the French *Code Civil* of 1804. This was divided into three parts, but the third only remained a miscellaneous one. It was really the German Pardectists who finally adopted a scientific or logical division of private law. At all events, after the reception of Roman law in Europe in the sixteenth century, the lawyers applied a learned type of Roman or 'civil' law, rather than the procedural devices invented by the praetor.

At that stage two crucial events occurred in Europe. The first was that, through the influence of the learned tradition, the Church was able to inject principles of justice into the practical solutions of Roman law. This is clear, for instance, when a French jurist, Loisel, in his book *Institutions coutumieres*, published in the seventeenth century, wrote "*On lie les boeufs par les cornes et les hommes par les paroles*; *et autant vaut simple promesse ou couvenance que les stipulations du droit Romain.*" This was certainly not the case in mediaeval French law.[16]

The other event of importance was the emergence of Natural law in the seventeenth century. It can hardly be denied that Rationalism and the movement of the Enlightenment had a role to play in the subsequent development of the Civil law. Henceforth, the Civil law constituted a body of abstract principles divorced from procedure. Still, these principles were superior to other local laws and full of good sense. It is not surprising that the world tended to look at these principles of the Civil law as self-evident truths. Indeed, at one stage it became possible for the itinerant scholar, who was also often a monk, to travel from Bologna to Paris or Leyden and, indeed, even as far as Oxford, to teach the very same principles of Roman law.

It is interesting that, after the break-up of this unity of the Civil law in the nineteenth century, following the emergence of nationalism, Europe has needed two World Wars to be convinced once again of the need to achieve this unity. In this respect, I am referring to the efforts towards the harmonisation of the law within the European Economic Community.

However, even the fragmentation of the Civil law in the nineteenth century did not completely destroy the Civil law. On the contrary, it added strength to its principles because these were seen as achievements of each nation rather than as an abstract body of rules imported from abroad. They were part of the universal principle of justice, which all civilised nations of Europe shared as a common heritage. Moreover, if the Codes were different, there was an underlying unity of method and of concepts. The method was deductive, that is, the process of reasoning was from general principles to specific cases, and the concepts were intellectual constructions, some, such as possession, of considerable complexity. It is no wonder that the Civil law eventually reached its apotheosis in the Pandectist movement, in nineteenth century Germany. With it the Professors' law (the so-called *Professorenrecht*) prevailed, for the Professors had the time and the ability to develop the concepts. Thus, the judge's role was minimised and he simply became part of the administration of justice. In this respect, it is interesting to contrast the importance of the English judge, who acquired Constitutional significance with that of the French judge. The latter, having allied himself with the King, lost when the French Revolution and, later, the French Civil Code, removed the judge from the exalted position he had acquired in the *Parlements*, that is, the Courts. Thus, the French judge became a mere administrator with strictly reduced power defined in articles 4 and 5 of the *Code civil*, judging only individual disputes between private persons and making no rules for the future. This does not mean that the development of a new legal technique in the Civil law world rendered that law in any way inferior to the Common law. Indeed, it may be claimed that the insistence on principles as against case-law permitted a rational and civilised body of principles to expand well beyond the confines of Europe. I believe it is this quality of the Civil law which is appreciated by nations across the seas and which led in the nineteenth century to the adoption, with some local variations, of European Codes as the law of those nations, from Japan to Chile.

It is interesting to note that the technique devised by the Civilians, which is based on the codification of principles, has found in modern times a further use. For, through the system of codification, it has become possible for some of the countries of the emerging, or so-called Third World, in Africa and Asia, to adopt European codifications and thus achieve a regulation of their private relationships of a high order. Such a regulation was only achieved in Europe after efforts extending over several centuries. It may be added that the convenience of a codified system of law has tended to displace any desire for a system of law based upon the Common law. Indeed, even in the Common law world, the expansion and sophistication of a complex modern society has tended to bring about a recognition of the value of codification. Witness the English Law Commissions Act 1965 which, for the first time, enjoins a newly-created reform-body to proceed to the codification of English law.

B. The Philosophy

Granted the technique, what is the philosophy of the Civil law? In this respect, it can be argued that the Civil law is on the side of authority and order. It was a Roman principle to be found in Justinian's Institutes that *quod principi placuit legis habet vigorem*.[17] If this principle is alarming, we need not be unduly worried about the philosophy of the Civil law as a whole. For order and discipline are essential elements if liberty is not to give way to anarchy. What the Civil law has sometimes found difficult is to draw the line which will permit a right mixture between liberty and order.

It can hardly be denied that, in some aspects, the Civil law tends to be paternalistic. This is not necessarily to decry paternalism, for we are all familiar with the utopian view that society consists of fully fledged adult, responsible and responsive individuals. Moreover, it can be a matter of legitimate argument whether individuals need protection against themselves in any given situation. Here I am aware of the danger of over-simplification. This danger is illustrated by reference to the Common law, which, with all its stress upon liberty, until the Homicide Act 1957 had retained suicide as a crime. But in the field of human relations, in which the State does not wish to punish but to regulate life, it can be argued that the Civil law carries a strong element of paternalism.

Thus, in the law of property and succession, which can only be segregated with difficulty, the Civil law tends to stress the rights of the family against its individual members. The law insists upon the duty of the owner of property and of the testator towards his family. For example, many Civil law systems have rules which oblige the testator to leave—through the compulsory share or *legitimate portion*—part of his property to his children, even though they may be grown-up, wealthy and fully capable of looking after themselves. There are also rules which prohibit the owner of property to resort to what his family and the Court may consider abusive disposal of his property. In family law parents exercise a greater control over their children and for longer—until they reach the age of eighteen, twenty or even twenty-five. They may refuse their consent to a young marriage and this refusal—as is the case in French law—may not be overruled by a Court. Parents may also use their children's own income whereas guardianship and, sometimes, a family council are set up to ensure proper control. The parents themselves are bound, in their turn, to a form of accounting to the Courts. A joint family property regime often comes into operation upon marriage and there are many complicated rules imposed by the law to ensure that such a property or fund is administered in accordance with principles recognised by the law. In the law of contract, general principles ensure that the freedom of the parties to enter into any contractual arrangement they wish is limited by the existence of general clauses. These permit the Court to interfere *ex post facto* with the wishes of the parties, as expressed when the contract was made. In other cases, the Courts assume wide powers to interfere or adjust contracts to new circumstances. Typical of such powers is the *Geschäftsgrundlage* of German law. In some systems the parties are not permitted to assume, as by article 1184 of the French Civil Code, a breach of contract without a declaration by a Court. In tort there is a greater readiness to accept strict liability and presume fault. For instance, strict liability exists in most systems in respect of motor accidents. On the whole, it may be argued that the Civil law interferes more with individuals, expects a higher standard of behaviour from them than the Common law does, and insists upon the need for discipline and control. With this view goes an extensive civil power given to the police to regulate behaviour, only allowing individuals a right to dispute police action after the event. Thus, the police may impose a ruling on my neighbour, say, on noise, without trial and it is up to him to seek the protection of the Court. This is often desirable, but it contrasts strongly with the Common law's insistence that the police should have no greater power than that of any individual. A similar power exists in European law. Thus, the European Commission may impose fines upon enterprises without trial.[18] It is not surprising that English lawyers (and I suspect businessmen) are strongly critical of such exercise of arbitrary power.

If this—no doubt partial—account of the Civil law tends, perhaps, to emphasise the control aspect of the system, it must not be thought that it necessarily implies a criticism in all cases. For, over a period of centuries, that system has managed to achieve a scale of civilised values which has been the envy of the world. Clearly, our society needs both the Civil law and the Common law in order to succeed. As the world becomes smaller by greater speed and through enormous but peaceful movements of population, a tendency may be detected to amalgamate the two in a new form of European law in which those features of the two systems are retained which have proved to be of enduring value. Thus in recent years Ireland, a Common law country, has introduced the compulsory share in the law of succession. England is contemplating the introduction of joint matrimonial property regime,[19] whereas Common law ideas of the protection of the individual are on the ascendancy in some Civil law countries. An example of the latter is the development of special rules of protection of the individual in the Federal Republic of Germany. These extend not only to the creation of a special Constitutional Court, which bears the characteristic features of the U.S. Supreme Court, but also in the field of private law through the development of the right to an injunction (the so-called *Unterlassungsklage*) in the law of defamation.

IV Socialist Law

When we turn to Socialist law we come across a novel and complex phenomenon upon which there can be some doubt as to whether it has been dispassionately analysed, or its underlying philosophy adequately understood. It can be argued that, as far as its technique is concerned, Soviet law belongs to the Romanistic systems, at least in a superficial way. Socialist lawyers have complained, with some justice, that their system has too often been classified as a derivative of the Civil law systems, whereas it can lay a claim to being a separate system in its own right.[20] Their complaint, in this respect, could be readily acknowledged and easily accepted, but for reasons other than those for which Socialist lawyers claim originality.

A. The technique

In the first place, and quite apart from its philosophical assumptions which will be considered presently, Socialist law involves a reduction of the traditional field of legal activity. Thus, it is a characteristic of the Socialist systems—and here I can only consider those of Eastern Europe—that they involve the creation of law outside the traditional structures, while maintaining in form the full extent of these structures. To take an example, in most Socialist countries there has been a codification of the Civil law. This codification retains and often improves provisions that existed previously but, in effect, through the growth of parallel law outside the Codes, those provisions have a far reduced area of application. This is the case with the contract provisions of Socialist Codes. These, though theoretically valid, will not apply in practice in any comparable degree, as they do in Western Europe. This is because a law of contract implies, in the Western sense of the term, wide control of wealth by private individuals who have the means and the occasion to indulge in private disputes and, therefore, in private litigation. This is not so in the Socialist countries and this can be seen by an examination of the Law Reports published in these countries. There, disputes as to property are scarce, though there are many instances of criminal prosecutions for the theft of Socialist property. Conversely, there is considerable regulation of contracts of public authorities which are dealt with outside the Codes. In this respect, litigation takes the form of pre-contractual arbitration by State Boards between two Socialist enterprises. The same is true of torts. Thus, there is, in practice, little room for private litigation in these fields. In early Soviet law strict liability was far more extensive than in Western law. Such liability has been reduced since the early days only to the extent that the law of social security has grown. But the central position that the Civil Codes occupy in the Socialist systems gives the impression that litigation is as important in Socialist societies as it is in Western societies. That this is not a personal interpretation can be seen by a basic principle accepted by Socialist legal systems. This principle is contained in an often quoted phrase by Lenin in a letter to Komsky, that "there is no longer any private law with us, everything has become public law."[21]

In the second place, the machinery of justice, designed to give effect to the law, differs fundamentally from that of the Civil law systems. For this machinery is not considered, though it often acts, as if it had a different function from that of the executive. It rather looks as a means of giving effect to the policies of the executive. In other words, the object of the law in the Socialist system is to protect the State and to enforce its objectives, not to protect private interests. As Article 1 of the earlier Soviet Civil Code of 1922 put it, rights are to be interpreted in accordance with their economic and social purposes. The more recent Civil Code of the RSFSR of 1964 in article 5 §1 states "Civil rights are protected by law except in cases where they are exercised in a manner which would be inconsistent with the progress of such rights in a socialist society during the period of the establishment of Communism." A similar view is also taken, for example, in articles 4 and 5 of the Hungarian Civil Code of 1959, in articles 4 and 5 of the Polish Civil Code of 1964, or in articles 6 and 7 of the Czechoslovak Civil Code also of 1964. It is not surprising that in the Socialist countries the role of the courts is not to adjudicate between the litigants but to improve social behaviour. Thus, Soviet law, which occasionally seems to insist upon confessions as a recognition of the errors of the accused, attributes to the Courts an educative role.[22] The Courts are there to make the litigants better citizens not to adjudicate objectively in a dispute.

This theory and practice in the Socialist systems is rendered possible because, unlike our own societies, the State through the wholesale take-over of private wealth and therefore of private power, has the monopoly of power which it can use to accomplish its purposes. This position reveals a totally different concept of the use of power from that expressed by Lord Acton, the English nineteenth-century philosopher, namely that "power corrupts and absolute power corrupts absolutely."

Thirdly, the Socialist systems appear to be using a technique familiar to the Romanistic systems through the use of well-established Romanistic terminology. But they subject that technique to a Marxist standpoint, namely, that law is merely a superstructure based upon unequal economic conditions. Once these conditions become equal, law and the State will wither away.[23] But, in practice, that utopian stage of the disappearance of the law has been indefinitely postponed to the end of the capitalist encirclement. This was first stated by Vyshinski[24] and has since been confirmed by Galenza who wrote in these terms in the Moscow University Journal as far back as 1957.[25]

However, it is inevitable that the complete subordination of legal concepts to economic categories is bound to distort the use of these concepts and therefore the legal technique which is based upon them. As these economic categories are flexible and lack precision they can only further complicate the application of law. They can also undermine its object, which is to be a guide to future conduct through providing a minimum of legal certainty and security. In order to illustrate the point it is sufficient to refer to the concept of private property, which is surely central in any legal system. But private property in the Western sense is only a small part of what property means in the Socialist systems. For in the Socialist systems private property is that part of property which does not belong to the State (called : State property) and does not belong to individuals for the satisfaction of their personal needs (called : personal property). In other words, the State allocates property according to an economic test, namely the rule that the means of production cannot be subject to private property. They cannot be allowed to belong to individuals. Only property for the satisfaction of personal needs—termed personal property—can belong to individuals. But the test of the means of production is an economic test. As such, it is too flexible and too uncertain to provide a sound basis for the legal definition of property and the attribution of legal rights. Thus, whether a thing is a means of production which would, in Marxist terms permit an individual to enrich himself, if he were allowed to use it, or personal property for the satisfaction of personal needs, can be a matter of chance which cannot easily be controlled by the State, unless it establishes totalitarian control. To take an example or two,[26] a family has a three-room flat which is in personal property. The child grows, marries and sets up home elsewhere. The parents take a lodger. Here, by the change in the use of the room in the flat, and to that extent only, personal property, has become a means of enrichment and therefore a means of production. Equally, an individual owns a barrow or a car. When he uses it for his personal purposes it is personal property ; when he plies for hire, which can happen informally, the barrow or the car becomes a means of production. But a legal system, by the nature of things, can seldom take account of such flexible changes in the use of property. Characteristic of the uncertainty that prevails in the Socialist systems, and which is reflected in their legal techniques, is the difficulty whcih the Yugoslav legislator has found, in attempting to define social property, which is the Yugoslav answer to Soviet-style State capitalism. The exact definition of social property, as a legal term, has long eluded the Yugoslav legislator and is still the stumbling block to the codification of Yugoslav law. In the last resort, the Socialist systems cannot maintain the consistency of definition which their systems require, for economic concepts are, and must remain, far more flexible than legal concepts which must necessarily exert a stabilising influence in society. In effect, in some cases, social realities have forced Socialist legal systems to give up total dependence of law upon economics. Thus, Socialist lawyers find it difficult to explain incentive schemes. For example, they cannot adequately explain why interest should be paid to Savings Accounts held by State banks, for it is difficult to square the Socialist principle "to each one according to his work" with the payment of interest which the depositor has done nothing to earn.

These considerations of technique give to the Socialist systems a special flavour which fully justifies their claim that these systems are entitled to a category of their own. There are, of course, misleading similarities with the Civil law systems. For, traditionally, the Socialist countries belonged to the Romanistic family of laws and the terminology and technique of Socialist law is superfically attached to the Civil law. But the similarity ends at that point.

B. The philosophy

When we turn to the philosophy that underlies Socialist law, the differences are even more striking. That philosophy may be summarised in two propositions. The first is that the total good is better than the good of the individual. The individual, in other words, has, in the main, value in himself but only to the extent that he is part of the whole. The second proposition is that government, and therefore law, based upon discretionary power, is better than the rule of law. In other words, the pursuit of the Socialist ideal must not be hampered by individual rights. Here it must be made clear that the reference is made to Socialist systems as they have developed in the East European countries. For, as Karl Renner has shown in his book on *The Changing Function of Property*,[28] there exists a view of Socialism which merely pleads for the adjustment of legal concepts to the need to take into account social changes. Consequently, a modified form of Socialism, in a non-Marxist sense, is not at all incompatible with the philosophical view that the individual has absolute value. It is this form of Socialism which has grown and flourished since the last War in some of the countries of Western Europe. But it is a Socialism which operates within the framework of the rule of law.

However, let us consider in more detail the two propositions in which the Socialist systems of the East European type express their philosophical aspirations. The first was that total good is better than the good of the individual. It is of course true that there is nothing new under the sun. The idea that the ultimate good is a matter of judgment for the ruler is of ancient origin. This idea of the supremacy of the Philosopher-King was first developed by Plato in his *Republic*. But there is a steady stream of political theory to the same effect that goes through the period of the Enlightenment down to Marx and Lenin. After all, it was Jean-Jacques Rousseau—the anniversary of whose death falls this year—who wrote, no doubt in an unguarded moment of rhetorical exuberance, for I do not share the view often propounded that Rousseau's philosophy leads to totalitarianism, that "*Il faut avoir pitie de notre espece plus que êue de notre prochain ; c'est une tres grande cruaute envers les hommes que la pitie pour les mechants . . . l'amour du genre humain n'est autre chose en nous que l'amour de la justice.*" But, as Pierre Gascar has recently pointed out,[29] "From these lines and others, such as these, we know that Robespierre and numerous other dictators down to our day have made an article of faith." As Robert Conquest has put it, Soviet law "ultimately regulates justice not in the interests of the individual or any objective norms but primarily in those of the Soviet State and the Communist Party, claimed to be the highest embodiment of both the individual and all the component parts of society."[30] What more lucid and brilliant accounts of the nefarious goals of such philosophy than the books of George Orwell—*Animal Farm*, a children's story for grown-ups—of Arthur Koestler's *The Yogi and the Commissar*, or Jean-Paul Sartre's *Les Mains Sales*.

There can be little doubt that this type of philosophical approach leads to the neglect of individual rights and eventually to their suppression.[31] Such neglect can even be dangerous when clothed in a pseudo-scientific dogma. It is not without reason that Marxism has been defined as the assertion of knowledge without investigation. It was Marx and, in particular, Engels in his example of ice-water-steam-who, not without some help from Hegel—attempted to trace Society's progress in automatic stages that inevitably led to Communism. But, as has since been amply demonstrated, especially by Karl Popper in his *Logic of the Scientific Method* and in his classical two-volume work *The Open Society and its Enemies*, the scientific method is no less haphazard or less subject to chance than the method of the physical sciences. Penicillin was not found by Sir Alexander Fleming by a logical process and the discovery of a cure for cancer cannot be predicted by deductive logic. It will most likely be, if and when it comes, a discovery due to an accident observed by a team of brilliant doctors. It is not surprising that those who, as lawyers, have formed an attachment to human rights, show a distinct preference for Aristotle's golden mean, the pragmatism of William James and the empiricism of John Locke as expressed in Anglo-American law, rather than for nebulous notions of unproven or unprovable ultimate justice.

However, Socialist law not only propagates the belief in the scientific truth of its philosophy, thus describing any different viewpoints as anti-scientific and reactionary, but it also subjects the individual good to the general good, as this happens to be doctrinally conceived from time to time. This willingness to adjust legal rights to the temporary purposes of the State may be shown by the rule that individual rights can only be exercised if they are in conformity with their social and economic purposes. It may also be shown by the continuing decrease in the elements of choice in the Socialist legal systems. Thus, in the field of matrimonial property, the choice available in other Civil law systems is eliminated and there is only one possible system to be adopted. In the field of family law there is an increase in the area of jurisdiction of the guardianship authority at the expense of the rights of the parents. In respect of the institution of divorce, after an initial period of freedom, the procedure has been, certainly in the Soviet Union between 1944 and 1965 difficult, cumbersome and complicated. This happened just as, in the West, divorce tended to become easier. Indeed, Western systems are rapidly moving towards a fundamental principle, boldly declared in the Preamble of the law of 20th September 1792 that, "*La faculte de divorce resulte de la liberte individuelle, dont un engagement indissoluble serait la perte.*" There has, indeed, been legislation in advanced European countries since 1969, including Italy, recognising in practice divorce by mutual consent. A Swedish law of 1974 goes as far as to lay down that the State no longer takes a position in favour of marriage—which all East European Codes do—and leaves this matter to the individuals concerned.

It would take too long to go through, or even partly fill, a list of cases in Socialist law in which there is a reduction of the field of choice in favour of discretion from above, in accordance with State-established criteria of social objectives. Let me just give two examples, in the important field of the exercise of human rights. Thus, article 39 §2 of the new Soviet Constitution of 1977 lays down that: "The utilisation by citizens of rights and freedoms must not inflict damage upon the interests of society and the State and the rights of other citizens." In a different context it is, no doubt, known that Western legal systems have recently tended to imitate the Swedish institution of the Ombudsman, that is, a person who is outside the administration, possesses considerable powers and has the function to ensure that the individual is protected, mainly against the State. In the Soviet Union and other Socialist countries, such as Hungary, the task of the protection of the individual against the State is entrusted to a state officer, the Public Prosecutor.

The second proposition—that government and therefore law—should best be based upon discretionary power is amply grounded upon the very principles of Socialist law. Thus, the law as such is considered to be bad because it is a means of coercion based upon a substratum of unequal economic conditions. Law must therefore wither away. The place of law will then be taken by the administration of things. However, such a view is either too naive, for it contains an implicit belief in the inherent good sense of the individual and takes no account of the complex and sophisticated society in which we live, or alternatively, it can lead, through the absence of the legal protection of the individual and of an appropriate enforcement or due process procedure, to the individual being placed at the mercy of the State.

That these are not fanciful claims may be seen when we turn to the criticism to which Western institutions have been subjected in the Socialist States. Marx himself thought that "it is a phantasy of jurists" to claim that society rests on law.[32] Soviet legal theory has condemned the idea of the rule of law and has developed the principle of 'socialist legality'. In this connexion, the Soviet legal dictionary has defined the rule of law as "An anti-scientific conception established in bourgeois legal literature, picturing the bourgeois state as if there is no room for arbirrary executive power and where allegedly law and legality reign."[33] But if the rule of law is unacceptable in Socialist societies, what do Socialist lawyers place in its stead? In this respect they have developed the concept of 'socialist legality', which is defined as "the precise observance and execution of the Soviet Constitution and the law."[34] But this is not intended to limit the leading role which the Soviet State attributes to the Communist Party. Nor does it prevent as we have seen from article 39 §2 of the Soviet Constitution of 1977 the interpretation of Soviet laws in accordance with the legally undefined social interests. In the last resort law, in the official Soviet view, still remains, in the words of two recognised authors Ioffe and Shargorodskii, "the expression of the will of specific, politically dominant classes, seen through the prism of dominance over relationships . . ." This definition, in the words of the same authors, "is also entirely applicable to the concept of Socialist thought in general."[35] As Vyshinski wrote, "The formal law is subordinate to the law of the Revolution. There might be collisions and discrepancies between the formal commands of the law and those of the proletarian revolution . . . This collision must be solved only by the subordination of the formal commands of law to those of Party policy."[36] In this way, Socialist legality also preserves the ultimate discretion of the rulers, as it is intended to ensure only one form of society: that which is officially approved. It matters not that this discretion, once firmly established, denies the possibility of change from below. Nevertheless, if anything is inevitable, it is change. Thus, the freedom of the individual to hold opinions and engage in peaceful actions which may lead to change, can only be seen as a threat. This view runs counter to the principle of the respect of the individual, of human tolerance and of the respect of minority or unofficial opinion, all of which constitute the foundation and fabric of European civilisation.

These are, in effect, the logical consequences of dogmas, even if it may be admitted that those in favour of such a system of law have opted for it for the best motives; namely because they believe, with Rousseau, that "*il fault avoir pitie de notre espece plus que de notre prochain.*"

V Conclusion

I started this essay with a modest objective, that is, with an attempt to draw some impressionistic strokes upon the canvas of the legal systems of the world in the hope that, if the full picture of the three legal systems eludes us, lawyers may, at least, recognise different trends and distinctive features of each legal system. I also stated at the outset that a full description can, at best, only be a personal point of view. At the practical level, I expressed the hope that the existence of different forms of regulation of society may reveal trends and possible generalisations, which ought to be left to the individual jurist for evaluation. I have tried to demonstrate, but laid no exclusive claim to the truth. It may be that the specific legal regulation in each of the three systems described reflects trends which are worthy of note and may be the object of choice. As you may imagine, the temptation to let you draw your own conclusions, as I draw mine, must be considerable. And, on the whole, I prefer not to argue but to communicate to you a reflexion which I believe is appropriate for the experience which we are undergoing at present. That reflexion is the following:

In the course of this essay it must have become obvious that it is not to the Socialist systems of law that we must look for a sound foundation for the future of a free and open society. Some may even have detected my distinct preference for a philosophy of individual freedom which the Anglo-American system of law enshrines in its precepts. But I can hardly deny the value of the Romanistic tradition of order and discipline for the preservation of that freedom. No doubt European civilisation needs both traditions. If this view is accepted, I believe we can look forward to the future with hope. For in our own time, a concerted effort is being made to build a system of European law, and here I refer to the European Economic Community—which is based on both the Common law tradition and on the tradition of the Romanistic systems. We note this every day in the present-day development of European law. In the need for overt control from the centre of the European Community; in the need for harmonisation of legislation which is expressly required by article 100 of the Treaty of Rome. But we also note the boldness in which European law is supplemented by principles which are outside the Treaty. I refer here to the acceptance of a full protection of human rights, which was never laid down in the Treaty but which the European Court, acting in this respect as a Common law court—the House of Lords or the U.S. Supreme Court—might well have done, has boldly recognised as forming part of European law. In this way European civilisation may recreate the unity of thought which prevailed in the period after the Renaissance. Perhaps like Marcel Proust we are also now engaged *a la recherche du temps perdu.*

NOTES

[1]J. Austin, *The Province of Jurisprudence Determined* (ed. by H. L. A. Hart) 1954, 9.

[2]*Op. cit.*, 15.

[3]H. Kelsen, 'The Pure Theory of Law and Analytical Jurisprudence', 55 *Harv. L. Rev.* (1942), 44, 54-57.

[4]*Op. cit.*, 53.

[5]J. Stone, *The Province and Function of Law* (1950), 105.

[6]Cited in J. Stone, *op. cit.*, 133.

[7]See generally, W. Friedmann, *Legal Theory* (3rd ed.), 1953, 50.

[8]See Holdsworth, *Some Makers of English Law* 1938, Lecture I, pp. 8-24, Plucknett, *A Concise History of the Common Law*, 1948, 246 ; Holdsworth, *Sources and Literature of English Law* 1928, 23-30.

[9]Quoted from A. L. Goodhart, *English Contributions to the Philosophy of Law*, 1949, 35.

[10]1953, 178 ff.

[11]Edward S. Corwin, *The "Higher Law" Background of American Constitutional Law*, 1957, *passim*.

[12]"After the Bible, Locke was the principal authority . . ." Corwin, *op. cit.*, 74.

[13]See mainly : O. W. Holmes, *The Common Law*, 1881 ; Cardozo, *The Nature of the Judicial Process*, 1921 ; Frank, *Law and the Modern Mind*, 1930.

[14]Quoted from Goodhart, *op. cit.*, 17.

[15]See for this comparison Peter, *Actio und Writ*, 1957.

[16]See Olivier-Martin, *Precis d'histoire du droit Francais* (4th ed.) 1945, S 525 : See also Lepointe et Monier, *Les obligations en droit Romain et dans l'ancien droit francais*, 1954, 450, 463.

[17]Inst. I, II, 6.

[18]See the Law Commission's Working Paper No. 42, Family Property Law (1971).

[19]Regulation 17.J.O.204/62. See articles 15 & 16. This Regulation was enacted by the Council in pursuance of article 87 of the E.E.C. Treaty.

[20]See for the similarities R. David, *Les grands systemes de droit contemporains* (6th ed.) 1974, §20. See also E. C. Johnson, *An Introduction to the Soviet Legal System*, 1969, 13-14 and Szabo & Pöteri, *A Socialist Approach to Comparative Law*, 1977, chapter by Eorsi ' Convergence in Civil Law ? ' 45 ff.

[21]Cited in R. David, *op. cit.*, §245.

[22]H. J. Berman, The educative role of the Soviet Court, 21 *Int. Comp. Law Quart.* (1972) 81 ff.

[23]See *The Essentials of Lenin*, 1947, Vol. II, 150.

[24]E. L. Johnson *The Soviet Legal System*, 1969, 74-75.

[25]*The Observer*, 27.2.1955, 4 ; see also Golunskii & Strogovich in Lloyd, *Introduction to Jurisprudence* (3rd ed.) 1972, 673 ff.

[26]I owe these to an unpublished text of a lecture given at King's College by Professor A. Gams of Belgrade University.

[27]Chloros, *Yugoslav Civil Law*, 1970, 174 ff.

[28]First published in 1949.

[29]*Le Figaro*, 22.1.1978, p. 19. Quotation from Rousseau in the same text.

[30]*Justice and the Legal System in the USSR*, 1968, 21.

[31]As Professor Kovarik has put it very recently ". . . the minority is being suppressed in the interests of millions of working people." See ' Development of the Socialist State and Socialist Democracy after the 15th Congress of the Communist Party of Czechoslovakia ' in 16 *Bull. Czech. Law* (1977) 8, 11.

[32]See Vyshinsky, *The Law of the Soviet State* 1948, 20 ff.

[33]*Juridical Dictionary* (in Russian) (2nd ed.) 1956. Vol. II, 196, quoted in No. 6 Bulletin of the International Commission of Jurists (Dec. 1956) 12.

[34]Chikhikvadze (ed.) *The Soviet State and Law*, 1969, 266. See also Kiralfy ' The Campaign for Legality in the USSR ' in 6 *Int. Comp. Law Quart.* (1957), 625.

[35]Quoted in Lloyd, *op. cit.*, 676.

[36]Cited in R. Conquest (ed.) *Justice and the Legal System in the USSR*, 1968, 17.

Part II
Common Law and Civil Law: Encounters

[5]

HESSEL E. YNTEMA

Equity in the Civil Law and the Common Law

THE FOLLOWING ARTICLE BY THE FORMER EDITOR-IN-CHIEF OF THIS *Journal* WAS WRITTEN FOR PUBLICATION IN SPANISH AT THE REQUEST OF THE SPANISH COMMISSION IN CHARGE OF THE COMMEMORATIVE VOLUME, *Centenario de la Ley de Notariado.* THE BOARD OF EDITORS WISHES TO EXPRESS ITS GRATITUDE TO THE *Junta de Decanos de los Colegios Notariales de España,* AND IN PARTICULAR TO ITS PRESIDENT, DR. RAFAEL NÚÑEZ LAGOS, FOR PERMISSION TO PUBLISH THE ORIGINAL ENGLISH TEXT POSTHUMOUSLY.

I

It is a fascinating but elusive task to sketch the place of equity in the civil law and the common law on comparative lines. The inquiry will soon reveal that the term has varied and shifting meanings; as remarked in the famous aphorism of John Selden, "Equity is a roguish thing."[1] It is a species of intellectual quicksilver that in one sense or another may be found in almost any branch of law in developed legal systems, and more concretely in the sphere of Anglo-American law, it forms a unique and multifarious counterpart to the common law, properly so-called. Consequently, the first problem in such an inquiry is to ascertain what is to be considered under the ambivalent head of equity in the respective legal systems.

One possibility has been suggested by a trenchant remark of Bentham in the *Rationale of Judicial Evidence;*

> "Taken by itself, or anywhere else than in company with the word *court, equity* is abracadabra: a word without meaning.
>
> "To give meaning to it, you must connect it with the word *court,* and say *court of equity.*"
>
> "What then is equity?" asks Bentham. "Answer, whatever has been done by a court of equity." And this he adds "is a sort of court peculiar to English jurisprudence."[2]

Leaving aside the vagueness of the conception of equity as what courts of equity have done in England and elsewhere—which speaks in terms strikingly akin to modern legal realism—such a topic is clearly insufficient for the present purpose. In this sense, equity is an indifferentiated congeries of historical elements, which for the purposes of comparison with developments in other legal systems should be

[1] THE TABLE TALK OF JOHN SELDEN, ch. *Equity* 143 (3rd ed. 1860).

[2] RATIONALE OF JUDICIAL EVIDENCE, Book VIII, Ch. XIX, § 3, in 7 WORKS 291–92 (Bowring ed. 1843).

defined and distinguished. Thus, it would be possible to examine the analogues in the civil law of particular doctrines of equity, relating for example to fraud, trust, or contract. Conducted in detail, this were a fruitful type of inquiry, but much too large for this occasion. Moreover, an exposition of this nature has been competently outlined in Buckland's *Equity in Roman Law,*[3] and need not be repeated. The same may be said of equitable remedies and procedure, which may well be left to the experts in such matters, particularly the canon law techniques taken over in the English Court of Chancery. These are of most interest in terms of their English setting, which Professor Dawson has recently and critically explored.[4]

Another theme that suggests a possible basis of comparison that might well attract consideration, one on which Bentham also energetically animadverted, is the effect of what he termed the "splintering" of jurisdictions, as most notably exemplified in the common law system of his time by the co-existence of courts of common law and of equity. This phenomenon of division in the judicial establishment, attended by a corresponding division in the common law, has a well-known parallel in the law of Rome. During the classical period of Roman jurisprudence, the *ius civile,* which applied to Roman citizens, was administered primarily in the court of the *praetor urbanus,* while the *ius honorarium,* which was to serve the needs of commerce with aliens, was the province of the *praetor peregrinus.* While the historical settings were in various respects dissimilar, the basic causes and effects of this bifurcation of jurisdiction and law in Rome and England present obvious analogies; in both instances, the earlier system of remedies, which had been evolved in terms of typical actions, became stereotyped and, instead of being enlarged to meet new needs, was supplemented by another system of remedies, administered in a separate court; in both systems, the relief provided in the two jurisdictions for causes that in considerable degree were similar, in this sense overlapped; in both developments, the Roman and the English, since the newer scheme of remedies was in many respects superior, there was a gradual infiltration of the more modern ideas into the older scheme of actions, a progressive integration of the law administered in the two separative jurisdictions, and when these were ultimately combined in a unified system of courts, a gradual coalescence, in Rome of the *ius civile* with the *ius honorarium,* in England of law and equity. In the modern civil law, there exists a somewhat similar distinction of civil and commercial law, which is still accompanied in France and a decreasing number of other countries by a corresponding vestigial division of the courts.

[3] London (1911).

[4] A History of Lay Judges 145–72 (1960).

But we must forego more detailed consideration of these instances of the translation of the more modern conceptions of justice, or in other words of equity, in the formation of jurisdiction and law during the creative stages of the two principal legal systems of the Western world. Instead of endeavoring to survey the multitudinous technical detail in which equitable notions have operated, which would undoubtedly demonstrate that, in the context of different legal systems, the ultimate effect of these notions in comparable situations will be similar, though reached by diverse means, it is proposed to consider the general conception of equity as it has at various times been envisaged. This will be attempted in a short series of brief vignettes presenting the concept of equity in different institutional settings. A superficial review of this character will present little that is new, but it is hoped that it may be of interest.

II

We look first to ancient Greece, where it has been said all things that move began. In the beginnings of Greek speculation concerning human society and the universe, nature and reason were not differentiated. As Erik Wolf has observed, in early Greece there were neither conceptless bodies (*Gestalten*) nor disembodied concepts; what the Greek saw, he thought, and what he thought, he saw.[5] The primitive scheme of thinking reflected in the epic literature had not differentiated the concepts of justice and law in abstract terms; the germs of these more advanced ideas were most nearly represented by the goddesses Themis and Dike. The former, born of Earth and Heaven and thus an elemental, Titanic divinity, embodied the principle of order, declaring by her counsel to the gods and by oracle to human beings the designs of destiny. Dike is close akin, being the daughter of Themis and Zeus; she personified what is straight and right in nature as well as in human society, her office being to regulate and dispense even-handed justice according to the divine will. Implicit in these representations in the theogony of early Greece is the idea that human society and the phenomena of nature are regulated by a cosmic order, which even the gods cannot change.

Homer, it has been said, made the gods seem like men, and men like gods. The mythical representations of justice as an unwritten code of conduct for the aristocratic elite in the loose tribal confederacy of Homer's time was fundamentally affected by the transition from clan to city that had taken place by the sixth century. In the succeeding efflorescence of Greek culture, the myths formed the stuff of great drama, showing that even the gods might err, but for the purpose of speculation, they had been superseded by critical discussion in the more

[5] 1 GRIECHISCHES RECHTSDENKEN, VORSOKRATIKER UND FRÜHE DICHTER 21 (1950).

sophisticated terms of philosophy. From this source, the concept of relativism, of change and growth in the universe, was introduced, with the related principle of the polarity of opposites. This seminal notion anticipated the Sophist doctrine of the *dissoi logoi, viz.,* that in every cause there are two opposed points of view and that, in disputing any question, it is therefore proper to argue from either side. These ideas naturally influenced Greek thinking about justice. In the democratic city-state, the emphasis shifted from the belief in an immutable order governing human affairs to the protection of the weak against the powerful and the privileged. The reforms of Draco and Solon assumed that the political constitution might be adapted to the needs of the particular city-state; that enactments might derogate from inveterate custom. It was even argued, in view of the diversity and disparity of the laws in different times and places, that these were mere conventions, which might conflict with and in any event were not predicated upon justice.

In consequence, as Jones has remarked, there was "a weakening of the force of *themis* from a direct expression of the divine will through oracle, or later king or judge, to a mere general indication that something ought or ought not to be done."[6] At the same time, the term *dike,* while retaining the sense of what is right and just, came also to denote in a more concrete meaning the legal process, as well as the claims of litigants and the judgments of the courts. Thus, while still referring to a suprahuman standard of conduct, *dike* was also regarded as binding on the citizens by reason of their membership in a city governed by its particular customs and enactments. In sum, in this evolution of ideas, the conception of justice in a sense resembling that of natural law was preserved, but it had been differentiated from unwritten law and positive enactments.

As this suggests, the problem that Aristotle was called upon to resolve in the leading passage in the fifth book of the *Nicomachean Ethics,*[7] in which Greek ideas on justice have been transmitted to posterity, was to synthesize the sense of right and the ultimate belief in a rational social order with the diversity of laws, customary and enacted, which varied from time to time and place to place and were subject to revision to meet new conditions. In *The Statesman,* Plato had pointed out that "the law cannot comprehend exactly what is noblest or just, or at once ordain what is best, for all. The differences of men and actions, and the endless irregular movements of human beings, do not admit of any universal and simple rule. No art can lay down any rule which will last forever."[8] To meet this criticism of

[6] JONES, THE LAW AND LEGAL THEORY OF THE GREEKS 32 (1956).
[7] 9 ARISTOTLE, WORKS 1129a–1138b (Ross trans., 1925).
[8] 294a (Jowett's translation).

the law, Artistotle introduced a theory, for which, as Hamburger has stated, "he can claim sole and first authority,"[9] integrating equity in the sphere of justice. Taking a term in common use, *epieikeia* or in Latin *aequitas,* which was promiscuously employed to designate goodness, clemency, indulgence, moderation, mitigation of the strict law, and the like, Aristotle redefined the term more precisely as denoting what is fair or reasonable. What is more important, while Plato regarded *epieikeia* as a deviation from the right and true law, Aristotle ascribed to equity the function of correcting, supplementing, and adapting laws that are inappropriate in practical instances or have become incompatible with current conditions. In this construction, equity, which previously was contrasted with strict law, is a necessary adjustment, an epiphenomenon, of legal justice. For this reason, a brief consideration of the Aristotelian conception of justice is pertinent.

In this conception, a primary distinction is made, on the one hand, between justice as the greatest of virtues, a disposition of character to exercise complete virtue not only in one's self but in relation to neighbors, or in other words to act fairly and lawfully, and on the other hand, particular or political justice in a more specific sense with which we are here concerned. This relates to the pleasure that comes from gain, to honor or money or security, but does not include all the objects that may concern a virtuous man. In this specific sense, justice is again distinguished: one branch, distributive justice, is manifested in the distribution of honor or money or other possessions among the members of the community; the second, corrective or commutative justice, has a rectifying role to perform in transactions between individuals. It will be recalled that, in Aristotle's exposition, the problem of distributive justice is to give every man his due according to his relative merit; it involves a species of geometrical proportion, the just being defined by the proportion and the unjust by what violates the proportion. This problem, it is frequently remarked, is to be resolved by the legislature. On the other hand, the problem of corrective justice is to compensate for a wrong, whether arising from a voluntary transaction or from what we would term a civil delict or tort. Here the just is equality between individuals regarded as equals, and without reference to their individual merits; the wrong, whether arising from violation of an agreement or an injurious act, creates an inequality of gain and loss, a disturbance of the equilibrium determined by distributive justice, that must be equalized in an arithmetical proportion. In sum, the basic principle of corrective justice is just, *i.e.,* equal, compensation for unjust enrichment or damage, which will restore equilibrium between the parties. It is of interest that in this connection Aristotle analyzes the subjective element of intention in defining just and unjust acts.

[9] Morals and Law: The Growth of Aristotle's Legal Theory 89 (1951).

Now, in the Aristotelian sense, justice exists only between men whose mutual relations are governed by law, not by a man, who will become a tyrant; and law exists for men between whom there is injustice. Legal justice is the discrimination of the just and the unjust as above defined. In this scheme, equity is generically the same as justice, but not absolutely so; equity is just and at the same time better than justice. It is a correction of legal justice, needed since the law is universal but in some cases it is not possible to make a universal statement which is correct for all situations. In such instances, the law takes the normal case to form the rule, and the function of equity is to correct the omission of the law to cover the unusual case, to provide for the gaps in the law due to the nature of practical affairs. As Aristotle remarks, where the subject matter is indefinite, the rule also must be indefinite, so that a decree adapted to the facts is necessary.

The doctrine set forth in the *Nicomachean Ethics* is more succinctly reproduced in Aristotle's *Rhetoric* [10] and, consistently with the purpose of the latter work, its practical consequences are indicated in more detail. As summarized by Coing, these include:

(i) leniency in appropriate cases, especially by distinguishing intentional wrong from violation of law through mistakes and cases of accident;
(ii) understanding of the human element;
(iii) reference not to the words of a statute but to the legislator and his intention;
(iv) consideration of the whole personality and not the particular act;
(v) preference for arbitration as against litigation.[11]

As Cairns has pointed out, this view has theoretical merits, but it involves a practical difficulty. As he states:

"Equitable principles in their application are governed by rules or they are not; if not, justice ceases to be uniform, one of its most valuable characteristics; if it is, equity itself soon becomes as rigid as the written law."[12]

The answer to this dilemma, it would seem, must be found in the relative balance needed from time to time between security and flexibility as requirements of justice.

Thus, the doctrine of Aristotle extended the conception of justice to include the dynamic element of equity, providing, in Pringsheim's

[10] I. 13–1374a, b.

[11] *Zum Einfluss der Philosophie des Aristoteles auf die Entwicklung des römischen Rechts*, 69 ZEITSCHRIFT DER SAVIGNY STIFTUNG FÜR RECHTSGESCHICHTE. ROM. ABT. 43 (1952). *Cf.* the summary in CAIRNS, LEGAL PHILOSOPHY FROM PLATO TO HEGEL 109 (1949).

[12] *Ibid.*

metaphor,[13] a bridge between the law that was and the law that is to be. It recognized the fact that, as indeed was exemplified by the wide discretion exercised by the Greek tribunals in the administration of justice, the conception of justice itself requires that the application of legal rules to particular cases and to changed conditions must be inspired by equity. Consistently enough, the term was undefined in various respects. Assuming the inherent validity of the laws as formulated, in Aristotle's view equity was apparently limited to the adaptation of general rules in specific instances, and did not envisage the questions that might arise when there was no applicable rule or when the rule itself conflicted with the sense of justice. On its face, the Aristotelian concept of equity is vague, sufficiently so to allow the term to be used in later times not only in reference to interpretation of the laws but also to characterize reformatory legislation and the institution of equitable tribunals. This indefiniteness is not necessarily a defect; Vinogradoff regarded this teaching as "one of the most instructive parts of Greek jurisprudence," which has had great influence on the development of modern legal theory.[14] But it is a source of difficulty in tracing the influence of the idea in later times, as will appear below.

III

The next stage is Rome; indeed, during the long evolution of Roman law extending over a thousand years, there were at least two stages in the reception of equity in legal thought: the period of the republican and classical jurisprudence and the period that commenced with Constantine in the fourth century A.D. This is a complex story; while it is clear that, through the schools of rhetoric, the teachings of Greek philosophy had been imported into aristocratic circles in Rome at least before the last century of the Republic, the nature and extent of the influence of the doctrine of equity as formulated by Greek philosophy upon the legal system leads into controversial territory.

To start as it were in midstream, in 1926 there appeared in the *Festschrift* of Paul Speiser-Sarasin a contribution in forty pages by Professor Johannes Stroux, entitled *"Summum Ius Summa Injuria."*[15] This monograph touched off an international tempest in the camps of the Romanists. Gerhard von Beseler, the archdetector of interpolations, declared that the work should be burned forthwith in the public square; Salvatore Riccobono, the Nestor of Romanist studies, retorted that to understand the development of Roman law the monograph was worth more than all the critical works of the preceding thirty

---

[13] *Aequitas und Bona Fides*, 33 Pub. Università Cattolica 183, 194 (1931).

[14] 2 Outlines of Historical Jurisprudence: The Jurisprudence of the Greek City 63 (1922).

[15] (1926). New edition included in Rechtswissenschaft und Rhetorik (1949).

years. As Professor Schiller remarked twenty years ago in a particularly instructive comparison of *interpretatio* in the Roman law and interpretation in Anglo-American law,[16] the publication of Stroux inspired a fruitful and more precise consideration by various authors of the extent to which *aequitas* and the system of interpretation developed on the basis of equity were incorporated into Roman jurisprudence.[17]

In retrospect, the thesis propounded by Stroux does not seem explosive. It was in sum that by the middle of the second century B.C., or in other words more or less contemporaneously with the procedural reform introduced by the *Lex Aebutia,* the Roman jurisprudence had received from Greece through the schools of rhetoric the conception of equity as a complement to the formalism characteristic of early law. Citing the remark of Kant that the adage *summum ius summa injuria* is the basic *motif* of equity, he pointed out that when law is reduced to written form, the legal rules must eventually and inevitably be interpreted on grounds of equity, so as to do justice to the individual case and in the light of changing conditions. The proof offered to show that this must have occurred in republican Rome is that references to the adage by Terence, Cicero, and Columela indicate that it was in common use in the later Republic; that the schools of rhetoric, in which the Roman elite were trained, had developed a refined theory of interpretation, in which the so-called "status" of *scriptum et voluntas,* of reference to the word as against the intention, embodied the Aristotelian doctrine of equity; and that in certain celebrated cases the more liberal construction was recognized. Unfortunately, as Stroux himself acknowledged, the witnesses that he adduced were not jurists. Indeed, the adage taken as the text, as Cicero made clear, denoted undue litigiousness, the abuse of legal rights as the height of malice or injury, and was not used as a criterion of interpretation. In this instance, Kant's legal history was inferior to his philosophy.

More recent studies concerning the influence on the evolution of Roman law of Greek philosophical ideas and more especially their systematic exposition in Aristotle's works have only in part sustained the thesis advanced by Stroux in 1926. It took several centuries to complete the process of assimilation that he proposed had been accomplished by Cicero's time; on the other hand, if he had limited the argument for Greek influence during the later Republic to those developments in the Roman legal system which corresponded with Aristotle's teachings, it would have approximated the results of later

[16] *Roman Interpretatio and Anglo-American Interpretation and Construction,* 27 VA. L. REV. 733, 753ff. (1941). *Cf.* Kisch, *Summum Ius Summa Injuria; Basler Humanisten und Juristen über Aequitas und "Epieikeia"* in SIMONIUS, AEQUITAS UND BONA FIDES. FESTGABE ZUM 70. GEBURTSTAG 195, 197ff. (1955).

[17] For a general review of the influence of Aristotelian philosophy on the development of Roman law, see Professor Coing's article, cited *supra* note 11.

more intensive investigations of the subject. However this may be, the results of these investigations, though in certain respects they are based on constructions from incomplete evidence and various details are subject to dispute, give a picture of the development during the republican and classical period which is plausible and sufficiently substantiated.

In the first place, it appears that from at least the establishment of the Republic, Rome was in the orbit of Hellenic influence. Even if the details of the expulsion of the kings and the events leading to the enactment of the XII Tables as narrated by Livy may be apochryphal, in essence they correspond with similar developments that had been occurring elsewhere in the Hellenic world. As Wieacker has observed,[18] the political establishment of the Roman republic as a city-state conformed to the pattern that had been followed in Greek, Etruscan, and Italian cities. A king with tenure for life was supplanted by a magistracy for a term of years, usually plural and elected annually; the expulsion of the king was the result of an understanding among those participating in the revolution that there should be equality, if not in the distribution of offices, at least in the political status of the citizens. Likewise, in attributing the enactment of the XII Tables to the decemvirs, the Roman tradition clearly conforms with the Greek *aisymnetie:* the introduction of legislation to appease social and political unrest by an extraordinary arbitral authority. For this purpose, experience had shown the necessity of laying down the fundamental law of the constitution in written form; without this the equality of all citizens under the law would not be secure. In this respect again, the tradition that a committee was sent to Greece to consult the laws of Solon and other Greek models, if not authentic, suggests Greek inspiration. The purpose of the reform was essentially political—to secure equality and security in the administration of justice against arbitrary application of the laws. This is attested not only by the traditional accounts of the political antecedents, by the lapidarian language of the XII Tables, but also by their specific provisions. These prescribe in detail all that is needed to regulate in the common interest—but no more—the affairs of the city in an agricultural community.[19]

If this construction of the establishment of the Roman city-state, predicated upon analogies to Greek antecedents, is plausible but not conclusive, there can be no doubt as to the extensive penetration of Greek influence among the Roman *élite* after the Punic Wars. It is a historic law that a superior culture commands the obeisance of those by whom it is conquered. Speaking of the Greek dialectical method,

---

18 VOM RÖMISCHEN RECHT 2, 47 ff. (2nd ed. 1961).

19 Wieacker gives an instructive summary of the provisions in the XII Tables. *Id.* at 54–56.

Schulz states that knowledge of the method "must be presumed" in the leading Roman lawyers from the second half of the second century onwards. "If they did not make its acquaintance by philosophy, they certainly did so by their studies in mathematics, rhetoric, and grammar, for in all these branches of knowledge they met the same dialectical method."[20] During this period, the Greek conception of equity was certainly known; the question with which we are concerned is when and how far it was received in the Roman legal system.

The answer to this question, as indicated by more recent studies correcting Stroux' *Wahnvorstellung* (Beseler) of 1926, may be briefly summarized as follows. First, it is to be noted that, from the time of Q. Mucius, Roman jurisprudence adopted, or rather adapted, for its purposes the Greek dialectic. As Schulz states, "The importation of the dialectical method transformed Roman jurisprudence into a systematic science, and was therefore of incomparable importance in the history of legal science."[21] More specifically with reference to a reception of the Aristotelian concept of equity, it has been suggested with some plausibility that the praetorian reforms introduced by the *Lex Aebutia* in the second century B.C. were inspired by this conception;[22] in any event, the *praetor* in the exercise of his *imperium* during this period introduced a number of actions that recognized current ideas as to the requirements of justice and enlarged the discretion of the *iudex;* by this means, the praetorian magistrate created a new body of law, the *ius honorarium,* fundamentally correcting and supplementing the older *ius civile* and employing as the standard of decision by the *iudex* terms that in a sense applied the Aristotelian conception of *aequitas: aequum et bonum, aequius melius, bona fides, inter bonos bene agere et sine fraudatione, dolus, metus, circumscriptio minorum.*

How far the ideas represented by these terms, which have had a profound influence on later law, are directly traceable to Aristotelian influence is another question which has been explored by Pringsheim in a notable series of articles, meticulously analyzing the texts.[23] Equity, he suggests, has two principal functions; on the one hand, as the conscience of the law, it is the motive of legal reform, the law that is to be; on the other hand, it supplies the basic principle of interpretation

[20] HISTORY OF ROMAN LEGAL SCIENCE (1946). *Cf.* also Coing's article on the influence of Aristotelian philosophy on the development of Roman law, cited *supra* note 11 at 26–27.

[21] *Id.* at 68. See generally pp. 62–69.

[22] WIEACKER, *op. cit. supra* note 18 at 113, 145.

[23] *Aequitas und Bona Fides,* PUB. UNIVERSITÀ CATTOLICA 183 ff. (Milan Conference, 1930); *Römische aequitas der christlichen Kaiser,* 1 ACTA CONG. JUR. INT. ROM. 119 (1935); *Ius aequum und ius strictum,* 42 Z. SAV. (ROM.) 643 (1921); *Bonum und aequum,* 52 *ibid.* 68 (1932). *Cf.* 5 ALBERTARIO, STUDI DI DIRITTO ROMANO 107 ff. (1937); Maggiore, *L'equità e il suo valore nel diritto,* 3 REV. INT. DI FILOSOFIA DEL DIRITTO 256 (1923); Wenger, *Zur christlichen Begründung des Naturrechts,* 69 Z. SAV. (ROM.) 5 (1952).

according to the intention, not only of legal enactments and rules but also of contracts, testaments, and other documents.[24] In the dual formulary procedure of the republican and classical periods, while, by virtue of his *imperium,* the praetor instituted new actions *ex aequitate,* this term was conspicuously absent in the formulae that were invented. In this ingenious system, the proceedings *in iure* before the praetor terminated in the *litis contestatio,* the agreement of the parties to accept the decision of the *iudex* on the terms prescribed in the formula, which was settled by the praetor after hearing and on the advice of jurists. Thereafter, there was no room for equity except as the formula itself prescribed. As Pringsheim has shown, clarifying the later confusion of concepts, the Roman jurists employed standards more concrete than *aequitas* in the classical formulary system of actions; in the actions on the important commercial contracts, sale, loan, *negotiorum gestio,* mandate, deposit, fiducia, etc., the standard was *bona fides,* the measure of integrity of a Roman citizen,[25] while in the ancient actions on account of *injuriae, i.e.,* for what we would call moral injuries, in which there was no clear basis for assessing compensation, the *iudex* was instructed in the *aestimatio* to decide *ex bono et aequo,* or in other words on the basis of a fair appraisal.[26]

In sum, in the light of modern textual criticism, it appears (1) that the praetorian reforms of the late Republic presumably were introduced *ex aequitate;* (2) that in the formulae introduced by these reforms the *iudex* was never authorized to decide *ex aequitate* but, when it was necessary to allow him a certain discretion, this was defined by a more concrete Roman standard of conduct; (3) that, while the jurists in the second century B.C. assimilated the Greek dialectic into their jurisprudence, the term *aequitas* does not appear in their works until the late classical jurists and then as an idea separate from *ius.* In other words, the Aristotelian concept of equity was not expressly employed in the most important and distinctive branch of the law, the *interpretatio* of the jurists.

How is this to be explained? The answer, it would seem, lies in a conjunction of various factors which conspired to produce a unique system for the elaboration of law centered in the *consulta* given by the jurists. In the first place, the system rested on the *auctoritas,* the knowledge and prestige of the individual jurists. They were recruited from the highest ranks of the nobility, from those who after distinguished public service and study of the law sought the honor of service without pay as jurisconsults.[27] In the second place, as members of the ruling

[24] *Cf.* Pringsheim, *Aequitas und Bona Fides, loc. cit. supra* note 23 at 194 ff.
[25] *Op. cit. supra* note 24.
[26] Pringsheim, *Bonum et Aequum, loc. cit. supra* note 23.
[27] *Cf.* WIEACKER, *op. cit. supra* note 18 at 128 ff.; KUNKEL, HERKUNFT UND SOZIALE STELLUNG DER RÖMISCHEN JURISTEN (1952).

class, they continued the traditional monopoly of the college of pontiffs in the interpretation of the laws. This explains the sporadic use of legislation to develop the law, except when necessary to reform the constitution or to deal with political crises. Through the *interpretatio*, they determined the application of the existing legislation both by the magistrate, a younger member of the ruling group, and by the *iudices*, drawn from a panel of senators. In the third place, since they were a group of professionals, whose power depended upon their prestige, they instinctively avoided innovation and continued the traditional casuistry of the *interpretatio* of the pontiffs; their opinions were given on specific cases, excluding all extraneous argument. By this method, the jurists developed consummate powers of analysis and concise statement; their *consulta* took no account of philosophy or history, of comparative law or sociological considerations, of family and commercial customs, or even constitutional law—all these were excluded by the pragmatic jurists who were concerned only to advise whether an action would lie.[28] In consequence, as Schulz has characterized the product:

> "Private Roman law as portrayed by classical writers attains an extraordinary, almost logical definiteness. The number of juristic conceptions which play a part in it is comparatively small, as all which pertain to special or non-Roman variations are set aside. The legal rules take on the character of apodictic truths, as any limitations imposed by public law or extra-legal duties are ignored. Often the jurists' statements almost give the impression of a mathematical treatise or rather of a treatise on a law of Nature, but one within the framework of Roman legislation and retaining certain traditional principles and axioms—in short, a Roman law of Nature lacking the speculative airiness of the Greek conception. The Roman jurists' aim is to find—within the specified framework —the rule arising out of the nature of the thing itself, out of conditions as they are."[29]

In this scheme, there was no place for Aristotelian equity, not merely since the Roman jurists were averse to abstract ideas[30] but also since it was expedient to eschew constructions that might hamper the adaptation of the system of remedies to new situations.[31] The unique position of the Roman jurisconsults enabled them to construct a body of doctrine respecting specific cases in which theory was united with practical experience, avoiding on the one hand, the rigidity of a traditional system of precedents and, on the other, the unreality and

[28] *Cf.* SCHULZ, *op. cit. supra* note 20 at 70–71; WIEACKER, *op. cit. supra* note 18 at 143 ff.

[29] PRINCIPLES OF ROMAN PRIVATE LAW 34–35 (1936).

[30] *Id.* at 40 ff.

[31] *Id., op. cit. supra* note 20 at 61.

excesses to which a rational projection of general principles may lead. They took from Greek philosophy only what was germane to their technique, but not the conception of equity, which was immanent in the law itself and therefore was difficult to conceive as a separate branch of justice. Even in the works of the last classical jurists, as for example in the well-known definition of *ius naturale* by Paulus,[82] the use of the Greek terms appears adventitious for purposes of exposition.

From Constantine to Justinian, with the conversion of the throne to Christianity, the legal order was fundamentally changed. There was to be one Empire, one law, one faith.[83] As a matter of fact, it was remarkable how long the traditional system of the classical jurisprudence, painstakingly constructed by methodical analysis of practical cases, had withstood the tide. Long since, Rome had become cosmopolitan—even the great jurists of the Dynasty were not Roman. The edict of the *praetor,* which once had been the chief source of legal development, had become perpetual; the authority of the great jurisconsults was stereotyped by the law of citations; supreme authority had been absorbed by the emperor, whose edicts and constitutions formed the law. The formulary procedure, on which the system of actions had been based, had been superseded by the *cognitio,* a unitary proceeding before an official judge; in consequence, the distinctions between *aequitas, aequum et bonum, bona fides,* had lost their *raison d'être* to limit the discretion of the lay *iudex.* The post-classical separation of *strictum ius* from *aequitas* was introduced, presumably under Byzantine influence, and the Aristotelian doctrine that equity is superior to law was gratefully adopted by the absolute monarchs, who regarded the strict law as an undesirable restriction on their authority. In 314 A.D., Constantine ordained that in all matters justice and equity should prevail over strict law;[84] this perhaps represented a propagandist effort of the imperial chancery to justify the numerous changes that were being introduced in the old law under Hellenistic and Christian influences. But the declaration of the subordination of strict law to equity doubtless had implications in the day-to-day administration of justice; in any event, two years later in 316 A.D. Constantine reserved interpretation as between equity and law to his own decision.[85] This need not be regarded as a *volte face;* in 314, it was decided that

[82] Dig.1,1,11 (Paul 14 ad Sab.): *Ius pluribus modis dicitur: uno modo, cum id, quod* [semper] *aequum et bonum est, ius dicitur, ut est ius naturale. Cf.* Vogensperger, Der Begriff des *"Ius naturale"* im Römischen Recht 85 ff. (1952) and more generally the references collected by Pringsheim, *Ius aequum und jus strictum, op. cit. supra* note 23 at 643 ff.

[83] *Cf.* Pringsheim, *Römische Aequitas der Christlichen Kaiser, op. cit. supra* note 23.

[84] C.3,1,8. *"Placuit in omnibus rebus praecipuam esse iustitiae aequitatisque quam stricti iuris rationem."*

[85] C.1,14,1: *"Inter aequitatem iusque interpositam interpretationem nobis solis et oportet et licet inspicare."*

justice and equity should prevail over law while in 316 it was made clear that the emperor should decide what is equity and justice. The gates at last were opened wide to Hellenistic, Christian, and universalistic ideas—to the Aristotelian conception of equity as a superior, more concrete form of justice, to the identification in the canonical conception of justice and equity with natural law, to the universal authority of the emperor to maintain on this earth justice, virtue, and the Christian faith. Equity here reached its apogee; the merger of justice, morals, and religion appeared to be complete.

The concept of equity in which the *bonum et aequum, bona fides,* natural law, and even justice, reason, and charity were compounded with the Aristotelian doctrine was thus made a discretionary prerogative of the imperial power by Constantine. It provided authority with a charismatic justification in terms broad and diffuse enough to satisfy the need for flexibility in the supervision of administration and for the reform of the strict law. For this reason, it was perpetuated in the *Corpus Iuris Civilis* of Justinian and became a cardinal element in the doctrine of church and state. But while the predominance of equity over law, in the canonical doctrine binding even the emperor himself, was of great moral significance as a principle of official conduct, encouraging liberal interpretation of the existing laws and their reform by legislation in accord with changing social conditions and ideals, the generality of the conception of equity made it vulnerable. The result was that in the codification of Justinian the more precisely elaborated constructions of the classical jurisprudence also survived and in the end prevailed as the basic component of the civil law. Moreover, the fact that the prerogative of equity was reserved to the emperor was eventually also to prove a weakness; such latitude of discretion placed in the hands of concentrated power—for which reason officialdom in England as in imperial Rome favored equity—was subject to abuse. And this is the reason why the grand imperial conception of Constantine and Justinian later succumbed to the democratic revolutions of the modern age.

The rest is epilogue, as a brief visit to the Middle Ages and in conclusion to more modern times will suggest.

IV

We pass first to the Middle Ages. Equity in various senses is then a term in common use; it may serve as a motive to justify legislation, as a general principle of interpretation, or, as in England in a later time, to signify a special jurisdiction. It is not possible in this paper to explore the manifestations of the conception of equity in all these directions through the variegated panorama of history since the time of Justinian. Hence, no attempt will be made to trace one of the obvious channels through which equity may influence the course of legal development, namely, legislation. The legislative power evidently includes the power to act on equitable considerations, and the extent to which these are reflected in the unnumerable variety of laws can only be inferred in each case from the attendant circumstances. For the present purpose, it is of more interest to consider, as an illustration of the influence of equity in interpretation of legal texts, the problem faced by Irnerius and his successors at the end of the 11th century upon the discovery of the manuscripts of the Code and the Digest, and more cursorily thereafter the development in England.

As Savigny observed,[36] the position of the Glossators was unique. Ordinarily, laws reflect the culture of the time in the place where they are enacted, but the *Corpus Iuris Civilis* was a monumental mosaic of legal prescriptions devised by the Roman jurists during several centuries to meet the needs of a highly sophisticated cosmopolitan civilization a millenium before Irnerius, and compiled over six hundred years before his time. The primary purpose of Justinian's codification was to restore the classical jurisprudence of Rome, enacted in imperial laws ordained to stand forever—*in omne aevum valituras*—comprising the Digests in which the writings of the jurists, excerpted and edited to conform to later changes in legal doctrine and procedure, were reproduced, the Institutes, a text for students, and the Code of imperial constitutions to 534 A.D., supplementing the earlier law. It is a question how far the body of legal provisions enacted in the *Corpus Iuris Civilis* was the actual law, even in Justinian's time; at least in the West, recent researches have disclosed the extent to which the refined distinctions of the classical law had been obliterated in common understanding during the later Empire.[37] The Roman jurists had expressed the living law of their time, but the task of the Glossators, undertaken before the renascence of learning in Western Europe, was to breathe life into the relics of an age that had long since passed into oblivion.

Moreover, at no time has legal science seemed so bound to the legal texts as the Glossators deemed themselves to be. Imbued with the idea that legislation is a prerogative of the sovereign, they received the *Corpus Iuris Civilis* as the authoritative general law. They had first to establish the text and then to ascertain the meaning of the multitude of individual provisions, not as did the Roman jurists, using them as a base to declare the living law, but in a flat logical plane, in which the disparate conceptions formed at different stages in the evolution of the law of Rome, expressing Byzantine as well as Roman constructions, could be coherently reconciled. To accomplish this, the Glossa-

[36] 1 SYSTEM DES HEUTIGEN RÖMISCHEN RECHTS 86 (1840).

[37] See especially, LEVY, WEST ROMAN VULGAR LAW. THE LAW OF PROPERTY (1951); *id.*, WESTRÖMISCHES VULGARRECHT. DAS OBLIGATIONENRECHT (1956).

tors had to contrive a technique of textual interpretation; as yet, the evolution of the doctrines which they developed in the process of interpreting the texts is for the most part unexplored. Fortunately, however, recent essays by Meijers[38] and Lange[39] reveal the significance of the conception of equity as a means not only to harmonize the texts but also to develop the law as a system of general principles. The remarks that follow are based on their findings.

In the first place, the Glossators added little, if at all, to the conception of equity; their interest lay in its application in specific cases as a principle of interpretation. As they conceived, equity is superior to justice and law, the *fons et origo iustitiae.* Justice is the disposition to recognize and to act in accordance with equity; this reflects Ulpian's definition of justice as the *constans et perpetua voluntas ius suum cuique tribuens.*[40] When reduced to precept, written or customary, it is termed law. After Guarnerius, it was common to make a threefold division of equity and justice as (a) *nondum constituta,* also termed *aequitas rudis,* equity not yet concretized in precept; (b) *constituta,* or *ipsum ius,* the positive law; and (c) *concepta,* namely, *id quod pro iure habetur,* the lawful will of men, living expressed in contracts, and dying in their testaments.[41] These distinctions neatly summarize the doctrines as to equity to be found in Aristotle and the Roman legal texts.

The applications of these ideas in specific cases by the Glossators is for our purpose of more interest than their characterization. There is little evidence, except at first, that they claimed discretion to amend or ignore the texts, but these contained numerous instances in which reference was made to solutions dictated by strict law in contrast to those inspired by equity. Indeed, the very texts that prescribed the relative effect to be given to equity and law—which the Glossators were bound to apply in their interpretation of other texts—presented a fundamental antinomy that had to be resolved, were the interpretation of the texts as authoritative to be tenable. The problem was presented by the enactments of Constantine in 314 and 316 A.D., to which reference has been made above. The first of these, the Constitution *Placuit,* declared that in all matters the reason (*ratio*) of justice and equity prevails over that of strict law;[42] the latter, the Constitution *Inter aequitatem,* prohibited interpretation as between equity and law except by the emperor.[43] Both were supported by other texts; the former, for

[38] *Le Conflit entre l'Equité et la Loi chez les premiers Glossateurs,* 17 TIJDSCHRIFT VOOR RECHTSGESCHIEDENIS 117 ff. (1941).

[39] *Ius aequum und ius strictum bei den Glossatoren,* 71 Z. SAV. (ROM.) 319 ff. (1954).

[40] D. 1. 1.10. pr.

[41] Meijers, *op. cit. supra* note 38 at 117.

[42] *Supra* note 34.

[43] *Supra* note 35.

example, by a provision in the Digest that in all things, especially in law, consideration is to be given to equity,[44] while the latter was reinforced by the fiat of Justinian that it is only appropriate for the sovereign to interpret the laws.[45]

To resolve this apparent conflict in the texts, two solutions were offered. The stricter view of Bulgarus and his followers was that, in the provisions generally declaring that equity should prevail over strict law, *aequitas* should be understood in the sense of *aequitas constituta* or *aequitas scripta,* and it seems that this view became generally accepted. On the other hand, Martinus, who may have been influenced by liberal Byzantine theories of interpretation, and those who accepted his position, maintained that the reservation to the emperor of interpretation as between equity and law covered only cases in which there is complete contradiction between equity and law, as distinguished from cases where a law includes situations to which in equity it should not apply or is less extensive than equity requires. In the former case, interpretation is reserved to the emperor, since only by a *general and necessary* interpretation, having the force of law, can the conflict be resolved. In the latter types of cases, interpretation is necessary but not general, and the judge therefore may construe the law in consonance with equity.

There is, however, a difference of opinion whether Martinus held that the edict *Placuit* enabled the judge to apply *aequitas rudis, i.e.,* equity not yet declared as law, as well as *aequitas constituta,* in preference to strict law. That such was the case, Meijers infers from a passage in which Rogerius, a disciple of Bulgarus, declaims against the *stulti* who would set their own opinion over the authority of the emperors clearly declared by law. Meijers takes the attack as directed against Martinus and cites various opinions, attributed to him in support of this conclusion.[46] However, as Lange has pointed out,[47] the conclusion does not seem plausible, not only since there is no gloss of Martinus to support it but also since his argument was always rested on a text, however liberally extended, which he regarded as equitable. The difference between the two schools of interpretation apparently turned on the degree of generality with which an equitable decision in a specific case, evidenced by a text, should be extended to other analogous cases, not on whether *aequitas rudis* could be a ground of judicial decision. Undoubtedly, Martinus went further than his contemporaries in drawing generalizations from particular texts on equitable grounds than ordinary canons of exegesis would allow. But it would not have

[44] D. 40.9.12.1 *in fine.*
[45] C. 1. 14. 12. 3.
[46] *Op. cit. supra* note 38 at 120, 126.
[47] *Op. cit. supra* note 39 at 328 ff.

been necessary to proceed in this manner, had he regarded *aequitas rudis* as a sufficient ground of decision.

While the more conservative doctrine of Bulgarus eventually won out, it should not be supposed that it led to a rigid positivistic technique of interpretation. Even restricted to the texts, legal science was left large leeway on account of the many references to equity which they contained to adapt the written law to new conditions. As Meijers has pointed out,[48] many of the solutions advocated by Martinus later were generally accepted, not on grounds of equity, but since they conformed to the spirit or reason of the law, a construction which in effect supposed that equity was immanent within the law itself. Hence, the dispute as to the relative force of equity and law, while of theoretical interest, was not so significant as the distinction which it caused the Glossators to draw between the *jus aequum* and the *ius strictum*. Recognition of the existence in the *Corpus Iuris Civilis* of both equitable provisions and provisions of strict law that might apply to the same cases, together with the generalizing method of the Glossators, employed to draw principles from particular instances, gave larger freedom in the interpretation of the texts.

To give a few illustrations:

1. *Harmonization* of conflicting texts. The distinction between *ius aequum* and *ius strictum* enabled the Glossators to reconcile conflicts in the texts and in so doing to supersede the more primitive conceptions. Thus, in case an animal has been promised and a *fideiussor* kills it before it is to be delivered, (D.4.3.19), it was advised by Neratius Priscus and Iulianus that, since the debtor was discharged, the *fideiussor* in consequence would not be liable; Papinian therefore held that an *actio doli* would lie against the *fideiussor*. On the other hand, in D. 45.1.88 an action *ex stipulatu* is held by Paulus, in an analogous case, to be available against the *fideiussor* although the defendant is discharged. The texts are reconciled by the *Glossa ordinaria* on the ground that the action *ex stipulatu* is *de aequitate utili*, the *actio doli* is *de rigore*.

Similarly, the merger of the action in the *litis contestatio* could have undesirable results under certain circumstances when alternative actions were available to the plaintiff or there were several debtors. Thus, if the plaintiff sued one of the debtors and he became insolvent after *litis contestatio*, the plaintiff would ordinarily have no relief. In this case, (D. 15.1.32.pr.), Ulpian stated that, although this was the result under the law (*iure*), *tamen aequitas dictat iudicium in eos dari, qui occasione iuris liberantur, ut magis eos perceptio quam intentio liberet.* Here the *Glossa* typically generalizes to the effect that the discharge

[48] *Op. cit. supra* note 38.

effected by *litis contestatio* is *stricti iuris,* while equity requires performance.[49]

2. Generalization from a particular case to allow an *actio utilis ex aequitate* in other cases not expressly provided for. Thus, Martinus held that an action of this nature would be available in the following situations:

(a) To the third party beneficiary under a contract. This was generalized from the exception to the rule *alter alteri stipulari non potest* provided by a rescript of Diocletian, allowing an *actio utilis propter aequitatem* to the owner of property, deposited by a third party, against the depositee.

(b) To one who without the authority of his principal or without the assent of the owner of property has incurred expenses. In this instance, Martinus allowed recovery of the benefit to the principal or the property owner, adducing the principle of equity enunciated by Pomponius (D. 12.16.14 and 50.17.206), that no one should be enriched to the detriment of another, a principle that may be traced back to Aristotle.

(c) To a volunteer who makes improvements on the land of another. Under the strict law, a possessor in good faith enjoyed only a right of retention. The *actio negotiorum gestorum utilis* was allowed to the volunteer by Martinus, presumably even if he were in bad faith, on the strength of the action provided in D.3.5.5.5 to recover any profit from one who conducts the business of another on his own account. In a somewhat different situation, Martinus extended the same action to the owner of a thing that has been sold by a bona fide acquirer and thereafter destroyed, by analogy to the action against the purchaser provided in D.3.5.48.

3. *Exception* to a general rule in a particular case. As Lange points out,[50] the predominance of equity in the technique of interpretation developed by the Glossators led them to prefer the exception as against the rule. In the case of the most important exception, the *exceptio doli,* Paulus had remarked that this was introduced by the praetor, *ne cui dolus suus per occasionem iuris civilis contra naturalem aequitatem prosit.* (D.44.4.1). Consistently with this, the Gloss to C.3.1.8 states generally that exceptions are *de aequitate,* rules *de rigore,* and hence an exception is to be followed.

There was a classic dispute among the Glossators whether the doctrine should be extended to give an exception to the repeatedly enacted interdiction of self-help, in case recourse to justice was not possible. In opposition to the opinion of Bulgarus that no exception should be

[49] See Lange, *op. cit. supra* note 39 at 333 ff., 341 for discussion of this case and other situations where analogous problems of interpretation were presented.

[50] *Op. cit. supra* note 301 at 342.

made, unless expressly allowed, Martinus maintained the contrary on the ground *cessante causa cessat effectus,* for the first time enunciating this celebrated axiom which was eventually accepted even by those in the tradition of Bulgarus.

The foregoing references, which are more fully discussed by Meijers and Lange, illustrate the degree of liberty that the concept of equity, regarded as superior to strict law, gave to the Glossators in interpreting and harmonizing the texts. As the distinction between *ius aequum* and *ius strictum* was employed to ameliorate and to reduce the application of rigorous rules, other distinctions, also derived from textual authority, gave the Glossators similar freedom to restrict overweening extensions of equity when this appeared in the public interest. A striking example is the exception admitted to the equitable principle against unjust enrichment in the case of *usucapio* or prescription. Here *publica utilitas* was given priority over equity, by analogy to the disposition in D.49. 14.3.10, awarding the *fiscus* one half of a treasure-trove found in a public or sacred place.

Brief as it is, the foregoing account of the problems encountered by the Glossators in the interpretation of the *Corpus Iuris Civilis* may serve to indicate the great influence of the doctrines concerning equity which they had inherited from the classical Roman jurists and thence from Aristotle in the development of a theory of textual interpretation. As a result of the antinomy presented by the edicts of Constantine of 314 and 316 A.D., they were constrained to give equity a dominant place in their theory. Even though the concept of equity was general and ill-defined, and the Glossators professed themselves exclusively bound by the authority of the received texts, the concept of equity encouraged them to develop a technique that almost from the beginning transcended mere exegesis—enabling them to harmonize conflicting texts by superseding those which were antiquated or were deemed to be *de rigore,* to generalize equitable doctrines from particular decisions, and thus to prepare the groundwork for the endeavors of their successors to systematize the civil law.

Apart from these achievements, the technique of interpretation elaborated by the Glossators, textbound in appearance and at the same time inspired by equity, exhibits in a particularly instructive setting, the fundamentally topical character of jurisprudence as an *ars boni et aequi,* in the elegant words of Celsus, and not a closed science, a scheme of mathematical deductions from axiomatic premises.[51] It is of particular interest that, to the contrary, the technique of the Glossators moved from particulars to generalizations that could be adjusted to new situations when this became desirable. In this they followed,

[51] See the writer's article, *Legal Science and Natural Law,* 2 INTER-AMERICAN L. REV. 207 (1960).

subconsciously no doubt, the admonition of Paulus, *non ex regula ius sumatur* (D.50.17.1). In consequence, while it became the prevailing view that only equity expressed in the texts should be applied as against the rigor of the strict law and without reference to *aequitas rudis* not yet concretized in positive statute, it was evident that the method of generalization left a place at every turn for rude equity to creep in. In sum, while the Glossators added little, if anything, to the general conception of equity, they set the basic lines for the elaboration of a flexible technique of textual interpretation, professedly controlled by authoritative texts and yet inspired by the immanent sense of equity, which has since characterized the method of the civil law.

V

While the conception of equity as a superior and individualized aspect of justice was thus employed by the Glossators and their successors to develop liberal techniques of interpretation of legal texts, the Canonists enlarged equity to include the Christian ethic and in effect sought in the courts Christian and, in the secular sphere, through the prerogative of the sovereign to enforce the higher law. We must by-pass this most influential channel for the perpetuation of equity in the Aristotelian sense, so influential it would seem that, on the Continent, equity has become a necessary presupposition of the interpretation and reform of law. As was observed in 1803 in the discussion of the *projet* of the French Civil Code:[52]

> *"En un mot, pour toute affaire, soit civile, soit criminelle, ou la loi parle, ou elle se tait. Si la loi parle, il faut juger encore, mais avec cette différence que, lorsqu'il s'agit d'une affaire civile, les juges doivent se déterminer par les règles de l'équité, qui consistent dans les maximes de droit naturel, de justice universelle et de raison; et que, lorsqu'il s'agit d'un procès criminel, l'accusé doit être renvoyé, vu le silence de la loi."*

While the same may be said of analogous aspects of the development in England, the fact that in the common law system equity was also institutionalized in a separate jurisdiction and a special jurisprudence, in some respects reminiscent of the *ius honorarium* of the peregrine *praetor,* deserves brief mention.

Before doing so, it may incidentally be queried whether the evolution on the Continent, which, in the course of time, included a more or less extensive reception of the ancient, alien laws of Rome and, in more modern times, has been centered in codes designed to enact *"Des règles positives, des principes lumineux et féconds en conséquences,*

[52] Fenet, 6 RECUEIL COMPLET DES TRAVAUX PRÉPARATOIRES DU CODE CIVIL 387–88 (1827) (Faure).

qui puissent être aisément saisis et appliqués à tous les cas ou au plus grand nombre,"[53] but at the same time, when the law is silent or obscure, allowing reference to equitable considerations in the administration of justice, is not more artificial than the creation of equitable tribunals in Republican Rome and in England to remedy defects in the ordinary course of justice. In this light, the controversy regarding the so-called *aequitatis iudicium* of the later Carolingian period is of interest.[54] The thesis advanced by Brunner in 1865, still widely accepted, that the royal courts instituted by the Frankish kings to render *aequitatis iudicia* in reclamations from proceedings in the popular courts were of this nature, appears to be refuted by more recent criticism, chiefly on the ground that, in the tenth century, *aequitas* was synonymous with justice and the antithesis of equity to strict law was not yet known. Apparently at the time, the royal courts were developing a system of appeals, but these as a rule were decided in accordance with law. The royal prerogative of legislation and interpretation doubtless included a measure of discretion, but there was no need for a separate court of equity, as the customs currently being reduced to written form at the instance of the crown spelled justice.

Hence, with the fragmentation of political power after the partition of the Frankish Empire, the organization of law in Western Europe was delayed, and an occasion for the institutionalization of equity did not come. In comparison with conditions on the Continent, however, Britain was favored after the invasions of the Norsemen and the Normans by its insular position and advanced culture. Geographically a small compact state, it had the fortune to be governed for a century and a half after the Norman conquest by a succession of astute rulers whose ministers fashioned the centralized institutions that introduced effective government at a relatively early date and fostered the creation of an indigenous common law. This, if it did not require, at least laid the stage for the apparition of equity as a separate branch of jurisprudence in the common law system. It is not feasible in this schematic survey to trace the vicissitudes of this development, and it is not necessary to do so—the history of the law of England from Anglo-Saxon times, thanks to the work of Maitland and his successors, is the most fully documented and the most extensively explored of the various systems of European law. The present modest concern is to note, in comparison with the conception of equity in the continental laws, certain salient features of what has been described as the unique history of equity in England.

1. In the common law system, the term "equity" in the sense ascribed

[53] *Ibid.*, at 375 (Grenier).

[54] For an excellent recent study of the question, with references to the source materials and the literature, see KAUFMANN, AEQUITATIS IUDICIUM (1959).

to it by Bentham, noted above,[55] ordinarily is used to designate the law administered in a so-called court of equity. This usage, as Story observed in reviewing the meanings of the term in his *Commentaries on Equity Jurisprudence*,[56] is not to be confused with the broader significance of equity derived in the Middle Ages from the Aristotelian doctrine.

2. It is clear that the medieval conception was common learning in England from the twelfth century. As previously remarked, the acceptance of the idea of equity in the common law was not dissimilar to its influence on the Continent. It has been pointed out, for example, that in the time of Glanvill the royal justices exercised wide judicial discretion in the course of both civil and criminal proceedings as would be *utilius et equius*.[57] Or, to speak of a later and important work, Saint Germain's *Doctor and Student,* in the early sixteenth century reproduced the Aristotelian doctrine of equity. As Vinogradoff has stated, "the definition of equity in the work is drawn through Gerson from Aristotle: equity comprises the guiding principles for the adaptation of general rules to particular cases,"[58] these principles being derived from conscience.

3. A special application of the conception of equity deserves mention, namely, the doctrine of equitable interpretation of statutes which was developed by the common law courts either to limit or to extend the application of laws on the equitable ground, *quia ratio legis est anima legis*. In the famous note in Plowden's Report,[59] numerous examples of such interpretation of statutory provisions in accordance with the sense and reason of the law, rather than the letter, are given, and this practice is expressly explained by references to Aristotle.

4. As the foregoing illustrates, Lord Bacon's remark quoted by Story, that "There is no law under heaven which is not supplied with Equity,"[60] supposing the Aristotelian sense of the term, is amply exemplified in the common law. From the beginning, its development has been influenced by equitable considerations, not only in the differentiation of cases and in statutory interpretation, but also in the invention of new remedies to provide for typical situations demanding relief. But the extent of the discretion allowed to take account of equitable, or as we would now say, policy factors has varied from time to time according to political, economic, and social conditions, as well

[55] *Supra* at p. 60.

[56] In Chapter I, pp. 1 *et seq*. of the 13th edition (1886).

[57] Hazeltine, *Judicial Discretion in English Procedure of Henry the Second's Time,* in FESTSCHRIFT OTTO GIERKE 1055–68 (1911).

[58] *Reason and Conscience in Sixteenth-Century Jurisprudence,* 24 L. Q. REV. 373, 378 (1908).

[59] Pp. 465–68. See Hammond's note on *Equitable Interpretation* in LIEBER, LEGAL AND POLITICAL HERMENEUTICS 283 (3rd ed. 1880).

[60] 4 WORKS 274, quoted in Story, *op. cit. supra* note 56 at 6 n. 4.

as the complexion of the law and the attitudes of its ministers. It was natural that the judges of the common-law courts developing from the *curia regis* during the twelfth and thirteenth centuries, while they enjoyed the confidence of the king, should have a latitude of such discretion in the formation of a legal system which was to supersede the local laws and become the common law of England, that would not be admissible when the system had been more perfectly developed. Witness, for example, the proliferation of writs,[61] the emergence of trespass, that "fertile mother of actions," and for a later time the elaboration of the action on the case in its varied forms.[62]

Indeed, during this period and until the fourteenth century, the royal courts gave relief on grounds and by procedures that, in the technical sense of the later law, would be regarded as equitable. In Bracton's time, it seemed that the beneficiary of a use or a devisee would be protected by the common law courts; in a variety of cases, before the expansion of trespassory actions, specific relief was available to recover a *res,* and orders or prohibitions were issued to prevent wrongful acts, such as nuisance or waste, affecting interests in land. There was similar flexibility in procedure; the parties could be interrogated to ascertain the truth, the *secta* examined by the court, and third parties allowed to intervene. As Holdsworth observes, "The judicial mind was distinguished for its intelligence rather than its ignorance."[63]

5. The "precocious fixity" of the common law and the inadequacy of its rules and procedures after the thirteenth century, doubtless opened the way for equity to form a separate branch of the law of England. But, considering the initial flexibility of the administration of justice in the central courts, this needs explanation. Plucknett has pointed out that the common law was essentially the law of the land, acting *in rem* and only rarely *in personam* and mainly concerned with records and documents or with notorious facts such as seisin, which were better proved by a jury than by interested testimony.[64] Conversely, the system based on the writs had developed a refined but dilatory technique of pleading, while the modes of proof and execution and especially the primitive scheme of actions were inadequate to deal effectively or justly with an increasing variety of transactions involving personal obligations. This of course does not show why the system itself was not reformed, but became stereotyped. Various explanations are given: the restriction on the creation of new writs by the Provisions of Oxford (1250) and the Statute of Westminister II (1285), the with-

---

[61] The classic summary is Maitland's *The Forms of Equity at Common Law,* originally printed with his LECTURES ON EQUITY (1909), and recently republished in a separate paper edition in 1962.

[62] See especially KIRALFY, THE ACTION ON THE CASE (1951).

[63] 2 HISTORY OF ENGLISH LAW 250 (3d ed. 1923).

[64] A CONCISE HISTORY OF THE COMMON LAW 177–78 (3d ed. 1956).

drawal of the judges from party politics during the War of the Roses, the monopolistic organization of the profession in the inns of court, not to speak of the inveterate indisposition of a professional group to change. But it would seem that the laicization of the bench and bar in the common-law courts, resulting from the differentiation that developed, not between lawyers and administrators but between the ecclesiastical and the secular administrator-lawyers, to which Plucknett has drawn attention,[65] must have been of great moment. As he remarks, "The new sort of law students for whom these works [the non-Bractonian literature of the later thirteenth century] were prepared, like their teachers, seem to have been thoroughly philistine, deliberately cut-off from the universities and from the Roman and clerical traditions which the universities fostered."[66] This narrow outlook of the nascent legal profession is a sufficient explanation of the long backwardness and insularity of the common law of England.

6. The extraordinary jurisdiction in equity to remedy the defects in the common law became centered in the hands of the chancellor for various reasons, conveniently summarized by Holdsworth[67]—the close connection of the chancellor and chancery with the king's council, the control of the chancellor over the issue of original writs and his supervision of the common-law courts, and especially the fact that chancery provided adequate machinery for dealing with petitions to the king for relief. Chancery thus became a court in which the chancellors, who invariably were ecclesiastics until Wolsey's deposition, introduced the more advanced procedure of the canon law, with the advantages of the *subpoena* to compel compliance, interrogation of the parties and depositions to ascertain the facts, and, while affecting not to subvert the course of the common law, decided in accordance with the requirements of conscience and good faith, which is to say, reason and equity. Since it acted *in personam,* equity was not deemed to conflict with the common law.

7. The doctrines of equity were thus introduced as glosses on the common law; it is one of the maxims of equity to follow the law. After the seventeenth century, as chancery came to be administered by professional lawyers and the doctrines of equity were established, elaborated, and extended by precedent and legislation, equity could be more accurately described as a particular branch of English jurisprudence, comprising a heterogeneous assemblage of topics, that grew into grounds of equitable jurisdiction, not as a logical system but in response to historical circumstances. Eventually, the Judicature Act of 1873 amalgamated the Court of Chancery with the three common law courts and the courts of Probate, Divorce, and Admiralty, and

[65] EARLY ENGLISH LEGAL LITERATURE 82 (1958).
[66] *Id.,* at 93.
[67] *Op. cit. supra* note 63, Vol. 1 at 395–416 (3d ed. 1922).

though chancery remains as a Division of the High Court, a judge in any division can adjudicate upon any question of equity or of law. Even after three-quarters of a century, it is mooted how far this reform has fused law and equity in a single substantive law.[68] As for the particular doctrines developed in equity, the enumeration in the early rhyme:

> "These three give place in court of conscience,
> Fraud, accident and breach of confidence,"

was largely extended, notably by the development of the trust, one of the major achievements of British jurisprudence. The subject matter still regarded as equity in England has been treated by Hanbury under the heads of trusts, other equitable interests, executors and administrators, equitable remedies. This classification scarcely adumbrates the varied ways in which equitable principles and remedies have supplemented or corrected the common law as such; for the details reference may be made to the modern English and American treatises on equity.[69]

VI

In conclusion, and here we touch the position in modern times, it should appear that the historic conception of equity provides a philosophic justification for legal reform and a guiding principle of legal interpretation. But its substance is too diffuse to serve as a term of art. In both the Roman and the common-law systems, the controlling factors have been specific needs for relief and not a general appeal to equity. It is time to restate the problem in modern terms.

The conception of equity expresses the two-fold dilemma of the legal order. On the one hand, however elaborate legislation may be, the law must be formulated in general terms, in which it is not desirable by redundant enactment, nor even possible in view of the uncertainty of human events, to include provision for exceptional or unforeseen instances. Hence, as Aristotle taught, justice imports an element of equitable adaptation in the application of the general rules to particular cases. On the other hand, the law must be stable and yet must conform to changing social needs. The crux of the problem of equity in modern eyes is not only to determine when and how the law should be reformed to correct abuses or varied in its application to new conditions, but also in whom this power should be vested. And on these questions, the vague response of equity is of little aid.

Today, the principal instrument of legal reform is legislation, and at least in the Western world the power to legislate is exercised, not as the exclusive prerogative of a sovereign monarch, but in the name of

[68] See discussion in HANBURY, MODERN EQUITY 20 *et seq.* (6th ed. 1952).

[69] A convenient summary will be found in Holdsworth, *op. cit. supra* note 63, Vol. 1, 466 *et seq.*

the people. In this manner, social needs and ideals find expression in the enacted law. In addition, the formal legislation is supplemented by a great proliferation of so-called delegated legislation, the regulations issued by executive departments or by independent agencies that define, administer, and adjudicate matters affecting the more technical activities of modern government.

More or less independent of these is the judiciary, which is called upon not only to determine private disputes but also to interpret the laws so as to control the executive and administrative agencies consistently with the constitution. It is in this area of adjudication that the problem of equity as here defined is most acute. It was not so long ago that this problem was in effect avoided by reserving equity to the sovereign legislator. This was the technique employed by Constantine and Justinian, and in modern times has been reflected in the belief that the law can be comprehensively stated in a body of legislation, which should be strictly applied by the courts of justice. The belief was presumably induced by the rational elaboration of natural law, patterned upon the logical development of modern science and enshrined in the dogma of the separation of governmental powers. Consistently with this principle, it has been assumed that only the sovereign legislature can create general rules of law, which the courts are bound to apply. But it has become apparent also that adjudication inevitably involves change in law, however slow and impalpable or sudden and dramatic. It has always been tacitly, if not expressly, recognized in Anglo-American jurisdictions that the law must be adapted by the courts to new conditions. And the same conclusion seems more recently to be admitted in the domain of the civil law; the evolution of the law of France since 1804, for example, in which the supremacy of enacted law is axiomatic, provides abundant evidence of the extent to which, without changing the letter of the law, new wine may be poured into old bottles by *doctrine* and *jurisprudence*. Here again the topic of strict law and equity reappears; the courts appointed to apply the law also of necessity must exercise equitable discretion in its interpretation. And to do this properly, we have no choice but to rely on the integrity, trained intelligence, and independence of the judges.

[6]

WHY NO TRUSTS IN THE CIVIL LAW?

In the field of property, the trust furnishes a striking antinomy between the common law and the civil law. The purpose of this comment is limited to an examination of the considerations commonly supposed to exclude this institution in the civil law. For the present purpose, it is unnecessary to survey the extent to which the trust nevertheless is recognized or paralleled in various civil law countries at the present time—a topic recently covered in a leading article in this Journal.[1] As there indicated, the basic obstacles, aside from the existence of domestic civil law institutions analogous to trusts, are: first and chiefly, that the principle of indivision of property, supposed to be fundamental in the Roman legal system and therefore presumptively also in modern civil law, precludes acceptance of an institution, such as that of the trust, by which property is divided into legal and equitable rights; and, secondarily, that the principle of registration of interests in property necessitates a *numerus clausus* of rights in rem, limited to the categories received in the modern codes and not including even traditional rights involved in fiduciary arrangements. As will appear, neither of these arguments is tenable in history or in logic, but the fixed beliefs which they represent are of consummate comparative interest.

The major premise that the Roman and civil law tradition does not allow division of the claims to a thing among several persons at the same time, is refuted by the record. This exhibits a long and flexible evolution of property rights in response to current social needs in the Romanic as well as in the English legal system, which cannot in reason be expunged by authoritarian efforts, however pretentious, to oversimplify the concept of property in terms of autonomous, absolute, abstract power, such as appear in the *Corpus Iuris*

[1] Joaquín Garrigues, "Law of Trusts," 2 American Journal of Comparative Law (1953) 25 *et seq.*

Civilis of Justinian and the *Code Civil* of Napoléon. The premise takes the nominalistic abstraction for the norm.

In the evolution of Roman law, the moving force was the long conflict between the patricians and the plebs, reflected in the distinction between the *ius quiritium* and the *ius honorarium*. The former comprised the original rights of the Roman *cives*, the *ius civile*; the latter was developed by flexible praetorian remedies which, in their enforcement reduced these quiritarian rights to a *nudum ius* without beneficial enjoyment. The basic contest between right and remedy was especially acute in the field of property law, where in case of suit the quiritarian owner was at a disadvantage. The bonitarian possessor, as factual owner, was relieved of the burden of proof of title[2] and was protected by a wide array of procedural remedies ranging from the *Actio Publiciana* to the various possessory interdicts, not to speak of the short periods of usucapion.[3]

It is strange how erroneous beliefs persist in human minds even in the face of proof positive to the contrary. In addition to the epochal invention of the distinction between *dominium* and *possessio*, by which rights *in rem* in a property could conveniently be divided, the evidences of common ownership, offered by the history, the institutions, and the authors of Rome, are undisputed. In Rome, lands were owned in community by the *gentes*[4]; originally the word *familia* meant the totality of ownership rights within the family,[5] until, at a later stage of development they were concentrated in the person of the *paterfamilias*. Gaius recognizes common ownership in slaves[6] and division of ownership generally.[7] But in modern doctrine all this has been superseded

[2] F. J. Thibaut, System des Pandekten-Rechts (1846) 195 *et seq.*; Savigny, Das Recht des Besitzes (1865) 27,36; D.VI.2.9.4: "... melior causa sit possidentis quam petentis..." The position of the *bona fide* possessor under the *Actio Publiciana* is comparable to that of the cestui que trust. W. Buckland, Equity in Roman Law (1911) 16.

[3] The periods established by the XII tables were, for immovables two years, for movables one year. To these was added the *praescriptio longi temporis* on provincial land running for ten years *inter praesentes* and twenty years *inter absentes*. These were available also to peregrines.

[4] Theodor Mommsen, 3 Römisches Staatsrecht (1887) 9,10, and n.2; Abriss des Römischen Staatsrechts (1907) 6; v. Jhering, 1 Geist des Römischen Rechts (1891) 179,180; F. Girard, Manuel Élémentaire de Droit Romain (1918) 266; Jörs-Kunkel, Römisches Privatrecht (1935) 240 *et seq.*

[5] Ernst Rabel, "Die Erbrechtstheorie Bonfantes," 50 Zeitschrift der Savigny-Stiftung für Rechtsgeschichte, Romanistische Abteilung (1930) 320–327; Gaius II.157: "Sed sui quidem heredes ideo appellantur quia domestici heredes sunt et vivo quoque parente quodammodo domini existimantur...;" Paul. D 28.2.11: "In suis heredibus evidentius apparet continuationem dominii eo rem perducere, ut nulla videatur hereditas fuisse, quasi olim hi domini essent qui etiam vivo patre quodammodo domini existimantur...."

[6] I.54: "Ceterum cum apud cives Romanos duplex sit dominium ... ita demum servum in potestate domini esse dicemus, si in bonis eius sit, etiamsi simul ex iure Quiritium eiusdem non sit...."

[7] II.40: "... sed postea divisionem accepit dominium, ut alius possit esse ex iure Quiritium dominus, alius in bonis habere."

by Celsus' authoritative *duorum quidem in solidum dominium vel possessionem esse non posse.*[8]

This maxim, however, did not prevent the classical period of Roman law from proceeding to elaborate two institutions with duplication of ownership rights. One of these was the "curious double ownership" in the *dos*, the wife's separate property, an institution which, contrasting with the exclusion of marital gifts,[9] shows, even according to Buckland,[10] a striking similarity to the legal and equitable interests in a trust; the other was the *peculium castrense*, the son's private property within the paterfamilias' property, the son having exclusive powers of administration and the paterfamilias latent rights of inheritance,[11] a privilege originally created for soldiers and later extended to civil servants.

Moreover, as Levy has demonstrated,[12] during the vulgarization of Roman law, the case law of the provinces, governed by social and economic rather than legal considerations, progressively operated with unconcern for traditional niceties. Gone were the strict analytical distinctions of classical jurisprudence; *iura in re aliena, servitus, ususfructus* were considered to be varieties of *dominium*, which lost the sense of exclusive title. Forms of co-existing ownership developed: the "corporation-bound" property of the *collegium*, the *emphyteusis* on the imperial domain, and the *bona materna* shared by the surviving father and his children.[13] The words *possessio* and *dominium* were indifferently used to describe legal ownership *or* factual control; either might mean ownership or a *ius in re aliena*, as well as actual enjoyment.[14]

In 1928, an eminent Hungarian jurist published a comparative treatise,[15] displaying the amazing similarity of the land laws of Hungary in the sixteenth century to those of Great Britain in 1914. Comparison of the wealth of Roman

---

D.13.6.5.15. In this discussion, the possible connections between common ownership and property held by a legal person, representing a group or collectivity, are not considered. Savigny drew attention to the possibility in Roman law that ownership by a corporation might be fictitious in cases where the purpose was to protect enjoyment thereof by the individuals forming the corporation. (2 System des heutigen Römischen Rechts (1840)288). More recently Planiol and others have developed the theory that all forms of legal personality are in reality forms of collective property. See Planiol—Ripert, 1 Traité Pratique de Droit Civil Français (1952) 82–83.

[9] F. J. Thibaut, Civilistische Abhandlungen (1814) 338–339; L.46 Ulpianus lib. 72 *ad edictum*: "Inter virum et uxorem nec possessionis ulla donatio est . . . ;" L.16 Ulpianus lib. 73 *ad edictum*: ". . . Quod uxor viro aut vir uxori donavit, pro possessore possidetur . . . ;" *cf.* the restrictive provisions of the French Civil Code, Arts. 1081–1100, on donations either directly or through marriage contract between wife and husband.

[10] Equity in Roman Law (1911) 18; also, Buckland-McNair, Roman Law and Common Law (2nd ed., revised by F. H. Lawson, 1952) 82, 83.

[11] Until Justinian accorded intestate succession in the *peculium*.

[12] Ernst Levy, West Roman Vulgar Law. The Law of Property (1951) 7.

[13] *Ibid.*, 67; also, Buckland-McNair, *op. cit.*, 83.

[14] *Ibid.*, 22, 24.

[15] Grosschmid Beni, Werbőczy és az angol jog, (Werböczy and the Law of Great Britain).

fiduciary transactions, initially enforceable only in conscience,[16] with the modern Anglo-American law of trusts would yield likenesses equally striking. In addition to the early *mancipatio familiae*,[17] which became the most popular form to cover a large number of transactions for the benefit of third parties, testamentary or inter vivos, with expressed or merely implied stipulations, there developed the *fiducia*, the *fideicommissum*, and the *legatum per damnationem*, the last in its provisions frequently exhibiting a remarkable similitude to the charitable trust.[18] The legal relations involved in such fiduciary transactions included the legal ownership of the fiduciary and the equitable interest of the beneficiary. The latter has been conceived as an *in personam* obligation of the fiduciary towards the beneficiary based upon *fides*; in addition a fairly complicated system of liens on the assets of the fiduciary and the *actiones famosae* which, in case of default, entailed dishonor and deprivation of citizenship,[19] ensured compliance with the trust.

These developments as incorporated in the Roman legislation of the fourth and fifth centuries, together with certain passages in the Digest,[20] were generalized by the Glossators in the conception of the *dominium directum* and the *dominium utile*,[21] which manifestly resembles the legal and equitable ownership of the common law. This conception typified the feudal property system of the Middle Ages, when the main form of ownership, that in land, was divided into a variegated order of estates in one and the same holding, all carved out of the ultimate dominion of the sovereign. These ideas, at a later date, influenced Grotius to describe ownership as including the possibility for two or more persons to own the same property together with either equal or different rights. His views on complete and incomplete ownership and on feudal tenure as a sum total of legal relations divided into reciprocal rights,

[16] Inst. II.23.1: "... et ideo fideicommissa appellata sunt, quia nullo vinculo iuris, sed tantum pudore eorum qui rogabantur continebantur. ..." Later, however, fideicommissa became regularly enforceable, *cf.* Windscheid-Kipp, 3 Lehrbuch des Pandektenrechts (1906) 575.

[17] H. Lévy-Bruhl, "Nature de la Mancipatio Familiae," Festschrift für Fritz Schulz (1951) 253 *et seq.*

[18] Buckland-McNair, *op. cit.*, 179; D.33.2.14,15,16; J. Voet, Commentarius ad Pandectas, Liber VII, Tit. I, XII.

[19] One of these *actiones* was the *actio fiduciae* brought by the debtor to recover his property given as security from the creditor after discharge of his debt. The creditor's obligation to return the security was merely fiduciary.

[20] Ernst Levy, *op. cit.*, 68.

[21] The contrary opinion derives the *dominium directum* and *dominium utile* from the Germanic *Nutz und Gewer*; *cf.* O. Gierke, 2 Deutsches Privatrecht (1905), 368 *et seq.*, and 369, n.5; Edouard Meynial, 2 Mélanges Fitting, 1908, 411 *et seq.* This opinion was represented in the United States by Justice Holmes, "Early English Equity," Collected Legal Papers (1920) 4 *et seq.*, who derived the origins of the British feoffee to uses and the subsequent fiduciary transactions from the Germanic *Gewere* and *Salman*. Max Radin, however, has ascribed the success of Holmes' theory in part to the predilection for Germanic rather than Roman origins that characterized the period in which Holmes wrote his famous article. *Cf.* Anglo-American Legal History (1936) 431.

duties, and privileges,[22] and not as mere derivatives of unitary power, anticipated the most significant analyses of legal relations in modern times.[23]

This tradition of flexible divisibility and duplication in the conception of property was interrupted by the *Code Napoléon*. It is highly significant that those civil law countries, which for historical reasons had remained unaffected by the revolutionary changes introduced by this codification in the field of property relations, upon close contact with the English law, have readily assimilated the trust concept. Such was the case in South Africa and Ceylon, territories of Roman-Dutch law, in the Province of Quebec in Canada, and in Scotland.

The establishment of the *Conseil supérieur* of Quebec in 1663 introduced in this French colony the laws of France generally, including the *coutumes* of Paris and the royal ordinances prior to this date.[24] Quebec was ceded to Great Britain in the Treaty of Paris in 1763 and thus remained free from the Napoleonic restrictions on donations. In consequence, Quebec conserved the liberal policies of pre-revolutionary French law with regard to fiduciary substitutions, testamentary and inter vivos donations, and marriage contracts in favor of *enfants à naitre*,[25] which, in conjunction with exposure to common law influence (illustrated by the wide liberty of testation accorded in the Province),[26] made the ground relatively easy for legislation adopting the trust in 1879, which has been incorporated in the Code of 1888 under the heading *De la Fiducie* in French and *On Trusts* in English. The Quebec experience was repeated in Ceylon, where the trust and the fideicommissum exist at present side by side.[27] In both countries, precedents recognizing the trust prepared the way, while in South Africa the trust has been introduced without specific legislative provision. In these jurisdictions, the courts have had no difficulties in interpreting instruments of trust in the light of their domestic institutions, such as the fideicommissum or the fiducia; the theoretical incubus of *dédoublement de propriété* has been avoided by construing the property rights under a trust—with an ease characterized as judicial rationalization amounting to legerdemain[28]—as including the apparent title of the fiduciary,[29]

[22] Inleidinge tot de Hollandsche Rechts-Geleerdheid (2nd ed., Leiden, 1952) 54, 151–152, 164 *et seq.*; also, The Jurisprudence of Holland, Translation, notes, and commentary by R. W. Lee (1926) 85, 223, 247.

[23] W. N. Hohfeld, Fundamental Legal Conceptions (1923) 35 *et seq.*

[24] P. B. Mignault, "La Fiducie dans la Province de Québec," Semaine Internationale de Droit (Paris, 1937) *Travaux*, at 37.

[25] *Ibid.*, 38.

[26] The first trusts established in Quebec were the results of this liberty of testation; they are McGill University and the Fraser Institute, both in Montréal.

[27] T. Nadaraja, The Roman-Dutch Law of Fideicommissa, (Ceylon, 1949) 239. The Ceylon law on trusts is Ordinance No. 9 of 1917.

[28] *Ibid.*, 241.

[29] Estate Kemp v. McDonald's Trustee, South Afr. L. R., 1915, A. D. 491, per Innes, C.J., at 504. The court held in this case that the share of one of the beneficiaries under a will, who died without issue, vested in her trustee in insolvency and not in the trustees or residuary legatees under the will.

but without *usus*, *fructus*, or *abusus*,[30] and the interest of the beneficiary in the proceeds of the property conformably to the terms of the trust. In the case of conditional fideicommissa, postponement of the beneficiary's enjoyment until the *dies venit* has been held not to preclude vesting of his rights.[31] The donor's intentions, whether expressed in common law or civil law terms, are interpreted according to the comprehensive and elastic provisions of domestic fideicommissary and other substitutions.[32]

In Scotland, the gradual operation of the combination of law and equity, aided by the system of public records, has led easily to the establishment of a regular system of trusts, in which the rights of all parties are regarded as vested in the trustee, as in deposit, with perfect security to those interested. The trust is construed as a combination of two contracts, deposit and mandate. The object in view is always some purpose to be established.[33]

The developments in Louisiana, a civilian island surrounded by common law, are peculiarly instructive.[34] The Louisiana Codes of 1808 and 1825, under the influence of the *Projet* of the *Code Napoléon*, prohibited the establishment of fideicommissa, in this respect going beyond the French Code, which contained no such prohibition. This provision was regarded by both the legislature and the courts as excluding admission of the foreign trust concept, identified with the domestic fideicommissum.[35] The traditional hostility to trusts was relaxed somewhat in 1882; in contemplation of the gifts about to be made by Paul Tulane to Tulane University, the legislature legalized donations mortis causa or inter vivos for educational, charitable, or literary purposes. After 1900, the alien quality of the trust gradually faded; subsequent legislation enabled banks to execute trusts (1902), allowed trustees to act for bondholders and noteholders (1914), and legalized trusts of limited duration (1920). Finally, the facility with which Louisiana wealth could be settled under trusts in other states, induced the enactment, after brief hesitation, of the present Louisiana Estates Act of 1938, which apparently has effectively buried the prejudice against trusts inherited from the Napoleonic era.

Except in jurisdictions which, as above indicated, remained outside the influence of the French Revolution, a profound deviation in the traditional doctrine of the civil law regarding property was introduced by the *Code Napoléon*. The chief features of interest for present purposes in this develop-

---

[30] Curran v. Davis [1933] Can. S. C. R. 283, per Rinfret, J., at 293.

[31] Jewish Colonial Trust Ltd. v. Estate Nathan, South Afr. L. R., 1940, A. D. 163. The bequest created a charitable trust to be established fifty years from the death of the testator. At the same time the payment of annuities to be paid out of the income of the fund should cease. Appellant requested payment before the *dies venit* of so much of the residue as was not required to provide for the payment of annuities. The holding of the lower court that the beneficial interest did not vest at the testator's death, was reversed.

[32] *Loc. cit.* n. 29, per Solomon, J.A., at 508.

[33] G. J. Bell, 1 Commentaries on the Law of Scotland (1870) 30, 32.

[34] F. F. Stone, "Trusts in Louisiana," 1 The International and Comparative Law Quarterly (1952) 368–378.

[35] Succession of Franklin, (1852) 7 La. Ann. 395, cited *ibid.*

ment, characteristic of the modern civil law, are: first, a unitary conception of ownership, inconsistent with duplication or division of rights in rem in the same thing; second, the supplementary notion, elaborated in the German doctrine, that public registration of rights in rem involves taxative codification of such rights, a *numerus clausus*; and, third, the appearance of a variety of devices, serving in a degree the same purposes as trusts and calculated for practical reasons to escape the procrustean bed prepared for the evolution of property law by the imperious logic of these conceptions. These three factors are the main obstacles to the reception of the trust in modern civil law.

The first and indeed basic obstacle to acceptance of the trust is the concept of autonomous and indivisible ownership. First formulated in the Justinian Code and then forgotten for centuries, it was again declared in Article 544 of the *Code Napoléon*, defining property as the absolute right to the enjoyment and disposition of things, not prohibited by law. In their respective codifications, Justinian and Napoleon both sought to simplify an intricate network of customs, precedents, and local ordinances. While Justinian's object in so doing was to restore the classic categories of a bygone capitalistic era, the *Code Napoléon* sought to consolidate the objectives of the Revolution, including notably the abolition of the feudal burdens of the *ancien régime*.[36] The social conditions for which it was drafted were receptive to the formulation of ownership as an absolute right, as the autonomous ownership in and management of capital were imperative for the beneficial development of *laissez faire* economy. Notwithstanding the credit due to the *Code Napoléon* for the clear logic of its legal analyses and its contribution to the theoretical refinement of modern civil law,[37] the fact that it imposed oversimplified and autocratic rules on the customary development of law has proved to be detrimental as well as advantageous.

This is also true of the German Civil Code. Gierke's warnings against discarding the truly Germanistic concept of divided ownership, which custom and local codes had introduced, even if "as a horrible logical blunder and a scientifically unmotivated notion,"[38] and its replacement by the classical Roman concept, which operates as an exclusive and arbitrary rule within the weak boundaries of a few positive exceptions[39] and will lead to the total aboli-

[36] The translation of property which was considered the basic motive and achievement of the Revolution (*cf.*, H. Taine, Origines de la France contemporaine, L'ancien régime, I, 386) was completed before the Revolution. *Cf.*, M. Planiol, 1 Traité Élémentaire de Droit Civil (1911) 723; also G. Morin, "Le sens de l'évolution contemporaine du droit de propriété," 2 Le Droit Privé Français au Milieu du XXe Siècle, Études Offertes à Georges Ripert (1950) 5.

[37] Hessel E. Yntema, "Roman Law and its Influence on Western Civilization," 35 Cornell Law Quarterly (1949) 78.

[38] O. Gierke, Der Entwurf eines bürgerlichen Gesetzbuchs und das Deutsche Recht (1889) 324.

[39] *Ibid.*, 323.

tion of private ownership, have proved prophetic. Suffice it to point to the gradual separation of ownership and control,[40] to the dissociation of legal ownership and actual use,[41] to the statutory restrictions imposed on private property by the welfare state,[42] to the legislative developments which deprive landowners[43] and owners of housing and commercial units[44] of free disposal over their property.

These developments are of course effects of fundamental changes in the entire social structure and not merely of the formulation of autonomous and exclusive ownership in modern codifications, as the example of Great Britain sufficiently displays. But the emphasis on the *change* in and the *departure* from an established ideology would be less accentuated had the modern civil law operated with an ownership concept more adaptable and less rigid. The ideology represented in the modern codes is the myth of and belief in the power of private capital, a word that became the symbol of ownership. The new ideology that is supplanting the old is the myth of the liberation of the masses from the oppressions of capital and their endowment with human dignity.[45] In the course of this liberating process legal values are being reversed; acquired riches have ceded their predominance[46] to the supreme value of the human individual[47] and to the basic rights inherent in this value. These rights, however, are stated in the form of the old myth; they are conceived of as new property rights of individuals. The right to life, the right to work, and the right to education (culture) are considered as commercial property, cultural property, or collective property of workmen in an industry. This process, dismembering property as envisaged in the codes, certainly does mark the end of the autonomous *dominium* of the individual over things;[48] at the same time it signifies the "proletarization of civil law" resulting from the collectivization of rights and the elimination of individual responsibility.[49] Its danger lies in "the new belief in the magic power of controlled economics over chang-

[40] Berle and Means, The Modern Corporation and Private Property (1932) 9. Cited in W. Friedmann, Law and Social Change in Contemporary Britain (1951) 14 *et seq.*

[41] R. Théry, "De l'Utilisation à la Propriété des Choses," 2 Le Droit Privé Français au Milieu du XXe Siècle, 18.

[42] W. Friedmann, Law and Social Change in Contemporary Britain (1951) 25.

[43] *Ibid.*, 26, British Agriculture Act, 1947, Pt. II.; French Law of April 13, 1946, discussed in R. Savatier, Les Métamorphoses Économiques et Sociales du Droit Civil d'Aujourd'hui (2nd. ed., 1952) chapter: *Fermages et Métayages.*

[44] *Ibid.*, at 73; Loi du 10 juin 1944. *Cf.* G. Morin, "Le Sens de l'Évolution Contemporaine du Droit de Propriété," 2 Le Droit Privé Français au Milieu du XXe Siècle, 9–10.

[45] It is doubtful, however, whether the liberating verbiage does not carry an unfortunate implication for those liberated. As Savatier has observed, the French farmers, for instance, assuredly possessed human dignity prior to the preamble of the Law of April 13, 1946, *cf. op. cit.*, 205, 223 *et seq.*

[46] *Ibid.*, 225.

[47] G. Morin, *loc. cit.*, 15.

[48] *Ibid.*, 16.

[49] R. Savatier, *op. cit.*, 297–299.

ing realities"[50] and mystical reliance on social and national over economic considerations.[51]

The second obstacle asserted against adoption of the trust in the civil law is the principle of publicity construed as requiring a *numerus clausus* or taxative enumeration of real rights. Investigation evinces that in this conclusion, theory, inspired by the nominalistic influence of a seductive name, has found in the absence of codified provisions a remarkable principle that violates the requirements of practical life.[52] In effect, this is the doctrine: (a) all transactions creating *iura in rem* must be entered in the official register; (b) the types of in rem transactions are stated in the Code; *ergo* (c) transactions not contained in the Code can not be entered, and (d) the number of ius in rem transactions is necessarily closed.

This doctrine was first formulated in Germany in the *Motive zu dem Entwurfe eines Bürgerlichen Gesetzbuches*,[53] published in 1888. Soon after its appearance, strong objections were voiced against this theory,[54] on the ground that there *might* be other rights in rem than those contained under the various headings of Book III of the BGB, as indeed there *are* already such rights within the BGB but under different headings.[55] Nevertheless, with amazing speed, the *numerus clausus* doctrine was taken at face value in the various commentaries on the German Civil Code[56] and by the Swiss theorists.[57] In the face of such authorities, it might be thought that the German and Swiss codes should contain corresponding restrictions, but they do not.[58] The basis of the rule is found elsewhere—in the allegedly strict division between *iura in rem* and *iura in*

[50] W. Friedmann, *op. cit.*, 33.

[51] G. Ripert, Aspects Juridiques du Capitalisme Moderne (1951) 263.

[52] O. Gierke, *op. cit.*, 315.

[53] Amtliche Ausgabe (1888) 3: "... die Betheiligten können nur solche Rechte begründen, deren Begründung das Gesetz zulässt. Die Zahl der dinglichen Rechte ist daher nothwendig eine geschlossene."

[54] O. Gierke, *op. cit.*, VI. Abschnitt, Das Sachenrecht des Entwurfes; E. Fuchs, Das Wesen der Dinglichkeit (1889); L. Jacobi, Entstehung und Inhalt des Entwurfs eines bürgerlichen Gesetzbuches für das Deutsche Reich. Vortrag gehalten in der Juristischen Gesellschaft zu Berlin (1888).

[55] Alfred Schultze, "Treuhänder im geltenden bürgerlichen Recht," 42–43 Jherings Jahrbücher für die Dogmatik des Bürgerlichen Rechts (1901) 25–27, mentions the husband's right of administration and to usufruct on the wife's separate property; the right of usufruct of the parent or guardian on the child's property; the future interests of the "*Nacherbe.*"

[56] E.g., Planck's Kommentar zum Bürgerlichen Gesetzbuch (4th ed., 1920) 7.

[57] *Cf.* Hermine Herta Meyer, "Trusts and Swiss Law," 1 International and Comparative Law Quarterly (1952) 379.

[58] The codified basis of this rule is Par. 137 of the BGB. It reads: "Die Befugnis zur Verfügung über ein veräusserliches Recht kann nicht durch Rechtsgeschäft ausgeschlossen oder beschränkt werden. Die Wirksamkeit einer Verpflichtung über ein solches Recht nicht zu verfügen, wird durch diese Vorschrift nicht berührt." [Translation—The power to dispose of an alienable right can not be excluded or restricted by a legal transaction. The effectiveness of an obligation not to dispose of such a right is not affected by this provision.]

Articles 970–977 of the Swiss Civil Code contain regulations merely with respect to the techniques of registration. Regarding the provisions of the French Civil Code, see p. 213 *infra*.

personam, which isolates the law of things (*Sachenrecht*) from the law of obligations and, indeed, from all other branches of law. While party autonomy is largely allowed in the field of obligations, it is excluded in the field of property.[59] In regard to trusts, since any arrangement between the parties to establish a trust would involve an in rem burden on the trust res and thus would extend the concept of property to the claims and future interests of the beneficiaries, such arrangement can have no *in rem* effects, as no continental code includes the trust among its types of *iura in rem*. This reasoning is considered logically, dogmatically, systematically, and teleologically correct, as well as *rechtssystematisch*.[60]

In France, public registration was introduced in 1855 as a practical measure for the protection of mortgagees and has subsequently been extended to other types of rights in rem and even certain personal contracts.[61] Until recently at least, there was no need to formulate the theoretical basis, no hint of a *numerus clausus*. To the contrary. Marcel Planiol, in the 1911 edition of his treatise[62] concurs with Gierke against conceiving a *ius in rem* as an exclusive relation between a man and a thing. Legal relations exist only between persons. A transaction establishing real rights is conceived of as a contract between the owner and the illimited number of individuals who are constrained to respect the owner's *ius in rem*. The 1926 edition of the *Traité Pratique de Droit Civil Français* similarly states that the pertinent legal provisions are merely enunciative, not prohibitive and that there is no legal obstacle to party autonomy in the creation of real rights. Such theoretical autonomy, however, is subject to the practical difficulty that publicity is provided only for a limited number of real rights.[63] But in the 1946 edition of the *Traité Élémentaire* of Planiol[64] it is stated on page 853 that the number of real rights is closed, while on pages 1050 and 1230, reference is made to the insufficient co-ordination of the legal rules on publicity on the one hand, and the merely theoretical interest in the matter on the other. The fact is, as evidenced by the trends of legal development in France, that the registration of title with allegedly *in rem* effects may be rendered null and void through the emerging *in rem* effects of possession (*occupation*) of the registered property.[65]

---

[59] Gierke, *op. cit.*, 281 *et seq.*

[60] W. Siebert, Das rechtsgeschäftliche Treuhandverhältnis (1933) 247–257.

[61] Code Civil (ed. Dalloz, 1950) 846–850.

[62] M. Planiol, Traité Élémentaire de Droit Civil Français (1911) 658 *et seq.*

[63] M. Planiol—G. Ripert, Traité Pratique de Droit Civil Français (1926) 52 *et. seq.*

[64] G. Ripert—J. Boulanger, 1 Traité Élémentaire de Droit Civil de M. Planiol (1946) 853, 1230, 1050.

[65] R. Savatier, Les Métamorphoses Économiques et Sociales du Droit Civil d'Aujourd'hui (1952) 72 *et seq.*; G. Morin, "Le Sens de l'Évolution Contemporaine du Droit de Propriété," 2 Le Droit Privé Français au Milieu du XXe Siècle (1950) 8 *et seq.* Hauriou taught the doctrine of administrative rights *in rem* as contrasted with civil rights *in rem* as early as 1908. *Cf.* Maurice Hauriou, 3 Notes d'Arrêts sur Décisions du Conseil d'État et du Tribunal des Conflits, (1929) 286.

Referring to the inalienability of property in the public domain, Hauriou states:

"En méditant cet exemple et quelques autres, on est conduit à formuler cette proposition

There is no doubt that official registration does offer protection to third parties. The prima facie validity of the official register however, may, and indeed at times does, serve as a cover for simulated transactions, usually transfers of property to fiduciaries. In such cases, the courts are bound to investigate the simulated deed. The general practice is to uphold the validity of the official registration, unless the simulated transaction violates public policy or a strict prohibition of law.[66]

If the legal mind were disposed to overcome those obstacles it has created,[67] neither the principle of publicity nor the rule of *numerus clausus would* be serious objections to the trust concept. The publicity of the official registers could well serve to protect the beneficiary under a trust, as is indeed the case in Quebec[68] and in Scotland.[69] The *numerus clausus* rule, on the other hand, which has no apparent practical value, might well be left to the museum of *Begriffsjurisprudenz*. The same result might be reached by granting parties the same autonomy in the creation of real rights as in the creation of obligations. As this seems unlikely in view of the departure from the classic concepts of liberalism with regard to individual freedom in contracting and the accentuation of legal positivism,[70] legislative enlargement of the list of real rights to include trusts with *in rem* effects is indicated. Or, as has been suggested for Germany,[71] the famous Article 137 of the BGB might be elaborated to provide for the *Treuhänder* rights of administration with *in rem* effects, subject to the *Vollrecht* of the settlor.

The activities of human beings, their basic motives and volitions, do not depend on the legal system under which they live. Both the Roman law and the common law have recognized and endeavored to realize by appropriate proceedings the essential purpose of the trust, namely, to protect third party beneficiaries through the activity of a disinterested intermediary. The fact that

générale, qu'il existe des droits réels de nature administrative, se distinguant des droits réels de nature civile, en ce qu'ils sont résolubles ou rachetables pour les besoins du service, et que si les droits réels civils non résolubles et non rachetables sont inconciliables avec l'inaliénabilité du domaine public, les droits réels administratifs, résolubles ou rachetables pour les besoins du service, sont parfaitement compatibles avec l'inaliénabilité, surtout lorsqu'ils constituent un moyen normal d'assurer une utilisation du domaine public qui soit dans le sens de sa destination." *Ibid.*, 286.

[66] BGE 72 I 334 (1946); BGE 72 II 67 (1946); *Ibid.* II 358 (1946); Trustee in Bankruptcy of Concustill Senlihy v. Moro Vallejo, 6 Jurisprudencia Civil, 2d Series, 1944, at 124,146; Pérez López v. Navarro Arranz, 6 Jurisprudencia Civil, 2d Series, 1944, at 788 (discussed by Joaquín Garrigues, "Law of Trusts," 2 American Journal of Comparative Law (1953) 32.)

[67] F. Weiser, Trusts on the Continent of Europe (1936) 9.

[68] R. H. Mankiewicz, "L'Assimilation du 'Trust' à Titre Gratuit dans la Province de Québec," Actes du Congrès International de Droit Privé (Rome, 1951) 251; also, *id.*, "La Fiducie Québécoise et le Trust de Common Law," 12 Revue du Barreau de la Province de Québec (1952) 18.

[69] *Cf.* n. 33.

[70] Hessel E. Yntema, " 'Autonomy' in Choice of Law" 1 American Journal of Comparative Law, (1952) 356.

[71] W. Siebert, *op. cit.*, 420 *et. seq.*

the need for transactions of this character has caused the modern continental systems also to admit various devices serving purposes similar to those of the trust is the source of a third obstacle to the reception of the trust concept in these systems. The domestic means are preferred, and the more nearly these approach the trust, the more effectively do they argue for the rejection of the alien institution. That these means, involving circumvention of existing legal provisions, are typically more complicated than the trust, may be illustrated by an illuminating development in French law, the *fondation*. This example is selected on account of the fundamental similarity of the charitable and cultural foundations in France to the common law charitable trusts and the cy près doctrine.

The Code Civil, preserving a "malevolent silence on the question,"[72] has no provision, providing for or prohibiting, foundations. These were generally abolished during the Revolution, but they commenced to revive as early as 1806, as the result of an *avis* of the Conseil d'État of that date recognizing the existence and the public utility of charitable societies, to which gifts might be made.[73] On the other hand, since Article 906 of the Code prohibits testamentary or inter vivos donations to persons not yet in being, such dispositions in favor of a foundation not yet established were invariably annulled by the civil courts, even if the authorization was granted subsequently by the Conseil d'État. Beginning with the middle of the last century, however, another divergent line of practice developed. As there is no legal prohibition against establishing a foundation by way of a legacy to one or several individuals in being, who are charged by the terms of the will to carry out such provisions, the courts, on the basis of their power to interpret testamentary provisions in the light of the intention of the donor, have validated such foundations, provided they are expressed in terms of *legs à charge de fonder*.[74] This practice of testamentary interpretation has been carried further, the primary emphasis being on the purpose and the beneficiaries of such bequests, while the foundation itself has been of secondary concern.[75] It is difficult to imagine that the dynamic genius

[72] For an excellent résumé of this topic see Professor Savatier's comment on the case *De Renesse c. Robineau et al.*, D. 1928.2.121; *cf.* R. Savatier, "La Fiducie en Droit Français," Semaine Internationale de Droit (Paris, 1937) *Travaux*, 57 *et seq.*

[73] Louis Canet, "Le Régime des Fondations en France," Le Conseil d'État—Livre Jubilaire (1952) 434.

[74] The distinguished French *Académie Goncourt* was founded by such means. Edmond de Goncourt left his property to a literary foundation composed of ten writers. First, he named Alphonse Daudet and Léon Hennique testamentary executors, but later, upon receiving thorough legal advice, he appended a codicil to his testament in which he named them residuary heirs. *Cf.* 3 Colin-Capitant, Cours Élémentaire de Droit Civil Français (1921) 694.

[75] *Cf. De Renesse c. Robineau et al.*, D 1928.2.121. The court validated a legacy for the creation of a foundation destined to provide for the poor widows and orphans of the Banque de France, and in case of a shortage in this category of beneficiaries—a fairly unlikely event considering the date of the testament:1918—to the poor orphans and widows of the Crédit Lyonnais. *Held*, that the unequivocal terms of the legacy left no doubt regarding the inten-

which thus has devised the *fondation* without statutory authority should be troubled by the idea of a trust.[76]

The French *fondation* is only one of an array of institutions analogous to the trust to be found in the modern civil law, in which funds are devoted to or a function is conceived in terms of a certain purpose. Examples of funds thus earmarked (*patrimoine affecté*, *Zweckvermögen*), or as we should say subject to a trust, include the assets of a variety of charitable, cultural, etc., foundations, bankrupt estates, decedents' estates, the Swiss family foundations,[77] and the property conveyed in Germany under a *Sicherungsübereignung* by the debtor to the creditor to be applied by the latter exclusively in discharge of the debt.[78] Likewise, the *interests* of the beneficiary of a *stipulation pour autrui* in French law, conceived as an abstract entity, are very similar to those of a beneficiary under an analogous common law trust.[79]

On the other hand, certain types of activities regarded as functions directed to the performance of a given purpose have been formulated in German legal theory as *Partei kraft Amtes*:[80] such for example are the functions of testamentary executors, administrators of estates, and administrators of funds in bankruptcy. This idea is carried further in the conception *neutrales Handeln*,[81] signifying activities quasi-detached from the acting individual and imputed to the fund on behalf of which they are performed. The latest German *Treuhänder* laws, enacted in Western Germany during the military occupation,[82] vesting

tions and the beneficiaries of the *de cujus*, and although the foundation was not yet in being at the time the legacy was made, the beneficiaries were, and so was their need for maintenance and care. Their need to this effect validates the legacy.

[76] Swiss law exhibits an analogous development based on precedents and not on codified provisions. It is the *fondation fiduciaire*, funds donated for certain charitable, etc., purposes to foundations already in being. The two outstanding decisions in this matter are, *Parti social-démocratique de Granges c. Grütli*, R. off. 1920, II, 25; and *Fehr c. Fondation de la Communauté suisse-allemande de Genève*, R. off. 1922, II, 158. *Cf.* F. Guisan, "La Fiducie en Droit Suisse," Semaine Internationale de Droit (Paris, 1937) *Travaux*, at 104.

[77] Erich Huber, "Trust and 'Treuhand' in Swiss Law," 1 The International and Comparative Law Quarterly (1952) 66; *id.*, Actes du Congrès International de Droit Privé (Rome, 1951) 209; Konrad Bloch, "Der anglo-amerikanische Trust und seine Behandlung im internationalen Privatrecht," 46 Schweizerische Juristen-Zeitung (1950) 68. But *cf.* Hermine Herta Meyer, "Trusts and Swiss Law," 1 The International and Comparative Law Quarterly (1952) 379.

[78] A. Nussbaum, "Sociological and Comparative Aspects of the Trust," 38 Columbia Law Review (1938) 416; W. Siebert, *op. cit.* 366 and n. 4; F. Weiser, *op. cit.*, 28 *et seq.*

[79] H. Batiffol, "The Trust Problem as Seen by a French Lawyer," 33 Journal of Comparative Legislation and International Law (1951) 24; *cf.* G. Ripert-J. Boulanger, 2 Traité Élémentaire de Droit Civil de Marcel Planiol (1949) 228.

[80] Lent, "Zur Lehre von der Partei kraft Amtes," 62 ZZP, 176 *et seq.*; cf. *loc. cit.* n. 81 *infra*, at 268 and n. 1.

[81] H. Dölle, "Neutrales Handeln im Privatrecht," 2 Festschrift Fritz Schulz (1951) 268 *et seq.*

[82] Bavaria: Gesetz Nr. 67 über die Bestellung von Treuhändern für Vermögen unter Vermögenskontrolle, 19 Juni 1947; Württemberg-Baden: Gesetz Nr. 218 (Treuhändergesetz) 4. März 1948; Bremen: Gesetz v. 25. Oktober 1948 (Treuhändergesetz); Höfeordnung für die Britische Zone, 24. April 1947.

the *Treuhänder* with administrative functions which the owners of the properties involved are not in position to discharge, have been thus construed. The lack of a clearly defined German *Treuhand* notion, blended with the influence of Anglo-American trust terminology, creates an amorphous legal situation as respects the various duties and responsibilities arising under these laws.[83]

Additional examples of trustee-like functions are those of the guardian,[84] the husband in dealing with the community estate,[85] the testamentary executor,[86] the executor in bankruptcy,[87] the German *Kommissionär*,[88] and the functions created by fiduciary transactions, including the French *prête-nom*[89] and those generically described in Germany and Switzerland as *Treuhand* activities.[90]

Continental courts are certainly not at a loss when presented with controversies arising from fiduciary, *Treuhand*, or acknowledged trust transactions.[91] Common law trusts are recognized,[92] and may even be considered as subject to domestic taxation.[93] In addition, in controversies involving questions of private international law, courts ascribing valid domestic effects to a trust, necessarily recognize its existence and validity.[94]

Why then are there no trusts in the civil law? If, as the record outlined above suggests, the principal obstacles offered in explanation are factitious, they must reflect underlying attitudes. Doubtless, among these are adherence to tradition and aversion to an alien concept on the part of those indoctrinated in the civil law, for fear that the existing structure of legal ideas might be unsettled by its admission. But these considerations do not explain how or why the distinctive contrast between the common law and the civil law with respect to trusts has occurred.

It may be suggested that the explanation is partly jurisdictional, partly ideological. On the one hand, the equitable jurisdiction of the chancellor for

---

[83] H. Dölle, *loc. cit.*, 281 *et seq.*

[84] F. Guisan, *loc. cit.*, 99, 100; P. Lepaulle, "Civil Law Substitutes for Trusts," 36 Yale Law Journal (1926–27) 1135 *et seq.*, F. Weiser, *op. cit.*, 17.

[85] A. Schulze, *loc. cit.*, 26; G. Ripert-J. Boulanger, 3 Traité Élémentaire de Droit Civil de Marcel Planiol (1951) 192 *et seq.*

[86] F. Guisan, *loc. cit.*, 102 *et seq.*; W. Siebert, *op. cit.*, 420 *et seq.*; P. Lepaulle, Traité Théorique et Pratique des Trusts (1932) 69, 70, n. 1.; A. Nussbaum, *loc. cit.*, 417; Max Rheinstein, "European Methods for the Liquidation of the Debts of Deceased Persons," 20 Iowa Law Review (1934–35) 472, 473, n. 77.

[87] W. Siebert, *op. cit*, 381 *et seq.*; F. Weiser, *op. cit.*, 17.

[88] F. Weiser, *op. cit.*, 18 *et seq.*, 42.

[89] *Ibid.*, 57 *et seq.*; A. Nussbaum, *loc. cit.*, 414; 72 BGE II 67, at 73 (1946).

[90] 72 BGE I 125 (1946).

[91] ERG 84, 217; ERG 91, 16; ERG 127, 8, 341; ERG 133, 84; Swiss cases cited in n. 65 *supra.*

[92] A. Nussbaum, *loc. cit.*, 424 and cases cited; P. Lepaulle, *op. cit.*, 365–368 and cases cited; F. Weiser, *op. cit.*, 69–70.

[93] 75 BGE I 315 (1949).

[94] Konrad Bloch, "Der anglo-amerikanische Trust und seine Behandlung im internationalen Privatrecht," 46 Schweizerische Juristen-Zeitung (1950) 68.

centuries formed a familiar and useful part of the English legal system, correcting or supplementing the basic common law. To the Anglo-American jurist, therefore, duplication of the ordinary remedies by relief in equity and consequent division of rights does not seem anomalous, as it must to the continental jurist, imbued with the unitary, logical scheme represented by the civil code, sharply distinguishing rights *in rem* and *in personam*.[95] This distinction of course had not troubled the chancellor in England, who, as Maitland observed,[96] was concerned merely to do equity in scandalous cases.[97, 98]

In addition, the *Code Napoléon*, followed by more recent civil codes, filled the vacuum created by the abolition of the complex and servile feudal law of property, with the simple, seductive concept of individual liberty, expressed as an absolute power of enjoyment and disposition vested in the owner. This not only fulfilled the political and economic convictions of the time, but it appealed to the profound instinct of human beings to have and to hold,—to their cravings for security and power. Mankind lives by fictions, by the ideas he constructs to build a tolerable world. Indeed, the survival of society depends in no small degree upon the capacity of legal rules to canalize power into its institutions. The definitions of property in the modern codes,[99] all in terms of

[95] Although not displaying such a sharp distinction between rights *in rem* and *in personam*, the common law notion of property is more abstract and analytical than that of the civil law. Indeed, in the course of time, the elaboration of ideas of property in the common law became like a mathematical calculus, effectively abstracted from its physical basis. *Cf.* F. H. Lawson, "Rights and Other Relations In Rem," Festschrift für Martin Wolff (1952) 114; *id.*, The Rational Strength of English Law (1951) 79; C. R. Noyes, The Institution of Property (1936) 518 *et seq.*

[96] Equity (1910) 29, 30.

[97] For description of the current trends in English equity and the increased rigidity of received concepts in its application, see especially, Lord Justice Denning, "The Need for a New Equity," Current Legal Problems 1952 (1952) 1 *et seq.*

[98] It is of interest to observe that, in France, the jurisprudence of the Conseil d'État has developed certain remedies alongside of the *voie ordinaire*, but these are too recent and the extent to which they parallel the civil remedies too limited to affect the basic approach of the civil law as such—where the two systems do impinge, as in the case of *fondations*, the ideas elaborated by the Conseil d'État are segregated as public law. *Cf. loc. cit.* n. 72.

[99] A few examples:

BGB § 854: "Der Besitz einer Sache wird durch die Erlangung der tatsächlichen Gewalt über die Sache erworben. Die Einigung des bisherigen Besitzers und des Erwerbers genügt zum Erwerbe, wenn der Erwerber in der Lage ist, die Gewalt über die Sache auszuüben."

§903: "Der Eigentümer einer Sache kann, soweit nicht das Gesetz oder Rechte Dritter entgegenstehen, mit der Sache nach Belieben verfahren und andere von jeder Einwirkung ausschliessen."

Code Civil, Art. 544: "La propriété est le droit de jouir et disposer des choses de la manière la plus absolue, pourvu qu'on n'en fasse pas un usage prohibé par les lois ou les règlements."

Art. 550: Le possesseur est de bonne foi quand il possède comme propriétaire, en vertu d'un titre translatif de propriété dont il ignore les vices."

Swiss Civil Code, Art. 641: "Le propriétaire d'une chose a le droit d'en disposer librement, dans les limites de la loi. Il peut revendiquer contre quiconque la detient sans droit et repousser toute usurpation."

Art. 919: Celui qui a la maitrise effective de la chose en a la possession. . . ."

USSR Law of August 7, 1932: "Preamble: public property . . . is the basis of the Soviet

power, are an outstanding illustration of this process. Thus, in a degree, property has been equated with power, symbolizing the increasingly mythical fiction of control, exclusive, unlimited, and inviolable. But England has shown that this idea is not necessary to preserve civil liberty.

VERA BOLGÁR*

regime. It is sacred and inviolable, and persons guilty of offenses against it shall be regarded as enemies of the people." *cited* in V. Gsovski, 1 Soviet Civil Law (1948) 562.

In addition to codified provisions, two samples from treatises: Vinding Kruse, The Right of Property (1939) 404, 424: "Possession is the external visible relation of power between a person and an external object at any given moment;... The external relation, possession, is easier for human thought to understand than the other relation, [legal] attribution.... We have seen that ideas of primitive law, to which mankind stubbornly clings in the field of property law more than in any other field, still obscure a free view."

Karl Renner, The Institutions of Private Law and their Social Functions, London, 1949, at 107: "We see that the right of ownership thus assumes a new social function ... a *de facto* right is added to the personal absolute domination .... This right is not based upon a special legal provision. It is the power of control, the power to issue commands and enforce them."

* Research Associate, University of Michigan Law School.

[7]

Quot judices tot sententiae: A study of the English reaction to continental interpretive techniques

By Shael Herman
Associate Professor of Law, University of Tulane

When the United Kingdom joined the European Economic Community in 1973, the English bench and bar must have perceived only dimly the challenges before them. Like contemporary descendants of Noah, they dropped into a Babel of languages and legal terms indispensable to the operation of the European Commission and the Court of Justice. Membership in the European Economic Community entailed the substantive harmonisation of English laws with those of other member states, and England's common law tradition could not have made the process easy. But the scope of the harmonisation task reached beyond substantive law to deeply rooted judicial attitudes toward the role of legislation and techniques of interpretation. In a recent editorial, Dr C. D. Ehlermann, Director of Legal Services for the European Commission, offered reasons for the English judiciary's potential resistance towards harmonisation of interpretative techniques.

'The United Kingdom has in relation to community legislation a special psychological problem. To "civil lawyers" law enacted by the State is something wholly familiar; membership of the community merely means that the originator of the enacted law changes. The United Kingdom, on the other hand, is proud of its historically developed common law. If even the statute law enacted at Westminster is regarded with scepticism, the institutions of Brussels are all the more certain to face mistrust, even aversion[1].'

In a sense, this paper concerns the English judiciary's mistrust of legislation and their nearly unanimous aversion to purposive legislative interpretation. Inevitably, Lord Denning, the chief proponent of purposive or liberal interpretation, figures prominently in the discussion along with his decision in *James Buchanan & Co Ltd v Babco*

1. C. D. Ehlermann, (1978) 15 Common Market Law Review 7. Interesting speculations on England's adjustment to membership in the European Economic Community appear in Chloros, 'English Law and European Law: The Problem of harmonisation' (1972) 36 Rabels Zeitschrift für aüsländisches und internationales Privatrecht 603. On legislative interpretation see N. S. Marsh, 'Interpretation in a National and International Context' (1974); C. D. Ehlermann and I. Sinclair, 'The Interpretation of Community Law' (1976) and Bredimas, 'Methods of Interpretation and Community Law' (1978). On the special question of English treaty construction, see Lipstein, 'Some Practical Comparative Law: The Interpretation of Multi-Lingual Treaties with Special Regard to EEC Treaties, (1974) 48 Tul L Rev 907. For an excellent treatment of the United Kingdom in the European Community, see Lord MacKenzie Stuart, (1977). The European Communities and the Rule of Law.

Forwarding & Shipping (UK) Ltd[2]. In clinical terms *Buchanan* is an ideal specimen, for it frankly displays a variety of consciously employed interpretive techniques and a remarkable judicial willingness to discuss these techniques. The case is also ideal for analysis because it concerns an unemotional, even mundane question of commercial liability, not an explosive issue that might cloud judicial perceptions.

Using the *Buchanan* decision as a springboard, this paper attempts to demonstrate two points; first, conceptual reasoning teleological reasoning are inevitable antagonists; and, second, conceptual analysis will remain a valid interpretive technique despite constant challenges by utilitarians and proponents of teleological techniques. As the paper later elaborates on these terms, a brief definition of them should suffice here. When we analyse a rule conceptually, we try to derive a concept from its words to discover what it commands. Then over the course of our experience with the rule, we apply our view of the command concept, usually quite literally. Teleological reasoning, etymologically from *telos*, the Greek word for 'end' or 'goal', seems antithetical to conceptual reasoning. It directs us to interpret a rule by focusing on its social purpose, even if we end up ignoring what it seems to command.

The first part of the paper analyses Lord Denning's judgment in *Buchanan* because it is so clearly committed to teleological techniques. Then, for contrast, it examines the opinions of Lord Wilberforce and Lord Edmund Davies because they typify the strict, conceptual analysis of the other judges. The second part of the paper traces the historical roots of conceptual and purposive techniques; the third speculates on reasons for distinctive interpretive techniques of English judges and the fourth and fifth parts examine in turn the application of conceptual and teleological techniques in selected continental decisions, and their political and philosophical implications.

I

The facts of *Buchanan*[3] were not contested. Buchanan had hired Babco to transport a shipment of whisky. En route, Babco's driver left his vehicle unattended over a weekend. When he returned on Tuesday of the following week, the whole shipment had apparently been stolen. The shipment was to have been trans-shipped to Europe and thence to Iran. Outside England its sale price was about £7,000. But the driver's fault, which was conceded by Babco, brought section 85 of the Customs and Excise Act 1952, into operation, requiring Buchanan to pay an excise duty of £30,000. Though Babco admitted liability, there was sharp disagreement on the amount of damages; Buchanan claimed the total £37,000 while Babco contended that it

2. Opinion in Court of Appeal, [1977] 1 All ER 518. Opinion in House of Lords, [1977] 3 All ER 1048.
3. Ibid.

owed only £7,000. The amount of damages, as everyone agreed, had to be fixed according to a carriage contract subject to CMR conditions. In other words, the contract incorporated the terms of an international convention enacted into English law by the Carriage of Goods by Road Act 1965.

The critical question in *Buchanan* was whether, in the language of section 23(4) of the Carriage of Goods by Road Act 1965, a substantial excise duty was 'a charge incurred in respect of the carriage of the goods'[4] and therefore refundable to Buchanan. According to Lord Denning, the quoted phrase, strictly interpreted, covered packing, insurance and certificates of quality, but it excluded the excise duty[5]. In his view, Buchanan had paid the £30,000 in respect of the non-carriage of the goods, not their carriage. But, asked Lord Denning, should the court be speaking strictly when the text at issue appears in an international convention, not in a traditional English statute? No.

'. . . It should be given the same interpretation in all the countries who were parties to the convention. It would be absurd that the courts of England should interpret it differently from the courts of France, or Holland or Germany. Compensation for loss should be assessed on the same basis, no matter in which country the claim is brought. We have for years tended to stick too closely to the letter – to the literal interpretation of the words. We ought, in interpreting this convention, to adopt the European method'[6].

Against resistance, Lord Denning advocated English adoption of a European method of interpretation as early as 1949. He described it more recently in an important decision, *H. P. Bulmer Ltd v J. Bollinger SA*[7]. There he pointed out that English statute drafters tried to legislate so as to foresee all possible circumstances that might arise; and English judges, following suit, interpreted the statutes literally as though they applied only to the circumstances covered by the very words of the statute. By contrast, the drafters of the Treaty of Rome had laid down general principles, aims, and purposes and European judges divined the spirit of the treaty and themselves filled the gaps. Finding a gap in section 23(4), Lord Denning emulated his European colleagues, filled it and elaborated on European interpretive method:

'They adopt a method which they call in English by strange words – at any rate they were strange to me – the "schematic and teleological" method of interpretation. It is not really so alarming as it sounds. All it means is that the judges do not go by the literal meaning of the words or by the grammatical structure of the sentence. They go by the design or purpose . . . behind it. When they come upon a situation which is to their minds within the spirit – but not the letter – of the legislation, they solve the problem by looking at the design and

4. [1977] 1 All ER 521-522.
5. [1977] 1 All ER 522.
6. Ibid.
7. [1974] 2 All ER 1226 at 1236-37.

purpose of the legislature – at the effect it was sought to achieve. They then interpret the legislation so as to produce the desired effect. This means that they fill in gaps, quite unashamedly, without hesitation. The ask simply: what is the sensible way of dealing with this situation so as to give effect to the presumed purpose of the legislation? They lay down the law accordingly'[8].

Eventually the House of Lords rejected Lord Denning's use of teleological reasoning, though Buchanan prevailed on the ground that 'other charges' was conceptually wide enough to include the excise duty. According to Lord Wilberforce (and his view was typical) there was no gap in section 23(4). The question was whether the loss should fall on the owner or the carrier. Somehow the words had to cover the case. Lord Wilberforce also took issue with Lord Denning's denigration of English methods and praise of continental ones. 'The assumed and often repeated generalisation that English methods are narrow, technical, and literal whereas continental methods are broad, generous, sensible seems to me insecure at least as regards interpretation of international convention'[9]. If the goal of the teleological approach was uniformity, it certainly had not been reached by the twenty-odd states that signed the Convention. One English decision showed that courts in six member countries had produced twelve different interpretations of particular provisions and Lord Wilberforce, to underscore the international disunity, examined two specific recent decisions interpreting section 23(4), one from Paris[10] the other from Amsterdam[11]. These cases, though factually similar to *Buchanan*, went for the carriers. They showed 'that there is no universal wisdom available across the channel upon which our insular minds can draw'[12]. And in Lord Wilberforce's view, it was pointless to characterise an interpretive style as liberal or strict as Lord Denning had done. One might as easily ask whose ox was being gored. According to Lord Edmund Davies, Lord Denning instead of reading the legislation, had legislated the result *on his own* and then justified the decision by reference to the intent of the drafter. Excise duty did not fit the category of charges in section 23(4) and 'liability to pay duty was not incurred in respect of the carriage of goods'. He conceded that a true gap might justify a continental approach, but in this case there was no gap. 'The literal approach [was] preferable to the schematic and teleological approach'[13]. And he drew attention to the misgivings about the teleological approach expressed in another decision.

'a possible danger of that approach . . . is not, indeed, that the judges

8. [1977] 1 All ER 522-523.
9. [1977] 3 All ER 1053.
10. *Cie L'Helvetia v Cie. Seine et Rhone* [1973] Bulletin des Transports 195.
11. *British American Tobacco Co (Nederland) BV v Van Swieten BV* (unreported) (30 March 1977).
12. [1977] 3 All ER 1054.
13. [1977] 3 All ER 1060.

become legislators, but that they may become legislators with widely differing, and perhaps unduly legalistic, views of the policy which is, or ought to be, behind the legislation. Hence the law, whatever it may gain in other respects, may in some cases suffer a loss in what has always been regarded as one of the essential features of law-uniformity; or, at least predictability. Sometimes, in relation to the judicial view of "the presumed purpose of the legislation", it may be a case of *quot judices, tot sententiae;* whereas in relation to what the legislation has actually said, it is unlikely that judicial opinion would vary so widely'[14].

It is hard to argue with Lord Edmund Davies's observations. A teleological interpretation might easily require the sacrifice of predictability to a deity of uniformity. Judging from varied treatments of section 23(4) by continental tribunals in France, the Netherlands and elsewhere, the god itself remains unappeased and unpredictable. And this unpredictability is expressed in the Latin maxim, *Quot judices tot sententiae.*

II

Laws, unlike many other forms of verbal expression, are dominantly instrumental in the sense that they incite us to action. They order, permit, and forbid; they announce rewards and punishments. In a positivist legal tradition, rules appear as statements, and they become commands when judges apply them to facts. The legal significance of a legislative text is the command the judge discovers in it, and discovery depends upon interpretation.

The debate in *Buchanan* about proper statutory interpretation was not isolated or accidental. On the contrary, the judges' literalism – sometimes called a search for plain meaning – is a hallmark of English statutory interpretation; it practically pre-ordained the shape of the decision in the House of Lords. For thirty years, Lord Denning himself unsuccessfully urged purposive techniques on his colleagues. In *Seaford Court Estates Ltd v Asher*[15], then a Lord Justice of only six months standing, he had to interpret the thoroughly ambiguous term 'burden' in a rent act. His fundamental insight in that case, one that often eludes both jurists and historians, was that history will always outstrip the imagination:

'Whenever a statute comes up for consideration it must be remembered that it is not within human powers to foresee the manifold sets of facts which may arise, and, even if it were, it is not possible to provide for them in terms free from all ambiguity . . . It would certainly save the judges trouble if Acts of Parliament were drafted with divine prescience and perfect clarity. In the absence of it, when a defect appears a judge cannot simply fold his hands and blame the

14. Ibid.
15. [1949] 2 KB 481.

draftsman. He must set to work on the constructive task of finding the intention of Parliament, and he must do this not only from the language of the statute, but also from a consideration of the social conditions which gave rise to it, and of the mischief which was passed to remedy . . .'[16].

Although the House of Lords eventually upheld the decision in *Seaford Court Estates*, the majority, as Lord Denning later recounted, rested their decision on traditional grounds[17]. And only a year later Denning's approach came in for heavy criticism. In *St. Mellons Rural District Council v Newport*[18], Lord Simonds 'poured scorn'[19] on the teleological approach, and accused Lord Denning of attempting a naked usurpation of the legislative function under the thin disguise of interpretation. Then in a succession of cases, teleological techniques arose only to be shot down. In 1974, Lord Denning, fortified with arguments based upon England's membership in the European Community, tried once again to introduce teleological interpretation. In *Bulmer Ltd v Bollinger SA* he characterised the Treaty of Rome as an incoming tide that 'flowed into the estuaries and up the rivers'[20]. To promote international uniformity, he argued, English judges had to construe the treaty purposively. His technique did not take hold in 1974, and it was rejected in *Buchanan*. His fellow judges' insistence leads us to ask several questions. First, was Lord Denning proposing anything new or revolutionary? Second, assuming he was correct about the English tendency to literalism, why was this so? Third, why did continental judges not share such literalism towards statutory interpretation?

This section attempts brief answers to the first two questions. The third must be postponed until we have first described and contrasted the roles of legislation in both civilian and common law contexts. If anything is clear from the literature on English statutory interpretation, it is the unrevolutionary nature of Lord Denning's proposed interpretive techniques. In *Seaford Court Estates* he acknowledged that the proposed purposive technique went back at least four centuries to *Heydon's* case[21] celebrated today for its articulation of the rule that correct interpretation requires a search for the equity of the statute. As the Barons of the Exchequer said, 'The sure and true interpretation of all statutes' required consideration of the 'true reason of the remedy'[22]. Though interpretation according to the equity of a statute was not novel, it was not the pre-eminent interpretive technique during four centuries either; it seems always to have

16. Ibid.
17 Denning, *The Discipline of Law* (1979) p. 13 (hereinafter cited as *Discipline*).
18. [1951] 2 All ER 839.
19. *Discipline*, supra, p. 14, n. 31.
20. [1974] 2 All ER 1226 at 1236-37.
21. [1949] 2 KB 481.
22. (1584) 3 Co Rep 7a. Quoted in Thorne, 'The Equity of a Statute and Heydon's Case, (1936). 31 Ill L Rev 202 at 214, n.44 (hereinafter cited as *Thorne*).

competed unsuccessfully with strict, literal interpretation, and the facts of *Buchanan* provided a contemporary arena for the contest. As Professor Thorne has shown, English judges traditionally refused to extend the words of a statute even when refusal might lead to injustice. Their attachment to literalism was a by-product of their commitment to the gradual case-by-case evolution expressed by a judge as early as 1342: 'We will not and cannot change ancient usages'[23]. In a system where decisions were the source of predictability and stability, statutes were understandably aberrational; they were 'in derogation of common law'.

Professor Thorne's description of an ancient cast of mind, characterised by literalism, has a distinctly modern ring:

'Statutes are to be taken as they stand; though they may be restricted in scope without comment, any extension, however slight, must be justified by reference to a definite doctrine of interpretation . . . The general attitude during the later Year Book period is one of jealousy for the common law which was not to be modified by statute more than could be avoided. Statutes will be held to do no more than they literally say in changing or adding common law rules . . . common law policy can be read into statutes to restrict general words that change common law principles too violently'[24].

Long before *Buchanan*, English judges had displayed an affection for strict interpretation. Predictably, teleological reasoning – call it equity of a statute, reason for the remedy – would run against the grain of most of Denning's colleagues. One could not expect them to abandon an 'ancient usage' because the legislation at hand was organic, not incidental or occasional. As two commentators said of *Buchanan* even before the decision in the House of Lords, a grammatical approach was 'inevitable. Teleology was clearly the last resort'[25].

This section explores the historical background of conceptualism and teleological reasoning, two interpretive techniques that figure prominently in the *Buchanan* case. Both techniques rest on the assumption that the legislation at issue is the primary source of law. This view contrasts sharply with the traditional Anglo-American notion that statutes derogate from common law. In a system dependent on the gradual evolution of rules in cases, full-blown interpretive theories would be unlikely. As long as the judge was his own interpreter, such theories, if they existed at all, were submerged in the judge's psyche; their emergence is due to the expanding reach of legislation. On the continent, however, such theories blossomed because of the separation of powers: judges had to explain how they applied legislation they had not authored. According to Professor Arthur Lenhoff, modern theories of legislative interpretation arose

23. YB 16 Edw. III, 1, 90, YB 19 Edw. III, 12. Quoted in Thorne, 'The Equity of a Statute and Heydon's Case', (1936) 31 Ill L Rev 202 at 214 n.44 (cited as *Thorne*).
24. *Thorne*, supra, pp. 208-209, 36.
25. Sacks & Harlow, (1977) 40 MLR 581.

with the bureaucratic state intent on providing judges with a codified standard[26]. Eighteenth century jurists portrayed monarchs and enlightened despots as absolute law-givers, and judges as their personal spokesmen. There is also a connection between the assumption of the supremacy of codified legislation and the rise of a natural law school established during the Enlightenment. According to an enlightenment dogma, sometimes attributed to Grotius and Pufendorf, a law drafter was to codify a few definite and immutable principles of human interaction buried among thousands of disparate rules in much the same way as natural scientists, by means of reason and detailed inspection, could discover the natural laws inherent in the universe[27]. Assuming the role of legal scientists, drafters and lawyers looked askance at sources of law other than legislation. They shared a general commitment to a strict separation of powers in which the judge was to decide cases by logical and scientific application of legislation to facts.

On the continent, a historical school led by the German scholar Savigny arose to legitimate civil codes as the source of law. The Civil Codes of both France and Germany were supposedly logical gapless systems, internally consistent documents whose logic appeared in the interaction of their provisions and the results derived from them. 'Every decision seemed to be a logical conclusion in a syllogism whose major premise was a rule and whose minor premise was the factual situation of the particular case'[28]. Since the keystone of the purely deductive theory of interpretation lay in the assumption that the Code was final and complete, the prevalent school of thought was satisfied by linking the decision to the code. This link was important whether the decision was based upon literal interpretation of a command in the code or logical deduction of its consequences. As Professor Lenhoff tells us,

'A legal technique was developed which often reminded the reader of the medieval scholastic disputes concerning the existence of God. For the case at issue, the decision is deduced from certain conceptions by way of subsumption . . . Notions are worked out from certain legal propositions and moulded into abstract conceptions from which, in turn, new concepts will be deduced through a similar logical-mechanistic process, and so on, *cum gloria in infinitum* . . . Thoël explained these methods as follows: "One has to find those rules which are not expressly defined in the statute by deducing them from general principles which, in turn, are to be discovered either by . . . abstraction, or by drawing consequences from those governing principles'[29].

26. Lenhoff, 'On Interpretative Theories: A Comparative Study in Legislation', (1949) 27 Texas L Rev 312 (cited hereafter as *Lenhoff*).
27. The relationship between techniques of natural science and legal science during the enlightenment is elaborated in Herman, 'Legislative Management of History: Notes on the Philosophical Foundation of the Civil Code', [1979] 53 Tul L Rev 380.
28. *Lenhoff*, supra, p. 313, 29.
29. Ibid., at 313-314.

In Germany, the scholastic conceptual approach described by Lenhoff came to be called *Begriffsjurisprudenz* while in France it was associated with the exegetical school. The chief virtues of conceptual jurisprudence were said to be predictability and certainty. Its chief drawback was that it eliminated the human element needed for the resolution of new social and economic problems. A German writer, Rudolph von Jhering, satirised the *Begriffsjurist* as a scholar who constructed a legal decision purely from texts and abstract concepts without taking into account its political impact[30]. By overemphasising conceptualism and literalism, *Begriffsjurisprudenz* had a petrifying effect. While the civilian scholar gained skill in detecting the faintest shades of meaning in statutory language, courts, challenged by changing social conditions, had to use verbal gymnastics and legal technicalities to adapt the codes to new circumstances. Inevitably, the judge's image as tender of a legal machine was destined to be transformed into that of law creator. Interpretive techniques supplied a basis for the transformation.

In retrospect the change seems natural because the scholarship harped on a variety of inter-related themes. To encourage the break from hairsplitting literalism, writers stressed important general terms in the codes, the purposive character of law, and the inevitable incompleteness of any legislation. The civil codes of Germany and France contained a number of sweeping general clauses. For example, German Civil Code, Article 242 provided that 'obligations of any kind are to be performed in such manner as good faith (guter Glaube) requires with due regard to the custom of the trade (Verkehrsitte)'. A German writer, Oscar von Bülow, argued that the use of these clauses gave judicial decisions a uniquely creative character, and he invoked Platonic metaphors to support the point. A judge, proceeding upon general clauses such as 'good faith', was said to be filling an abstract vessel with particular content; he was thus writing a particular rule for a particular case[31]. As we shall see shortly, the general clauses of Article 242 became the basis for a revolutionary turn in German private law. On the western bank of the Rhine, meanwhile, the French Cour de Cassation generated a theory of strict liability and tomes of decisions from flexible terms like 'fault' in a handful of tort articles. The following is a celebrated text of the French Civil Code:

'Art. 1382. Any act of a person which causes damage to another makes him by whose fault the damage occurred liable to make reparation for the damage.'

Once the scholarship had rationalised the leap from literal interpretation to the general clauses, the incompleteness of civil codes arose as a corollary. Paradoxically some codes codified the

30. Ibid., at 315-316. Translations of lengthy passages by Jhering, Heck and other continental scholars appear in *Jurisprudence of Interests* (M. Schoch ed. & trans. 1948).

31. Ibid., at 317.

corollary, offering convenient hooks to a judge who sought to decide a case outside the code's literal framework. For example, Article 7 of the Austrian Civil Code (1811) provided:

'Where a case cannot be decided either according to the literal text or the plain meaning of a statute, regard shall be had to the statutory provisions concerning similar cases and to the principles underlying other laws or similar matters. If the case is still doubtful, it shall be decided according to the principles of *natural justice* after careful research and consideration of all the individual circumstances'[32].

'And the first article of the Swiss Civil Code, enacted a century later, provided:

'The Civil Code applies to all cases as to which it contains provisions either according to its letter or its spirit. In default of an applicable provision, the judge shall decide according to customary law, and in default of a custom, according to such rules as he would enact if he were the legislator. He may inspire his decision by solutions sanctioned by doctrine and by the course of judicial decision'.

One can imagine Lord Denning's delight if such provisions appeared at the begining of the Carriage of Goods by Road Act 1965. To Lord Edmund Davies's charge that he was legislating in *Buchanan*, he would respond that he did it because the pertinent legislation authorised it. Even when broad directives were unstated, they constituted an integral part of a continental judge's interpretive baggage. As scholars quickly noted, Austrian Civil Code Article 7 furnished a road map of techniques for the resolution of cases otherwise unprovided for within the confines of the code itself. It distinguished judicial recourse to rules expressly provided for similar cases (*Gesetzesanalogie*) from a method that seeks a solution implicit in the spirit of the law, that is, the general principles on which the entire legislation is based (*Rechtsanalogie*). A judge, armed with such an arsenal of analogical techniques, was well equipped to settle many ambiguities. If he still could not solve a particular problem, he might then refer to the 'natural justice' clause, presumably a reference to the natural law school that viewed certain principles as innate in human nature and superior to any municipal law. In constitutional law such principles might include the right of privacy and the right against self-incrimination. In the *Buchanan* decision, several judges almost fastened on a maxim of natural justice that is a commonplace in tort law: If one of two parties must suffer, let it be the one whose negligence contributed to the damages.

The step from analogical reasoning to purposive reasoning is illuminated by reference to Article 1 of the Swiss Civil Code, for this article literally provided a basis for the judicial filling of a legislative gap. Of course it did not authorise a judge to fill a gap with his own privately held social ideals. Instead, according to Swiss legal doctrine, it called upon the judge to seek a fuller articulation of principles

32. Ibid.

embodied in the code itself. Lenhoff traced Article 1 of the Swiss Civil Code to a passage in Aristotle's *Nichomachean Ethics:* 'Where a law is not specific enough and therefore lacks a rule applicable to the case, one should fill the gap as the lawgiver if present and faced with the case would have formulated the rule[33]. Equally convincing is Professor Jaro Mayda's claim that Article 1 of the Swiss Civil Code was inspired by a modern French writer, Francois Gény, whose *Méthode d'interpretation et sources en droit privé positif* was a devastating assault on the formalistic code exegesis prevalent in France well into the twentieth century[34]. Gény was the foremost exponent of *'libre recherche scientifique'*, the view that the judge, having found neither an appropriate formal norm nor guidance in doctrine and decisions, must freely and objectively search for a rule in social realities and values. Gény sought to demolish the positivist myth that legislated law was exclusive and self-sufficient. He attacked the methods of *Begriffsjurisprudenz* that 'erected on a legislative text a system of concepts handled in closed circuit by means of formal logic, independently of the changing world of facts[35]. Inspired by Von Jhering, a prime mover in the teleological school of *Interessenjurisprudenz*, Gény envisioned a civil code as a structural frame that did not *a priori* establish the limits of judicial interpretation. Recognising that history would always outrun the imagination, he elaborated the concept of the insufficiency of written law that Portalis, chief architect of the Code Napoleon, had expressed a century before him: 'It is for experience gradually to fill up the gaps we leave. The codes of nations are the fruit of the passage of time: properly speaking we do not make them'[36].

For Gény, the judge's first task was interpretation of the legislative text pursuant to a subjective theory that aimed at discovering the legislator's actual will. If, by means of this approach, the interpreter discovered that the legislator had expressed no intention regarding the precise situation at hand, either because the specific problem did not come to his mind or had been overlooked, then he should find the basis for the decision in sources beyond the confines of the legislation. For Gény, a legislative provision was a general rule or norm enacted for a general type of situation, although the provision might be couched in terms of specific facts. If the interpreter could not subsume a given set of facts within a general conceptual category, then he could project the norm beyond its original scope. In the context of *Buchanan*, Lord Denning accomplished this projection by reference to the overall scheme and purpose of the Act as well as the general goal of uniformity among the member states' courts.

33. Ibid., at 318. Aristotle, Nichomachean Ethics.
34. Mayda, *Francois Gény and Modern Jurisprudence* (1978) 31-32 (cited hereafter as *Mayda*).
35. Ibid., at 7.
36. Author's translation in Levasseur, 'Code Napoleon or Code Portalis', (1969) 43 Tul L Rev 762 at 773.

For analytical purposes, Gény had assumed the command element of a provision could be severed from its purpose; and because command and purpose were often antagonistic, the assumption was convenient. However, other proponents of teleological reasoning argued this division was artificial because the two elements were in reality inseparable. In other words, a command in positive law could be regarded as an objectification of subjective purpose. The German scholar, Philip Heck, founder of the school of *Interessenjurisprudenz*, made this point when he suggested that every legal norm has on one hand its logical place in a conceptualistic framework of legal precepts. On the other hand, it aims at a balancing of conflicting private interests by drawing a line of demarcation between one party's interest and those of others. According to Heck, conceptualism was onesided and mechanical because it missed the connection between a norm and the conflict of human interests for whose settlement it was enacted. Heck attributed the onesidedness of conceptualism to the fallacious idea that a rule for every case ultimately must be derived from a legislative provision. Though legislation might be the primary source of law, it was not the only one. Heck did not argue for the destruction of conceptualism; instead he sought to emphasise the indissoluble links between command and purpose, norm and interest. According to Lenhoff, the fallacy of conceptualism was a logical inversion; it ignored that rules are formulated deductively from concepts that were themselves formed to establish the rules[37]. Although, to all appearances, a judicial opinion generally omits allusion to a process of valuation of interests in the case, the true reasons for the decision lie in the perception of and the significance given to the manifold interests in the balance[38]. According to the school of *Interessenjurisprudenz*, the judge was no mere legal automaton operated by logical mechanics. He could not focus strictly on the words of a text and derive concepts logically from it without attending to the provision's purpose. A creative assistant to the lawmaker, he had to lay bare, to articulate and to classify what a statute might express inarticulately. To fashion a rule appropriate for the case he had to evaluate the interests involved in the case, not enshroud the process in mechanical, formalistic deductions.

III

Having explored briefly two interpretive techniques for civil codes, we can return to a question posed earlier: Why do English judges and their continental counterparts not share literalistic attitudes toward statutory interpretation? This is not a new question, but perhaps we can offer some new explanations.

Long before England joined the European community, commentators warned against impatience with the English for their distinc-

37. *Lenhoff*, supra, p. 330.
38. Ibid.

tive attitudes toward statutory interpretation[39]. Dr Ehlermann's explanation, quoted at the beginning of this article, explains these attitudes[40]. For an English lawyer, unlike his continental counterpart, an exploration of the limits of judicial interpretation might seem a vain exercise. Conditioned to attach great weight to judicial decisions, he might wonder why anyone would bother to debate the values of judicial lawmaking. To complicate matters, a continental jurist might wonder why English judges, by their own admission capable of creating law, insist on reading statutes literally (uncreatively?). Answers to these questions will take us some distance toward understanding why Lord Denning's teleological approach fell like a hand grenade among his brothers. As we have seen, the reasons for their rejections are institutional, not personal. The explanation requires a sketch of English and continental assumptions about the separation of powers and the roles of statute and precedent as sources of stability. It will be recalled that modern continental theories of legislative interpretation arose with the bureaucratic state intent on providing judges with the stability of a codified standard. By definition, a codified standard entailed the glorification of the legislator. Equally important, it also required the denigration of the judicial function, a trick that could easily be played because judges in the precodification era had been traditional objects of distrust. Civil law dogma asserted legislative supremacy; and a corollary of the assertion was that judicial decisions were not law. The products of judges in courts had no place in the hierarchy of recognised sources of law.

By contrast, English common law had no significant tradition of distrust of the judiciary, at least since the time of Coke. Thus it placed no particular emphasis on restricting the judicial function. To the contrary, judicial decisions were the principal means of developing the law; unlike continental codes, English statutes played a minor uneven role in legal development. From this basic contrast between continental and English experience with statutes and decisions flowed other differences that influenced their perspectives. As noted previously, the civil law tradition entrusted to the legislature the task of assuring predictability and stability. Thus, a civil code, a visible sign of predictability, was necessarily characterised as a comprehensive scheme, complete in its field and logical in its arrangement. In the common law tradition since the Glorious Revolution, predictability was a responsibility of the judiciary rather than Parliament. While the demand for predictability virtually precluded the development of a doctrine of binding precedent on the continent, the same desideratum of the English common law demanded it. Precedent was the soil from which predictability was mined, and stare decisis was its visible sign. Even today, the English lawyer, though

39. Chloros 'English Law and European Law: The Problem of Harmonisation', (1972) 36 Rabels Zeitschrift für ausländisches und internationales Privatrecht 603.
40. See text accompanying note 1.

he is aware of the growing role of statute, is bound by a traditional view that legislation is abnormal and occasional. It is law made outside the usual and traditional developmental machinery of the legal sysem. It arose in derogation of the process whereby predictability was achieved, and therefore was not fully assimilated into the legal system until the judiciary legitimated it. English statutes, from a practical standpoint, must also have been outside the traditional machinery. Until the nineteenth century, English enactments, some dating back to the 1200s, 'were disorderly to an almost incredible degree'[41]. If the importance of statutes to a legal system can be gauged by their disarray and imcompleteness, English enactments must have rated pretty low.

English and continental perspectives on the role of statute and precedent entailed differences in judicial and legislative methods. Lord Cooper summed up these differences well:

'A civilian system differs from a common law system much as rationalism differs from empiricism or deduction from induction. The civilian naturally reasons from principles to instances, the common lawyer from instances to principles. The civilian puts his faith in syllogisms, the common lawyer in precedents; the first silently asking himself as each new problem arises, "What did we do last time?" . . . The instinct of the civilian is to systematise. The working rule of the common lawyer is *solvitur ambulando*'[42].

Differences between continental and English interpretation suggest a fundamental difference between continental and English legislation per se.

As Portalis, the chief drafter of the French Civil Code noted, the fundamental task of civilian legislation is to establish general principles of law 'fertile in their effects' from which particular applications might be deduced. Thus, the civilian separation of powers model presents a distinctive division of labour between judge and legislator: 'There is a legislative skill as well as a judicial skill and the two are quite distinct. The skill of the legislator is to discover the principles in each area which most conduce to the common weal: the skill of the judge is to put these principles into action'[43].

41. C. K. Allen. *Law in the Making* (7th edn, 1964).

42. Cooper, 'The Common Law and the Civil Law – A Scot's View', (1950) 63 Harv L Rev 468 at 470, See also, R. Pound, What Is the Common Law? in the Future of the Common Law (1937) 3: 'Behind the characteristic doctrines and ideas and technique of the common law lawyer there is a significant frame of mind. It is a frame of mind which habitually looks at things in the concrete, not in the abstract . . . It is a frame of mind which is not ambitious to deduce the decision for the case in hand from a proposition formulated universally . . . It is the frame of mind behind the sure-footed Anglo-Saxon habit of dealing with things as they arise instead of anticipating them by abstract universal formulas'.

43. Portalis, 'Discours preliminaire pronuuncé lors de la présentation du projet de la commission du gouvernement', in 1 P. Fenet, *Recueil complet de travaux préparatoires due code civil* (Paris 1827) 470, translated by S. Herman in Levasseur, *Code Portalis*, supra, p. 769, n. 50. See the translation by T. Weir in 1 Zweigert & Kötz, *An Introduction to Comparative Law* at 82.

The common law tradition presents a strikingly different division of labour. During the formative periods of English law, general principles of law were drawn inductively from existing decisional law, not deductively from legislation. Thus the division of labour between common law judge and legislator is almost the converse of that embodied in the civil law tradition. Not surprisingly, the judicial approach to statutory construction in the two traditions differs significantly. For English lawyers, legislation has traditionally consisted of ad hoc enactments to alleviate particular social or economic mischief. English empiricism, in combination with a conception of decisional common law as a seamless web, reacts with suspicion to such enactments: the common law judge senses that legislation is itself a kind of mischief, a nagging disturbance of the 'lovely harmony of the common law'[44]. English statutory interpretation, even when applied to a modern convention like the Carriage of Goods by Road Act, reflects a conviction that the mischief of legislative interference should be confined within a narrow compass[45]. Statutes in derogation of the common law are to be strictly construed and limited to the particular situations they address unquestionably. This assumption of strict construction would exist even in the face of the most comprehensive legislative scheme, and as Lord Denning learned, even if the scheme is a multilateral commercial treaty. If the particular facts do not fit into the unquestionable coverage of the legislation, the judge turns away from it, confident that he will somehow turn up a solution from common law. Even when he denies the application of common law, he does not seem concerned over the potential chaos that might result from a defect in legislation. Unlike his civilian counterpart, he does not exhibit a strong commitment to maintaining the myth that legislation is logically complete and perfect. This absence of commitment is predictable because the English judge, even when he says otherwise, believes he works with a safety net. If he falls through the superstructure of a legislative scheme, he believes he will land safely in the seamless, stable web of the common law[46]. Even Lord Denning, the most 'liberal' of statute readers, justified his reading of section 23(4) of the Carriage of Goods by Road Act on the ground that it coincided with the common law rules that would have applied without the legislation.

44. 1 Zweigert and Kötz at 269: 'The judges saw statutes as being an evil, a necessary evil, no doubt, which disturbed the lovely harmony of the common law . . .' The restrictive attitude towards statute is well documented in Plucknett, *Statutes & Their Interpretation in the First half of the Fourteenth Century* (1922), Thorne, 'A Discourse upon the exposition and Understanding of Statutes (1942).

45. F. Pollock, 'Essay upon Jurisprudence and Ethics' 85 (1882).

46. The English judge 'has no feeling that, if he fails to provide a remedy through the statute for the particular set of fact with which he is presented, he is failing in his duty, that he is leaving a gap in the law. There is always, apart from the statute, the common law, the law developed by the judges themselves, which will govern the legal relations of the parties'. N. S. Marsh, 'Interpretation in a National and International Context' (1974) 67.

Civil law tradition presents a model of the judge at work diametrically opposed to the description above. For a continental judge, a body of law is by definition legislative in character; he is in partnership with the legislator and the guardian of the integrity of the legislation. Hence their functions are complementary, not antagonistic. Unlike his English counterpart, he instinctively tries to avoid the legislative gap or explain it away. His use of analogy and teleological method reflects a desire always to save the legislation, for tradition requires the assumption that it is the fountainhead of predictability in law. No matter how much he engages in judicial lawmaking he will not easily admit he is doing so. For him, unlike his English counterpart, there is no safety net, no extra-legislative stability. His interpretive techniques tend to expand rather than restrict the reach of legislation. For him, expanded structure is safer than a void.

IV

Conceptualism and literal interpretation have been fashionable targets of scholarly criticism at least since the inception of legal realism. The criticism probably had its seed in the United States in Holmes's statement that the life of the law was experience, not logic[47]. But judicial method is more than a matter for scholarly discourse. Both conceptualism and teleogical interpretation have political implications evident in microcosm in the *Buchanan* decision. I argue here that conceptualism is inevitable and desirable in legislative interpretation if there is to be legitimacy to the rule of law. As Montesquieu taught us, certainty can positively affect the citizenry: if private actors know in advance the incidence of state intervention, they can adjust their activities to account for it, thereby avoiding the effect of sporadic legal catastrophes[48]. Thus, in criminal statutory interpretation we have not subscribed to purposive interpretation. Even in interpreting organic civil statutes like the Uniform Commercial Code, we normally try to subsume cases within categories established by the various sections[49].

I do not argue that there is a cause-effect relationship between conceptualism and liberal democracy on one hand or between teleology and totalitarianism on the other, but judicial preference for one of

47. Holmes dictum was probably borrowed from Jhering who said in *Der Geist des Römischen Rechts*, 'Life is not here to be a servant of concepts, concepts are here to serve life . . . What will come to pass is not postulated by logic but by life'. Zweigert & Siehr, 'Jhering's influence on the Development of the Comparative Method', (1971) 19 AJCL 215, 225-226. I am indebted to Professor Mary Ann Glendon for the connection between Holmes' dictum and Jhering's statement.
48. About the plight of peasants in the Ottoman Empire in the eighteenth century, Montesquieu wrote: 'Ownership of land is uncertain and thus the incentive for agricultural development is weakened: Neither title nor possession is good against the rulers' caprice'. *Lettres Persanes* (1721) 65 (author's translation).
49. See, e.g., Hawkland, 'Uniform Commercial Code Methodology', 1962 U Ill L Forum 291.

these techniques at a given period is a remarkably sensitive weather vane of political currents. Once political forces establish a dictator or tyrant, he can feed on an anti-conceptual judicial method with an entrenched tradition of gap filling by teleological reasoning. In this section, it will be helpful to liken reading a text to sticking to a footbridge over a chasm. Security and predictability are possible if one looks straight ahead. As we shall see in a brief contrast of Swiss and German judicial experiences in the twentieth century, peering down into the chasm may induce vertigo.

Professor Mayda, after meticulous analysis of a number of Swiss decisions, concluded that Swiss Courts, in the first thirty to forty years after the enactment of the Swiss Civil Code, 'exuded confidence in the judge's suppletary mission'[50]. This confidence appeared in a variety of cases reflecting 'substantial broadening of the scope of the gap in a teleological direction'[51]. In 1925, for example, a Swiss court declared that 'where the text is insufficient to resolve a question, the judge should complement it according to his judgment'[52]. And the court went on to declare itself guardian of both the word and spirit of a text.

'The existence of a gap to be filled judicially must be admitted not only when a given fact situation is not covered by any statutory provision. It must be admitted also when there is such a provision, but its application to the specific case obviously does not correspond to the true ratio of the statute according to its meaning, its text and content. In such a case one cannot speak of simple equity lying outside the positive legal system, which could be considered only in the presence of a clearly and categorically expressed legislative will. On the contrary, the true content of the law, which the judge must find and apply, is at issue'[53].

About ten years later a Swiss court further elaborated the judge's role as gap filler in *Haus v Graber*. This case involved a creditor's right to sue an original debtor and a surety for the unpaid remainder of a debt, a situation not expressly regulated in Swiss civil law. Eugen Huber, the principal draftsman of the Swiss Civil Code, had written that a solution to the case could be derived from the Swiss Code of Obligations. Huber's opinion and a consistent ninety year line of decisions from the canton of Zurich (where *Haus v Graber* originated) were both unfavourable to Haus' appeal. But the Swiss Bundesgericht reversed, on the ground that the lower courts had ignored the spirit of the legislation. Inspired by this spirit, the judge was bound to 'supplement the law'[54].

Haus was a landmark. For a decade after it, Swiss courts showed a willingness to invoke the judge's creative power authorised in Article 1.

50. Mayda, supra, p. 42, n. 37.
51. Ibid.
52. Ibid.
53. Ibid.
54. Ibid., at 43-44.

According to Mayda's careful analysis of more recent Swiss rationes and dicta, however, Swiss judges, relying on a strict separation-of-powers doctrine, have hesitated to exercise their pretorian lawmaking powers. The judicial retreat from pretorian use of Article 1 was already clear in the *Suisa* case decided in 1948. In *Suisa*, plaintiffs argued that the Swiss copyright law of 1922 had a gap because it could not have been intended to cover talking films. The plaintiffs argued that this gap should be filled by reference to custom and technological progress. In the course of the opinion, the court elaborated on gap filling techniques:

'The existence of a gap must not be assumed lightly. The judicial exercise of the lawmaking power, . . . provided for in cases of extreme need (Art. 1, ZGB), represents a violation of the principle of separation of powers, a fundamental principle of modern democracy. The judge must therefore proceed with the making of new rules only where there is no doubt that a norm cannot be derived from the statute. If it is possible to solve a new fact situation through analogous use of existing legal prescriptions, the claim of a gap in the statute must be normally denied even if the resulting order is not the most expedient one. For expedience alone is not the factor that determines the existence of a gap'[55].

Mayda attributed the 'atrophy' of teleological method partly to Swiss psychology and technique. On a political plane, however, such atrophy seems to have been associated with the rise of authoritarian regimes after 1933 and the 'vertigo caused by the recognition of where a deviation from respectful deference from the texts might lead[56]. Mayda expressed disappointment that the Swiss Bundesgericht slipped backward from the technique of teleological gap filling, generally associated with the purposive interpretation of *Interessenjurisprudenz*, and fell into mechanical conceptual jurisprudence. The 'slip backward', if that is what it was, is understandable: Exaggerated judicial deference to the texts was a predictable response for a nation that witnessed judicial tyranny beyond its borders. The judges of the Nazi regime, in response to demands of the new social order, ran roughshod over teleological gap filling techniques. A brief look at German judicial behaviour from 1920 to 1945 reveals reasons for the Swiss judiciary's retreat.

Lenhoff reports that in the early 1900s techniques of *Interessenjurisprudenz* had gained ground in Germany, and German courts between the World Wars showed a tendency to escape from a technical scholastic approach. Many cases arose out of one of the greatest currency devaluations of modern times, proportionally like the plunge of confederate money. One celebrated piece of litigation concerned a pre-war lease with a clause permitting the landlord, at the end of the lease, to recover livestock for an amount fixed in Reichsmark. When the case reached the highest court, the German

55. Ibid., at 47.
56. Ibid., at 51.

Reichsmark had lost 90% of its foreign market value. Because the lease ended at a time when the Reichsmark's value was skidding, the tenant naturally objected to the enormous loss threatening him if his compensation were computed by face value of the mark. On the other hand, the prices of livestock had skyrocketed, so that the tenant, if he were compensated on the basis of then current prices, would reap enormous profit from the changed circumstances. The German Reichsgericht declined to follow the conceptualists' tenet that a proper result could be derived from the legislative text alone. 'Viewed in the light of reality, all legislation, not excepting the [German] Civil Code, is only patch-work . . .'[57]. Neither jurisprudence nor the parties' intentions supplied a basis for the decision, as the case was a matter of first impression and the disputed clause did not provide for the situation. Thus, the court, legitimately seeking to do equity, sought a middle course:

'A middle course [between the two diametrically opposed interpretations offered by the parties] must be charted to strike a balance between the two conflicting interests . . . Where the statute fails to offer a solution, the judge replaces the law-maker for the particular situation. One often speaks in such a case of a gap; but the expression is inappropriate because it conveys the idea that it would be possible to restrict the multifariousness of life within the confines of a code. Such a thing is impossible. Every day produces new aspects of legal significance, the creative power of life is infinite and the *judge has to find the law in all such cases*'[58].

This judicial revaluation case prefigured dramatic interpretive developments. According to Professor John Dawson, the disruption of private transactions, occurring on a vast scale, was traceable to one primary cause: the capricious fluctuations of the currency as a helpless government financed itself through the printing press. 'Disparities of value became so enormous as in themselves to stamp the results as unjust, by any measure of injustice'[59]. Only in the case of debts arising from original money loans did judicial relief seem precluded. This was so because pre-war legislation, admittedly valid, had made the paper mark legal tender at its normal par – 'one mark equalled one mark' – for the purpose of discharging a money debt. As the inflation progressed, this legislation enabled a debtor to pay in money whose purchasing power was a thousandth or a millionth of the purchasing power he had acquired through the original loan. In a case involving a mortgage debt contracted before World War I, the court concluded that payment tendered in 1920, under appropriate circumstances, would not be 'performance in good faith'. This conclusion was supported by two arguments, by then predictable tools in the teleologists' toolchest: First, the framers of the legal tender

57. *Lenhoff*, supra. p. 331, n. 29, citing Reichsgericht 26 May, 1922; [1922] Juristische Wochenschrift 1910.

58. Ibid., at 332.

59. Dawson, *The Oracles of the Law* (1968) 468-69, (hereinafter *Dawson*).

legislation could not have foreseen the vast depreciation of the mark that had occurred after the war. Second, a conflict had arisen between Article 242 of the German Civil Code and the legal tender legislation, and in this conflict the latter must give way. Though these arguments sounded reasonable enough, the result was remarkable. The court concluded that a general clause of the Civil Code, effective in 1900, could invalidate a *subsequent* statute [60].

Within two months after rendition of this decision, German courts, in overturning pre-war transactions, would explicitly say that inflation had destroyed the foundation of a transaction, and had distorted the equivalence in a bilateral contract. Nevertheless, the balance could be restored; and the good faith clause of article 242 demanded a fair sharing of the burden of revalorisation[61]. In 1933, the German courts' attraction to the general clauses was publicised by a German jurist, Justus Hedemann, in a well-known tract, *'The Flight into the General Clauses, A Danger for Law and State'*. Hedemann saw the flight as a magnification of judicial power. In his view, its greatest danger was that it would obliterate legal rules as restraints on power, leaving discretion uncontrolled. For all of its drawbacks, the conceptual framework of a legislative text hemmed a judge in, preventing him from arrogating power from the legislature to himself. Hedemann linked the flight into the general clauses to disintegration of Germany's public order and conflicts between power groups that had nearly paralysed government. Investing 'neutral' judges with discretion through new interpretations of general clauses would accelerate the dilution of governmental restraints. A week before Hedemann's book appeared, Hitler acquired command of the state; and with his rise came a new general clause, the will of the Führer. It rivalled all other clauses and could fill any gap. Hedemann's judgment was accurate: the advent of the Nazi regime further accelerated the flight into the general clauses. 'Judges were to promote the "togetherness" of the Volk, its racial purity, common good above private good, the world view of Nazism'[62]. The general clauses, especially 'good faith' and 'good morals', were to be main ports of entry for these principles of the new order. The inflation and revalorisation cases were the channels to the ports, though by the mid-1930's 'good faith' had been invoked for labour contracts, literary property, corporations, civil procedure, the right of neighbouring landowners, taxation and public administration. In 1936, the Great Senate for Civil Matters declared that a contract could be void as offensive to 'good morals' if the values exchanged were unequal and 'in its content, motive and object it offends the sound sense of the people'[63].

60. This paragraph paraphrases Dawson's account in *Dawson*, 469-470.
61. *Dawson*, supra, p. 474, note 54.
62. *Dawson*, supra, p. 476, note 54.
63. *Dawson*, supra, p. 474, note 54. On abuses of judicial interpretation committed by the Nazi court, see Lowenstein, 'Law in the Third Reich', (1936) 45 Yale LJ (cited hereafter as *Lowenstein*).

Notably, not one line of the German Civil Code had to be repealed for the Nazis to establish their new order. The Great Senate merely had to fill old bottles with new wine:

'The concept of an "offence against good morals" as contained in articles 138 and 826, Civil Code, includes in essence the content of the National Socialist world outlook, which has become since the revolution the prevailing sense of the people (*Volksempfinden*). Filled with this content, article 138 is to be applied also to transactions of the period preceding that have not yet been performed. When a transaction offends good morals according to the views that now prevail no legal protection can be accorded it by any German court'[64].

According to Dawson, Nazi ideology may have pervaded the Reichgericht's tests of good faith and good morals in many transactions, and he illustrates this point by reference to beer franchise cases.

'The official Nazi vocabulary had numerous ways of expressing sympathy for hard-pressed, small-time businessmen. One of the stray currents in that turbulent stream was the impulse to help the little man against the big, especially Big, Inc., this being one of the means for curbing the abuses of "monopoly capitalism". So the Reichsgericht must have counted on some nods of approval by heads in high places when in 1936 it described with indignation the unjust terms imposed by a great brewery, having vast resources and "paramount power," on a struggling retailer who must invest his scanty resources and all his efforts in an enterprise that could be cut off at any time, for a whim. This was condemned, it was said, by the German people's "conscience" and "sound sense of right" which had come to incorporate the whole national socialist world outlook'[65].

On the whole, however, Dawson reports that the permanent deposit of Nazi ideas on German private law and procedure was remarkably small. 'Even the continuing resort to the general clauses was in large part a working out of ideas that had germinated before 1933'[66]. Judicial departure from the conceptual framework established by the Civil Code was a response to the rampant inflation of the 1920s. Ironically, the Nazi courts did not invent new techniques to achieve their goals; they merely had to twist well entrenched judicial methods, filling gaps with the ideals of the new order. They justified this subversion of the rule of law on the spurious ground that they had

64. Ibid., Lowenstein's observation is noteworthy. 'Legal intepretation may . . . change the application of the old statutes without changing their textual formulation. National Socialist 'equity' seized upon those general clauses of the codes which already provided for equity as an integral part of positive law'. *Lowenstein*, supra, p. 804, note 58.

65. Dawson, 'Unconscionable Coercion: The German Version', (1976) 89 Harv L Rev 1041 at 1090.

66. *Dawson*, supra, p. 478, note 54. The damage of Nazism, viewed without benefit of historical perspective, seemed much greater. *Lowenstein*, supra, p. 794, note 59. But Lowenstein himself predicted that the abuses of the Third Reich would not cause permanent damage to German law. Ibid., at 814.

uncovered the 'true' purpose of the law in the ruling spirit of the people.

V

According to Montesquieu, predictability and certainty, the chief virtues of conceptualism had a positive effect on the citizenry: if private actors could know in advance the incidence of state intervention they could adjust their expectations and activities to account for it. These virtues must have been especially appealing to the jurists of post-Revolutionary France. Because judges of the ancien régime tended to ignore express commands of law, the drafters of the Code Napoleon put a premium on clear legislation. Division of legislative and judicial functions was the essence of Montesquieu's doctrine of separation-of-powers. Today Montesquieu's argument is implicit in criminal law: if someone were indicted for a crime not clearly prohibited at the time he was alleged to have acted, he would have legitimate due process objections. Predictability and certainty were high on Karl Llewellyn's list of values when he argued for a commercial code. Llewellyn, as though he were a modern Montesquieu, asked rhetorically:

'What does it cost a polity in delay and uncertainty in legal discomfort or injustice to have the making or review of a rule wait upon the chance raising and appeal of issues one by one by dragging one? Consider, in contrast, what a Uniform Commercial Act or a Uniform Commercial Code does in making available in a jurisdiction where rulings are sparse the experience and wisdom of the whole country – all at a single stroke'[67].

We cannot know for sure if a strongly entrenched conceptualist tradition would have robbed Nazi officials of the opportunity to base decisions on criteria never articulated by the pertinent legislation. But an anti-conceptual strain committed to gap-filling appears to have made their rise to power easier. By contrast, Italian jurists during the same period resisted the Fascist onslaught by invoking the values of conceptualism and certainty and coupling them with a commitment to rigid separation of powers. Italian jurists saw a rigid separation of powers as a bulwark against executive interference in the judiciary. When Fascists suggested the abolition of legal technicalities and relaxation of insistence on certainty so that judges could 'decide in accordance with the facts of the case and the needs of the corporative order, the traditional legal value of certainty became the symbol for defense of the legal order'.

'The example of Germany, where the abolition of legality had gone forward under the theory of "free decision" or by reference to the *Führerprinzip*, was before the Italian jurists, and its tendency to make the law merely another branch of the administration was evi-

67. Llewellyn, *The Common Law Tradition: Deciding Appeals* (1960) 518.

dent. Many Italian jurists strongly resisted the tendency in the name of the traditional values of the doctrine, among which certainty tended to dominate'[68].

Thus far I have argued that conceptualism and teleological reasoning are based upon different political assumptions. They also represent different epistemological assumptions. The conceptualist approach derives its strength from the intuition that the human mind operates according to innate ideas or intelligible essences. For a conceptualist words have fixed definite meanings. To assert the virtues of flexibility and adaptability, proponents of teleological reasoning must view the words of a rule as elastic vessels of variable content to be filled and emptied to achieve a right or good result. In opposition to the teleologists, the conceptualists assert that there is no necessary link between a rule and its purpose. They decry speculation about legislative policy and the arbitrary assignment of values to interests as tricks for destabilising the plain meaning of the rule. As outsiders, we may not feel a strong preference for any particular view in *Buchanan* because a minimal change of terms in a commercial statute like the Carriage of Goods by Road Act seems innocuous enough. Lord Denning's decision had an understandably disquieting effect on his colleagues because a matter of principle, symbolised by a verbal quibble, was at issue. And the reaction of Lord Denning's colleagues was summarised in the motto '*quod judices tot sententiae*'.

The conflict between conceptualism and teleological reasoning symbolises an important aspect of the human condition: a contemporary doubt about the capacity of language to convey meanings precisely. This issue requires the serious attention of the legal community because law is the instrumental language *par excellence*, and past research does not fully address it. Because jurists of the great codification era did not share the doubt, their interpretive techniques did not embody contemporary epistemological assumptions.

Although the period of French codification was characterised by rampant irrationalism at the guillotine, it was also marked by exaggerated rationalism, among lawmakers. The French *philosophes* thought human reason capable of analysing and recomposing the constituent meaning of complex terms of a language; in their view, the human mind could attain precise understandings of nature and experience by moving from simple, narrow notions to broader ones by way of logical operations. The Abbé de Condillac, for instance, devoted extensive efforts to developing *une langue bien faite* in his *Essai sur l'origine des connaissances humaines*[69]. He was con-

68. Merryman, 'The Italian Style I: Doctrine' (1965) 18 Stanford L Rev 39 at 62.

69. A Condillac, Essai sur l'origine des connaissances humaines (2nd edn 1771 Paris, (1st edn. 1746, Paris). More background on the rationalism of civil codification appeared in Herman, 'Command Versus Purpose: The Scylla and Charybdis of the Code Drafter', (1977) 52 Tul L Rev 115 and Herman, 'Legislative Management of History: Notes on the philosophical Foundation of the Civil Code', (1979) 53 Tul L Rev 380.

vinced that a lucid, well constructed language, simple in its elements but comprehensive as well, was the fundamental desideratum of human thought. The notion of *une langue bien faite* was transferred to the arena in which the Code was drafted. According to rationalist notions of codification, the complex feudal restraints of the *ancien régime* could be abolished by coherent, organic legislation in which each institution was carefully delineated and each article precisely crafted in a simple, straightforward style. An outgrowth of the commitment to rationalism was the utopian viewpoint that the Code Napoleon was to be a manual of general commands that a French judge could read to determine proper relations among citizens. The French historian Sagnac summarised the rationalist view of codification.

'The Civil Code should be simple and clear, like the laws of nature. It must be reduced to a small number of articles which flow logically from general principles of the new democratic society. The individual will know the laws that govern him; he will be delivered from the subtleties and infinite complications that chicanery invents at his expense'[70].

If the Civil Codes had fully realised the rationalists' hopes, and laws were objectively knowable, then judges might still be characterised as legal automatons. But our era, in contrast to the codificatory period, seems wedded to the view that there are no objective truths. In an address at Cambridge University in 1944, Friedrich Hayek, the economic theorist, argued that the 'most difficult thing to re-create in Germany (after World War II) will be the belief in the existence of an objective truth, of the possibility of a history . . . not written in the service of a particular interest'[71]. He went on to criticise German historians for their 'extreme ethical neutrality which tended to 'explain' – and thereby seemed to justify – everything by the 'circumstances of the time'[72]. In his view these historians were afraid even 'to call black black and white white'[73]. As much as their political colleagues, they inculcated into their fellow Germans the belief that political acts cannot be measured by moral standards, and that ends justify means. Thus, Heyek argued, future historians needed the courage to say Hitler was a bad man; otherwise the time spent explaining Hitler would only glorify his misdeeds.

Hayek was arguing against extreme ethical relativism, a dangerous doctrine a step removed from nihilism, Nietzche's description of an attitude that would permit everything. If a historian could not call black black and white white, then perhaps he could not distinguish them either. And if he could not distinguish them, then perhaps he

70. P. Sagnac, La legislation civile de la Revolution Françoise (1789-1804) 385 (1898) (author's translation).
71. Hayek, 'Historians and the Future of Europe', *Studies in Philosophy, Politics and Economics* 135 at 140.
72. Ibid., at 141.
73. Ibid.

would not think the distinction mattered. Equally nihilistic was the assertion of the eminent existentialist philosopher, Martin Heidegger, that speech and silence were indistinguishable. From Heidegger, such a statement would be predictable, for he seems to have been infected by a nihilist strain. As rector of Frieburg University in the early 1930s, 'he delivered a number of speeches . . . that may be fairly described as an effort to justify national socialism by assimilating the terms of his own philosophy to those of the popular Nazi vocabulary'[74].

Ethical relativism, like unfettered teleological reasoning, borders on nihilism. Some legal scholars have suggested as much in their criticism of cases such as *Roe v Wade*[75]. For conceptualists and teleologists alike there would be neither legitimacy nor predictability in law if words had no meanings, or only the meanings that eventually emerged from a conflict of subjective incommensurable interests. And the Nazi experience has shown us the danger of granting judges the discretion to be the arbiters of meaning. Hölderlin once said that 'what has always made the state a hell on earth has been precisely that man has tried to make it his heaven'[76]. Assuming the state, through judges, is a permanent fact of life, we would be well advised to avoid the chaos suggested by the maxim *quot judices tot sententiae*. I do not want to be misunderstood as saying that we should abandon teleological reasoning, conceptualism or any other interpretive technique. We are probably doomed to use all these techniques so long as there are cases to be decided under statutory schemes. But the far reaching political implications of the techniques suggests that we employ them soberly and prudently. Otherwise Hoelderlin's hell might be the consequence.*

74. Rosen, *Nihilism: A Philosophical Essay* (1969) 121: '. . . the ease with which Heidegger succeeded in accommodating the teaching of *Being and Time* to the resolute choice of Hitler and the Nazi party provides us with an essential clue to the political philosophy implicit in this ontological analysis of human existence'. Ibid.
75. According to Laurence Tribe, 'nothing in the Supreme Court's opinion provides a satisfactory explanation of why the fetal interest should not be overriding prior to viability'. Tribe (1928) American Constitutional Law 927. The ethical dilemma of balancing incommensurables is well discussed in Ely, 'The Wages of Crying Wolf: A Comment on Roe v Wade', (1973 82 Yale L J 920.
76. Quoted in Hayek, *The Road to Serfdom*, 24 (2nd edn, 1956).

*The author gratefully acknowledges a debt to Professor Mary Ann Glendon, Boston College Law School, for suggesting the theme of this article; and to Professors Cynthia Samuel, Thomas Schoenbaum and Mr Ian Forrester for helpful criticisms of early drafts.

Part III
Variations for Cultures of Law

[8]

NATURAL JUSTICE IN AFRICA*

Max Gluckman

THIS ESSAY presents evidence which shows that Africans always had some idea of natural justice, and of a rule of law that bound their kings, even if they had not developed these indigenous conceptions in abstract terms.[1] Their failure to do so is accounted for by their lack of writing; a written language is to a large extent necessary if people are to elaborate conceptions into some kind of theory.

I

UP UNTIL the end of the eighteenth century there existed in the present area of Natal, in South Africa, several hundred small tribes, living in some degree of peace with one another and waging only periodical wars which did not lead to conquest of one by the other. Towards the year 1800 some of the more powerful tribes, for reasons into which I need not enter, began to conquer their neighbors and to build small kingdoms. After 1816 the pace of

* This article is based on a lecture delivered to a public audience at the University of Aberdeen, by invitation of the Principal, the late Sir Tom Taylor, a distinguished student of natural law in Scots law. A helpful bibliography: PAUL BOHANNAN, JUSTICE AND JUDGMENT AMONG THE TIV (London: Oxford University Press for the International African Institute, 1957); BENJAMIN CARDOZO, NATURE OF THE JUDICIAL PROCESS (New Haven: Yale University Press, 1928); EDWARD EVAN EVANS-PRITCHARD, THE NUER (Oxford: Clarendon Press, 1940); Max Gluckman, *The Kingdom of the Zulu of South Africa,* in MEYER FORTES & EDWARD EVAN EVANS-PRITCHARD (eds.), AFRICAN POLITICAL SYSTEMS (London: Oxford University Press for the International African Institute, 1940); GLUCKMAN, ESSAYS ON LOZI LAND AND ROYAL PROPERTY (Rhodes-Livingstone Paper No. 10, 1943); GLUCKMAN, CUSTOM AND CONFLICT IN AFRICA (Oxford: Blackwell, 1954, 1963); GLUCKMAN, THE JUDICIAL PROCESS AMONG THE BAROTSE OF NORTHERN RHODESIA (Manchester: Manchester University Press; New York: Humanities Press; Glencoe, Illinois: Free Press, 1955); Gluckman, *The Technical Vocabulary of Barotse Jurisprudence,* 61 AMERICAN ANTHROPOLOGIST 743-59 (1959); GLUCKMAN, ORDER AND REBELLION IN TRIBAL AFRICA (London: Cohen and West; Glencoe, Illinois: The Free Press, 1963); GLUCKMAN, THE IDEAS OF BAROTSE JURISPRUDENCE: STORRS LECTURES AT THE YALE LAW SCHOOL, 1963 (New Haven and London: Yale University Press [in press, 1964]); GLUCKMAN, RULE, LAW AND RITUAL IN TRIBAL SOCIETIES (Oxford: Blackwell; New York: New American Library; Chicago: Aldine Press [in press, 1964]); KARL LLEWELLYN & E. ADAMSON HOEBEL, THE CHEYENNE WAY (Norman: University of Oklahoma Press, 1941); John G. Peristiany, *Pokot Sanctions and Social Structure,* 24 AFRICA 17-25 (1954); VICTOR W. TURNER, SCHISM AND CONTINUITY IN AN AFRICAN SOCIETY: A STUDY OF NDEMBU VILLAGE LIFE (Manchester: Manchester University Press, 1957).

1. This essay is devoted, as far as possible, to indigenous African conceptions. On the rule of law in the new states of Africa, see AFRICAN CONFERENCE ON THE RULE OF LAW (Proceedings published by the International Commission of Jurists, 1961).

these wars of domination accelerated, and a certain chief Shaka, head of the small Zulu tribe, emerged as ruler over the whole region of Natal, while his armies were raiding far beyond his own borders. The Zulu achieved fame during their war against the British in 1879, particularly by their defeat of a British corps at the Battle of Isandlwana, which opened the campaign; and their then king Cetshwayo became a byword for savage tyranny. Their first king, Shaka himself, was, in my opinion rightly, regarded by whites as a monstrous tyrant. This is how he acted when the first party of English traders came to visit him. Shaka had assembled tens of thousands of warriors and dancing girls to stage a great exhibition for his visitors. After an exchange of gifts and of welcoming speeches, the English began to converse with him. Suddenly, Shaka made a signal, and a man standing by was seized by his neighbors and executed. This happened to several men; and the English could not find out what offense these men had committed. I am myself inclined to think that Shaka was impressing on the English that he could have them killed as easily as his own people; if so, he succeeded only in scaring one elderly trader who became so fearful (the wonder is that all did not!) that he fell ill and had to leave. Nonetheless, this eyewitness account shows us the picture of a tyrant, killing men at his personal whim; and elsewhere we are told of his ordering the execution of men and their families, and of his confiscating their property.[2]

At its inception, therefore, it appears that there was no rule of law above the king in the Zulu kingdom. Yet Zulu history, even while it exhibits the extent to which the ruler could act outside the law, also gives the best example of how an African king was bound by law — in a legend which at the same time illustrates his power to behave tyrannically. One of the tribes defeated by the Zulu was the Ndwandwe — indeed the Ndwandwe were Shaka's greatest rivals on his road to supreme hegemony in the region. The defeated Ndwandwe fled in many directions: some sections drove northwards to establish their own distant kingdoms by conquest. The main chief of the Ndwandwe founded an independent state nearby, whence a great army returned to attack the Zulu, who defeated it. I give these details to emphasize the acute enmity between Zulu and Ndwandwe. Some Ndwandwe settled among the Swazi, to the north of Zululand. The son of one of these returned many years later to Zululand, in the reign of King Mpande, and was welcomed back. He found that his father's brother, who had remained behind after the tribe's defeat, had taken over his father's cattle; and he sued for these cattle

2. The rise of the Zulu state, and the following legend, are briefly analyzed in Max Gluckman, *The Kingdom of the Zulu of South Africa,* in M. Fortes & E. E. Evans-Pritchard (eds.), African Political Systems 25f. (1940).

and their offspring. His uncle was by that time a favorite of the king, and he pleaded that if the cattle were awarded to his nephew he would be ruined. The king told his favorite that he had no choice; he was bound by the law and had to award the cattle to the rightful owner. But — or so the story goes — that night the king sent a troop of warriors to kill the successful litigant and all his family, so that the favorite might become rightful heir under the law to the cattle. The king's senior son heard of the order, and warned the nephew, who then fled and escaped; and when challenged by his son, the king said he knew nothing of the order to kill, which must have been issued by his councillors. Zulu frequently told me this story to illustrate that the laws of the nation bound the king, as well as his subjects, and that the king could not alter or apply the law to meet his own wishes, or the nation would fall into ruins. They also pointed out that kings could find ways around the law, and were always likely to do so.

This legend — if legend it be — brings out dramatically that even in a recently established African nation there was a conception of "law" as such, of a body of rules which were binding on rulers and subjects alike. Belief in, and adherence to, this body of rules persisted despite the frequent occasions on which some ruler might break the rules. For it was clear to the people that the ruler was acting in a wrongful way, and that he was acting in breach of the law when he committed some capricious action outside the procedure and the scope of the law. The actions of kings were constantly assessed against these procedures and rules; and if they broke the law too frequently, rivals for the kingly power might genuinely raise rebellion against the king to defend the rules, or at least might exploit subjects' grievances to lead an attack on the king for his lawless and tyrannical behavior. Or a section of the nation might for this reason move away into independence from the king. We can only understand the course of African tribal history if we see that men were moved to fight in the name of law and justice against a tyrant. Even the great king Shaka, founder of the nation, was eventually assassinated by two of his brothers and his closest body servant, egged on by his aunt, who was revolted by his constant executions. They justified their action to the nation by pointing to Shaka's tyrannies; and they promised to stop these arbitrary executions and to amend his harsh laws. The assassins even felt compelled to justify their murder, and their future course of action, by messages to this effect to the English traders who had settled where Durban now stands.

I could give examples from the histories of many African tribes to show that they likewise constantly exhibit these contradictory tendencies — belief in a rule of law and justice which bound the king, kings acting tyrannously in disregard of the law and thus provoking rebellion against themselves or their advisers. In these respects African history is not unlike the history of Europe. But I propose now to take this for granted, and to concentrate on the doctrines of the laws, rather than on the practice of kings. When I do this, we shall have an idealistic picture of the situation: for men lived up to the law as little in Africa as elsewhere — and as much.

II

BEFORE WE examine the doctrines of African law, we must first appreciate the general social and economic background within which that law operated. African tribesmen lived mainly in association with their kinsmen of one kind or another, and they fulfilled most of their purposes in life by cooperating with the same sets of fellows. In these small communities they bred, reared, and educated their children; they made their living; they formed a political group, and a religious congregation attending on the same spirits. Hence, any breach of rules in one set of activities provoked disturbance in wide ranges of activity. If a man defaulted in his obligations to his brother, this might affect the production of crops and the herding of cattle; conversely, a quarrel over ownership of land or a cow within this kind of group might lead to severe disruption of general social relationships, and even ultimately to the breakup of the group. Thus, when a case came to be argued before the judges, they conceived their task to be not only detecting who was in the wrong and who in the right, but also the readjustment of the generally disturbed social relationships, so that these might be saved and persist. They had to give a judgment on the matter in dispute, but they had also, if possible, to reconcile the parties, while maintaining the general principles of law. It is in this process of achieving reconciliation, while abiding by the law, that I believe we can see most clearly the doctrine of natural justice present in Africa. It it thus best exhibited in trial cases, and unfortunately few anthropologists or lawyers have recorded these in detail. Perhaps I may then be forgiven if I begin with citations of cases I myself heard tried in the courts of the Barotse of Northwestern Rhodesia.[3]

The dominant tribe of the Barotse dwells in a great flood plain on the Upper Zambezi; and they exploit a variety of arable soils, pastures, and fishing sites from villages built on small islands in the plain. When I asked them for the laws of land tenure, they told me again and again that under their law a man had to live in a village to use the land resources

3. I have cited numerous cases with an analysis of each in MAX GLUCKMAN, THE JUDICIAL PROCESS AMONG THE BAROTSE OF NORTHERN RHODESIA (1955).

attached to it: if he left the village, he lost his rights to the land in it.[4] Here are two contrasting cases arising out of this situation. In the first case,[5] three nephews of the headman of the village sued for their rights to work gardens which belonged to the village. They had left the village and built new homes nearby. They argued that trouble for them in the village had begun when their cousin, the headman's son, had seduced the wife of one of them, and then failed to pay the damages awarded by a court. When his cuckolded cousin complained, the adulterer insulted him; and when the cuckold and his brothers went on to complain to the headman, they alleged that he told them to get out of the village. They left the village. They now found that their cousin was working their land and taking the fruits of their trees. The cousin's defense was an admission that he had committed the adultery, but he counterpleaded in excuse that the eldest of the three plaintiffs had himself also committed adultery with the wife of a kinsman. He denied that they were driven out of the village, but asserted that they left it in the night. He then complained of a long series of actions by the plaintiffs in which they stinted his father, who had been their guardian since their own father's death. He then went on:

> After they left, they told me that they had put magical substances against thieves on the mangoes, so the children should not enter [lest they get bitten by snakes]. Can you do this, get your child bitten by a snake? . . . [And] how can a man who has moved work gardens that he has left? There is the law of the Whitemen, about cleaning the village of weeds: will they be clearing in the village, or my wives? Is it fair for them to have gardens there, and live elsewhere? My hens and children and calves will enter their gardens. If they live in the village it balances out, for theirs will enter my gardens. But it is not the same if they live elsewhere.

The headman began his own evidence with a diatribe against the wickedness and irresponsibility of modern youth. He described how he had raised his nephews after his brother's death, complained that they stinted him of many things and of help, and denied that he had driven them out of the village.

After some attempt to get at the truth of these various allegations (which I have shortened considerably), both through witnesses and through cross-

4. Full data on land tenure are given in MAX GLUCKMAN, ESSAYS ON LOZI LAND AND ROYAL PROPERTY (1943), while I analyze Barotse relations of property holding in *The Technical Vocabulary of Barotse Jurisprudence,* 61 AMERICAN ANTHROPOLOGIST 743-59 (1959). This essay is to be published shortly, with others dealing with Barotse juristic conceptions, in THE IDEAS OF BAROTSE JURISPRUDENCE: STORRS LECTURES AT THE YALE LAW SCHOOL, 1963.

5. This case is reported fully in GLUCKMAN, *op. cit. supra* note 3, at 37-45.

examination, one judge asked the headman: "Do you want your nephews back?" He said he did; and they then affirmed they wanted to return. Their cousin also said he wanted them back. The judges got the old man to admit that his son was in the wrong, as well as his nephews. On this basis, the various judges all entered judgment that the nephews lost their gardens unless they returned to the village; but they accompanied this clear statement of the law with homilies to all the parties: to the old headman that he should not favor his own son against his nephews instead of enquiring impartially into disputes between them; to the headman's son for committing adultery with his kinsman's wife and for trying to treat his kinsmen as serfs, on the possibly unwarranted assumption that he would succeed his father as headman; to the three plaintiffs for not being generous and helpful to their uncle. Around the main judgment there were therefore woven sermons on living together in parental, filial, and brotherly love, and on taking the chances of the depredations of each other's stock and children and crops in mutual tolerance. The nephews were ordered home, and all were warned they would be fined if they started quarrelling again.

In this case, we see the court applying the law that you cannot work gardens unless you live in a village, in such a way as to bring about a reconciliation between kinsmen who were in danger of quarrelling irremediably. They did so in terms of a rule of law, clearly stated. In another case, the court applied the same rule of law in a quite different way.

This second case[6] also involves the rights of persons, not resident in a village, to use its resources, which are vested in the title of the village headman. There was a certain village headman named Mahalihali, who was so quarrelsome that his bad temper drove many people out of the village. He personally expelled one of his daughters, whom he had accused of sorcery. Eventually he died and his son inherited his position, and took his title as Mahalihali the Second. He found himself with a village, and few villagers. His nephew, son of his sister expelled from the village by their father as a sorceress, was using some of the trap sites in a fish dam belonging to the village, but was living with his widowed mother in her mother's village. Another sister of the new headman had married into a nearby village, and her sons were using a fish dam which her father had let her have. The new headman brought suit that his sisters and their sons must stop using the fish dam unless they moved into his village. The judges satisfied themselves that the one sister, accused of sorcery, had been badly wronged when she was driven out of the village. Since then she and her son had behaved with

6. This case is fully reported in *id.* at 178-187.

proper respect to their kinsman, the headman. Hence the judges found themselves in a dilemma. The law was clear: if you do not live in the village, you lose your rights in its land. By this rule the headman was right in his claim that the others join his village or cease to use its fish dams. But the defendants had not done him any wrong, and the headman was behaving unjustly — like the dog in the manger in our fable. The resident villagers had more fishing sites than they could use. How did the judges solve this dilemma?

In Barotse courts when the judges come to give their decision, the most junior judge speaks, and then his seniors in turn, until the head of the court gives judgment. This is the binding decision — as in our courts-martial — even if it contradicts the verdicts of all other judges, though it is referred to the king in his palace for confirmation. The first three judges felt themselves to be bound by the basic premise of their land-tenure law: the dog-in-the-manger headman was entitled to expel his sisters and their sons from the dams unless they moved into his village. But they all stressed that he ought not to treat his relatives in this niggardly way since there was more land than his villagers could use; being rich, he ought to help his relatives. Nevertheless, the dams were his. The next set of judges were reluctant to apply the letter of the law in favor of the headman, against people who, in their words, had "done nothing wrong." Many judges told the headman, "If they had done wrong, you would have a case." Most judges therefore contented themselves with stating the moral issue, that he ought to let his relatives fish. One said that the fish dams had passed out of his control, though this opinion broke with the basic law of Barotse landholding. But the senior judge sitting in court returned to this basic law: the dams were the headman Mahalihali's. He too exhorted the headman to be generous and let his kin fish them; but he insisted that "We cannot change the law against Mahalihali." Like us the Barotse consider that "hard cases make bad law." They say, "It is hard, but it is the law." As it happened, the head of the court was busy on administrative business elsewhere. Next day he came to deliver his decision on the basis of reports of evidence and judgments made to him by other judges. He found the headman still insisting on his right to take the dams unless the others moved to join him, as laid down in the last decision. In this dilemma the head of the court found a brilliant solution. The dams clearly belonged to the title Mahalihali; but if the present incumbent of that title were not upright and generous to his kin who did not live with him, the court would discharge him from the headmanship and appoint a more generous successor.

What happened here was that the judge achieved a just and equitable solution by stressing a new kind of sanction. He invoked the administrative powers of the court to discharge unsatisfactory headmen, in order to compel a headman to be generous in exercising his rights. In this way, the judge enforced standards of generosity on the headman in favor of defendants who had done no wrong, while he maintained the basic law of land tenure. The fish dams remained vested in the headman's title.

I have argued[7] that we can understand the rebellions against tyrants which were frequent in African kingdoms, only if we understand that the people thought that those who are powerful should be just and merciful, fair as well as law-abiding: thus they had general standards for assessing royal actions. Similarly, I maintain that we cannot understand how judges come to a decision on a case unless we recognize that they operate with certain values which enable them to take a moral position on the issues, and that they then try to state the law in terms of those issues. Only in this way can we explain why in the first dispute over resources the judges should unanimously have insisted on the imposition of the rule that a man cannot work land of a village and live elsewhere; they had come to the conclusion that all the litigants, including the headman, had defaulted from the standards required of them, but that a statement of the law in favor of the headman could be used to induce the departed young men to return, while they brought pressure on the headman to receive them. In the second case, they were faced by a real dilemma: enforcement of the rule would have entailed inflicting loss on people who had done nothing wrong; but not to enforce the rule would have been going against a fundamental part of the land-tenure system and the social relations based upon it. To vary the law to meet hard cases is recognized as leading to uncertainty and insecurity in social life. Happily, the head of the court saw a just way out, in which the righteous would be defended while the law would be maintained. This kind of "hunch" of where the moral merits of a case lie, and the manner in which judges follow this hunch to choose between the alternatives open to them, embody those ideas of justice which are current in a particular society at a particular time.

We must start by recognizing that the rules and custom of a society — its body of law — do not form an internally consistent and logically interdependent set of principles. The whole trend of recent research on tribal societies by social anthropologists is to emphasize the independence of social rules and principles of grouping, and to analyze the manner in which they

7. The argument is set out more fully, with reference to the works of other anthropologists, in MAX GLUCKMAN, ORDER AND REBELLION IN TRIBAL AFRICA (1963) and in RULE, LAW AND RITUAL IN TRIBAL SOCIETIES (in press, 1964), where it is applied to a greater variety of states.

set discrepant and even conflicting processes of action at work.[8] Tribal society is no longer seen as structured by harmoniously balanced principles; instead, the customs and values which associate persons in the pursuit of their goal are also seen to produce conflicts of interest between them. This is something that is inherent in the very nature of social life; and we can see it more clearly in tribal cultures than in our own, because the tribes have a higher development of custom which creates and exaggerates differences between people as well as the links between them. For example, there are in tribal societies a whole series of customs which exaggerate the biological difference between sexes, by rigidly defining the division of labor between men and women and tabooing any breach of this division. Beyond this, beliefs such as those of some tribes in an inherent antagonism, yet essential interdependence, between the sexes with femininity containing the polluting evil of menstruation and witchcraft as well as the good of fertility, stress the conflict as well as complementariness that resides in so basic a social group as the family.

These beliefs emphasize for us that the roles of persons and groups in any society force upon them independent action under various rules. Hence we should not expect the laws of any tribe to form a consistent logical system, any more than do the laws of England. Lord Halsbury said of English law:

> A case is only an authority for what it actually decides. I entirely deny that it can be quoted for a proposition that may seem logically to follow from it. Such a mode of reasoning assumes that the law is necessarily a logical code, whereas every lawyer must acknowledge that the law is not logical at all.[9]

Given the variety of rules of law, and the fact that many of them are independent of another, how do judges select what rules to apply in a particular case? In the Barotse cases I have just cited, there is no logical association between the rules involved. One rule states that the resources of a village are vested in the title of its headman; another that a man should live in a village if he is to use its resources; another that any kinsman is entitled to use the wealth of one of his ancestral villages; another that a person who leaves a village loses his rights to resources in it; another that when a woman leaves a village to marry she is going to what Barotse call "her work"; another that a woman expelled for alleged sorcery is driven from

8. This view has been developed by many anthropologists, and has been applied to a variety of problems in popular exposition by MAX GLUCKMAN, CUSTOM AND CONFLICT IN AFRICA (1954, 1963) and also RULE, LAW AND RITUAL IN TRIBAL SOCIETIES. The fullest development in analysis of an African society in these terms is in VICTOR TURNER, SCHISM AND CONTINUITY IN AN AFRICAN SOCIETY (1957).

9. In Quinn v. Leathem, [1901] A. C. 495, 506, as quoted by BENJAMIN CARDOZO, NATURE OF THE JUDICIAL PROCESS 32 (1928).

the village, and does not leave it; another that the law must not be altered to meet the circumstances of a hard case; another that the court may discharge an unsatisfactory headman; and still another that a person should not be penalized unless he has committed some wrong. The judges had to select which of these rules they would apply in a particular dispute, and how they would combine those selected. The dominant factor influencing their choice was their judgment of who was in the right and who in the wrong. The rules were therefore arranged in a hierarchy of a kind, and in the cases here the supreme rule was that no one should be penalized unless he has done wrong.[10]

III

IN THE VOLUMINOUS literature on the law of nature, the law of nature is divorced from the process by which judges apply law to particular situations of dispute: the main discussion is on the rules of law extant at any time, and whether these can be assessed against any general law. This discussion raises problems of the relation between state and law; and it shows how in different eras the law of nature has been invoked by various protagonists to argue for preservation of the status quo or for the revolution of society. I am here not concerned with these important problems, since I am discussing relatively stable societies and their law. Perforce I concentrate on the problem of how far the systems of African law embody general principles of ethics which Africans themselves conceive of in the way that Europe's tradition spoke of as natural law. As far as this aspect of the problem is concerned, I wonder why more attention has not been paid to the judicial process by at least Anglo-American lawyers in discussions of natural law. It is true that the idea of natural law seems to be an importation into English law from Roman law, canon law, and in recent centuries continental jurisprudence; and the indigenous English parallel conception is that of "equality."

The long tradition of writing about the fundamental nature of law in Europe has been divorced from the application of law to specific disputes, perhaps because the writings that survive are the books of ethical and legal philosophers, and treatises on the rules of law, rather than detailed records of how decisions were taken in particular disputes. When judgments survive, from ancient and medieval times, they are usually the bare bones of decisions. Moreover, it may have required the development of a highly hetero-

10. On this hierarchy see GLUCKMAN, *op. cit. supra* note 3, at 295f. The same impression emerges from KARL LLEWELLYN & E. ADAMSON HOEBEL, THE CHEYENNE WAY (1941).

geneous society, with widespread acknowledgment of varied social interests and values, to focus investigation on the nature of the judicial process — on what judges actually do in court with the law. This kind of investigation is a comparatively recent line of full-blown research; and significantly it has produced, particularly in the United States, highly iconoclastic studies of law, many of which seem to throw out the idea of certainty of law. As an anthropologist, I made it my duty to sit in African courts and record the full details of cases, from the point before they came to court, through pleas and evidence, to final judgment. This experience made me concentrate on how far in judgments on particular disputes Africans were influenced by general principles of ethics. Among the Barotse at least this influence seemed a marked feature. Judges — good judges — were moved to come down on one side rather than the other by what they call *ngana,* which can be translated as "sense" or "reason"; and they explained to me the principles which guided their reason as *milao yabutu,* the laws of humankind, which I think are fairly equivalent to the law of nature in our tradition.[11]

I may, therefore, be using natural law and natural justice in a rather heterodox sense. I have some authority for doing this. Justice Cardozo in his analysis of the nature of the judicial process pointed out that it is in decision making that the sense of natural justice comes into its own. The sense of justice, he says, moves a judge so that, in the words of a French jurist whom Cardozo quotes, "One wills at the beginning the result; one finds the principle afterwards; such is the genesis of all juridical construction. Once accepted, the construction presents itself, doubtless, in the ensemble of legal doctrine. . . ." It is true that the ability of the judge to follow his sense of justice may be restricted by legal rules, and may be influenced, to quote Cardozo himself, by his own "likes and . . . dislikes . . . predilections and prejudices, the complex of instincts and emotions and habits, which make the man, whether he be litigant or judge."[12] But there is in every judgment a balancing of decisions, and a choice between alternatives, in which judicial creativity comes to the fore; and it is here that certain wide principles of morality enter into the law. I consider that they enter even in those cases where the judge feels compelled by the rules of law to find for a litigant even against what he feels to be justice in the particular case. He is here obeying the moral principle that the law must not be altered to meet the hard facts of a particular case; and a good judge in these circumstances will take care to point this out to the successful litigant, and to deliver an exhortation on the moral merits of the case. In the Barotse case of the headman who reclaimed

11. See, for a fuller exposition, GLUCKMAN, *op. cit. supra* note 3, ch. IV.
12. BENJAMIN CARDOZO, NATURE OF THE JUDICIAL PROCESS 178, 179 (1928).

his fish dams from his sisters, even those judges who said the dams were his, emphasized that he ought not to take them; the genius of the last judge was that he saw the court had lawful power to compel the headman not to insist on his rights against justice.

I am not arguing that all laws are in every sense just, and that every case in all lands is solved in such a way as to achieve a just result, in terms of some ultimate discoverable body of ethical rules common to all mankind. In many systems of law, both simple and complex, certain rules have a rigidity that constrain judges to apply them in all circumstances. Most systems of law have rules which appear to inflict constant hardship on certain categories of persons, in defiance even of their own principles of ethics — such as the laws about slavery, or about the position of women. Usually societies with these laws also evolve elaborate arguments to justify the special positions of such persons, by reconciling, often in terms of a pseudoscientific theory, their special position with a society's own general principles of ethics; and many of these principles of ethics are indeed common to all societies of men. Nevertheless the rules operate within a specific type of social organization, which controls what Kohler has called the "jural postulates" of a system of law — the principles and presuppositions of that system.

IV

THESE OFTEN contradictory tendencies can be further illustrated by another African society, very different in type from the Barotse. Dr. Peristiany has reported a vendetta which developed among the Pokot of East Africa. The Pokot are a tribe which has not developed any administrative system or governmental apparatus, so that they do not have judges who can sit on disputes and give enforceable decisions. The tribe contains a number of clans which have themselves to redress wrongs done to their members; and each clan is required, under a duty of blood vengeance, to demand compensation for the killing of one of its members. Each killing is liable to start a vendetta. The best account of a vendetta which Peristiany collected began some sixty years earlier when a man of one clan killed a member of another clan during night fighting against foreign invaders. The killer's clan admitted guilt and liability; and they offered a minimum of compensation as a gesture, maintaining that since the murder occurred by accident in a fight against common foes, the full payment should not be claimed. The dead man's clan insisted on full compensation, though they were adjured by neutral elders to take much less. The killer's kin paid in full; but this event started a rankling state of hostility which lasted over sixty years, with each side seizing the slightest excuse to make demands on the other.[13] Since this was the best account of a vendetta which Peristiany obtained, sixty years later, under pax Britannica, clearly unusual circumstances have sharpened the attention paid to it: and these circumstances were that a man who had not done wrong, had been threatened as if he had. Notice that the killer's clan did not deny guilt and liability to pay compensation: that is, they did not attempt to deny the law, or its requirement that compensation be paid. This had to be met; but they felt that the innocence from murderous intent of their man and the fact that he killed by accident while defending a joint homeland against hostile invaders, should be recognized by acceptance of token payment. And neutral elders affirmed that this was just.

There is a folk tale which Professor Evans-Pritchard tells me is current over the whole of Northeast Africa and the Middle East which summarizes the manner in which a sense of justice may be outraged by the rigid application of the law of vengeance — the demand of an eye for an eye and a tooth for a tooth. A man once fell out of a tree on top of a member of a different clan, who was killed. The killer's clan offered compensation of blood money, but the victim's kin insisted on their claim to kill the killer. They persisted in this claim before the judge, who then ordered that they were entitled to do this; but the law required that the killer be killed in exactly the same way as his victim. Hence he ordered the killer to walk to and fro under the tree while the victim's kin took turns in falling on him until he was killed. Indeed, here was a Daniel come to judgment. Those demanding blood of vengeance said they would now prefer to take blood money; but the judge said they had lost their opportunity to do this. Those who have refused mercy under one alternative in the law cannot then expect, when this turns to their disadvantage, to avail themselves of other remedies.

Barotse would call the reasons which guided this judge of the folk tale, "wisdom" and "sense"[14] — just as when I asked them why they thought the final judgment that the dog-in-the-manger headman must be generous or he would be discharged, was a good judgment, they said because the judge decided by "truth" and "reason" and "wisdom." My own attendants explained to me that everyone could see that the headman was wrong, the defendants in the right: those judges who held therefore that the dams belonged to the headman's kin were weak judges, lacking the courage to face the consequences of maintaining the rules of law through hard cases; those judges who said the dams were the headman's had this courage, an essential attribute of the good judge, but they lacked the wisdom of the judge who saw how the law could

13. John G. Peristiany, *Pokot Sanctions and Social Structure,* 24 AFRICA 17-25 (1954).
14. GLUCKMAN, *op. cit. supra* note 3, ch. III.

be maintained while truth and right was served. This "truth," my informants told me, was that a man who had done no harm should not be penalized; and when I asked them where they got this, they said it was a law of God, and a law of mankind. Furthermore, they said that all peoples recognized that this was right, even the Whites; hence they also called it a "law of nations." It was to them a self-evident proposition, and they could not see why I bothered to try to work out how they arrived at it. Was it not obviously just? Similarly, how could I expect them to justify to me the proposition that "if you are invited to a meal and a fishbone sticks in your throat, you cannot sue your host"? — the equivalent of the Roman Law maxim, *volenti non fit injuria.*[15] Again, they thought this came from the very *ngana,* the reason, of men. In their own activities, this meant that if a man went on one of those fishing parties where crowds of men enter a pool and throw bundles of spears blindly into the bottom to get mudfish, he could not sue if he got a spear in the foot — unless he could prove malice. If a man goes in a dugout on the waters, to fish or to travel, he is doubly debarred from suing for injury, for in addition to the voluntary risk taken, the Barotse hold that it is self-evident that "fire and water are other lords," i.e., the dangers of river and fire are so swift and terrible that no action can be founded on accidents arising from them.

I could give other examples of fundamental ethical rules which the Barotse hold to arise from the very reason of men, from the fact that they are human beings and not animals. Not all these rules are found in all African tribes: for example, in Central Africa only the Barotse bar suits arising from accidents caused by fire and river. Many rules are common to large areas of Africa; and like the rule on assumption of risk, some are common to other systems of law. The Barotse, for instance, say in effect,[16] again like the Romans, that *ex turpi causa non oritur actio* (no action arises from an immoral agreement), and *in pari delicto potior est conditio defendentis* (in equal guilt the position of the defendant is stronger). But in suits involving this kind of judgment, Barotse judges are likely to fine all the parties; in their unspecialized courts, a civil suit can be converted by the judges into a criminal action. If wrongdoers have been foolish enough to appeal to the law to protect them in their wrongdoing, they run the risk of punishment.

Besides this body of rules, springing from reason itself, the Barotse think that certain kinds of social institutions are necessarily common to all mankind, in all societies. All men, they say, must have laws enforcing respect for chiefs and elders, controlling marriage, tabooing sexual relations between certain kinds of kin though these may vary from tribe to tribe, ordaining respect to

15. *Id.* at 206, 252n., 325.
16. *Id.* at 204f.

and avoidance of senior in-laws. Without these institutions, men would not be men, but animals. I once heard a group of Barotse men discuss whether the Bushmen hunters who live in Western Barotseland were human beings. One man said they were not, for they neither cultivated nor tended cattle. As soon as I described Bushman marriage and taboos on marriage to near kin, and their funeral rites, he said: "They are indeed men, with laws of humankind." Similarly when this point was discussed in the king's palace, the king said: "They are men. Once in Liuwa I shot a giraffe. The Bushmen came and hovered on the edge of the forest. We offered them meat: they came running, crouched before us as chiefs, cut up the meat and cooked it for us. They know kingship, and so they are of humankind."

The Barotse to a large extent use the phrases "law of humankind" and "law of nations" interchangeably in many contexts — as the Romans used *ius naturale* and *ius gentium*. These phrases cover both this generality of certain basic human institutions which all men must have, and certain principles of ethics which Barotse believe all men must see. If anyone lacks these institutions and does not see the ethical principles, then he is not of humankind. But they distinguish between rules of ethics and institutions, by referring also to the rules of ethics as "laws of God." Unfortunately, the early missionaries who recorded Barotse ideas in the last century did not cover these ideas: it may well be that these formulations are influenced by Christian doctrines which have been preached among Barotse and widely accepted by them. The Barotse say that after God had created the world and begotten men, He was so horrified and indeed frightened by the cunning of the first man and his way of murdering animals that He withdrew into heaven and ceased to take an active interest in the affairs of men. This story may well have been held together with the belief that God gave reason and perception of morality to men: the Barotse would not be the first people to hold inconsistent ideas. Nevertheless, it is possible that we are here dealing with an association of morality with God that was influenced by Christianity, though the evidence indicates that the idea of laws of humankind is genuinely indigenous.

Barotse talk today about their widest conceptions of morality as "laws of God," and they use the same phrase to cover both the regularities of the natural environment in which they live and the physiological and psychological processes of men and women. For them too, as for the ancient world, there is a close similarity between what we think of as the physical laws of nature and the fundamental rules of social morality. It is worth emphasizing that the physical laws of nature, insofar as their knowledge goes, provide a framework within which their judges make decisions on evidence: they assess facts against their knowledge of the growth of crops, the rise and fall of the flood, the periods of gestation and "normal" fertility rates of women and animals, their presumptions about the psychology of men and women, fathers, spouses, mistresses and their lovers.[17]

Though all mankind that they know have the same basic social institutions, the Barotse, dominating as they do over twenty-five tribes of alien culture, recognize that there is considerable variation in the form of these institutions. Their own secular and ritual customs and beliefs differ in many respects from those of other tribes, and there is no wrong in most of the practices of those tribes. Thus while Barotse favor succession through males, though succession through females is frequent, they recognize that under the law of other tribes succession is only in the female line; and they will adjudicate these tribes' cases in terms of this law. Again, some tribes marry the daughters of a father's sister, and of a mother's brother, women who rank as "sisters" in Barotse law and are tabooed as spouses; but they do not deny the validity of such marriages among these tribes. As the head of a court once said to a foreign litigant: "There is no path of slavery in this court. . . . A foreigner sues by the customs of the foreigner; a Barotse sues by the customs of the Barotse."[18] Some alien practices, like wife-lending, they forbid, as against public morals.

The morality and institutions of the Barotse nevertheless embody certain inequalities. In theory, all persons who come to court are equal before the law, in that they will be listened to carefully and allowed to lead evidence for their case without interruption. A judge should not take a decision after hearing only one side of a case; and he must judge impartially. Indeed, if he has an interest in the case, he should excuse himself. But each litigant comes before the court in terms of the inequalities which are involved in his or her social position. Thus, under the divorce laws, a man who tires of his wife can divorce her simply by sending her home to her people under escort of one of his kin. A woman has to sue in court and establish grounds for divorce, if she wishes to break with her husband. After all, he paid cattle to gain rights over her, and some rights over her children; and while he can abandon these rights himself, she is subject in some respects to his demands. I have heard many wives claim that their husbands neglected them and did not treat them properly, and that therefore they were entitled to divorce, but they had their suits rejected. Yet the husband must convince the court that he regards the woman as his wife and will treat her as such. Thus, when a husband refused to appear in court to answer his wife's suit, the court heard her evidence and held that he no longer cared for her, but was holding on to her so that he could secure cattle as damages if she committed adultery. Judgment was

17. *Id.* at 268f.
18. *Id.* at 211.

given against him in default, on the grounds that "no one shall place [a woman] in slavery, to make her a trap, in order to get cattle from people."[19]

There were serfs — prisoners of war — in Barotseland, till they were freed under pressure from the British. In general, serfs were regarded as quasi-kinsmen, and were supposed to be treated as children by their master. One of their disabilities was that they could not leave their master's village, and theoretically their master also held power of life and death over them, and could treat them as he pleased. But I met serfs whose masters had treated them so badly that they ran to the palace to claim the king's protection; and after hearing the case, the king had ruled that the master was unfit to own serfs and would never again be allowed to do so, because serfs were entitled to be treated as human beings. The king took the abused serfs under his own protection.

V

WHEN I DISCUSS the general principles which pervade Barotse law, and cite certain key cases to illustrate these, I necessarily give an idyllic picture of Barotse law, whereas their life was full of hardship and often of cruelty. Kings dealt with their enemies severely; and accusations of witchcraft and sorcery to account for people's misfortunes led to many executions. Some rich and powerful persons would in need try to pillage the poor and escape the consequences of their actions. But we must remember that Barotse law was applied in circumstances where commercial traffic had developed little, and where rich and poor lived at approximately the same standard, since there were neither luxuries nor other means for the rich to elevate their own standard of living. Hence they distributed their land to acquire dependents, and they dispensed of their plenty to acquire social power. In this situation, the main grounds for tyranny and caprice on the part of kings lay in the exercise of power itself, and arose from fears, real and fancied, of intrigues against their persons. Even the most tyrannical kings had reputations for great generosity with their goods. Meanwhile, as far as judges were concerned, their central task was, as we have seen, to adjust disputes between closely related people; and their judgments were — and in this kind of case still are — veritable sermons on the importance of living together in generous loving kindness, sharing the vicissitudes of life in a spirit of mutual helpfulness and give-and-take.

19. Many of the cases cited in MAX GLUCKMAN, THE JUDICIAL PROCESS AMONG THE BAROTSE OF NORTHERN RHODESIA, deal with these problems. The position of women, in inequality, is summarized at 216f.

Bohannan, who studied the judgments of the Tiv of Nigeria, has shown that this situation produced a somewhat complex evaluation of the concept of "truth," a point that I missed among the Barotse. To get to the heart of a dispute, at what the Barotse described as its *niti,* a word which also means "truth" in our sense, is to see the solution that establishes and proclaims settled law and achieves justice, yet at the same time reconciles the disputing parties and prevents the breaking-up of their relationship. In this sense, the head of the court saw "the truth" of the dispute in the case of the headman's fish dams.

The Tiv whom Bohannan studied are a tribe that had no instituted governmental system before the coming of the British who established courts. Bohannan tells us that they have a word *yie,* which can mean a "lie" or a "broken promise." But to tell a *yie* is also "to say something or make a remark which disturbs the even flow of social relationships." "It make no difference," Bohannan says, "whether the remark is true or false, in the sense that we use these words in English, *unless* it be to someone's detriment, in which case it is worse to tell a false *yie* than a true one." Set against *yie,* are two words. One of them, *mimi* in Tiv, is used in contexts where we speak of morally good things, and means to tell that version of the story which does least damage to social relationships from one's own point of view. In this version each litigant is likely to be doing damage to the relationships from his opponent's point of view. But the Tiv also use the word *vough,* which describes a truly straight row in making a farm mound or setting something upright, to cover a statement of the precise facts in a story. A witness, as against a litigant, should speak *vough,* i.e., straightforwardly. Bohannan states, however, that no one would blame a witness if he did not tell the precise facts, and indeed told untruths, if by so doing he smoothed social relationships and enabled judges to give a verdict in which both litigants could concur. Hence Bohannan concludes from this that "truth" in Tivland is an

> elusive matter because smooth social relationships are deemed of higher cultural value than mere precision of fact. We must not judge Tiv litigants or witnesses by our standards. They are not liars, as they are sometimes called: their truth has other referents than has European truth.[20]

I consider that Bohannan here raises an important problem in understanding the process of reconciliation — the idea of avoiding the rupture of social relationships — which is one of the dominant moral principles that should guide a good African judge. Among the Barotse, a judge who, in a lawsuit between kin, rushes into cross-examination and judgment on the apparent issue of dispute, without drawing out the parties so as to try to

20. Paul Bohannan, Justice and Judgment Among the Tiv 50 (1957).

reconcile them, is a bad judge, so estimated by the people. In order to reconcile, a judge must be cautious, discreet, and tactful; and a witness may well exercise considerable discretion and tact so as not to exacerbate disturbed relations between the parties. For this, the Barotse would approve him, even while they demand from him the precise truth or facts. I would suggest that Bohannan has been misled in his comparison, because while he has worked with the several contexts in which the Tiv words are used, he has contrasted them with only two English concepts — truth and untruth. But other concepts in English deal with the same phenomena as he finds in Tivland: the white lie, tact, and discretion are but three. I wish to insist on this equivalence as against Bohannan, because he represents a school which stresses mainly the differences between African law and European law, and overlooks similarities. I think that on this point he has gone astray. Moreover, he has compared Tiv acting in courts established by the British with witnesses and litigants in our own courts. I wonder what standards a lawyer sets for those who are acting as witnesses when he attempts to achieve a family settlement, or an arbitrator trying to settle an industrial dispute. Here too I suspect that truth is often advisedly tempered with discretion, if a settlement is to be achieved. There are ways of stating facts so as to exacerbate relationships, and ways of stating facts so that these relationships are smoothed. We have to take lawyers and arbitrators into account as part of our whole system of law, and not insist on studying courts of law alone. And African courts are in some respects like family councils, even though the judges lay down authoritative decisions — which does make them courts.

I have said that I would like to insist on making a comparison of the Tiv concepts with the full range of our own concepts, because only then do we arrive at the heart, the truth, of what is involved in processes of law in Africa. I consider that there we find certain principles of morality which arise from the very fact that men live together, cooperating and conflicting. Their cooperation demands that men be discreet, that society aim at not penalizing those who have done no wrong and attempt to assist those judged to be in the right, that when a dispute is heard truth tempered by discretion is valued. Institutions and inequalities vary from society to society, and the study of these differences is most important. In some societies, people may not even be aware of hardships falling on certain classes of people, though often there is an explicit attempt to reconcile this unequal treatment with another theory which holds all people equal before the law. They may be foreigners, not neighbors, for all peoples say, "love thy neighbor as thyself"; or there may be a myth to justify their position — as among the warlike Masai, who hold blacksmiths in despite because they make the weapons which kill men. History is full of injustice and cruel afflictions perpetrated by men on men; and African history is no less full of these than is the history of the rest of the world. Yet I think that our studies of African law demonstrate that all men, because they live in society, have some theory of rules of justice which they believe arise from reason itself; and my own evidence on the Barotse — the only evidence we have — suggests that Africans may well have formulated, in embryonic form at least, a theory of natural justice, coming from human-kindness itself.[21]

21. E. E. Evans-Pritchard, in his study of the Nuer, whose fierceness and quarrelsomeness he has described vividly, also writes (THE NUER 171 [1940]):

> The Nuer has a keen sense of personal dignity and rights. The notion of right, *cuong,* is strong. It is recognized that a man ought to obtain redress for certain wrongs. This is not a contradiction of the statement that threat of violence is the main sanction for payment of compensation, but is in accord with it, for a man's kinsmen will only support him if he is right. It is doubtless true that if a man is weak it is unlikely that his being in the right will enable him to obtain satisfaction, but if he is in the right he will have the support of his kin and his opponent will not, and to resort to violence or to meet it the support of one's kin and the approval of one's community are necessary. One may say that if a man has right on his side and, in virtue of that, the support of his kinsmen and they are prepared to use force, he stands a good chance of obtaining what is due to him, so long as the parties to the dispute live near one another.

I.e., so long as they are neighbors. Even in waging the vendetta, and in enforcing rights by self-help, a judgment of right and wrong guides alignments and judgments.

[9]

THE RULE OF LAW VERSUS THE ORDER OF CUSTOM*

BY STANLEY DIAMOND

Creon: Knowest thou the edict has forbidden this?
Antigone: I knew it well. Why not? It was proclaimed.
Creon: But thou didst dare to violate the law?
Antigone: It was not God above who framed that law,
Nor justice, whispering from the underworld,
Nor deemed I thy decrees were of such force
As to o'er ride the sanctities of heaven;
Which are not of today or yesterday.
From whom—whence they first issued, no one knows.
I was not like to scant their holy rites
And brave the even justice of the gods
For fear of someone's edict.

(Sophocles, *Antigone*)

The lowest police employee of the civilized state has more "authority" than all the organs of gentilism combined. But the mightiest prince and the greatest statesman or general of civilization may look with envy on the spontaneous and undisputed esteem that was the privilege of the least gentile sachem. The one stands in the middle of society, the other is forced to assume a position outside and above it.

(Friedrich Engels, *Origin of the Family, Private Property and the State*)

There's too much due process of law. The electric chair is a cheap crime deterrent to show these criminal elements that law and order is going to triumph.

(Detective Sergeant John Heffernan, current vice-president of the International Conference of Police Associations and head of the New Jersey State Police Benevolent Association)

I

We must distinguish the rule of law from the authority of custom. In a recent effort to do so (which I shall critically examine because it is so typical), Paul Bohannan, under the *imprimatur*

* Author's Note—This article, in slightly different form, appears in *The Rule of Law*, Robert Paul Wolff, ed., New York: Simon & Schuster.

of the *International Encyclopedia of the Social Sciences*,[1] contends that laws result from "double" institutionalization. He means by this no more than the lending of a specific force, a cutting edge, to the functioning of "customary" institutions: marriage, the family, religion. But, he tells us, the laws so emerging assume a character and dynamic of their own. They form a structured, legal dimension of society; they do not merely reflect, but interact with given institutions. Therefore, Bohannan is led to maintain that laws are typically out of phase with society and it is this process which is both a symptom and cause of social change. The laws of marriage, to illustrate Bohannan's argument with the sort of concrete example his definition lacks, are not synonymous with the institution of marriage. They reinforce certain rights and obligations while neglecting others. Moreover, they subject partners defined as truant to intervention by an external, impersonal agency whose decisions are sanctioned by the power of the police.

Bohannan's sociological construction does have the virtue of denying the primacy of the legal order, and of implying that law is generic to unstable (or progressive) societies, but it is more or less typical of abstract efforts to define the eternal essence of the law and it begs the significant questions. Law has no such essence but a definable historical nature.

Thus if we inquire into the structure of the contemporary institutions which, according to Bohannan, stand in a primary relation to the law, we find that their customary content has drastically diminished. Paul Radin made the point as follows: "A custom is, in no sense, a part of our properly functioning culture. It belongs definitely to the past. At best, it is moribund. But customs are an integral part of the life of primitive peoples. There is no compulsive submission to them. They are not followed because the weight of tradition overwhelms a man . . . a custom is obeyed there because it is intimately intertwined with a vast living network of interrelations, arranged in a meticulous and or-

[1] Paul Bohannan, "Law," *International Encyclopedia of the Social Sciences* (New York, 1968), pp. 73–78.

dered manner."[2] And, "What is significant in this connection," as J. G. Peristiany indicates, "is not that common values should exist, but that they should be expressed although no common political organization corresponds to them."[3]

No contemporary institution functions with the kind of autonomy that permits us to postulate a significant dialectic between law and custom. We live in a law-ridden society; law has cannibalized the institutions which it presumably reinforces or with which it interacts.

Accordingly, morality continues to be reduced to or confused with legality. In civil society we are encouraged to assume that legal behavior is the measure of moral behavior, and it is a matter of some interest that a former Chief Justice of the Supreme Court proposed, with the best of intentions, that a federal agency be established in order to advise government employees and those doing business with the government concerning the legal propriety of their behavior. Any conflict of interest not legally enjoined would thus tend to become socially or morally acceptable; morality becomes a technical question. Efforts to legislate conscience by an external political power are the antithesis of custom: customary behavior comprises precisely those aspects of social behavior which are traditional, moral, and religious, which are, in short, conventional and non-legal. Put another way, custom *is* social morality.[4] The relation between custom and law is, basically, one of contradiction, not continuity.

The customary and the legal orders are historically, not logically

[2] Paul Radin, *The World of Primitive Man*, New York, 1953, p. 223.

[3] J. G. Peristiany, *The Institutions of Primitive Society*, Glencoe, Illinois, 1956, p. 45.

In the words of V. C. Uchendu, writing about the Ibo: ". . . the use of force is minimal or absent; . . . there are leaders rather than rulers, and . . . cohesion is achieved by rules rather than by laws and by consensus rather than by dictation. In general, the Igbo have not achieved any political structure which can be called a federation, a confederacy, or a state." V. C. Uchendu, *The Igbo of Southeast Nigeria*, N.Y. 1965, p. 46.

[4] Sydney P. Simpson and Julius Stone, *Law and Society in Evolution*, Book I, Saint Paul, 1942, p. 2.

related. They touch coincidentally; one does not imply the other. Custom, as most anthropologists agree, is characteristic of primitive society, and laws of civilization. Robert Redfield's dichotomy between the primitive "moral" order and the civilized "legal" or "technical" order remains a classic statement of the case.

"The dispute," writes William Seagle, "whether primitive societies have law or custom, is not merely a dispute over words. Only confusion can result from treating them as interchangeable phenomena. If custom is spontaneous and automatic, law is the product of organized force. Reciprocity is in force in civilized communities too but at least nobody confuses social with formal legal relationships." [5] Parenthetically, one should note that students of primitive society who use the term "customary law" blur the issue semantically, but nonetheless recognize the distinction.

It is this overall legalization of behavior in modern society which Bohannan fails to interpret. In fascist Germany, for example, laws flourished as never before. By 1941, more edicts had been proclaimed than in all the years of the Republic and the Third Reich. At the same time, ignorance of the law inevitably increased. In a sense, the very force of the law depends upon ignorance of its specifications, which is hardly recognized as a mitigating circumstance. As Seagle states, law is not definite and certain while custom is vague and uncertain. Rather, the converse holds. Customary rules must be clearly known; they are not sanctioned by organized political force, hence serious disputes about the nature of custom would destroy the integrity of society. But laws may always be invented, and stand a good chance of being enforced: "Thus, the sanction is far more important than the rule in the legal system . . . but the tendency is to minimize the sanction and to admire the rule." [6]

In fascist Germany, customs did not become laws through a process of "double institutionalization." Rather, repressive laws, conjured up in the interests of the Nazi Party and its supporters,

[5] William Seagle, *The History of Law*, Tudor, 1946, p. 35.
[6] *Ibid.*, pp. 19–20.

cannibalized the institutions of German society. Even the residual customary authority of the family was assaulted: children were encouraged to become police informers, upholding the laws against their kin. "The absolute reign of law has often been synonymous with the absolute reign of lawlessness." [7]

Certainly, Germany under Hitler was a changing society, if hardly a progressive one, but it was a special case of the general process in civilization through which the organs of the state have become increasingly irresistible. It will be recalled that Bohannan takes the domination of law over custom to be symptomatic of changing societies. But the historical inadequacy of his argument lies exactly here: he does not intimate the overall direction of that change and therefore fails to clarify the actual relation between custom and law. Accordingly, the notion that social change is a function of the law, and vice versa, implies a dialectic that is out of phase with historical reality.

Plato, it deserves note, understood this well enough when he conceived the problem of civilization as primarily one of injustice, which he did not scamp by legalistic definition. His remedy was the thorough restructuring of society. Whether we admire his utopia or not, *The Republic* testifies to Plato's recognition that laws follow social change and reflect prevailing social relationship, but are the cause of neither. Curiously, this view of the relationship between law and society accords with the Marxist perspective on the history of culture. Customary societies are said to precede legal societies, an idea which, semantics aside, most students of historical jurisprudence would accept. But Marxists envision the future as being without laws as we know them, as involving a return to custom, so to speak, on a higher level, since the repressive, punitive and profiteering functions of law will become superfluous. Conflicts of economic and political interest will be resolved through the equitable reordering of institutions. Law, for the Marxists and most classical students of historical jurisprudence, is the cutting edge of the state—but the former, insisting on both a historical and normative view of man, define the state

[7] *Ibid.*

as the instrument of the ruling class, anticipating its dissolution with the abolition of classes and the common ownership of the basic means of production. Whatever our view of the ultimate Marxist dynamic, law is clearly inseparable from the state. Sir Henry Maine equates the history of individual property with that of civilization: "Nobody is at liberty to attack several property and to say at the same time that he values civilization. The history of the two cannot be disentangled. Civilization is nothing more than the name for the . . . order . . . dissolved but perpetually re-constituting itself under a vast variety of solvent influences, of which infinitely the most powerful have been those which have, slowly, and in some parts of the world much less perfectly than others, substituted several property for collective ownership."[8] In the words of Jeremy Bentham, "Property and law are born together and die together."

Law, thus, is symptomatic of the emergence of the state; the legal sanction is not simply the cutting edge of institutions at all times and in all places. The "double institutionalization" to which Bohannan refers needs redefinition. Where it does occur, it is an historical process of unusual complexity and cannot be defined as the simple passage of custom into law. It occurs, as we shall see, in several modes. Custom—spontaneous, traditional, personal, commonly known, corporate, relatively unchanging—is the modality of primitive society; law is the instrument of civilization, of political society sanctioned by organized force, presumably above society at large, and buttressing a new set of social interests. Law and custom both involve the regulation of behavior but their characters are entirely distinct; no evolutionary balance has been struck between developing law and custom, whether traditional or emergent.

II

The simple dichotomy between primitive society and civilization does not illustrate the passage from the customary to the legal order. The most critical and revealing period in the evolution of

[8] Henry Maine, *Village Communities and Miscellanies*, New York, 1889, p. 230.

law is that of *archaic societies,* the local segments of which are the cultures most often studied by anthropologists. More precisely, the earlier phases of these societies, which I call proto-states, represent a transition from the primitive kinship-based communities to the class-structured polity. In such polities, law and custom exist side by side; this gives us the opportunity to examine their connections, distinctions, and differential relationship to the society at large. The customary behavior typical of the local groups —joint families, clans, villages—maintains most of its force; the Vietnamese, for example, still say: "The customs of the village are stronger than the law of the emperor." Simultaneously, the civil power, comprising bureaucracy and sovereign, the dominant emerging class, issues a series of edicts that have the double purpose of confiscating "surplus" goods and labor for the support of those not directly engaged in production while attempting to deflect the loyalties of the local groups to the center.

These archaic societies are the great historical watershed; it is here that Sir Henry Maine and Paul Vinogradoff located the passage from status to contract, from the kinship to the territorial principle, from extended familial controls to public law. One need not be concerned with the important distinctions among archaic societies, or with the precise language or emphases of those scholars who have recognized their centrality for our understanding of the law. The significant point is that they are transitional. Particularly in their early phase they are the agencies that transmute customary forms of order into legal sanction. Here we find a form of "double institutionalization" functioning explicitly; we can witness, so to speak, what appears to be the *emergence* of a custom, in defense of the kinship principle against the assault of the state, and the subsequent shift of the customary function into its own opposite as a legal function. The following example from the archaic proto-state of Dahomey, prior to the French conquest in 1892, will make this process clear.

Traditionally, in Dahomey each person was said to have three "best" friends, in descending order of intimacy and importance.

This transitional institution, a transfiguration of kin connections, of the same species as blood brotherhood, reinforced the extended family structure, which continued to exist in the early state, but was being thrown into question as a result of the political and economic demands made by the emerging civil power. So, for example, the best friend of a joint-family patriarch would serve as his testator, and, upon the latter's decease, name his successor to the assembled family. It seems that the ordinary convention of succession no longer sufficed to secure the family's integrity, since the central authority was mustering family heads as indirect rulers. In this instance, the institution of friendship was assimilated to the form and purpose of customary behavior. On the other hand, the best friend of a man charged with a civil "crime" could be seized by the king's police in his stead. However, these traditional friendships were so socially critical, so deeply held that the person charged, whether or not he had actually committed a civil breach, would typically turn himself in rather than implicate a friend in his punishment. The custom of friendship was thus given a legal edge and converted by the civil power into a means of enforcing its will. This example of "double institutionalization" has the virtue of explicitly revealing the contradiction between law and custom; but there are others in which law appears as a *reinforcement* of customary procedure.

In eleventh century Russia, for instance, Article 1 of the codified law states, "If a man kills a man . . . the brother is to avenge his brother; the son, his father; or the father, his son; and the son of the brother (of the murdered man) or the son of his sister, their respective uncle. If there is no avenger (the murderer) pays 40 grivna wergeld . . ." [9]

Similarly, circa A.D. 700, the law of the Visigoths states, "Whoever shall have killed a man, whether he committed a homicide intending to or not intending to (*volens aut nolens*) . . . let him be handed over into the potestas of the parents or next of kin of

[9] George Vernadsky, *Medieval Russian Laws*, 1947, pp. 26–27.

the deceased. . . ." [10] In these instances, a custom has been codified by an external agency, thus assuming legal force with *its punitive character sharpened.* Such confirmation is both the *intimation* of legal control and the antecedent of institutional change beyond the wish or conception of the family. "Whatever princes do, they seem to command," or, as Sir Henry Maine put it, "What the sovereign permits, he commands." [11] Maine had specifically in mind "the Sikh despot who permitted heads of households and village elders to prescribe rules, therefore these rules became his command and true laws, which are the solvent of local and domestic usage." Simpson and Stone explain this apparent reinforcement of custom by the civil power as follows: "Turning then to the role of law in the emergent political society . . . it is true that political institutions, independent of the kin and the supernatural, had risen to power; yet these institutions were young, weak and untried. Their encroachment on the old allegiance was perforce wary and hesitating. Social cohesion still seemed based on non-political elements, and these elements were therefore protected. It is this society which Pound has perceived and expressed when he says that the end of law envisaged in his period of strict law, is the maintenance of the social *status quo.* In modern terminology this means the primacy of the interest in the maintenance of antecedent social institutions." (italics added)[12]

This sort of confirmation, which betrays the structural opportunism of the early civil power, inheres in the limitations of sovereignty, and is further apparent in the sovereign's relation to the communally held clan or joint-family land. In Dahomey, for example, where the king was said to "own" all property, including land, it is plain that such ownership was a legal fiction and had the effect of validating the pre-existent joint-family tradition. That is, the king "permitted" the joint families, by virtue of his fictional ownership, to expand into new lands and continue trans-

10 Quoted by Simpson and Stone, *op. cit.*, p. 78.
11 Henry Maine, *Early History of Institutions*, 1897, p. 383.
12 Simpson and Stone, *op. cit.*, p. 177.

mitting their property intact, generation after generation. The civil power could not rent, alienate or sell joint-family property, nor could any member of a joint family do so.[13] This is borne out by A. I. Richards, who informs us that "in Northern Rhodesia (Zambia) the statement that 'all the land is mine' does not mean that the ruler has the right to take any piece of land he chooses for his own use . . . I have never heard of a case where a chief took land that had already been occupied by a commoner." [14] The same point is made by Rattray on the Ashanti [15] and Mair on the Baganda,[16] among others. Civil validation, then, expresses the intention but not yet the reality of state control. We might more realistically formulate Maine's epigram as: What he cannot command, the sovereign permits.

Ultimately, local groups have maintained their autonomy when their traditional economies were indispensable to the functioning of the entire society. They could be hedged around by restrictions, harassed by law, or, as we have seen, they could be "legally" confirmed in their customary usage; but, so long as the central power depended on them for support, in the absence of any alternative mode or source of production, their integrity could be substantially preserved. This certainly seems the case during the early phases of state organization in the classic nuclear areas (e.g., Egypt, Babylonia, Northern India) before the introduction of large-scale irrigation and analogous public works, and it was true of precolonial Africa. But in all archaic societies, whether incipient, as in sub-Saharan Africa, florescent, as in the ancient peasant societies of the Middle East or China, or in cognate contemporary societies which probably still embrace most of the world's population, the extensive kin unit was more functional, in spite of varying

[13] Stanley Diamond, *Dahomey, a Proto-state in West Africa*, Ann Arbor, Microfilm, 1951, p. 109.

[14] Quoted by Max Gluckman, "Studies in African Land Tenure," *African Studies*, Vol. III, 1944, pp. 14–21.

[15] R. S. Rattray, *Ashanti, Law and Constitution*, London, 1929.

[16] L. P. Mair, "Baganda Land Tenure," *Africa*, Vol. VI, 1933.

degrees of autonomy, than the family in commercial and industrial civilization.

As the state develops, according to Maine, "the individual is steadily substituted for the family as the unit of which civil laws take account." [17] And in Jhering's words, "The progress of law consists in the destruction of every natural tie, in a continued process of separation and isolation." [18] That is to say, the family increasingly becomes a reflex of society at large. Hence, one might add, the legal stipulation that spouses may not testify against each other appears as one of the last formal acknowledgements of familial integrity, and the exception that proves the historical case. Clearly, the nuclear family in contemporary urban civilization, although bound by legal obligations, has minimal autonomy; obviously, the means of education, subsistence and self-defense are outside the family's competence. It is in this sense that, given the absence of mediating institutions having a clearly defined independent authority, the historical tendency of all state structures vis-à-vis the individual may be designated as totalitarian. Indeed, the state *creates* the disaffiliated individual whose bearings thus become bureaucratic or collective; the juridical "person," who may even be a corporation doing business, is merely the legal reflection of a social process. If "totalization" is *the* state process, totalitarianism cannot be confined to a particular political ideology but is, so to speak, *the* ideology, explicit or not, of political society.

This étatist tendency has its origins in archaic society; we can observe it with unusual clarity in the proto-states of sub-Saharan Africa. In East Africa, pastoralists, competing for land, and in West Africa, militaristic clans, catalyzed by the Arab, and, later, the European trade, notably in slaves, conquered horticulturalists, thereby providing the major occasions for the growth of civil power. Since the basic means of exploiting the environment in these polities remained substantially unchanged, and, to some extent, survived under colonialism, we can reconstruct through

[17] Henry Maine, *Ancient Law*, p. 140.

[18] R. von Jhering, *Geist des Romischen Recht*, 1866, Vol. II, p. 31.

chronicles extending back for centuries and by means of contemporary field work, the structure of early state controls, which evolved in the absence of writing and the systematic codification of law. The absence of writing *should* relieve the scholar from that dependence on official records that has so thoroughly shaped our sense of European history; unfortunately, rubbing shoulders with the upper class in a non-literate state creates equivalent distortions.

In such societies, Rattray tells us, referring to Ashanti, "the small state was ever confronted with the kindred organization which was always insidiously undermining its authority by placing certain persons outside its jurisdiction. It could only hold its own, therefore, by throwing out an ever-widening circle to embrace those loyalties which were lost to it owing to the workings of the old tribal organization which has survived everywhere." [19] Further, "the old family, clan and tribal organization survived in the new regime which was ever striving to make territorial considerations, and not the incidence of kinship, the basis of state control." Rattray concludes that "corporate responsibility for every act was an established principle which survived even the advent of a powerful central public authority as the administration of public justice." [20] Nadel asserts, concerning the Islamized Nupe of the Nigerian Middle Belt, that what emerged from his analysis was "a much more subtle development and a deeper kind of antagonism (than interstate warfare), namely, the almost eternal antagonism of developed State versus that raw material of the Community which, always and everywhere, must form the nourishing soil from which alone the state can grow." [21] And Engels refers to the "irreconcilable opposition of gentile society to the state." [22]

I have documented this conflict in detail in a study of the Dahomean proto-state. There, as elsewhere, it is apparent that the

[19] Rattray, *op. cit.*, p. 80.
[20] *Ibid.*, p. 286.
[21] S. F. Nadel, "Nupe State and Community," *Africa*, Vol. VIII, p. 303.
[22] Engels, p. 133 (see N. 58).

contradictory transition from customs to specified laws, "double institutionalization," if you will, *is by no means the major source of law*. Whether the law arises latently in "confirmation" of previous usage, or through the transformation of some aspect of custom, which the law itself may have, in the first instance, provoked, as in the example of the "best friend," neither circumstance brings us to the heart of the matter. For we learn by studying intermediate societies that the laws so typical of them are *unprecedented;* they do not emerge through a process of "double institutionalization," however defined. They arise in opposition to the customary order of the antecedent kin or kin-equivalent groups; they represent a new set of social goals pursued by a new and unanticipated power in society. These goals can be reduced to a single complex imperative: the imposition of the inter-related census-tax-conscription system. The territorial thrust of the early state, along with its vertical social entrenchment, demanded conscription of labor, the mustering of an army, the levying of taxes and tribute, the maintenance of a bureaucracy, and the assessment of the extent, location, and numbers of the population being subjected. *These were the major direct or indirect occasions for the development of civil law.*

The primary purpose of a census is indicative. Census figures (in non-literate societies, pebbles, for example, would be used as counters) provided the basis on which taxes were apportioned among the conquered districts and tribute in labor exacted from the constituent kin units. The census was also essential for conscripting men into the army. This information was considered so important in Dahomey that each new king, upon his enstoolment, was escorted by his two leading ministers to a special hut in the royal compound and there admonished as he knelt: "Young man, all your life you have heard Dahomey, Dahomey, but you have never until today seen the true Dahomey, for Dahomey is its people and here they are." [23]

[23] M. J. Herskowitz, *Dahomey, an Ancient West African Kingdom*, New York, 1938, p. 73.

With this declaration, the two elders pointed to sacks of pebbles, each pebble representing a person, each sack representing a sex or age group. The young king was then told that he must never allow the contents of the sacks to diminish and that every year the pebbles would be counted to see whether their number had increased or declined. He was then given an old gun (in earlier times a hoe handle) and advised, "Fight with this. But take care that you are not vanquished." [24]

The census figures represented the potential power of the state and were carefully guarded; perhaps they were the first state secret. The act and intent of the census turned persons into ciphers, abstractions in civil perspective; people did all they could to avoid being counted. Suspicion persists; even in the United States the authorities during the period of census taking find it necessary to assert that census information will not be used to tax or otherwise penalize the individual, and, in fact, to do so is said to be against the law.

The double meanings of certain critical terms in common English use—"custom," "duty," and "court," reveal this conflict between local usage and the census-tax-conscription system of the early state. We have been speaking of custom as traditional or conventional non-legal behavior, but custom also refers to a tax routinely payable to the state for the transportation of goods across territorial borders. All such taxes are clearly defined legal impositions, frequently honored in the breach, and they do not have the traditional command of custom. In Dahomey, the "Grand Customs" held at the unveiling of a new king, presumably in honor of his ancestors, were the occasion for the payment of taxes, the large-scale sentencing and sacrifice of criminals, and the prosecution of other state business. Camus has Caligula describe such an event in a passage that could have been extrapolated from a Dahomean chronicle: "It's only the Treasury that counts. And living is the opposite of loving . . . and I invite you to the most gorgeous of shows, a sight for gods to gloat on, a whole world

[24] *Ibid.*

called to judgment. But for that I must have a crowd—spectators, victims, criminals, hundreds and thousands of them. Let the accused come forward. I want my criminals, and they are all criminals. Bring in the condemned men. I must have my public. Judges, witnesses, accused—all sentenced to death without a hearing. Yes, Ceasonia, I'll show them something they've never seen before, the one free man in the Roman Empire." [25] Along with the annual "customs," the "Grand Customs" paralleled the form of local ceremonies, but the substance had entirely changed. Fiscal or legal coercion, political imposition were not the purpose of these ancestral ceremonies which ritually re-enacted reciprocal bonds. The "customs" of the sovereign were laws, the ceremonies of the kin groups were customs.

Similarly, the term "duty" implies a moral obligation on the one hand and a tax on the other. Naturally, we assume that it is the duty of citizens to pay taxes: the paradox inherent in the term becomes more obvious, as one might imagine, as we examine archaic civilizations.

The term "court" is analogously ambivalent. On the one hand, it refers to the residence or entourage of the sovereign; on the other, to a place where civil justice is dispensed, but at their root the functions fuse. The prototypical juridical institution was, in fact, the court of the sovereign where legislation was instituted, for which no precedent or formal analogue existed on the local level. Peristiany, speaking of the Kipsigis, sharpens the latter point: "One of the most significant differences between the . . . council of elders and a European judicature is to be found in the relation between officer and office. The Council elders do not hold their office from a higher authority. They are not appointed . . ." [26] As Seagle, among others, indicates, the court is the first,

[25] Albert Camus, *Caligula and Three Other Plays*, Stuart Gilbert (trans.), New York, 1958, p. 17.

[26] Peristiany, *op. cit.*, p. 42.

The contrast is well remarked by V. C. Uchendu: "Under a constitution like that of the Igbo, which does not provide for a specialized court, judicial matters are ad hoc affairs. The injured party takes the initiative. He may appeal to the head of

most important, and perhaps the last legal artifact. In Montaigne's words, "France takes as its rule the rule of the court." [27] Put another way, the court is a specialized legal structure and it embraces all those particular and determinate legal bodies which are peculiar to civilization.

Clearly, the function of the court was not primarily the establishment of order. In primitive societies, as in the traditional sectors of proto-states, there already existed built-in mechanisms for the resolution of conflict. Generally speaking, as Max Gluckman, among others, has shown, in such societies conflicts generated by the ordinary functioning of social institutions were resolved as part of the customary ritual cycle integral to the institutions themselves.

With regard to more specific breaches, we recall Rattray's observation on the Ashanti: "Corporate responsibility for every act was an established principle which survived even the advent of . . . the administration of public justice." That is to say the kin unit was the juridical unit, just as it was the economic and social unit. Furthermore, "Causes which give rise to the greater part of present 'civil' actions were practically nonexistent. Inheritance, ownership of moveable and non-moveable property, status of individuals, rules of behavior and morality were matters inevitably settled by the customary law, with which everyone was familiar from childhood, and litigation regarding such matters was . . . almost inconceivable. Individual contract, moreover, from the very nature of the community with which we are concerned, was also unknown, thus removing another possible, fruitful source of litigation." [28]

The primary purpose of the historically emerging court, the sovereign's entourage and habitation, was to govern. The distinguished British jurist Sir John Salmond has observed, "Law is

the compound of the offender or to a body of arbitrators. . . . Since the arbitrators have no means of enforcing their decision, for it to be respected it must be acceptable to both parties." Uchendu, *op. cit.*, p. 43.

[27] Montaigne, (see N. 56 for full citation) p. 197.

[28] Rattray, *op. cit.*, p. 286.

secondary and unessential. . . . The administration of justice is perfectly possible without law at all." [29] And Sir William Markby writes, "Tribunals can act entirely without law." [30] The perhaps unintended point here is that justice, commonly defined, is neither deducible from the law, nor was the legislation of the court a measure of justice, but of the political thrust of the early state, and that flowed from the implementation of the census-tax-conscription system.

In the census-tax-conscription system, every conceivable occasion was utilized for the creation of law in support of bureaucracy and sovereign. We observe no abstract principle, no impartial justice, no *precedent,* only the spontaneous opportunism of a new class designing the edifice of its power. It should be re-emphasized, however, that in certain instances formal analogues for civil imposition existed on the local level, but no formal or functional precedents. Civil taxation, for example, can be rationalized in the context of reciprocal gift-giving in the localities, but the latter was not confirmed by law, or specifically used by the sovereign; similarly, corvée labor is a political analogue of local cooperative work groups. But such evolutionary, and dialectical, relationships are most important for their distinctions.

Stubbs writes about the Norman kings that "it was mainly for the sake of the profits that early justice was administered at all." [31] Burton relates that at Whydah, in native Dahomey, in the event of a financial dispute the Yevogan, the leading bureaucrat in the district, sat in judgment. For his services, he appropriated half the merchandise involved, in the name of the king, and another quarter for various lesser officials. The remainder presumably went to the winning contestant in the judicial duel.[32] Among the Ashanti, the central authority relied on the proceeds of litigation

[29] Sir John Salmond, *Jurisprudence,* 1920, p. 13.

[30] Sir William Markby, *Elements of Law,* 1905, p. 21.

[31] William Stubbs, *The Constitutional History of England,* London, 1890, Vol. I, p. 48.

[32] Burton, Richard F., *A Mission to Gelele, a King of Dahomey,* London, 1864, Vol. II, p. 211.

as a fruitful means for replenishing a depleted treasury. Litigation, Rattray notes, came actually to be encouraged.[33]

Tolls were an important source of revenue. In Ashanti, the king had all the roads guarded; all traders were detained until inquiries were made about them, whereupon they were allowed to pass on payment of gold dust.[34] W. Bosman writes that in early eighteenth century Whydah, the king's revenue "in proportion to his country is very large, of which I believe, he hath above one thousand collectors who dispose themselves throughout the whole land in all market roads and passages, in order to gather the king's toll which amounts to an incredible sum, for there is nothing so mean sold in the whole kingdom that the king hath no toll for it. . . ."[35]

The punishment for the theft of property designated as the king's was summary execution by "kangaroo courts" organized on the spot by the king's agents.[36] This is echoed in the code of Hammurabi: "if a man steals the property of a god (temple) or a palace, that man shall be put to death; and he who receives from his hands the stolen (property) shall also be put to death."[37] Where the king's property was concerned, no judicial duel was possible. In these instances, which could be endlessly multiplied, we witness the extension of the king's peace, the primary form of the civil "order," actually the invention and application of sumptuary law through the subsidiary peaces of highway and market. In Maitland's words, "the king has a peace that devours all others." If, in these proto-states, the sovereign power is not yet fully effective, it nonetheless strives to that monopoly of force which characterizes the mature state.

The purpose and abundance of laws inevitably provoked

[33] Rattray, *op. cit.*, p. 292.

[34] Rattray, *op. cit.*, p. 111.

[35] W. Bosman, *A New and Accurate Description of the Coast of Guinea*, London, 1705, p. 362.

[36] R. Norris, *Reise nach Abomey, der Hofstadt des Königs von Dahomey an von Guinea im Jahr 1772*, Leipzig, 1790, p. 221 ff.

[37] *Code of Hammurabi*, Harper translation, 1904, paragraph 6, p. 13.

breaches. The civil authority, in fact, continually probed for breaches and frequently manufactured them. In Dahomey, for example, a certain category of the king's women were distributed to the local villages and those men who made the mistake of having intercourse with them were accused of rape, for which the punishment, following a summary trial, was conscription into the army.[38] Thus, rape was invented as a *civil* crime. If rape had, in fact, occurred in the traditional joint-family villages—and such an occurrence would have been rare, as indicated by the necessity of civil definition—the wrong could have been dealt with by composition (the ritualized giving of goods to the injured party), ritual purification, ridicule, and, perhaps, for repeated transgressions, banishment; the customary machinery would have gone into effect automatically, probably on the initiative of the family of the aggressor. Such instances as this only sharpen the point that in early states crimes seem to have been invented to suit the laws; the latent purpose of the law was punishment in the service and profit of the state, not prevention or the protection of persons, not the *healing* of the breach. As Seagle indicates, "The criminal law springs into life in every great period of class conflict," and this is most obviously the case during the initial phases of state formation.

In its civil origins, then, a correlation existed between law and crime which partook of entrapment. One may even state that the substantial rationale for law developed *after* the fact of its emergence. For example, civil protection of the market place or highway was certainly not necessary to the degree implied in the archaic edicts at the time they were issued. Joint-family markets and village trails were not ordinarily dangerous places, if we are to believe the reports of the earliest chroniclers, as well as those of more contemporary observers. Moreover, if trouble had developed, the family, clan or village was capable of dealing with it. But, in an evolving conquest state, the presence of the king's men would itself be a primary cause of disruption. Indeed, as M.

38 A. Le Herisse, *L'Ancien Royaume du Dahomey*, Paris, 1911, p. 72.

Quénum, a descendant of Dahomean commoners, informs us in a remarkable work, the soldiers were referred to as bandits and predators who victimized many people. Sometimes their forays were confined to a single compound, where someone, whether man, woman or child, resided who had spoken badly of the sovereign or whom the king suspected.[39] In common parlance, the very names of the elite army units became insults; one meant "nasty person," another "arrogant person," and one would say of a tragic event that it was worthy of yet another military cadre. It is, therefore, understandable that the peace of the highway became an issue.[40]

As the integrity of the local groups declined, a process which, in the autochthonous state, must have taken generations or even centuries, conditions doubtless developed which served as an *ex post facto* rationalization for edicts already in effect. In this sense, laws became self-fulfilling prophecies. Crime and the laws which served it were, then, co-variants of the evolving state.

Just as entrapment was characteristic of early civil law, the idea of protection, in the sense of a protection racket, also inheres in its origins. In Dahomey, we are told by Norris and others, prostitution was encouraged by the civil power and prostitutes were distributed through the villages, the price of their favors being set by civil decree. They were obliged to offer themselves to any man who could pay the moderate fee and once a year were convened at the "annual customs" where they were heavily taxed.[41] Skertchly notes that the prostitutes were licensed by the king and placed in the charge of the Mew, the second leading bureaucrat, who was entrusted with the task of "keeping up the supply." [42] Bosman observes at Whydah that "for every affair that can be thought of, the king hath appointed a captain overseer." [43] *What the king permits, he commands; what he "protects," he taxes.*

[39] M. Quénum, *Au Pays des Fons*, Paris, 1938, p. 7.
[40] Quénum, pp. 21–22.
[41] Norris, *op. cit.*, p. 257.
[42] Skertchly, *Dahomey As It Is*, London, 1874, p. 283.
[43] Bosman, *op. cit.*, p. 361.

The intention of the civil power is epitomized in the sanctions against homicide and suicide, typical of early polities; indeed they were among the very first civil laws. Just as the sovereign is said to own the land, intimating the mature right of eminent domain, so the individual is ultimately conceived as the chattel of the state. In Dahomey, persons were conceived as *les choses du monarque.* Eminent domain in persons and property, even where projected as a fiction, is, of course, the cardinal prerequisite of the census-tax-conscription system. We recall that Maine designated the individual the unit of which the civil law steadily takes account. Seagle stated the matter as follows: "By undermining the kinship bond, they (the early civil authorities) made it easier to deal with individuals, and the isolation of the individual is a basic precondition for the growth of law." [44]

Homicide, then, was regarded as an offense against the state. In Rattray's words, "The blow which struck down the dead man would thus appear to have been regarded as aimed also at the . . . central authority." [45] In Ashanti homicide was punishable by death in its most horrible form; in Dahomey, by death or conscription into the army. There is a nuance here which should not be overlooked. By making homicide, along with the theft of the king's property, a capital offence, the sovereign power discouraged violent opposition to the imposition of the civil order.

Traditionally, murder in a joint-family village was a tort—a private, remediable wrong—which could stimulate a blood feud, not to be confused with the lex talionis, until redress, which did not imply equivalent injury, was achieved. But a breach was most often settled by composition. As Paul Radin put it: "The

[44] Seagle, *op. cit.*, p. 64. Quénum had a poor opinion of the ethnographers who claimed to understand and interpret his country. They failed, he believed, because of inadequate sources of information, and (or) ignorance of social customs. "Most of our ethnographers," he wrote, "have had as collaborators princes and ex-ministers of state and have believed their tales." He adds that ignorance of the native language and deficient sympathy compounded the problem. The point to note here is that Quénum is objecting to the view from the top which is a critical issue in the writing of all political history.

[45] Rattray, *op. cit.*, p. 295.

theory of an eye for an eye . . . never really held for primitive people . . . rather it was replacement for loss with damages."[46] And this is echoed by Peristiany: ". . . they claim restitution or private damages and not social retribution."[47] In any case, the family was fully involved. "The family was a corporation," said Rattray, "it is not easy to grasp what must have been the effect . . . of untold generations of thinking and acting . . . in relation to one's group. The Ashanti's idea of what we term moral responsibility for his actions must surely have been more developed than in peoples where individualism is the order of the day."[48] This more or less typical anthropological observation makes it clear that the law against homicide was not a "progressive" step, as if some abstract right were involved which the state, coming of age, finally understands and seeks to establish. "Anti-social conduct (is) exceptional in small kinship groups," writes Margery Perham of the Ibo.[49] Crimes of violence were rare, Richard Burton reported of Dahomey, and "murder virtually unknown."[50] Of course, as with other crimes defined by civil law, they may have increased as the social autonomy, economic communalism, and reciprocity of the kin units weakened. But this is much less important than Dalzel's observation that in Dahomey "many creatures have been put to death . . . without having committed any crime at all,"[51] thus exemplifying the power of the sovereign

[46] Radin, *op. cit.*, p. 252.

[47] Peristiany, *op. cit.*, p. 43.

[48] Radin, *op. cit.*, p. 62.

[49] Margery Perham, *Native Administration in Nigeria*, London, 1962, pp. 229 ff.

[50] Burton, *op. cit.*, p. 56.

Acts of violence must be distinguished from *crimes* of violence. The incidence, occasions for, and character of violence in primitive, as opposed to civilized societies, is a subject of the utmost importance, which I have discussed elsewhere (see footnote 52). But the question here has to do with crimes in which violence is used as a means for, e.g., the theft of property. In contemporary societies unpremeditated acts of personal violence which have no ulterior motive, so-called crimes of passion, may not be penalized or carry minor degrees of guilt, that is, their status as legally defined crimes is ambiguous. This would certainly seem to reflect a historically profound distinction between crime and certain types of violence. In primitive societies violence tends to be personally structured, nondissociative, and, thereby, self-limiting.

[51] A. Dalzel, *The History of Dahomey, an inland kingdom of Africa*, etc., London, 1793, p. 212.

literally to command the lives of his citizens. The threat and example of summary execution, especially but by no means exclusively evident at the mortuary celebrations of "Grand Customs" on the enstooling of a king, encouraged obedience to civil injunctions.

The law against suicide, a capital offense, was the apotheosis of political absurdity. The individual, it was assumed, had no right to take his own life; that was the sole prerogative, presumably, of the state, whose property he was conceived to be.

The fanatical nature of the civil legislature in claiming sole prerogative to the lives of its subjects is conclusively revealed among the Ashanti, where, if the suicide was a murderer, "the central authority refused to be cheated thus and the long arm of the law followed the suicide to the grave from which, if his kinsmen should have dared to bury him, he was dragged to stand trial."[52] (One recalls Antigone's defiance.) This contrasts remarkably, if logically, with the behavior of the more primitively structured Ibo, as reported by Victor Uchendu, an anthropologist who is himself an Ibo: "Homicide is an offense against ala—the earth deity. If a villager is involved, *the murderer is expected to hang himself,* after which . . . daughters of the village perform the rite of . . . sweeping away the ashes of murder. If the murderer has fled, his extended family must also flee, and the property of all is subject to raids. When the murderer is eventually caught, he is required to hang himself to enable the daughters of the village to perform their rites. It is important to realize that the village has no power to impose capital punishment. In fact, no social group or institution has this power. Everything affecting the life of the villager is regulated by custom. The life of the individual is highly respected; it is protected by the earth-goddess. The villagers can bring social pressure, but the murderer must hang himself."[53]

It can hardly be argued that the purpose of the civil sanction

[52] Rattray, *op. cit.*, p. 299.
[53] Uchendu, *op. cit.*, pp. 42–43.

against suicide was to diminish its incidence or to propagate a superior moral consciousness. Dare we say, as with other crimes, that attempts at suicide increased as society became more thoroughly politicized? The law against suicide reveals, in the extreme, the whole meaning and intent of civil law at its origins. In the proto-state, the quintessential struggle was over the lives and labor of the people, who, still moving in a joint family context, were nonetheless conceived to be *less choses du monarque.*

III

If revolutions are the acute, episodic signs of civilizational discontent, the rule of law, in seven millennia of political society, from Sumer or Akkad to New York or Moscow, has been the chronic symptom of the disorder of institutions. E. B. Tylor stated, "A constitutional government, whether called republic or kingdom, is an arrangement by which the nation governs itself by means of the machinery of a military despotism." [54]

The generalization lacks nuance but we can accept it if we bear in mind Tylor's point of reference: "Among the lessons to be learnt from the life of rude tribes is how society can go on without the policeman to keep order." [55] When he alludes to constitutional government, Tylor was not distinguishing its ultimate sanction from that of any other form of the state: all political society is based on repressive organized force. In this he was accurate. For pharaohs and presidents alike have always made a public claim to represent the common interest, indeed to incarnate the common good. Only a Plato or a Machiavelli in search of political harmony, or a Marx in search of political truth, has been able to penetrate this myth of the identity between ruler and ruled, of equality under law. The tradition of Plato and Machiavelli commends the use of the "royal" or "noble lie," while that of Marx exposes and rejects the power structure (ultimately the state) that

[54] E. B. Tylor, *Anthropology*, Vol. II, London, 1946, p. 156.

[55] *Ibid.*, p. 134.

propagates so false a political consciousness. On this issue, I follow Marx.

Tylor distinguishes the civilized from the primitive order. Such a distinction has been made at every moment of crisis in the West but nowhere so pertinently as in Montaigne's contrast of a primitive society with Plato's ideally civilized republic: "This is a nation, I should say to Plato, in which there is no sort of traffic, no knowledge of letters, no science of numbers, no name for a magistrate or for political superiority, no custom of servitude, no riches or poverty, no contracts, no successions, no partitions . . . no care for any but common kinship. How far from this perfection would he find the Republic he imagines!"[56] The issue of law and order implicit in Montaigne's contrast between primitive and civilized societies has been a persistent underlying theme for the most reflective and acute minds of the West. The inquiry into the nature of politics probably demarcates most accurately the boundaries of our intellectual landscape. The evolution of the state toward what Max Weber called maximally politicized society, the unprecedented concentration of bureaucratic and technological power, which economically and culturally dominates the rest of the world, creates a climate in which all problems cast a political shadow. We may flee from the political dimension of our experience or we may embrace it in order to do away with it, but we are obsessed by politics. It was perhaps Plato's primary virtue that, at the very origin of the Western intellectual tradition, he understood that, in civilization, all significant human problems have a political aspect and he insisted upon the solution of the latter as a coefficient of the creative resolution of the former. *The Republic*

[56] Michel de Montaigne, *The Complete Essays,* trans. Donald Frame, Stanford, 1965. In ignorance of Montaigne's contrast between primitive society and Plato's ideal republic, I published an article, "Plato and the Definition of the Primitive," *Culture in History,* New York, 1960, which explicates some of the points briefly noted above. For a more comprehensive model of primitive society see my "The Search for the Primitive" in *Man's Image in Medicine and Anthropology,* New York, 1963, edited by I. Galdston, pp. 62–115. In order to understand the functioning of custom in primitive society fully, one should have such a model in mind. Unfortunately, in this article I can only suggest its outlines.

is the first civilizational utopia, and it maintains its force both as a model of inquiry and as antithesis to all projections of the nature of primitive society. Any contrary view of the possibilities of human association must take *The Republic* into account.

The legal order, which Plato idealized, is as Tylor maintained and Marx understood, synonymous with the power of the state. "The state," writes Paul Vinogradoff, "has assumed the monopoly of political co-ordination. It is the state which rules, makes laws and eventually enforces them by coercion. Such a state did not exist in ancient times. The commonwealth was not centered in one sovereign body towering immeasurably above single individuals and meting out to everyone his portion of right." [57] And Engels, reflecting on the origins of the state, asserts: "The right of the state to existence was founded on the preservation of order in the interior and the protection against the barbarians outside, but this order was worse than the most disgusting disorder, and the barbarians against whom the state pretended to protect its citizens were hailed by them as saviors." [58] Moreover, "The state created a public power of coercion that did no longer coincide with the old self-organized and (self) armed population." [59] Finally, in a passage that epitomizes the West's awareness of itself, Engels writes: "The state, then, is by no means a power forced on society at a certain stage of evolution. It is the confession that this society has become hopelessly divided against itself, has estranged itself in irreconcilable contradictions which it is powerless to banish. In order that these contradictions, these classes with conflicting economic interests may not annihilate themselves and society in a useless struggle, a power becomes necessary that stands apparently above society and has the function of keeping down the conflicts and maintaining 'order.' And this power, the outgrowth of society, but assuming supremacy over it and becoming more and

[57] Paul Vinogradoff, *Outlines of Historical Jurisprudence*, Vol. I, London, 1920, p. 93.

[58] Friedrich Engels, *Origin of the Family, Private Property and the State*, Chicago, 1902, p. 179.

[59] *Ibid.*, p. 207.

more divorced from it, is the state. . . ."[60] In a word, the state is the alienated form of society: and it is this process which has fascinated the Western intellect and which may, in fact, have led to the peculiar intensity of the reflective, analytic, and introspective consciousness in the West, to our search for origins and our inexhaustible concern with secular history. A knowledge of one's present, as Montaigne maintained, implies not only a knowledge of one's past but of one's future.

However we project, imagine, or reconstruct the past, we recognize the division, the objective correlate of the division within ourselves, between primitive and civilized society, between moral and civil order, between custom and law. Interpretation of the nature of the primitive and the civilized has, of course, not been uniform. Hobbes versus Rousseau is paradigmatic. But most theorists tend to see civilization as a kind of fall from a "natural," or at least more natural, to a legal or more repressive order. No matter how the virtues of civilization are weighed, the price exacted is inevitably noted. This is as true of Plato as of Freud or Engels. Plato, for example, notes, however inadequately, a condition of existence prior to the city-state, a type of rusticity which he views nostalgically and whose destruction he maintains was socioeconomically determined. I suspect that even the great majority of anthropologists, despite professional illusions of dissociated objectivity, sense that primitive societies are somehow closer than civilized societies to the realization of "natural" law and "natural" right. I believe this emphasis in the Western tradition to be the sounder, and it serves as the basis of my own thinking. There is, as Montaigne noted, an "amazing distance" between the primitive character and our own. In the contrast between these two sides of our historical nature, which we existentially re-enact, we come to understand law as the antonym and not the synonym of order.

60 *Ibid.*, p. 206.

IV

I agree with Nadel that in the transition from primitive to political society the means of control and integration employed were, in a wider sense, "all . . . deliberately conceived and (executed): they are agencies of an assimilation conscious of itself and of the message which it carries."[61] Finally, we are led to ask, as did Nadel about the Nupe: "What did the tax-paying law-abiding citizen receive in return for allegiance to king and nobility? Was extortion, bribery, brutal force, the only aspect under which the state revealed itself to the populace? The people were to receive, theoretically, on the whole, one thing: security—protection against external and internal enemies, and general security for carrying out the daily work, holding markets, using the roads. We have seen what protection and security meant in reality. At their best, they represented something very unequal and very unstable. This situation must have led to much tension and change within the system and to frequent attempts to procure better safeguards for civil rights."[62]

The struggle for civil rights, then, is a response to the imposition of civil law. With the destruction of the primitive base of society, civil rights have been defined and redefined as a reaction to drastic changes in the socioeconomic structure, the rise of caste and class systems, imperialism, modern war, technology as a means of social exploitation, maldistribution and misuse of resources, racial hatred. The right to socially and economically fruitful work, for example, which did not come into question in a primitive society or in a traditional sector of an early state (and therefore was not conceived to be a stipulated right) becomes an issue under capitalism. The demand implies a need for profoundly changing the system and indicates that our sense of the appropriately human has very ancient roots indeed. However, we are reminded by the struggle for civil rights, that legislation alone has no force

[61] S. F. Nadel, *A Black Byzantium*, London, New York, Toronto, 1942, p. 144.
[62] Nadel, "Nupe State and Community," *Africa*, Vol. VIII, p. 287.

beyond the potential of the social system that generates it. From the study of proto-states we also learn that the citizen must be constantly alert to laws which seek to curb his rights in the name of protection or security. Restrictive legislation is almost always a signal of repressive institutional change, but is, of course, not the cause of it.

The major focus of the defense of the citizen as a person can only be on procedure or, as we call it in our own society, due process. Quénum reports, of the early state of Dahomey, "There was no penal code promulgated . . . punishment had no fixity . . . the Miegan (leading bureaucrat, chief judge, and executioner) would become restive if capital punishment would be too long in coming."[63] In the words of Dalzel, "There was a vast disproportion between crimes and punishments."[64] And in early states, most if not all civil breaches were what we would define as crimes, just as in primitive societies "civil crimes" were considered, where they were not unprecedented, torts or private remediable wrongs. As every intelligent lawyer knows, the substance of the law can hardly be assimilated to morality. It is clear, therefore, why Jhering insisted that "Form is the sworn enemy of unlimited discretion (of the sovereign power) and the twin sister of freedom."[65] The degrees of theft or homicide, the question of double jeopardy, habeas corpus, the right to counsel, the question of legitimate witness, trial by jury and the selection of jurors, protection against summary search and seizure, the very division between civil and criminal law—these intricacies of procedure are the primary, but far from absolute, assurance of whatever justice can be obtained under the rule of law.

For example, the only way dissidents in Russia can defend themselves against summary punishment and make their cases universally understandable is by calling attention to abuses of pro-

[63] Quénum, *op. cit.*, p. 22.
[64] Dalzel, *op. cit.*, p. 212.
[65] Jhering, *op. cit.*, Vol. II, p. 471.

cedure. The spirit of the laws, mummified in the excellent constitution of 1936, is irrelevant, abstract. The tribunal that discharges the intentions of the state can discard, suspend, reinterpret, and invent laws at will. The court, not the constitution, is the primary legal reality. And the politically inspired charge of insanity, which can remove dissidents from the body politic altogether, is the ultimate étatistic definition of the person—a nonbeing incapable of autonomy. And that, I should note, is foreshadowed in the consummate anti-Socratic Platonism of the Laws, the heavenly city brought to earth, wherein the ordinary citizen is "to become, by long habit, utterly incapable of doing anything at all independently."

Procedure is the individual's last line of defense in contemporary civilization, wherein all other associations to which he may belong have become subordinate to the state. The elaboration of procedure then, is a unique, if fragile, feature of more fully evolved states, in compensation, so to speak, for the radical isolation of the individual. In the proto-states, the harshness of rudimentary procedure was countered by the role of the kinship units which, as we recall, retained a significant measure of functional socioeconomic autonomy and, therefore, of local political cohesion.

But "law has its origin in the pathology of social relations and functions only when there are frequent disturbances of the social equilibrium." [66] Law arises in the breach of a prior customary order and increases in force with the conflicts that divide political societies internally and among themselves. Law *and* order is the historical illusion; law versus order is the historical reality.

In the tradition of Rousseau, Lévi-Strauss, in a moment of candor, declares, "We must go beyond the evidence of the injustices and abuses to which the social order gives rise, and discover the unshakable basis of human society . . . Anthropology shows that base cannot be found in our own civilization, ours is indeed perhaps the one furthest from it." [67]

[66] Seagle, *op. cit.*, p. 36.

[67] Claude Lévi-Strauss, *A World on the Wane*, New York, 1961, p. 390.

The progressive reduction of society to a series of technical and legal signals, the consequent diminution of culture, i.e., of reciprocal, symbolic meanings, are perhaps the primary reasons why our civilization is the one least likely to serve as a guide to "the unshakable basis of human society."

[10]

The Chinese Conceptions of Law: Confucian, Legalist, and Buddhist

By LUKE T. LEE*
WHALEN W. LAI**

Introduction

THREE PHILOSOPHICAL traditions affecting the legal systems in China stand out in clear relief: the Confucian, the Legalist, and the Buddhist. Although the legal system in China grew out of the thoughts of the Legalists, who helped found the first empire, Ch'in (221-206 B.C.), under Han, the immediately following dynasty (207 B.C.-220 A.D.), a Confucian-Legalist synthesis was struck. The only other independent concept of "law" in any sense of the word belonged to the Buddhist establishment. The major Chinese traditions may be characterized in terms of their conceptions of law, man, and the cosmos as follows: the Legalist believes in man, or rather, the king, as the agent in the creation of law; the Confucian trusts in the natural harmony between man's ritual propriety and the natural principles of the universe; and the Buddhist believes in the sacred transcendental law, with a historical but superhuman origin in the teachings of one man—the Buddha. Because much has already been written on the Confucian-Legalist traditions, this Article will only briefly summarize them, devoting the main discussion to an examination of the Buddhist conception of law and to the impact of the various religious traditions upon the current Chinese state.

---

* Professor Lee is currently the Director of the Office of Population Affairs, Department of State. B.A. 1944, St. John's University (Shanghai), M.A. 1947, Columbia University; Ph.D. 1954, Fletcher School of Law and Diplomacy; J.D. 1963, University of Michigan.

** Assistant Professor, Asian Religious Studies Program, University of California, Davis. B.A. 1968, International Christian University (Tokyo); Ph.D. 1975, Harvard University.

The Confucian-Legalist Traditions

There is a widespread belief that Chinese law is not "law" in the Western sense at all. Escarra, the French jurist, once remarked, "Where it is anything else but a fiction, the opposition traditionally established between Orient and Occident is met nowhere more clearly than in the domain of law."[1] He went on to contrast the Confucian society of China with Western civilization, dominated by the Greco-Roman conception of law carried along with the spread of Christianity.[2] The Westerner, according to Escarra, views the law as almost sacrosanct, as the regulator of the social conduct of all people. In contrast, the Chinese traditionally hold the law in low esteem.[3]

Even in the West, however, law is defined many ways. The Austinian definition of law is a command, prescribed or dictated by a superior, which an inferior is bound to obey under threat of punishment. Eugen Ehrlich, on the other hand, discusses the "living law of the people." Under that concept legal regulation and enforcement based on the political state are only a fraction, albeit an increasing fraction, of the sum total of this living law, the balance being comprised of norms which result from the influence of family, religion, and other social organizations and associations.[4] The Chinese equivalents of these two approaches to law are *fa* and *li*, terms representing a conceptual dichotomy which is traditional in China. *Li*—translated variously as propriety, ethics, or moral rules of correct conduct and good manners—embodies chiefly the teaching of Confucius, in particular the "five relations": ruler and subject, father and son, husband and wife, elder and younger brother, and friend and friend. *Liki* (The Book of Li) describes *li* as "a regulator of human desires that has been devised for the protection of the people."[5] It is a form of social control over unrestrained expression of human desires. It "forbids trespasses *before* they are committed, whereas

1. ESCARRA, LE DROIT CHINOIS 9 (G. Browne trans., reproduced by Harvard Law School 1961) [hereinafter cited as ESCARRA].

2. *Id.* at 10.

3. *Id.* at 11.

4. E. EHRLICH, FUNDAMENTAL PRINCIPLES OF THE SOCIOLOGY OF LAW 373, 493 (1936).

5. *Li and Law*, 2 CHINESE CULTURE No. 4, at 4 (Chang Chin-tsen, trans. 1960).

fa punishes criminal acts *after* their commission."[6] *Li* is closely related to *tao,* the natural order, and this emphasis on moral rules and natural order is not unlike the emphasis on natural law in the West,[7] which is frequently concerned with the problem of how actuality is related to the normative order.[8]

Fa, although it has been translated as "law," is actually much narrower in scope. It is chiefly associated with the Legalist school of Han Fei-tze, which reached its zenith in the despotic Ch'in dynasty during the Third Century B.C. The Legalists rely on the force of sanctions to obtain obedience to and compliance with the law, and therefore they stress government by *fa* or decree, as opposed to the Confucian emphasis on government by man and *li.* The Legalists insist on complete equality before *fa,* as opposed to the Confucian acknowledgment of the inequality of people. The Legalists enforce objective and unvarying rules of conduct, in contrast to the Confucian acceptance of different rules for different relations and positions. Although the Ch'in dynasty was short-lived, Legalist thought continued to influence subsequent dynasties, as evidenced by centralized bureaucracies and official codes.

If one discards *li* and identifies only *fa* with "law," using the criteria of codification and enforcement by government authorities, one must reject, for example, the validity of customary international law because it lacks these qualities. Although *li* does not fulfill Austin's definition of law, it certainly fits into the broader definition of law given by Ehrlich. In fact, *li* can be described as a code enforced by society rather than by government.[9] *Li* and *fa* were commingled in the T'ang Code, which provided: "That which deviates from '*li*' comes within the competence of legal penalties. Violations of *li* are subject to punishment."[10] In the Code of Law drawn up by Prime Minister Hsiao Ho and in the Court Ceremonials formulated by Shu Sun Tung, *li* and *fa* were made to coordinate and complement each other, a principle which was to endure 2,100 years to the present century.[11]

---

6. *Id.*

7. *See* 2 NEEDHAM, SCIENCE AND CIVILIZATION IN CHINA 544 (1956).

8. Schwartz, *On Attitudes Towards Law in China,* in GOVERNMENT UNDER LAW AND THE INDIVIDUAL 29 (1957).

9. *See, e.g.,* Address by Franz H. Michael, American Society of International Law Pacific Northwestern Regional Meeting (Spring 1961).

10. *Li and Law,* 2 CHINESE CULTURE No. 4, at 15 (Chang Chin-tsen, trans. 1960).

11. *Id.* at 13.

Even Confucius did not totally reject the role of *fa*.[12] *Li* comprehends *fa* as one facet of the law, even though the converse is not true. If Ehrlich's definition of law is accepted, Wigmore was correct when he said in 1935 that the Chinese legal system is "the only one that has survived continuously to date—a period of more than 4,000 years; in comparison, the other living systems of today are but children."[13]

In any conflict between *li* and *fa*, traditional Chinese society preferred *li*. The reason for this resolution was eloquently explained by Confucius:

> If the people are guided by *fa*, and order among them is enforced by means of punishment, they will try to evade the punishment, but have no sense of shame, but if they are guided by virtue, and order among them is enforced by *li*, they will have the sense of shame and also be reformed.[14]

Confucius noted the value of this system when he said: "As a judge, I decide disputes, for that is my duty; but the best thing that could happen would be to eliminate the causes for litigation."[15] In fact, the highest ideal of *chün-tze* (gentleman) is to show oneself capable of exact proportions and moderation in all circumstances. Compromise or yielding with propriety is always far more important in China than invoking personal rights and privileges.

Li traditionally dominated not merely domestic society but also interstate relations. For example, in one instance Confucius praised the action of the Marquis of Ch'i, a leader of a league, in convening a congress of states to conclude a new league in 651 B.C. and thus uniting the lords by peaceful means instead of military force.[16] In another instance, the Duke of Hsüang and the Marquis of Ch'i tried to reconcile a conflict between the states of Ch'ü and T'an. The people of Ch'ü were unwilling to be reconciled, and so the Duke invaded Ch'ü and took the city of Hsiang. The classic history, *Tso Chuan* condemned the Duke's act as not being in accord with *li:*

---

12. *Id.* at 14.

13. C. Wigmore, Panorama of the World's Legal System 141 (1936).

14. Confucian Analects, bk. II, ch. III.

15. Confucius, *The Great Learning*, ch. IV.

16. The event was recorded in *Tso Chuan* as follows: "They assembled at K'wei-ch'iu to renew the league and to cultivate the good relations among the princes themselves; which was proper." *Duke Hsi*, bk. V, yr. IX, in 5 Chinese Classics 154 (2d ed. J. Legge 1966) [hereinafter cited as Chinese Classics].

> States must be reconciled by the rules of propriety, and not by disorder. To attack Ch'ü, without regulating [the differences by those rules] was creating disorder. By disorder [*sic*] to attempt to reconcile disorder, [it] left no room for the [proper] regulation; and without such regulation, how could any rule of propriety be carried out?[17]

In another historical episode, the powerful state of Tsin, upon defeating the state of Cheng, tried to impose a harsh peace settlement. Cheng protested that peace terms should be based on *li* and should not be imposed arbitrarily. Tsin conceded the propriety of this claim, acknowledging that a coerced settlement would be contrary to *li*. *Tso Chuan* noted the statement from a Tsin leader:

> We indeed have not virtue, and it is not proper to force men to covenant with us. Without propriety, how can we preside our covenants? . . . If we are without virtue, other people will cast us off, and not Cheng only; if we can rest and be harmonious, they will come to us from a distance.[18]

Accordingly, Tsin agreed to a revision of the terms and withdrew its forces.

Above all, *li* is concerned with sincerity (*ch'eng*) and trustworthiness (*hsin*), for which Western legal equivalents are good faith and *Pacta sunt servanda*. The concepts of *ch'eng* and *hsin* are extensions of the Confucian concept of the proper relationship between friend and friend. Mencius, a Chinese thinker, said: "Between father and son, there should be affection; between sovereign and subject, there should be righteousness; between husband and wife, there should be respective duties; between the elder and the younger, there should be order; between friends, there should be sincerity."[19]

The dominance of *li* in the Chinese law of treaties was manifested when China was forced to enter the modern family of nations. The Chinese of the mid-nineteenth century viewed the 1842 Sino-British Treaty of Nanking,[20] known as the *Wan-nien Ho-yüeh* (the Peace Treaty of Ten Thousand Years), as unalterable and forever

17. *Duke Hsiang*, bk. VII, yr. IV, in 5 CHINESE CLASSICS, *supra* note 16, at 296.
18. *Duke Hsiang*, bk. IX, yr. IX, in 5 CHINESE CLASSICS, *supra* note 16, at 441.
19. *Mencius*, bk. III, pt. I, ch. 4, § 8, in 2 CHINESE CLASSICS, *supra* note 16, at 251-52.
20. 30 BRITISH AND FOREIGN STATE PAPERS 389 (1841-42).

valid. The Tsungli Yamen wrote in 1867 that once an item enters into a treaty, every word of it becomes ironclad.[21] Li Hung-chang was convinced that once a treaty had been ratified, nothing could be done to change it.[22] Even the xenophobic monarch, Emperor Hsien-feng, did not unilaterally abrogate any treaty. The closest he came to doing so was to encourage the obstructionist tactics and tendencies of his Canton viceroy, Yeh Ming-ch'en, and the Canton populace.[23]

Li continues to be a strong influence in modern China, in both interpersonal and interstate relations. Specific rules of conduct decreed by the government and constituting *fa* continue to be dominated by *li*. *Li* and *fa* are two of the major religious concepts that have become ingrained in the Chinese legal system. They are not, however, the only religious ideas to have affected that system. This Article now turns to a consideration of other important religious concepts that originated not from Confucian or Legalist tradition but from Buddhism as it developed in China.

The Buddhist Concept of Law

The Buddhist tradition constitutes the third major legal tradition in China. As a religion seeking liberation from *samsāra* (rebirth), Buddhist legalism is not legalism in the usual sense of the word. This section of the Article focuses, not on the internal structure of Buddhist law, but on the general Buddhist concept of "law" and its historical consequences in China. We focus on the concept in order to reveal the ethos of Buddhism and the spirit of its rational life style.[24]

Levels of Law in Buddhism

Buddhism is, strictly speaking, the *Buddha-Dharma*, the Law of the Buddha. Law is only one meaning of the word "*dharma*," which also means truth, virtue, righteousness, and duty. The word "*dharma*" is rooted in *rta*, the cosmic norm followed by the Aryans who

21. Hsu, China's Entrance into the Family of Nations 6 (1960).
22. *Id.*
23. *Id.*
24. The schematization will lend some clarity to law in Buddhism although it might not do justice to all the finer aspects in this tradition.

invaded India and founded the Brahmanical culture. In Hinduism, *dharma* oversees the society and therefore encompasses the duties of caste. When the Buddha discovered the *dharma* (truth) he understood it outside the caste context. His teaching is referred to as *Buddha-Dharma,* the Law of the Enlightened One. Corresponding to the Greek *logos* or the Chinese *Tao, dharma* is both the correct and the actual norm of the universe. *Dharma* is reality and truth. Inasmuch as the truth is embodied in his teachings (*dharma*[25]), the *Buddha-Dharma* is truth itself. In Christian thought, Jesus Christ is seen as the *logos* personified. Similarly, in Mahayana, the Buddha is said to be the *dharma,* and all Buddhas, enlightened ones, are one in the *Dharmakāya,* the Law-body.

The Chinese were converts to the *Buddha-Dharma* beginning some time in the first century A.D. A consensus was soon reached to translate the Sanskrit term to "*fo-fa*": *fo* stood for the Buddha, and *fa,* for the *dharma.* Although it may appear peculiar that the Buddhists would settle on the word *fa* (law) in the face of the traditional Confucian stigma against law and against the Legalist, at that time the term "*fa*" had a more general meaning than law. *Fa* connoted method and therefore teaching or school. It thus functioned to convey the law as well as the teachings of the Buddha in the translation. *Fa* may also mean model, pattern, or, perhaps in Mohist usage,[26] shared characteristics. Thus, Lao-tzu's *Tao-te-ching* at one point says:

> Man patterns (*fa*) after Heaven.
> Heaven patterns (*fa*) after Tao.
> Tao patterns (*fa*) after Nature.[27]

The word *fa* (pattern) conveys the sense of cosmic pattern which is also basic to the word *dharma.* The choice was therefore not legalistic.

The Development of the Legal Institution: Śīla and Vinaya

Śīla (precepts) and *vinaya* (disciplines, monastic rules) correspond most closely to law in the Buddhist tradition. The Buddha

25. *Dharma* in the sense of a *personal* "teaching" is a Buddhist innovation.
26. *Tao* also had the meaning of "way," "teaching," "school."
27. LAO-TZU, TAO-TE-CHING, ch. 25.

set down for the lay congregation the five basic precepts, *pañcasīla.*[28] The novice (*śramaṇa*) follows, in addition, five more *śīlas*. *Vinaya* is the monastic code designed specifically for the full monk. It grew out of the early fortnight confessions, *prātimoksa,* when the brethren would publically confess their transgressions. The Chinese term for vinaya was "*lü*" (regulations), a legal term. The mature legal system known as *lü-ling,* "regulations and commands," evolved in the seventh century. *Lü* pertains to administrative regulations or decrees; *ling* pertains specifically to commands or orders from above. *Lü-ling* became the general term for legal code. One Japanese scholar has speculated that the Buddhist institution of *lü* and its corresponding mentality might have influenced the T'ang creation of an objective, bureaucratically more efficient administrative and legal system.[29]

The Buddhist *lü* was introduced into China relatively late. Comprehensive awarness of *lü* began in the fifth century. The Chinese probably never adopted the harsh rules of a full monastic life, because most monks at that time were only *śramaṇas,* barely initiates. By the time Chinese Buddhists became familiar with the full Buddhist teaching, they had created their own Ch'an (Zen) monastic code known as *ch'ing-kuei* or "pure rules." Nevertheless, beginning in the fifth century, there were identifiable masters of the *vinaya* known as "*lü-shih,*" a term now used to designate legal counsel or jurists. Although the *lü-shih* in Buddhism did not approach being modern jurists, and although their impact at that early date was probably minimal, they may represent the first legal specialists in China. Famous *lü-shih* studied more than one recension of the *prāktimokṣa,* compared the teachings, formulated their own interpretations, and settled disputes in the monastic community.[30]

Basic Legal Principles

There are different levels of law operating in the *Buddha-Dharma.* The most basic one is the law of *karma* (action), which is accepted

28. *Ahiṃsa* (nonviolence to life) is the first rule. The other rules forbid lying, stealing, adultery, and alcohol consumption.

29. The suggestion is that *lü* and *ling* were differentiated from the more compact notion of *fa* (law) used in the Han dynasty. Due to the complexities involved in this issue, such a discussion is beyond the scope of this Article.

30. T'ang monk, Tao-hsün, is the acknowledged master and founder of the *lü* sect. He developed rules for the Chinese monasteries patterned upon Indian precedents.

without question by Buddhist and Hindu alike and which forms the basis for all Indian philosophy. After the Buddha sought and found an escape from the karmic cycles of *saṃsāra* (rebirth), he charted the Buddhist law of causation. The Buddha believed in the rationality of the universe, rejecting the concept that the world is structurally *adharmic* or lawless. Even if the ultimate wisdom (*prajñā*) is not open to rational analysis, the path (*mārga*) leading to it may be constructed. A summary of various laws appears below.

Karma

The law of *karma* is the law of action and reaction: all deeds will generate, inevitably, their proper rewards and punishment whether immediately, in the next life, or in lives ahead. *Karma* (action, deeds) includes all action, "good, evil or indifferent," physical or psychic, overt or covert, or large or small.[31] Nothing falls outside the law of *karma*.[32] *Karma* is therefore the most general of laws. Originally, *karma* referred to magical actions at Brahmanical sacrificial rites,[33] but during the period of social chaos and instability around the sixth century B.C., its meaning was expanded to include *all* actions.

The Buddha, furthermore, uncovered the power of latent actions (actions unperformed) and recognized the centrality of *citta-karma*, the *karma* of the mind. Just as the religious principles of Jesus emphasized that sin could be committed in the heart, the Buddha's doctrine also underlined the perilous nature of the mind. Both religious founders introduced a new "ethics of motivation" into what previously had been predominantly an ethics of consequence. Jesus said that a man who lusted in his heart had already committed adultery. Buddha was certain that good and evil follow faithfully from the actions of the mind.[34]

31. This theory of action is much more comprehensive than the Western concept of moral action. Even the ethically neutral movement of a blank thought constitutes *karma* that will generate a minute momentum toward one's rebirth.

32. More accurately, nothing in the material world falls outside the laws of *karma*. Transcendental realities like *nirvāṇa* or *Buddha-Dharma* may fall outside this domain.

33. This meaning of *karma* appeared in the Vedic *Brahmaṇas* (priestly lore) prior to the time of the Buddha.

34. The opening verse of the popular *Dharmapada* speaks of good and evil, following closely upon the mind like the track and the wheel of a cart. Also, both in Christianity and in Buddhism, will or *saṃskāra* becomes a new focus of moral concern in matters of salvation or enlightenment.

Historically, religious concern about ethics of motivation usually led to a rational and critical review of traditional morals. Lore, custom, and taboo which constituted law or part of the sacred law before were refined, redefined, or rewritten by the resulting moral criticism. The early Christian church, for example, challenged Hebraic rules of dietary cleanliness. The Buddha, too, rejected old ideas about caste uncleanliness, opening his fellowship to the *śūdra*, the lowest caste, and to women. This focus on ethics of motivation perhaps also led to a redefinition of the Chinese concept of legal responsibility. Sharper distinctions were made between the intent to do evil, actions committed with intent, and acts committed mindlessly or accidentally. This distinction was a clear advance beyond the innocent guilt and subsequent punishment that previously was visited upon an unaware taboo-breaker.[35] Above all, a culture influenced by ethics of motivation insists on personal responsibility. A person will not be punished for sins committed by a brother. So, too, the Buddha emphasized that a person is a Brahmin not by birth but only because of his actions and present virtue. Birth (ascription) is secondary to merit (achievement). *Karma* in Buddhist understanding is therefore not passive fate; to resign oneself to karmic fate is in fact a sin in Buddhist thought.[36]

The Buddha emphasized free will and karmic consequence. In the earlier tradition, preserved in Theravāda (Hinayana), *karma* was entirely individualistic and could not be transferred.[37] Each man was required to earn his salvation by his own actions. This idea was fairly alien to China because even the Taoist community had the idea that the sins or the blessings of ancestors would visit upon and be borne by their children.[38] Similarly, Chinese familism could not free itself from communal responsibility. Only the Legalist tried to insist on strict personal responsibility, at the same time preserving the idea of guilt by association. The impact the Buddhist empha-

35. For a comprehensive treatment of this issue, see P. RICOEUR, THE SYMBOLISM OF EVIL (1967).

36. Thus, there is both active *karma* and passive *karma*, depending on emphasis, and the Buddhist tradition is highly critical of the latter, referring to it as the "poison" of indolence or lassitude.

37. Māhâyna modifies this with the notion that one pays for one's own sins but works for the good of all.

38. This concept is called "carrying the burden" in the *T'ai-p'ing-ching* and is comparable to the concept of *nemesis* in Greek myth and drama. Both boon and burden sent down by ancestors may undermine the ideal of individual responsibility.

sis on individual responsibility had upon the Chinese notion of justice and the legal system in the medieval period is difficult to ascertain. Buddhism did not appear to change much of the traditional practice of assigning liability on the basis of responsibility, a practice that was most severe in cases of crime against the state.[39]

The shortcomings of the ethics of motivation arise precisely because of the subjective nature of such ethics. Pushed to its extreme, this ethic would make the administration of justice in society impossible. No judge can charge and sentence all men who lust in their hearts on the grounds that they have, thereby, committed adultery. A monk's concern about any unbecoming thought, however minute or private, should not be duplicated into a society's paranoia about hidden evils. In contrast, laws based on the ethics of consequence, tend to allow greater privacy to the individual because only those of his actions that have public consequence will be judged. Ethics of motivation generated in the puritan West and in the Neo-Confucian China regrettable witch-hunts seeking to control and punish private behavior. The moral common law of the people made life difficult for many people.

In India the law of *karma* was wedded to Buddha's concept of *anātman* (no-self, no-soul, no-actor). The philosophical contradiction of insisting on moral retribution while denying the reality of a self was more acute in India than in China. The harshness of this contradiction was mitigated by the Chinese acceptance of the doctrine of an immortal soul that transmigrates from one life to another. This development was attributable to the Confucianist emphasis on morality and to the Taoist emphasis on immortality of the spirit. In India, the evil of a socially reprehensible deed may be counteracted by the practice of private austerities or *yoga*. In Confucian China, the dialectic of *karma* was more narrowly defined as moral good and evil to be rewarded or punished publicly. Thus in the Ming and Ching periods, Chinese authors produced numerous treatises on the inevitability of moral retribution, often within this life. These moralizing tales preached that where human justice fails, divine justice will ultimately triumph with total impartiality. "The net of Heaven (justice) is wide; though thinly woven, it never lets the evildoer escape."[40]

39. The most severe punishment was execution "up to nine tribes (lineages)."
40. Chinese idiom. The Divine Law is thought to be supportive of, but more

One Buddhist answer to the paradox of moral retribution without a lasting self is given by the formula of *pratyaya* or "condition." Although there is no permanent selfhood, there are conditions that create an everchanging self identity. The physical self does not transmigrate to the next life, but subtle psychic forces might. Similarly, actions are accounted for, not by a permanent actor but by a set of conditions permitting those of actions to arise. The classical formula is the Buddhist theory of causation, *pratītya-samutpāda*: "when this is present, that is present." The theory is also called "conditioned co-arising" or "dependent origination." The Buddha is said to have discovered, under the *bodhi* (enlightenment) tree, that whenever there is craving, there is suffering; whenever craving ceases to be, there is the cessation of suffering. This law of causation is more a law of concomitancy than a mechanical law of cause and effect.[41] Technically, only when the proper conditions exist, usually in the moment just preceding the action to be analyzed, will the result occur. For example, in murder the murderous act can be committed only when the correct conditions are present: the intent, the presence of the victim, the timeliness, and the availability of a weapon. In theory, the Buddhist law of causation is similar to the modern liberal theory of environmental determinism, a view that imputes social responsibility to extrapersonal conditions, for example, a high crime rate in the ghetto. It appears, however, that the Confucianists and the Legalists never openly accepted the theory of condition as a mitigating circumstance. The theory of *yüan*, when wedded to a doctrine of no-self, would easily shift moral responsibility entirely away from the moral agent to surrounding factors.

An understanding of conditioned co-arising can lead to a counteraction of the law of *karma*. If one knows that craving leads to suffering, this knowledge can free him from suffering. The Buddha, after discovering this formula, mapped out a path of *mārga*, describing the karmic chain that produced suffering in *saṃsāra*. His teaching, his Law, can transcend the law of *karma*.[42] This Law may either depict the path to *nirvāna* or may, because of the Buddha's

---

comprehensive than, the laws of men, who are often only agents of Heaven, *karma*, or Tao.

41. *See* Lai, *Chinese Buddhist Causation Theories*, 27 PHILOSOPHY EAST AND WEST No. 3, at 241-64 (1977).

42. In Chinese and Japanese Buddhism, *karma* and *Dharma* are often set up as opposite poles. The burden of life's *karma* is said to be lifted by the infinite mercy of the *Buddha-Dharma*.

great power in Mahayana, liberate the devotee through merely his faith in the *Buddha-Dharma*. The latter case involves the theory of merit transference from the Buddha to the believer and touches upon the irrationality of grace. The more rational path is seen in the classic program of *śīla, samādhi,* and *prajñā* (precepts, meditation, and wisdom). These three steps correspond to the Western spiritual path of purification, contemplation, and illumination practiced by medieval mystics. Adherence to the precepts in combination with the practice of meditation will lead to enlightenment. This law or path counteracts the effects of *karma*. Contemplation of enlightenment defies the rational parameters of this Article and the supernatural laws governing the Buddha's grace and the flight of spirit during meditation are also beyond the scope of consideration. The *vinaya* (*lü* in our earlier discussion), however, merits further examination.

Monastic Regulations

The *lü* or monastic precepts are the body of rules to which monks should adhere. The Buddha reputedly authored or authorized this second "basket" (division) in the *tripiṭaka*, the Buddhist "three-basket" canon in Theravāda. The Buddha, in rejecting the caste duties and founding his own community, outlined these communal laws and regulations. Different sects have slightly different versions of the basic 250.[43] The *vinaya* governs both personal and official conduct of individual monks and monks-in-fellowship. The rules are extremely detailed because they are designed to cover all conceivable misdemeanors, including even the private contents of dreams. They must have appeared at an early date because in the second council after the death of the Buddha, such minor misdeeds as storing salt were important enough to split the community. Compared with the monastic codes of the West or the canonical law of the Church, the Buddhist *vinaya* is older and much more detailed. Its substantial impact on Chinese culture is traced below.

The Buddha's act of establishing a semipermanent community of *sannyāsins*, or ascetics, was a break with the previous individualistic tradition of eremites. Responsible for organizing a new communal life for individual hermits, the Buddha founded the *saṇgha*,

43. *See* C.S. Prebish, Buddhist Monastic Disciplines: The Sanskrit Prātimoksha Sūtras of the Mahāsanghika and the Mūlasarvāstivādins (1975).

fellowship of monks, the first large-scale "tertiary group" beyond the traditional family, village, and state. Custom, lore, and taboos were pushed aside to create an atmosphere conducive to the rational search for enlightenment.

The *saṅgha* institution, introduced into China in the fifth century,[44] was distinguishable from even the Taoist experiment in the third century. The religious Taoists of the T'ien-shih-tao were the first to create a tertiary group but even they accepted the Confucianist commitment to the family (the primary group). In Taoism, filial piety was affirmed as the basic precept. Filial piety was rejected, however, in the early Chinese *saṅgha*. The Buddha, the *bhikṣu* (ordained monks), and even the *śramaṇas* (novices), as teachers of the Dharma, were seen as more important than parents. The community even called its members brothers, sisters, mothers, sons, and other family appellations not unlike the primitive Church. The rational lifestyle of the independent brotherhood may have affected secular institutions. Later Zen monastic codes, without historical precedent, created a previously unknown organizational ability. The Zen simplicity in lifestyle, its devotion to task (*kungfu*), and its faithful reverence toward teachers (regarded as living *Buddhas*) influenced the Neo-Confucians. The Neo-Confucian private academies were, like monasteries, removed from the secular world. Rules governing student life and master-disciple relationship were sparklingly clear, concise and structured so as to be spiritually edifying. The members of those academies then produced, from the 12th century on, popular family laws, bureaucratic codes of behavior, and the moralizing treatises.[45]

The *vinaya* was regarded as the word of the Buddha, on the same level of sacredness as the *sūtra*.[46] For perhaps the first time in Chinese history, there was a code that was inviolable because no man, not even the precept-master, was above the law. The seriousness of the rules of the *vinaya* can best be illustrated by the example of Hui-yüan. This gentry monk died after refusing to take any medicine containing alcohol, a forbidden substance.

The *vinaya* inculcated the ideal of uniformity and equality before the law. This ideal is contrary to the Confucian *li*, ritual pro-

44. About three centuries after the initial acceptance of the *sūtras*.

45. In their detailed regulations, puritanical overtones, rigidity, and evangelical zeal, the Neo-Confucianists seem to have been indebted to the Buddhists.

46. The same claim is not made by the Christian monastic codes.

priety, which recognizes grades of deference and addresses itself primarily to the cultured classes. According to Confucian thought, the common people should not be bound or burdened by the decorum and etiquette of the gentlemen. The Buddhist spirit of law is also contrary to the Legalist tradition. The Legalist desires total objectivity in law and dreams of a country ruled automatically by clear, understandable decrees. Notwithstanding this dream, the Legalist must cater to the wishes of the king who is above the law. Legalist *fa* is also positive law, changeable at will and dependent on power and craft of the ruler, who is the ultimate source of the definitions of right and wrong. In contrast, the law of the Buddha, created by a man, is neither arbitrary nor coercive. Anchored in the transcendental *dharma,* the *vinaya* is impersonal and therefore objective.[47] Designed for *sannyāsins* brought together in a fraternity, the *vinaya,* unlike Canon Law, is nonhierarchial and insists on obedience to the letter of the law and not, as in Christian monasticism, personal obedience to the superior or abbot. Only in Zen monasteries is the master seen as a living Buddha, a representative in the unbroken transmission of the *dharma* and, therefore, one who may flout the rules for expedient purposes.

Autonomy is the goal the *vinaya* seeks to inculcate because the goal of the Law of the Buddha is not justice but discipline, especially self-discipline. Self-discipline is the implicit goal in any *yoga,* the art of perfect self-control. The Chinese term to describe this is *tzu-lü,* self-regulation. This ideal may be new in view of the Confucianist belief in *li,* an interpersonal and societal standard, although Confucianism does insist on introspection. The Neo-Confucianists, who came *after* the Buddhist era, stressed, even more, the independence of spirit. Confucianists, however, also trust in *te,* the virtue and the power of sages and illustrious ancestors. *Te* exerts an almost magical influence upon their fellow men.[48] The ideal of self-regulation, or *tzu-lü,* was foreign also to the Legalist way of thinking. In the Legalist-Taoist outlook, law, *fa,* may be self-regulating to such a degree that the king could withdraw into *wu-wei,* nonaction. Legalist *fa* insists on fear of punishment as a basic prerequisite to law-abidance and utilizes coercion to get its way. The Legal-

47. Compare the impersonal *Torah* of the Jewish religion as the word of God and the subjective Grace sought by Christians through the person of Christ.

48. The Buddha, however, is comparable in this incidence to the sage's *te*; and monks are thought to generate waves of friendliness in the world.

ist would not accept Buddha's last instruction: "Be a lamp unto thyself; strive on in diligence." The idea of autonomy for the people suggests to the Legalist only anarchy and lawlessness.

The foregoing discussion illustrates the ascetic rationality in the *Buddha-Dharma*. Despite Buddhism's otherworldly goal (*nirvāna*) and the transrationality of *prajñā* (wisdom), the Buddhist believes in a structured universe and a structured lifestyle.

Sociological Impact of the *Buddha-Dharma*

The *Buddha-Dharma*, which calls a person to leave family and home to join the *saṇgha* and seek enlightenment, created the first real tension between a church and the Chinese state. Loyalty to the Buddha was incompatible with the Confucian and Legalist ideal of "one king, one ideology." The Confucian concept of state is paternalistic; the king is theoretically replaceable if he fails to fulfill the moral mandate of Heaven. The Legalist idea of the state is absolutistic; the king "owns" his domain and his subjects and is not answerable to anyone. In the Buddhist period, there suddenly arose in China a class of people who forsook the sacred family, pledged a new loyalty to Buddha and declared themselves his sons, *shih-tzu*.[49] Young men reaching the age of majority, eighteen, wanted to join the *saṇgha* as novices and become monks at twenty-one, the Buddhist age of majority.[50] *Sūtras* declared that a "master" was more precious than parents.[51] Filial piety was losing its status as the most important virtue in the Six Dynasties.[52] An enduring controversy among Buddhists, Legalists and Confucianists ensued from these conflicts.

The conflict between *fo-fa*, the Law of the Buddha, and *wang-fa*, the Law of the King, flared up many times. The initial Buddhist position rejected the laws of the state. It conceived of the monk as having left home and country and having accepted the new laws within the *saṇgha* instead. Hui-yüan was successful in defending

49. All Chinese monks adopt *Sakya*, *Shih*, as their new clan name.

50. Buddhist *vinaya* recognizes human laws and would discourage the sole son of a family, for example, from joining the fellowship.

51. *See* *T'i-wei Po-li ching* (*Sūtra* of *Trapusa* and *Bhallika*) (recently recovered manuscript).

52. Later, in the T'ang Dynasty, Buddhism reaffirmed this virtue. *See* K. Ch'en, The Chinese Transformation of Buddhism 15-50 (1973).

this position.[53] The more liberal Mahayana followers espoused another view grounded in the *sūtra's* notion that being King constituted a contract that could be rescinded if the king was unruly. It taught that the state existed for the common good and for the glory of the Buddha.

Saṇgha and state coexist in peace. The Buddhists were granted privileges, and the monks maintained a generally apolitical profile. The state did not intrude into the *saṇgha's* traditional rights through legislation but expected the *saṇgha* to be a passive and ascetic community. The rights had been granted from the inception of the monastic way of life. This broad grant of rights to the institution—the *saṇgha* "jewel"—rather than to the individuals—set a precedent. Through this action the state recognized the sanctity of a separate reality, a "City of Buddha" on earth.[54] Previous to this recognition, the Chinese emperor had only recognized the sanctity of individual sages, holy men, and descendants of sages and had granted them privileges out of his own free will and without undermining his claim to absolute control. Such favors were also given in return for their subtle contributions to the state. In granting exemption from searches by any imperial troop to Master Lang, a Buddhist hiding in T'ai-shan, the king still exercised this prerogative. When the king recognized the sacredness of the *saṇgha*-jewel as an institution, however, it was a much greater concession because the charisma of the individual was no longer relevant. Abuses of the new system proliferated, and repeated persecution through special edicts charging the abuses became the standard method of controlling the Buddhist "state within a state." Both the Legalist and Confucianist camps recognized the danger of the Buddhist claim to *tzu-lü*, or autonomy.[55] During the sixth century in the north, the *saṇgha* actually ran its own monastic bureaucracy alongside the civil Confucianist bureaucracy, collected its own tax in the form of grain and administered its own justice, except in murder cases. Not until the T'ang dynasty were the temples returned to civil control, accompanied by a decree requiring monks to take "placement examinations."

53. *Id.* at 72-77.

54. The *sangha* is being compared to the Christian concept of the Church as the City of God on earth.

55. The Chinese Buddhist apologists, under attack, naturally defended the compatibility of the *Buddha-Dharma* with the law of the family and the state. *See* K. CH'EN, THE CHINESE TRANSFORMATION OF BUDDHISM 65-124 (1973).

The Mahayana community in China did have some positive influence on secular law. Compassion is a key prerequisite to the bodhisattvic career, and in those dynasties in which the rulers were sympathetic to Buddhism, the number of tabooed days in which beheading could not be done increased.[56] Emperor Wu of the Liang dynasty was famous for his leniency in this area. Mahayana encouraged its followers to mitigate the harshness of punishment, because compassion required the suspension of human laws for the sake of enlightening lost souls.

Mahayana, however, also has a concept of the End of the Law stemming from the perceived corruption of the authentic teachings of Buddha as a result of their transmission from men to men. This corruption is only related to the transmission of the teachings and not to the eternal purity of the *dharma* as such. In contrast to the Hindu concept of cyclical decay and regeneration of the universe,[57] Buddhists perceive only one sequence of decay interrupted by moments of revival. Different dates have been predicted for the commencement of the last age. Because the degeneration of the *Buddha-Dharma* means not just the decay of the doctrines, but also the nature of humanity, family, state, cosmos, and universe, the arrival of total lawlessness in this period can sometimes be met with "intentional lawlessness" (flouting of all conventions)[58] and eschatological expectations of the arrival of the Future Buddha. The Ming dynasty was founded in expectation of the reign of Light (*ming*), a *Manichaean* motif that had infiltrated Buddhism. Because of such eschatological expectations, in the recent dynasties there have been repeated uprisings among peasants whose members deny all current laws and institutions. The political impact of this folk Buddhist discontent registered in the mobilization of the peasant masses in the Communist revolution. This religious underground, often violent, apocalyptic, and a law unto itself, was nurtured by communalistic hopes to serve the oppressed. This late Buddhist tradition was no longer the parasitic, withdrawn, and passive piety of the otherworldly monks.

56. *See* CHÜ T'UNG-TSU, LAW AND SOCIETY IN TRADITIONAL CHINA 15-90 (1961). The tabooed days occur when the *karma* accounts are being made. They are often determined by Chinese calendar calculations of "crisis days."

57. Hindu *Dharma* is cosmic, but the *Buddha-Dharma* is based on a historically unrepeatable event.

58. One famous Japanese text says that laws in fact are made to be broken and any pretense at keeping the *vinaya* is prideful and impossible.

The contemporary scene may now be evaluated from the historical perspective gleaned from the preceding survey of the Buddhist tradition.

Impact on the Present

The Buddhist "ethics of motivation," as opposed to "ethics of consequences," is echoed in the present-day People's Republic of China, where "thought reform" and "self-criticism" have assumed a religious fervor. The strong note of egalitarianism in Chinese communism reflects the Buddhist emphasis on universal brotherhood, on a life of service, and on personal merit (achievement) over birth (ascription). Even the forsaking of families by the Red Guards recalls the similar actions of Buddhist monks in leaving behind earthly cravings and belongings. Revolutions often produce their own brand of asceticism.

The dichotomy between *li* and *fa* in the Chinese legal system and the dominance of *li* over *fa* in the event of a conflict have continued from Imperial China through the Nationalistic era to the People's Republic of China. In conflicts between the heavily Western-oriented laws and Constitution of the Nationalist period and *li*, *li* prevailed.[59] The inheritance law is one example.[60] The traditional *li* would, in the interest of continuing the cult, pass everything from a deceased father to the eldest son of the legitimate wife. Other offspring, whether younger sons or daughters, married or unmarried, would not have any right of succession to the patrimony, although the deceased or his heir could relinquish a share of the hereditary property to the heir's brothers and sisters. Under the Nationalist Civil Code, equality of the sexes was the proclaimed policy of the State, and all of the deceased's children, sons and daughters, married or unmarried, were allowed equal shares of the property. Nevertheless, Escarra quotes the following remark, made to him by a high Kuomintang official:

---

59. *See Dien in China and Vietnam*, 17 J. ASIAN STUDIES 403, 411 (1958); *Suginchara Shun' ichi, Ten No Hotcki: Seishihtsu*, 19 HORITSU JIHO 32 (1947); McAleavy, The People's Court (1961) (unpublished).

60. For a discussion of inheritance law in China today, see VAN DER VALK, THE LAW OF INHERITANCE IN EASTERN EUROPE AND IN THE PEOPLE'S REPUBLIC OF CHINA (1961).

> According to law, my interlocutor told me in substance, my wife would have the right, on the death of her father, to claim a share of the property equal to that of her brothers. Perhaps, according to the circumstances, she would have an understanding with them to obtain a share. But one fact is certain. That is, that she will never exercise her right (although it is inscribed in the Code) and that I will never permit her to plead on this point. For in so doing I should act contrary to the rites and I, as well as my wife, should have against me the unanimous disapproval of public opinion.[61]

It is important to realize that the content of *li* is not immutable. Just as Han Fei-tze, founder of the Legalist School, had no monopoly over the specific rules of *fa*, so Confucius could not dictate the content of *li* for all generations to come. *Li*, in a broad sense, may be interpreted as custom that has acquired the force of law, characterized by moral teachings, the use of persuasion, the appeal to reason and good sense, and the exemplification of good conduct and behavior. Its metamorphosis into law depends upon its widespread and unvaried acceptance by society, but its specific content may change with the times. Just as customary law may change over the ages, so some rules of *li*, appropriate in Confucius' time, may not be relevant in the twentieth century. Anyone able to instill a new *li* into the spirit and mind of the people would succeed in remolding the social behavior of millions in the same way Confucianism has done in the past. The Kuomintang had the *San-Min-Chu-I*[62] and the New Life Movement but, for a variety of reasons, their goals remained unfulfilled.

The guiding spirit of Chinese Communist Law is Maoism, the new *li* which replaced the Confucian *li*. Fully aware of the danger of a discrepancy between *fa* and the new *li*, the Communist Party, renowned for its mass organizational ability, mobilized all the human resources at its disposal—party members, cadres, and students—to reshape public opinion into accepting the Communist *li* based on Mao's New Democracy. Mass meetings were convened and study groups formed for the purpose of re-educating the people. Furthermore,

61. ESCARRA, *supra* note 1, at 31.

62. The *San-min Chu-I* were the Three Principles of the People: Nationalism, Democracy, and the People's Livelihood. Formulated by Dr. Sun Yat-sen around 1905, these three principles formed the dogma of the Kuomintang which Sun Yat-sen founded.

the promulgation of important laws, including the 1954 Constitution and the Marriage Law of 1951, was preceded by intense public discussion and debate, and the public was invited to make comments and suggestions.[63] Although it appears that basic policies and doctrines are predetermined by the Communist Party, there is always room for a change on a technical level. There is no doubt that such measures have been instrumental in giving the public a sense of identity with the new legislation and thus in bridging the gap between the Communist *li* and *fa*.

When a conflict does exist, the Chinese Communists have not hesitated to follow the centuries-old tradition of elevating *li* over *fa*. For example, despite the guarantee of religious freedom in article 88 of the Constitution of the People's Republic of China, such freedom is at best restrictively interpreted and at worst severely impaired because of its incompatibility with dialectical materialism. In addition, article 78 of the Constitution, providing that courts must be guided by law alone when deciding cases, is designed to ensure judicial independence, but this provision for independence has been construed to mean that courts must follow national policy, must be controlled and supervised by the people, and must be in harmony with local governmental activities.[64] A third example of the predominance of *li* over *fa* is the vestigial nature of article 10 of the Constitution, which guarantees capitalists the right of ownership of the means of production, and of article 87, which guarantees freedom of speech, publication, assembly, association, procession, demonstration and the Government's material assistance in their implementation.

A question may be raised concerning the compatibility of China's habit of elevating *li* over *fa* with its meticulous observance of treaty obligations, even those which conflict with Chinese principles of justice and equity.[65] Cynics may attribute this apparent inconsistency to temporary military expediency in the face of the overwhelming nuclear superiority of the United States and the Soviet Union.

---

63. *See* Mizuno, *The Judicial System*, in CHUGOKU NO HO TO SHAKAI 51 (1959) (Report of the Japanese jurist's mission to China); *id. passim*.

64. WEI WEN-PO, TUI-YU "CHUNG-HUA JEN-MIN KUNG-HO-KUO JEN-MIN FA-YUAN TSU-SHIH-FA" CHI-PEN WEN-T'I TE JEN-CHIH 7 (1956).

65. *See* L.T. LEE, CHINA AND INTERNATIONAL AGREEMENTS (1969); Lee, *Treaty Relations of the People's Republic of China: A Study of Compliance*, 116 U. PA. L. REV. 244 (1967).

The teaching of Confucius may, however, shed some light on this question.

The last of the five relationships which dominate Confucian society is the relationship between friends, a relationship characterized by sincerity. This trusting relationship is based on equality. It is the one that diplomatic relations most closely resemble, governed as they are by *Pacta sunt servanda* or good faith—the equivalent of sincerity on the interstate level. A discussion of the contrast between China's relations with North Korea and those with Tibet may illustrate the validity of the above analogy.

The suzereign-vassal relationship that has traditionally existed between China and Tibet may be analogized to the relationship between an elder and younger brother in a Confucian society, rather than that between a sovereign and a subject or between friends. Because brotherly relations in a Confucian society call for a strict maintenance of order, the rights and duties between brothers transcend mere observance of agreements. Thus, regardless of the personal preference of a younger brother, the elder brother has, in the interest of the family, certain obligations toward him which cannot be shirked without violating the Confucian code of conduct. Transformed into the international sphere, this duty might form the basis for Peking's institution of land reform and other programs in Tibet, notwithstanding the provisions of article 11 of the Sino-Tibetan agreement of 1951 against the use of compulsion on the part of the central authorities to effect reforms.[66]

---

66. The legal relationship of Tibet to China dates from the 13th century when Kublai Khan, a Mongol Emperor of China, ceded temporal authority over Tibet to the Dalai Lamas, and continued through the Manchu dynasty and the Republican era to the 1951 Agreement of the Central People's Government and the Local Government of Tibet on Measures for the Peaceful Liberation of Tibet. For an English translation of the Agreement, see A.L. STRONG, TIBETAN INTERVIEWS 200-05 (1959). For further discussion of Sino-Tibetan relations, see INTERNATIONAL COMMISSION OF JURISTS, THE QUESTION OF TIBET AND THE RULE OF LAW (1959); A. LAMB, THE CHINA-INDIA BORDER (1964); Alexandrowicz, *Comment on the Legal Position of Tibet*, 5 INDIAN YEAR BOOK OF INT'L AFFAIRS 172-73 (1956); Green, *Legal Aspects of the Sino-Indian Border Dispute*, CHINA Q., at 43 (July-Sept. 1960); Rubin, *A Matter of Fact*, 59 AM. J. INT'L L. 586 (1965); Rubin, *The Position of Tibet in International Law*, CHINA Q. No. 35 at 110 (July-Sept. 1968); Sharma, *The India-China Border Dispute: An Indian Perspective*, 59 AM. J. INT'L L. 16 (1965); Tieh-Tseng Li, *The Legal Position of Tibet*, 50 AM. J. INT'L L. 394 (1956). Neither India nor the United States, nor, indeed, any state, has recognized Tibet as anything other than Chinese territory.

In the case of Korea, however, its centuries-old, vassal-suzereign relationship with China was terminated by the Sino-Japanese War of 1895. It was formally annexed by Japan in 1910 and, after World War II, it became divided but independent. Korean relations with China have resumed as those between friends in a Confucian society, characterized by sincerity. This turn of events might explain Peking's meticulous compliance with promises made to North Korea, including that concerning the withdrawal of Chinese troops in 1958.[67]

Because of the predominance of *li* over *fa*, the study of Chinese law must be all-embracing. To a much greater extent than is true of Western law, it must include the study of philosophy, religion, classics, history, politics, economics, sociology, and psychology. Preoccupation with scrutinizing, analyzing, and comparing statutes and court decisions—a skill that Western lawyers employ with dexterity and felicity—is futile and misleading[68] because such an approach, devoid of insight into the makeup of Chinese society, would at best deal with symptoms and not causes. Yet the mastery of the Chinese language, let alone the mastery of the Chinese culture, is a life-long process for non-Chinese. Although the efforts of a few American universities to initiate Chinese legal studies and a few law professors who have begun the study of the Chinese language serve as encouragement, the tasks ahead are arduous and full of pitfalls.

---

67. *See* L.T. Lee, China and International Agreements 46-58 (1969).
68. *See* Lee, Book Review, 12 Am. J. Comp. L. 606-09 (1963).

[11]

WESTERN LAW IN A TRADITIONAL SOCIETY KOREA

by Dai-Kwon Choi*

I. Introduction

Koreans, perhaps more than others, used to say that there is a gap between the law and the reality. For some the gap borders on an outright lawlessness as seen in the high rate of traffic violations on the streets of metropolitan cities, in the number of public officials dismissed or prosecuted on a bribery charge, and in the business practices believed as invariably associated with tax evasions, reckless discharge of pollutants, etc. For others the gap represents an attribute of human nature. An ideal is always not fulfy realized; in a sense, the harder to realize, the more ideal. In fact, there is no society in which there is no gap between the law and the reality. For still others the gap is symptomatic of social malaise afflicted with by a society in rapid transition such as Korea.

For some others the gap is actually between Western and Oriental cultures. In this shrinking world a tension and conflict between two cultures is only natural according as Korea is extensively exposed to Western influences. The formal Korean law is based on Western concepts, particularly German ones, which were forcefully introduced by the Japanese for their colonial rule at the turn of the century—American influence is also felt in its ideological contents, following the World War II.

Traditional Korean culture was greatly influenced by two thousand years of Confucian teachings. Naturally, Confucian notions of propriety and law became deeply ingrained in Korean attitudes toward law. In the Analects, Confucius says:

> "Lead the people with governmental measures and regulate them by law and punishment, they will avoid wrongdoing but will have no sense of honor and shame. Lead them with virtue and regulate them by the rules of propriety (*li*), and they will have a sense of shame and, moreover, set themselves right."

*Currently Professor of Law (Assistant Professor), Law School, Seoul National University; Associate Director of the Korea Law Research Institute of Seoul National University. LL.B., 1960, Seoul National University; M.C.L., 1967, University of Michigan Law School; LL.M., 1969, University of California School of Law at Berkeley; Ph.D., 1976, University of California at Berkeley.

Even at the level of ordinary persons, the most popular expression toward an upright neighbor or a good colleague today is "a person who can live without law." One's insistence on the formal law tends to make a Korean frown upon him.

Apart from the formal law, there is a remarkable orderliness. This stands out especially when the formal law completely collapses because of a political upheaval or a disaster. The kind of orderliness showed up right after the fall of President Syng Man Rhee's regime and the accompanied collapse of the formal law apparatus that followed the students' revolt of April 19, 1960. The same students that took to streets to revolt had promptly organized themselves to do the job of cleaning streets, controlling traffic, and patrolling neighborhoods. The same orderliness prevailed a few years ago in the town of Iri where there was a giant explosion of the freight train carrying a large amount of explosives at night. The explosion caused heavy damages to humans and properties accompanied by a total blackout like a town devastated by a severe earthquake. Thus one is reminded of the newspaper articles that carried a contrasting picture of New York when the city had a blackout. In Korea, the orderliness resides in the persisting traditional social structure.

What is said above of the gap, the traditional Korean cultural patterns, and the social orderliness, all has truth about law in Korean society. The gap between the law and the reality in Korea is more complex than the simple gap in any normative system; the former gap has three dimensions of conflicts: between the social norms residing in the persisting social structure and their reality; between the formal Western law and its reality; and between the Western values embodied in the formal law and the social norms embodied in the social structure. However, the last dimension is more significant than the other two; it highlights one of the core problems with the gap between the law and the reality in Korea today.

Even with the last dimension of the gap, a thorny issue is how to approach it. Understanding of the entire scope of the dimension is not tried here. In this paper, only an attempt is made to bring a more focused light on five antinomies around which tensions, conflicts, interactions, and interrelationships between Western formal law and the persisting traditional social structure manifestedly evolve. These are: (1) universalism vs. particularism, (2) impersonal vs. personal relationships, (3) competition vs. cooperation, (4) individual vs. collective responsibility, and (5) conflict vs. harmony. Modern Western law incorporates the first variables of these five antinomies as overarching principle and underlying values. The second variables of these five antinomies are embodied in the Korean traditional social structure. No doubt, the five characteristic features of Western law considered here have their historical roots in Western society. Likewise, the five traits of the traditional Korean social structure have their historical roots in Korean society. Even this simple historical consideration makes apparent the presence and pervasiveness of the five antinomies in various social contexts. It obviously precludes the idea that the imposition of a Western, modern, formal legal system on a non-Western—and non-Communist—society such as Korea will alone transform a traditional social structure into one with modern characteristics. At the same time, however, there is a danger of overdichotomizing the five antinomies against which we must guard. A closer examination will reveal a complicated combination of the variables involved in the dichotomies.

II. Universalism vs. Particularism

Since particularism is defined as interchangeable with ascriptive principle or with status, universalism is in our scheme defined as a principle negating particularism. Thus understood, universalism differs from uniformity. Even a particularistic (or ascriptive) rule can be perfectly uniform throughout a society or a state. Uniformity—that is, generality or regularity—is an inseparable feature of law whether it applies to group, nation, or state. Of course, there is room for local variation (localism or federalism) in territorial uniformity to some extent within certain areas of human activity. But in other areas territorial uniformity is the rule. Even the kind of social and/or political-institutional localism that once prevailed in China and feudal Japan never existed in Korea. In law of nationality (naturalization and immigration), a personal principle is the rule in the Continental Europe and in Korea. In the Anglo-American world, a territorial principle is the rule. In a conflict of law situation, the law of nationality (or of domicile) is relied on for certain issues whereas the law of the forum is for other issues, according to the forum's choice of law rule.

Historically, particularism is associated with class, race, and religion. In this connection the evolution from status to contract best describes the present state of universalistic law. In the transformation the French revolution is the symbolic and political turning point in Europe. The introduction of the Western formal legal system in Korea at the turn of the century marks the start of universalistic law in this society at least in formal legal principle. In dynastic Korea, particularism was the rule.

Social and (formal) legal norms were structured along official class lines and order of rank among *yangban* officials.

In dynastic Korea, for example, there were sumptuary laws that differentially regulated one's mode of life with respect to clothing, housing, and rituals in accordance with one's social and legal status.[1] Scholar-officials for the centralized bureaucratic organizations were recruited exclusively from the ruling yangban class on the basis of performance at the royal examinations for civil and military officials. As the philosopher-king producing ruling class, the yangban received differential treatment legally from other classes with respect to both privileges and obligations. For example, members of this class were not subject to compulsory military service and labor—corresponding to the Western corvée. These obligations were borne entirely by the commoners. On the other hand, more exacting behavioral rules and standards, based on Confucian moral norms, were required of yangbans than of non-yangbans. These included rules against extravagance,[2] making a profit, corruption,[3] immoral behavior,[4] superstition including practices in Buddhism,[5] and sexual promiscuity.[6] This latter included prohibitions against taking a wife with-

1. As for clothing, for example, see *Kyongkukdaejon* (The Great Codes of Governance), a modern Korean translation, (Seoul: Bopjaech'o, 1962), I; 216 ff. and II, 166; *Sokdaejon*, a modern Korean translation, (Seoul: Bopjaech'o, 1965), 202; as for housing *Kyongkukdaejon*, II, 210; *Han'guksa* (History of Korea), (Seoul: Kuksa p'yonch'an wiwonhoe, 1974), XI, 393–396; as for rituals, *Kyongkukdaejon*, I, 233 ff., 261, and 266–268.

2. For example, it constituted a crime entailing a flogging of 100 strokes for a yangban lady to have a picnic in a wood or on a beach. *Kyongkukdaejon, ibid.*, II, 165. Similar prohibitive rules had existed against various forms of "extravagance."

3. Like a yangban lady who had "befouled her virtue" (see note 6 *infra*), a yangban (official) who had embezzled public funds, taken bribe, or illegally enriched himself was also recorded in the public records which were kept by various ministries and offices. *Kyongkukdaejon, ibid.*, II, 167. He was not only punished but also permanently barred from taking another official position and from taking the royal examination. His son and grandson were also barred from taking the royal examination as well as from being appointed to major official positions specified in the Code. *Kyongkukdaejon*, I, 23 and 201.

4. A yangban whose behavior was "against the proper human relations" was also in the official records kept by various ministries and offices. *Kyongkukdaejon, ibid.*, II, 167.

5. It also constituted a crime entailing 100 strokes for a Confucian scholar (or a lady) to go to a Buddhist temple. *Kyongkukdaejon, ibid.*, II, 165.

6. It was prohibited for a yangban man to marry within three years after his former wife had died, and for a yangban lady to marry for the second time. For the

in three years after a previous wife had died and against a yangban lady marrying for a second time, and the requirement of three years of mourning at the death of a parent,[7] during which period a yangban had to live a monk-like ascetic life by the parent's graveyard. Due to this requirement any official who had an official position had to resign, and any misconduct unworthy of a yangban, especially sexual misconduct, during the mourning period entailed harsh punishment.[8] A yangban in mourning who

former prohibition, see *Kyongkukdaejon, ibid.*, I, 267. Probably the former rule must have been more effective than the latter, even though there was no negative formal legal sanction for the former rule. The social censor against a yangban who violated the former rule, however, must have been extremely strong among the yangban class especially when he was ambitious in the officialdom. For the latter rule, there were official records in which a yangban lady who had "befouled her virtue" by having married for the third time was recorded. These records were kept by the Ministry of Officiais (*Ijo*), the Ministry of Armed Forces (*Pyongjo*), and the two censorial offices. *Kyongkukdaejon*, II, 167. Descendants (son or grandson) of a lady who had married for the second time or otherwise "befouled her virtue" were not only allowed to take the royal examination for civil officials (*Kyongkukdaejon*, 1, 201), but also were barred from their being appointed to major official positions specified in the Code of Officials (*Kyongkukdaejon*, I, 23). See also Yi Sang-paek, "Chaeka kumji supsokui yurae-e daehan yon'gu" (A Study of the Origin of the Prohibition against Ladies' Second Marriage), *Han'guk munhwasa yon'guron'go* (Studies on Korean Cultural History), (Seoul: Eulyumunhwasa, 1954), Chapter 3, 205–248.

Having a concubine was socially tolerated. But there was the strong sanction against taking a concubine in the form of permanently disqualifying descendants of a concubine from taking the royal examination for civil officials and thus barring them from becoming officials. *Kyongkukdaejon*, II, 201. See also Yi Sang-paek, "So-ol ch'adaeui yonwon-e daehan ilmunjae" (A Problem of the Origin of Discrimination Against Descendants of a Concubine), *Han'guk munhwasa yon'guron'go*, Chapter 2, 172–204. Descendants of others than common law wives were generally classified among the middlemen class even though their father was a yangban.

An official's going to a prostitute constituted a crime entailing a flogging of 100 strokes. If a son of an official was caught for committing the crime, his name went to an official record for consideration in the future official appointment. *Daemyongnyul jikhae*, a Modern Korean Translation of the Ming Codes in Use during the Yi Dynasty, (Seoul: Bopjaech'o, 1964), 479.

7. *Kyongkukdaejon, ibid.*, I. 233 ff.; *Han'guksa* (History of Korea). (Seoul: Chindan hakhoe, 1962), III, 333 ff.

8. One who married, had a party, or did not wear mourning clothes and wore instead ordinary clothes during the mourning period, among others, was regarded as having committed a crime of being not filial, and a wife who did the same thing at her husband's death was regarded as having committed a crime of being not righteous.

came personally to the court to institute a lawsuit was punished, and his suit would not even be received.[9] These rules were neither required nor expected of commoners. As centuries passed, however, certain yangban practices, notably rituals related to ancestor worship, were diffused among members of other classes to a great extent.

On the other hand, different rules were applied for crimes committed by a yangban. The punishment for identical crimes was more favorable to yangbans than to non-yangbans in kind and degree,[10] different procedural rules were followed for members of this class, and extra care was taken in cases involving yangbans.[11] Furthermore, an outcaste—i.e., a servant or slave—who committed a crime such as battery or adultery

These two crimes are listed in the ten most heinous crimes. *Daemyongnyul jikhae, op. cit.* (note 6), 51–52.

9. *Sason'gyuch'wi* in *Wonsinbo Sukyojiprok–Sason'gyuch'wi*, a modern Korean translation, (Seoul: Bopjaech'o, 1964), 483. If he did not have a servant or other who could proceed on his behalf, he was allowed to institute the suit after the funeral. If the defendant was in mourning, the hearing would be had also after the funeral.

10. For officials, eunuchs, sons of a certain level of the former high–ranking officials, and those who had passed the royal examination for civil officials, punishment by flogging was as a rule substituted by payment of redemption money, unless they had committed one of the ten most heinous crimes such as high and petty treasons, or adultery, stealing, murder, or bribery. *Kyongkukdaejon, op. cit.* (note 1); Suh Il-kyo, *Choson wangjo hyongsajaedo ui yon'gu* (A Study of the Criminal System of the Yi Dynasty), (Seoul: Han'guk bopryong p'yonch'anhoe, 1968), 188. In sentencing, yangbans were generally spared their lives as far as possible. They were instead sent into exile to a remote place for their crime. *Han'guk Il–bo*, Feb. 17, 1974.

11. Those who came under one of the eight specified groups of royal family members, prominent military men who had performed meritorious services in war, great wise men, extra–talented scholars, high–ranking civil and military officials, etc., could be subpoenaed for criminal investigation only upon the king's special instruction; facts investigated and relevant legal rules were required to be reported to the king for instruction of sentencing, and sentence of punishment was to be decided upon the concurrence of a number of high–ranking officials concerned and then upon the king's approval, unless the crime under consideration was treason. *Daemyongnyul jikhae, op. cit.* (note 6), 53–56. Civil and military officials and ascendants, descendants, wife, and other relatives of those who came under one of the eight specified groups of persons were also provided the special treatment of similar nature even though the requirements were less and less vigorous as the rank order of the official under investigation became lower and as the family relationship of the criminal suspect to one of those eight groups of persons became distant. *Daemyongnyul jikhae*, 56–60. See also Suh Il–kyo, *ibid.*, 292–293.

against a commoner incurred a heavier degree of punishment, and, conversely, a commoner was visited by a degree lighter punishment than usual for a crime against an outcaste.[12]

The ruling-class work ethic that existed in Korea was in fact geared to the scholar-officialdom. The whole political and social system was so arranged that once one became a scholar-official, one could have power, wealth, and prestige. These benefits were invariably conferred on both the individual official and his extended family. The division of labor was organized so that the three other classes formed supporting classes for the yangban scholar-officials. Being a scholar-official was the only career choice for a yangban. A member of this class would go jobless rather than become a professional such as a herb doctor, a jurist, an interpreter, an accountant, or a meteorological observer, or engage in a productive activity such as farming, craftmanship, or commerce. Moreover, a yangban would not take a low-ranking official position in the civil or military hierarchy. These professional careers and low-ranking official positions were held exclusively by members of the middle men class, not because yangbans were excluded but because they regarded them demeaning for a yangban. Commoners engaged in farming, craft, and commerce. The outcaste produced sailors, butchers, shamans, actors, and private and official servants who were sold or inherited like slaves.

The major material burden of support for the yangban class and the bureaucratic political organization of the state fell upon the shoulders of the commoners among others. The absolute majority of these commoners were peasants. Peasants were tied strongly to the land. In fact, it was almost impossible for a peasant to leave the land. The stability of the whole system depended upon the ties that held all classes to their respective professions, especially peasants to the land. It was crucial for the system to maintain the ties undisturbed. There were, for example, the *hopaebop* which required everyone to carry his ID card showing, among others, status and vocation, the *hokubop* (a kind of household census law), and the *okajaktongbop* which made five households a unit for mutual cooperation and collective crime prevention. These devices were in the main designed to discourage peasants from leaving their land.[13] Craft industry and commercial activity were also equally under strict governmental control, which was extremely unfavorable for their prosperity.

12. *Daemyongnyul jikhae*, *ibid.*, 426–427 and 478–479. See also *Kyongkukdaejon*, *op. cit.* (note 1), I, 164.

13. See *Han'guksa* (History of Korea), *op. cit.* (note 1), X, 635.

Since it was (and it is) racially and linguistically homogeneous, Korea did not have any problems with ethnic minorities. Because of its Confucian bias, however, discrimination did exist against Buddhism.[14] This discrimination existed in the various forms of governmental control. In the early stage of Yi dynasty, Buddhism underwent a drastic reorganization which resulted in its reduction to a less important social force. The matters related to Buddhism that were under the governmental control had once included the nation-wide Buddhist hierarchy organized on the basis of performance at the Buddhist national examination and promotion thereafter, the size of the landed Buddhist property, and building and repair permits of Buddhist temples. For another example. a special license was once required to become a Buddhist monk. In the later stage, however, the license system was abolished, and, officially albeit ineffectively, no one was allowed to become a monk. Confucian alone enjoyed the monopoly of patronization by the ruling yangban class and the government.

Upon introduction of the Western formal legal system, under the aegis of the Japanese, law in Korea became a universalistic one, at least formally. Particularism as a formal legal principle disappeared with the Japanese so far as the former official class distinctions were concerned. When it came to matters between Japanese and Koreans, however, discrimination against Koreans in favor of the Japanese was legal and systematic. This amounted to a reinforced particularism. Socio-economically, Korean society was reorganized into one composed of the ruling Japanese landlord and Korean sharecropper classes. In the reorganization of Korean society into the two socio-economic classes, however, the former yangban officials were politically *de facto* favored over other former classes among Koreans.

Under the Land Reform Act of 1949 following the liberation of Korea and the founding of the democratic republic, even the landlord class as a readily identifiable socio-economic class, disappeared from the Korean social scene. Today, social discrimination based on former class distinctions—especially in favor of the yangban and against the outcaste —does not exist beyond preference being given to a former yangban descendant and conversely low preference being given to a former out-

14. See *Han'guksa, op. cit.* (note 7), III, 707 ff.; *Han'guksa, ibid.*; IX; 144–151; Yi Sang-paek, *Han'guk munhwasa yon'guron'go, op. cit.* (note 6), Chapter I, 1–170; Kim Yong-tae, "Han'guk pulkyosa" (History of Buddhism in Korea), *Han'guk Munhwasa daekye* (Korean Cultural History Series), (Seoul: Korea University Research Institute of Korean Culture, 1970), VI. 269–364.

caste descendant as a marriage partner if one's origin is ever known. Thus in this respect Korean society is perhaps more egalitarian than Japanese.

Traditionally in Korea, government towers far above the rest of society. This situation in dynastic Korea was associated closely with its centralized bureaucratic political organization, the predominance of Confucianism, and the pre-eminence of the yangban ruling class. The prevailing system was so entrenched that no other organization, ideological or learning system, and no other social group or class that the ones that dynastic Korea actually had was able to compete with or to change the overtowering position of government in society into something else: nothing existed in society that could effectively challenge, or overthrow, its political organization, Confucianism, or the yangban class. All the wealth, power, and honor in society centered around the three elements. Moreover, there was only a single channel to any combination of these. Upward mobility was perceived and attained through this channel alone. To reach the top of the societal hierarchy, one had to become a yangban official, which position could be attained through successful performance at the royal examination.

The door to a cherished governmental position was open only to yangbans. A civilian position was especially coveted and monopolized exclusively by yangbans. Among yangbans, moreover, technically only those who could prove that one of their ancesters at least within the last three generations was an appointed official were allowed to take the royal examinations. Only in the royal examination for military officials could persons of lower class origins compete. There was considerable pressure for persons of common origins to become a yangban—or even to become an outcaste—to avoid the enormous burdens and disadvantages of being a commoner.[15] Toward the end of the Yi dynasty, there are indications that the ratio of the yangban of the total population had remarkably increased and the commoners became considerably thinned. A study even shows that the yangban constituted 68.8% of the population of a community—Taegu—in the middle of the 19th century.[16] Of course, there

15. See *Han'guksa, op. cit.* (Kuksa p'yonch'an wiwonhoe, 1974, note 1), XIII, 446–487 and 492 ff.; Kim Yong-mo, *Choson jipaech'ung yon'gu* (A Study on the Ruling Class of Yi Dynasty), (Seoul: Iljokak, 1977), 42 ff.

16. Shikata Hiroshi, "Richojinkoni kansuru mibunkaikyubetsuteki kansatsu" (An Observation of the Population of Yi Dynasty on the Basis of Status-Class Distinction), *Chosenkeizaino kenkyu* (Study of Korean Economy), Keijoteikokudaikaku hogakkai (Seoul Imperial University, Law Society), X, (Tokyo: Iwanami, 1938), 363–482, especially 387–417. See also Kim Yong-mo, *ibid.*; 43–52.

must have been a natural attrition of the commoner population, caused by famine, epidemic disease, and wars. But a vertical mobility is also involved, although its precise picture is difficult to draw. Many apparently took a military career to facilitate their upward mobility. A fabrication of yangban *chokpo* (family geneology record usually associated with yangban families) to support one's claim to yangban status has been a clandestine trend ever since. There is a number of classical novels and folktales about bribing to get or purchasing a yangban title.[17] During wars or famine many took advantage of being granted a yangban title upon performing a meritorious military deed or turning in a required amount of grain. There are also tales of commoners pretending to be or taking refuge among outcastes such as slaves, Buddhist monks, and travelling entertainers. We have here a picture showing that upward mobility was visualized in terms of buying a yangban title or smuggling oneself into the yangban class rather than in terms of becoming a rich farmer, merchants, or successful craftman or manufacturer who was to form the middle class challenging the privileged class or the political power held by the upper class. At the later stages of the Yi dynasty, Korea became a top-heavy class society in a class analysis. Consequently, it became an easy prey to the Japanese. By toppling the top, Japan took over Korea with relative ease. Within the greatly expanded yangban class, a considerable degree of stratification took place. Only a small number of yangban families virtually monopolized the top-ranking governmental positions, landed wealth, and honor.[18]

The centralized bureaucratic political system closely associated with Confucianism and the yangban class was thoroughly permeated with, and supported by, universal variables such as the work ethic, ability, and performance—initially, among yangbans. The overarching position of the political system in society helped make these universalistic variables permeate the society's value system. Today, these values and the work ethic in the cultural system, and the towering importance of the state in the social structure, remain as two elements from the past that are related to the universal-particular variable, even though the former class lines have disappeared and the social base has been broadened with respect to upward mobility. To the extent that persons of yangban origin were alone allowed to take the royal examination, the Yi dynasty's system was

17. For example, *Yangban chon* (The Tale of a Yangban) by Pak Chi-won (1737–1805) in *Upper-Class Culture in Yi-dynasty Korea*, (Seoul: International Cultural Foundation, 1973), 17–25.

18. Kim Yong-mo, *Choson jipaech'ung yon'gu*, 130–159.

particularistic. However, no official title or position was ever inherited. There was no primogeniture institution in Korea. The social structural picture in which the state is large and in which government officials monopolize power, wealth, and honor in society is, however, inherited by contemporary Koreans from their past. In this particular sense, Korean society is structured by a particularistic principle. Among yangban families, there was an internal hierarchical order. Passing the royal examination was necessary for a highly regarded governmental appointment. This was especially the case for a yangban of lower-family status. For those yangbans whose father or grandfather was a meritorious minister or whose family background was otherwise influential, there was even a chance that they might acquire an appointment without passing through the royal examination.[19] But the top posts were beyond the reach of those who were thus appointed without examination. It was absolutely necessary for one to pass the examination to acquire an appointment in the top notch. At the same time, however, the higher one went on the hierarchical ladder of bureaucratic organization, the more decisive one's family ties were for promotion even among those who passed the examination.[20] One's ability and performance both in the examinations and in the bureaucratic hierarchy[21] were critically important for one's initial status and promotion. But one's family ties were critically important for later stages of promotion. Both the universal norms and traditional primary group ties are still decisive for upward mobility in contemporary Korea.

The family was the "holy community" in the Confucian ideological system upon which the yangban scholar-official dominated centralized political system was based. The family was regarded as the basic social unit. Family relations received not only the moral and ideological but also political and legal spotlight. Differential legal treatment in accord-

19. Kim Yong-mo, *ibid.*, 94-97; *Han'guksa*, Chindan hakhoe, *op. cit.* (note 8), III, 203-296. See also note 51 *infra*.

20. Kim Yong-mo, "Yissi wangjosidae ui jipaech'ung ui hyongsong kwa idong e kwanhan yon'gu" (A Study of the Formation and Social Mobility of the Power Elites in the Yi Dynasty), *Chung-ang University Theses Collection*. No. 11, 167-199, and No. 12, 127-178.

21. Merit system was the integral part of the centralized bureaucratic organization. Performance and ability not only in the royal examination but also on the job in the official hierarchy, along with restrictions on the basis of status distinction, were critical for appointment, job assignment, and promotion. For example, there was an elaborate system of job performance evaluation of officials which was made twice a year. *Kyongkukdaejon, op. cit.*, I, 144.

ance with one's status in the family was the rule. Essentially the same treatments and spotlight were extended to the relationships between teacher and his students, and between the officials representing the king as the parent of people and the subjects. The legal codes of the Yi dynasty included criminal provisions of *high treason* and *petty treason* which were met with the most severe forms of punishment.[22] This situation is comparable to that in the ancient English law.[23] Unfilial behavior such as filing a lawsuit, a criminal charge,[24] or making abusive or defamatory statements,[25] against parents or grandparents, having a separate household from one's parents or grandparents while they were alive,[26] failing to support them or to obey their orders,[27] and marrying or indulging in sex during the mourning period after their death, constituted punishable crimes. A husband who killed his wife or concubine for beating and using abusive language against one of his parents or grandparents incurred only floggings.[28] A parent or grandparent who had beaten his son to death for disobeying his order was punished only with floggings or servitude.[29] Entering into a compromise settlement with the killer who killed one's parent or grandparent constituted a punishable criminal conduct.[30] Taking revenge was a morally imposed obligation on the part of the victim's son or grandson sanctioned by the law.[31] Similar

22. *Daemyongnyul jikhae, op. cit.*, 381–382 and 405–496.

23. In the ancient English law, petty treason was malicious homicide which involved a killing of husband by wife, master by servant, or prelate by clergyman. In England, it was abolished in 1828 by statute. Sir James Fitzjames Stephen, *A History of Criminal Law of England*, (London: Macmillan, 1883), III, 34–35; Rollin M. Perkins, *Criminal Law*, 2nd ed., (Mineola, New York: Foundation Press, 1969); 9–10.

24. *Kyongkukdaejon, op. cit.*, II, 164. The punishment was death by hanging which could be contrasted with exile plus floggings in the Ming Codes. A Chinese son or grandson incurred capital punishment only when he filed a false accusation against his parent or grandparent. Cf. *Daemyongnyul jikhae, op. cit.*, 451–453. See also *Sokdaejon, op. cit.*, 286.

25. *Daemyongnyul jikhae, ibid.*, 440.

26. It constituted one of the ten most heinous crimes. *Daemyongnyul jikhae, ibid.*, 51–52 and 202.

27. *Daemyongnyul jikhae, ibid.*, 454–455.

28. *Daemyongnyul jikhae, ibid.*, 411–412.

29. *Daemyongnyul jikhae, ibid.*, 433–434.

30. *Daemyongnyul jikhae, ibid.*, 415–416.

31. *Daemyongnyul jikhae, ibid.*, 437. One who had beaten another who was beating one's parent or grandparent did not incur any punishment, and if one inflicted a serious injury upon another, one's punishment was commuted by three degrees. If

rules existed with regard to relationships between officials and the ruled and between teachers and students. For example, a subject who killed the magistrate under whose jurisdiction he lived, or an inferior official who killed his superior, or a student who killed his former teacher was visited by heavier punishment than one would have been in the absence of such a relationship.[32] A subject who filed a lawsuit or a criminal charge against the magistrate under whose jurisdiction he lived was punished with floggings and servitude, and the suit or charge was dropped.[33]

Petty treason in Korea included acts of beating or killing committed by a wife against her husband, or against her husband's parents. It also included acts of beating or killing committed by a servant against his master. The crime of filing a lawsuit or a criminal charge against one's own parents included a wife filing one against her husband or against her husband's parent. The crime also included a servant's filing a lawsuit or criminal charge against his master. Conversely, a parent, grandparent, husband, or master, who committed the same crimes against son, wife, or servant would, in fact, or by written provisions, be given lighter punishment or no punishment at all.[34] The rules determining

one killed the murderer who killed one's parent or grandparent, one would incur only 60 strokes. If one killed the murderer on the spot, one would go free.

32. *Daemyongnyul jikhae, ibid.*, 405, 422–424, 425, 438–439; etc.; *Kyongkukdaejon, op. cit.*, II, 164.

33. *Kyongkukdaejon, ibid.*, II, 174.

34. For example, a son (grandson or wife) who filed a criminal charge against a parent (grandparent, or husband) before the court had incurred capital punishment, even though the criminal charge was true. See note 24 *supra*. And the criminally charged parent (grandparent or husband) was not to be punished because he was officially treated as if he voluntarily surrendered himself to justice. *Daemyongnyul jikhae, op. cit.*, 452. On the other hand, a parent (grandparent, or husband) who filed a criminal charge against his (or her) son (grandson, wife, or servant) did not incur any punishment, even though it was a false accusation. *Daemyongnyul jikhae*, 454. A similar differential treatment did exist in connection with the crime of using abusive or defamatory language, battery, and killing, depending on the family relationship. Those kinds of crimes committed by a son, grandson, wife, or servant against a parent (grandparent, husband, or master) were regularly met by heavier punishment than ordinary. The same kinds of crimes committed by a parent (grandparent, husband, or master) against a son (grandson, wife, or servant) were met by ordinary, much commuted, or no punishment at all. Punishment of a parent using abusive language against his son and punishment of a husband beating his wife or older brother (or sister) beating his younger brother (or sister) were out of the question unless the beating was followed by serious injury or death (for the latter

degree of punishment on the basis of hierarchical rank in the family were extended to include to some degree the more extended family relations, such as the older-younger brother relationship, the uncle—i.e., father's brother—nephew relationship, and relationships between cousins.[35] The rules were even extended to former family relations in one case, specifically, to an ex-wife who killed her ex-husband's parent or grandparent.[36] A husband who killed his adulterous wife and her paramour on the spot was exempted from all punishment.[37]

Larceny committed by one against his relative or by a servant against his master or fellow servant incurred commuted punishment the degree of which depended upon the determination of whether their family relationship was close or remote and upon that of whether they were members of the same household.[38] Hiding a criminal who was one's relative or master, or helping him escape from arrest by giving the fugitive a tip needed for escaping or in other way entailed likewise commuted punishment for the one who gave the help to the criminal or fugitive.[39]

To a great extent, legal particularism in accordance with one's status in the family has survived Japanese rule and the subsequent political and socio-economic transformation of Korean society. Actually, it was reinforced during Japanese rule by the Japanese version of familial particularism which ran from the worship of the emperor to the institution of patriarchal family headship. Legal particularism finds its most eloquent expression in the criminal and family law. At this point, it will suffice to cite only a few examples which include a differential legal treatment of patricide or infanticide from an ordinary murder in the criminal

crime). *Daemyongnyul jikhae*, 427–434. There is no specific provision for punishment of a parent killing his son (or husband killing his wife). It is hard to believe that a parent (or husband) regularly went unpunished. It seems that he was punished probably lightly. See Suh Il-kyo, *op. cit.* (note 10), 94–98.

35. For example, in case of a crime of using abusive language, *Daemyongnyul jikhae, ibid.*, 439–440; in case of a crime of filing a criminal charge, *Daemyongnyul jikhae*, 453–454; in case of battery, *Daemyongnyul jikhae*, 430–433.

36. *Daemyongnyul jikhae, ibid.*, 407. And ex-servant or ex-employee who beat, use abusive language against, or filed a criminal charge against, his ex-master or ex-employer regularly incurred punishment two degrees heavier than ordinarily the case would be. *Kyongkukdaejon, op. cit.*, II, 164.

37. *Daemyongnyul jikhae, ibid.*, 406. This is contrasted with the ancient Roman criminal law in which not her husband but her father had the right to kill his adulterous daughter and her lover on the spot. Stephen, *op. cit.* (note 23), I, 14–16.

38. *Daemyongnyul jikhae, ibid.*, 393–394.

39. *Daemyongnyul jikhae, ibid.*, 95–97.

law.[40] The same differential rule is extended to other violent crimes committed against one's parents or grandparents.[41] The rule for the exemption of punishment on the ground of familial relation also obtains for stealing, perjury, and hiding or helping fugitives.[42] The proscription against filing a criminal charge against one's parents or close relatives is also retained in criminal procedure law.[43] The family law amendment of 1977 deleted from the Civil Code a number of particularistic legal rules which were related to sexual inequality. But other particularistic rules still remain in the family law. These include the institution of family headship and the broad definition of the exogamous group.

Particularistic social norms in accordance with one's station in the family and other primary social organizations, as we have defined these, are adhered to in society. Rarely are two persons equal in Korean social interactions when they are related to each other by way of either traditional primary social group or a formal organization. It is more likely that they understand their relationship in terms of father-son, superior-subordinate, leader-follower, teacher-student, and senior-junior contrasts. It is apparent that, to some extent, particularism in social norms overlaps personal considerations when they are related to the formal legal rules. Since in legal theory particularist social norms beyond those provided for in the formal law are *de facto* practices, they, as well as personal considerations, are reflected either legitimately or illegitimately in the administration of the formal law. There are formal legal channels through which particularist social norms, as well as personal considerations, are legitimately reflected in the administration of the formal law. These include a number of the "general clauses" such as "good morals"[44]—the public policy—, the public welfare,[45] faith and sincerity,[46] and extenuating, or mitigating, circumstances,[47] involving a good deal of a judge's discretion. There is room for particularism and personal considerations in situations in which a judge, public prosecutor, or other decision-maker exercises his discretionary powers.

40. Criminal Code(1956), Articles 250, Section 2 and 251.

41. Criminal Code, Articles 257, Section 2; 258, Section 2; 259, Section 2; 260, Section 2; 271, Section 2; 273; 276, Section 2; and 283, Section 2.

42. Criminal Code, Articles 151, 155, 328, 344, etc.

43. Code of Criminal Procedure(1954), Article 224.

44. Civil Code(1958), Article 103.

45. Constitution(1972), Article 32, Section 2.

46. Civil Code, Article 2.

47. Criminal Code, Article 53.

III. Impersonal vs. Personal Relationships

It seems that the "impersonal" variable overlaps the "irrational" variable to a great extent, even though these two are not identical. The impersonal-personal contrast is related to subjective states of minds of actors whereas the rational-irrational contrast is related to the objective nature of actions which are, or will be, taken by actors. It is questionable whether absolute rationality exists. Rationality appears to be a relative term. An economically unsound decision can be rational in relation to the actor's aesthetic or moral perceptions, or an official's illegal action can be rational in relation to his felt need for political survival. It seems that rationality is a predominantly Western middle-class, value-laden term. Rationality is largely related to scientific-economic variables and to Weberian legal rational variables. What is scientifically and/or economically sound is rational. What is other than scientifically, economically, or legally rational is irrational, and, moreover, morally wrong. A rational action is morally right to take. Thus defined, rationality dictates that "personal" considerations must not be taken into account in scientific, economic, and legal judgments because it will be irrational. When it does not affect rational judgments, however, personal considerations do not cause problems. But when they do affect rational judgments, personal considerations cause a normative problem of choice between rational actions and irrational but personal approach. Of course, there can be a conflict between scientific rationality and legal rationality. Furthermore, there is a conflict between substantive rationality and formal rationality in law.[48] Naturally, there can arise a problem of choice or preference among conflicting rational actions to take.

The impersonal-personal contrast seems to be related to an actor's orientation in its cognitive, emotional, evaluative, and behavioral aspects. In the West, an impersonal-rational action in which nothing but scientifically or economically rational considerations are taken into account is not only morally but also religiously endorsed as, for example, in the Protestant ethic.[49] A scientifically or economically rational legislation is also judged as morally right. Once legislated, formal legal rationality is stressed, and relatively little room is left for substantive legal rationality.

In Korea, a substantial rationality in relation to the Confucian es-

48. Max Weber, *Economy and Society*, ed. by Guenther Roth and Claus Wittich, (New York: Bedminster Press, 1968). II, 809 ff.

49. Max Weber, *The Protestant Ethic and the Spirit of Capitalism*, trans, by Talcott Parsons, (New York: Charles Schribner's Sons, 1958).

sential truth (tao) of human being, of nature, and of society has traditionally been emphasized. Formal rationality has been devalued. In traditional Korean law, substantive rationality was the rule. The essential truth of human being, nature, and society is inseparably associated with such concepts as propriety (禮), virtue (德), humanity or benevolence (仁), righteousness or justice (義), faithfulness and loyalty (義理), and their contrasts, dignity or "face" (体面), and shame or disgrace (羞恥). Moreover, these concepts are defined not abstractly but in concrete human terms represented by the five relations—of prince and subject, father and son, husband and wife, brothers, and friends. Consequently, personal considerations related to these concepts are required to be seriously taken in relation to actions and judgments. Personal considerations, for example, an action motivated purely by selfish economic interests, that disregard the concepts are completely another matter. They are regarded as other than virtuous, humane, righteous, faithful, loyal, and graceful. They are shameful and disgraceful. It is in this sense that traditional Korean social structure is "personal."

It is particuluarly the ruler's obligation to practice virtue, benevolence, righteousness, and faithfulness, and to avoid disgraceful or shameful acts. It has been sufficiently embedded in the on-going social structure, although, on the level of popular perception, it is not so clearly articulated as in the Confucian intellectual conceptions. In interpersonal transactions such as negotiation, mediation, and conciliation, and in formal official and legal settings, personal considerations such as humaneness, selflessness, faithfulness, loyalty, "face," disgrace, apology, begging humbly, and repentant attitudes are extremely important. To that extent, particularistic ties are as important in official transactions as they are in private ones. They can be determining elements for an action. But they take forms which appear to be inseparably intertwined with those personal considerations.

Not only intellectually—in terms of Confucianism—but also popularly, "the man is more important than a formal institution" has been a consistent theme, negating formal rationality. It is apparent that since there are few formal institutional guidelines and controls substantive rationality demands an extra strong moral achievement or discipline on the part of actors. Otherwise, this type of system with the emphasis on substantive rationality can be an arbitrary one. This is particularly so with respect to the ruler. The legal system of the Yi dynasty was a system which for its success depended critically upon the moral achievement of the ruler. It is no wonder that Confucian teachings were essentially addressed to the rulers. The rulers were supposed to be able to detach themselves sufficiently from mundane concerns, private personal interests, and private ties, and thereby to maintain a serenity and peace of mind "when being alone" (愼獨).[50] Overall social harmony and solidarity were to be achieved through moral exemplary deeds taken personally by the rulers and through their morally well-balanced governmental actions. Otherwise, the judgment of what is virtuous, humane, righteous, faithful, and/or graceful would be difficult to make in concrete situations, and confusion of private interests with virtue, righteousness, and humanity would be inevitable, and a compartmentalization would be likely along the lines of private and factional interests. The king and his yangban scholar-officials were teachers of morals at the same time. Even in contemporary Korea a leader is expected to be morally superior to others, especially his followers. To a great extent, this expectation intertwined with cross-cutting primary social ties is an antidote to the possible moral depredation and social divisiveness. Finally, it must be pointed out that there was no concept of "rationality" as such in the intellectual vocabulary of traditional Korea.

Certain aspects of substantive rationality and certain personal traits were newly experienced—and even further reinforced—under the Japanese rule. Whatever actions that were considered rational for the Japanese colonial rulers of Korea were readily taken without being hindered by moral principles or by the principles of formal rationality that were engrained in Japanese Westernized formal law. Substantive rationality guided by the principle that political need justifies anything and everything was the norm. Particular personal considerations such as submissive attitudes toward the authority, repentant attitudes in criminal processes, shame, and face were the critical factors in transactional relationships between the Japanese rulers and their Korean subjects.

IV. Competition vs. Cooperation

It seems that competition and cooperation are a universal phenomenon. However, their pattern, conceptualization, and relative importance vary from society to society. It is characteristic of modern Europe that unparalleled intellectual and ideological light has been shed exten-

50. Chong Yak-yong, *Kukyok Mokminsimso* (A Modern Korean Translation of *Mokminsimso*), (Seoul: Minjok munhwa ch'ujinhoe, 1969, originally 1818), III, 361; *The Great Learning* in *A Source Book in Chinese Philosophy*, trans. and compiled by Wing-tsit Chan (Princeton University Press, 1963), 89.

sively and intensively on competition both as a pervasive social phenomenon and as a moving force for social progress. As inseparably interwoven with liberal and democratic ideas and practices as an expression of liberty, competition is presupposed by Western democratic political systems and market economies as one of their indispensable elements. The principle of competition is also a basic presupposition of Western judicial ideas, practices, and procedures involving litigation. This is especially the case in the Anglo-American legal system. Competition, however, presupposes an equality of socio-economic and political powers between competitors. It is therefore natural that Western political and economic ideas and practices revolve around matters of attaining substantial socio-economic and political equalities between individuals, social strata, and political groups as much as around competition as such. A few examples of such ideas and practices include those of pluralism, the general franchise, civil rights, progressive taxation, welfare state, equal justice, legal aids and state-appointed counsel or public defender system. Moreover, Western ideas and practices of competition coupled with those of equality presuppose individualism and a closely related individualistic nuclear family social structure. Competition again coalesces with universalism. Competition is not regarded as a goal but only a means to attain a higher goal such as social harmony, equilibrium, or justice. Equality is also not a final goal. Equality is regarded as consisting in equality of opportunity. Intellectually and ideologically, however, both equality and competition are exalted to the point of their being almost the final goal to achieve in society.

In dynastic Korea, the notion of competition did not receive as much intellectual and ideological attention. Competition failed to be conceptualized as an important social, economic, and political idea. Since the royal examinations and the bureaucratic political organization occupies the central place in society, it may be said that competition received indirect conceptual attention as part of the universalistic values and formal legal and social norms that were associated with the examination system and the governmental bureaucracy. Consequently, individual performance and ability rather than competition as such stood out in social and political concepts and ideas. No doubt, there were individual competitions in the royal examinations and in governmental appointments, on the formal political organizational level. But there were no ideological and social bases to conceptualize individual competition. Confucian teachings, as the official ideology, stressed the obligation of the rulers to exercise a parental care for the people. Litigation was visualized not as a competition between individual parties but as a personal appeal of aggrieved parties to the magistrate for his parental care. Social harmony and peace were envisioned as being realized by the moral achievement of individual rulers through their exemplary deeds and wise decisions. Even today, Korean culture is elitist. Intra and inter group harmony and peace are visualized as attainable through the roles of leaders rather than through competition between individuals and groups. On the other side of the same coin, leaders are seen in their leadership role which includes, among others, that of bringing intra and inter group harmony and solidarity.

The pattern of competition is affected by the traditional social structure. Competition in Korea is as much group or organizational competition as it is competition between individual members of society. It is conducted both as an individual and as a group phenomenon along lines of traditional primary social groups and formal organizations.

Whether conceptualized in terms of ability, performance, competition, or all of these, the traditional themes that are closely associated with passing the major examinations, such as great honor and prestige awarded to an individual examination passer and to his family and as a promised future, are deeply engrained in the value system today. These themes are now associated with passing an entrance examination to a prestigious university, the national bar examination or the national higher civil service examination, and governmental positions. These themes were in fact reinforced during the Japanese rule even though only a few Koreans were able to pass the prestigious Japanese universities'—namely, imperial universities'—, bar, and civil service examinations.

V. Individual vs. Collective Responsibility

Because of strong tradition of liberalism and individualism, the principle of individual responsibility has been the rule in the modern West. In relatively recent years, however, particularly following the two world wars, a growing socialism or welfare state, that is, a form of collective responsibility borne by whole society for the well-being of individual members, has been witnessed in the West. It is fair to say that as the fact of human interdependency is recognized more and more the idea of collective responsibility will grow stronger in this quarter of the world.

In Korea, collective responsibility has been the rule because of the strong influence of the traditional social structure and notions of government developed within its patriarchal political organization. With the introduction of the Western formal legal system, however, individual responsibility became the formal legal rule.

The variable of individual-collective responsibility is related to goal achievement, competition, social harmony, social control, legal consequences of actions, individual well-being, and other social phenomena. In the broad spectrum of social phenomena with which this variable is associated, legal responsibility is an important facet. It is characteristic of modern Europe that the notion of individual responsibility has received more attention as an overarching principle governing legal consequences of actions than as one governing also other social phenomena such as goal achievement, individual material well-being, competition, and social control. In traditional Korea, however, collective responsibility stands out as the legal as well as social principle governing the broad range of social phenomena. It is an aspect of the traditional group social structure. Individual well-being is a matter of group responsibility. Social control is also a group oriented phenomenon. In dynastic Korea, those aspects of collective responsibility that were regarded as essential to the functioning of the centralized bureaucratic political organization and to social harmony as envisioned by Confucian scholar-officials were conceptually and practically more attended to.

Examples of such collective responsibility include the following: High ranking officials were privileged and also required each year to recommend three learned and able persons for governmental appointment. If an official committed a crime or other irregularity, however, liability fell upon the one who recommended him for governmental appointment as well as upon himself.[51] A formal legal principle of collective family responsibility by which not only the criminal but also his family

51. In the spring each year, high-ranking military as well as civil officials were privileged and also obligated to recommend up to three able persons for official positions or the magistrate or local garrison commander's position. A high-ranking official who recommended a person for a position was collectively responsible for the crime of corruption (embezzlement of official funds, taking bribery, or illegally enriching himself) or the "crime against the fundamental moral rules" that were committed by the officials thus recommended and appointed. *Kyongkukdaejon, op. cit.* (note 1), 140–141. See also *Daemyongnyul jikhae, op. cit.* (note 6), 90–92; *Kyongkukdaejon*, II, 131. When "crime against the fundamental moral rules" was committed, i.e., when a son, wife, or servant killed his parent, husband, or master, his wife and children were made slaves, his whole property was confiscated, his house was demolished, the title of the town or village in which he lived was downgraded, and the magistrate was to be fired. *Sokdaejon, op. cit.* (note 1), 174.

members were subjected to punishment was practiced rather widely. An extreme example was the rule that one's three families (families on his father's, mother's, and wife's side) as well as he himself were to be perished in case he was convicted of treason. Finding a spouse for one of marriageable age under one's protection was not only social but also legal responsibility of family, especially borne by the one who played the parental role.[52] A son was socially and even legally responsible for debts incurred by his father, and a father was responsible for debts incurred by his son.[53] Certain taxes in kind were levied on villages as collective entities. Default of a family to pay its share of these taxes resulted in an increased share of the total by the rest of the member families of the village.[54]

Some examples of legally relevant collective responsibility today include the case of security clearance for governmental appointment and for issuance of passports. A governmental appointment or issuance of a passport is refused to one whose father was a communist who, for instance, went north. Another example includes a disciplinary demotion or dismissal of a ranking official if a subordinate commits a certain crime or has made a serious mistake in his official duties. Collective responsibility

52. The ministry of rituals was required to report to the king for instruction regarding daughter of a yangban family who was not able to get married because of poverty, and also required to provide her with proper amounts of necessary goods and articles for her marriage. If her family was not that poor and yet did not have her get married by age 30, the household head of her family would be subjected to punishment. *Kyongkukdaejon, ibid.*, I, 286. Matching unmarried bachelors and spinsters into couples was part of the governmental business, and usually the duty to match devolved upon the magistrate. A magistrate within whose jurisdiction there were unmarried bachelors and especially spinsters were officially even reprimanded. In folktales, those who died unmarried became bad spirits haunting the magistrate. The magistrate would usually make efforts to match bachelors and spinsters in his juridiction, sometimes by using coercion (e.g., flogging the household head who had an unmarried son, daughter, nephew, or niece), sometimes by persuation; or some other times by providing for expenses or granting funds if those unmarried were poverty-stricken. See Yi Tae-kyu, *Kaehwa paekkyong* (Hundred Scenes of Modernization), (Seoul: Sint'aeyangsa, 1969), II, 284-285 and 382.

53. *Kyongkukdaejon, ibid.*, I, 188, *Sason'gyuch'wi* in *Wonsinbo Sukyojiprok-Sason'gyuch'wi, op. cit.* (note 9), 498. When public debts of a certain amount or more were in default, the debtor's wife and children all would be even made servants in substitution for the debts. *Sokdaejon, op. cit.* (note 1), 110.

54. *Han'guksa*, Chindan hakhoe, *op. cit.* (note 7), III, 430 ff.; *Han'guksa*, Kuksa p'yonch'an wiwonhoe, *op. cit.* (note 1), X, 502-503.

as a principle of after-the-fact responsibility in discipline or social control (deviation control), especially that practiced in the army as a collective disciplinary measure, have been receiving critical attention in Korea. It is so because it collides with the formal legal principle of individual responsibility governing consequences of actions. In general, however, collective responsibility is widely practiced as an intrinsic element of the social structure. This is particularly so with regard to goal achievements, associated with groups, large organizations, and the nation as a whole. To a great extent, the recent Korean industrialization efforts were an expression of collective responsibility geared to a goal achievement with the nation as the collectivity.

Some aspects of collective responsibility were reinforced by the Japanese because of their wide use. Collective disciplinary measures consisting of corporal punishment practiced in the Japanese army and even in schools were notorious. This is one reason why collective disciplinary measures are discredited, at least ideologically, today in Korea. The Western idea of individual responsibility is also responsible for this development. As for Korean nationalist activities under the Japanese rule, a whole village and family were brutally retaliated. But it was also a collective preventive measure.

VI. Conflict vs. Harmony

Dispute and harmony are also universal social phenomena whose patterns and conceptualization vary from society to society. Disputes, conflicts, struggles, and revolutions are not only recognized but are given positive roles to play in the modern West. They are regarded as important means for social change. Ideologically, moreover, they prevail over harmony, cooperation, and equilibrium to a great extent. Many social theories and social and political institutions are built on the basis of these facets of social life, positively recognized. Western legal system and jurisprudence are also built on the same ideological basis. Dispute, conflict, struggle, and revolution in the West are more or less individualistic in their pattern as affected by individualism. On the other hand, they generally center around individual (convictional), religious, and socio-economic cleavages and divisions.

Because of the strong influence of Confucian ideology, closely associated with the yangban-dominated centralized bureaucratic political organization, dynastic Korea presented an opposite intellectual picture. Intellectually and ideologically, harmony and equilibrium were predominant, and themes of dispute and conflict found no positive place. At the individual level, disputes, conflicts, struggles, and revolutionary changes were unusually negatively depicted. Confucius' saying, "The superior man is conciliatory but does not identify himself with others; the inferior man identifies with others but is not conciliatory"[55] was the motto. In the Oriental world, political changes involving the ruling group or sector was alone recognized in the periphery of intellectual awareness. Even there the legitimacy of political change alone was the major issue, which was debated in accordance with the intellectually articulated theme of "voice of people" equated with "voice of the Heaven." The theme of orthodoxy vs. heresy was also an intellectual tool for dealing with political change. Even such political changes had relatively less relevancy to Korea because of the dynastic stability that had prevailed for many centuries, as compared with, for example, China. Individual, religious, ideological. and socio-economic cleavages and divisions did not loom large in dynastic Korea.

Theory is one thing, and a culture which is engrained in social structure and in individual personalities is another thing. Individual, religious. ideological and socio-economic cleavages and divisions, especially those of the West, are widely known to educated Koreans as knowledge. They—or their appearance—do exist to some extent in Korea. It is characteristic of Korean culture, however, that in emotional and evaluative orientation disputes, conflicts, and revolutions are conceived negatively, and harmony and equilibrium are conceived positively. In Korea, for example, both disputants in a conflict tend to be viewed as morally wrong regardless of the material issues involved. The same observation applies to litigants. Loss of face, or shame, is usually imputed to both participants in dispute or in litigation. Change is also deplored as seen in such a popular slang expression as "changing one's face" (anmyonul bakkunda). A conciliatory and harmonious person is highly regarded as "one who can live without law." Being conciliatory and harmonious does not mean that as a disputeless or conflictless person one is morally unprincipled, but, on the contrary, principled and morally committed. As an element in personality, this political (legal) culture is widely and uniformly distributed. As an element in social structure, however, it is affected by morphological structural considerations. The culture is strong among those who share common traditional social ties. Among those who do not share such ties, the culture is not necessarily a controlling factor. A dispute or conflict may become more furious than otherwise, when two parties share the

55. *The Analects* in *A Source Book in Chinese Philosophy*, *op. cit.* (note 49), 41.

same social group tie. In such a situation, hatred may run high, and a dispute may become more difficult to mediate, harmonize, or settle.

VII. Concluding Remarks

Both universalism and particularism exist in the traditional social structure in Korea. Moreover, particularism in social norms is closely associated with the morphological elements of the social structure, including the state. The primacy of personal approaches which stand out in Korean interpersonal relationship overlaps the traditional emphasis on both substantive rationality and particularism to some extent. The primacy of collective responsibility, social harmony, and cooperation in social norms is imprinted in the traditional social structure of which personal approaches are integral parts.

As to the relationship between morality and law, morality in Korea is associated with the kinds of particularism (interwoven with the kind of universalism), personal approaches, substantive rationality, collective responsibility, cooperation, and social harmony that are prominent in the Korean traditional social structure. On the other hand, law in Korean conception is associated with the denial of the kind of particularism, lack of personal considerations (like merciless individualism, competition, and dispute or litigation oriented attitudes), and lack of the primacy given to cooperation, harmony, and collective responsibility. Consequently, law represents undesirable, necessary but evil, elements in social norms while morality represents desirable, proper elements of the antinomies. In the Korean value system, formal rationality is lowly evaluated. In the West. morality and law reinforce each other, and both are intertwined with universalism, impersonal approaches, and formal rationality, individual responsibility, competitively oriented values, and the positive recognition given to disputes in society.

The critical question is that of whether a modern society capable of coping with contemporary problems such as nation building and industrialization, on the one hand, and the creation of a modern legal system, on the other, are impossible with the kinds of particularism, personal approaches, collective responsibility, and the primacy of cooperation that prevail in the traditional Korean social structure? In particular, are the kinds of particularism, personal approaches, and substantive rationality that exist in Korea incompatible with a modern society when they are incorporated into a formal legal system?

A positive answer without resort to a revolution may be possible.

And the recent industrialization of Korea may indicate what that is. A growing awareness of human interdependency, the need for fraternal love, and primacy of collective responsibility, social harmony, and cooperation are on the horizon in the West in the form of welfare state or socialism. The other end of the continuum—e.g., individualism, competition, impersonal approaches—alone is obviously not the only controlling principle for human relationships. Since collective responsibility is already a part of the social structure, it may be easier to realize the idea of a welfare state in Korea. Danger of compartmentalization along the lines of traditional primary groups is a problem in Korea. A solution to the question of how to overcome the danger of compartmentalization and yet to realize an overall community in which traditional principles prevail seems to hinges on roles of leaders to a greater extent in Korea than in a Western society. Substantive rationality may be ideologically better than formal rationality when (or if) a mechanism can be invented or developed to prevent a substantive-rational system from degenerating into an arbitrary one. As a humane, emotionally and evaluatively responsive system, a legal system into which personal approaches are integrated may be desirable. For we are too much deprived of personal touches in many aspects of our contemporary life. This kind of particularism cannot be eliminated in a stroke by a piece of legislation because they are very much part of society. We have to discover ways to live with this aspect of social life instead of ignoring it. Finally, the main question is what mechanism we can have or we can develop to restrain governmental power? This issue is particularly important in view of the fact that the state component and its related leadership roles in society have been traditionally strong, on the one hand, and substantive rationality has been a traditional formula for law, on the other. We cannot provide a definite answer. But some answers may be found in traditional social structure, too.

No doubt, an understanding of the gap between the law and the reality in Korea will not be complete without an appreciation of its dimension of the conflict between the Western and Oriental cultures. This appreciation must go beyond a condemnation of one set of variables as totally bad or as far better than the other without a discriminating assessment. One difficult problem arising from the conflict, however, is that in Korea there are two sets of social standards for action neither of which is triumphant over the other or diminishing its social relevancy. Naturally, one is easily led to rely on one set of the standards at one time and on another at other time without consistency as situation dictates. Consequently, the final question is how to cope with the inconsistency that borders on arbitrariness which arise from the double standards.

[12]

THE LAW OF THE SUBTLE MIND: THE TRADITIONAL JAPANESE CONCEPTION OF LAW

By

CHIN KIM *

and

CRAIG M. LAWSON **

" They don't like law in Japan." [1] This is one scholar's summary of the traditional Japanese attitude to law. Though oversimplified, it is substantially true.

Japan's growing economic, political and cultural importance is prompting Western lawyers and legal educators to study Japanese traditional [2] and contemporary law.[3] They are likely to be startled. Westerners are accustomed to the idea of justice under a system of rational and impersonal laws. Western society is litigation-oriented; social problems become legal problems, thrashed out in open court, and lawyers are everywhere. Japanese traditionally abhor lawsuits. Why do they? Ten thousand Japanese lawyers serve a major industrial nation with a population of 100 million.[4] How can they? [5] The answers are not to be found in the law books alone; owing partly to the traditional Japanese aversion to law, book law in Japan does not accurately reflect the social mechanisms which adjust tensions and resolve disputes,[6] and may not adequately reflect the state of the living law itself.[7] To answer these questions we must put aside our Western conception of law and try to understand the traditional Japanese conception of law.[8]

* Professor of Law, California Western School of Law, San Diego, California.

** Assistant Professor of Law, University of Nebraska College of Law, Lincoln, Nebraska. Member of State Bar of California.

1 " On n'aime pas le droit au Japon." Y. Noda, *Introduction au Droit Japonais* (1966) p. 175.

2 For a useful brief guide and excellent bibliography to Japanese legal history, see Ryosuke Ishii, " Japan," in Vol. E, *Bibliographical Introduction to Legal History and Ethnology*, s. 13 (J. Gilissen, ed., 1964).

3 For a bibliographic guide to Japanese law in Western languages, see *An Index to Japanese Law*: 1867–1973 (Coleman and Haley, eds., 1975). Since 1975 this excellent work has been annually supplemented in *Law in Japan: An Annual*.

4 F. Gibney, " 10,000 Lawyers vs. 350,000," 8 *Center Report* 7–10 (Center for the Study of Democratic Institutions, Report of the President, 1975).

5 On the reasons for the small number of lawyers in Japan, see Henderson and Anderson, " Japanese Law: A Profile," in *An Introduction to Japanese Civilization* (A. Tiedemann, ed., 1974).

6 See pp. 506–7, *infra*.

7 See pp. 507–511, *infra*.

8 Law is a reflection of socio-cultural phenomena in a polity. As we think of law in the West, its three most general features are that it is normative, institutionalised, and coercive. It is normative in that it serves, or is meant to serve, as a guide for human behaviour. It is institutionalised in that its application is to a large extent carried out by institutions or

The two differ fundamentally. Noda, for instance, refers to Western law as the " law of the geometric mind " and to Japanese law as the " law of the subtle mind."[9]

In writing this article on the traditional Japanese conception of law, we have tried to abstract a set of attitudes towards law, attitudes that seem to have characterised Japanese culture as a whole. We have not attempted the difficult task of tying them to a particular era or social class. Because these attitudes seem to have flowed deep in the springs of Japanese thought, we think we can legitimately speak of them as if they had a life of their own, beyond precise location in class and time. We have divided our article into three parts. First, as background, we will briefly discuss the external and internal forces that have shaped the traditional Japanese conception of law. Secondly, in examining the conception itself, we will try to identify non-legal forces that ensure social order and we will try to clarify the common notion of aversion to the formal legal process. Thirdly, to illustrate and evaluate the effects of the traditional Japanese conception of law, we will try to show it at work in the living law (or law in action) of Japanese society.

I. JAPANESE THOUGHT: A BACKGROUND TO TRADITIONAL JAPANESE ATTITUDES TOWARD LAW

The major forces that have shaped Japanese thought in general, and the traditional Japanese conception of law in particular, might be characterised as external—physical, historical and cultural conditions —and internal—important features of Japanese thought or the Japanese character.[10] We wish to present only the briefest summary possible of these internal and external social forces, for we do not intend to deal in detail with the birth of the traditional Japanese conception of law.

A. Physical, Historical and Cultural Conditions

Traditional Japanese social attitudes have been fostered in part by Japan's physical and historical circumstances.[11] As an island nation, Japan enjoyed relative isolation, which produced a national ethnic cohesion and helped to preserve it for thousands of years.[12] Although

social organs. And it is coercive in that obedience to it, and its application, are internally guaranteed, ultimately, by the use of sanction or social compulsion. In discussing the traditional Japanese conception of law, we will generally and loosely use the word " law " in this sense. Other definitions might do. See generally Sawer, " The Western Conception of Law," in 2 *International Encyclopedia of Comparative Law*, Chap. 1, at p. 10 (1973). But the definition of law is a difficult problem of jurisprudence, see G. Paton, *A Textbook of Jurisprudence* (4th ed., 1972) pp. 66–98, and we are neither inclined nor qualified to attempt its solution here.

[9] Noda, " The Far Eastern Conception of Law," in 2 *International Encyclopedia of Comparative Law*, Chap. 1, at p. 120 (1971).

[10] Noda so characterises them, *ibid.*, at p. 120.

[11] *Ibid.*, at p. 129; Y. Noda, *Introduction to Japanese Law* (1976) p. 171.

[12] Noda, *op. cit. supra*, n. 10, at p. 129.

many of her basic cultural innovations were inspired by other cultures, Japan's isolation enabled her to digest these foreign cultural influences gradually, and to adapt them to, and integrate them with, her own culture at will. Until the last century, Japan was a rural agricultural nation whose people were largely settled in localised farming communities. Rice cultivation demanded an unvarying annual calendar of planting, tending and harvesting, and a consequently stable society of families living in one place generation after generation.[13] Social relations tended to be face-to-face, highly particularised and long in duration.[14] Centuries of Japanese feudalism were founded on the extremely stable hierarchical social structure permitted by these physical and historical conditions.[15] Although the peaceful surface of Japanese society was marred by civil wars, these came to an end at approximately the end of the sixteenth century, with the beginning of the Tokugawa Shogunate.[16] During two-and-a-half centuries of Tokugawa feudalism, Japan was isolated, her society stable, her life unchanging. One scholar has vividly described the period:

> For the successive generations of Tokugawa bureaucrats and "judges" then, Japan was almost everything; other vague lands furnished curiosities, but really did not matter much. The whole country was one big rice estate, with daimyō sub-estates. Every bag of rice was precisely alloted before it was planted; each person was classified before he was born and registered soon thereafter. After the chaos and strife of times past, peace and security seemed quite enough to give one's retainers. All was now administration; there was no political activity worth noticing, just a bit of graft and intrigue to be rooted out by an occasional confiscation or by diligent application of ancestral moral precepts. Movement was slow, change imperceptible; efficacy of human effort to refashion their world was negligible. Such a caricature of the Shogunate structure and thinking is of course oversimplified, but we suggest that it does nevertheless capture the main stream and general tone of official thought in Edo.[17]

Shintō, Buddhism, and Confucianism have also affected traditional patterns of thought.[18] Shintō is Japan's indigenous pantheistic faith, a faith which intuitively perceives divinity in nature.[19] Shintō deities are generally associated with nature and regular natural cycles of birth, growth, change and death.[20] Buddhism, by contrast, teaches that all things are changing and impermanent, and that one can attain an absolute non-dual reality of perfect quietude by losing desires for

[13] Nakamura, "Basic Features of the Legal, Political and Economic Thought of Japan," in *The Japanese Mind: Essentials of Japanese Philosophy and Culture* (Moore, ed., 1967), pp. 147–148.

[14] Kawashima, "The Status of the Individual in the Notion of Law, Right and Social Order," *ibid.*, p. 262.

[15] Wren, "Legal System of Pre-Western Japan," (1968) 20 Hast.L.J. 217, 220.

[16] C. Dunn, *Everyday Life in Traditional Japan* (1969) p. 5.

[17] D. Henderson, *Conciliation and Japanese Law: Tokugawa and Modern* (1965) Vol. 1, pp. 47–48.

[18] Wren, *op. cit. supra*, n. 15, at p. 217.

[19] Shunzō, "Shintō: Japanese Ethnocentrism," in *The Japanese Mind: Essentials of Japanese Philosophy and Culture* (C. Moore, ed., 1967), pp. 24–26.

[20] *Ibid.*

pleasure in the world of change and by realising the Self.[21] As we shall see, the Shintō intuitive sympathy with nature and the Buddhist emphasis on attainment of a perfectly quiet inner reality seem to survive in the Japanese character[22] and in Japanese ideals.[23]

Chinese Confucianism stands out as the single most important intellectual influence on traditional Japanese thought.[24] In the Confucian view the world of nature follows certain immutable laws (*dào*), which man must strive to follow.[25] Rites (*li*) governing human behaviour were elaborated to imitate these natural laws.[26] The Confucian emphasis is pragmatic, not transcendental[27]:

> The basic Confucian virtue of *jen* (translated variously as "compassion," "human-heartedness," or "man-to-man-ness") is not a world of transcendental reality, but of immediate experience. Man achieves *jen* through the relationships which he has with other members of the society.
>
> The emphasis is on the *relations* between men, not on individuals.[28]

This emphasis on the concrete particulars of a human relationship accords with a general emphasis on conduct conforming to a wise intuitive understanding of the particulars of life itself, and not to a set of logical and abstract general rules.[29] In this view, good conduct following the *dào* establishes social harmony; disputes are disturbances of the natural peace of the social order caused by deviating from the *dào*.[30] The moral man and social leader is a peacemaker,[31] and justice flows from his virtue, not from a set of written laws.[32] A dispute, a disturbance of social peace and harmony, is therefore to be resolved through respectable compromise,[33] by "making both parties understand what is their duty, in order to restore the peace they have disturbed."[34]

These borrowings—the extensive adoption of Buddhism and elements of Chinese culture in the late sixth century, the imposition of Confucianism upon Japanese society as a whole during the Tokugawa period (1600–1867), and the selection and adaptation of various elements of Western culture during and after the Meiji period (1868–1912)—have been carried out with a distinctly Japanese flavour. The elements borrowed are firmly embedded in Japanese culture.

[21] See generally Shinsō, "Buddhism of the One Great Vehicle"; Teitarō, "Reason and Intuition in Buddhist Philosophy"; Teitarō, "An Interpretation of Zen Experience", all in *The Japanese Mind: Essentials of Japanese Philosophy and Culture* (C. Moore, ed., 1967) at pp. 33, 66 and 122, respectively.

[22] See pp. 495–8, *infra*.

[23] See pp. 498–501, *infra*.

[24] Wren, *op. cit. supra*, n. 15, at p. 223.

[25] Noda, *op. cit. supra*, n. 10, at p. 122.

[26] *Ibid.*

[27] *Ibid.*; Wren, *op. cit. supra*, n. 15, at p. 221.

[28] Wren, *op. cit. supra*, n. 15, at p. 221.

[29] *Ibid.*

[30] Noda, *op. cit. supra*, n. 10, at p. 128.

[31] F. S. C. Northrup, "Asian Mentality and United States Foreign Policy," in *Philosophical Anthropology and Practical Politics* (1960), pp. 155, 159.

[32] Wren, *op. cit. supra*, n. 15, at p. 222.

[33] *Ibid.*

[34] Noda, *op. cit. supra*, n. 10, at p. 128.

The Tokugawa period saw the formation and consolidation of the social patterns that seem most to characterise contemporary Japan. Contemporary Japan is Tokugawa Japan transformed, but not rejected. True, Japan has grown from an isolated, feudalistic, agrarian society into a modern, urban, industrial one, and in little more than a century. But this transformation has been accomplished rapidly and completely, and with relatively little social upheaval.[35] Every foreign adaptation, every modernisation, has been embraced by Japan, without fundamentally altering her national character.[36]

B. The Japanese Character

Any attempt to describe generally a people's character or mental life must necessarily ignore a rich diversity of thought which that people's culture displays. And the nature of national character is disputed. Some argue that national character is primarily conditioned by physical, historical and cultural forces, and that it therefore changes as society does.[37] Others argue that national character is primarily hereditary and so " rooted in the unconscious part of mentality " [38] as to resist all but the most gradual change.[39] We recognise these problems, but we do not offer any complete general theory of the Japanese character. Benedict,[40] Maruyama,[41] Nakamura,[42] Devos,[43] Doi [44] and others [45] have already done so. We do, however, feel that typical general features of Japanese thinking are revealed in Japanese attitudes towards law

[35] See p. 512, *infra*.

[36] Indeed, Japan's willingness to adopt elements from other cultures may be due to her national character. *Cf.* p. 512, *infra*.

[37] Tanaka and Takeuchi, " The Role of Private Persons in the Enforcement of Law: A Comparative Study of Japanese and American Law," (1974) 7 *Law in Japan: An Annual* 34, 48; Kawashima, *op. cit. supra*, n. 14, at p. 271.

[38] Noda, *op. cit. supra*, n. 10, at p. 120.

[39] *Ibid.*

[40] Benedict is remembered for her controversial thesis that Japan is a " shame (*haji*) culture ": see her brilliant pioneering study, *The Chrysanthemum and the Sword: Patterns of Japanese Culture* (1946).

[41] Maruyama identifies " face " and status as important Japanese cultural themes: M. Maruyama, *Thought and Behaviour in Modern Japanese Politics* (1963); *Studies in the Intellectual History of Tokugawa Japan* (1974).

[42] Taking a psycho-cultural approach to Japanese character, Nakamura feels that the Japanese way of thinking is characterised by non-rational tendencies, by an acceptance of actuality, and by a preference for operating within a limited social nexus. See p. 496, *infra*. Nakamura's major work is *Ways of Thinking of Eastern Peoples: India, China, Tibet, Japan* (1964).

[43] Devos advances an achievement-motivation theory based on his study of Japanese psycho-culture; he feels that the concept of *on* (" indebtedness ": see p. 499 *infra*) is the key motivating element: *Socialisation for Achievement* (1973).

[44] Doi holds that dependence is a basic human need. His penetrating analysis of the Japanese mind revolves around a Japanese concept akin to dependence—*amae*, a feeling easily expressed in everyday Japanese life: *The Anatomy of Dependence* (1973). For a discussion of the effect of *amae* on law, *see* D. Mitchell, *Amaeru: The Expression of Reciprocal Dependency Needs in Japanese Politics and Law* (1976), pp. 173–202.

[45] See, *e.g.* Kokuminsei Chōsa Iinkai, Tōkei Sūri Kenkyūjo, *Nihonjin No Kokuminsei* (3 vols., 1961–1975) (an extensive study of the ways of thought of the Japanese people at large, conducted by the Research Committee of the Study of Japanese National Character of the Institute of Statistical Mathematics, Tokyo).

and social organisation. For this reason we shall attempt to highlight here several of those typical features.

Nakamura, for instance, lists the main elements of Japanese thought as follows [46]:

> 1. *The acceptance of actuality*: (a) apprehension of the Absolute in the phenomenal world; (b) this-worldliness; (c) acceptance of natural human qualities; (d) the spirit of tolerance; (e) cultural stratification; and (f) weakness of the spirit of direct criticism.
>
> 2. *The tendency to emphasise a particular social nexus*: (a) emphasis on human relationships; (b) human relationships as of greater importance than the individual; (c) absolute view of limited social organisation; (d) reverence for family morality; (e) emphasis upon hierarchial relations of status; (f) the supremacy of the state; (g) absolute obedience to some particular person; (h) emperor worship; (i) closed character of sects and cliques; (j) protection of the particular social nexus by force; (k) emphasis on activity in society; (l) sensitivity to moral introspection; and (m) lack of self-consciousness in religious reverence.
>
> 3. *Non-rational tendencies*: (a) non-logical tendencies; (b) weakness in ability to think in terms of logical consequences; (c) intuitional and emotional tendencies; (d) lack of ability to form complex representations; (e) fondness for simple symbolic representations; and (f) weakness in knowledge of objective processes.

Let us explore some of these elements.

Logic has no place in Japanese thought. Indifference to logic has apparently characterised Japanese thinking from the earliest periods of Japanese history.[47] Life is an organic whole, to be accepted and lived as it is; it is not to be cut by logic into analytically neat pieces, for to do so is artificial and removed from the natural state of things.[48] Life is indeterminate, immensely varied, and subtle.[49]

> [T]he Japanese do not like logical solutions to any problem because this appears to them too decisive and too distant from the actual state of things. They prefer seeing things as they are. They have little interest in knowing if A can at the same time be not A. The clarity and precision of thought which is so dear to the French seem to the Japanese to be incompatible with the integrity of existing things. To clarify and to give logical precision to things is to limit them, and therefore to denaturise them, from a Japanese point of view.[50]

This antipathy to logic may result from Japan's racial and cultural homogeneity, which fosters homogeneity of thought.[51] So much is common experience, that things are felt to be self-evident. As one commentator has noted, " the Japanese people have a naive belief that everyone thinks alike. . . . To understand one another, it is unnecessary to resort to a discussion proceeding according to rules agreed upon in

[46] Nakamura, *op. cit. supra*, n. 13, at pp. 143–144.

[47] Noda, *op. cit. supra*, n. 11, at p. 169.

[48] Noda, *op. cit. supra*, n. 10, at p. 133.

[49] Kawashima, *op. cit. supra*, n. 14, at p. 262.

[50] Noda, *op. cit. supra*, n. 11, at p. 164.

[51] Noda, " Nihon-Jin No Seikaku To Sono Hō-Kannen " (" The Character of the Japanese People and their Conception of Law "), in H. Tanaka, *The Japanese Legal System* (1976) pp. 295–299.

advance, *i.e.* logical rules. One simply looks to this community of spirit."[52] Tied to this antipathy to logic is a more general antipathy to the precision of thinking that logic promotes; traditional Japanese thought finds no room for black-white distinctions.[53] " Harmony consists not in making distinctions; if a distinction between good and bad can be made, then there *wa* (harmony) does not exist."[54]

Life is to be lived as it is given, to be lived as it is immediately perceived:

> When we look at the traditional notions of the Japanese people about Nature as well as society, what impresses us most in contrast with the prevailing view of contemporary Western society is the fact that, in the traditional culture of the Japanese, nature and society are accepted as they appear to the senses in their empirical immediacy. The indeterminateness of nature and society with immense variety and subtle nuances is therefore their everlasting attribute, and, hence, it is to be valued because it is in its very nature unlimited and contains infinite possibilities for development and expansion.[55]

Men appear clothed in infinite variety, each man with his own separate status and value. Relations between men are necessarily subtle and distinct, and social relations are by nature indeterminate.[56] Rooted in these assumptions, traditional Japanese law and ethics aim to maintain the actual statuses of men, subtle and complex as such statuses are.[57] The ideal is willing acceptance. In the West our lives are constructed; we have made ourselves what we are. In the traditional Japanese view one's life is given; it is to be accepted as it is.[58] Here is a traditional quiet faith in nature, in the nature of things as they are, a faith produced by a society in which human life was shaped by the natural agricultural calendar. " This way of life has embedded in the spirit of the Japanese people a special conception of nature, according to which everything is good if you accept it as it is. To meddle with things given by nature is to distort or to spoil them.[59] Justice inheres in the natural order: " What is, is for that reason just."[60] Any absolute or ultimate reality is not beyond, but is within the phenomenal world, within the world immediately touched by the senses.[61]

The traditional Japanese spirit is emotive, tends to subjectivity, inwardness, fantasy.[62] This emotionality, and the traditional Japanese reverence for nature as it is, produce feelings of integration into the natural order.[63] Emotional impulse, not careful reasoning, motivates action.[64] We now discover another reason for the absence of theoretical

[52] Noda, *op. cit. supra*, n. 10, at p. 130. [53] *Ibid.* at p. 132.
[54] Kawashima, *op. cit. supra*, n. 14, at p. 264, *quoting* Ono, *Nihon Hōri No Jikaku Teki Tenkai* (" Self-conscious Development of Japanese Philosophy of Law ") (1942) at p. 300.
[55] Kawashima, *op. cit. supra*, n. 14, at p. 262.
[56] *Ibid.* at p. 264. [57] *Ibid.* at p. 263.
[58] Noda, *op. cit. supra*, n. 10, at p. 135.
[59] *Ibid.* at p. 131. [60] *Ibid.* at p. 133.
[61] Nakamura, *op. cit. supra*, n. 13, at p. 144.
[62] Noda, *op. cit. supra*, n. 11, at p. 163. [63] Noda, *op. cit. supra*, n. 10, at p. 131.
[64] R. David, *Les Grands Systemes de Droit Contemporains* (5th ed., 1973), pp. 565–566.

or systematic thought—logic—in the traditional Japanese character. Logic is a solvent that strips life of feeling. Logic can find no place in a culture based upon the " aesthetic and intuitive and concrete."[65]

II. TRADITIONAL JAPANESE ATTITUDES TOWARDS LAW AND SOCIETY

A. Important Non-legal Social Forces

Feudal Japan, especially in the Tokugawa era, was a society both orderly and stable.[66] One late nineteenth century American visitor to Japan came away with the impression that " there was probably no country in the world where the mass of people, down to the smallest farmer in the possession of a few square yards of land, were more familiar with their rights and duties. . . ."[67] Let us turn to some of the non-legal forces that secured this order.

Japanese tradition, like millenial Asian and African traditions, emphasises the ascendency of the group interest over the individual interests of its members.[68] An individual is a part of the social body,[69] not an isolated atom, but part of a molecule. This emphasis on the social whole, with its corresponding de-emphasis on the individual, may be traced at least in part to Confucian thought, with its emphasis on the human relationship, not on the individuals who compose it.[70] In the Confucian view, society is built upon five basic human relationships: (1) ruler and subject, (2) father and son, (3) elder and younger, (4) husband and wife, and (5) friend and friend.[71] " It is unthinkable that one will insist on his ' rights,' so as to place a focus on the individual rather than the relationship."[72] As a result, the individual interest is not fixed and independent, but is merged in the group interest.[73] An individual who asserts his own interest thereby steps outside the group, hurting the feelings of others.[74] The primacy of the group is also closely tied to Japan's traditional homogeneity of thought. As Nodà has observed, " As everyone thinks alike, everyone spontaneously behaves in the same way."[75] Noda sees this at work in collective Japanese behaviour, which often proceeds without a clearly defined design or control by a leader:

> Another characteristic is the peculiar pattern of behaviour bearing the imprint of a spontaneous group. In other words, the Japanese people always and un-

[65] Nakamura, " Consciousness of the Individual and the Universal Among the Japanese," in *The Japanese Mind: Essentials of Japanese Philosophy and Culture* (C. Moore, ed., 1967), p. 179.

[66] Henderson, *op. cit. supra*, n. 17, at pp. 47–48.

[67] Wren, *op. cit. supra*, n. 15, at p. 226, *quoting* Simmons and Wigmore, " Land Tenure and Local Institutions " (1891) 19 T.A.S.J. 50.

[68] A. Bozeman, *The Future of Law in a Multi-cultural World* (1971), p. 162.

[69] Noda, *op. cit. supra*, n. 10, at p. 126.

[70] See p. 494, *supra*.

[71] Wren, *op. cit. supra*, n. 15, at p. 221.

[72] *Ibid.*

[73] Kawashima, *op. cit. supra*, n. 14, at p. 264.

[74] Nakamura, *op. cit. supra*, n. 13, at p. 148.

[75] Noda, *op. cit. supra*, n. 10, at p. 131.

consciously behave collectively, a pattern one might call the village-bent of our behaviour.

. . .

As we have seen so far, collective actions taken by the Japanese are neither based on a clearly defined design nor controlled by a leader. They somehow move in one direction as a group. Without being conscious why, each individual moves in one direction on his own but it turns out that these individuals, when taken as a group, move in one and the same direction. And such a phenomenon serves to show that there is a homogeneity in their thinking. It is very interesting that a vast mass of individuals not consciously guided by a centrally defined goal should involuntarily move in unison in a certain direction.[76]

The family plays the central role in this traditional Japanese group consciousness, and Japan has therefore been called a familial society.[77] Social relationships are modelled on family relationships, even in emotional content; the rules governing the family are regarded as the ideal rules by which other social relationships should be governed.[78] A business firm is still often felt to be analogous to a family, and family ideals therefore colour the field of labour relations.[79] The employment relationship, like family blood relationships, lasts the worker's lifetime, virtually eliminating mobility in the Japanese labour market.[80] Government itself, probably following the Confucian model, is often seen as an extension of family authority, the ruler enjoying the status of father.[81] In Japan, the family tie is so close, the family bond so indivisible, that the family as a unit is disgraced by, and prior to modern times, was sometimes as a unit punished for, the misdeeds of its individual members.[82]

The family and the larger social order are protected by the rules of *giri* [83]—a subtle set of rules of conduct—and the obligations of *on*.[84] Both *giri* and *on* promote *wa*, " harmony " or " concord," and

[76] Noda, *op. cit. supra*, n. 51, at p. 299. [77] Nakamura, *op. cit. supra*, n. 13, at p. 148.

[78] Noda, *op. cit. supra*, n. 10, at p. 134.

[79] von Mehren, " Some Reflections on Japanese Law " (1958) 71 Harv.L.Rev. 1486, 1493.

[80] See J. Abegglen, *The Japanese Factory: Aspects of its Social Organization* (1958).

[81] Strayer, " The Tokugawa Period and Japanese Feudalism,"in *Studies in the Institutional History of Early Modern Japan* 3, 8 (J. Hall and M. Jansen, eds., 1968), pp. 3, 8.

[82] Wren, *op. cit. supra*, n. 15, at p. 232.

[83] See pp. 500–1, *infra*.

[84] The obligations of *on* are intangible debts one is under a duty to repay (*hōon*). According to Azumi, ". . . a person's conduct in social life is governed by the obligations of *on* and *giri*. In contrast to America where people consider themselves ' heirs of the ages,' the Japanese consider themselves debtors to the ages. Men are indebted not only to the past but also to the emperor, the nation, parents, and teachers. It is the need to repay these debts which furnishes the motivations for a person's actions. *On* refers specifically to the obligations passively incurred toward important benefactors such as the emperor, the nation, the law, parents. It is one's *gimu* (duty) to work hard to repay these benefactors, but the debt is life-long and is never considered to be fully paid. One is obliged, however, to repay the mathematical equivalent of *on* (whether the original benefaction be money, a favor, or a gift) within certain time limits if the benefactor is less closely related. Toward friends, workmates, distant relatives, and other persons of a status equal to or inferior to oneself one is said to have incurred *giri*. Though one may not be genuinely willing to do so, the *giri* relationship will nevertheless oblige one to come to the aid of these persons if ever the need should arise . . . ": Azumi, " Japanese Society: A Sociological View," in *An Introduction to Japanese Civilization* (A. Tiedemann, ed., 1974), pp. 525–526.

harmony in human affairs, *wa*, is a particularly important traditional value. An ideal human relationship is characterised by *wa*, as are properly filled social roles.[85] *Wa* is a supple concept, ideally suited to the closeness of social relationships and to the indeterminateness of social obligations, both of which it idealises.[86] The traditional spirit of *wa* is emotionally rich, and undoubtedly contains some notion of love and benevolence.[87] The spirit of affection in which a duty is performed is itself traditionally highly valued, reflecting again the emotional nature of Japanese thought. This spirit of affection is called *ninjō*, translated as " natural human affection,"[88] or " human feeling."[89] *Ninjō* is a concept often misunderstood in the West, and looked on by the Japanese as specifically Japanese.[90] Social obligations are ideally to be filled by a voluntary act suffused with *ninjō*, with particular friendliness or benevolence.[91] The emotional warmth of *ninjō* seems to reflect the assimilation of social relationships to family relationships, for social relationships are thereby given a warm emotional colour. *Ninjō* also reflects a traditional reverence for nature as given, a reverence for the " givens " of human nature.[92] " The love of human beings seems to be closely connected with the love of the beauties of Nature, which is as old as the Japanese people themselves." [93]

Ninjō is not only the basic cement that secures observance of the subtle rules of conduct known as *giri*. *Ninjō* is also the emotional content of conduct according to *giri; giri* and *ninjō* are so closely related that one often encounters the compound " *giri-ninjō*." [94] Although the emotional, intuitive Japanese temperament, with its aversion to precise logical distinctions, is clearly antithetical to any systematic and conceptually arranged system of rights and duties, traditional Japanese society always possessed a pervasive social order.[95] *Giri-ninjō* is one of the foundations of that order. *Giri* has been defined as follows: " *Giri* (*gi*, just or right; *ri*, reason or reasonable behaviour) means the manner of behaviour required of one person to others in consequence of his social status." [96] Although *giri* is tied to bonds of moral obligation, *giri* is more than moral, since it is intended to insure the social order.[97] More than moral, rules of *giri* are for all that less than legal,

[85] Kawashima, " Dispute Resolution in Contemporary Japan," in *Law in Japan: Legal Order in a Changing Society* (A. von Mehren, ed., 1963), pp. 41, 43.
[86] Kawashima, *op. cit. supra*, n. 14, at p. 264.
[87] *Ibid.* at pp. 264–265.
[88] Noda, *op. cit. supra*, n. 11, at p. 176.
[89] H. Tanaka, *The Japanese Legal System* (1976) at p. 303.
[90] Doi, " Giri-Ninjō: An Interpretation," in *Aspects of Social Change in Modern Japan* (R. Dore, ed., 1967), pp. 327, 329.
[91] Kawashima, *op. cit. supra*, n. 14, at p. 263.
[92] Nakamura, *op. cit. supra*, n. 13, at p. 144.
[93] *Ibid.* at p. 145.
[94] Noda, *op. cit. supra*, n. 11, at p. 176. One also encounters the compound " *on-giri-ninjō*," sometimes " *giri-on-ninjō*" or " *giri-ninjō-on*."
[95] See p. 498, *supra*.
[96] Noda, *op. cit. supra*, n. 11, at p. 175.
[97] Noda, *op. cit. supra*, n. 10, at p. 134.

lacking generality and exteriority.[98] Noda has identified six important characteristics of *giri*.[99] First, *giri* is both the duty and the state of a person bound to a prescribed manner of behaviour towards a certain other person. It varies from situation to situation, according to status. Secondly, a person to whom a duty of *giri* is owed must await its voluntary fulfilment. If a person demands conduct owed to him under the rules of *giri*, he in his turn violates his *giri*. Thirdly, *giri* partakes of a feudalistic hierarchical order of social statuses. The *giri* of a socially inferior person will not be the same as that of his superior, even though each will bear *giri* duties towards the other. Fourthly, *giri* relationships are perpetual. Fifthly, the system of *giri* rules is not enforced by public constraint. The violation of one's *giri* is sanctioned only by a feeling of dishonour. He who has failed to uphold his *giri* loses face. Sixthly and lastly, *ninjō* is the foundation of *giri; giri* thus has an important affective content, as we noted earlier. Although the Western mind often separates the bond of love from the bond of social duty, often indeed finds them opposed, *giri* and *ninjō* are necessarily interpenetrating concepts, each giving content to the other[100]:

> An obligation is considered valueless, if, although it is fulfilled by the obligated person, he does not fulfil it in addition with a special friendliness or favour toward the other party. In other words, the actual value of social obligations depends upon the good will and favour of the obligated person.[101]

B. Aversion to the Legal Process

> To an honourable Japanese the law is something that is undesirable, even detestable, something to keep as far away from as possible. To never use the law, or be involved with the law, is the normal hope of honourable people . . . In a word, Japanese do not like law.[102]

The Japanese dislike for law is a commonplace. Let us now turn to some of the elements of the traditional Japanese conception of law. As we have seen, intuition and emotion are the dominant tones of Japanese thought. Logic jars against the gentle aesthetic life. Life is organic and whole; it is indeterminate. By contrast, the resolution of problems through recourse to law entails a mechanical reduction into unliving legal parts, leading to a determinately precise outcome. This makes the legal solution of social problems seem unnatural to the Japanese, whose " emotional nature requires a more harmonious reconciliation of the interests of all parties—what the Japanese call a ' full and round ' solution." [103] The traditional Japanese mind is an accepting one, in

98 *Ibid.*

99 Noda, *op. cit. supra*, n. 11, at pp. 175–177.

100 But see H. Varley, *Japanese Culture: A Short History* (1973) p. 124. Varley finds that " one of the most important themes in all of Tokugawa literature is the conflict between human feelings (*ninjō*) and the heavy sense of duty (*giri*) imposed on the individual by the feudal laws and mores of the age."

101 Kawashima, *op. cit. supra*, n. 14, at p. 263.

102 Noda, *op. cit. supra*, n. 11, at pp. 159–160.

103 Noda, *op. cit. supra*, n. 10, at p. 133.

favour of taking life as life presents itself to the senses; it is against meddling, against artifices. Nature's goods are given to the willing recipient, not taken by artificial—hence unnatural—enterprise. If things are simply allowed to follow their own course, they will work themselves out. Regulation by legal rules, being manipulative, is therefore to be avoided.[104] What is worse, the law is impersonal, abstract, general. Japanese thought emphasises the personal, the concrete, the particular. For all these reasons the round emotional nature of the Japanese character is offended by the square rational nature of law and the legal process. Some didactic poem cards (*karuta*) on conciliation illustrate this [105]:

> Better talk based upon *giri* (social obligation) and *ninjō* (human feeling) than argument on points of logic.
> Never talk in formal language when discussing rights and duties.
> Forget about a smattering of legal argument.
> The aroma (of conciliation) lies in reaching a solution without saying which is black and which is white.

Society is built upon the spirit of *wa*, harmony or concord. It is expected that in a society permeated by the spirit of harmony disputes will not arise. If they should arise, disharmony has arisen. The resolution of disputes thus requires the restoration of harmony and mutual understanding.[106] Lawsuits, on the other hand, pit one party against the other and determine which one shall win, thereby further straining the relationship and further injuring the delicate spirit of *wa*.[107] The spirit of harmony and the social tie (*en* [108]) that binds all relationships act together on the Japanese mind, which therefore tends not to view a dispute in terms of personal rights and duties. The harmonious settlement of disputes through mutual understanding is virtuous; the fight to the finish in the courtroom is shameful. As Northrup has observed, in the Confucian view, the moral man is a peacemaker, not a litigation maker.[109] Justice is therefore associated, not with rights and duties, but with righteousness.[110]

The rules of *giri* also play their part. First, they demand that one graciously await the fulfilment of a duty owed to one. The beneficiary

[104] Noda, *op. cit. supra* n. 51, at 300–301.

[105] Tanaka, *op. cit. supra*, n. 89, at pp. 494–495.

[106] Kawashima, *op. cit. supra*, n. 85, at p. 44.

[107] Kawashima, *op. cit. supra*, n. 14, at pp. 266–267.

[108] According to Kawashima, *en* is a buddhist-originated concept that social relationships are predestined by the past lives of individuals. Thus the parties to a contract are predestined to their relationship: they are not merely " persons who pass one another by on the street." Thus also the Japanese proverb, " When people's sleeves brush one another, it is by the *en* (tie) in their past lives." Kawashima, " The Status of the Individual in the Notion of Law, Right and Social Order in Japan," in *The Status of the Individual in East and West* (C. Moore, ed., 1968) at p. 432.

[109] Northrup, *op. cit. supra*, n. 31, at p. 159.

[110] Kōsaka, "The Status and Role of the Individual in Japanese Society," in *The Japanese Mind: Essentials of Japanese Philosophy and Culture* (C. Moore, ed., 1967) pp. 245, 258.

of a duty who demands its fulfilment has thereby violated his own *giri*; to sue violates one's *giri*. Secondly, when one has been offended, the amount of reparation and the terms of punishment are secondary; what is primarily sought is the offender's change of heart, the sincere attitude worthy of *giri-ninjō*.[111] Thirdly, resort to law carries the shameful implication that the plaintiff thinks his opponent is an unworthy or an abnormal person with whom mutual understanding cannot be reached through ordinary discussion.[112] The shame that accompanies litigation may be one of the most important elements of the Japanese aversion to the legal process. Japan has been called a " shame culture," [113] and the idea of shame has been said to be " the keystone to the system of Japanese civilisation." [114] In the traditional Japanese view, it is shameful to be brought into court, even on a civil matter, even, indeed, to be mentioned in court.[115]

Not surprisingly, traditional Japanese thought has often been observed to lack any consciousness of rights. The Japanese word for law, *ho* (or *horitsu*), means only the corpus of legal rules; it carries no connotation either of subjective law or of personal rights.[116] And the non-individualistic emphasis on the group in Japanese society has been reflected in the historical fact that the law rarely ever functioned to protect individual rights.[117] As we have seen, conduct was subject to *giri*, rules not dependent on any notion of defined and delimitable rights. The dictates of *giri* were well known and closely observed, sometimes giving the impression of a people conscious of their rights and duties,[118] but the concept of subjective rights simply did not exist in traditional Japanese thought.[119] The concept closest to " right " was that of entitlement or one's entitled interest. The word *kenri*, corresponding to the French *droit*, or " right," was introduced in the Meiji era by one of the Japanese translators of the French Civil Code.[120] The rules of *giri* and the intangible debts of *on* [121] necessarily implied a concept of social obligation, but the concept was not balanced by any countervailing concept of rights.[122] Traditional Japanese thought can find no place for it. This does not mean that the individual was unprotected and subject to unfair treatment by those more powerful than he. As was observed above, the content of *giri*, social duty, is *ninjō*, human affection, and *wa*, the spirit of harmony, implies love and

111 Noda, *op. cit. supra*, n. 11, at p. 181.
112 Noda, *op. cit. supra*, n. 10, at p. 133.
113 R. Benedict, *The Chrysanthemum and the Sword: Patterns of Japanese Culture* (1946).
114 Noda, *op. cit. supra*, n. 11, at p. 160.
115 *Ibid.*; David, *op. cit. supra*, n. 64. at p. 565.
116 Noda, *op. cit. supra*, n. 11, at p. 159.
117 *Ibid.*
118 See p. 498, *supra*.
119 Noda, *op. cit. supra*, n. 51, at p. 305.
120 *Ibid.*
121 See p. 495 *supra*.
122 Kawashima, *op. cit. supra*, n. 14, at p. 264.

benevolence. Traditional Japanese thought includes a special reverence for human life, and grants it a natural dignity. But it does not accord the individual any set of rights.

For these reasons, the Japanese shun litigation; it cannot conceivably fit their traditional character. There may also be other historical reasons for the Japanese abhorrence of the courtroom. First, the stability of Japanese society, and the pervasive influence of *on-giri-ninjō* may have resulted in less need and fewer occasions for the intervention of law.[123] Secondly, the actual codes in Japan, prior to modern times, were regarded as manuals for the magistrates and were not to be seen by anyone else.[124] This may have given the legal process an air of mystery, removing it from the familiar world. Finally, Japanese law descended from the early Chinese Codes,[125] which were almost exclusively penal. This may explain how the law came, early on, to be associated with constraint. Law still connotes pain and penalty, and is still primarily conceived of as the instrument by which the State imposes its will.[126] The punishments in these early codes were, like the Chinese punishments they descend from,[127] always humiliating, often barbarically harsh. Something of this unpleasant image survives in the mind of the ordinary citizen, who views law and lawyers as primarily related to the criminal law.[128]

As a consequence of these unfriendly attitudes toward law, the legal process is felt to be an expedient means of keeping society orderly, but nothing more. When all else has failed, law comes into play, but only because it must. Law is an expedient, not an end in itself.[129] This follows the Confucian view, within which the machinery of justice is an evil last resort.[130] A society in which disputes never arose would be the Confucian and the Japanese ideal. In such a society there would simply be no need for law.[131]

Countervailing views of law have existed in Japan. A Japanese strain of legalism, not unlike Chinese legalism [132] can be detected in some of the literature. The following passage may be its most recent and clearest statement:

> I hope you will think at this point about whether strict enforcement of law is really " contrary to *ninjō* " or inhuman . . . Condoning a small offence, when repeated, tends to dull the sting of the law, and people may be misled into

123 To this effect, see David, *op. cit. supra*, n. 64, at p. 561.
124 Wren, *op. cit. supra*, n. 15, at p. 230.
125 *Ibid.* at p. 226.
126 Noda, *op. cit. supra*, n. 11, at p. 159.
127 See Kim and LeBlang, " The Death Penalty in Traditional China " (1975) 5 Ga.J.Int. & Comp.L. 77.
128 Tanaka, *op. cit. supra*, n. 89, at p. 261.
129 Noda, *op. cit. supra*, n. 10, at p. 134.
130 Northrup, *op. cit. supra*, n. 31, at pp. 160, 164.
131 Noda, *op. cit. supra*, n. 10, at p. 134.
132 On Chinese legalism generally, *see* Kim and LeBlang, *op. cit. supra*, n. 127, at pp. 81–82.

> thinking nothing of violating laws, short of serious crime. By the time one realises the serious criminal or civil consequences of one's act, one has already reached a point of no return. In order to nip the culpability in the bud, there is no substitute for a harsh but reasoned punishment. Permissiveness in relation to small offences could thus in the long run amount to an inhuman consequence. A harsh punishment meted out against a small crime in its incipient stage would deter the would-be offender from larger crimes.[133]

It is interesting that this is a legalism tailored to traditional Japanese thought, for it suggests " harsh but reasoned punishment " in the interest of *ninjō*, or humanity. Although this view does find a place for legalism in the Japanese character, it is an uncommon view nonetheless. Japanese thought is generally averse to the strict exaction of legal penalties.[134] However, there is in the Japanese attitude toward law one view as common as it is paradoxical. This view is that law carries substantial moral force and commands respect for its moral authority, and it is firmly rooted in Japanese legal history. Japan's first constitution, promulgated in the seventh century A.D. by Prince Shotoku, is composed of 17 articles that resemble moral injunctions more closely than statements of law. Article I begins: " Above all else esteem concord (*wa*); make it your first duty to avoid discord." [135] Centuries later, during the Tokugawa era, it became customary for each *shogun*, at the beginning of each new regime, to re-enact all the prior law, symbolising the importance of law as the foundation of all propriety.[136] The traditional Japanese notion of law does not differentiate law, justice and morality as we do in the West.[137] The law of man is simply a part of the larger law,[138] and, for this reason, human law is to be received and revered. In the prevailing view, a statute in Japan is regarded as *denka no hoto* (a sword handed down from ancestors as a family treasure), not for actual use, but for symbolic effect.[139] Here is a clue that helps us understand the place this respect for law might find in the general aversion to the legal process discussed earlier. The respect accorded to the statute as a family treasure is not a respect for its application in a particular case, but a respect for its symbolic value. The Japanese aversion to law is really an aversion to the use of law in the legal process, to the shame of the courtroom, to the judgment that blames:

> Japan has long emphasised the law's prescriptive function as distinguished from its function in the resolving of concrete problems. . . . [T]he codes are today among the chief expressions of the society's values and as such, carry considerable moral force. . . . Japan has a long tradition of seeing in the body of law a statement of morals; the government always used the codes as a basis of moral

[133] Noda, *op. cit. supra*, n. 51, at p. 303.
[134] Noda, *op. cit. supra*, n. 10, at p. 134. *See* text accompanying n. 147, *infra*.
[135] Nakamura, *op. cit. supra*, n. 13, at p. 145.
[136] Wren, *op. cit. supra*, n. 15, at p. 230.
[137] Kawashima, *op. cit. supra*, n. 14, at p. 265.
[138] Henderson, *op. cit. supra*, n. 17, at p. 48.
[139] Kawashima, *op. cit. supra*, n. 14, at p. 267.

> education—*shushin*—and law is still so regarded today by the people. Thus members of the legal profession generally, and particularly professors and judges are considered teachers of morals.[140]

The law is highly regarded as a moral statement prescribing good conduct. It is abhorred, as we have seen, when applied in the courtroom to particular disputes. Perhaps the sense of this distinction is best captured by Noda: "We want the law to reign, but not to rule." [141]

The traditional Japanese attitude toward law is more than a simple aversion to law. The legal resolution of disputes is clearly abhorred; the lawsuit is opposed to most elements of Japanese thought. The spirit of *wa* and *on-giri-ninjō* are far better adapted to the needs of day-to-day relationships than is the spirit of litigation. Still, the law itself, as doctrine, is a respected teacher of morals.

III. TRADITIONAL JAPANESE ATTITUDES AT WORK IN THE LIVING LAW

Beginning in the Meiji era (ca. 1868), Japan effectively borrowed her entire legal system from the West, and Tokugawa feudal law was formally abolished.[142] But centuries of tradition are not so easily put to sleep. Western legal shapes and concepts have been filtered through the Japanese mind, and the living law continues to reflect traditional Japanese thought. Western law has been bent to an Eastern task. For this reason, numerous students of the Japanese legal system have noted that the written law "gives a far less accurate picture of how the society adjusts disputes and harnesses human energy and capacity for mutually beneficial activity than does Western book law." [143] Let us examine some instances in which the Japanese mind has given the law and legal institutions a Japanese twist.

As their traditional aversion to the lawsuit might lead one to expect, the Japanese resort to litigation much less frequently than do citizens of the West.[144] The Japanese traditionally do not sue. The number of civil suits *per capita* has been estimated to be between 4 per cent. and 10 per cent. of those in many Western countries.[145] Disputes are generally settled out of court, and attorneys are rarely used in these extra-judicial settlements.[146] Lawsuits begun are often settled by conciliation prior to judgment.[147] The law is just far less pervasively used as a dispute resolver than it is in the West. Disputes ought to be resolved by restoring a missing harmony, but litigation divides the parties

140 von Mehren, Commentary in *Law in Japan: The Legal Order in a Changing Society* (A. von Mehren, ed., 1963), p. 190.

141 Noda, *op. cit. supra*, n. 10, at p. 134.

142 See generally Noda, *op. cit. supra*, n. 11, at pp. 41–62.

143 von Mehren, *op. cit. supra*, n. 79, at p. 1494. *See also* Wren, *op. cit. supra*, n. 15, at p. 244; Tanaka, *op. cit. supra*, n. 89, at p. 254.

144 For a statistical evaluation, see Kawashima, *op. cit. supra*, n. 85, at p. 42.

145 Tanaka, *op. cit. supra*, n. 89, at pp. 255–260.

146 *Ibid.*

147 Kawashima, *op. cit. supra*, n. 85, at. p. 48.

definitively into winner and loser. Social relationships are indeterminate, but litigation demands a determinate analytic precision. To sue, to demand one's rights, is a cold-hearted violation of *on-giri-ninjō*. The fighting spirit of litigation shocks the Japanese mind. For all these reasons litigation is relatively uncommon in Japan.

Far better suited to the Japanese temperament, and hence far more common, is conciliation. Conciliation, mediation, and compromise are characteristic of Far Eastern culture.[148] Conciliation agrees with the Confucian spirit. Disputes result from having fallen from the way (*dao*), from having deviated from one's social duties. To re-establish the lost harmony between the parties, both must " understand what is their duty in order to restore the peace they have disturbed." [149] Conciliation serves this didactic function, and teaches both parties their duties in order to restore harmony between them. This didactic emphasis can be found as many as 13 centuries ago in the teachings of Prince Shōtoku:

> Prince Shōtoku did not teach that the people shall merely follow or obey but that discussion should be carried on in the atmosphere of concord or harmony, so that one might attain right views. Earnest discussion was most desirable. If we discuss affairs with the feeling of harmony, desisting from anger, difficult problems will be settled spontaneously in the right way. In this way alone is it possible that decisions may be reached at conferences.[150]

Conciliation revives the parties' feelings of integration with the community and is thus better calculated to satisfy their sense of *giri-ninjō*.[151] Through conciliation, both parties participate actively in the resolution of their dispute, and the compromise reached can therefore reflect the particulars of their relationship. The Japanese do not share our Western assumption that disputes ought to be resolved without reference to the social and economic statuses of the persons involved.[152] Dispute resolution techniques must be flexible enough to embrace the detail and the uniqueness of any of life's infinitely varied relationships. This flexibility is also suited to the Japanese view of the indeterminateness of the social order.

Extra-judicial compromise may be effected through direct reconciliation, in which the parties meet, confer and reach a mutually acceptable resolution, or through conciliation, in which the parties are reconciled through the help of a third person in whom they trust.[153] Conciliation procedures, however, are not exclusively extra-judicial, but are now also an important part of the enacted procedural law.[154] One Japanese

[148] See Noda, *op. cit. supra*, n. 10, at p. 128.
[149] *Ibid.*
[150] Nakamura, *op. cit. supra*, n. 13, at p. 146.
[151] Noda, *op. cit. supra*, n. 10, at pp. 133–134.
[152] von Mehren, *op. cit. supra*, n. 79, at p. 1496.
[153] Kawashima, *op. cit. supra*, n. 85, at pp. 50–51.
[154] *See* D. Henderson, *Conciliation and Japanese Law: Tokugawa and Modern* (1965) Vol. 2, pp. 200–234.

legal scholar lists the reasons for enacting such laws as follows:

> (i) to avoid the delay and cost accompanying formal adjudicative procedures, (ii) to reach a better solution where the literal application of existing law would have led to an undesirable result . . . and (iii) to avoid the stiff antagonistic sentiments between the parties that often follow black-or-white, clear-cut decisions reached through ordinary adjudicative procedures. More basically, what made possible the full-scale introduction of conciliation was the traditional respect for the spirit of " harmony " (*wa*). . .[155]

The image of the traditional Japanese mind is clearly etched into the purposes of these conciliation laws. Article 2 of the Conciliation of Personal Affairs Act provides: " The main object of conciliation lies in reaching a solution to a case based upon morals (*dogi*) and with a warm heart (*onjo*)." [156] Similarly, Article 1 of the Law for Conciliation of Civil Affairs provides: " This Law is to aim at effecting a settlement consistent with reason and befitting actual circumstances by mutual concession of the parties concerned in respect of disputes relating to civil affairs." [157] Neither statement of purpose refers to dispute resolution according to law. Instead, resolution is to be based upon morals[158] or reason, is to be reached with a warm heart, and is to fit the particular circumstances of the problem.

These broad principles of moral or reasoned dispute resolution, based on a warm heart and befitting actual circumstances, may seem unusual to the Western legal mind. Not only do they give law an emotional tone, but they also lack the precision of content we look for in a legal rule. They are, to be sure, only statements of principle, and we would expect them to be broad for that reason alone. Nonetheless, the Japanese mind does not demand precise law. Few Japanese statutes have been overruled for vagueness, because indeterminateness is taken for granted.[159] Since the nature of human relationships is indeterminate, ought the law not to reflect that indeterminateness? A certain amount of indeterminateness will also allow greater leeway within which to widen or narrow the meaning of the statute,[160] softening its mechanistic universality, allowing it to be applied more flexibly to the particulars of each case, better satisfying the particularistic orientation of Japanese thought. Given the rationalistic Western sources from which Japanese statutory law was taken in large blocks, and given the millenial non-rationalistic traditions of the highly civilised culture to which that law was to be applied, we should not be surprised to discover creativity in statutory interpretation. As one commentator has noted:

155 Tanaka, *op. cit. supra*, n. 89, at p. 494.

156 *Ibid.*

157 (1975) 2 *Eibun-Horei-Sha Law Bulletin Series*, MA.

158 For an interesting discussion of the moral elements of four well-known Japanese pollution cases, *see* Upham, " Litigation and Moral Consciousness in Japan: An Interpretative Analysis of Four Japanese Pollution Suits " (1976) 10 L. & Soc.Rev. 579.

159 Kim, " Constitution and Obscenity: Japan and the U.S.A." 23 Am.J.Comp.L. 255 (1975).

160 *Ibid.*

> The people live by their daily customs. They would be very worried or dissatisfied if their disputes were settled strictly according to the rules of law of the Civil Code when those disputes are brought before judges. To satisfy not only the parties to the suit, but also all citizens and to bring them to understand the spirit of the Civil Code we must apply many diverse techniques of interpretation. Only in this way will our rules of civil law be able to develop peacefully.[161]

Moreover, statutes requiring government enforcement are enforced with great reserve. As we noted earlier,[162] a statute is nothing but *denka no hoto*, an inherited family sword, a treasured symbol of force, morally revered, but not to be used. The first prosecution under the Prostitution Surveillance Law, enacted in 1956, was not brought until 1958.[163] When the law is enforced, it is often enforced leniently. The judge who enforces the law leniently is felt to act with an understanding heart, and stretching the law in favour of a violator is considered a virtue.[164] The strict exaction of punishment according to the letter of the law is often felt to be contrary to *ninjō*. Law is always measured against these traditional ideals. Does it or does it not fit the facts of men's lives? Is it proper in the light of human experience?[165] One foreign observer has noted that:

> The Japanese word, *ningen*, or humanity, is widely used and is apt to turn up anywhere, like the joker in a deck of playing cards. A judge's verdict may be described as "full of humanity," or a good person may be "richly human," of "mature humanity," and "truly human." A bad person is "inhuman," or does not seem human at all.[166]

This may seem backward to the Western mind, for in the West human affairs are judged against the law, whereas in this traditional Japanese view the law is judged against human affairs. Because we in the West expect human beings to chart their courses by the law, we use law extensively to regulate conduct in advance through elaborate contractual arrangements engineered by lawyers. Japanese contracts, by contrast, are usually short, and lawyers, rarely used outside the courtroom,[167] play a minor role in this preventive law setting.[168] After two

[161] "Les gens vivent selon leurs coutumes quotidiennes. Ils seraient très inquiets ou mécontents, si leurs conflits étaient tranchés strictement selon les règles de droit du Code civil quand ces conflits sont portés devant les juges. Pour contenter non seulement les parties au procès, mais aussi tous les citoyens et pour les amener à comprendre l'esprit du Code civil, nous devons appliquer bien des techniques diverses d'interpretation. De cette façon seulement, nos règles de droit civil pourront se développer pacifiquement": Taniguchi, "Loi et La Coutume au Japon," in *Études Juridiques Offertes à Leon Julliot de la Morandière* (1964), pp. 571, 582.

[162] See p. 505, *supra*.

[163] Kawashima, *op. cit. supra*, n. 14, at pp. 267–268.

[164] Tanaka, *op. cit. supra*, n. 89, at p. 303.

[165] I. Ben-Dasan, *The Japanese and the Jews 101* (1972), *excerpted in* Tanaka, *op. cit. supra*, n. 89, at p. 293.

[166] *Ibid.*

[167] The infrequent use of lawyers outside the courtroom and the relative infrequency of litigation are among the features of the Japanese legal culture that enable Japan to have such a small number of lawyers. *See* p. 491, *supra*. For a fuller treatment of the factors affecting the small number of lawyers in Japan, *see* Henderson and Anderson, *op. cit. supra*, n. 5.

[168] Tanaka, *op. cit. supra*, n. 89, at pp. 255–261.

years' experience in the United States, one Japanese observer, Shirō Hattori, drew the following interesting comparison between American and Japanese contracts:

> Americans carefully observe the law, regulations and contractual agreements, and they make full use of these legal forms. Japanese do not have a sufficiently clear conception of such legal forms but honour and trust *jōjō* [the surrounding circumstances], *giri* [moral or social obligation to others], *ninjō* [human feeling], *yujō* [friendship], *magokoro* [sincerity] and so forth. . . It is perhaps well known that Americans observe contractual obligations more closely than Japanese. Conversely, an American will say that he is not responsible for what he did not agree to. When a Japanese makes an agreement with another person, the *goodwill and friendship that gave rise to the agreement is more important to him than the agreement itself.* If there is sincerity, it does not matter if the contract itself is not executed according to its terms. To Americans legal agreements and feelings of friendship are completely different things. In these circumstances Japanese tend to be preoccupied with a *friendly atmosphere and are not careful to see that the agreement itself is thorough.* [Emphasis in original.][169]

According to Kawashima,

> In many Japanese contracts there are clauses such as:
>
> > If in the future a dispute arises between the parties with regard to the rights and duties provided in this contract the parties will confer in good faith (*sei-i o motte kyōgi suru*).
>
> or, in a similar situation,
>
> > . . . will settle the dispute harmoniously by consultation (*kyogi ni yori enman ni kaiketsu suru*).[170]

Traditional Japanese thought rejects the assumption " that a high degree of predictability is to be assured as to the consequences of particular conduct long before the conduct has occurred or the dispute has arisen." [171] Life is better left to flow as it will; regulation by outside rules is artificial.[172] Furthermore, since disputes are regarded as abnormal disruptions of the natural harmony of life, not to be foreseen in human affairs, human affairs being secured by bonds of love and benevolence, the anticipation of a dispute in, for instance, a contractual choice-of-law clause, certainly would seem to tread heavily on the parties' sense of *on-giri-ninjō*. Social relationships are dictated by *giri*, rules that are imbued with feudal principles of a hierarchy of social statuses. Merchant and client are not equal parties bargaining at arms-length; the client is superior, so the merchant ought to exhibit the deference appropriate to his inferiority. And *ninjo* fills the relationship with an affectionate or benevolent content. Thus an executive ought not only to direct his subordinates in their work; he also ought to have an empathic interest in their personal and domestic affairs.[173] Indeed, *ninjō* may sometimes effectively exclude the law from a subject matter

[169] *Ashihi Shimbun* (morning edition), Dec. 20, 1952, at p. 6; *quoted in* Kawashima, " The Legal Consciousness of Contract in Japan " (1974) 7 *Law in Japan: An Annual* 1, pp. 6–7.

[170] Kawashima, " The Legal Consciousness of Contract in Japan," *ibid.*, p. 16.

[171] von Mehren, *op. cit. supra*, n. 79, at p. 1496.

[172] Tanaka, *op. cit. supra*, n. 89, at pp. 300–301.

[173] Noda, *op. cit. supra*, n. 11, at pp. 177–178.

that we regulate by law in the West. For example, the marriage contract is a rarity in Japan, and only a small number of articles of the Civil Code deal with matrimonial property regimes. It is contrary to *ninjō* to think of marriage in commercial terms.[174]

A last illustration of traditional Japanese attitudes reflected in law is the principle of *kenka ryōseibai* ("both parties are to blame," or "both disputants are to be punished"). Disputes arise only when persons have stepped outside the community of thought, hence all parties to the dispute are to blame, all parties must be at fault.[175] Harmony is to be restored by reconciling the parties, not by determining which party was right and which was wrong. Accordingly, the principle of *kenka ryōseibai* is traditionally applied in both mediation and arbitration.[176] It is often pointed out that Japanese courts readily apply the rule of comparative negligence, and some scholars have felt this to be a reflection of the "both parties are to blame" attitude.[177] The principle of *kenka ryōseibai* was also seen in the criminal law in the interesting 1932 case of *Osada* v. *Japan*.[178] In *Osada* the accused had committed a homicide in the course of a quarrel, through fear that his victim was about to attack him with a knife. The court rejected both his self-defence argument and his argument that because of apprehension for his life he could not have formed the intent necessary to be guilty of an intentional homicide. *Kenka ryōseibai* was regarded as the governing principle:

> This court believes, however, that in a quarrel, the law considers that each of the parties is attacking the other. A quarrel cannot be regarded as a situation in which one side is launching an unjust attack and the other is defending against such attack. There is no room for the concept of self-defence to come in relation to acts committed by either party to a quarrel. In our country there is a proverb saying, "In a quarrel, both parties are to blame" (*kenka ryō-seibai*).[179]

IV. CONCLUSION

These are but a few illustrations of the adaptation of law to Japanese legal cultural patterns. As we have seen, it is not quite true that "they don't like law in Japan,"[180] since the law is respected as a teacher of morals. There is, however, a widespread antipathy to litigation, and to the attempt to squeeze life into the law's logical compartments. Western students of contemporary Japanese law must appreciate the general features of the traditional Japanese conception of law if they wish to come to understand the living law of Japan.

[174] *Ibid.* at p. 176.

[175] Noda, *op. cit. supra*, n. 10, at p. 133.

[176] Kawashima, *op. cit. supra*, n. 85, at p. 51.

[177] Tanaka, *op. cit. supra*, n. 89, at p. 315.

[178] Great Court of Judicature Judgment, Jan. 25, 1932, 11 Keishū 1; edited English translation in Tanaka, *op. cit. supra*, n. 89, at pp. 312–315.

[179] *Ibid.* at pp. 314–315.

[180] See p. 491, *supra*.

The growth of the living law in Japan has been more an adaptation to foreign law than an internal evolution, and necessarily so, because in the late nineteenth century Japan eclectically borrowed most of her legal system from European nations. Thorough adaptation was necessary if there was to be any accommodation between Western law, founded on Aristotelian logic, and Japanese society, founded on a non-rational, intuitive philosphy of life. It ought not to surprise us, then, to find that the manner in which Japanese law and legal institutions function is quite dissimilar to the manner in which their Western counterparts do so. Instead it ought, perhaps, to surprise us to find that this borrowing and adaptation have been so successful. Japan has developed her own law from elements borrowed from other cultures, yet, as von Mehren has remarked, she has managed to preserve " much of value in her own tradition: a profoundly aesthetic perception of life, a well-knit social structure, a capacity to accept man's mortality and to honour age for its mature wisdom." [181] Japan's successful accommodation of her traditional cultural values to the law of the West is probably due, at least in part, to the history—more than one thousand years long—of her reception of foreign law, dating from her earliest codifications, which were verbatim copies from the Chinese.[182] Even the character *ho*, meaning law, though centuries old, is Chinese in origin and did not evolve from the Japanese character.[183] And this readiness to borrow elements of another culture may extend beyond the law. Both Japanese [184] and American [185] scholars have noted that "(t)his willingness to fuse elements of a borrowed culture with one's own to form a blend that is different from its component parts has always characterised Japanese history." [186]

The reception of Western law was but one part of a national modernisation, in many respects a Westernisation, of Japanese culture.[187] Today neither Japanese thought nor Japanese law is standing still; both continue to move towards the West. Newer types of suits are being brought, and the popular press pays more attention to law and litigation.[188] In 1957, *Osada* v. *Japan* was overruled, removing the " both parties are to blame " bar to a plea of self-defence during a quarrel.[189] The consciousness of *giri* seems to be declining, especially among the young.[190] Several different factors—the post-war democratisation of government,

[181] von Mehren, *op. cit. supra*, n. 79, at p. 1492.
[182] Wren, *op. cit. supra*, n. 15, at p. 226.
[183] Tanaka, *op. cit. supra*, n. 89, at p. 301.
[184] Kōsaka, *op. cit. supra*, n. 110, at p. 253.
[185] Wren, *op. cit. supra*, n. 15, at p. 218.
[186] *Ibid.*
[187] On the specific stimulus to the reception of Western law during the Meiji period, see Tanaka and Takeuchi, *op. cit. supra*, n. 37, at p. 38.
[188] Tanaka, *op. cit. supra*, n. 89, at p. 263.
[189] Supreme Court Judgment, Jan. 12, 1957, 11 Keishū 31; *see* Tanaka, *op. cit. supra*, n. 89, at p. 315.
[190] Noda, *op. cit. supra*, n. 11, at p. 183.

the land reform demolition of the traditional rural order, the concentration of population in big cities, the changing structure of family relationships, and radical changes in other social conditions—" have all combined to shake from its very foundation the traditional mental attitude and values which the Japanese people held toward law."[191] Newer, more democratic attitudes are arising, and one observer has suggested that these new attitudes will probably foster a consciousness of rights and duties and a greater reliance on general rules administered by legal institutions as functionally appropriate for a society tending toward Western atomistic individualism.[192] Many see such a change occurring.[193] According to David, the trend could eventually implant in Japanese thinking the notion that the rule of law is a necessary condition of justice. But he points out that this is still only a hypothesis.[194] There are some indications, however, that Japan is not, as might appear, simply being swept westward. Noda has remarked that in rural areas community conscience generally remains, and resistance to modern law is therefore strong.[195] He even feels that the essence of *giri* survives among the young, for although they ignore its specific dictates, they still show a fascination with the idea of the social tie.[196] Perhaps it can only be said that Japan is in a time of transition:

> Despite their remarkable national progress in the last century, the Japanese remain strongly enthralled by their own unique heritage and uncertain, as they have been since Perry's squadron first arrived in 1853, of their moorings in the cultural gulf that still separates East and West in the modern world.[197]

The student of comparative law, wishing to know how closely the Japanese living law will come to resemble that of the West, can only await the outcome of Japan's social changes. Until then, and perhaps even then, Japanese law and legal institutions will be appreciated more fully by those who appreciate her traditional attitudes toward law. Even today, her law remains the law of the subtle mind.

191 Tanaka, *op. cit. supra*, n. 89, at p. 262.

192 von Mehren, *op. cit. supra*, n. 140, at p. 192.

193 *See e.g.* Tanaka and Takeuchi, *op. cit. supra*, n. 37, at p. 48; Kawashima, *op. cit. supra*, n. 85, at p. 57.

194 David, *op. cit. supra*, n. 64, at p. 569.

195 Noda, *op. cit. supra*, n. 11, at pp. 179–180.

196 Noda, *op. cit. supra*, n. 10, at p. 134.

197 Varley, *op. cit. supra*, n. 100, at p. 212.

[13]

Islam and Appeal*

Martin Shapiro†

Appeal is a legal phenomenon that Westerners tend to accept without question. The orthodox view is that appeal serves to correct trial errors and thus protect individual rights. Uniformity of law is also commonly advanced as a purpose of appeal. Yet appeal is encountered even in autocratic and totalitarian regimes that have no particular regard for due process or the rights of individuals. Moreover, in such regimes appeal is typically employed to allow the highest political authorities to dispense "personal" justice, or, in other words, to give special and nonuniform treatment to those favored by those in authority.

It is the hypothesis of this Article that the basic explanation for the almost universal adoption of appeal by various legal systems lies not in a commitment to individual rights and legal uniformity as general values, but rather in the benefits that appeal mechanisms provide to centralizing regimes engaged in the solicitation of political loyalty and the facilitation of hierarchical control. It is contended that political hierarchy is the wellspring of appellate processes. This hypothesis will be applied to the legal system of Islam, which stands alone among major legal cultures in its failure to employ appellate mechanisms.

After a brief survey of the primary political implications of appellate processes in general, various explanations for the absence of appeal in Islamic law will be critically examined. It will be argued that the cultural peculiarities of Islam alone do not explain the absence of appeal in Islamic legal cultures, since such mechanisms have developed in similar societies. In addition, this Article will explore the institutional factors that may better explain the absence of appeal, including the existence of dual judicial structures and the weak hierarchy of Islamic political and religious organizations. Finally, in a focused analysis of the Ottoman Empire's legal system it will be asserted that appellate procedures flourished as political power became concentrated and, conversely, waned as that power was dispersed.

---

* This Article will appear in slightly different form as a chapter of Martin Shapiro's forthcoming book, COURTS: A COMPARATIVE AND POLITICAL ANALYSIS, to be published by the University of Chicago Press. It is printed here by permission of the Press.

† Professor of Law, Boalt Hall School of Law, University of California, Berkeley. B.A. 1955, University of California, Los Angeles; Ph.D. 1961, Harvard University.

I

Political Implications of the Appellate Process

There appears to be a strong historical affinity between the supreme authority in any given political system and appellate jurisdiction, whether the sovereign be personal autocrat or tripartite constitutional government. Wherever ultimate political authority lies there also tends to lie the ultimate forum for appeals. Contemporary Western societies have tended to approach appeals from the bottom up in terms of opportunities available to the loser at trial. Most political regimes are likely to have looked at the matter from the top down, however, in terms of what appeal could do for the rulers. It is a bit difficult for contemporary Americans to adopt this perspective because we assume a separation of powers in which the highest appeals court is somehow independent of the governing "political" institutions, so that the political power of the rulers does not seem to be enhanced by appeal. A legislature which allocates funding for a supreme court is seen to be increasing someone else's political power, not its own. Leaving aside the political naiveté of this vision, it need only be said here that appellate processes were invented and became nearly universal long before separation of powers lines were initially employed. The proposition that the origins of appeal lie in the exercise of authority by unified sovereigns—chiefs, kings, emperors, or even the "people" acting as a whole—provides a useful framework for an analysis of how rulers benefit from appeal.

First of all, appeal to a supreme political authority tends to recruit political loyalty to the regime. It focuses the attention of the people scattered over the countryside upon their ruler in the capital. It provides a framework in which persons may ask the ruler for something and in which he may grant their requests. In England, for instance, distinct appellate mechanisms were slow to develop precisely because the trial courts were themselves the King's courts, centralized in the King's capital of Westminster. This had the effect of casting the fate of the litigants with the central regime even at trial stage.[1] Every king and emperor was careful to preserve his own ultimate power to "correct" the trial courts, just as he was careful to preserve many other means of reminding his people that those who were loyal to him could look to him for benefits.

The second advantage of appeal for the central government is rooted in the fact that judging and administration have historically been merged rather than separated activities in most political regimes. Most empires employ district officers or provincial governors or

1. Shapiro, *Judicial Independence: The English Experience*, 55 N.C.L. Rev. 577 (1977).

proconsuls who are committed to keeping the territorial region assigned them functioning in the interests of the Empire. The Roman governor, the British district officer in Africa, as well as the Imperial Chinese magistrate collect the taxes, keep the peace, mend the roads, and adjudicate legal disputes. In this setting, appeal becomes one of many modes of hierarchical control over scattered administrative subordinates. Just as the central political authority requires its local officials to send in many reports of their activities and dispatches inspector generals into the field to review the performance of the local officials, it also provides an appeals channel. When a central regime hears appeals, it essentially is reviewing the administrative performance of its local subordinates. In this context appeal involves error correction in the interest of the central regime rather than in the interest of the loser at trial. In both Imperial China and Tokugawa Japan, where central regimes were anxious to exercise very detailed control over their local subordinates, every serious case was reviewed by higher authorities whether either of the parties wished to appeal or not.[2] Thus the most rigorous and complete systems of appeal in history were conducted with little or no thought to the welfare of the individual litigant and every concern for assuming central government control over local administrative performance.

Appeal at the instance of the parties becomes an especially attractive device for regimes that cannot afford the very high levels of surveillance over administrative subordinates' practices employed by the Chinese and Japanese. If one cannot inspect every unit produced, an obvious alternative strategy for achieving quality control is to pull samples from the production line and inspect them. To avoid the possibility of the production workers presenting only their best work for inspection, the sampling should be either random or managed so that the least polished product will be available for inspection. Appeal is such a sampling process, insofar as the appellate authorities inspect some but not all of the decisions reached by local administrators. They do so not through the medium of review of a summary report prepared by the administrator himself which may be designed to hide his shortcomings, but rather through a particular case of a subject dissatisfied with the administrator's performance. Consisting of whatever cases litigants—as opposed to local administrators—choose to remit for inspection by higher authorities, the sample is essentially random. Alternatively, it is biased toward poor administrative performance, insofar as cases are less likely to be appealed when the local judge has produced a commendable judgment. When a central regime hears an

2. *See* D. Bodde & C. Morris, Law in Imperial China 113-43 (1967); 1 J. Wigmore, Law and Justice in Tokugawa Japan 48-49 (1969).

appeal, it effectively has scrutinized a particular slice of countryside life to see how well its local government has performed in that specific situation.

Similar points could be made about legal uniformity. Where appeal is employed to achieve uniform local application of law, central regimes may be far more concerned with the increment to their political power that is derived from the uniform transmission and enforcement of their commands than they are with any abstract devotion to legal uniformity as a due process value.

While these propositions about appeal are extremely general, one mode of testing them is an examination of the one major legal system which does not employ formal appeals procedures. If the propositions offered here present an adequate explanation for the absence of appeal in Islam, their validity will be somewhat enhanced. On the other hand, if Islamic regimes exhibit strong centralizing tendencies and nonetheless do not develop appeal processes, then the adequacy of essentially political explanations of appeal will be correspondingly impaired.

II

The Legal Culture of Islam

Two basic explanations—one cultural, the other political or institutional—can be advanced to explain the unique absence of appellate procedures in Islamic law.[3] This section will explore possible cultural

3. An initial caveat is necessary. Western perceptions of Islamic courts were seriously distorted when Max Weber, in his seminal work on legal systems, employed what has become a famous construct: "*kadi* justice." Max Weber on Law in Economy and Society 213 (M. Rheinstein ed. 1954). The term evoked the image of a somewhat scruffy Moslem holy man sitting under a tree and deciding cases on a purely ad hoc basis as the morality or equities of the conflict struck him. *Kadi* justice was to be contrasted with justice dispensed by a Western judge deciding cases according to fixed, general legal rules. Like so many of his constructs, "*kadi* justice" was for Weber an "ideal type," whose value lay in its analytical utility rather than its correspondence to the actual behavior of any particular set of people in any particular society. Weber was not summarizing empirical findings about the actual behavior of real *kadis*, but rather was seizing upon a colorful figure of speech in order to dramatize the contrast between rational-legal judicial decisionmaking and highly particularized decisionmaking based on religious inspiration.

The figure of speech was memorable, however, precisely because it appealed to a set of Western prejudices, and particularly central European ones. In Weber's day, Europeans' general vision of the Islamic world had been shaped by their contact with the Ottoman Empire in its final stages of decay in the turn-of-the-century Balkans. Because Weber has been so powerful in shaping subsequent thinking about law, his figure of speech has more or less accidentally transformed the popular prejudices of his day into a pervasive image which most Western students of law and courts retain about Islamic judicial institutions.

Weber's picture of the *kadi* has its roots in three aspects of Islamic law. First, Islamic law is often highly particularized. It does not treat of contract in general, for instance, but has one provision for contracts of sale for dates and quite another for sale of houses. Second, Islamic law treats not only of what is legally right or wrong but also of what is morally good, better, and best. The *kadi* may punish any act that seems to him to merit punishment. Third, since Islamic law

reasons for this phenomenon.[4]

A. Absence of Legislation

A brief sketch of the evolution of Islamic law (the *Shari'a*) provides the necessary backdrop for an appreciation of the cultural explanation. In Islam, the words of the Prophet as recorded in the *Koran* and in the sayings ascribed to Mohammed by certain authenticated traditions are the sole body of legislation. While the interrelation between secular and religious authority is complex, and has fluctuated over the course of Moslem history, in theory at least, the Caliphs, who were the highest authorities of Islam, were merely protectors of the faithful and not sovereigns. In the early years of the Abbasid Caliphate (following A.D. 750), there were proposals for codification and legislation, but they were conclusively rejected. Thus, aside from the Prophet and his words, legislators or legislation are foreign to Islam.

This rejection of legislation either causes, or at least is an integral part of, a number of distinct characteristics of Moslem law. Most bodies of law show a distinct disinclination to change. Deprived of the opportunity consciously and openly to make new law, Islamic law has been especially conservative. Perhaps more important, as a system of law it has never had to respond to the kind of single, central direction and unification that would flow from a sovereign wielding acknowledged lawmaking power.[5] Deeply embedded in Islamic legal and theological thought is the notion that what is true in law and religion is determined by the consensus of the faithful rather than the command

---

does not generally recognize appeal, the judgment of the *kadi* is usually final. These three factors, taken together and seen through the eyes of an outsider, tend to create a picture of the *kadi* as deciding each case on an ad hoc basis without the need to rationalize his decision on the basis of any general body of law. This stereotype is inapplicable to the ideas presented in this Article.

4. The survey of the Islamic legal system that follows is drawn largely from N. COULSON, HISTORY OF ISLAMIC LAW (1964) [hereinafter cited as COULSON]; D. MACDONALD, MOSLEM THEOLOGY, JURISPRUDENCE, AND CONSTITUTIONAL THEORY (1913); J. SCHACHT, INTRODUCTION TO ISLAMIC LAW (1964) [hereinafter cited as SCHACHT]; E. TYNAN, HISTORIE DE L'ORGANISATION JUDICIAIRE EN PAYS D'ISLAM (1944). *See also* N. COULSON, CONFLICT AND TENSIONS IN ISLAMIC JURISPRUDENCE (1969); AHMED BIN MOHAMMED IBRAHIM, SOURCES AND DEVELOPMENT OF MOSLEM LAW (1965); M. KHADDURI & H. LIEBSENY, LAW IN THE MIDDLE EAST (1955); D. LEV, ISLAMIC COURTS IN INDONESIA (1972); J. SCHACHT, THE ORIGINS OF MUHAMMEDAN JURISPRUDENCE (1950).

The proper English spelling of Arabic and Turkish words presents linguistic difficulties. I have employed common English spellings in the singular and added "s" for plurals (*e.g.*, *"beys"* instead of the more proper *"beyis"*).

5. The well-known "codification" efforts of the Ottoman Sultans were basically collections of the administrative regulations (*kanuns*) that they issued. In all but name many of these were laws, but they were denied the official status of law and so did not enter the *Shari'a*. While they were administered by a partnership of a *kadi* and a military official, they were actually a part of the secular legal system described in text accompanying notes 22-27. 1 S. SHAW, HISTORY OF THE OTTOMAN EMPIRE AND MODERN TURKEY 62, 83, 88, 100-03, 139 (1976).

of any living being. The Moslem treats such a consensus as a blessing, but a rare one. The absence of a sovereign other than Mohammed himself is part of a deeper cultural acceptance of great diversity of opinion within the overall consensus of the community of the faithful. For the Moslem it is neither particularly strange nor particularly offensive that two or three or six different versions of the law of the Prophet should exist side by side.

The absence of legislation subsequent to the words of the Prophet also has resulted in a highly particularized body of law. While Mohammed did attempt some relatively systematic and general comments on some legal topics, most of his law consists of highly specific utterances on the day-to-day disputes brought to him for settlement by his immediate followers.[6] Thus there are no general statutes on tort or contracts, for example, but only a body of particular sayings of the Prophet.

The absence of legislation does not mean, however, that Islamic law confines itself to the bare words of the *Koran*. Indeed, the legal pronouncements in the *Koran* are so sporadic, particularized, and incomplete that they could not serve as the body of law even for a relatively simple village society. The first great body of supplementary law consists of the authenticated "traditions" of the Prophet. After the death of the Prophet, his followers treasured memories of his sayings and actions and passed them on to their descendants. An enormous body of traditions thus arose, many no doubt invented to be employed in the sectarian conflicts that constantly racked the Moslem world. The elaboration of traditions, and selection among them, were methods of filling out and clarifying the fragmentary legal materials of the *Koran* itself. For several hundred years this was the principal task of legal commentators. The development of a more or less complete body of law through the "discovery" and "authentication" of traditions was enthusiastically pursued. It even was held that where conflict or uncertainty existed, the traditions were to be considered more authoritative than the words of the *Koran* itself.

B. The Schools

Shortly after the death of Mohammed, Islamic legal commentary began to proliferate at a dramatic rate. Hundreds of commentaries appeared on the words of the Prophet found in the *Koran*. The search for the true traditions of the Prophet resulted in an enormous amount of

6. For instance, Mohammed denounces *ribā*, transactions in which the amounts of gold, silver, wheat, barley, dates, or raisins exchanged are unequal or delivery is delayed. But the *Koran* states no general rule as to what kinds of commodities are subject to *ribā* prohibitions or even an explanation of what these particular six commodities have in common.

quasi-historical and pseudohistorical authentication and elaboration. This work usually sought to trace the traditions from their most recent advocates through an unbroken chain of earlier authorities and holy men to the Prophet himself. These commentaries on the *Koran* and the traditions were produced not by judges but by jurisconsults, who were independent scholars learned in the law.

As a result of early dynastic quarrels among the heirs and successors of the Prophet, Islam has almost from its first triumphs been divided into two major (the Sunni and the Shi'ite) and numerous minor sects. The vast Moslem empire and sphere of influence once stretched from the Philippines in a broad belt through India, Persia, the Arab lands, and across North Africa, with offshoots into East Africa and Spain. Different regions were dominated by different sects although, in some, members of various sects lived side by side. The Shi'ites and a number of the minor sects each had their own school of legal commentators. The main or orthodox body of believers (the Sunni Moslems) recognizes four major schools of legal commentary.[7] By the second half of the eighth century, six or more schools had established firm control of the law. The four major Sunni schools were each identified with the name of a single great commentator (Hanifa, Malik, Ash Shafi'i, and Hanbal). But it was the collective writings of all the commentators belonging to a given tradition, not a single synthetic work by a single author, that constituted the law of any given school. Just as the consensus of all the faithful, when it could be found, defined religious and legal truth, so the consensus of the commentators of a given school constituted the legal truth of that school. When one scholar is identified as the leading member of a school and his work cited as authoritative, it is because his writings are seen as representing the mean or consensual position within his school. The diversity of opinion within a given school was often great, and opinion was often graded as "dominant," "preferable" in certain circumstances, or "weak." While in theory the *kadi* would follow the dominant opinion of his own school, in practice he might follow the preferable or weak opinion in order to do justice in a particular case.

A lack of consensus between schools on a particular legal point was regarded by the faithful as a blessing from God. Each school might continue to assert its own differing legal holding.[8] Every Moslem fell under the legal authority of one—but no more than one—

7. There were in addition a number of others that did not quite achieve full status, although at least one, the *Zabirite*, lasted for centuries. D. MacDonald, *supra* note 4, at 110.

8. Indeed, the continuing diversity of the schools is sometimes described as a tree whose beautiful network of branches and twigs all spring from the same trunk and roots. *See generally* Coulson, *supra* note 4; Schacht, *supra* note 4.

school. In some areas adherents of various schools lived side by side, each under their own law. Where there was no consensus on a point of law, each school might continue to assert its own position.

The four major schools differ on many specific points of law, but it is not easy to generalize about their differences. The school of Abu Hanifa arose in Kufa, one of the new barracks or garrison cities created by and for the warriors of Islam as they conducted the conquest that shaped a vast empire in the course of a hundred years. The school of Malik flourished in Medina, a holy city associated with the Prophet and a settled commercial community with its own legal traditions predating the birth of Mohammed. Hanifa jurisprudence tended therefore to be more militant and in some senses more purely Moslem. Maliki jurisprudence borrowed heavily from the pre-Moslem customs and usages of Medina, particularly in its receptiveness to commercial practices which might, under the most rigid interpretations of the words of the Prophet, be considered illegal.

Ash-Shafi'i was a later figure, one of the great synthesizers of Moslem law, who sought to settle the quarrels between literalists and those commentators inclined toward more speculative and creative jurisprudence.[9] He was a skilled casuist who typically saved the letter of the *Koran* by demonstrating that the letter could be interpreted to meet practical exigencies. Ash-Shafi'i stressed the agreement of the faithful as a test of legal correctness. The school of Ash-Shafi'i is the most complex, subtle, and synthetic of the schools. To a certain extent it is the dominant school in the sense that the others have tended to accept its general methodology of cross-comparison and integration of the *Koran*, the traditions of the Prophet, and the agreement of the faithful. All of the major schools also seem to accept the method of analogy widely practiced by the Shafi'ites to expand their limited initial materials into a fuller body of law.

The Hanbali school shuns the synthetic sophistication of Ash-Shafi'i. Ahman ibn Hanbal was a fundamentalist theologian who taught that there should be no human commentary on the words of the Prophet. A martyr to his beliefs and a hero to the street mobs of Bagdad, his legal commentary consists simply of a massive collection of the traditions of the Prophet.

C. Lawmaking and the Schools

The vast body of legal scholarship created by the schools became the operative law of Islam. It elaborated and proliferated the skeletal

9. Shafi'i's great work, the *Risala*, is translated into English with an instructive introduction in M. KHADDURI, ISLAMIC JURISPRUDENCE (1961).

legal pronouncements of the *Koran*. Although a few of the traditions of the Prophet collected in the writings of the schools may actually be traceable to Mohammed himself, most of them must be new law made by the schools and legitimated by ascription to the Prophet. Furthermore, at the earliest stages a great deal of local custom (*urf*) was undoubtedly incorporated into the commentaries. The Hanafi school, which relied on the traditions of bedouin warriors, and the Maliki, with their tendency to legitimate Medinan commercial practice, were particularly prone to this process. Although later the schools came formally to reject custom as a source of law, it clearly was important initially. Shafi'ite reliance on analogy (*giyas*) is common to most of the schools. Analogy is an extremely powerful lawmaking method in legal systems, such as Islam, where the original corpus is a series of highly particular and incomplete legal pronouncements.[10]

Beyond tradition and analogy, most Islamic schools, with the notable exception of the Hanbali, engaged in various lawmaking practices labelled opinion (*ra'y*), preference (*istihsan*), consensus (*ijma*), and public interest (*istislah*). Schools differ on the legal authority of these techniques. In general, however, their existence is tacit acknowledgment that the koranic and traditional materials are incomplete and often contradictory, as are the subsequent commentaries. Thus, the latest commentator on occasion must choose between various applicable—but incomplete or conflicting—preexisting rules. In doing so, he may be guided by his own preference, tempered by his perception of the views most consistent with the general teachings of Islam and his school. He may seek to discover the consensus of the faithful or of his own school and declare it to be the law. Alternatively, he may choose the one of two conflicting or potential rules that appears to best satisfy the needs of the community, particularly as expressed in their own customary practices.[11] Thus in Islam there is a mixture of rational, legalistic, democratic, and utilitarian bases for supplementary lawmaking by commentators.

Finally, Islamic law, like most other legal systems, employs a set of special technical usages to allow the legal profession to modify some legal rules in order to meet unforeseen circumstances or to ease the burdens of legal administration. In the West, legal fictions or presumptions are frequently designed for these purposes. In Islam, the strict letter of the *Shari'a*, for example, contains prohibitions on interest, and

10. *Riba* again provides a good example. An endless series of analogies were drawn between other commodities and the original six. Those that were held to be like gold, silver, wheat, etc., fell under the prohibition against uneven or delayed exchange. Those that were held to be unlike them did not.

11. *See* A. IBN' ABD AL-HALLIM, IBN TAIMIYAH ON PUBLIC AND PRIVATE LAW IN ISLAM, OR PUBLIC POLICY IN ISLAMIC JURISPRUDENCE (1968).

derivatively on any uncertain or speculative elements in contracts, as well as several other doctrines that would render commercial activity impossible. Devices (*hiyal*) are designed to circumvent these doctrines.[12]

The schools obviously engaged in lawmaking, although the opportunities for commentators to make law were limited very early. The schools also did a certain amount of synthesizing, at least when great scholars like Malik or Ash-Shafi'i sought to integrate various sources and methods of lawfinding and harmonize conflicting interpretations. But the schools did not systematize, generalize, or codify Islamic law. For the most part the scholars commented upon secondary *Koran* commentaries and the early collections of traditions of the Prophet. The commentators engaged in detailed exegesis on a particular saying of the Prophet, usually by posing an imaginary fact situation that approximated the one for which the Prophet first shaped his pronouncements. The books of commentaries show only rudimentary attempts at systematic arrangement by subject matter, and little or no attempt to frame general rules or categories. In typical form the Prophetic text is announced, together with the particular situation in which it arose, such as the exchange of dried figs by weight. The commentator indicates how other commentators of his school have interpreted this saying and extended it to other very similar fact situations. Then he provides his own applications. Each book of commentaries is a long series of such exegetical commentaries on discrete rules and their attendant fact situations. There is no assurance that all of these discrete discussions add up to a complete code of law, nor any assurance that the rules for various specific fact situations are in harmony with one another.

Moreover, by approximately the tenth century, the basic collections of traditions (*hadith*) had been frozen. At about that same time, the "closing of the gate" of legal theorizing (*Ijtihad*) occurred.[13] After that time the orthodox consensus of the various schools was fixed and little scope for further innovation remained. This development appears to be largely the result of the work of Ash-Shafi'i. He emphasized that the traditions (*sunna*) of the Prophet must dominate the orthodox consensus (*sunna*) of each individual school. He also placed great emphasis on the consensus (*ijma*) of the whole community of the faithful. This dual emphasis may have been designated to unify Islamic law. In actuality, however, each school managed to identify its own particular

12. Consider the loan by double sale. *A* purchases an object from *B* at a lower price on date 1. *B* would at the same time agree to buy the same object back from *A* on date 2, at a higher price. *A*'s purchase price is a loan. *B*'s purchase price is repayment. The difference between the two prices is the interest. COULSON, *supra* note 4, at 139-40.

13. After the "closing of the gate" legal scholars were no longer permitted to advance new interpretations or doctrines. *Id.* at 80-81. *See* K. FARUKI, ISLAMIC JURISPRUDENCE 27-29 (1962).

teachings with the traditions of the Prophet and to preserve many interschool differences above and beyond the points of interschool agreement (*ijma*). The end result was that the law of Islam was frozen in the tenth century through its identification with the unchangeable *sunna* of the Prophet and unchallengeable *ijma* of the scholars. The divided legal teachings of the schools were some of the central features that became fixed. After that point the schools continued to produce new manuals for the guidance of judges and students, but their compilers ceased to employ the lawmaking techniques used by earlier commentators. The medieval manuals remained the basic corpus of Islamic law until various reform movements of the twentieth century. Until recently, Islamic commentators were committed to the doctrine of strict adherence to the teachings of their school as expressed in its medieval manuals (*taglid*). Given that even the compilers of those medieval manuals had themselves already forsworn the conscious use of such methods as preference and opinion, basic Islamic law retained its tenth-century substance and structure.

The jurisconsults (*muftis*) continued to offer opinions (*fatwas*) on disputed points of law, both to private litigants who went into court armed with as many *fatwas* as they cared to purchase, and to the *kadis* themselves. Indeed, official *muftis* were attached to many courts, but their opinions had no official sanctions, and the *kadi* were not required to accept them. Nevertheless, particularly in the nineteenth century, compilations of *fatwas* acquired some authority as legal texts complementary to the medieval manuals.[14] They undoubtedly contained a good deal of covert lawmaking.

D. *The Inadequacy of Cultural Explanations*

In Western legal systems, uniformity of law is typically achieved through the announcement of general legal definitions, concepts, and doctrines by the highest courts. These pronouncements provide guidance for future decisions of lower courts. But the legal environment of the *kadi* was far removed from these Western principles. The *kadi* functioned in a world of highly particularized legal rules rather than general legal concepts. His job was to find which among hundreds of specific and detailed rules most closely fitted the particular facts before him. In doing so he was removed from the original wording of the *Koran,* Islamic traditions, and the great scholarly texts. Instead, he referred only to the frozen medieval manuals of his school. He was for-

14. The Ottoman Empire was officially Hanafi and its law was defined by *The Pearls* and *The Confluence of the Seas*, works produced in the fifteenth and sixteenth centuries respectively. 1 H. GIBB & H. BOWEN, ISLAMIC SOCIETY AND THE WEST 22-23 (1957) [hereinafter cited as GIBB & BOWEN].

bidden to work by preference, public interest, or any kind of independent legal theorizing (*ijtihad*). He was limited instead to the most narrow kind of analogy in the interstices of already highly detailed and particularized rules. The work of Ash-Shafi'i and others had, by the tenth century, clearly identified the legitimate sources (*usūl*) of law to be the *Koran*, traditions, consensus of the schools, and analogy. Thus, no legal authority beyond the immediate case could attach to the pronouncements of any legal tribunal.

In such a system, appeals courts would be deprived of many of their major functions. They could not announce uniform legal rules or doctrines, which could only occur through the words of the Prophet or the consensus of the community of the faithful. In other words, in a legal culture that rejects all lawmaking, appellate lawmaking is not feasible. Moreover, since Islamic legal culture rejects generalization, the license for broad conceptualization and direct reinterpretation of basic law accorded Western appellate courts is lacking under Islam.[15] In such a culture, even the most difficult case turns upon a rather arbitrary choice among numerous highly concrete and particularized rules. Since there is little opportunity to rationalize this choice, there is no reason to believe that a second choice by an appellate court would be more just than the initial one made by the trial *kadi*.

Islam would also deprive appellate courts of their ultimate weapon in the struggle for institutional legitimacy. In Western legal systems it is theoretically unacceptable for two trial courts applying the same statute to arrive at contradictory interpretations of the applicable law. Because appeal is the major insurance against such nonuniformity, Westerners are generally committed to the principle of appellate jurisprudence regardless of how much they are opposed to the policies being pursued by the appellate judiciary at any given time.

In Islam, however, uniformity of law is not a central value. The multiple sects and schools are, of course, the most dramatic evidence of Islamic toleration of diversity.[16] More fundamentally, however, Islamic culture regards *both* consensus and diversity among the faithful as gifts from God. This belief is echoed in the recurring metaphor of diversity as branches springing from the great tree of Islam. Even the Islamic notion of consensus is generally one of spontaneous and evolving agreement rather than imposition of uniformity. Thus, appellate

15. The Hanbali tradition is the extreme statement of rejection of broad reasoning upon the words of the Prophet, but that rejection runs deeply through all of Islam.

16. Of course, sectarianism may exist in religious traditions that show little or no tolerance for diversity, as for example in Western Christianity. But unlike Islam, each Christian sect has historically tended to deny that the others are sharers in the true faith.

courts need not be available to reconcile nonuniform law since legal nonuniformity is accepted by this legal system.

The absence of appeal in Islamic law can therefore be traced to three basic cultural peculiarities: the particularization of legal rules, the rejection of institutional lawmaking beyond the words of the Prophet, and the notion of consensus as the mode of discovering the Prophet's true words. Explanations of the absence of appeal in Moslem courts based on the legal culture, however, are not entirely satisfactory for a number of reasons. First, Imperial China had a comparably particularized legal code equally adverse to the formation of general legal concepts or doctrines.[17] It also functioned by small step analogies from particularized and fixed legal provisions. Despite these similarities to Islamic legal culture, Imperial China had a highly elaborate system of appeal.

Second, there is no satisfactory explanation for the failure of appellate processes to develop before the body of law became immutably fixed in the tenth century. While the existence of the schools during even the earliest period might have precluded a single system of appeal, why was there not a highest appeals court for the *kadis* of each school? The fact that the enunciation and development of law during the early period was the responsibility of jurisconsults rather than the *kadis* themselves would not have precluded the formation of appellate courts advised by leading jurisconsults in the same way that trial *kadis* were advised by such jurisconsults. In short, during the formative period of Islamic law, when independent legal theorizing (*ijtihad*) was very much in evidence, appellate court lawmaking would have been appropriate to the contemporary legal culture. Its absence cannot be explained by reference to the historical phenomenon.

Third, even after the closing of the gate of *ijtihad*, a number of factors might have combined to encourage judicial lawmaking. Legal rules were particular and incomplete. Analogizing retained currency as a judicial technique, and a large body of commentary literature was in existence. These factors might have left room for considerable appellate judicial lawmaking, at least within each of the schools. Certainly many other legal cultures, most notably the Anglo-American, have witnessed the considerable growth of appellate lawmaking despite a theoretical commitment to reasoning by analogy in the judicial lawmaking process.

Fourth, even if the formal doctrines of each of the schools were theoretically fixed, each *kadi* still had to "apply" this large body of formal rules to the cases before him, many of which could not be liter-

17. *See* D. Bodde & C. Morris, Law in Imperial China 113-31 (1967).

ally accommodated by the highly particularized rules. This is a classic breeding ground for judicial lawmaking and, by extension, for appellate procedures to correct trial courts which have chosen the "wrong" rule or made the "wrong" analogy. Here again the Imperial Chinese practice is revealing.[18] Indeed, in the Maghreb, the western island of Islam running across North Africa, the practice of court decisions (*annal*) assuming an independent legal force was prevalent.[19]

Finally, the notion of the consensus of the community or the consensus of the jurisconsults is deeply embedded in many legal cultures. The German "reception" of Roman law is one example of this principle. Yet, substantial lawmaking at appellate court levels occurs in many such cultures. The appellate judge or the jurisconsult simply announces himself as the spokesman for the consensus of the community. The requirement of popular consensus need not be a bar to the announcement of law by a single high source. Instead, the cultural need for consensus may become one of the values supporting an appellate court that announces uniform rules in the form of "discovering" the consensus latent in the community. This need for consensus might have served as a strong weapon of appellate court discipline against the tolerance of diversity that characterizes Islamic culture.

In summary, then, the presence of one or more of the same features in other societies with appellate procedures suggests that the cultural peculiarities of Islam do not adequately explain the absence of appeal in Islamic law. Institutional factors may provide a more convincing explanation for the absence of appeal in the Islamic legal system.

III
Institutional Explanations for the Absence of Appeal in Islam

A sketch of the growth of Islamic legal, political, and religious institutions reveals two basic institutional factors that are relevant to the absence of appeal in Islam. The first is the simultaneous existence of both a secular and a religious judicial system. The second is the weakness or absence of hierarchical structures in the political and religious organization of Islam.

A. Religious and Secular Courts

The law of Islam (*Shari'a*) cannot simply be called either a purely religious law or a universal law governing both secular and religious

18. *Id.*

19. Coulson, *supra* note 4, at 145-47.

affairs. The *Shari'a* is the path to righteousness. It guides the faithful to an ideally pure existence rather than prescribing minimums of acceptable conduct. It is concerned with the believers' duties to God, and most of it is concerned with what Westerners would call religious obligations such as prayer, pilgrimage, and various kinds of abstinence. Substantial portions concern marriage, divorce, and inheritance, which were initially considered in the West to be essentially within religious jurisdiction. In this sense the *Shari'a* is religious rather than secular law. But the *Shari'a* also contains prohibitions against a number of major forms of crime, stipulations about the validity of various kinds of commercial transactions and agreements, and provisions about the holding and transfer of various kinds of personal and real property. In that sense it had the potential for governing a wide range of social interactions that Western cultures would label secular.

1. The Umayyads

Islam did not actually develop a single, unified body of law or court system, however, but instead created two parallel legal systems. One of these legal systems can be labeled religious, and the other secular. The first Islamic dynasty, the Umayyads (A.D. 661-750), who controlled a rapidly expanding empire, evidenced an institutional pattern that is typical of imperial rule.[20] Both judicial and administrative power were vested in the Caliph. His judicial powers were then delegated to the host of subordinates who exercised territorial or functional administrative control, such as provincial governors, army commanders, treasury officials, market inspectors, and water supply officials. Provincial governors were the principal judicial officers, but they left actual dispute settlement to the *kadis*. At this point, however, the *kadi* was simply the legal secretary to the governor, appointed by him and exercising his delegated authority. Decisions by the *kadi* were reviewable by the governor. The *kadi* replaced the *hakan*, the triadic figure whom Arabs engaged in a dispute had selected by mutual consent to mediate their differences. Thus at first the *kadi* handled only "private" disputes voluntarily brought to him by both parties. This is a typical pattern of a new central political regime supplanting purely private triadic dispute settlers with public officials. The police (*shurta*) were in complete control of investigation, arrest, trial, and punishment in criminal matters.

Before the end of the Umayyad Caliphate, however, the *kadi* ceased to be simply an administrative officer offering dispute settlement services on behalf of the territorial governor. By about 715, the custom

20. *See generally* GIBB & BOWEN, *supra* note 14.

of appointing *kadis* only from among the scholar specialists in the *Koran* was in evidence.[21] Thus, the *kadi* began to become a religious expert rather than simply an administrative subordinate.

2. *The Abbasids*

This tendency, begun under the Umayyads, was rapidly carried to its extreme under the next dynasty, the Abbasids. The Abbasids represented a militant religious reaction to the incipient secularism of the Umayyads. Abbasid policy emphasized the central role of the faith in the new Arab empire. One wing of that policy involved the formation of the *kadis* as a separate profession of religious scholars. The *kadis* ceased to be administrative subordinates of the governor and became specialized judges confining themselves entirely to the *Shari'a*. In this sense the *kadi* increasingly became an independent religious judge rather than the kind of secular subordinate administrator he had initially been.

It must be remembered, however, that the Caliph's regime itself was not a secular one in the Western sense. The Abbasid emphasis on Islam was at the same time an elevation of Islam and an elevation of the Caliph, who as defender of the faithful wielded both religious and secular authority. While nominally supervised by a chief *kadi*, the *kadis* actually served at the pleasure of the political authorities. In practice that political authority generally still was the Caliph's territorial governor.

3. *The Secular Courts*

At the same time that the *kadi*'s religious aspects were emphasized, and indeed partly because of this emphasis, a second body of law and courts arose. The trial jurisdiction of the *shurta* was far more extensive than the police court jurisdiction for minor offenses that are encountered in many legal systems. The caliphate took over from the Byzantines the institution of "inspector of the market" (*muhtasib*), a local official responsible not only for maintaining the orderly operation of the marketplace but also for settling commercial disputes according to the local customs of the market.[22] In Islam, as in Medieval Europe, the inspectors could play a particularly important role because religious objections to profit and interest on loans were deeply embedded in the general law. This is not to say that the inspectors of the market were totally isolated from *Shari'a* and employed a totally distinct body of

21. SCHACHT, *supra* note 4, at 24-27.

22. We also encounter this pattern of special merchants courts applying customary commercial law in the English pie powder courts. *See* 5 W. HOLDSWORTH, HISTORY OF ENGLISH LAW 106-14 (1924).

law. As with most older institutions taken over by the faithful, this one was Islamicized. The *muhtasib* was generally regarded as an inferior of, if not a subordinate to, the *kadi*.[23] On the other hand, a great many of the "devices" of Islamic law are designed to reach a compromise between the *Shari'a* and customary commercial practices. Thus, although the inspector of the market jurisdiction was not a repository of antireligious law, the inspector was not a *kadi* and his decisions were not pronouncements of the *Shari'a*.

From the earliest times the administrative side of the caliphate employed an official in charge of complaints (*Sahib al Mazālim*).[24] *Mazālim* jurisdiction included complaints against government officials, land law, and any other matters the government chose to define as a complaint. *Mazālim* courts could and did announce doctrines of substantive law additional and supplemental to the *Shari'a* in the form of administrative regulations or policies of the government. The relation between this *mazālim* court system and the *kadis* varied greatly in various situations. It is clear that the Sahib al Mazālim was totally independent of the court of the *kadi* and indeed could hear complaints against the *kadi* as against all other government officials. But in some instances *kadis* held both *Shari'a* and *mazālim* jurisdiction and many *mazālim* courts had a *Shari'a* jurisconsult in attendance. On the other hand, particularly in active military zones, the *mazālim* courts might take on almost complete jurisdiction.

The authority of the *mazālim* courts was derived from that of the Caliph. The caliphate expanded its own lawmaking powers, and thus the powers of the *mazālim* and the police courts, in two ways. First, under the name "*siyasa*" (which roughly means administration or public policy), the Caliphs did in fact legislate, particularly in the areas of police, taxation, and criminal justice.[25] The *Shari'a* condemned only a few offenses, for which it specified particularly severe punishments (*haad*). Prosecutions for other offenses, and even for *Shari'a* offenses when the authorites wanted something less than *haad* punishments, were brought in the secular courts. The Caliph defined both the substantive and procedural aspects of the non-*haad* criminal law. Moreover, the Caliph might impose whatever punishments (*ta'zir*) he thought were necessary to serve as a deterrent to bad conduct even in noncriminal disputes.[26]

23. COULSON, *supra* note 4, at 131.

24. E. TYNAN, *supra* note 4, presents the most complete account of the non-*Shari'a* courts available in a Western language. A second edition of his work was published in one volume in Leiden by E. J. Brill in 1960.

25. SCHACHT, *supra* note 4, at 53-54. *Siyasa* is the Arabic term. The Ottoman Sultans exercised their *siyasa* authority by issuing *Kanuns*. *See* note 5 *supra*.

26. COULSON, *supra* note 4, at 132-33.

Land and tax litigation were normally brought before the Master of the Treasury. The *Shari'a* had little or nothing to say about such matters. The seizure and reassignment to the faithful of great tracts of conquered land was a key feature of the Islamic political economy of conquest. Since the Caliphs assigned this land, major land disputes ended up in the *mazālim* courts rather than before the *kadi* because they were essentially problems of military administration rather than ownership. The scope of the Caliph's administrative powers was therefore very substantial.

Moreover, as Defenders of the Faithful, the Caliphs attributed to themselves the status of religious scholars. They could announce their personal interpretations of the *Shari'a* in the same manner as any other legal scholar. Thus, the vast administrative discretion of the caliphate could be given a gloss of *Shari'a* legitimacy by the Caliphs themselves.

It is inaccurate to make a sharp distinction between secular and religious authorities or jurisdictions in analyses of traditional Islam. Until the fall of the Ottoman Empire after the First World War, the Islamic world knew no purely secular governments, except in countries such as India and Indonesia, where Moslems were conquered and reduced to the status of a protected religious minority. Nevertheless, a large body of law and courts, basically involved in the secular administrative sector of the caliphate's vast authority, were apparently operating separately and parallel to the courts of the *kadis*. These courts conceived of themselves as applying the rules and policies of the Caliph and other territorial rulers rather than confining themselves to the *Shari'a*. In this sense a secular legal system exists side by side with the religious law of the *kadis*.[27]

The growth of an alternative system of law and courts was encouraged by two aspects of the *Shari'a*. The first was its incompleteness, which has been discussed above.[28] The second was its strict and demanding rules of evidence.[29] These evidentiary problems were so severe that they spawned a special official (*sahib ar-rodd*) whose function was to hear cases rejected by the *kadi* because the claimant could

27. GIBB & BOWEN, *supra* note 14, at 79, 115. The Ottoman Sultans officially proclaimed this distinction by codifying a body of *kanun*, *see* note 5 *supra*, separate from the *Shari'a*. While for reasons that will be discussed later the *kadi* enforced both the *Shari'a* and the *kanun*, a clear distinction was maintained between the two, and by the eighteenth century the *kadis* had entirely lost their secular "law and order" jurisdiction to the police authorities. *Id.* at 87.

28. *See* text accompanying note 6 *supra*.

29. Under *Shari'a* procedure it is almost always both necessary and sufficient that two male adult Moslems testify orally to the truth of the claimant's (*mudda'ī*) position. If two such witnesses cannot be produced, the defendant (*mudda'ā alayhi*) wins by taking an oath of denial. If two such witnesses do appear, about the only option open to the defendant is to attack their moral and religious character. There is no cross-examination, and *kadis* do not normally weigh opposing evidence.

not meet *Shari'a* standards of proof, although he appeared to be justified in his claim. The police courts and the *wali al-jarā'* (official in charge of crimes) heard evidence from dubious witnesses, cross-examined, extracted confessions, and heard and weighed circumstantial evidence. The *mazālim* courts used discretionary procedures outside the *Shari'a*. Thus the Islamic institutional structure appears to have been composed of two judicial systems: one which was essentially secular and linked directly to the political and administrative authorities, and another which was religious and linked directly to the *Shari'a* tradition as embodied in the teachings of the schools of jurisconsults.

B. Appeal as Hierarchical Control

Because two distinct judicial systems existed in Islam, some of the uses of appeal are not relevant to the *Shari'a* courts of the *kadis*. Appeal as a sampling of administrative performance was irrelevant because the *kadis* were not in the main line of administration. Appeal as a means of hierarchical control and coordination was irrelevant for the same reason. To the extent that the Caliphs and subsequently the Ottoman Sultans did exercise control over their domains, it was through a chain of territorial administrators and tributory monarchs to which the *kadis* were only loosely connected.[30] Appeal as an instrument of hierarchical control was, therefore, far more relevant to the secular side of Islamic institutions than to its system of religious courts.

Although relations between church and state have been extremely complex througout the history of Islam, it has nevertheless always been apparent that the law of *Shari'a* pertained to the religious aspirations of the faithful, while the police and administrative law and courts of the Caliphs and Sultans[31] were the principal governors of the more mundane aspects of public policy. Yet to label the *Shari'a* religious is not in itself a satisfactory explanation for the absence of appeal as a form of hierarchical control. In the ecclesiastical law and courts of the European Roman Catholic Church, where far clearer lines are drawn between religious and secular law than in Islam, an elaborate system of appeals heavily freighted with the function of maintaining papal control over widely dispersed subordinates is much in evidence. It is the nature of Islam as a religious community, rather than the fact that *kadi* courts are religious, that explains the absence of appeal.

The Islamic religious community, unlike that of Roman Catholi-

30. It is true that in the declining days of Islamic empire the *kadis* took on more and more of the duties of local government, but that was precisely because the hierarchical chain of government administrators was disintegrating.

31. The Ottoman Sultans, who were the successors to the authority of the Abbasid Caliphs, are discussed in Part V *infra*.

cism, has only the weakest hierarchical structure. The Caliph is in theory both the successor of Mohammed and the chosen of the people, but in practice he is considered only Defender of the Faithful and not proclaimer of the faith. There are no equivalents of Apostolic succession, dogma or papal infallibility, or of canon law made by the church as subsidiary to divine law. The Caliph or Imam may make no law on the central questions of religion. At best he is one among the many jurisconsults.

In some of the Islamic sects, a particular religious leader achieved the status of prophet or even a kind of god. This development led to absolutist regimes, combining full religious and secular powers, such as the Fatimids in Egypt and the Persian monarchy. But in the Sunnite mainstream no such dominant religious authority emerges. Islam has no ultimate human provider of religious law, nor any hierarchical organization of priests and bishops culminating in such a supreme source of law.[32] For a religious community that lacks both the doctrine of a single, central, dominant human source of religious truth and a hierarchical structure of priests and religious institutions, one of the principal attractions of appeal—its hierarchical control dimension—is missing.

The *Shari'a* courts did not need to be mustered in a hierarchical fashion to achieve the secular tasks of territorial rules, since those rulers enjoyed a second legal and administrative system for such purposes. Moreover, they did not need to be hierarchically organized to support the hierarchical structure of the religious community because no such structure existed in the religious community.

The religious fragmentation of Islam is a part of its more general fragmentation. Although political institutions such as the caliphate and the Ottoman Empire often claimed centralized authority, in practice Islam was usually divided into a large number of independent territorial states. Even within areas that acknowledged the nominal rule of a single Caliph, Imam, Sultan, or Emperor, there were typically a series of city-states or praetorian provinces with few lines of authority running from local to central authorities. Because *kadis* were appointed by the government authorities, *Shari'a* judicial organization reflected the general lapses in hierarchy of the political regime. In practice, unified corps of *kadis* or any single central appointing authority rarely existed.

The *kadi*'s law was a segment of a universal religion. The *kadis* were officials appointed by city or state secular regimes, but as purveyors of the universals of Islam, they could not be totally incorporated into the existing local political hierarchy. On the other hand, the *kadi*

32. GIBB & BOWEN, *supra* note 14, at 74, 117.

was also not incorporated into any universal religious hierarchy since such a hierarchy is nonexistent in Islam. Although governing authorities did sometimes try to discipline *kadis*,[33] these attempts were relatively rare and usually unsuccessful. Since the *kadi* was usually appointed by local authority, and his duty was to one of the schools of a religious law in which neither the school nor the religion had a single central authority, the *kadi* lived in an essentially nonhierarchical world where the absence of appeal is hardly surprising.

IV

Elements of Appeal in Islam

This close linkage between the vicissitudes of Islamic political and religious hierarchy and the absence of appeal can be further demonstrated through an examination of the elements of appeal actually in existence in Islam. Those elements are in fact substantial. Initially, no distinct appeal mechanism was necessary in Islam because of a constitutional theory of delegation apparently inherited by the Arabs from the Byzantines. All political, legal, and religious authority adhered to the Caliph. He might delegate portions of that authority to subordinates. They in turn might redelegate it. But the delegator retained full and complete jurisdiction and authority over all matters delegated. Thus, the Caliph and his governors retained full judicial authority even when delegating judicial tasks to the *kadis*. The notion of a level of appeals courts superior to the *kadis* did not develop due to the fact that a litigant dissatisfied with the *kadi*'s decision or initially reluctant to seek a *kadi*'s judgment could place his case directly before the highest political authority. A system of appeal by trial de novo conducted by the delegating authority therefore implicitly existed. There are scattered recorded instances of Caliphs reversing the decisions of a *kadi* or sending a case back to him with new instructions. Because initially the political authorities retained such complete judicial jurisdiction, they had no need for special appellate courts. Subsequently, two interacting forces intervened to disrupt this appellate system. First, as the *kadis* came to be seen as servants of the *Shari'a*—experts in a religious law rather than simple legal subordinates of Caliph and governor—they became increasingly independent of short term control by the political authorities. Second, as the central political, military, and religious authority of Caliphs and their governors decayed, rulers tended to relinquish personal exercise of their judicial authority.

33. There are instances in which regimes attempted to apply test oaths and purge the ranks of the *kadis* in order to achieve religious uniformity or compliance to the regime's policies. D. MacDonald, *supra* note 4, at 153-58.

A paradox is therefore apparent. Precisely because the Caliphs were initially the repositories of such enormous religious and secular judicial authority, they needed no special appellate institutions. As a result, once the powers of the central authorities waned, Islam ended up with no appellate institutions at all.

Closely connected to their personal judicial powers to try cases, the Caliphs, Sultans, and governors also exercised the authority of complaints (*mazālim*). As previously discussed,[34] *mazālim* jurisdiction was part of the second and "secular" line of Islamic courts. Three elements of the *mazālim* jurisdiction coalesced to form, in practice, an appellate procedure from *kadi* jurisdiction. First, the *mazālim* is a court of complaints against all government officials, including the *kadi*. Second, it is a kind of equity court designated to do substantial justice where the *kadis* have failed to that end.[35] Third, the *mazālim* jurisdiction is peculiarly connected to the head of the regime. It is a device for correcting the misconduct of his own lesser officials. It is also a device for bringing the full power of authority to bear against powerful individuals who resist the jurisdiction and judgments of the *kadi*'s courts. *Mazālim* jurisdiction inheres in the Caliph, Sultan, or governor, as does the general power to hold court. The two powers are often not distinguished, or are seen as additive or supplementary to one another. The *mazālim* jurisdiction, therefore, empowers the head of the regime to hear and remedy complaints against a *kadi* brought by those who have lost cases in the *kadi*'s court or otherwise suffered from his conduct.[36]

Whenever a Caliph, Sultan, territorial governor, or *wazir* (prime minister, mayor of the palace) was in the ascendancy, concentrating political power in himself, he tended actively and personally to exercise *mazālim* jurisdiction. It is significant that in such instances *mazālim* jurisdiction tended to expand so far that it not only supervised but sometimes also displaced the *kadis*' jurisdiction. Whenever central government was in disarray, however, the governing authority ceased to personally exercise *mazālim* jurisdiction and instead delegated it to a special corps of subordinate judges. When *mazālim* jurisdiction was exercised by such subordinates, appeals from the *kadis*' courts were usually specifically proscribed. Moreover, in the weakest periods of central authority, the *kadis* themselves often were granted the *mazālim* jurisdiction.[37] In short, a survey of the major appeals institutions of

34. *See* text accompanying note 24 *supra*.

35. Typically this incapacity arose because the procedural or substantive rules of the *Shari'a* were too rigid or narrow to remedy the injury. Sometimes the transgressor was a person so powerful that the *kadi* was unable to reach him. The failure of the *kadi* to reach a *correct* legal decision, however, was also viewed as an incapacity remedial by the *mazālim* court.

36. COULSON, *supra* note 4, at 120-24.

37. 2 E. TYNAN, *supra* note 4, at 141-281.

Islam over time reveals that appeal tended to flourish as political power became concentrated and wane as political authority was dispersed.

V

THE OTTOMAN EMPIRE: A CASE STUDY IN ISLAM, HIERARCHY, AND APPEAL

If the absence of appeal in Islamic law is indeed related to the absence of centralization rather than to the lack of concern for the loser at trial, appeal should have been introduced where Islamic institutions did become centralized. The Ottoman Empire, which dominated much of the Moslem world from the fourteenth through the nineteenth centuries,[38] witnessed the greatest incidence of centralizing tendencies under Islam. With the exceptions of Persia and the interior of Saudi Arabia, the Ottomans either directly or indirectly ruled the entire Islamic faith. The Sultan was both the emperor and caliph,[39] and the religious capital as well as the secular capital of most of Islam was Istanbul (Constantinople).

The Ottoman Empire only temporarily achieved its ideal of complete centralization of authority in the Sultan. This centralization gradually disappeared over the centuries. Nevertheless, the ideal of centralization did exist during the reigns of some of the great early Sultans. The ideal of centralization was reflected in the judicial institutions of the Empire. The *kadis* held the Sultan's commission. They enforced both the *Shari'a* and the secular laws enacted by the Sultan (*kanun*). The *kadis* played a major role in territorial administration, not only in the levying of criminal penalties, but also in supervision of the tax system and in the management of the large religious trust funds that were an important feature of Moslem life. The *kadis* and local governors (*beys*) shared authority as conveyors and enforcers of the

38. The discussion of the Ottoman Empire that follows is drawn largely from GIBB & BOWEN, *supra* note 14; H. INALCIK, THE OTTOMAN EMPIRE (1973); A. LYBYER, THE GOVERNMENT OF THE OTTOMAN EMPIRE (1966); S. SHAW, *supra* note 5.

The Ottomans were originally nomadic Turkic tribesmen from central Asia who settled in what is now the western portion of Turkey. From that base they gradually built their empire at the cost of both the European Christian lands to their west and north and the Moslem lands to their east and south. At its zenith, the Empire swept from the Balkans and Greece into the Caucasus, through Turkey, and subsequently along the eastern and southern shores of the Mediterranean all the way to Algeria and Tunisia.

39. The caliphate is a complex and often uncertain concept and institution, particularly subsequent to the early period when the Abbasid Caliphs held both political and religious authority. *See* T. ARNOLD, THE CALIPHATE (1924). The capacity of the Caliph to proclaim authoritative religious doctrine was usually referred to yet another title or office, that of *Imam*. Secular Moslem rulers often assumed the title Caliph as an honorific, usually on the event of some great military victory, but subsequently they might or might not actually claim religious authority as *Imam*. The Sultans proclaimed themselves to be Caliphs but rarely sought to exercise the dominant religious-doctrinal role implied by the title *Imam*. *See* GIBB & BOWEN, *supra* note 14, at 26-38.

commands of the Sultan.[40]

The judicial personnel system was centralized and hierarchical. Under the ultimate authority of the Sultan, the two military *kadis* (*kaziasker*), one for the European and the other for the Near Eastern sectors of the Empire, appointed all the *kadis* for their respective territories. Later, some of the authority of the *kaziaskers* was partially lost to the new office of *seyhulislam* (chief of Islam), or Grand Mufti. This *mufti* not only appointed and supervised lesser *mufti* and the general body of the *ulema* (the learned men of the faith) but also appointed the more important *kadis. Kadi* positions were hierarchical in nature, with appropriately graded salaries, honors, and approximately five hundred territorial jurisdictions in the eighteenth century. In short, the corps of *kadis* exhibited the standard pyramidal organization extending from rank and file local *kadis* through the *kaziaskers* and the *seyhulislam* who were appointed by and responsible to the Sultan. Moreover, the *kadis*, like other imperial officers, were subject to the scrutiny of the roving inspectors periodically dispatched by the Sultans. The Sultan and his high officers could and did summarily remove local *kadis* from office.

A. Appeal in the Ottoman Empire

Appellate institutions and procedures did begin to surface in the wake of the imperial thrust toward centralization and hierarchical organization of judicial personnel in the Ottoman Empire. Specialized appellate institutions, however, were noticeably absent. This absence was perhaps due in part to the fact that when Islamic law was taken over by the Ottomans such institutions were already formally proscribed. However, as in the development of English law,[41] appeal was stunted essentially because another mode of judicial centralization—centralized trial courts—was currently being employed. Like many sovereigns close to their tribal origins, the Sultans personally were the supreme font of justice. The Sultan held court wherever he was, as did the Grand Vizier, highest officer of the Sultan and the delegate of his authority. The Divan or Council of the Sultan and the Divan of the Grand Vizier, like the Privy Council or Star Chamber, were both administrative cabinets coordinating the business of government and important courts. Since all of these persons and groups reflected the personal and complete justice of the Sultan, each could hold trials at their discretion.

In the Ottoman Empire every court was a court of first instance for

40. *See* U. Heyd, Studies in Old Ottoman Criminal Law (1973).
41. *See* Shapiro, *supra* note 1, at 595-96.

those cases appropriate to its level of prestige. The two Divans were in a sense supreme courts, but they served as courts of first instance for cases important enough to attract their attention. The Grand Vizier personally decided those cases he wished to hear with the advice of the *kadis* who attended the Divan if the case involved the *Shari'a*. Other *Shari'a* cases were turned over to these *kadis* for trial. The Defterdar (Head of the Financial Office) had a court of his own to deal with all monetary disputes between the government and individuals. The Admiral heard all cases involving the fleet. Most important, the *kaziaskers* had trial jurisdiction over all cases of inheritance, marriage, and emancipation in which soldiers (*askeris*) were involved, and had direct personal jurisdiction over all members of the standing military forces. Given the basically military character of the Empire, nearly everyone above the rank of peasant and artisan and outside the *ulema* (the body of religious scholars) was an *askeri*. Moreover, because most of the land of the Empire was held as military fiefs (*timar*), almost all land disputes arose between persons who technically were members of the standing military forces. As a result, the courts of the two *kaziaskers* heard nearly all major real property cases and a substantial share of all cases involving the political and social elite of the Empire. Elaborate appeal mechanisms were therefore unnecessary as a device for centralization since the most important cases were likely to be heard directly by the central government itself.

While technically forbidden by Islamic law, a party dissatisfied with the judgment of one *kadi* could try another. Traditionally, the *kadis* summarily made their decisions without lengthy written or oral opinions. Given these two practices, an appeal was not necessarily differentiated in any way because it was an appeal. No special procedures or courts were necessary when a litigant, dissatisfied by the decision of a local *kadi*, went to a regional or provincial *kadi*, and then, still dissatisfied, proceeded to one of the highest courts of the realm sitting in the capital, or indeed to the Sultan himself. For each of the courts involved, the trial was a trial de novo rather than a "review" of what had been adjudicated below.

In spite of the absence of special appeals mechanisms, numerous authorities testify to the existence of appeal and to the fact that the Sultan, the Grand Vizier, and their respective Divans, stood at the apex of appeals.[42] After sessions of the Divan itself, the high officials who attended it customarily split up, each to hear further business of particular concern to him. Cases would also be heard at these sessions. The

42. A. Heidborn, Manuel de Droit Public et Administratif de l'Empire Ottoman 389 (1909); H. Inalcik, *supra* note 38, at 74-75, 89-97; A. Lybyer, *supra* note 38, at 41-42, 219-21 (citing 16th-century Western sources); S. Shaw, *supra* note 5, at 26, 136, 139.

two Divans sat both as trial courts in regular lawsuits and as administrative superiors hearing complaints against their subordinates, including the *kadis*. Appeal took the form either of a trial de novo or a complaint against the corrupt or unjust acts of a lower *kadi*. This was yet another reason why appeal does not appear distinctly in the Empire. It was often merged with the general complaints jurisdiction of various mixed judicial and administrative bodies. The *kaziasker*, for instance, heard appeals not only in the Divan but also from decisions of the military governors of towns and provinces concerning the affairs of their subordinate government officials.[43]

B. The Scope of Sultanic Power

Although in practice it is probable that the decisions of the local *kadis* were very rarely reversed, nevertheless the hierarchical ambitions and surface accomplishments of the Ottoman Sultans suggest a more explicit and institutionally distinct role for appeal than that which actually developed. The Ottoman constitution presents several clues concerning why such a role never evolved in the Ottoman Empire.

The Ottoman Sultans claimed absolute political authority and constructed a system of government to wield that authority. At the capital, the Sultans built a large, functionally specialized, hierarchical bureaucracy that culminated in the Divan of the Sultan which was an almost daily meeting of the highest officers of the realm. The Divan was dominated either by the Sultan or his Grand Vizier, the highest political officer of the realm.[44] The Divan not only sought to coordinate, announce, and enforce the policies of the central government, but also served as a high court both of first instance and appeal. The *kaziasters* sat in the Divan. With their participation, the Divan became the highest court of the *Shari'a*.

The hierarchical and centralized administration of the capital was mirrored by a comparable territorial organization. With exceptions resulting from the conquest of certain of its parts, this organization was fairly uniform. The land was divided into basic units called *timars*, each of which was supervised by and supported an armed and equipped cavalryman (*sipahi*) and his horse. The holders of the larger *timars* were also responsible for providing one or more cavalrymen in addition to themselves. There were intermediate ranks, roughly de-

43. As personal representatives of the Sultan, provincial governors heard and decided cases. The local *kadis* and other religious men were encouraged to memorialize the Divan concerning the misconduct of such officials, including their judicial misconduct. Here again, little distinction was made between the appeal of a case and the hearing of a complaint against an administrative official. *See* GIBB & BOWEN, *supra* note 14, at 201.

44. For the purposes of this Article the historically shifting power relations that made sometimes the Sultan and sometimes the Grand Vizier the actual head of state need not be traced.

fined, of captain (*subashi*) and colonel (*alay bey*) who served in wartime as commanders of small and intermediate size units and in peacetime as territorial police officials. They held even larger *timars* (zeamets). The *sipahis* and their *subashis* and *alay beys* were grouped territorially under *sanjac beys*, each of whom had his seat in a town and governed his district, as well as serving as general of the cavalry division composed of his *sipahis*. Above them were the *beylerbeys*, or *beys* of *beys*, who were governors of their provinces and commanders of the major wings of the army under the direct command of the Sultan and Grand Vizier.

This neat structure of centralized empire looks rather like that of the Chinese Empire[45] and might be expected to exhibit comparable judicial structures. Indeed, since there was a *kadi* in nearly every town, a provincial *kadi* of higher rank in each provincial capital, and a *kaziasker* to match each of the two most important *beylerbeys*, the judicial corps followed the territorial pattern of the general government and culminated like it in the Divan. At the height of sultanic powers in the fifteenth and sixteenth centuries, great emphasis was placed on the *kadis* as appointees of the Sultan administering the Sultan's *kanun*, rather than as entities drawing their authority solely and directly from the *Shari'a*.

It is apparent that the Ottoman Sultans nevertheless failed to achieve the political centralization of the Chinese emperors. One commentator concludes that "it was only in the nineteenth century, as the result of Western influence, that Ottoman government in fact secured the kind of autocracy and centralized power that Europe traditionally assumed it had."[46] The Ottoman state was confronted with so many obstacles to centralization that each merits individual scrutiny.

First, much of the neat hierarchy of the Ottoman government was actually a military structure that became quiescent during most of the year. Indeed, in Islam the title "Sultan" means military leader. In the tribal, Turkish traditions of central Asia from which the Ottoman Sultans emerged, a military leader (*bey*) was simply what that title suggests. In peace the Turkic tribes had no chiefs. It is apparent that the Ottoman Sultans never escaped these traditions. They wielded absolute authority only over a campaigning army. This is one of the basic reasons that the Sultans undertook a campaign nearly every summer. The vast bulk of the population (*raia*) was exempt from military service. It remained almost totally immune to the Sultan's authority as long as it paid its taxes. The neat territorial organization that ran from *timar* holder up to a *beylerbey* actually only operated when the army

45. *See* T. Chu, Local Government in China Under the Ch'ing (1962).

46. S. Shaw, *supra* note 5, at 165.

gathered for its summer campaigns.[47] For the rest of the year each *timar* holder administered his own lands as an almost entirely independent feudal fief. Each *bey* or *subashi* reverted to ruling his own headquarters town as if it were his *timar*, which in many respects it was.

Second, the Ottoman Sultans had come to power as tribal *beys* who were only first among equals. Their coequals were their Turkic lieutenants, who were fellow nomadic horsemen and fellow Moslems. Turkish Moslem notables continued to be an important independent power in the empire. To counter them the Sultans developed a unique feature of the Ottoman Empire known as the slave family of the Sultan. From the families of his conquered European Christian subjects, the Sultan drafted young boys, who were then rigorously educated in Islam and trained as servants and soldiers of the Sultan. A professional army and mandarinate of governing officials therefore grew up alongside the old Turkish Moslem elite of notables. Each was composed of men who were European and Christian in origin and remained throughout their lives the personal slaves of the Sultan. These slaves of the Sultan were mingled with the old Moslem notables at many points. For instance, many of the *timar* holders and *beys* were the Sultan's slaves, but old Moslem notables held many governorships and their retainers held many *timars*. Some civil servants of the capital were old Moslems and some were slaves.

The central political arm of the capital, however, was recruited almost exclusively from the Sultan's slaves. It consisted of the palace staff of the Sultan, the Grand Vizier and his immediate staff, and the central professional core of the army (the *Janissaries*). Much of what appeared to be absolute government, therefore, was in effect only absolute control by the Sultan over his slave family. As the sultanate declined, of course, even this absolutism often proved illusory. During these periods the Grand Vizier or the *Jannisaries* often controlled the Sultan rather than vice versa. It is apparent, nevertheless, that absolute and arbitrary sultanic power existed largely within the slave family, which was totally dependent upon the Sultan and isolated from the tribal and Moslem roots of Ottoman society. In contrast, the Sultan's authority in reference to the old Turks and the old Moslems was limited. Although it may be an overstatement to depict the Ottoman ruling institution as neatly split into two parts—the ex-Christian slave family of the Sultan, living at his pleasure, and the Moslem warriors and learned men living under the *Shari'a* and custom—in practice it

47. Both weather and unavailability of food limited most campaigns to the summer months. The soldiers returned home between campaigns.

appears that much of Ottoman centralization was really only a family affair.

Third, the centralizing and hierarchical tendencies of the empire were tempered by a vague constitutional balancing of powers. The three highest advisors to the Sultan were the Grand Vizier (military-political matters), the *nicansi* (chief scribe on administrative matters), and the *seyhulislam* and *kaziasker* (religious matters). The balancing function was most explicit in territorial administration. The *kadis* were responsible for both the *Shari'a* and the administrative regulations of the Sultan (*kanun*). The *beys* could therefore not act in many matters without the legal authorization of the *kadis*. On the other hand, the *kadi* had no sword to enforce his judgment and relied on the *beys* for such enforcement.[48]

More generally, the ruling establishment of the Empire consisted of two parts. One was military and political and centered on the Sultan's slave family. The other was religious and cultural and centered on the body of Moslem religious and legal scholars (*ulema*). In theory they both met at the pinnacle in the person of the Sultan-Caliph. The sultanate was, however, essentially a military-political institution, and the *ulema* was seen as a counterbalance to the secular authority of the Sultan. The Ottoman Sultans actually only began to insist on their status as Caliph in the waning days of the empire in an attempt to bolster their sliding political authority.

Finally, the seemingly absolute power of the Sultan was both limited and superficially dramatized by the Ottoman view of personal responsibility. Within the strict boundaries of the role or status that society had prescribed for him, each individual was supposed to be personally autonomous and responsible for his own acts. The kind of supervision that entailed issuing continuous corrections of a subordinate's errors ran counter to this cultural ideal. Thus, Ottoman administrative control was directed largely into personnel measures. A subordinate was to be left alone to do his job. If he failed, he was to be dismissed, or executed and replaced by someone else who would be left alone until he failed. Under a strong Sultan it was said that a hundred heads of those who had failed sometimes arrived for his viewing pleasure on a single day. The Ottoman government thus was characterized by dramatic hiring and firing policies but evidenced little detailed control

48. The basic governmental territorial unit below the *sanjac* was the *kada*, or judicial district, presided over by a *kadi*. Each *kada* had a *subashi*, whose dual role as military and police official has been explained earlier. The *kadi* depended on the *subashi* for enforcement of his judgments. In theory, the *subashi* could not punish without authorization from the *kadi*. In practice, he often did.

over day-to-day administration.[49]

C. *The Sultan and the Kadis*

The *kadis* were concerned primarily with civil and religious affairs and were deeply rooted in the culture of the old Moslem Middle Eastern notables. The *ulema* maintained its separate authority. At times of crisis a Sultan or Grand Vizier might overwhelm it by sheer force or threat of force. On a day-to-day basis, however, it maintained its independent tradition of learning and law. It provided the *muftis* and *kadis* who followed that tradition with a special reserve of authority against whatever pretentions to absolute authority the Sultan might have.

Given the Ottoman penchant for supervising administration by personnel policies rather than by direct daily supervision, the appointment process for *kadis* was crucial. The early and strong Ottoman Sultans sought in this instance to centralize the appointing power. In Islam the holder of political power traditionally had the right to appoint the *kadis*. As noted above,[50] the Ottoman Sultans established a carefully graded, hierarchical personnel system for *kadis* in which higher *kadis* appointed and dismissed their subordinates while the highest *kadis*, the *kaziaskers*, and later the *seyhulislam*, appointed and dismissed the principal territorial *kadis*. The Sultan himself appointed and dismissed the highest *kadis* and the *seyhulislam* and so in theory controlled the whole corps.

As in other aspects of Ottoman administration, it was this hierarchical control of appointment and dismissal rather than detailed daily supervision and correction of the errors of subordinates that was emphasized. Because appeal is part of a system of detailed supervision and correction of errors, a regime which does not choose to engage in detailed control of the performance of its judges does not need appeal. In familiar Western terms, the Ottoman political regime preferred to control its judicial product by reducing the independence of its judiciary rather than instituting a thoroughgoing system of appeal. The trial judge was held in check not by the fear of reversal on appeal but by the fear of loss of his job or even his head.

Ultimately, however, the personnel tactic of the Sultans failed precisely because the *kadis* were necessarily embedded in a traditional Moslem community that was at the periphery of his authority. The Sultan was not in a position to challenge the proposition that the *kadis*

49. It is noteworthy that, in spite of elaborate financial and accounting staffs and procedures, the Ottomans had no overall budget and exercised almost no supervision over the spending of individual government officials. S. SHAW, *supra* note 5, at 264.

50. *See* text accompanying note 45 *supra*.

must be men learned in the wisdom of traditional Islam. As a result, the *ulema* continued to dominate the education and the appointment of the *kadis*. The Sultan could in some sense ultimately appoint, but he could appoint only those whom the *ulema* had proposed on the basis of their demonstrated allegiance, not to the Sultan, but to the Islamic religious community.

In short, while the *kadis* played an extremely important role in the Ottoman constitution, they were far removed from the central channels of the Sultan's authority, which consisted of the army and the slave family.[51] They were deeply embedded in that portion of Ottoman society most insulated from the Sultan's absolutist pretensions, the traditional Islamic community of notables and learned men. Although the Sultans did, nonetheless, seek to impose their control over the *kadis* by both a hierarchical personnel system and an appeals system culminating in the person of the Sultan, these devices were relatively ineffective precisely because they operated at the farthest and weakest reaches of sultanic power.

In summary, then, despite the absence of appeal from the central Islamic juristic tradition which the Ottomans absorbed, there was an appellate process in the Empire, closely associated with the institutions through which the Sultan sought to centralize political authority. While this appellate process has been somewhat obscured by the use of trial de novo on appeal and the intermingling of litigation and complaint jurisdiction, the fact remains that appeal existed in Islamic cultures where Islamic law and hierarchical government intersected in a relatively stable and enduring manner. The appeals process is attenuated and obscured, however, primarily because it operated in the sphere in which the government's claims to hierarchical authority were weakest.

51. The essentially religious character of the *kadis* of the Ottoman Empire is somewhat obscured by the strategy of the early Sultans. Essentially, that strategy was to recognize and reinforce the fundamental split between government and religion and to balance one against the other under his own ultimate authority. In the provinces the *kadi* was given authority over both the *Shari'a* and the *kanun* and officers of the civil-military government were forbidden to punish without his approval. The *kadis* were also encouraged to report the misconduct of government officials to the capital. Thus, the *kadi* was to serve as a check on the Sultan's government. In the capital, no Grand Vizier could hope to survive without the cooperation of the *seyhulislam* and *fatwas* from the *ulema* legitimating his policies. At the same time, the *kadis* were set to watch the civil governors and, as holders of government offices, they were used as intermediaries between the Sultan's government and the *ulema*. Indeed, among the more orthodox the office of *kadi* was disesteemed because it involved compromise with the civil authorities. This policy of exploiting the dual nature of the *kadi* as religious man and government official to increase sultanic control over both the civil and religious establishment was more or less successful at various times, but it was neither intended to, nor did it in practice, result in the conversion of an essentially religious judge into a secular administrator. *See* GIBB & BOWEN, *supra* note 14, at 149, 153-55, 201; 2 *id.* at 79-80, 86-87, 115, 117, 119-21.

CONCLUSION

Legal rules and a commitment to procedural justice are not absent from the Islamic legal tradition. To the contrary, Islamic law is marked by a multitude of rules, a desire to apply them uniformly, and a strong antipathy to arbitrary judgment. If appeal is a minor element of Islamic justice it is not because the society was indifferent to whether trial courts did justice under law. Rather, the simplest explanation for the absence of appeal in Islamic law is that the *Shari'a* and the courts of the *kadis* are essentially religious, and that Islam as a religion was not organized hierarchically. Without hierarchical organization much of both the opportunity and incentive for appeal is absent. And most of the pressure for appeal as a lawmaking device was absent because adjustments in law to meet new circumstances could be accomplished by the secular wing of Moslem legal institutions. More generally, the Moslem world experienced great difficulty in establishing or maintaining any kind of unity or hierarchy over its vast domains. Where, as for instance in the efforts of the Abbasid Caliphs and the early Ottoman emperors, we do encounter attempts at centralization of authority, we do encounter appeal.

In the final analysis the *kadis* escaped appeals supervision for the same reasons they escaped all hierarchical supervision. Their special identification with the *Shari'a* insulated them from the central political authorities. Their religious dimension provided a shield from the hierarchical authority that normally would have been exerted over them as local legal officials of a central regime. That religious dimension did not in turn lead to their subordination to a central religious hierarchy because such a hierarchy was lacking. Indeed, in the recurrent collapse of central authority in the Islamic world, the local mosque and its *kadi* became the only constant and ever-present receptacle of the religious and political authority of the faith. More often than not the local *kadis* extracted various degrees of political, economic, religious, and administrative authority from the central regime. Quite apart from their judicial functions, they seemed to be the only officials with sufficient stability to wield that authority successfully. Where local authorities flourish on the confusion of central regimes, and the local authorities happen to be judges, it could hardly be expected that institutions of appeal would flourish. In Islam a peculiar institutional combination of dual legal systems and absence of hierarchy accounts for the absence of the institution of appeal present in almost all other legal systems. The Islamic experience suggests, therefore, that concern for political control rather than justice under law is the basic motivation for the implementation of appellate institutions.

Part IV
Comparative Legal Methods

[14]

LOGIC AND EXPERIENCE IN ROMAN AND COMMON LAW

PETER STEIN*

FOREWORD

*By Richard E. Speidel***

Charles Phineas Sherman, late Distinguished Professor of Roman Law at Boston University, agreed with the dictum of Anatole France that "Rome is not dead, because she is living in us."[1] For Professor Sherman, Rome's legacy of law was "incomparably the greatest and grandest gift of them all."[2] It was his generosity, in honor of his great uncle, M. L. Sykes, which led to the establishment of the Charles P. Sherman Lectureship in Comparative Law at Boston University.

Peter Stein, Regius Professor of Civil Law, University of Cambridge and Fellow of Queens' College, Cambridge, is eminently qualified to meet the expectation that the Sherman Lecture emphasize Roman law and the legal contributions of the Roman state to the common law and statutory development of American jurisprudence.[3] An internationally recognized scholar in Roman and comparative law, Professor Stein received his B.A., LL.B. and M.A. from Cambridge University and his Ph.D. from Aberdeen University. In addition to his impressive scholarship,[4] Professor Stein has served as Dean of the Faculty of Law at Aberdeen University, Chairman of the Faculty Board of Law at Cambridge and, since 1974, Fellow of the British Academy. He has just completed a year as Visiting Professor at the University of Virginia School of Law. We are proud to publish his Sherman Lecture, *Logic and Experience in Roman Law and Common Law,* which was delivered at Boston University on March 29, 1979.

---

*Regius Professor of Civil Law, University of Cambridge and Fellow of Queens' College, Cambridge. This article is the text of the Charles P. Sherman Lecture on Roman and Comparative Law delivered at the Boston University School of Law on March 29, 1979.

**Dean and Professor of Law, Boston University School of Law.

[1] C. Sherman, Roman Civilization in the Modern World 7 (1942).

[2] *Id.* at 125. Professor Sherman's legacy was his three volume work, Roman Law in the Modern World (3d ed. 1937).

[3] Previous lecturers include Professor Rudolph W. James, University of Dar es Salaam, Tanzania, 1973-74; Professor Jacques Vanderlinden, Université Libré de Bruxelles, Belgium, 1970-71; Professor A. Arthur Schiller, Columbia University, 1966; and Professor F. H. Lawson, Brasenose College, University of Oxford, 1965. *See* Lawson, Roman Law as an Organizing Instrument, 46 B.U.L. Rev. 181 (1966) and Schiller, The Nature and Significance of Jurists Law, 47 B.U.L. Rev. 20 (1967).

[4] In addition to publishing numerous books and articles in law journals, Professor Stein also edits Buckland, Textbook of Roman Law (3d ed. 1963) and was co-editor of Adam Smith's Lectures on Jurisprudence (1978).

Professor Stein presents a study of adjudication in the classical period of Rome, which extended roughly from 150 B.C. to 235 A.D. He explores two schools or approaches to adjudication which evolved in the leading jurists' commentaries upon particular legal questions referred to them by a *iudex* or praetor.[5] These responses were important, for the jurists gave order to the legal system and became the custodians of the Roman legal tradition. Over time, these jurists mastered a Roman case law system which embodied principles reflecting the external power and influence of the ascending Empire and the secure internal relations of its stratified society unencumbered by excessive legislation or decree.[6] Defining the essence of the conflict between the two juristic schools as that of experience versus logic, of stability versus change, Professor Stein illustrates the Roman adjudicatory process with specific cases and describes how a workable synthesis gradually emerged from the competing methods within that process. The classical period was followed, of course, by ever increasing challenges to the external power of Rome, the gradual decline of the case law system, a sharp acceleration of internal strife and the exercise of imperial authority over the subjects. When central authority was at its peak and the Empire was near its fall, Roman law was collected and codified by the Emperor Justinian in 535 A.D. According to Professor John P. Dawson, the result—the *Corpus Juris Civilis*—was an authoritarian document intended to be a "complete code of laws without contradiction or imperfection."[7] Yet it was more than a code. In Dawson's words, it was a "monumental design for a whole society transmitting to the men of the middle ages the experience and values of the ancient world"[8] when it was rediscovered and studied at Bologna in the twelfth century.

Professor Stein, by selecting a particular focus in a limited time frame, has continued and advanced scholarly inquiry into the development of the Roman legal system.[9] But more importantly, he compares the approaches to adjudication of the Roman classical period with those of the late nineteenth and early twentieth century period of American common law

---

[5] *See* Schiller, Jurists' Law, 58 Colum. L. Rev. 1226 (1958) and Schiller, *supra* note 3. *See also* Stein, The Two Schools of Jurists in the Early Roman Principate, 31 Cambridge L.J. 8 (1972).

[6] For a highly readable account, see J. Dawson, The Oracles of the Law 100-19 (1968). According to Professor Dawson, the jurists, in advising the praetor or *iudex*, worked with a given and unalterable system: "their assumptions were fixed, the main purposes of the social and political order were not to be called in question, the system of legal ideas was too well known to require much discussion." *Id.* at 115.

[7] *Id.* at 122.

[8] *Id.* at 124. *See also* Berman, The Origins of Western Legal Science, 90 Harv. L. Rev. 894 (1977) (arguing that the rediscovery in the twelfth century of the enormous collection of legal materials compiled under Justinian was an important contribution to the development of law as a science). This excellent article repays careful study.

[9] *See* A. Watson, Legal Transplants: An Approach to Comparative Law (1974); The Law of Actions and the Development of Substantive Law in the Early Roman Republic, 89 L.Q. Rev. 387 (1973); Watson, Morality, Slavery and the Jurists in the Later Roman Republic, 42 Tul. L. Rev. 289 (1968); Acquisition of Possession and Usucapion *per Servos et Filios*, 78 L.Q. Rev. 205 (1962).

development.[10] Not surprisingly, Stein has found evidence in the writings of Holmes and Cardozo of a tension between, and later a synthesis of, logic and experience in American adjudication like that in Roman legal development. The comparison is not fully developed. For example, the focus is upon the Americans' writings rather than upon their judicial opinions. But this comparison of adjudicatory methods, rather than a study of the influence of Roman law upon American substantive legal development,[11] is especially intriguing since Holmes placed Roman law "high among the unrealities" for an American lawyer.[12]

How much potential for further development exists in this incomplete but thought-provoking comparison? There is, of course, danger in undertaking a segmented comparison which focuses upon a few writings somewhat divorced from both their contemporary context and the historical continuum. Professor Stein has selected for study the two characters, Holmes and Cardozo, who played a major part in the transition from what Grant Gilmore has called the "Age of Faith" to the "Age of Anxiety" in American law.[13] The "Age of Discovery" was past, American legal realism was incipient and America was moving toward a fifty-year period that would feature a depression, wars, technological advancement, international tension and interdependency and a society increasingly dominated by regulatory legislation.[14] How these conditions will affect the American adjudicatory process and its underlying framework and value structure is not clear. What does seem clear is that if we are to learn anything from the Romans it is that logic, experience, or adjudication[15] will not necessarily save the fundamental structure of our society from the stresses and strains of the future. Perhaps it is enough to say at this point that Professor Stein illustrates how legal change through adjudication

---

[10] Professor Schiller recognized that useful comparisons between the Roman and other case law systems could and should be made. *See* Schiller, *supra* note 3, at 39.

[11] The work of Professor Mitchell Franklin of Tulane University is instructive. *See* Franklin, Some Considerations on the Existential Force of Roman Law in the Early History of the United States, 22 Buffalo L. Rev. 69 (1972); Franklin, Bracton, Para-Bracton(s) and the Vicarage of the Roman Law, 42 Tul. L. Rev. 455 (1968); Franklin, Concerning the Influence of Roman Law on the Formulation of the Constitution of the United States, 38 Tul. L. Rev. 621 (1964). *See also* Re, The Roman Contribution to the Common Law, 29 Fordham L. Rev. 447 (1961); Kessler, On the Value of Roman Law for Twentieth Century Law Students, 12 J. Legal Educ. 377 (1960).

[12] Lawson, *supra* note 3, at 181.

[13] G. Gilmore, The Ages of American Law 19, 41, 68 (1977). Interestingly, Holmes, for Gilmore, is more the symbol of logic and Cardozo is the revolutionary. For Stein, the labels appear to be reversed. *See* Stein, Justice Cardozo, Marcus Terentius Varro and the Roman Juristic Process, 2 Ir. Jur. 367, 369 (1967).

[14] For an insightful treatment of the intellectual themes during this period of transition, see White, From Sociological Jurisprudence to Realism: Jurisprudence and Social Change in Early Twentieth-Century America, 58 Va. L. Rev. 999 (1972). *See also* White, The Evolution of Reasoned Elaboration: Jurisprudential Criticism and Social Change, 59 Va. L. Rev. 279 (1973).

[15] The limitations of adjudication in a changing society are sharply outlined by R. Dworkin, Taking Rights Seriously (1977) and by his many critics, *e.g.* Levinson, Book Review, 30 Stan. L. Rev. 1071 (1978); Lyons, Book Review, 87 Yale L.J. 415 (1977).

occurred at critical times in Roman and American law and how leading jurists, whether they were advisors or judges, were important architects in developing the methodological framework within which the tension between logic and experience was mediated. This effort at any time in any society demonstrates one meaning of law—the process, in Gilmore's words, "by which a society accommodates to change without abandoning its fundamental structure."[16] Professor Stein has advanced our understanding of this process and illuminated the instrumental role legal players assume in times of change. We are in his debt.

---

[16] G. Gilmore, *supra* note 13, at 14.

I.

The title, of course, recalls the famous Boston lectures on *The Common Law* by Oliver Wendell Holmes, Jr., in which he said, "The life of the law has not been logic; it has been experience."[1] Holmes was not denying that logic has a place in the common law; rather he was arguing that it should not have too great a place—that law is not a set of mathematically certain rules. Too much emphasis on the systematic aspects of law is dangerous, but that does not mean that those aspects should be eliminated altogether. As Holmes said:

> It is something to show that the consistency of a system requires a particular result, but it is not all. . . . The felt necessities of the time, the prevalent moral and political theories, intuitions of public policy, avowed or unconscious, even the prejudices which judges share with their fellowmen, have had a good deal more to do than the syllogism in determining the rules by which men should be governed. The law . . . cannot be dealt with as if it contained only the axioms and corollaries of a book of mathematics.[2]

The lectures on *The Common Law* took place in 1881. Two years earlier, in 1879, Holmes had been reading Rudolph von Jhering's great work on the Roman law.[3] There is a passage in that work which expresses the same point in remarkably similar terms to those of Holmes. Jhering says:

> This desire for logic that turns jurisprudence into legal mathematics is an error and arises from misunderstanding law. Life does not exist for the sake of concepts but concepts for the sake of life. It is not logic that is entitled to exist but what is claimed by life, by social relations, by the sense of justice—and logical necessity, or logical impossibility, is immaterial. One could have considered the Romans mad, if they had ever thought otherwise, if they had sacrificed the interests of life to the dialectics of the school.[4]

Whether or not Holmes, consciously or unconsciously, had Jhering's passage in mind, we can only guess.[5] What is significant is that when they made such similar statements they were writing of different laws. Jhering was writing of Roman law; Holmes of the common law.

The most remarkable feature of Roman private law is the fact that it developed without any revolutionary interruption over a period of a thousand years. The customary law of a primitive tribe in Central Italy in 500 B.C. was very different from the sophisticated law of the Byzantine

---

[1] O.W. Holmes, The Common Law 1 (1881).

[2] *Id.*

[3] M. DeWolfe Howe, Justice Oliver Wendell Holmes, II: The Proving Years 152 (1963).

[4] Der Geist des römischen Rechts (1852); French translation—that used by Holmes—by O. Meulenaere, 4 L'Esprit de Droit Romain 311 (3d ed. 1888). There is no English translation of the complete work, although an English version of the preface was published by B.T. C[rump] in 4 Va. L.J. 453 (1880).

[5] M.D. Howe, *supra* note 3, at 155 (citing another passage of Jhering, but not referring to the one quoted).

Empire in 500 A.D.; yet the seeds of the latter are readily recognizable in the former. The only other legal system whose development is documented in such detail over such a long period is the Anglo-American common law. One of the main reasons for such continuity in the two systems is that when they each were reaching maturity they adopted similar mechanisms of development, and in addition they were each subject to a tension deriving from the contrasting forces of logic and experience. This is the theme that I propose to illustrate.

When we think of civil law systems today, we think of coherent bodies of rules purportedly deduced from general principles and arranged systematically in codes having fixed and authoritative texts. These texts can be interpreted in new ways, but the formulation remains the same. By contrast, the common law appears more as a set of rules inferred from decisions in particular cases. This legal formulation is always provisional in its continual restatement through the broadening or narrowing of terms as new cases arise. The rules are working hypotheses which await testing by the courts. In this respect, the ancient Roman law resembles the common law much more than it does the modern civil law. To the continental observer, ancient Roman law and modern common law share the same baroque or disorderly appearance.[6] It is true that our knowledge of Roman law derives from the sixth-century codification by the Byzantine Emperor Justinian and that the texts as authorized by Justinian have been regarded from medieval times as having quasi-biblical authority. But the most important part of that codification, the Digest, is an anthology of extracts from the writings of jurists of the much earlier classical period—roughly the first two and a half centuries of the Christian era. It was during the classical period that Roman law reached its highest point of technical development, and when we speak of the inner similarity between Roman law and common law, we refer to the law of that earlier time.

II.

Where does this similarity reside? The most important resemblance is that both the classical common law and the classical Roman law were action-oriented rather than right-oriented. Legal discussion in those systems was not in terms of whether a party had a right which the law would protect, but in terms of whether there was a recognized form of action which fitted the facts of the case, what the limits of that action were, and so on.

During the classical period, a Roman action was divided into two stages. The first stage, held before an official magistrate, the praetor, was de-

---

[6] H. Peter, Römisches Recht und Englisches Recht (Sitzungsberichte der wissenschaftlichen Gesellschaft an der J.W. Goethe Universität Frankfurt/Main, Band 7, Nr. 3), *reviewed by* Stein, 38 Tijdschrift voor Rechtsgeschiedenis 585 (1970); *see* Pringsheim, The Inner Relationship between English and Roman Law, 5 Cambridge L.J. 347 (1935).

signed to settle what the issue between the parties was—to categorize their dispute in legal terms. The parties then chose a private citizen to be a type of single juryman, the *iudex,* to conduct the second stage. The *iudex* heard the evidence, listened to arguments on behalf of the parties and decided the issue referred to him by the praetor. The praetor's instructions to the *iudex* were set out in a memorandum called a formula, which told the *iudex* in what circumstances he was to condemn the defendant and in what circumstances he was to absolve him. In the edict which the praetor issued on taking up office, he published the formulae of the standard actions, from which the parties in a typical case would select an appropriate one for themselves. In a novel case, however, the praetor could grant a new formula if he felt the case justified it. A formula was thus similar to the English writ issued by the Chancery[7] and the praetor's edict was something like the English *Register of Writs.*[8]

The odd feature of the formulary procedure was that neither the praetor nor the *iudex* nor even the advocates who represented the parties were professional lawyers. However, at each stage of the proceedings there were legal experts, the jurists, ready to advise on the legal implications of what was proposed. The jurists had no formal role to play in the legal drama, yet the actors' constant requests for their advice evidenced their intimate connection with the day-to-day administration of the law. It was the jurists' concern with actual problems put to them by praetors, *iudices* and litigants which gave them the opportunity not only to expound the law but also to change it.[9]

Thus Roman law, like English law, was developed by legal experts concerned with its application rather than by legislators. Just as the judges who developed the common law shared a common professional background, so the Roman law was in the hands of a similarly small, closely-knit group of men from upper class backgrounds who shared the same social values. Admittedly the advice of a Roman jurist was never a binding precedent like the decision of an English judge, but the opinion of a jurist who had acquired a recognized authority would carry great weight. The

---

[7] H. Peter, Actio und Writ (1957), *reviewed by* Nicholas, 9 IURA 235 (1958) *and by* Stein, 24 Studia et Documenta Historiae et Iuris 335 (1958).

By virtue of the Statute of Westminster II (1285), the Chancellor could vary slightly the forms of the writs in order that justice might be done. Those in the Chancery made much use of this power, so that later the Chancellor became regarded as an official who could do justice when the common law afforded no remedy. The common law courts could, however, quash new writs of which they disapproved. 1 W.S. Holdsworth, A History of English Law 397 (7th ed. 1956).

[8] The Register, a compilation of the forms of original writs most generally in use, was not official but developed out of collections made by anyone—private person or Chancery official—who cared to undertake the task. Thus the authorship of the Register of Writs remains largely in doubt. Particularly in view of the Chancellor's power to issue new writs supplemental to the existing forms, it was an "extremely variable and shifting collection." T. Plucknett, A Concise History of the Common Law 276 (5th ed. 1956).

[9] Schiller, Jurists' Law, 58 Colum. L. Rev. 1226, 1227 (1958); Schiller, The Nature and Significance of Jurists' Law, 47 B.U.L. Rev. 20, 27 (1967); *see* L. Vacca, Contributo allo studio del metodo casistico nel diritto romano (1976), *reviewed by* Stein, 24 Labeo 57 (1978).

traditional Roman jurist's view, like the traditional English judge's view, was that law was not something created, but rather was a set of permanent and unchanging customary rules that were part of the heritage of the people. These rules were mostly unwritten and were revealed and declared by experts only when the occasion required it. Legislation was at first treated as the declaration and clarification of what had always been the law. Even when it was recognized that legislation and praetorian control of remedies created new law, there was still a tendency to talk of the law as something unalterable.

However, the procedure in Rome, as in England, provided that at the point of final decision the interpretive views of the legal expert should be tempered by lay experience. Like the common law jury, the Roman *iudex* provided an input of nontechnical experience of life. This experience was harnessed in both systems through the use of standards.[10] Standards are specially appropriate for application by laymen since they are not formulated absolutely but are relative to time and place and circumstance. They call not for technical knowledge but for a judgment of conduct based on common sense about common things. The counterpart of the English standard of reasonableness was the Roman standard of good faith—*bona fides*. For example, when the main commercial contracts like sale, hire and partnership were first made enforceable, the content of the obligations which they imposed on the parties was determined by the standard of good faith. When a dispute arose over such a contract, the praetor's formula instructed the *iudex* to condemn the defendant to whatever sum he ought, in good faith, to pay the plaintiff. The phrase enabled the *iudex* to permit any defense or counterclaim which he thought affected the matter. The jurists monitored the application of the standard and, by following court practice, they gradually enunciated a series of duties. These duties included those that the good faith standard, required by the contract of sale, imposed on the seller and buyer respectively. They advised the *iudex* of these duties, but he had the last word on their application in a particular case.

Another feature of the formulary procedure was that it provided scope for the introduction of equity when the law became too strict. In England law and equity were administered by separate courts, whereas in Rome they were both administered by the praetor.[11] Despite this procedural unity, the Romans distinguished clearly between the traditional *ius civile*, based on custom and codified custom, where the praetor's formula enforced established law, and the *ius honorarium*, which owed its origin to new remedies introduced by the praetor on the advice of the jurists. For, as we have noted, the praetor could grant a new formula, or modify an existing formula, on his own authority.

An early example of praetorian equity was based on the recognition

[10] P. Stein & J. Shand, Legal Values in Western Society 93 (1974).
[11] *See* Buckland, Praetor and Chancellor, 13 Tul. L. Rev. 163 (1939).

that those who seriously enter into transactions should have their intentions fulfilled, even though they have failed to comply with the particular forms prescribed by the law.[12] The praetor recognized that the legal forms for transferring property were instrumental rather than ends in themselves. He could not change the law and validate an informal transfer, but he could protect the intended beneficiary by granting him appropriate relief. Thus, where a buyer had received that which he had bought without observing the appropriate form of ownership transfer required by the law, and the seller—who was still the owner at law—attempted to recover it, the praetor gave the buyer a special defense to the seller's action. If the buyer lost control of the property, the praetor gave him an action to recover it based on the fiction—which the *iudex* was instructed to assume—that the buyer had held it for the period necessary for him to become owner by prescription.

On the other hand, when the parties' intentions were vitiated by fraud, duress, or mistake about a fundamental element in the transaction, the praetor would refuse to enforce a transaction, even though it was valid according to law. Provided the requisite form had been complied with, the old law looked no further. It treated the legal obligation as deriving from the form. However, the praetor gave a defense to the victim of fraud or duress, if the other party tried to enforce the transaction, and he treated a transaction vitiated by mistake as void *ab initio.* Later he allowed the victim *restitutio in integrum,* which was a decree restoring a prejudiced party to the position he had been in before the tainted transaction took place, notwithstanding that the transaction had satisfied the requirements of the law. If the praetor had used this power of ordering *restitutio* too enthusiastically, he would have undermined public confidence in the law and its forms. It is a testimony to the restraint of praetors and of the jurists who advised them that the power was only exercised in certain limited classes of cases and then only after the praetor himself had investigated the circumstances and satisfied himself of the truth of the complainant's allegations.

The result of the Roman legal development by juristic advice was similar to that of the common law development by judicial decision. Both produced a chaotic jumble of rulings, and those who sought to discern a rational structure beneath the intractable mass of legal opinions often looked in vain. This was the stage reached by English law in the early part of the nineteenth century. Jeremy Bentham and his follower, John Austin, drew attention to the uncertainty and unpredictability of English case law and argued in favor of its codification, or at least its systematic restatement on orderly principles.

III.

It is a situation similar to the nineteenth century English debate on the form of the law which in my view provides the key to one of the mysteries

[12] P. Stein & J. Shand, *supra* note 10, at 97; Stein, Equitable Principles in Roman Law, in Equity in the World's Legal Systems 75 (R. Newman ed. 1974).

of Roman legal history. In the first century A.D., the jurists of the early Empire were divided into two schools, called the Proculians and the Sabinians. The nature of this division has been a perennial problem of legal history. Pomponius, as excerpted in Justinian's Digest, tells us that although the Proculians were named after the jurist Proculus, they regarded an earlier jurist, Labeo, as their founder. The Sabinians, who were named after Sabinus, followed Capito. These two jurists, said Pomponius, "made, as it were, two sects: for Ateius Capito held fast to what had been handed down to him, whereas Labeo, a genius, with confidence in his own scholarship, a man who had studied several other branches of knowledge, set out to make many innovations."[13]

Although Labeo is depicted as an innovator by comparison with the traditionalist Capito, when we consider the various individual controversies that divided the schools,[14] that of Labeo—the Proculians—does not seem to champion doctrines which are particularly progressive nor do the doctrines espoused by the school of Capito—the Sabinians—seem especially conservative.[15]

There has, therefore, been a tendency to conclude that the difference between the schools was personal rather than doctrinal.[16] But we *are* told by Pomponius that Labeo innovated. My view is that his innovations were not so much in substantive law as in legal method and technique,[17] and that Labeo used his recognized expertise in other disciplines, mentioned by Pomponius, to introduce more rigorous forms of argument into Roman law than those favored by earlier jurists. We have a good deal of evidence of Labeo's particular methods. About five hundred of his opinions are mentioned in Justinian's Digest, approximately one half of which contain reasoning or justification of his decisions.[18] We have little evidence of the methods of his rival, Capito. However, since he is characterized as a traditionalist, we may assume that he opposed Labeo's innovations and preferred the ways of the earlier Republican jurists. Capito's successor, Sabinus, after whom the school was named, left over two hundred opinions. From the arguments which he raised against Labeo's views we can infer the beginnings of a Roman legal theory.[19]

---

[13] Iustiniani Digesta 1.2.2.47 (T. Mommsen & P. Krueger eds. 1954) [hereinafter cited as Digest]. The word *innovare*, innovate, seems to appear for the first time in this text, so indicating the strength of Pomponius' judgment. Nörr, Zum Traditionalismus der römischen Juristen, in Festschrift für Werner Flume 163 (1978).

[14] Approximately thirty of these controversies are known. They are listed by H. J. Roby, Introduction to the Study of Justinian's Digest cxxxi (1884). Most are discussed in Stein, The Two Schools of Jurists in the Early Roman Principate, 31 (1) Cambridge L.J. 8 (1972), *noted in* Liebs, Rechtsschulen and Rechtsunterricht im Prinzipat, in Aufstieg und Niedergang der römischen Welt 197 (H. Temporini & W. Haase eds. 1976).

[15] Stein, *supra* note 14, at 8.

[16] H. Jolowicz, Historical Introduction to the Study of Roman Law 389 (2d ed. 1952).

[17] Stein, *supra* note 14, at 9, tested this idea.

[18] 1 F. Horak, Rationes Decidendi: Entscheidungsbegründungen bei den älteren römischen Juristen bis Labeo (1969), *reviewed by* Stein, 36 Studia et Documenta Historiae et Iuris 460 (1970).

[19] Stein, Sabino contra Labeone: due tipi di pensiero giuridico romano, 19 (3d ser.) Bulletino dell' Istituto di Diritto Romano 55 (1977).

The seeds of Labeo's methodological innovations were planted in the century before he wrote, when the influence of Greek philosophy became dominant in Roman intellectual circles. In the area of law this influence was not directed towards given solutions to specific problems, as it was in other disciplines, but was rather a general, climatic influence. From Greek philosophy the Romans learned that any worthwhile knowledge ought to be organized as a science. Aristotle's work demonstrated the evolutionary development of a body of knowledge into a science. First the common elements which unite individual experiences are identified and then propositions which state those elements in principles are formulated.[20]

One of the bodies of knowledge which had become a science in this sense was grammar. Among grammarians, or students of the science of language, there was a controversy between two groups—the analogists and the anomalists.[21] Analogists considered that language was inherently orderly and argued that nouns and verbs could be classified into declensions and conjugations on the basis of similarity of form. Anomalists rejected the idea that language was governed by general rules. They argued that language was the product of usage and practice, observing that the rules postulated by the analogists were riddled with exceptions. By the last century B.C., however, compromise views developed. The compromises were grounded in the realization that only through the acceptance of some of the analogists' basic premises was a scientific study of language possible. For one can only recognize exceptions and anomalous forms on the assumption that there are regular forms in the background.

We know that Labeo was an analogist in matters of grammar and that he used his linguistic expertise to solve knotty problems of law.[22] It would therefore be understandable if the Proculians, whom he inspired, adopted analogist methods. But the battle between the two schools of jurists is not just the analogist/anomalist controversy transferred to the area of law. It was a much more complex affair than that.

The Proculians wanted to make law a science. They therefore sought to make it more clearly defined, more logical, more rational, more systematic and so more certain.[23] They brought to the surface and made explicit many aspects of the law which earlier lawyers had left unarticulated because those earlier lawyers had not felt it necessary to decide more than the limited issues that the case in hand required.

It was Labeo who introduced the method of reasoning by analogy into Roman law and the Proculians who developed it[24] in their efforts to

---

[20] P. Stein, Regulae Iuris: From Juristic Rules to Legal Maxims 33 (1966).

[21] *Id.* at 53; Stein, Justice Cardozo, Marcus Terentius Varro and the Roman Juristic Process, 2 Ir. Jur. 367, 371 (1967).

[22] Aulus Gellius, Noctes Atticae 13.10.1; Stein, *supra* note 14, at 15.

[23] Bentham, as a protagonist of the great reform movement in England, similarly sought to have legal rules and institutions submit to the tests of utility and of logic, primarily through constant legislation. T. Plucknett, *supra* note 8, at 73, 75.

[24] "This method presupposes that the law is based on a set of coherent rational principles, but it is only applied in those areas where the relevant rule is in doubt." Stein, *supra* note 14, at 15; P. Stein, *supra* note 20, at 61; Stein, The Relations between Grammar and Law in the

articulate underlying legal principles. We are so familiar with analogy as a technique of legal reasoning that we are apt to assume that it was part of the equipment of jurists from the earliest times. But as Sir Henry Maine recognized, "analogy, the most valuable of instruments in the maturity of jurisprudence, is the most dangerous of snares in its infancy."[25] Thus, those jurists outside Labeo's sphere at first avoided its use.[26] For example, it was understood that in the case of damage to property, which was a statutory tort, a very young child, one who could not understand the nature of his actions, could not be sued. However, it was not clear whether an *impubes*, one who was near the age of puberty, was liable or not. Labeo argued that he must be liable because he was liable for theft.[27] Theft was an institution of the customary law rather than of statute, but Labeo taught that the same principle must apply to both wrongs. It would be irrational to have different rules in respect of age of liability in theft and in property damage, and Labeo assumed that the law was rational. In a parallel controversy, the schools of Labeo and Sabinus disagreed over the moment when a male child reached the age of puberty, at which point he potentially had legal capacity and was freed from guardianship. The Proculians argued that puberty must be judged by age alone and that a boy should be regarded as legally reaching puberty when he became fourteen years old.[28] This demonstrated their analogist preference for one objective rule for all cases.

The Proculians also made considerable use of the argument of *reductio ad absurdum*, sometimes even to avoid the consequences of the literal interpretation they urged. For example, suppose A sold B a piece of land, reserving for himself all beds of stone lying under the land. Later, a new bed of stone that the parties had not known about came to light. Did it belong to A, the seller, or to B, the buyer? Labeo held that it went to B, notwithstanding the reservation to A. His first supporting argument was based on analogy. Since there was a rule that no sale of nonexistent things could take place, he argued that one could not reserve such things in a contract of sale either. Things that were not known to exist were also nonexistent for the purposes of contractual liability. Labeo's second argument was a *reductio ad absurdum*: if all the land were to turn out to rest on beds of stone and be awarded to the seller under the reservation, he would be able to keep it all and have the price as well. Therefore, the reservation could not apply to any unknown beds of stone.[29]

Early Principate: The Beginnings of Analogy, in La critica del testo, Atti del II congresso internazionale della società italiana di storia del diritto 75 (1971); F. Horak, *supra* note 18, at 242.

[25] H. Maine, Ancient Law 11 (Everyman's Library ed. 1917).

[26] Stein, *supra* note 21, at 373.

[27] Digest 9.2.5.2.

[28] Gai Institutionum Libri IV 1.196 (F. de Zulueta ed. 1946) [hereinafter cited as Gaius]; Epitome Ulpiani 11.28, in 2 Fontes Iuris Romani Anteiustiniani 276 (J. Baviera ed. 1968).

[29] Digest 18.1.77; D. Daube, Roman Law: Linguistic, Social and Philosophical Aspects 176 (1969); F. Horak, *supra* note 18, at 271.

The Sabinians countered the Proculian emphasis on logic by stressing the importance of custom and practice. It was more important to them that the law should conform to the facts of life, both in the physical and in the social sense, than that it should be rational. Where the Proculians appealed to the *ratio*, the logic, of the civil law, the Sabinians justified a rule by reference to the nature of things, *natura rerum*.[30] In the disagreement mentioned above over the moment when a male child reached the age of puberty and of legal capacity, the Sabinians said that it depended on the individual's physical development. In doubtful cases an inspection of his body was needed, but in the case of those who were naturally impotent, the usual age of puberty was assigned.[31] This anomalist, empirical principle stands in clear contrast to the objective rule favored by the Proculians. The basic difference in the respective methods of approaching cases will now be more elaborately demonstrated.

The Proculians distinguished between two types of cases for decision. The first type consisted of cases turning on the meaning to be attributed to a fixed authoritative text, which they called *interpretatio verborum*.[32] The second class of cases involved the meaning and scope of a rule of the civil law which was not formulated in such a text, although it might have been discussed in the writings of jurists. Where the jurist's task was to attribute a meaning to a fixed text, *interpretatio*, it made no difference whether he was dealing with the words of a statutory provision, or the words of a contract or a will. In each such case Labeo and the Proculians sought a precise objective meaning of the words used and then applied it rigidly without regard to whether or not that interpretation represented the original intent of the parties responsible for the text. Labeo's followers rejoiced in being strict constructionists. For example, the interdict *unde vi* was a remedy which enabled the possessor of land who had been evicted by force to recover his land. Labeo refused the remedy to a man who had hurriedly left his land on hearing that armed men were moving in, without waiting to be actually physically ejected by them.[33]

In interpreting a legacy, if a testator bequeathed a designated fraction of his goods—*bonorum pars*—the Proculians regarded it as a bequest of the designated fraction of the goods themselves, whereas the Sabinians regarded it as a bequest of a fraction of the value of the goods. The Proculians argued that there was no obscurity in the words and had the testator intended the legatee to receive the value of the goods, he could easily have said so. The Sabinians, in contrast, considered that the words were capable of a more convenient interpretation than that provided by

---

[30] Stein, The Development of the Notion of *Naturalis Ratio*, in Daube Noster: Essays in Legal History for David Daube 305 (A. Watson ed. 1974).

[31] *See* authorities in note 28 *supra*.

[32] Digest 32.29pr. *Interpretatio* was an appropriate field for using the standard "topoi" of rhetoric: letter and spirit, ambiguity, contrary provisions, etc. Stein, The Sources of Law in Cicero, 3 Ciceroniana 25 (1979).

[33] Digest 4.2.9pr.

their precise objective meaning.[34] For these Sabinians the same expression could mean one thing in one testament and another thing in another. The attributed meaning depended upon the usage adopted by the particular testator. For instance, some people used the word wine—*vinum*—in a limited sense which excluded vinegar—*acetum*, while others used it in a looser sense which included vinegar. So, according to Sabinus, a legacy of wine included everything which the testator considered to fall within the category.[35] What was contained in a category depended upon a person's disposition and usage. In emphasizing the intention of the testator as a criterion of interpretation, Sabinus showed that he was more concerned with arriving at a reasonable decision in the particular case than he was with maintaining consistency of meaning whenever a form of words was given legal effect.

In regard to contracts, what mattered, said Labeo, was what the parties had transacted—*quod actum est*—and not what they had intended.[36] He felt that certainty was all important, and that parties who failed to utilize the potentialities of language to express themselves as clearly as they might have should expect no indulgence from the law. In a formal contract, if one party exacted from the other party the promise of a fixed sum for himself and for a third party, Titius, it was accepted law that no benefit could accrue to Titius since he was not a party to the contract. But what was due to the promisee? The Sabinians thought that he was entitled to the whole amount due, just as if Titius had not been mentioned. The Proculians held instead that the promise was made to the promisee and to Titius equally. Since the part of the promise referring to Titius' half was void, the promisee was entitled only to the other half. The Proculians reasoned that he should have been more careful in stipulating the terms of the contract.[37]

The Proculians regarded even the formula itself as a fixed and authoritative text to be strictly interpreted. Where the defendant in an action paid the plaintiff the sum claimed after the formula had been granted, but before final judgment, the Proculians would permit the *iudex* to acquit the defendant only if the formula contained a clause, such as a reference to what was due "in good faith," which specifically empowered the *iudex* to absolve the defendant if he thought it right to do so. Where the formula contained no such words, the *iudex* had no power formally to acquit the defendant. This was true even though the defendant had paid the debt, since all the powers of the *iudex* derived from the formula. He had, therefore, to confine himself to preventing the plaintiff from claiming payment twice over. Such sophistries irritated the Sabinians, who said

---

[34] Digest 30.26.2.
[35] Digest 33.6.9pr.
[36] Digest 18.1.77.
[37] Gaius 3.103.

that every action admits of acquittal at all stages, and thus that the *iudex* could in all cases absolve the defendant.[38]

Whether the case involved a legal provision, a will, a contract, or a procedural formula, the Proculians consistently adopted a strict approach to *interpretatio verborum.* The Sabinians, by contrast, were less interested in giving precise weight to words and tended to deal with problems in what they thought was the plain man's common sense way. One of the most famous disputes between the schools concerns *specificatio,* when A made something new out of materials belonging to B, for example, when A carved a statue out of B's marble. The Proculians held that the statue belonged to A, the maker. The Sabinians said that it belonged to B, the owner of the materials. The Proculians' reasoning was probably grounded in the technicalities of procedure. In an action to claim the statue, the plaintiff would have to describe it as his property. Only A could claim that he owned a statue, since all B had owned was a lump of marble. The Sabinians countered this subtlety by reference to nature, the facts of life and common sense. A thing is a thing is a thing, they said. Without the material of which it is made, there can be no thing. To them, the statue was still just a lump of marble even though its outward form might have been altered by A.[39]

When a legal problem involved the unwritten customary law rather than the interpretation of a fixed text, Labeo and the Proculians assumed that even this customary law consisted of a set of rules with definable limits. They further believed that the limits of this law, and more particularly of the actions by which the law was enforced, could be precisely stated. Their school determined the scope and extent of a rule of unwritten law by divining the underlying principle which justified it and which indicated its relationship to other rules. So the Proculians were not content merely to state the effect of the law; they wanted to know its *ratio,* or rationale. They assumed that beneath the rules of customary law was a substructure of rational principles waiting to be defined.

The Sabinians' approach to customary law was quite different. Instead of looking for the principle behind a rule of unwritten law, they looked for evidence of its antiquity. Sabinians felt instinctively that the validity of the law was somehow connected with its observance from time immemorial. They made frequent references to the views of jurists of earlier generations as authority for the views they themselves defended.[40] Labeo rarely referred to the authority of earlier jurists and when he did, it was often to criticize their views. Whereas Sabinus seemed sometimes to look back nostalgically to former times as a simpler and better age than his own, Labeo was conscious of the barbarity of ancient Rome. In one passage Labeo commented that he was ashamed to speak of the primitive rule of

[38] Gaius 4.114.
[39] Gaius 2.79; Digest 41.1.7.7; P. Stein, *supra* note 30, at 306.
[40] Aulus Gellius, Noctes Atticae 5.19.13; Digest 12.5.6.

the ancient Roman law permitting a creditor who had obtained a judgment which was not satisfied literally to carve up his debtor.[41]

An area of traditional law in which the schools clashed on a number of occasions was obligations, both contractual and delictual. The Proculians rigorously confined the scope of each contractual action to its proper field. Yet, if a set of facts did not fall clearly within the limits of a recognized form of action, they were quite ready to create a special action. Thus where the owner of goods had contracted with the captain of a ship to carry his goods, but it was not clear whether he had hired the whole ship, the contract of *conductio rei*, or had entrusted the goods to the captain for carriage, that of *locatio operis*, Labeo refused to allow the action for either contract. Rather he granted a special action with a formula which set out the particular facts of the case and expressed a duty at civil law.[42]

Sabinus was reluctant to create new actions. He and his school preferred to deal with new fact situations by pressing them into the already recognized forms of actions. As a result, Sabinians showed little respect for the limits of contractual or delictual actions and were prepared to extend them as convenience required. For example, Sabinus had no qualms about extending the notion of theft to include the stealing of land as well as moveables. The Proculians, however, refused such a proposition probably because the word for theft—*furtum*—implied originally that the thief carried away the owner's property.[43]

Labeo, not unreasonably, considered that the action ordering the production of a thing by the defendant could not be brought against one who did, in fact, produce the thing in question. Sabinus, on the other hand, thought that one who produced the thing, but in a deteriorated condition, could be said not to have produced it at all. So he allowed the action against such a defendant. The fact that he had to stretch the meaning of "produce" almost to breaking point in order to include "restore in good condition" was irrelevant. It was convenient to allow that action in order to accord the plaintiff a remedy which he deserved. That it was not the appropriate remedy did not disturb him.[44]

The famous dispute over whether the price in a sale had to be delivered in the form of money was an example of a dispute over the limits of a particular type of contract. In essence, the argument concerned the question whether barter could be regarded as a form of sale. Sabinus held that it could, citing in support of his view the arguments of antiquity, ancient usage and the authority offered by the poet, Homer. His point was that from time immemorial people in everyday life have treated barter and sale as the same transaction, and thus it would be artificial for the law to

[41] Aulus Gellius, Noctes Atticae 20.1.19.

[42] Digest 19.5.1.1.

[43] Aulus Gellius, Noctes Atticae 11.18.13; A. Schiavone, Studi sulle logiche dei giuristi romani 109 (1971).

[44] *actio ad exhibendum*: Digest 50.15.246pr.; Digest 10.4.9.3.

do otherwise. According to Sabinus, the law should reflect the nature of things, the character of social life. The Proculians rejected the assimilation of barter and sale on the ground that the contract of sale imposed different duties on the buyer and on the seller, and that there is no buyer-seller distinction in barter. Barter was a distinct type of contract which should have a distinct form of action.[45]

Labeo was adept in identifying the essential element which distinguished the legal institution he was considering from other legal institutions. The field which was later called that of quasi-contractual obligations provides examples. Roman law recognized that even an unauthorized act done by one party in behalf of another could create a duty in the party for whom the act was done to reimburse the "agent" for the expenses which he had incurred. But the precise limits of that duty were debated. It was Labeo who laid down the test as whether the unauthorized act performed by the agent was *utiliter gestum*, or objectively beneficial to the principal at the time the agent performed it. If so, he could recover his expenses.[46] By contrast, it was almost certainly Sabinus who caused embarrassment to later lawyers by including in the category of contract the duty of a person who has innocently accepted a payment which was not owed to him to return it to the payer.[47] Sabinus did not recognize that contract should be confined to obligations deriving from prior agreement. Such limits were theoretical and of no concern to him.

In some cases the Sabinians fictionally regarded a new situation as an old situation and thereby were able to extend the ambit of available legal remedies. The Proculians, with their concern for the limits of language and the proper scope of each form of action, thus appeared to be creating unnecessary difficulties, even when they would have granted a new remedy to cover the case. On occasion, however, the Proculians could use their emphasis on precise rules to produce a more liberal result than their rivals. It was trite law that a will was invalid if a testator made the will and just passed over his son, who was in the father's power, without either instituting him as heir or expressly disinheriting him. But suppose the son died in the father's lifetime. The Sabinians held that the will was invalid, *ab initio,* at the time when the father made it. The son's death could not validate it. The Proculians upheld the validity of the will in this situation. They emphasized that a will takes effect only on the testator's death, and at that moment, since the son was dead, there was nothing standing in the way of its validity.[48]

The differences between the two schools were brought into sharper focus in the dispute Labeo had with Sabinus over the character of legal rules. The traditional word for a legal rule was *definitio.* This *definitio*

---

[45] Gaius 3.141; Digest 18.1.1.1.
[46] Digest 3.5.9(10).1.
[47] Gaius 3.91.
[48] Gaius 2.123.

indicated a summary description of the existing state of the law by looking backward and generalizing the effect of past practice. Labeo introduced the term *regula*, which implied something more than a mere description. *Regula* was a normative proposition which governed all situations falling under its rationale. The word was taken over from the language of grammar, where it had definite analogist overtones. Unlike a *definitio*, a *regula* looked ahead to the future, for its reasoning was applicable to a whole range of cases that had not yet occurred in practice and could only be imagined. It was thus potentially an instrument of vigorous legal development. Sabinus did not accept this notion of *regula*. His reply to its use appeared in the famous text, Digest 50.17.1, in which he argued that the law was not, as Labeo had suggested, derived from the *regula* but rather that the *regula* was made from the existing law. A *regula*, he opined, was merely a description of the law like a *definitio*, and if shown to be wrong in any particular, that *regula* lost its function. The language of Sabinus was that of an orthodox believer attacking a heresy, for that was indeed how Sabinus regarded Labeo's innovations in the field of legal technique.[49]

Once the two schools had become established, the rivalry between them engendered its own momentum. They continued to exist separately into the second century A.D.[50] However, neither school won a final victory over the other. In some controversies the Proculian view prevailed and in others the Sabinian did. Gradually, the contrast between the methods of the early protagonists grew blurred. Julian, the head of the Sabinian school in the early second century, adopted many of Labeo's techniques as his own. By the end of that century, when Roman law reached its full maturity, the schools were written of no more. The jurists no longer had to choose between the methods of one or the other. Instead, they accepted the idea that they had a variety of techniques at their disposal; that in some cases it would be appropriate to rely on established practice or authority, whereas in other cases logical reasoning and analogy were more useful. If the clash between the two methods had not come when it did, however, Roman law would have been very different. Had it not been for the Proculian emphasis on logic, the classical Roman law would not have acquired that particular characteristic of empiricism resting on a firm framework of basic principles which has proven its fascination for later ages.

IV.

The common law at the beginning of the present century reached a similar compromise after the upheaval Bentham and Austin caused as

[49] P. Stein, *supra* note 20, at 67. When two parties agreed to submit a case to an arbitrator Sabinus considered the matter to be outside the law and therefore of little interest. Labeo, however, recognized the innovation and gave a series of rulings on the limits of a reference to arbitration and on the extent to which the praetor could compel obedience to an arbitrator's award. Stein, Labeo's Reasoning on Arbitration, 91 S. Afr. L.J. 135 (1974).

[50] For the reasoning of the later Proculians, see Ussani, Ermeneutica, diritto e "valori" in L. Nerazio Prisco, 23 Labeo 146 (1977).

they sought systemization, through orderly principles, of the often uncertain state of the English law. Austin, who studied law in Germany, said that turning from the English to the continental law, one "escape[s] from the empire of chaos and darkness to a world that seems by comparison the region of order and light."[51] The mid-nineteenth century, through the impetus of Bentham and Austin, thus saw a movement to make the common law more certain, more conceptual, more mathematical. The parallel of their work with that of Labeo and his followers is remarkably close. It was the excesses of the Benthamite movement that Holmes, in this a modern Sabinus, attacked in the opening passage of *The Common Law.* But without that movement the common law would have lacked the rational strength which it showed at the end of the nineteenth century.

Sometimes we common lawyers rely on logic and at other times on experience. Whereas Holmes in 1881 saw logic as a threat, Cardozo in 1921 saw it as one of a number of techniques available to judges. As Cardozo put it,

> My analysis of the judicial process comes then to this and little more: logic, and history, and custom, and utility, and the accepted standards of right conduct, are the forces which singly or in combination shape the progress of the law. Which of these forces shall dominate in any case, must depend largely on the comparative importance or value of the social interests that will thereby be promoted or impaired.[52]

The Roman jurists of the second century would, I believe, have accepted Cardozo's statement. They referred to custom or authority, or utility or analogy, as and when the occasion demanded.[53] It is the mark of a great Roman jurist, as of a great common lawyer, to know when each method is most appropriate. That is a lesson that can be learned only from history.

---

[51] Lectures on Jurisprudence 58 (5th ed. R. Campbell 1885); *see* Schwarz, John Austin and the German Jurisprudence of His Time, 1 Politica 178 (1934); Stein, Continental Influences on English Legal Thought, 1600-1900, 3 La formazione storica del diritto moderno in Europa, Atti del III congresso internazionale della societa italiana di storia del diritto 1119 (1977).

[52] Cardozo, The Nature of the Judicial Process, in Selected Writings of B.N. Cardozo 153 (M. Hall ed. 1947).

Justice Cardozo would not readily ascribe to the extremity of either the Sabinian or the Proculian assumption, as evidenced in his statement that "[t]he common law does not work from pre-established truths of universal and inflexible validity to conclusions derived from them deductively. Its method is inductive, and it draws its generalizations from particulars." *Id.* at 114. Yet the blended influence of both schools is apparent in the description Cardozo quoted of the judge's law-finding process: "'The principles themselves are continually retested; for if the rules derived from a principle do not work well, the principle itself, [or the judge's explication of it] must ultimately be re-examined.'" *Id.* (quoting M. Smith, Jurisprudence 21 (1909)).

[53] Stein, *supra* note 21, at 367.

[15]

LEGAL REASONING IN ROME AND TODAY

PROFESSOR A. M. HONORE*

I INTRODUCTION

A SCHOLAR interested in Roman law is sometimes asked to say in what the contribution of Roman law to our modern legal culture consists. When I am asked this I think first of the *rules* of Roman law which, through the various sorts of ' reception ', have found a niche in modern European legal systems. Then I turn to the *concepts*, like ownership, which have become embedded in our thinking and in our social ways. But perhaps one should attach equal or greater importance to a third area of influence, namely the *method of reasoning* which modern legal cultures have inherited from Roman law.

To talk about legal reasoning is to hear with trepidation the echoes of von Lubtow's remark that Roman jurists did not talk about method because they knew that a legal science which has occasion to be concerned with methods must be sick. If von Lubtow is right our modern Roman legal science is certainly in decline. Since the Second World War Romanists have shown a great deal of interest in legal method. The two works that stand out are those of *Viehweg* (1953) and *Horak* (1969). Viehweg's little classic Topik und Jurisprudenz (1953) is well known. It had a certain *succès de scandale*, because it totally devalued systematic reasoning as a tool of legal decision and suggested that the actual method followed by Roman jurists and their successors right up to the present day was non-systematic and non-deductive. He characterised it as a dialectical method based on *topoi*, a term taken from Aristotle and Cicero to denote a non-demonstrative sort of argument, in which the conclusions could only be called probable, not certain, and which is based on received or standard arguments, *topoi, sedes a quibus argumenta promuntur* (Cicero). This type of reasoning is not merely in general non-deductive but it centres round the individual problem to be resolved, the *Grundaporie* in such a way that the problem-solving element overrides deductive considerations. If the deduction creates a result which is unsatisfactory as an answer to the basic question, it is interrupted by an *invention* (i.e. a new rule is propounded or a new argument adduced) . . . by taking account of a recognized ' topos '. Hence when the will theory (under the BGB) suggests an unsatisfactory conclusion it is supplanted by a *topos*, that one who reasonably relies on another should be protected (*Vertruauensschutz*), which is not explicitly mentioned in the code and so cannot be deductively derived.

Viehweg's contribution, despite the criticism levelled at it, seems to me in retrospect to constitute not merely a famous but an important element in the debate about the character of legal problem-solving. Two of his themes are especially important : the notion of *topoi* as informal arguments, something distinct from an appeal to rules of law ; and the notion of the backlash, a dialectical movement backward from solution to reason or (to use more traditional language), from conclusion to premise.

*Regius Professor of Civil Law in the University of Oxford.

Not that there was anything fundamentally new about this idea of a reverse movement in the reasoning. Indeed the realist movement (in its American version especially) continually harped on the same theme and treated legal reasoning as essentially justificatory ; something produced in order to show why a decision reached independently should be accepted, or to make explicit intuitive assumptions which have gone to the making of the decision. What Viehweg showed was how the backlash from decision ro reason fitted into the more normal forward deductive movement of legal argument, by interrupting it in certain cases and causing a reconsideration of the premises on which a provisional conclusion had been based.

A great deal of criticism has been levelled at the work of Viehweg. Much of this is summarized in Horak's recent book *Rationes decidendi* 1 (1969). He and others have said that it is impossible to contrast, as does Viehweg, a problem-solving sort of legal argument with a systematic, deductive or axiomatic one. Every judge, every legal adviser giving an opinion, every legal writer considering a decision or anticipating a case that has not yet arisen is engaged in problem-solving. Only the methods adopted to solve the problem can differ. The distinction should therefore be between deductive, etc. and ' topical ' methods of problem-solving, not between problem solving and deductive or systematic reasoning as such. Secondly the notion of *topos* is said to be too vague to be of much assistance : in some lists it comprises almost every conceivable type or argument, and includes concepts as well as maxims, principles and *regulae*. Thirdly *topoi* are relevant only to law-finding, the formulation of a rule or decision, not to justification. Viehweg, one way and another, has been carried away, the critics say, by enthusiasm for his toy. The first two criticisms seem to me correct. It is important to appreciate the restricted character of the arguments which can be adduced in order to solve a legal problem. The third criticism does not convince.

The precise function of the *topos* is to justify a decision, a rule or a subsumption : indeed it could be defined as an argument which in the context serves in the absence of contrary arguments as an adequate justification for a decision. However, there is no need to be wedded to the somewhat archaic terminology of *topoi*. Though Cicero wrote a book on the subject addressed to the jurist C. Trebatius Testa it is uncertain how much notice Trebatius took of it. The Roman jurists probably had no conscious theory about the way in which they reasoned. This does not prevent us from trying to give a systematic account of what they were doing, any more than the fact that in ordinary speech the notion of ' cause ' is used unreflectively prevents us from giving a systematic account of the principles on which that unreflective use tests.

II Types of Reasoning Employed by the Roman Jurists

Consequently, before proceeding further with the theoretical debate I first describe the sorts of argument which Roman classical jursits deployed or did not deploy in order to justify the decision they reached in particular cases. The sort of decisions we are concerned with are decisions *according to law*, where that term covers decisions which are made in accordance with some pre-existing law, those decided according to a law which is declared simultaneously with the decision by virtue of a power to declare or make the law vested in the decider, and those which are made by virtue of some such power without reference to any pre-existing and simultaneously declared law : in the latter categories one can think of *responsa* of authorised jurists under the Roman system (compare judicial decisions under the Anglo-American system of precedent which are or are not combined with a stated *ratio decidendi*). Finally we may include the decisions resulting from the discussion of a *quaestio* in the Roman system (compare the discussion by a modern text-writer of a disputed or possible case which has not yet been the subject of legal determination). Here it is perhaps more accurate to speak of a recommendation than of a decision, and this recommendation is combined with an element of prediction—that such-and-such will be decided when the case arises—and justification, the giving of reasons for the recommendation.

If then we take as the matter to be analysed *decision making by solving a problem according to law*, we must admit that this activity formed a large part of the work of every Roman jurist as it does of every modern jurist and especially every judge. This is true even of a system which operates more systematically than the Roman or the English, e.g. of German law. Coming then to the types of argument to be found in the Corpus Iuris I propose to take examples only from the Roman law of unjust enrichment, the *condictiones*. This is a fairly well-known and up-to-date branch of the law, in the sense that it has not to any great extent become oscolete, and it has in fact exercised a great deal of influence on modern systems all over Europe. The first task is to list the main types of argument found in the texts, then to see what they have in common.

The analysis which follows is meant to apply to decision making at all its stages. Thus it is not merely the final stage, at which the judge or decider decides that the plaintiff should or should not, recover, that we are concerned with. The analysis applies equally to the formulation of a rule of law which is put forward as the reason for the decision.

The analysis we have to undertake therefore applies to a decision or a series of decisions (concerning the formulation of rules, subscumptions, non-subsumptions or the final disposal of the issue) backed by reasons or arguments, either expressed or implied.

The decisions that we find in the Roman jurists either (*a*) rest on rules of law or (*b*) rest on open arguments (topoi, principles) or (*c*) appeal to the facts of the case or (*d*) appeal to auhtority or (*e*) are unmotivated.

(*a*) *Appeal to rules of law.* The first category is that of decisions which rest on rules of law. This expression I use in a rather broad sense. It covers every sort of formulation which is intended to have a prima facie universality, that is, to be applied, subject to exceptions, in every case which it appears to cover. The most important type of rule is the norm, e.g. the norm that a payment for a given purpose must be returned if the purpose fails. But 'rules of law' also includes *definitions*, e.g. that payment of what is not owing includes payment of something which could not have been recovered by the payee because there was a valid defence to the claim. (Ulp. 26 ed. D. 12.6.26.3)—in the sense in which 'definition' extends to all directions to subsume certain classes of case or not to subsume them under a general term—and also *predicative statements* whereby legal consequences are directly or indirectly attached to fact situations, e.g. that a thief is always in *mora*, always guilty of delay and so liable to the various legal consequences of that condition. (D. 13.1.8.1. Ulp 37 ed. *semper enim moram fur facere videtur*.)

Julian is a jurist who often argues by appeal to a formulated rule (not necessarily a *regula* in the various senses distinguished by Stein, *Regulae Iuris*). Thus D.12.1.19 pr (Jul. 10 Dig.) "Not every payment creates an obligation in the recipient, but only when the sense of the transaction is that (an obligation shall immediately be created). Hence in a gift *mortis causa* an obligation to repay comes into existence only when the event contemplated takes place, e.g. when the donor recovers, in which case the money is recoverable". The rule is first formulated, then applied.

The same formulation might constitute a rule of law in the mouth of one jurist and not in the mouth of another. For example that no one should be enriched to the detriment of another (Pomponius 21 Sab., D.12.6.14) might be taken by someone as an appeal to a rule of law, though I should construe it as an open argument. The intention of the person deciding is crucial here. Does he mean this to apply prima facie to every case of enrichment at the expense of another, so that the recipient will have to show why he should not return the enrichment in the particular instance, or is it that this is simply an argument which justifies (not requires) a decision in favour of return in the absence of considerations to the contrary? This very crucial distinction is central to an understanding of legal reasoning.

It should be noted that the rule of law may be implicit in the argument rather than stated, and that it may be already established or newly formulated.

(*b*) *Open arguments*. The second type of argument is the open argument, *topos* or principle. What I have in mind is something very like the 'principles' '*Grundsätze*' explicated by Esser in his classic *Grundsatz und Norm in der richterliche Fortbildung des Rechts*.

They can however be broader than anything which would ordinarily be called a principle in English: for example an appeal to justice, utility or good faith is an open argument in the sense I am using. These open arguments have the following characteristics, partly formal and partly of substance. (i) They are, unlike rules of law, not prima facie universal in scope. Thus, the appeal to utility, *utilitas*, which is common in the Roman jurists of the early third century does not imply that in all cases the solution which has the greatest utility, which will probably bring the greatest advantage to citizens as a whole is to be selected. It is rather that in the absence of contrary reasons utility will *justify* the choice of a particular solution and that it will sometimes justify making an exception to a rule of law: (*ii*) They embody social values; I am content to follow Esser here and say that they incorporate the purposes of rules of law, *Gesetzzwecke*. These open arguments are therefore drawn both from legal discourse (previous arguments, professional tradition, etc.) and directly from everyday life, from moral or social discourse in the society in question. However, the argument need not take the form of a direct appeal to the social value in question. Often it does so, and in Roman law we find that such notions as *utilitas*, *bona fides*, *aequum et bonum*, *ratio*, *humanum*, *natura* and so forth figure prominently in arguments at certain periods. There is an element of fashion about this, and there is no doubt, for example, that whereas the heydey of *natura/naturalis/naturaliter* was the Spanish dynasty, Trajan and Hadrian, the acme of *aequum* and its cognates came with Marcus Aurelius and that of *utilitas* under Severus and his successors. These social values to which appeal is naturally made outside the law also can be encapsulated in maxims, apothegms, *regulae* (in the Roman sense) and the like. An example is the statement that one who suffers loss through his own fault is not regarded as suffering loss (the basis for many centuries of the rule which debarred a negligent plaintiff from recovering in a tort action). This rule (D. 50.17.203) is by Pomponius who is fond of the encapsulations I am describing; *quod quis ex culpa sua damnum sentit non intellegitur damnum sentire*. Pomponius is here appealing to a fundamental nation of responsibility. Everyone is responsible for his own fault and should not try to shift the consequence of it to another. However this notion of responsibility (for which there was no Latin expression) was not directly appealed to: it is filtered through the more specific maxim. (*iii*) Thirdly the open arguments are related to the rules in that they provide the justifications for the rules and justify the making of exceptions to them. And since the operation of a legal system is above all concerned with argument, is dialectical, the open arguments form an essential part of the legal system. To fulfil these functions the open arguments must be relatively broad in character. They are capable of yielding by way of justification a number of detailed rules and conversely of being distilled by what is miscalled an inductive process from the content of a number of rules. Estopped is an open argument since the English legal system contains a number of rules based on it—estopped by representation and by record for example. But the principle can be elaborated by an appeal to rules which do not mention it and are not expressly based on it, like *autrefois convict*.

The arguments I have in mind I call open because they have a wide but indeterminate scope of operation. A Roman jurist who was fond of appeals to such open arguments is Celsus. Thus D. 12.4.3.7 (Ulp 26 ed.) deals with a case where a slave owner dies giving his slave freedom by will if he pays 10 but by a later codicil giving the same slave freedom unconditionally. The slave does not know of the codicil and pays the heir ten. He later discovers, and sues for the 10. Celsus' father held he could not recover but Celsus the son, our Celsus, allows recovery on the ground of *naturalis aequitas*, natural equity.

(*c*) *The facts*. Next there is the appeal to the facts of a case. Very often this is coupled with a distinction: if the facts are, or were so-and-so the result is X, if not, Y. Thus D. 12.4.3.3 I give you money to manumit Stichus, a slave, Stichus dies. Can I recover the money? Proculus says, if he died after he could have been manumitted, I can, if not I cannot. The reason is implicit: the recipient is at fault in the first case in not manumitting the slave promptly. The appeal is therefore implicitly to the open argument, that the person at fault bears the risk or pays: i.e. to responsibility for one's own actions. Proculus favours this type of argument.

(*d*) *Appeals to authority*. Notoriously appeals to authority in this sense were abundant in Roman law. These appeals were made quite independently of any doctrine that the *responsa* or rescripts cited were binding, which in certain cases and at certain periods they were. Labeo says this, Celsus that, Julian the other (D. 12.6.6); quite apart from whether one is convinced by their reasons, and whether their opinions are binding, they are to be respected as lawyers. In listing the types of argument which underlie the various styles, then, we must make a place for arguments based on personal authority. In modern English practice arguments from precedent function in much the same way. The doctrine that precedents are binding is not an essential feature of a system based on precedent. English law functioned as such a system for many hundreds years without a formal doctrine to that effect. What is necessary for a system of precedent is that arguments from example should be admissible in the sense that an appeal to a previous instance or example is an adequate justification for decision, not necessarily that it compels decision. The status of precedent in England is derived from the high status of judges. If we look for a moment behind the veil of the technical doctrine that cases make law we find a mode of argument that depends on the authority of judges past and present, just as in Rome the appeal was to the authority of lawyers or emperors, including sometimes to the consensus of learned opinion, *quod constat*.

The appeal to authority, in the case where the opinion or precedent is not technically binding, is a way of adducing a particular type of open argument, based on the social value of keeping to trodden paths, or at least to the path trodden by some man of wisdom and repute. Some Roman lawyers overdid this sort of argument, as do some English lawyers the appeal to non-binding precedents. But it clearly has a place in every system.

(*e*) *No reasons given*. The unmotivated type of decision was supposed by Schulz to be in some sense characteristic of Roman lawyers, to bring out their real attitude to the business of dicision. In his Roman Legal Science (p. 17) he says that the pontifical jurisprudence was based on the notion *stat pro ratione auctoritas*, authority replaces reason, and of republican jurists he says (p. 61) that their *responsa* were brief and in principle disdained to give reasons. This is only a half truth, as Horak has shown in his recent study of Republican decision making in *Rationes decidendi*. Even at that period in about a third of the cases reported decisions are in fact supported by some form of reasoning. There was nothing to prevent a lawyer or legal writer giving reasons for his views on a given situation. Alfenus Varus (c. 40 B.C.) gives plenty. Nevertheless there is something in what Schultz says. All through the classical period it was quite common to decide a point without giving reasons. Some late classical jurists made a point, when they gave a *responsum*, of refraining from any explanation. Cervidius Scaevola, prefect in 175 A.D. is an example, and he was followed by his pupil Marcianus and by a pupil of Ulpian's, Modestinus. He will often reply to a questioner that there is no reason why the plaintiff should, or should not recover, *nihil proponi cur non agat* etc. For example (D. 12.6.67.1 Scae. 5 dig.) a tutor pays his ward's creditor more than he owes the creditor but fails to include the extra amount in his claim for expenses against the ward. Can the tutor recover against the creditor. *Scaevola respondit habere* (*condictionem* . . . "he can". No reason : the reason is treated as obvious viz. no estoppel arises (as we should say) from a transaction with a third party, the ward.

What sort of reasoning is implicitly appealed to in this unmotivated type of decision ? Although no reason is stated, clearly there is one hovering in the background. It may be that the rule of law applicable is so obvious that it needs no stating. It may be that it is so recherché that the lay audience would not understand it. It may be, to be sceptical, that if expressed it would sound unconvincing. Scaevola and his followers (Beseler is a modern devotee of the method) may be saving themselves from criticism. Nevertheless in most instances the implication of an unreasoned decision is that the decider could if he would appeal to a rule of law in support of his decision ; more rarely that he could point to some open argument in support of it.

Schultz says, rightly in a way, that his style of decision rests on authority and he connects it with the supposedly authoritarian character of Roman law and Roman lawyers. I am not now concerned with this general thesis which contains too many strands to be unravelled at one sitting. It may be worth noting that Horak in his thorough study of the republican decisions comes to the conclusion that the jurists of that period, who might *a priori* be supposed to show aristocratic authoritarian, tendencies do not argue in an authoritarian manner even when they fail to give reasons for their decisions, but argue rather within a technical or professional framework. But no doubt in a certain sense there is an appeal to authority in these cases. What does this mean ? When the decider is said to appeal implicitly to authority, what may be meant is either that he is trusted to know the law, so that he could if he would state explicitly the rule on which he relies, or else that even if there is no rule in point he can be trusted to decide wisely. In the second case it is his reputation for wisdom, common sense and the like that is the implicit justification for the decision ; in the first, the rule of law which he is taken to know. From a dialectical point of view it is the second case which is the more interesting since the first is already covered under heading (*a*). Instead of relying on soneone's else authority he relies on his own knowledge of the law or his own supposed wisdom.

III The Canon of Acceptable Arguments

Hence all our five categories of presentation reduce to two : open arguments and appeals to rules of law. But in many ways the most important feature of Roman and modern legal argumentation has been omitted from the catalogue so far discussed : it is this feature which constitutes the essence of the Roman gift to modern western civilisation. I am referring to the existence of a canon of unacceptable arguments. If we compare Greek and Roman civilisation and ask wherein the inferiority of the Greek lies from the point of view of legal culture we may be inclined to answer on the following lines. The Greeks had laws and constitutions and conducted arguments before juries and the like, but their mode of argument was determined by rhetorical and not specifically legal considerations. To them any arguments was grist to the mill : in particular arguments *ad hominem*, that one's opponent was a scoundrel or that one had oneself performed notable services to the city ; and arguments which appeals directly to philosophical or religious principles or to political considerations. The Greeks had in fact a notion of rhetoric, of the art of persuasion, and a theory or catalogue of types of arguments, in other words a notion of ' topic '. But what they lacked either in theory or in practice was the discipline to set up a canon of acceptable arguments proper to legal discourse. This involves a narrowing of the scope of the discussion with a view to strengthening within certain limits their persuasive power and so the stability of the conclusions reached. The appeal to rules of the law is of course the first type of argument to be listed as acceptable : this in turn involves the existence of a canon of recognition, to use Hart's excellent term, which defines the categories of admissible rules.

Secondly, there are conventions concerning the range of acceptable open arguments. The creation of these conventions depends on a certain professionalisation of the law. Now it is true that there are senses in which Roman law remained the preserve of amateurs until, in the middle of the fifth century, a law degree was made an essential qualification for admission to certain bars and public offices. Officially jurists were supposed to be unpaid amateurs—a theory which bore little relation to reality, not merely because payment was usual but because it was customary for young lawyers to follow a *cursus honorum* leading from the treasury counsel's office—*advocatus fisci*—to the prefectures. More important, lawyers from the republic onwards formed a relatively choesive group which accepted a common dialectical discipline. They were united by their training which taught them to accept certain types of argument and to reject others. The canon of acceptable arguments was gradually extended to include social considerations, utility and the like, in the late classical period which were but sparingly referred to in the republic. The beginnings of this professional discipline which marked off law from the evil influence of rhetoric almost certainly go back to the pontifical jurisprudence of the middle republic. Certainly in Cicero's day the distinction between lawyers and rhetoricians was firmly established, though Cicero himself, despite his acquaintance with leading lawyers, failed to grasp that the narrowness of legal dialectic was the source of its strength.

Given, then, intellectual professionalism it is possible for certain issues to be considered not in isolation from the moral, social, political and religious issues affecting society at large but in such a way that these are allowed to be taken into account only on certain terms and within certain limits. The terms are, I think, really twofold. The first is that open arguments resting on social values most ultimately give way to rules : in the last resort the argument that the decision proposed is onconsistent with a rule compelling the contrary decision, must be accepted. This in turn entails that the arbiters of society are in the last resort the legislators. The second is that the positive values which are the basis of open arguments are system—neutral and person—neutral, that is to say that they are indifferent to the idiosyncratic features of religious, moral, philosophical or political thought systems and are not conceived *ad hominem*. The system—neutrality of which I speak is of course not Kelsenian purity. The open arguments are the window through which the law looks at society and by which the values of society filter through to the law. By them the law absorbs the values of the people : utility, equity, nature and the like. But they enter in that very general form in which they would be likely to be endorsed by the mass of people, rather than as specific programmes, and they are filtered through a professional mesh which reduces them to technically manageable principles and maxims : no one should be enriched to the detriment of another. The argument from utility *tout court* is therefore in order : the argument that the contrary decision would interrupt the corn supply is not. An argument from deterrence is in order. An argument that a particular defendant will be deterred if the law is settled in a certain sense is not. This impartiality as between persons and systems is crucial to western legal culture ; it is the specific legacy of Roman law to our civilisation and it is alien to

Greek culture. Modern examples of its operation are of course well-known for example the canon which excludes from legal discourse the particular interpretation put on a statute by a minister or member of Parliament; or which prevents the courts in tort cases from taking account of the particular insurance situation of the parties, as opposed to the general likelihood that one or other of them will be insured; or which restricts the extent to which sociological and statistical arguments can properly be addressed to a court, and so on. In certain countries, such as the U.S.A., attempts are being made to destroy the separateness of legal discourse and to reduce legal issues to issues in which every sort of social, political and moral consideration ir relevant. In my opinion this modern Hellenistic movement is to be resisted: fear the Greeks bringing gifts, even if they are disguised as devotees of the American Supreme Court.

The Romans therefore bequeathed to us a form of legal culture in which the closed and the open are combined. Law is a separate sphere of discourse: it is closed in the sense that all arguments adduced must be person and system—neutral. On the other hand it is open in that open arguments, if they conform to the above criteria, are acceptable, subject to the ultimate test of consistency with binding rules. The openness of their legal culture varied from time to time. In particular arguments drawn from utility (what we whould call public policy, or the policy underlying certain rules and statutes) seem to increase in the late classical period. Arguments drawn from philosophy, e.g. from Stoicism are acceptable if couched in a very general form, as in an appeal to *natura* or *aequum*. This is a point which Stein (36 SDH1 463) has brought out very well: philosophical influence did exist, but it was a general, climatic sort of influence, not something specifically directed towards a given solution to a problematic case.

IV Roman and Modern Legal Concepts and Reasoning

My original aim was to demonstrate the contribution of the Roman world to modern legal concepts and nodern legal reasoning. It will now be clear how I should like to do this. The Roman contribution to our civilisation consisted in an important way in the professionalisation of the law: that is, in the creation, necessarily within a restricted group of persons trained in the same general ideas, of conventions restricting the scope of permissible arguments in relation to given problems, so that the discourse of the law is in one way independent of and in another way open to influences drawn from other streams of social life, moral, political, religious and (in the modern age) sociological: the law looks at society through a half-open window. The Greeks, garrulous and undisciplined, were incapable of devising such an instrument of social control and social cohesion. The Romans succeeded and owing to the *tour de force* of Justinian's codification luckily transmitted sufficient examples of the technique for the mediaeval and modern world to absorb the essentials of this institution, and at the same time to add to it the discipline of systematic legal science. This, though it has been guilty of grevious intellectual sins, especially of a tendency to become self-centred and narcissistic, is a necessary adjunct to the Roman discipline: one which classifies and systematises the rules and decisions in such a way as to bring out inconsistencies at a deeper level than the decision making process itself permits and so to suggest changes and adjustments.

The Romans did not get far with the systematising of the law. Gaius, building on rather feeble earlier efforts, took the first steps : but he is not a mainstream Roman lawyer. The mainstream lawyers are not systematisers but casuists and expositors. They are united by their practice of argument, which conforms to a professional tradition. But within that tradition they supply abundance and variety by each doing his own thing. Proculus likes to argue from the facts, Julian to formulate rules, Pomponius to appeal to open arguments, Ulpian to cite authority, Scaevola disdains giving reasons. Professional discipline does not preclude personal idiosyncrasy, and strong opinions are shaped by common standards. These tensions have not ceased to bear fruit.

[16]

LEGAL ONTOLOGY AND LEGAL REASONING *

Chaim Perelman **

By "legal ontology" I mean the religious or philosophical view which is the basis of a system of law and by "legal reasoning" I mean the totality of techniques which legal theorists and lawyers use to adjust that system to the requirements of adjudication; these requirements essentially being security and justice. Since the role of the judge is to proclaim the law in each specific case, we want his decisions to be not arbitrary, to be predictable in that they treat cases which are basically similar in the same way. We also want them to be seen as equitable, appropriate to the circumstances, the ways and the customs of the community. In reconciling stability and flexibility, the various systems to be compared in this article, i.e. Jewish law, Continental European law and Common law, allocate differently the powers of judge and legislator, regarded as complementary to one another. It will be seen that this division of powers changes at different times, while at the same time the ontology according to which the allocation of powers is effected becomes more flexible.

Clearly a detailed historical study of these differing systems would require many volumes; in this article only a short description can be offered, but it is one that is most illuminating in the sharp contrasts which it presents.

Jewish law as it is drawn from the Bible and the Talmudic interpretation[1] of the Bible made Moses the sole prophet-legislator.

The body of his legislation is indeed accompanied by a command which renders it unalterable forever:

* This paper will also appear as a contribution to the forthcoming *Festschrift* to Professor Julius Stone, to be edited by Professor A.R. Blackshield and published by Butterworths.

** Professor Emeritus, Faculty of Law and Philosophy, University of Brussels; Visiting Professor, Faculties of Law and Philosophy, Hebrew University of Jerusalem.

1 As to this see my paper "La Bible et son interprétation juridique par les talmudistes" at the Louvain colloquium (10 Nov. 1975) published in the proceedings of the colloquium *Oral and Written Tradition*, L. Dequeker, ed. (Institutum Judaicum, Brussels), 42–62. For more detailed treatment see Ḣ. Cohn, *Jewish Law in Ancient and Modern Israel*, (Ktav Publishing House, New York, 1971).

> Now, Israel, listen to the statutes and laws which I am teaching you, and obey them; then you will live, and go in and occupy the land which the Lord the God of your fathers is giving you. You must not add anything to my charge, nor take anything away from it. You must carry out all the commandments of the Lord your God which I lay upon you. (*Deut. 4;* 1–2, New English Bible translation).

The law of Moses was revealed to him on Mount Sinai by God. Emanating from divine authority, it binds all believers; emanating from a just God, its precepts are just: it will not be necessary to amplify them nor to amend them.

We know that the law given to Moses in the 13th century B.C. was reinstated by Esdras in 532 B.C. after the return from the Babylonian captivity. Did the law remain unchanged during these seven centuries? Should it remain unchanged forever? Was it necessary to integrate customs and ancestral traditions with it? According to the evidence of Flavius Josephus, the Pharisees, who represented popular feeling, were on this point fiercely opposed to the Sadducees, who represented the aristocratic class and especially the priests:

> The Pharisees have delivered to the people a great many observances by succession from their fathers, which are not written in the law of Moses; and for that reason it is that the Sadducees reject them, and say that we are to esteem those observances to be obligatory which are in the written word, but are not to observe what are derived from the tradition of our forefathers; and concerning these things it is that great disputes and differences have arisen among them, while the Sadducees are able to persuade none but the rich, and have not the populace obsequious to them, but the Pharisees have the multitude on their side. (*The Antiquities of the Jews,* transl. by William Whiston, Book XIII, ch. x, § 6.)

The Pharisees won. They were responsible for the traditional distinction between written and oral law. So that it would not be confused with the written, more holy, law, it was forbidden to put it in writing until the time when Rabbi Akiba, the most outstanding interpreter of law who lived in the first century of the modern era, managed to give the unwritten law the same ontological status as the written law; it was only a commentary or repetition of it (*Mishna*).

The *Mishna*, the first codification dating from the second century of the modern era, declares at the beginning of *Pirke Avot* (The Precepts of the Elders I: 1) that the oral law had been received by Moses on Mount Sinai at the same time as the written law and that it was transmitted orally by generations of interpreters without interruption. In the fifth and sixth centuries of the Christian era, the Talmud of Jerusalem and the Talmud of Babylon were written: they included the discussions by the scholars of the text of the *Mishna*. What should be done when the interpreters disagree? In the first century of the Christian era, the disagreement between the School of Hillel, the more liberal school, and the School of Shammai, the stricter school, had already become proverbial. In reply to the question put by Rabbi Samuel, how to know which interpretation was right, "a voice from above replied that both interpretations expressed the word of the living God" (Babylonian Talmud, *Erubin* 13b). How then is it to be decided? In a dispute about a ritual oven, Rabbi Eliezer, the only voice opposed to the great majority of Scholars, calls on God as witness in a kind of reference to the legislator. God declared himself by performing miracles and even a heavenly voice was heard, each time proclaiming that Rabbi Eliezer was right. The Babylonian Talmud reports (*Baba Metziah* 59b) that Rabbi Joshua, spokesman for the majority, said that "the Torah is not located in heaven" and explained the statement, according to Rabbi Jeremiah, thus:

> ...that the Torah had already been given on Mt. Sinai; we pay no attention to a heavenly voice, because Thou hast long since written in the Torah at Mt. Sinai (*Exod.* 13:2) after the majority must one incline.

If the law has a divine origin, its interpretation, although made by man, must be respected in the same way, since the oral law was handed down to Moses on Mt. Sinai at the same time as the written law.[2] If the plurality of interpretations does not controvert the holiness of these laws (and that is why the Talmud reports all the dissenting opinions) there must, nonetheless, be some criteria for taking a decision.

The first criterion is that of the majority. When the opinions of two scholars contradict one another, then the opinion of the scholar of greater authority must be adopted: the opinion of Hillel contradicting that of Shammai, the opinion of Rabbi Akiba, contradicting that of any other adversary. The third rule takes into account the worth of the arguments: a rule supported by reasoning is to be preferred to one which is groundless, unless the latter can be based on a tradition deriving from Moses and the prophets. The fourth criterion grants precedence to the authority of most recent date. The fifth says that one should follow the established custom

[2] *Cf.* This quote from the *Jerusalem Megillah*, IV, 74d, was given to me by Professor Julius Stone: "Whatever a competent scholar will yet derive from the Torah, that was already given to Moses on Mt. Sinai".

or usage. The sixth distinguishes between rules laid down by the written law as to which a more strict interpretation is adopted, and rules which are based on rabbinical decisions, for which a more lenient interpretation is adopted. Finally, the ultimate rule as it applies to the post-Talmudic judges is based on a text of *Deut.* (17: 8–11) where it is prescribed that in difficult cases, recourse should be had to "the levitical priests, or to the judge then in office... Act on the instruction which they give you, or on the precedent that they cite; do not swerve from what they tell you, neither to right nor left." It was on the basis of this latter text that the authority of the courts, and particularly of the Sanhedrin established in 141 B.C., was founded.

Here is a system of law which, in the absence of legislative power, could only evolve through the work of commentators and judicial decisions. Their ruling could only be modified by someone whose moral authority prevails "in wisdom and number", i.e., by his moral authority and the number of his supporters. It is for that reason that, in a difficult case, the rabbinical tribunals used to consult the great authorities of the age, whose *responsa* permitted a softening of the rabbinical law. The institute for the Study of Jewish Law at the Hebrew University of Jerusalem has, in its archives, 300,000 of these *responsa.*

Besides the evolution of law by textual interpretation, two other interpretative techniques can be recognized: the use of fictions and of general principles of law.

The best-known fiction was that proposed by Hillel which permitted the bypassing of the rule in *Deut.* (15: 1–2) requiring the remission of debts at the sabbatical year, which occurred every seven years. According to the fiction devised by Hillel, the courts became the fictitious creditors, the real creditors becoming the court's agents: from that point on, debtors were no longer freed from their debts (*Makkot,* 3a). By means of other fictions, it was possible to by-pass the prohibition of loans with interest, establish testamentary succession for which there was no provision in the Bible, and so on.

Recourse to general principles of law was based on biblical texts whose import was generalized. From the fact that the rule had been ordained by God "that you may live" (*Deut.* 4: 1) the general principle was derived that one could violate the most imperative rules where a human life is at stake. On the basis of the text "Do not move the ancient boundary-stone which your forefathers set up" (*Proverbs* 22: 28) the general rule as to respect for customs was drawn. And following the rule "judge your fellow-countryman with strict justice" (*Lev.* 19: 15) the unacceptable results of legal formalism could be controverted.

Despite the prohibition of legislation, the value or regulations of subordinate status was admitted, within temporal and spatial limits. Thus the prohibition of polygamy on pain of excommunication decreed in the 11th century by Rabbi Gershom of Mainz, was only valid for Jews living among Christians and for a period of 1000 years.

From the 11th to the 16th century, there were four codifications of Jewish law which has, since that era, evolved very little until the creation of the State of Israel.

*

In contrast to Jewish law which offers the extreme example of a system of law without a legislator other than Moses, Continental law since the French Revolution represents the other extreme, where there was an attempt to regard the whole of the law as the expression of the will of the legislator.

The State-oriented and legalistic ideology of positivism was a consequence of combining the ideas of Montesquieu with those of Rousseau.

The doctrine of separation of powers gave the power to make laws to the legislative arm, judges being only "*la bouche qui prononce les paroles de la loi*: *des êtres inanimés qui n'en peuvent modérer ni la force ni la rigueur*".[3] However, for Montesquieu, the laws, since they must respect equity which pre-exists positive law by which they are laid down,[4] should be the expression of reason rather than of a sovereign and arbitrary will. J.J. Rousseau, regarding the laws as the expression of the will of the sovereign, i.e. the nation, was to develop a theory of generalized will which is "always in the right"[5] when it is motivated by the general interest. The law-making which derives from it must be just; the "admirable agreement between interest and justice gives to the common deliberations an equitable character which at once vanishes when any particular question is discussed, in the absence of a common interest to unite and identify the ruling of the judge with that of the party".[6]

The elevation of the law and the distrust of the judges is exhibited by Art. 12 of the Organic Decree of 16–24 August 1790, setting up the referral of a general nature, and forbidding the courts to make regulations: "they will, on every occasion which they find necessary, whether for the interpretation of a law or the making of a new one, address themselves to the Legislature". The courts were required to give reasons for their

3 *De l'esprit des lois,* Part I, Book I, Ch. III. 6.

4 *Op. cit.* Part I, Book I, Ch. I.

5 *The Social Contract,* Book II, Ch. VI.

6 *Op. cit.* Bk. II; Ch. IV.

decisions by reference to the law, and the Court of Cassation was established "with the duty of ensuring that the judges did not break the law which they were supposed to apply. The Court of Cassation was seen as a policeman, delegated by the legislative power to supervise the judiciary, and bound to account periodically to the legislature on the way in which it accomplished its task."[7]

The conception according to which the whole of the law is contained within the written law led certain professors in France in the first half of the nineteenth century to say that they were not teaching the civil law, but the Napoleonic Code. Consider, too, the speech of Dean Aubry, at the opening session of the Faculties of Strasbourg in 1857:

> The task of the teachers called on to dispense legal education on behalf of the State is to protest, temperately of course, but also firmly, against any innovation which would tend to replace the will of the legislator with some other intention foreign to it.[8]

The accepted practice was to induce in the students an almost holy reverence for the written law, as is witnessed by these lines taken from the book, *Written Exercises on the Civil Code*, published by Mourlon in 1846:

> A good judge submits his reason to that of the written law, for it is established to be judged by and not to be judged. Nothing is above the law, and it is prevarication to sidestep its provisions with the excuse that the sense of justice objects. In making judicial decisions, there is no, there cannot be, reason more rational, justice more just that the reason or justice of the law.[9]

We know that the inconveniences of the reference to the legislator, which were very soon observed, obliged the drafters of the Code Napoleon to introduce the famous Article 4, which forbids the judge to refuse to give judgment "with the excuse that the law is silent or unclear or inadequate". He must act—even if he is forbidden to interpret, in the spirit of the elected representatives when the text is clear (*interpretatio cessat in claris*)—where there is a gap, antinomy or ambiguity. It is by these means that the judges have gradually increased their power while nevertheless sheltering behind a written provision of the law as far as possible.

[7] *Cf.* Ch. Perelman, *Logique Juridique, Nouvelle Rhétorique,* (Dalloz, Paris, 1979), 16.

[8] *Cf.* Bonnecase, *L'école de l'exégèse,* pp. 133–134, cited by L. Husson, "Analyse critique de la méthode de l'exégèse", in *Nouvelles études sur la pensée juridique* (Dalloz, Paris, 1974) 182.

[9] Cited by L. Husson, *op. cit.,* at 183.

That was the technique of adapting the texts advocated by Ballot-Beaupré, first Chairman of the *Cour de Cassation* in 1904 in his speech commemorating the centenary of the Civil Code. We know how French judges, under the influence of the historical school and of sociological trends, are adopting more and more a teleological interpretation of law, invoking the values which the legislator sought to protect (referring to the spirit of the law) and making more and more room for general principles of law and legal topics.[10]

At the moment the judge is expected not only to respect the written law but to reconcile it with the requirements of justice in such a way that the judge's decisions are at one and the same time in conformity with the law in force and accepted by enlightened public opinion. The judge will use all the techniques of legal reasoning in reconciling security and justice, in carrying out his task of pronouncing the law in the particular cases which come before him. We will see that the Common Law which has a quite different legal ontology has reached a not dissimilar synthesis.

*

While the written law in Jewish or Continental law is the expression of will, either of God or of the nation, the legal ontology of the Common Law as it was developed first in England and then in the English colonies, assumes the existence of an objective, rational and just law which is evident in judicial decisions. This we call *case law*, defined by the American jurist Karl Llewellyn thus:

> Case law is found in decided cases and enacted by judges in the process of solving particular disputes... These generalizations contained in, or built upon, past decisions, when taken as normative for future disputes, create a legal system of precedent. Precedent is operative, however, before it is recognized. Toward its operation drive all those phases of human makeup which build habit in the individual and institution in the group. The force of precedent in the law is heightened by an additional factor: that curious almost universal sense of justice which urges that all men are properly to be treated alike in all circumstances. As the social system varies we meet infinite variations as to which men or treatments or circumstances are to be classed as 'like'; but the pressure to accept the views of the time and place remains.[11]

10 See on all these matters Ch. Perelman, *Logique Juridique, Nouvelle Rhétorique*, (Dalloz, Paris, 1979).

11 K. Llewellyn in *Encyclopaedia of Social Sciences* (Macmillan, New York, 1930), vol. III, p. 249 (see *Case Law*).

According to this view, already to be seen in the writings of Bracton in the 13th century, the judges do not make the law, they only discover it. In a significant contribution of Professor L. Chafee, Jr. of the Harvard Law School titled "Do Judges Make or Discover Law?"[12] we find the following characteristic quotations from Blackstone[13] where he says of judges:

> They are the depositaries of the laws; the living oracles who must decide in all cases of doubt, and who are bound by an oath to decide according to the law of the land.

and further on he states that judicial decisions are

> ...the principal and most authoritative evidence, that can be given, of the existence of such a custom as shall form a part of the "common law".

The ontology in which the judge discovers the law, but does not make it, makes it possible to reconcile the stability of a system based on precedents with its evolution. For even if it is conceded that the judges, as a normal rule, decide cases submitted for their consideration in a just way, it may be that the way in which they formulate the decisive rule (the *ratio decidendi*) is not adequate, because it is expressed too widely or too narrowly. This was the origin of a basic distinction made within the doctrine of *stare decisis*, i.e. to follow judicial precedents, a doctrine which was strongly espoused in the nineteenth century. The distinction was made between *dicta*, the rule as expressed, and the *holding*, the rule which was a prerequisite for the judge to reach the decision which he did on the facts established. It is for the judge in a later case to reformulate the rule followed by the prior judge where necessary, using the technique of distinguishing the case by showing how the instant case differs from the precedent. The rule of *stare decisis* binds all lower courts, and the appellate courts, while the House of Lords, acting as final court of appeal, regarded itself from 1898 to 1966 as bound by its own decisions. During that period only an act of Parliament could alter by statute, the rules of law already established in the common law.[14]

[12] *Proceedings of the American Philosophical Society* (1947), vol. 91, pp. 405–420.

[13] Commentaries I, (Oxford, 2nd ed., 1776) 69.

[14] On *case law cf.* A.R. Cross, *Precedent in English Law* (Clarendon Press, Oxford, 3rd ed., 1977) and Neil MacCormick, *Legal Reasoning and Legal Theory* (Clarendon Press, Oxford, 1978). In an illuminating article, Professor Julius Stone shows the limited importance of the Practice Statement made by Lord Chancellor Gardiner in 1966. See his "1966 And All That: Loosing the Chains of Precedent" (1969) 69 Colum. L.R. 1162, esp. 1189–1199.

The advantage of this system is that it satisfies the need for security and formal justice because of the obligation to follow decided cases and to treat similar cases in the same way. The disadvantage is that each new judgment, each reinterpretation of the rule works retroactively, the new formulation of the rule being regarded as the only adequate statement of the common law. The advantage of statute law, of a legislative rule, is that it is prospective, only having validity, in theory, for the future.

For this reason, Bentham, and later Austin, scorned the fiction that judges do, like the legislator, make law, but instead of proclaiming the law in advance, they state it after the event, at least each time that they formulate it. Bentham considered that the judges established the common law the way a man trains his dog:

> When your dog does anything you want to break him of, you wait till he does it, and then beat him for it. This is the way you make laws for your dog; and this is the way the judges make law for you and me. They won't tell a man beforehand what it is he *should not do*—they won't so much as allow of his being told: they lie by till he had done something which they say he should *not have done* and then they hang him for it.[15]

The application of the common law created some problems in the United States where the Constitution set up, besides the Supreme Court, federal courts with jurisdiction to judge conflicts between inhabitants of different states by applying the common law. What happens when the judges of one state frame a rule which is rejected by a federal judge? Should e.g., the principle of commercial law concerning the effects of trade, be made by the judges of each state, which would lead to intolerable diversity, or should the law be uniform? In this connection, a distinction has been made between legislation of a local nature with which federal courts should not concern themselves, and law of general relevance which is stated by the federal courts. From this stems the problem described by Professor Chafee:

> ...two different sets of legal rules prevailed in a given state over great areas of the law, depending on whether the litigation got before a state court or a federal court.[16]

This major problem was a weighty argument for those like John Chipman

[15] J. Bentham, *Works*, Bowring (ed.) (Edinburgh, 1843) vol. V., p. 235, cited by Chafee, *op. cit., supra* n. 12 at 410–411.

[16] Chafee, *op. cit.*, p. 413.

Gray or Oliver Wendell Holmes who preferred a conception of law as the expression of the will of a competent authority.

In a 1928 decision Holmes expressed himself thus:

> Law is a word used with different meaning, but law in the sense in which courts speak of it today does not exist without some definite authority behind it. The common law so far as it is enforced in a state, whether called common law or not, is not the common law generally but the law of that State existing by the authority of that State without regard to what it may have been in England or anywhere else.[17]

From that point is was a short step to the statement of Justice Brandeis in a 1938 Supreme Court decision:[18]

> Except in matters governed by the Federal Constitution or by Acts of Congress, the law to be applied in any case is the law of the State. And whether the law of the State shall be declared by its Legislature in a statute or by its highest court in a decision is not a matter of federal concern. There is no federal common law.

Once this is conceded there is nothing to stop the courts acting as the legislator and giving notice in a decision that the doctrine previously applied will not be applied in the future.[19]

A similar evolution, i.e. a gradual liberation from the baleful results of legal ontology, can be seen in the attitude of the common law judges to statutes, i.e. laws made by the legislator.

Their initial reaction to statutes was to regard them as an intrusion to which the judge is required to submit, but which he must interpret in a restrictive way wherever the statute is contrary to the common law. Thus the renowned English lawyer, Sir Frederick Pollock, described the approach of the common lay judges in these terms: their attitude

> ...cannot be well accounted for except upon the theory that Parliament generally changes the law for the worse, and that the business of the judge is to keep the mischief of its interference within the narrowest possible bounds.[20]

[17] *Black and White Taxicab Co.* v. *Brown and Yellow Taxicab Co.*, 276, *United States Reports* (1928), pp. 533–534 (cited by Chafee, *op. cit.*, pp. 413–414).

[18] *Erie Railroad Co.* v. *Tompkins*, 304 U.S., 64, 78.

[19] Margaret Hall, (ed.) *Selected Writings of Benjamin Cardozo* (New York, 1947) 36–37.

[20] Sir F. Pollock, *Essays in Jurisprudence and Ethics* (Macmillan, London, 1882) 85.

Again in 1908 in an article with the title "Common Law and Legislation", Roscoe Pound mentions four possible approaches to statute law:

1. They might receive it fully into the body of the law as affording not only a rule to be applied but a principle from which to reason, and hold it, as a later and more direct expression of the general will; as superior authority to judge made rules on the same general subject, and reason from it by analogy in preference to them.
2. They might receive it fully into the body of the law to be reasoned from by analogy the same as any other rule of law, regarding it, however, as of equal or co-ordinate authority in this respect with judge made rules upon the same subject.
3. They might refuse to receive it into the body of the law and give effect to it directly: refusing to reason from it by analogy but giving to it, nevertheless, a liberal interpretation.
4. They might not only refuse to reason from it by analogy and apply it directly only, but also give to it a strict and narrow interpretation, holding it down rigidly to those cases which it covers expressly.[21]

It was the fourth approach which he considered delineated the orthodox attitude of the common law judges although the third just missed being adopted; but the first two would have seemed ridiculous to the common law lawyer.

Since that time there seems to have been a development towards the third approach, that a statute ought to be put on the same footing as the rules devised by the judges.

On this point, I would like to draw attention to an important article of Charles D. Breitel, former Chief Justice of the New York Court of Appeal. He accepted that statutes constituted a new source of principles and rules, along with customs and usages. But there cannot be a single way of dealing with them.

> All statutes are not alike, in fact, are not treated similarly... What is required is an acknowledged pluralistic treatment... the scope for creative adaptation... varies directly with the degree of generalization... Because perfect generalization for the future is impossible, no generalization is complete. Aware of this impossibility, legislators often do no more than propose to lay down the most general state-

[21] (1908) 21 Hvd.LR. 383.

> ments of law, intending that the courts and other law applying agencies shall creatively adapt the general principle to specific cases. Thus, every time a statute uses a rule of reason, or a standard of fairness without specification, there is conscious and deliberate delegation of this responsibility to the courts.[22]

Furthermore, various codifications and restatements have been undertaken in the United States with the object of unifying different branches of the law and achieving codes similar to the Napoleonic Code: thus we come to the domain of codified law, to the primacy of statutory law. Depending upon the type of code and the area of law the greater importance may be attributed to the work of the legislator or that of the judge. Indeed, their roles are complementary, and judges will be more active where it is relatively difficult to achieve an analogous result by legislation, e.g., where a constitutional amendment would be required.

Thus can be seen, in this search for a synthesis between the will of the legislator and the acceptable or fair result in each factual situation, the ideological vision faded in order to make the solutions reached acceptable to the community concerned.

I have chosen, on purpose, three essentially different legal ontologies as examples in order to be able to show how, in each case, the scholars and judges found a way to liberate the law from the logical consequences of the religious, philosophical or ideological legal ontology when it became indispensable to cope with "the felt necessities" of the legal situation.

[22] Ch. D. Breitel, *The Courts and Lawmaking*, in *Legal Institutions Today and Tomorrow*, M.C. Paulsen, ed., (Columbia University Press, New York, 1959) 2–9.

[17]

COURTS AND CODES IN ENGLAND, FRANCE AND SOVIET RUSSIA

BERNARD RUDDEN*

Stanley Kowalski was a true civilian. For him life's difficulties were lightened because, as he frequently insisted, "In the State of Louisiana we have the Napoleonic Code."[1] Professor Lawson, on the other hand, is a true comparativist who has wisely observed that "it is not . . . at all necessarily the mark of Civil Law systems that they are or should be codified, or of Common Law systems that they are or should not. Nor is there any profound difference between codified and uncodified systems as such. Like nature, law knows no sharp divisions between species."[2]

It is the purpose of this paper to draw some comparisons of the role of the courts, the style of judgment, and the place of civil legislation in England, France and the RSFSR. The words "role" and "style" are meant to cover, not merely the constitutional position and verbal skills of the judges, but also their consciousness of their own function, and of the creative nature of their activity; and the extent to which this is made explicit by the tribunals themselves. For reasons of space, I shall focus largely on the higher courts and on questions of private law. Furthermore, the method will be to describe what appear to be the distinctive traits of English law and to show the differences; and to suggest that, in terms of the role and style of the courts, the English and French systems are the extremes, with that of Soviet Russia falling in between.

THE INSTITUTIONAL STRUCTURE

Of the three countries, England's particular features are that there are no comprehensive codes and that the judges overtly make the law. Of course in some fields—those, for instance, of sale of goods or bills of exchange—there is virtual codification; but the basic topics of property and obligations are not to be found in the statute book. Indeed, on the part of the legislature, there is a pronounced aversion to deal with them. Thus the Law Reform (Frustrated Contracts) Act of 1943 begins, "When a contract . . . has become . . . frustrated" without attempting to define the notion; and section 1 of the Misrepresentation Act of 1967 begins by tin-

---

* Fellow of Oriel College, University of Oxford. B.A. 1956, M.A. 1960, University of Cambridge; Ph.D. 1965, University of Wales; Solicitor 1959.

[1] Tennessee Williams, A Streetcar Named Desire, Act I, Scene 2.

[2] F. H. Lawson, A Common Lawyer Looks at the Civil Law 52 (1953). What this paper owes to all of Lawson's work will be obvious, as is its debt to J. Dawson, The Oracles of the Law (1968).

kering about with basic rules which, in any rational Civil Code, would have been set out at the start. Furthermore, even in property, that area where English law—as Lawson has so brilliantly demonstrated[3]—is both the most conceptual and the most subject to enactments, the latter never attempt to define the basic notions, clear though they be.

English judges have, from time to time, denied that they make law and have spoken of it as if it were something there which could, with sufficient learning, assiduity, and insight, be descried and brought forth to the people. This view is no longer popular; and, even if it were, it would be true that the courts are a source of law whether they make it or find it. The best argument for this is simply the absence of any other source for those basic concepts mentioned above: on them there are no statutes; but there is law aplenty. The creative function of English courts is, of course, strengthened by the doctrine of precedent by which courts are bound as to the law by the decisions of superior tribunals with only the House of Lords being free to overrule itself.[4]

There is one further point about the English system which might be taken to be of merely procedural significance but has, in fact, a great effect on both substantive law and the role of the courts. In order to appeal to the House of Lords *leave* is needed;[5] the highest court deals with only 30-40 cases a year and so has time enough to devote to its law-making function. Thus it will not hesitate to consider facts, and inferences therefrom, at much greater length than its Continental counterparts; it will decide, for instance, what one word in a contract between two private parties means—a role that both the French and the USSR Supreme Courts would be loth to undertake. One perhaps unfortunate result of this is that many propositions of fact tend to become elevated into rules of law.

The French constitutional structure is quite different. Firstly, there is the great *Code Napoléon* whose task, in the words of Portalis, one of its draftsmen, was "to fix, in broad perspective, the general maxims of the law; to lay down principles rich in consequences, and not to descend into the details of questions which may arise on each topic."[6] Those details, he said, were to be dealt with by judge and jurist.

---

[3] F. H. Lawson, The Rational Strength of English Law (1951); F. H. Lawson, An Introduction to the Law of Property (1958).

[4] Statement of Lord Gardiner, L.C., [1966] 3 All E.R. 77.

[5] Administration of Justice (Appeals) Act 1934, 24 & 25 Geo. 5, c. 40, § 1; Administration of Justice Act 1969, ch. 58, Pt. II.

[6] Portalis, *Discours Préliminaire,* in 1 P. Fenet, Recueil Complet des travaux préparatoires du Code civil 464 *et seq.* (1830).

The courts, however, may not make law. This prohibition stems from the doctrine of separation of powers and finds formal expression in article 5 of the Code: "Judges are forbidden to decide the cases submitted to them by laying down general rules." (*Il est défendu aux juges de prononcer par voie de disposition générale et réglementaire sur les causes qui leur sont soumises.*) We shall consider later how far the Supreme Court—the *Cour de Cassation*—obeys this rule, but meanwhile it should be said that the tribunal never, of course, openly admits to flouting it, and that the majority of French jurists still hold the view that the court is not a source of law.[7]

It follows from the constitutional position of the French courts that there can be no formal doctrine of precedent. The *Cour de Cassation* is not bound by its own decisions and no lower court is strictly bound by those of a superior; indeed, a lower court to whom the *Cour de Cassation* has remitted a case on the grounds that the previous decision got the law wrong is not, the first time, bound by the Supreme Court's ruling.

The final preliminary point to be made is that, provided the motion alleges a misapplication or misunderstanding of law, no leave is needed to bring the case before the *Cour de Cassation.* The result is that that Court—sitting in six chambers—deals with, not 40, but over 4,000 cases a year. The effects of this pressure are manifold; they reinforce the French judges' natural inclination to terseness; they leave no time for a contemplation of past decisions or an analysis of policy choices; and they are one cause of the Supreme Court's resolute refusal to deal with issues of fact.

The Soviet system falls midway between these positions. As in France there are codes: Basic Principles enacted at the Federal level and then expanded into the Codes of the constituent Republics.[8] Further, as in France, there is no express or implied grant of law-making power to the courts. It is perfectly clear that a single decision or even a series thereof, does not formally bind other

---

[7] For the debate see F. Gény, Méthode d'interprétation et sources en droit privé positif Nos. 46 *et seq.* (2d ed. La. State L. Inst. transl. 1963); Waline, *Le pouvoir normatif de la jurisprudence*, in 2 La Technique et les principes de droit public: études en l'honneur de G. Scelle, 613 *et seq.* (1950); Maury, *Observations sur la jurisprudence en tant que source de droit* in 1 Le Droit Privé français au milieu du XXe siècle: études offertes à Georges Ripert 28-50 (1950); Esmein, *La jurisprudence et la loi* [1952] Rev. trim. dr. civ., 17 *et seq.*; Boulanger, Jurisprudence, [1950] Encyclopédie Dalloz, (Civil III) 17 *et seq.*; G. Ripert, Les forces créatrices du droit (1955).

[8] For our purposes the main statutes are: Basic Principles of Civil Legislation of the U.S.S.R., 1962; and the R.S.F.S.R. 1964 Grazh. Kod. (Civil Code). Translations may be found in Law in Eastern Europe (Leyden) No. 7, 1963, and No. 11, 1966.

courts in like cases; although a ruling on appeal or protest will bind the lower court in the particular instance.

The Soviet codes, however—especially those of the 1920's—were far from perfect, and the courts soon found themselves confronted with situations that cried out for judicial remedy but were not provided for by statute. Examples will be given later to show that the Supreme Court filled the gaps in the Code, that their decisions were then treated virtually as if part of the Code, and that they were later enacted as such with no discernible difference to their actual operation.

The Full Bench of the Supreme Courts of the USSR and RSFSR come nearer to the English system in two other ways. Firstly, unlike the *Cour de Cassation*, they are protected against a flood of appeals, since proceedings may be initiated before them only by superior officials of the judiciary or Procuracy and not by any private litigant. Secondly they are given power to issue "guiding explanations"—pronouncements based, not on the facts of one particular case, but from a survey of judicial practice in particular areas.[9] There is the usual dispute among jurists as to the normative effect of these utterances but the quasi-official authority of the journal *Soviet State and Law* asserts that "guiding explanations are normative by their general character and are law-creating."[10] Moreover—and more importantly—the Supreme Courts, whether or not they have normative power, *act as if they do.*

JUDICIAL METHOD

Torstein Eckhoff has pointed out that "[t]he characteristic features of judicial decision-making are to a considerable extent conditioned by the *professional training of judges.* Belonging to a profession makes for dependence in the sense that the person concerned is left to rely upon the body of theory and the ways of handling problems in which he is trained. Dependence on a field of learning which one masters is, however, usually not felt as a constraint, but as a source of satisfaction and strength."[11]

9 U.S.S.R. Supreme Court Act 1957 art. 9; R.S.F.S.R. Court Organisation Act 1960. The power was formally given in 1938.

10 O iuridicheskoi prirode rukovodiashchikh ukazanii plenuma VS SSSR, 1956 Sovetskoe Gosudarstvo i Pravo [hereinafter cited as S.G.P.] 8 13. Other main articles are by: V. Kaminskaia, 1948 S.G.P. 6 33; I. Tishkevitch, 1955 S.G.P. 6 29; N. Zeider, 1958 Pravovedenie 2 79; A. Kats, 1964 Pravovedenie 2 87; V. Akimov, 1969 Pravovedenie 3 110; S. Polenina 1969 S.G.P. 4 49; A. Pigolkin, 1970 S.G.P. 3 49 [hereinafter cited as Pigolkin]; K. Komissarov 1971 S.G.P. 3 71; V. Tolstoi, 1971 S.G.P. 10 37; S. Alekseev & I. Diuriagin, 1972 Pravovedenie 2 25; V. Lazarev, 1973 S.G.P. 2 20.

11 Eckhoff, *Impartiality, Separation of Powers and Judicial Independence*, 9 Scandinavian Studies 11, 32-33 (1965) [hereinafter cited as Eckhoff].

To this I would add that, not only is the individual judge conditioned by his background, but that the decades, or even centuries, of a traditional training, of particular methods of recruitment, even of the physical characteristics of the place where the job is done, create a corpus of professional habits and assumptions which affects judicial method and, through it, the legal order, and does so all the more strongly for being so rarely made articulate.

Nowadays the word "court"—at least to a lawyer—may mean either the institution or the place; but in the latter sense it conveys the idea of a room—indeed in the United States one speaks of "the court room." But, even as descriptive of a place—in England a relatively modern usage—a glance at its earlier connotations may assist both comprehension and comparison. The typical *court* of the English system—there is one still in Oxford—is not a room but a box. At one end, slightly elevated, is, quite literally, a *bench* for the judges; in front of that, a large table; and, surrounding the table on three sides, is a kind of wooden wall or—and the sight will be familiar to anyone who has visited an English pub—a *bar.*

A brief contemplation of this structure explains a great deal about the common law. In the first place it is small; and one recalls that, until the last century, when the courts sat in Westminster Hall, the picture was not one of several rooms but of one large hall with boxes by each pillar. Secondly the nearness of the *bench* and the table makes it clear that rhetoric, or oratory, would have been quite inappropriate. It was a place for argument of course; but by way of conversation, not set speeches; and nothing was easier—in physical and spatial terms—than for the judge to interrupt the advocate, or for counsel sitting on opposite sides of the table to conduct their case through a discussion with each other and with the Bench. This facility combines with the effect of recruiting judges from the bar—so that the move is only one of a couple of yards—and with the court's awareness of its creative role to produce the distinctive features of the common law style: the four dialogues.

First dialogue: Bench and Bar

The fact that the process of arriving at a decision involves argument and discussion among the judges and advocates leaves its mark on judicial style. Far from being Olympian, detached, "the mouth that enunciates the words of the Law" (in Montesqieu's phrase[12]) the judge is forced to come to terms, openly and explicitly, with the views of counsel; to present, in short, his own assessment

[12] L'Esprit des Lois, Tome I, Livre XI. ch. VI (1842).

of them and, where necessary, his counter-argument. Virtually any reported judgment will contain such phrases as "in deference to the argument of counsel for the plaintiff" or "counsel for the defendant sought to persuade me . . ." and the like. Thus the judge is led to see his own role as not altogether different in kind from that of the bar. His final task is to decide, but as, on the way, he has to deal with the arguments advanced, it is clear on the surface of the judgment that there was a choice as to the result. And further, since the bar know him as a man who was once one of them, they know his strengths and weaknesses; and he knows that they know. He can thus admit his role as judge and yet retain a certain detachment which enables him to assess both his own contribution and that of counsel. Thus Sachs, L.J., after spending years as a judge of the Queen's Bench Division, found himself, after his elevation to the Court of Appeal, faced with a Chancery action. His judgment includes the following passage:

> There is, however, a further matter to which I would advert with the natural diffidence of one who has for the first time entered the hallowed fields of trusts and powers, of uncertainties, and of perpetuities, and has incidentally found roaming there one no less than the Attorney-General seeking to achieve on the construction of a short document the one result which could be manifestly contrary to the legitimate intentions of the dead man and also contrary to the interests and wishes of each and every one of all others concerned.[13]

Second dialogue: among the Bench

At first instance a judge sits alone, but in any higher court there will be more than one judge. The usual practice, at any rate in non-criminal cases, is for each to give judgment. It is thus possible—even when all members of the court agree on the result—to discern differences of approach and argument. This is facilitated when the Court takes time for consideration for then draft judgments are circulated; but—as is common in the Court of Appeal—even when judgment is delivered as soon as counsel have concluded their arguments the judges who speak after the first are able to comment on, and differ from, their colleagues. For instance: "I agree that this appeal should be allowed although the legal route which has led me to this conclusion is not at all points identical with that traversed by the Master of the Rolls. After all, that is the beauty of the common law; it is a maze and not a motorway."[14]

---

[13] Re Leek, [1968] 2 W. L. R. 1385, 1396 (C.A. 1967).

[14] Morris v. C.W. Martin & Sons Ltd., [1966] 1 Q.B. 716, 730 (C.A. 1965) (Diplock, L.J.).

If a diversity of approaches to the same result is a commonplace of English law, the presence of the dissenting judgment is even more striking. Its author will analyse, dissect, and attempt to refute the arguments of the majority; so the court, far from being unanimous, anonymous, laconic and poker-faced is visibly displayed as divided. The dissent may vary from the courteously devastating: "[For the majority] to proceed thus does not accord with my conception of the proper administration of justice,"[15] to the wryly baffled as where MacKinnon, L.J., on the construction of a difficult statute, confesses:

> [H]aving once more groped my way about that chaos of verbal darkness . . . I have come to the conclusion, with all becoming diffidence, that the [lower] court judge was wrong in this case. My diffidence is increased by finding that my brother Luxmoore has groped his way to the contrary conclusion.[16]

The dissenting judgment has two main effects. Firstly it makes it perfectly clear to the world that the court had a choice; that it was not a matter of fitting facts to law and getting that answer as from a slot-machine. Secondly it highlights those areas of the law which are developing and uncertain. It is no accident that those parts of private law in which the lower courts of France and the USSR most frequently diverge from the decisions of the Supreme Courts—in the field of automobile and industrial injuries—are precisely those in which the House of Lords is likely to be divided 3-2.

The judicial candour of the dialogue among the judges has never seemed alien to the common law. In the civil tradition of both France and Russia it has been strongly opposed. Thus Odilon Barrot argued: "It would, no doubt, be possible to compel each judge to state his reasons. This would make each judge responsible . . . but would entail the serious disadvantage of reducing the weight of the decision by revealing to the public the diversity of opinions that went to make up that decision."[17]

Third dialogue: with the past

The English judge converses with the dead. He has to, for several reasons. As there are in general no codes, the law is what his predecessors have laid down; and the rule of precedent obliges him to come to terms, in public, with arguments from the past. While the *Cour de Cassation* or the USSR Supreme Court can

[15] Bedson v. Bedson, [1965] 2 Q.B. 666, 698-99 (C.A.) (Russell, L.J.).

[16] Winchester Court, Ltd. v. Miller, [1944] K.B. 734, 744 (C.A.)

[17] De L'organisation judiciaire en France 69, *quoted by* S. Kucherov, Courts, Lawyers and Trials Under the Last Three Tsars 39 (1953).

reverse itself completely on a fundamental issue without ever admitting this, the House of Lords in such a situation would feel bound to analyse and evaluate the older decision, to accord it respect and to overrule it only by producing compelling reasons.

The most frequent instance, of course, is not of overruling but of extending, refining, and applying. Virtually every tort case of the present day contains a reference to Lord Atkin's speech, forty-two years ago, in *Donoghue v. Stevenson.*[18] Lord Diplock has recently paused, as it were, in the middle of deciding a case, to give an analysis of this type of dialogue. "[T]he judicial development of the law of negligence rightly proceeds by seeking first to identify the relevant characteristics that are common to the kinds of conduct . . . involved in the case for decision and the kinds of conduct . . . which have been held in previous decisions of the courts to give rise to a duty of care . . . . The choice to extend [liability] is given effect to by redefining . . . in more general terms. . . ." His Lordship then describes the decisions of his predecessors Ashurst, J., Blackburn, J., Willes, J., and Lord Atkin—in cases spanning a century and a half—as "landmarks in the common law . . . instances . . . where the cumulative experience of judges has led to a restatement in wide general terms of characteristics of conduct and relationships which give rise to legal liability."[19]

Fourth dialogue: with the future

Because the English judge—especially of an appellate court—knows that his judgment will be cited as authority in arguments yet to come, he must be conscious of the effect of today's case on tomorrow. He will, in consequence, often adopt the approach: if I decide this way, what will be the likely effect on future conduct in this sphere. For instance, in imposing liability on a council whose building inspector had carelessly certified a privately-built house as safe, and where the plaintiff was the second purchaser, Lord Denning candidly admits "This case is entirely novel. . . . It seems to me that it is a question of policy which we, as judges, have to decide. . . . I ask: If liability were imposed on the council, would it have an adverse effect on the work? Would it . . . hold up work unnecessarily? . . . I see no danger. If liability is imposed on the council, it would tend, I think, to make them do their work better, rather than worse. In some cases the law has drawn the line [because] . . . if no limit were set there would be no end to the money payable. But I see no such reason here for limiting dam-

---

[18] [1932] A.C. 562.

[19] Dorset Yacht Co. v. Home Office, [1970] A.C. 1004, 1058-59.

ages. . . . Finally I ask myself: If we permit this new action, are we opening the door too much? Will it lead to a flood of cases . . . ?"[20]

In contrast to the features just described, the judgments of the *Cour de Cassation* and—though to a lesser extent—of the Soviet Supreme Court are terse, addressed to the one issue, and apparently, as it were, instantaneous; they hold few echoes from the past and do not set out to reverberate into the future. In both countries the judges, from the beginning of their professional training, form a separate career-group from that of the bar, becoming at first something the equivalent of the American judge's "clerk," then taking a seat on one of the lower or provincial tribunals and so working up. The effect of this separate training interacts with the constitutional role of the courts as will be shown later.

Thus the four dialogues described above leave no traces on a French or Soviet law report. There is, however, one relationship of which the common law knows little: that with the public power. In France its representative is the Procurator-General of the Republic, with his staff of advocates-general. Technically, theirs is a judicial office—the *magistrature debout* as opposed to that *du siège* and there is some career movement between the two branches; but the *parquet*—so called because their table used to stand on the floor at a lower level than that of the *bench*—does not have the same guarantee against removal as do the judges proper. The corps derives from a long tradition of independence; it is not a watchdog of State—as opposed to individual—interests but, according to the traditional formula was "instituted to watch over the observance of statutes and decrees, see that judgments and decisions are enforced, and defend the interests of the incapable and of charitable bodies."[21] Thus the Procurator-General or his staff act as a kind of institutionalised *amicus curiae* and, as such, intervene in all kinds of civil actions the outcome of which can have no possible political or public significance. It is in their submissions to the Court that one finds the features so familiar to a common-law judgment: a review of previous cases and of academic opinion; a discussion of policy factors such as insurance; and observations on the possible future effect of the course proposed. But the Court is in no way bound by these submissions; and, whether they are adopted or rejected, the judgment will usually do so without counter-argument.

In the USSR the name is the same—Prokuror-General—and his office was, in fact, copied from the French.[22] His functions are far wider than those of his French counterpart but, for our pur-

[20] Dutton v. Bognor Regis U.D.C., [1972] I Q.B. 373, 397-98 (C.A. 1971).
[21] Vincent, Procédure civile No. 177 *et seq.* (1969).
[22] G. Morgan, Soviet Administrative Legality (1962).

poses, his important powers are those of taking a case *proprio motu* by way of "protest" to a higher court for reconsideration, and of presenting his submissions to the tribunal. Unfortunately these are rarely published, but one comes across many cases of his acting as a watchdog on behalf of individual parties and of his asking the court—not always, of course, with success—to think again.

JUDICIAL STYLE

In the style of judgments as reported are to be found reflections of the constitutional position of the courts; of their relationship with other bodies; of their role as presented by academic writers; and of the judges' training, selection and self-awareness. It is the actual words used by the judge which set the tone of the system and reveal the nature of law as a social institution. The point is best made by extracts.

An English style: from Gray v. Barr (1971)[23]

> LORD DENNING, M.R. Mr. and Mrs. Barr have a prosperous business at Tooting in ladies' blouses, which they run together. In 1965 they bought a country home at Warlingham. About a quarter of a mile away there was a farmer and his wife, Mr. and Mrs. James Gray, of Farleigh Court Farm. The Barrs had three boys. The Grays had a boy and a girl. On Guy Fawkes day the Barrs had a bonfire party for the children and the Grays brought their children to it. The families became friends. But the results were disastrous. Mr. Gray and Mrs. Barr fell in love with one another. By May 1966, Mr. Gray had become so infatuated with Mrs. Barr that he wanted to make his life with her. He left the farm and his wife and children—all without a word—and went out to New Zealand. He gave Mrs. Barr £240 to buy her ticket out to join him. But, before she went out there, Mr. Gray's father told him that he must come back for the sake of the farm. So, in October 1966, he returned to England and ran the farm. But he still kept seeing Mrs. Barr. So much so that Mrs. Gray could not stand it any longer. She separated from him. He bought her a house in Edenbridge, 15 miles away. She had the children there with her. Mr. Gray entered into a deed of maintenance providing for her and the children. He stayed on alone in the farmhouse running the farm, but no doubt still seeing Mrs. Barr. In May 1967, he took Mrs. Barr to Scotland for a week's holiday. When they came back Mrs. Barr went to her mother's for three days and then returned home to her husband. At first she told him that she wanted to stay with him, but also that she still loved Mr. Gray. But on Tuesday evening Mr. and Mrs. Barr went out to dinner at the country club and then she told him to his great delight that she did not love Mr. Gray

[23] [1971] 2 Q.B. 554, 564-65 (C.A.).

any more and was coming back to live with him, Mr. Barr. They went back to their home hand in hand.

Now comes a tragic sequence of events. Mr. Barr went into the kitchen of his house to make up the boiler, and afterwards to the lavatory. His wife, he thought, had gone upstairs. But when he went up to join her, she was gone. He looked everywhere for her, but could not find her. He thought that she must have gone back to Mr. Gray. He got out the car and drove first towards her mother's and then back to Mr. Gray's farm. He drove in the gates, but turned round and went back again to his own house. He asked his cousin who was there: "Have you found Ethel?" She said, "No." Mr. Barr by this time was in a terrible state. He was crying and praying at the same time. He thought that his wife must have gone to Mr. Gray at the farm. He went to the dining room and picked up his shotgun. (He had bought it from Mr. Gray six months earlier.) His cousin said to him: "You don't need that, Bill." He said nothing. He took up a handful of cartridges and loaded two of them. He asked his cousin to come with him. She would not. He went out with the loaded gun. He drove up to the farm. He got out of the car, leaving the engine running. He opened the front door. There at the head of the stairs he saw Mr. Gray. Mr. Gray said: "Come in, Bill." He called out: "Is Ethel here, Jim?" Mr. Gray said: "No, she is not." Mr. Barr said: "I want to see for myself." He went up the stairs, holding the gun at the port. He was determined to see into the bedroom. But Mr. Gray stood in the way. He said: "Put that bloody thing down and get out." Exactly what happened next is not clear. Two shots went off. The first went up through the ceiling. The second killed Mr. Gray.

It was all a mistake. Mrs. Barr was not in the bedroom. She was not even in the farmhouse. She was lying in the woods 100 yards from her home, unconscious, having taken an overdose of sleeping tablets. She had attempted to commit suicide. She was found early next morning, taken to hospital, and recovered in three weeks. She and her husband are now together again, with their family and their business.

A literary critic might well classify this as the style of Simenon. The sentences are short, the words simple and, if possible, monosyllabic. Facts are given—the ladies' blouses or the bonfire party, for instance—which are quite irrelevant to the legal issues involved but whose mention is revealing: they build up the impression that the judge, far from being a detached, Olympian figure is acutely conscious of his role in helping out in the aftermath of a very human affair. The structure of the paragraphs is deliberately dramatic: "Mrs. Barr was not in the bedroom. She was not even in the farmhouse. She was lying in the woods. . . ." There is an important sense in which this shows the judge as involved, even as enjoying the story; *not* as a mere spectator, there for the thrill, but as a judge who perceives—and reveals—that it is in the sad tangles of human life that the law is secreted.

This section is headed "*an* English style" since there are as many different versions as there are men on the bench. Unlike their Continental brethren the English judges make no attempt to write a "judicial" prose in the sense of one accepted medium. Lord Denning, M.R. is perhaps unusual in his treatment of facts and in his candour as to the legal choices open to him—the latter is shown in the earlier extract. One weapon he never uses is irony; but to his brethren it often comes naturally as a handy tool of argument. A judgment of Megarry, J., for instance, will be studded with such phrases as: "This may be the law; it might even be equity; but it is indisputably remarkable."[24]

But, whatever the individual differences of formulation, it is generally true that the English style is closely tied to—and indeed relishes—the facts; that it uses exaggeration, irony, and other devices to make its point; that it accepts the need to meet and rebut argument; and that it is candid as to the options open.

The French Style: Cour de Cassation 1.12.69[25]

> THE COURT;—On the single ground:—Whereas it appears from the findings of the judgment complained of that Sandrock, being near to a collision between the automobile of Veidt and the moped of Martin, in the course whereof the latter's engine caught fire, attempted to put out the flames with an extinguisher but was wounded when the petrol tank exploded;—Whereas it is complained that the court of appeal ordered Martin to compensate the damage caused to Sandrock on the ground that a rescue contract had been formed between the parties, but there can be no agreement without the consent of the parties and the judgment did not mention that of the victim;—But whereas the court of appeal did not have to find the express consent of the victim since, when an offer is made in his exclusive interest, the offeree is presumed to have accepted it; that having, within their sovereign power, concluded that a rescue contract had been formed between Sandrock and Martin the judges of appeal were quite right to hold that the victim was obliged to compensate the damages sustained by one who lent assistance through benevolence; therefore the ground cannot be accepted; For these reasons, reject.

The French style is evident from the very beginning of the report. The case is referred to by its date and, although the parties' names are reported, it is not by them that the judgment will be remembered. It is "THE COURT" and not a single judge which is

[24] Re Figgis, [1969] 1 Ch. 123, 149 (1968).
[25] D.S.1970.422, note by Puech.

presented as speaking. Its whole judgment is cast in one sentence, and this is true of all French judgments no matter how lengthy the facts or how complex the law. This verbal style is at once a symptom and a technique. It is a reflex of the precept of article 5 forbidding the judge to lay down general rules and of the whole tradition that it is for the legislature and not the courts to make law; so, by expressing the judgment in that particular grammatical form, an impression is given that all is an easy deduction from the principles of enacted law.

The very act of decision implies a choice; but the French grammatical technique enables the judge to conceal this. If one looks at this particular case in the round, certain policy considerations appear. It is in the interests of accident victims that they should receive help; and of rescuers that they should be indemnified against risks. Were the decision to go the other way there is a danger that, in future emergencies, prudent passers-by will emulate the Priest and the Levite. The defendant is insured. An action in tort might lie but there are problems of proving fault; whereas by construing a contract—"I offer to help you if you recompense any injury I sustain"—the plaintiff wins with, presumably, some influence on future behaviour in like situations. But the only hint of this that appears in the judgment is in the final reference to the kind of moral considerations associated with the word "benevolence." Other particular omissions may be noted. Firstly, the failure to cite an article of the Code. The trouble here is that the only relevant rule is that of article 1108 which requires *consent* as an essential condition for the validity of an agreement. Clearly the defendant's case was based on this; but the second omission is of any argument in rebuttal. Indeed—and thirdly—the Court, in saying that acceptance is "presumed" appears to be acting in flat defiance of article 5, though this is not even remotely acknowledged. And finally one notes the absence of any findings as to the behaviour of the automobile driver, whose role in responsibility is not discussed at all; and that there is no discussion of the general policy considerations outlined above.

There are many other examples of the French style of handling injury. When Madame Dehen picked up a bottle in a supermarket and was injured by its explosion before reaching the check-out the choice was clearly between tort—which might involve questions of fault—and sale, under which liability is strict. The Court of Cassation devotes one phrase to the issue: "the liability of [defendant] to the victim could only be contractual."[26] In another recent case the defendant bloodbank supplied blood to a hospital which gave

[26] Cass. civ., Oct. 20, 1964, D.S. 1965.62.

the plaintiff patient a transfusion. The blood turned out to be infected with syphilis. The lower court's finding of fault—sufficient for the tort action in which the case was brought—was doubtful, as, had the blood been checked by the defendant, the incubating disease would not have been discovered. The Court of Cassation noted this but averred that "it is for [this] Court to *restore their true character to the legal relationships deduced* from the facts found by the judge . . ." and found a contract (with strict liability) for the benefit of the third party, the plaintiff.[27]

This paper is not concerned with the results of such cases but with their style of expression. It will be seen from the three examples given that the language is of assertion, not of argument. But more than this, it is existential and descriptive, not normative and prescriptive. The supermarket's liability "can only be" contractual; the Court of Cassation *restores* relationships to their *true* character. It is a clear example of Eckhoff's observation that "expressions associated with knowledge and perception (*e.g.*, 'examine' 'see' 'find' and 'is') occur much more frequently than do expressions associated with evaluation, preference and choice."[28]

The Soviet Style: RSFSR Supreme Court Plenum 28.6.26[29]

> The principle of mixed liability is unknown to the Civil Code. Life, however, creates circumstances of harm arising which are significantly more complex than those provided for by law. In many cases it would be quite wrong to place responsibility in full on the tortfeasor, while in others it would be no less mistaken that he should be entirely exonerated from liability. Particular difficulties in judicial practice have arisen when, along with the gross negligence of the victim, there occur equally gross carelessness, indifference and so on on the part of the tortfeasor. For instance the court in this case finds that the victim was in a state of intoxication at the moment the damage (injury) was caused but at the same time the railroad employees failed to observe the rules on sounding a warning whistle, cutting speed and so on. In such cases the courts have ordinarily either ignored the victim's gross negligence and imposed liability for the injury in full on the railroad or [other defendant] or have denied the victim any redress.
>
> The Court considers the application of the principle of mixed liability necessary in such cases. Its essence is the following: in so far as the harm is caused by the incorrect, careless or negligent actions of both tortfeasor and victim,

27 Cass. civ., Dec. 17, 1954, D. 1955.269, note by Rodière (emphasis added).
28 Eckhoff, *supra* note 11, at 19.
29 Sbornik raz'iasnenii Verkhovnogo Suda R.S.F.S.R. 149 (Stuchka ed. 1931) [hereinafter cited as Stuchka].

the liability for the damage must be 'mixed' that is it must be placed equally, or in some proportion, upon both.

It will be seen that the Soviet style falls between the personal and idiosyncratic judgments of the common law and the elegant austerity of the French. This is partly due to the institutional role of the court. In the extract above, while it is dealing with a particular fact situation, it takes the opportunity to review similar cases. It freely admits its creative role and that the Code is insufficient to cope with life's problems. Homely illustrations are given and the remedy is laid down in simple language. The style is, admittedly, largely that of officialdom (and the phrase "mixed liability" might displease a purist) but the tone is that of a tribunal admitting the existence of problems, acknowledging the possibility of different solutions, and buttressing its proposed remedy, if not by formal argument, at least by example and by an appeal to common sense.

The extract was taken from a case of the 1920's because that was the heyday of the Supreme Court's creative power. In several other situations it reproached lower courts with taking a "formal" stand on the words of the statute—perhaps its most striking creation in this field was to broaden the tort law for industrial injuries. The relevant statute permitted such an action—for the excess of earnings lost over social security payments—only where the employer was guilty of "a *criminal* act or omission"[30] but the Supreme Court simply read the word as "negligent."[31] Similarly, in rescue cases involving State property and injury to the rescuer, the Court invented liability in defiance of what it again referred to as a "formalist" position.[32]

If the Soviet higher courts appear less creative today, one reason is that they did their work so well that many of their earlier decisions have simply been elevated into articles of the more recent civil codes.

The Paradox of Precedent

Within the common law world, the English have been the high priests of precedent. But, as any lawyer knows, even the strictest doctrine leaves a good deal of leeway; and it is within this leeway and through the tensions between a perfect theory and a developing society that the new law grows.

---

[30] R.S.F.S.R. 1922 Grazh. Kod. (Civil Code) § 413(2).

[31] Decisions of June 9, 1924 and July 18, 1927, reported in Stuchka, *supra* note 29, at 174, 176.

[32] Pigolkin, *supra* note 10, at 56.

The vital effect of the extreme English position, however, when taken with the institutional position of the courts, the training of the judges, and the role of the bar, is that any higher tribunal is forced, openly and in public, to come to terms with itself both past and future. Precisely because Blackburn, J., or Lord Atkin were making law, today's judge must reckon with them; precisely because he is making law, he must look to his successors. The paradox is that a constitutional system which gives great power to the judges finds it necessary, by a doctrine of precedent, to make responsible the exercise of that power; while a system which denies the creative role of the judge sets him free to legislate. This cannot, however, be shown by any one facet in isolation; it emerges only from a consideration of all the elements discussed above.

The "legislative" power of the French judges can be demonstrated easily. The following case—translated in full—deals with the issue of enforcing injunctions. The problem is that there is no power to commit for contempt; that article 1142 declares that *damages* is the remedy for breach of a duty to act or refrain; and that they may not exceed the loss sustained and (in appropriate cases) profit foregone by the plaintiff. The case turns on the legality of the *astreinte*—a monetary penalty fixed by the court for non-compliance and payable to the plaintiff even though far in excess of his loss.

> THE COURT;—On the single ground in its two branches:—Whereas it is complained that the judgment under attack, in assessing the total of an *astreinte* ordered earlier to ensure performance of an obligation to act, took into consideration the culpable resistance of the debtor without taking into account the damage caused to the creditor by the delay in performance, while, according to the motion, the judge who assesses an *astreinte* is bound not to exceed the total damage, a finding as to which is indispensable to justify the order;—
>
> But whereas, in deciding that the provisional *astreinte*, a measure of constraint entirely distinct from damages and, in the final analysis, nothing more than a means of overcoming resistance to the execution of a court order, is not designed to compensate the damage caused by the delay and is normally assessed in terms of the gravity of the fault of the recalcitrant debtor and of his means, the court of appeal, whose judgment is reasoned, has legally justified its decision; For these reasons, reject.[33]

Once again the points of comparison are obvious. The Court discusses no facts. In fact the defendant was carrying on an indus-

[33] Cass. civ., Oct. 20, 1959, D. 1959.537, note by Holleaux. The decision has now been codified into Law No. 72-626 of July 5, 1972; D.S.L. 1972.361.

trial process and was presumably committing some sort of nuisance, the profits of which exceeded his neighbour's loss. No article of the Code is cited—none could be—and the one article to the contrary (1142), far from being distinguished, is not even mentioned. Counsel's arguments are not met. Only six years previously the same court—though in a different fact situation—had announced precisely the contrary rule of law.[34] And finally the Court gives no thought to the future: what is to be done where the defendant is not making that extra profit?

Thus the Court of Cassation can act more decisively and more boldly—not less—than the English court. The case just quoted is perhaps peculiar to France; but one cannot envisage the English judiciary construing supermarkets, bloodbanks, or accident rescues as contractual situations so as to make it easier for the plaintiff.

Once again, the Soviet court occupies an intermediate position. Compared with an English report its style is dull; compared with the French it is helpful. For instance, the interminable litigation in the latter country on the strict liability of a "*gardien*" was largely obviated in the USSR by a guiding explanation as to what is meant by the "guardian" (*vladelets*) of a source of increased hazard. Thus the driver, the machinist and the like do not fall within the category; nor is one who proves that the source left his control through no fault of his own but through the illegal act of a third party; in that case the latter is strictly liable.[35]

A 1971 case demonstrates that the Federal Supreme Court is still anxious to get things right. The plaintiff's eye was injured by a splinter of metal while he was working on a vice. The Court undertakes a fairly full review of the facts and directs a finding for him, saying "[r]egardless of the experience and qualifications of the worker, the creation . . . of conditions enabling him to carry out his work in safety is the job of the administration, which is required also to check the workers' observance of technical safety regulations, including the use of protective measures . . . when jobs are being simultaneously carried out in one place the benches should have safety grids. . . ."[36] At first sight there may seem nothing unusual in this review of the facts. But nowhere does the Court mention a date or an article of the Code. In fact the decision is a reversal of that of the RSFSR Supreme Court taken *ten years earlier* which had denied recovery on the ground that the plaintiff's own experience should have made him wear goggles.[37] Thus we find,

---

[34] Cass. civ., Feb. 27, 1953, S. 1953.I.196.

[35] Decree of U.S.S.R. Sup. Ct. Plenum of 23.10.1963, Sbornik postanovlenii plenuma Verkhovnogo Suda 1924-70, 109 (1970).

[36] U.S.S.R. Sup. Ct. Bull. 311 (1971).

[37] R.S.F.S.R. Sup. Ct. Bull. 42 (1961).

in 1971, the Plenum of the Federal court interpreting, *sub silentio*, a Civil Code then repealed; so that the plaintiff's justice, though long delayed, was not, in the end, denied.

CONCLUSION

In attempting a brief comparison of the judicial method of three countries I have tried to emphasise the interrelationship of many factors: the position in constitutional theory, the training and background of the bench, the demands made on judges, and the way in which they see their role. It seems that the systems all require some area of tension within which the judges can act. In England this is provided by the play of precedent; in France by the way in which the courts pay literal lip-service to their restrictions and, by the very style so imposed, free themselves from the Code. In the USSR the fecund tensions come from several sides. The Federal Principles of Civil Law, for instance, give the *plan* as one of the sources of civil rights and duties. Further, there is a potential creative conflict between article 88 al.4—"Harm caused by lawful acts must be compensated only in cases provided for by statute"—and article 5 al.2: "In exercising rights . . . citizens . . . must . . . respect the rules of socialist cohabitation and the moral principles of a society which is building communism."

The final point is merely a tentative suggestion. The Soviet system is seen by the judges as developing and responsive to change and so as part of a process. The striking contrast is between English and French law and lies in the attitude to *time*. Thus in substantive law the classic preoccupations of the civilians have been —following an old tradition—the law of sale and—in modern times —that of tort. But both of these are, by and large, instantaneous incidents which produce their results here and now. The *typical* creations of the common law are the estate and the trust. The former welds the notion of time into its concept of "ownership"— "for an estate in the land is a time in the land, or land for a time, and there are diversities of estates which are no more than diversities of time. . . ."[38] The trust, likewise, is an institution designed to endure and within whose temporal structure the concepts of estate and fund can interlock.

A similar point may be made about legal method. The French judgment—like the contract of sale—appears as instantaneous, new-minted; it no tomorrow has, nor yesterday. The English judge seems to feel that his role this morning is no bar to a conversation with his predecessors nor is it without relevance to the future; and

[38] Walsingham's Case, 2 Plowden 547, 556 (1579) (Barham).

he must accept both the facilities *and the limits* of that position. It was suggested that a helpful insight into the common law might be afforded by imagining the judge in the box described above. But the point is that it is the same box.

[18]

Japanese Way of Legal Thinking

by *Takeyoshi Kawashima**

Ladies and gentlemen, it's a very great honor for me to be able to speak to you on the subject entitled, *The Japanese Way of Legal Thinking.* As you probably know, many westerners believe in a myth which has developed concerning the psychology of the Japanese people. The myth tells us that many things in Japanese culture are completely opposite to everything in the western society. There is some basis for this belief. For example, when we want to call someone to come toward us, we use a wave of the hand for this purpose. However, in western society this signal is almost universally interpreted to mean waving good-bye to the person. Since the end of World War II with increased contacts between Japanese and westerners there has been a greater understanding about the psychology of the Japanese. Today, there seems to be less and less basis for this myth. At the same time, there does, however, exist a way of legal thinking which is specific to Japanese culture and her people.

As many of you already know, much of the law of contemporary Japan was originally imported from western society. Its initial influence came from French legal education and legal institutions. After the Meiji constitution was promulgated, the German school of legal thinking predominated the writing and thinking of Japanese lawyers and scholars. With the end of World War II and particularly during the post-war period of occupation, the ideas of Anglo-American law gradually came into our legal thinking. Despite these many influences, I would say, however, that the basic structure of the Japanese legal thinking of today is predominantly influenced by German legal thought. But this does not mean that the legal thinking of Japanese lawyers is completely western through and through. This is not the case. Upon examination, we can find significant elements which illustrate non-western ways of thinking. This "traditional way" of thinking permeates the doctrines of law, the decision making of judges and the practice of law generally.

Today, I want to take up only one aspect of this subject which I would call the semantic tradition of Japanese language and law. There are, of course, numerous other aspects which I would say are specifically Japa-

* Takeyoshi Kawashima, Professor Emeritus, University of Tokyo Faculty of Law.

nese in their spirit and context. I might, for example, point to aspects such as the weakness of the notion of legal right, or the spirit of ideal harmony in human relationships, or the relationship between law and morality. Keep in mind that my topic represents only one aspect of the Japanese way of legal thinking.

In European society and in America, every word has a definite meaning. In western societies, it is presupposed, expected or even taken for granted that the meaning of every word should be clear, limited and fixed. If it were otherwise, communication would be confusing and our way of thinking would be disturbed. In Japan, however, the tradition is just the opposite. In Japan the traditional notion or expectation concerning language is that every word has some meaning which represents only the core of its many possible meanings. Around this core there lies rather an area of ambiguous meaning which fades away into zero through the process of interpretation. The meaning of a word is not expected to be definite, limited and fixed. It is intended to undergo change according to its use and application in a wide variety of possible situations. In this connection it is important to understand something about the correlation between non-normative assumptions or epistemology and legal ethical theory. It is also important to understand the contrast between the epistemology of naive realism and that of logical realism.

Naive realism is the special characteristic of the Japanese culture, while logical realism is much more characteristic of western thought. The naive realist views the images of man and society through his senses with a certain degree of empirical immediacy without resorting to abstractions. Ideas and feelings are suggested by concrete objects rather than being represented by abstract concepts. On the other hand, the logical realist construes the images of man and society through abstractions and concepts. For instance, in its beginnings, the aboriginal Japanese language itself did not have words through which an abstract idea or concept might be conveyed or communicated. When it was necessary, such words were borrowed from Chinese symbols and combined with Japanese characters. Thus, in contrast with contemporary western society is the fact that in the traditional culture of the Japanese, nature and society are accepted as they appear to the immediate empirical senses. The indeterminate quality of nature and society with its subtle and infinite variety is regarded as a welcome attribute. It is to be valued because by its very nature it is unlimited and contains infinite possibilities for development and expansion. This basic assumption not only permeates traditional Japanese culture, but is equally evidenced by the Japanese language which is not a suitable vehicle for detailed and determinate expression or precision in communication. For example, many of our writers have to be translated into English with much longer sentences than in the original Japanese, requiring numerous detailed expressions so as to make it understandable to western readers. In the English manner of writing, although the meaning of words is much clearer, at the same time such attempts at precise definition makes the language appear to be more limited and shallow. We do not make such an effort in our writing. The Japanese uses words which allow sufficient leeway to suggest various things and permit the reader to supplement the rest with that which is not expressed but only possibly suggested. The sentence of the westerner tries to restrict its meaning as narrowly and in such detail as possible so that there is no room at all for the imagination of the reader. In Japanese literature and in our daily communication the author or speaker tries to say something with very few words and with very vague meanings. The rest is supposed to be interpreted or supplemented by listeners and readers through associations. An example from Japanese literature is the very short form of poetry called haiku, which consists of three phrases with each phrase consisting of five syllables, seven syllables and five syllables respectively. In other words the whole poem consists of only seventeen syllables. An example might be translated as "Frog, a frog jumped into an old pond." My guess is that most western society people would not understand it. As a Japanese I feel to some extent that I can understand it, though I am not sure why it is considered a masterpiece. For the Japanese people it has greater meaning through the association it suggests or implies. For the Japanese, this haiku creates a rather mystic atmosphere which is completely quiet. Then the only sound is the splash made by the frog. The quietness comes back and the poet feels himself to be very lonely but spiritually purified. For the Japanese such associations are important. The only problem may be that such stimulus could cause too great a series of associations in the minds of readers of this poem. But if the western people read this, it is very likely that this kind of association would not occur.

Perhaps this explanation of the Japanese language has been too long, but I think it is important because language and words are very important elements of the law in civilized societies. In the legal traditions of western societies the law is made up of general norms or principles which are verbal statements consisting of terms artifically elaborated by logical reasoning or defined through a high degree of abstraction. It seems to me that is the very essence of the legal propositions or precepts expressed in European continental law. In its essence the law of Anglo-American society appears to be similar since it also represents logical thinking through words which have very specific and limited definitions. This creates some problems since very strictly stipulated definitions of legal terms appear to be incomprehensible to laymen in Anglo-American societies with the result that lawyers are blamed for using very strange jargon. I think this may be inevitable in European societies as well. For instance, the French are very proud of their Code Civil because it uses only words harmonious to laymen. Actually, the meanings of those words are not easily understandable by laymen even though most of the terms used are simply taken from daily images and a common vocabulary.

To me the question of legal thinking based on words with very strictly defined concepts is very interesting since in Japan legal reasoning is based on verbal propositions with ambiguous, changeable, and elastic meanings. In Japan the meaning of words used in legal principles or in statutes is taken for granted by Japanese people as being necessarily ambiguous and elastic. Here, the people would not be surprised to discover that the meaning of law sometimes is changed, shaped and sometimes distorted by policemen, prosecutors, lawyers and by judges during the legal process. It is inevitable, of course, in every society that lawyers and judges have to change the meaning of law in order to adjust the existing law to a new set of circumstances after the original legal norms have appeared. In European or Anglo-American societies, however, the scope and manner in which lawyers or judges can change or adapt the meaning of the law to a particular situation or set of circumstances is limited. However, in Japan it seems to me that the limit itself is not as clearly established. Let me give you an example which illustrates the Japanese legal mind or consciousness in this respect.

When I was in California the parking meters permitted parking only for five minutes for five cents or ten cents. During my visit, a policeman gave me a parking ticket even though the meter had registered a violation only by a minute or less. The policeman told me that the meter had passed the limited time and therefore, the fine had to be paid. When I told this story in Japan, my friend who is a prosecutor laughed. In Japan, if you apologized very, very politely, you would be dismissed from the violation. But if you were absolutely arrogant, then you would have to pay the fine. In Japan everything depends upon each particular situation and circumstance. While we have definite rules and limits in our laws, I think that the basic difference lies in our attitudes toward the language of the law and its enforcement. It is taken for granted by lawyers, prosecutors and judges that the meanings of words of law are subject to change by interpretation. As I stated earlier, in every society the interpretation of words of law or statutes is inevitable, particularly at a time of change. However, in western society, this kind of change through interpretation appears to be possible only as a last resort and not at the beginning of an instance or situation. In Japan it is understood from the beginning of a legal enactment that the meaning of law is changeable and not definite. This appears to be a peculiarly Japanese characteristic of legal thinking. Thus, when the parliament debates some legal enactment, often there are heated discussions about the meaning of terms. Yet, once the measure is enacted into law such debates lose their importance. This is due to the fact that traditionally Japanese lawyers and scholars do not regard the debates of legislators as being binding upon judges. In Japan the records of debate in the Diet have no particular meaning for retrospective interpretation.

Along the same lines, I should like to make one final point regarding the Japanese way of legal thinking and its relation to code revision. In Japan, once a measure is enacted into law, revision is very difficult and such instances are actually very rare. The reason for this is very simple. Code revision is not felt needed or to be desirable because change is always possible and accepted through interpretation. In this respect, I often like to say that the written provisions of Japanese law are just like the Cinderella story. Interpretation is the magic wand with which everything needed can be accomplished through some kind of semantic manipulation.

In summary, I would like to point out my belief that this semantic tradition in Japan is really contradictory to the basic values which are required for a modern, democratic society which needs predictable judicial decisions. Sooner or later we will have to change our traditional attitude toward the meaning of words, especially in our laws. Although our semantic tradition serves our literature well, it does not function with the needed precision and limits in our laws. Thank you.

[19]

LEGAL REASONING IN ISLAMIC LAW AND THE COMMON LAW: LOGIC AND METHOD

THE LOGIC OF LEGAL REASONING IN RELIGIOUS AND NON-RELIGIOUS CULTURES: THE CASE OF ISLAMIC LAW AND THE COMMON LAW

WAEL B. HALLAQ*

I. INTRODUCTION 79
II. ROLE OF LOGIC 81
III. TYPES OF ARGUMENTS USED IN BOTH THE COMMON LAW AND ISLAMIC LAW 82
A. *Deduction* 82
B. *Legal Analogy* 85
C. *Induction* 91
IV. CONCLUSION 95

I. INTRODUCTION

It is only reasonable to assume that dissimilar legal systems possess dissimilar patterns of legal reasoning. Inasmuch as two legal systems differ in their structure and function, they also differ in the types of arguments they employ in their service. It may well be argued that law is, in the final analysis, the product of the premises and methods from and through which it is derived. Two such legal systems which display a vast difference in their overall structure and function are Islamic law and the common law.[1] This paper proposes to shed some light on the logic of legal

*Assistant Professor of Islamic Law and Theology, Institute of Islamic Studies, McGill University, Montreal; B.A., Haifa University, Israel; M.A. and Ph.D., University of Washington. I should like to record my thanks to Professors Marjorie Rombauer, John Haley, and James Hardisty of the University of Washington Law School for their helpful comments on the common law part of this paper.

[1] Islamic law and the common law are treated here synchronically rather than diachronically. The convenient point of departure, insofar as this paper is concerned, is the phase of intellectual maturity of both systems falling in Islamic law, in the period after the tenth century A.D., and in common law, in the end of the last century and the present one. It is not implied that common law could reach intellectual maturity only toward the end of the nineteenth century; the concern of this paper is with analytical jurisprudence and the role of logic in law. Therefore, one cannot speak of such mature theory in common law before the latter part of the past century.

reasoning in both orders as well as to analyze the reasons and background which give rise to differences and similarities in their methods of reasoning. This will be done with the intent of bringing out some of the major factors which operate on the level of the judicial process and which contribute to the creation of differences in legal orders. The focal comparison in such a study must be the relationship between the logic of the law and the amount of emphasis given to social change in secular and religious cultures.

This, it must be pointed out, is a preliminary investigation which awaits a more thorough and comprehensive study—primarily because legal logic in Islam has not yet been analyzed, and our knowledge of the methods of legal reasoning subsumed under what is commonly known as *qiyās* is still rudimentary. This is particularly evident from the fact that, with very few exceptions, modern scholars of Islamic law translate *qiyās* as analogy without realizing the existence of other arguments (e.g., *a fortiori* argument in both its forms, the *a minori ad maius* and *a maiori ad minus*, *reductio ad absurdum* and induction) which are comprised by that nomenclature. This paper is not aimed at arguing for the existence of these arguments in *qiyās*; rather, it presupposes them. This presupposition, however, is fully justified by the sources cited herein.[2]

By way of introduction, it must be noted that the general attitude of Islamic and common law lawyers[3] towards logic cannot be described as positive. Although lawyers from both systems find logic an indispensable tool for the systematization and consistency of legal concepts and doctrines, logic generally remains suspect.[4] Surely, in each case, this attitude is the result of different causes. The Islamic lawyer resists logic because he views it as an offshoot of Greek philosophy. For him the unqualified acceptance of logic entails the acceptance of metaphysical conclusions which run against the fundaments of his belief as Muslim. Only when logic is stripped from its theological implications and used merely as a tool does the Islamic lawyer consider it legitimate.

In common law, logic is also rejected whenever it is conceived as a

---

[2] Subsequent to the submission of this Article to press, further investigation of the arguments subsumed under *qiyās* led to the conclusion that, to the exclusion of the *argmentum e contrario*, which was considered as a linguistic argument, *qiyās* encompassed the arguments enumerated above. For a documented account of this investigation, see the author's *Non-Analogical Arguments*, in SUNNI JURIDICAL QIYAS (forthcoming).

[3] For purposes of convenience, the terms "lawyers," "judges," and "jurists" will be used loosely in this paper. The judges are primarily responsible for the development of common law, while the jurists undertake such a responsibility in Islam. Islamic law, like Roman law, is jurists' law. Despite usages such as "the Islamic lawyer," this distinction must always be kept in mind. On Islamic law as jurists' law, see J. SCHACHT, AN INTRODUCTION TO ISLAMIC LAW 209 (Oxford 1964); Weiss, *Interpretation in Islamic Law: The Theory of Ijtihad*, 26 AM. J. COMP. L. 199, 201-03 (1978).

[4] H.J.M. BOUKEMA, JUDGING 180 (1980); Goldziher, *The Attitude of Orthodox Islam Toward the "Ancient Sciences,"* in STUDIES ON ISLAM 198-209 (M.L. Swartz ed. & trans. Oxford 1981); Guest, *Logic in the Law*, in OXFORD ESSAYS ON JURISPRUDENCE 176 (1961); Simitis, *The Problem of Legal Logic*, 3 RATIO 1, 94 (1960).

rigorous tool of inference. Of great concern are the results to which logic may lead against the constantly changing social reality. Law, Justice Holmes said, is "the resultant of a conflict at every point between logic and good sense—the one striving to work fiction out to consistent results, the other restraining and at last overcoming that effort when the results become too manifestly unjust."[5] By this statement, Justice Holmes implied that logic brings about formal consistency of concepts irrespective of the consequences when applied to concrete matters of fact. The heart of the problem, common law lawyers argue, is compromising the necessary logical deduction from non-contemporaneous premises with contemporary problems, while simultaneously taking into account social and ethical questions.[6] Although this is a major problem facing the common law lawyer, the question of the serviceability of logic in law as a normative system[7] constitutes yet another insurmountable difficulty. To this last point we shall return later.

II. Role of Logic

Although the notion of "high authority" as a source of law lingers in the background of the common legal tradition, it would be accurate here, for all intents and purposes, to state that common law is rooted in, or grafted to, sociology. As such, it is to be construed in sociological terms. Common law is an instrument of social control and its relevance to society is an ever-present element in the mind of counsel as well as of the court. On the other hand, law in Islam is conceived not as a means employed in the service of society, but, rather, in the service of God, who alone knows what is best for society. Islamic law delineates the dictates of divine will, and it is perceived as the ideal way in which man can worship his Creator. It is an all-encompassing law which covers every conceivable human act, from liturgical forms to neighborly conduct, to partnership and homicide. Its sources are the Quran, the Sunna of the Prophet, the consensus of the community and its scholars, and the method of inference known as *qiyās*. Through the latter, which is the primary concern of this paper, the law is derived from the former three sources. Whatever these sources dictate becomes the law governing all Muslims. The changing social reality, at least in theory, has no effect whatsoever on the process of judicial reason-

---

[5] Dewey, *Logical Method and Law*, 10 Cornell L.Q. 17, 20 (1924).

[6] J. Stone, Legal System and Lawyers' Reasonings 285-86 (1964); J. Stone, The Province and Function of Law 170 (1946).

[7] As a normative system, law contains propositions which function as major premises in syllogistics. Norms are not statements; therefore, they are neither true nor false. The difficulty stems from this very fact because the validity of deductive logic hinges on the necessary relation between the truth of the premises and the truth of the conclusion. *See* C. Wellman, *Deduction in Legal and Moral Reasoning*, in Reasoning on Legal Reasoning 193 (A. Peczenik and J. Uusitalo eds. Helsinki 1979); Guest, *supra* note 4, at 183-86. For a general discussion of the normative character of law, see F. Castberg, Problems of Legal Philosophy 24 (Oslo 1957).

ing. Only when these religious sources enjoin the protection of a certain human need does the law allow for that need and for those analogous to it. Should this need change because of new circumstances and conditions, the Islamic lawyer stands helpless in the face of the omnipotent sources. For example, one cannot alter a rule based on an explicit textual injunction and still characterize that rule as Islamic. Islamic law is not a law enacted by Muslims; rather, it is enacted by God, for Muslims. Human reason cannot make law; it only functions as the means by which law is discovered. Thus, instead of being organically tied to social exigencies, Islamic law is rooted in divine volition and authority, whether or not this authority takes cognizance of social reality.

Legal reasoning in common law thus differs from its Islamic counterpart in that it is bound by facts and norms which, while relevant to the conclusion, are not entirely intrinsic to the premises. Reasoning in common law recognizes the validity of a legal norm (conclusion) although such norm may not follow entirely from the given, established rules (premises). Admittedly, this somewhat lax procedure is often insisted upon in common law in exchange for a more mutable and flexible law. In Islamic law, on the other hand, the jurist is bound only by those premises which are prescribed by the religious sources, and, unless a certain ambiguity in the premises allows the inclusion or exclusion of certain material facts, nothing that does not follow from the premises can or should be joined to the conclusion.

Common law lawyers conceive logic as the organ by which one seeks to discover the conditions under which a conclusion follows from given premises. In other words, logic is viewed as concerned with the validity of the conclusion as it relates to the premises from which it is derived. Common law lawyers, interested as much in the truthfulness and validity of the legal premises and their relevance to changing situations, have always attempted to curb the overuse of formal logic in law. Although to a certain extent Muslim lawyers expressed their own reservations about logic, they have been considerably less successful in resisting the influence of logic on law.

III. Types of Arguments Used in Both Common Law and Islamic Law

A. Deduction

Admittedly, both legal systems use deductive logic, particularly when general principles and rules are laid down.[8] Under a broad principle, the

---

[8] O.C. Jensen, The Nature of Legal Argument 25 (1957); R. Cross, Precedent in English Law (3rd ed. Oxford 1977); Abu Ḥāmid al-Ghazāli, Mi^c^yār al-^c^Ilm fi Fann al-Manṭiq 154 (H. Sharāra ed. Beirut 1966); Ibn al-Ḥājib, Mukhtaṣar al-Muntaha al-Uṣūli 9-16 (Cairo 1326 H.); Abdel-Rahman, *La Place du Syllogisme Juridique dans la*

judge subsumes the case which needs a solution, and applies the general legal principle to that particular case. Such an operation, though purely deductive, seems so intuitive that one need not be thoroughly familiar with logic to conduct it. When it is established, for instance, that things intoxicating are forbidden in the Quran, little analysis is needed to reach the rule that whisky, vodka, etc., are forbidden by law. Similarly, it takes common sense to deduce from Quran V:96 which reads, "And I permit to you the catch of the sea . . .," that feeding on fish, shellfish, and other animals which inhabit the sea is permissible. Judge Cardozo has asserted that, when the Constitution or a statute supplies the rule which fits the case, "the judge looks no further."[9] In the works on Islamic legal theory and jurisprudence, the role of deductive logic in the process of legal reasoning is seldom discussed. Perhaps this is because Muslim jurists reckon that there is little mental endeavor involved in deductive-legal operations. For them it is simply a question of subsumption. In cases where deduction is used, however, the role of the judge is still significant. To reach a decision, the judge must first undertake the difficult task of establishing the exact meaning of the relevant law, and then ascertain its applicability to the new case from a purely legal standpoint.

Perhaps as a result of the impact of modern formal logic, common law lawyers, as well as other Western legal theorists, have gone well beyond their Muslim counterparts in discussing the relevance of deductive logic to law. An articulate treatment of this subject has not been undertaken in Islam,[10] although Western lawyers have dealt with it somewhat unsuccessfully. The judgment that *A* is guilty of offense *X* and must therefore be punished by *Y* can be a conclusion of a syllogism in which the major premise is a statute and the minor premise is a set of facts about *A*. This conclusion certainly differs from the conclusion in the classic syllogism "All men are mortal; Socrates is a man; therefore, Socrates is mortal." The latter conclusion is a factual statement, whereas the former's factuality hinges upon several conditions yet to be fulfilled. Such a distinction between legal and non-legal syllogism does not seem to disturb some common law lawyers. Sir Rupert Cross, for instance, has observed that "[o]ne allowance must certainly be made for this distinction, but it may yet be the case that there is a sufficient resemblance between the methods by which the conclusion is reached to justify the description of each of them as an example of deductive reasoning."[11] The acceptance of non-factual or

Méthode Exégétique chez Gazali, in LE RAISONNEMENT JURIDIQUE 185-94 (H. Hubien ed. Bruxelles 1971). *See also infra* note 43 (further on the deductive character of some *qiyās* arguments).

[9] B. CARDOZO, THE NATURE OF THE JUDICIAL PROCESS 14 (1964).

[10] Two of the few jurists who discussed this problem are Abu Hâmid al-Ghazâli and Taqi al-diǹ Ibn Taymiyya. *See supra* note 8 and *infra* notes 37 & 48.

[11] R. CROSS, *supra* note 8, at 178.

normative statements in legal deduction is the result of the fact that the logic of norms has not yet been worked out.[12]

The lack of a practical solution for this and other problems[13] in deductive legal reasoning has prevented common law lawyers from dwelling too long on them. Deduction remains the most central, though by no means the only, method by which general legal principles are applied to questions of fact. Notwithstanding all difficulties, both legal systems find deduction an indispensable tool of legal reasoning.

In addition to syllogistics, both Muslim and common law lawyers use other arguments which take the form of deduction. The first is *reductio ad absurdum*, which is often used to reach a conclusion about a case by making a certain assumption and then proving that this assumption contradicts an established legal norm. The judge asserts, for instance, that *X* is a goal that the law *ought* to promote; but *Y* impedes, or would impede, the realization of *X*; therefore, *Y* ought to be prevented by law. Another instance of this argument may be the assertion that *X* is a goal which the law ought to promote; accepting *Y* as legal would defeat the realization of *X*; therefore, *Y* ought not be legally recognized. This argument abounds in both legal systems.[14] Also very common is the *a fortiori* argument by which a law governing a certain situation is extended to another more obvious situation. This is of two types: *a minori ad maius* and *a maiori ad minus*. An example of the first type is the inference from the Quranic injunction "Say not 'fie' to them (i.e., to parents) nor repulse them, but speak to them graciously"[15] that mistreating or beating parents is forbidden. Here the legal norm is transferred from a limited act to a more general one. The second type requires a reversal of this process, i.e., from the general to the particular. For instance, from the rule that the consumption of large quantities of wine is prohibited, it is ruled that the drinking of the smallest particle of wine is also prohibited.[16]

---

[12] Guest, *supra* note 4, at 185; Summers, *Logic in the Law*, 72 MIND 257 (1963).

[13] Following Aulis Aarnio, Carl Wellman has succinctly analyzed eight problems which arise in legal as well as moral deductive reasoning. *See* C. WELLMAN, *supra* note 7, at 193-98.

[14] M. GOLDING, LEGAL REASONING 55-60 (1984). Muslim jurists term this argument *qiyās al-ᶜaks*, and logicians *qiyās al-khulf*. *See* SAYF AL-DĪN AL-ĀMIDI, III AL-IḤKĀM FI UṢŪL AL-AḤKĀM 3 (Cairo 1968); ABU ḤĀMID AL-GHAZĀLI, *supra* note 8, at 118-19; IBN AL-ḤĀJIB, *supra* note 8, at 15; IBN ABI AL-ṢALT AL-DĀNI, TAQWĪM AL-DHAHN 48 (C.G. Palencia ed. Madrid 1915). The application of this argument is also evident in the formulation of the general principle of *maqāsid* (or *maqṣūd*) *al-sharᶜ* (the aims of the law). *See, e.g.*, ABU-ISḤĀQ AL-SHĀṬIBI, II AL-MUWĀFAQĀT FI UṢŪL AL-AḤKĀM 127-28 (Cairo 1970); SAYF AL-DIN AL-AMIDI, III *al-Iḥkām fi Uṣūl al-Aḥkām* 71-76 (Cairo 1968); MUḤAMMAD B. ᶜALI AL-SHAWKĀNI, IRSHĀD AL-FUḤŪL ILA TAḤQĪQ AL-ḤAQQ MIN ᶜILM AL-UṢŪL 214 (Cairo 1909).

[15] Quran XVII:23.

[16] Later Muslim scholars often refer to the *a fortiori* argument as *bil-aḥra*. Shāfiᶜi, the "master architect" of Islamic jurisprudence, uses it but under the general term *qiyās*. *See* S. RISĀLI, ISLAMIC JURISPRUDENCE 307-08 (M. Khadduri trans. 1961) (It is to be cautioned that Khadduri consistently translates *qiyās* as analogy); IBN ḤABIB AL-MAWANDI, I ADAB AL-

The nature of law and its sources in the Islamic and common legal traditions make it difficult to work out legal concepts solely by means of formal arguments. Lawyers from both systems have acknowledged that deduction is only one of several arguments employed in legal reasoning.[17] Primarily, the lack of universal or general principles contributes chiefly to the relegation of strictly formal arguments to a secondary, often negligible, position. Despite the increasing entrenchment of the legislature on the common law, case law still constitutes the major segment of the common law system. Similarly, Islamic law is characterized by its concern with individual cases rather than with general precepts, a resultant manifestation of the material structure of its two primary sources: the Quran and the Sunna. The Quran was revealed to Muhammad piecemeal in order to fulfill and answer the specific needs which arose during the period of his Mission. Likewise, the Sunna, expressed in a collection of reports of the utterances and deeds of the Prophet, came to answer similar needs in later times. Characteristically, these two sources deal with specific issues and, strictly speaking, contain relatively few general legal principles. It is therefore clear that, like common law, Islamic law is, in a large measure, case law. This fact determines the type of argument and logic which best fits and serves common case law and Islamic law.

B. *Legal Analogy*

One of the most commonly used arguments in both systems, and one which answers most of the law's needs, is reasoning from part to part or case to case, an argument known as legal analogy.[18] The basic course of reasoning is the extension of a legal rule from one case to another due to a similarity which is deemed by the judge to be a material similarity. The form of this argument is as follows:

> *A* has the properties *X*, *Y* . . . .
> *B* has the properties *X*, *Y* . . . .
> *A* has the rule *J*.
> *X*, *Y* . . . are relevant properties in inducing *J*.
> ———————————————
> Therefore, *B* must have the rule *J*.

Such an argument gives rise to serious problems. For the logician, this argument, however meticulous it may seem, remains imperfect at best.

QĀḌI 587-92 (Baghdad 1971); IMĀM AL-ḤARAMAYN AL-JUWAYNI, AL-WARAQĀT (printed with the commentary of Jalāl al-Dīn al-Maḥalli, on the margin of SHAWKĀNI, *supra* note 14, at 199-200) (Cairo 1909)).

[17] C. WELLMAN, *supra* note 7, at 193. See the types of arguments as discussed by ABU HĀMID AL-GHAZĀLI, *supra* note 8, at 102-37.

[18] SAYFAL-DĪN AL-ĀMIDI, *supra* note 14, at 3-10; L. CARTER, REASON IN LAW 12 (1984); E. LEVI, AN INTRODUCTION TO LEGAL REASONING 1-2 (1949).

Muslim logicians and philosophers discard it because it is conjectural and merely leads to probable (*ẓannī*) knowledge. The Muslim and common law lawyers, while realizing its shortcomings, have no choice but to accept it. Undoubtedly, they have striven, within the limits imposed by the nature of such an argument, to strengthen it by supporting arguments with a view toward realizing its utmost potential. The crucial problem posed is determining the element of similarity which justifies the transference of the rule of one case to another. For it is this element which determines the validity of the conclusion.[19] How, in light of such considerations, the common element in analogy is decided in Islamic and common law is perhaps the most illustrative differentiation, not only of the legal reasoning in both systems, but also of their function and goal.

Whether it is taken to be "[t]he ground or reason of decision," or "[t]he point in a case which determines the judgment,"[20] or, as the Muslim jurist would put it, "that which induces the judgment,"[21] the *ratio decidendi* and the Islamic *ᶜilla* (the relevant similarity which justifies the transference of the judgment from the precedent to the new case) have remained the most illusive doctrines in common law and Islamic law. In Britain and the United States, this doctrine has been a major concern of a number of experts since the beginning of this century; in Islam, it occupied major portions of jurisprudential theories for several centuries. The first major attempt at defining the rules for finding the *ratio* of a case was made by Professor Goodhart in 1930. He concluded that the *ratio* is neither found in the reasons given in the judge's opinion nor in the rule of law set forth in that opinion. Nor is it necessarily found by a consideration of all the ascertainable facts of the case and the judge's decision. Rather, Goodhart argued, the *ratio* is to be found by taking account of (1) the facts treated by the judge as material, and (2) his decision as based on them. In finding the *ratio* it is also necessary to establish what facts are held to be material by the judge.[22] In other words, Goodhart proposes that a later court is bound by the presumably applicable precedent and its ruling, as an outcome of the judge's consideration of the material facts determined in the earlier case.

---

[19] The German scholar Urlich Klug properly remarked that the difficulty in using analogical argument lies in the obscurity of the distinction between essential and unessential respects. *See* J. HOROVITZ, LAW AND LOGIC 32 (1972).

[20] BLACK'S LAW DICTIONARY 1135 (rev. 5th ed. 1979). *See also* R. CROSS, *supra* note 8, at 76-79 (adopts any rule of law expressly or impliedly treated by the judge as a necessary step in reaching a conclusion and discusses means of ascertaining the *ratio decidendi* from a case).

[21] *See, e.g.*, ABU ḤUSAYN AL-BAṢRI, II AL-MUᶜTAMAD FI UṢŪL AL-FIQH 704-05 (Damascus 1964-65); MUḤAMMAD B. ᶜALI AL-SHAWKĀNI, *supra* note 14, at 207.

[22] Goodhart, *Determining the Ratio Decidendi of a Case*, 40 YALE L.J. 161 (1930). A summary of this article may be found in Goodhart, *The Ratio Decidendi of a Case*, 22 MOD. L. REV. 117 (1959).

After lengthy polemics in the *Modern Law Review* about the *ratio decidendi,*[23] Professor Julius Stone argued that Goodhart was attempting to set forth a prescriptive theory rather than a descriptive account for determining the *ratio decidendi.*[24] Stone found this unacceptable. He maintained that in each precedent there is implicit a number of *ratio decidendi,* and it is left to the deciding judges to determine, in light of current exigencies (e.g., public policy, ethics, justice), the "appropriate level of generality" in the precedent which must prevail in the new case.[25] It is not the material facts in the earlier case which must dictate the decision of the later court but rather "the analogical relevance of the prior holding to the later case," which requires "the later court to choose between possibilities presented by the earlier case."[26] Representing what may be termed "the sociological school of jurisprudence," Stone emphatically argued that the later court is the final arbiter of which *ratio* is applicable to the case in question.[27]

> In short a "rule" or "principle" as it emerges from a precedent case is subject in its further elaboration to continual review, in the light of analogies and differences, not merely in the logical relations between fact situations, and the problems springing from these; but also in the light of the import of these analogies and differences for what is thought by the later court to yield a tolerably acceptable result in terms of "policy," "ethics," "justice," "expediency" or whatever other norm of desirability the law may be thought to subserve. No ineluctable logic, but a composite of the logical relations seen between legal propositions, of observation of facts and consequences, and of value-judgments about the acceptability of these consequences, is what finally comes to bear upon the alternatives with which "the rule of *stare decises*" confronts the courts, and especially appellate courts. And this, it may be supposed, is why finally we cannot assess the product of their work in terms of any less complex quality than that of wisdom.[28]

Thus, "wisdom" and, as Justice Holmes stated, "good sense," must be employed in determining the *ratio* rather than a mechanical or fixed set of

---

[23] Some of the articles include: Goodhart, *The Ratio Decidendi of a Case*, 22 MOD. L. REV. 117 (1959); Montrose, *The Ratio Decidendi of a Case*, 20 MOD. L. REV. 587 (1957); Montrose, *Ratio Decidendi and the House of Lords*, 20 MOD. L. REV. 124 (1957); Simpson, *The Ratio Decidendi of a Case*, 20 MOD. L. REV. 413 (1957); Simpson, *Ratio Decidendi of a Case*, 21 MOD. L. REV. 155 (1958).

[24] Stone, *The Ratio of the Ratio Decidendi*, 22 MOD. L. REV. 597 (1959). For a useful summary of the main thesis of this article, see J. FARRAR, INTRODUCTION TO LEGAL METHOD 69-71 (1977).

[25] Stone, *supra* note 24, at 618.

[26] *Id.* at 604-05.

[27] *Id.* at 618.

[28] *Id.*

logical rules.[29] The lack of serious attempts in the Anglo-American legal tradition to "prescribe" methods by which a *ratio* of a case can be decided is an eloquent testimony to the disinterest of common law lawyers in a permanently defined and inflexible set of rules which might control and limit the ability of law to adapt itself to the changing reality.[30]

On the other hand, the Islamic lawyers, being acutely conscious of the religious character of their law, stress the dictates of the sources of law rather than the needs of the new cases to which they seek to find the "sound" solutions. Divinity has expressed its will in the Quran and sunna which are deemed not only the ideal guides in man's life but also the final revelation to mankind. Thus, insofar as deciding a new case is concerned, the Muslim jurist can operate on two levels which are determined by the nature of these two sources. On the first level, the jurist is bound by the explicit textual statements and commands. What determines the judgment in the new case is solely the explicit *ratio* in the original text, i.e., the precedent. There is little latitude for deciding the case in light of current exigencies. On the second level, however, the jurist is allowed a certain, although limited, freedom of interpretation in deciding the new case, due to the ambiguous nature of the textual precedents.

This paper is not concerned with the linguistic principles which come into play in determinating the *ʿilla*; it focuses on the logical and perhaps semi-logical tools employed for this purpose. The first condition set forth for finding and establishing the *ʿilla* is its efficiency, that is, its causal relationship with the judgment. The property or properties which constitute the *ʿilla* must bring about a judgment. Joining an inefficient property to the *ʿilla* will no doubt spoil that *ʿilla*. Intoxication, for instance, is an efficient property which necessitates the judgment of prohibiting the consumption of wine. Should it be assumed that redness is a property which together with intoxication effects the judgment of prohibiting red wine, it must then always be assumed that in any judgment of prohibiting

---

[29] *Id.* at 619.

[30] The increasing concern with the flexibility of law brought about certain changes in the effect of precedent in the House of Lords. In 1966, Lord Gardiner, the Lord Chancellor, representing the Lords of Appeal in Ordinary, declared the following:

> Their Lordships regard the use of precedent as an indispensable foundation upon which to decide what is the law and its application to individual cases. It provides at least some degree of certainty upon which individuals can rely in the conduct of their affairs, as well as a basis for orderly development of legal rules.
>
> Their Lordships nevertheless recognize that too rigid adherence to precedent may lead to injustice in a particular case and also unduly restrict the proper development of the law. They propose therefore to modify their present practice and, while treating former decision of this House as normally binding, to depart from a previous decision when it appears right to do so.

M. Zander, The Law-Making Process 104 (1980).

intoxicants the property of redness must be present in conjunction with the property of intoxication. Otherwise, the *ᶜilla* which is extended to a new case, say white wine, becomes invalid because the property of redness is inefficient due to its absence from white wine, while the same judgment of prohibition remains in effect. Since part of the *ᶜilla* has no efficiency beyond the case of red wine, the *ᶜilla* as a whole is rendered invalid.[31]

The second method is coextensiveness (the presence of the *ᶜilla* when the judgment is present) and coexclusiveness (the absence of the *ᶜilla* when the judgment is absent).[32] Like efficiency, this method seeks to emphasize the causal connection between the judgment and its *ᶜilla*. A valid causal relationship must have both the coexistence of the cause and its effect and the absence of one when the other is absent. This method also guarantees the exclusion of an additional, unnecessary *ᶜilla*. If two different *ᶜillas* are claimed to induce the judgment, it is inconceivable that when one *ᶜilla* becomes absent, the judgment becomes absent as well.[33]

In conjunction with these methods, Muslim jurists employ a third theory which may be termed the "joined method of difference and agreement."[34] By the method of difference, it is demonstrated that certain properties, say *A, B, C* . . ., constitute the only difference between the *ᶜilla* in the precedent and the *ᶜilla* in the new case. It is then proved that these properties are inefficient and irrelevant in inducing the judgment. In other words, such an analogy first assumes the total sum of differences between the *ᶜillas X* and *Y* are *A, B, C* . . . . The second premise is that *A, B, C* . . . have no weight insofar as the judgment, *J,* is concerned. Since *X* and *Y* are identical save for *A, B, C* . . ., *J* is the judgment.

As a prerequisite to the method of difference, the method of agreement must come into play. By this method, the similarity between *X* and *Y* is found. Then the judgment of the precedent is transferred to the new case.[35] The method of difference and agreement can be implemented only by use of what the logicians call disjunctive and conjunctive syllogism. Put schematically, the course of reasoning by analogy is as follows:

> *P* has properties *A*, *B*, *C*, *D*, *E*, *F*.
> *Q* has properties *A*, *B*, *C*, *D*, *E*.
> *P* has the rule *J*.
> *F* is not a property in *Q*.
> *A*, *B*, and *C* are not relevant similarities.
> *D* and *E* are relevant similarities and efficient in *J*.

---

[31] ABU ḤUSAYN AL-BAṢRI, *supra* note 21, at 789-90.

[32] ᶜALI SĀMI AL-NASHSHĀR, MANĀHIJ AL-BAḤTH ᶜINDA MUFAKKIRI AL-ISLĀM 111 (Cairo 1966).

[33] *Id.* at 112.

[34] This is reminiscent of Mill's methods of agreement and difference. *See* E. NAGEL, JOHN STUART MILL'S PHILOSOPHY OF SCIENTIFIC METHOD 211 (1974).

[35] MUḤAMMAD B. ᶜALI AL-SHAWKĀNI, *supra* note 21, at 213-14, 219, 220-22.

D and *E* are present when *J* is present and absent when *J* is absent.

Therefore, *Q* has (or must have) the rule *J*.

The effort expended in establishing the *relevant* similarity which, in turn, determines the validity of transferring a judgment of one case to another must be seen in light of the conflict between formal logic and the actual needs of the law. Both Western and Muslim lawyers recognize the insuperable difficulties encountering conclusions by analogy. Some idealists in the West have gone so far as to say that a conclusion by analogy can be valid only after *modus barbara*.[36] The Muslim logician, Farabi, also argued that to be valid, analogy must be converted to the following syllogistic form: All *S*'s are *X*'s; all *A*'s are *S*'s; therefore, all *A*'s are *X*'s. This is so, he insisted, because valid analogy amounts to syllogistic inference. And when a syllogism cannot serve, analogy cannot be valid.[37] However, the imprecise nature of legal propositions and the law's actual requirements prevent jurists from accepting, much less adopting, such arguments. In real life it is rarely possible to ascertain conclusively the exact similitude between all aspects of two cases. Thus, to convert an analogy to strict syllogism would be tantamount to forging a link which is justified neither by the facts in the precedents or in the new case.

Another argument to which Muslim and common law lawyers resort is *argumentum e contrario*.[38] In analogy, the two cases possess a similarity which justifies extending the rule from the precedent to the new case. In the *argumentum e contrario*, the absence of such a link and the diametrical opposition of the two cases brings about a conclusion.[39] The argument may take one of two forms. The first is "*S* is a *P*; therefore, no non-*S* is a *P*." An example of this may be the following: From the rule that several legal residences are allowed for private persons, it is inferred that several legal residences are not allowed for corporations.[40] The second

---

[36] See the discussion in Simitis, *supra* note 4, at 70; Abu Naṣr al-Fārābi, *Kitāb al-Qiyās al-Saghīr*, in 16 REVUE DE LA FACULTÉS DES LANGUES, D'HISTOIRE, ET DE GÉOGRAPHIE DE L'UNIVERSITÉ D'ANKARA 266-68 (1958); AL-FARABI'S SHORT COMMENTARY ON ARISTOTLE'S PRIOR ANALYTICS 93-98 (N. Rescher trans. 1963).

[37] Abu Naṣr al-Fārābi, *supra* note 36, at 267-68; AL-FARABI'S SHORT COMMENTARY, *supra* note 36, at 95. Also see the argument of ABU ḤĀMID AL-GHAZĀLI, *supra* note 8, at 123-25; ABU-ḤĀMID AL-GHAZĀLI, MIḤAKK AL-NAẒAR 31 (Cairo ——). Urlich Klug also argues that in sound analogy the minor premise is subsumed under the major premise just as in any syllogism. Horovitz agrees and argues that analogical inference eventually reverts to syllogism and has no special logical structure of its own. *See* J. HOROVITZ, *supra* note 19, at 33.

[38] SAYF AL-DĪN AL-ĀMIDI, *supra* note 14, at 3; J. FARRAR, *supra* note 24, at 50-51; J. HOROVITZ, *supra* note 19, at 44.

[39] ABU ḤUSAYN AL-BAṢRI, *supra* note 21, at 698-99; ABU ḤUSAYN AL-BAṢRI, KITĀB AL-QIYĀS AL-SHARᶜI, printed with AL-MUᶜTAMAD 1031-32.

[40] J. HOROVITZ, *supra* note 19, at 44.

form, often claimed to be the most important argument in Islamic law after analogy,[41] may be best illustrated by the well-known example about the purity—or impurity—of pets. The ruling that dogs are impure is reached on the basis of a Prophetic report making the Prophet refrain from visiting a residence in which a dog is present, but allowing him to visit another residence in which there is a cat. The Prophet then remarks that "(the cat) is not impure." This statement, coupled with the fact that he withheld his visit to the residence of the dog's owner, led to the conclusion that dogs are impure.[42]

C. Induction

The last of the major arguments common to both systems is induction[43] which, unlike deduction or analogy, bases itself more often than not on conclusions reached by other arguments. Except for a relatively few cases in the Quran and the Sunna where ready-made solutions are given, cases in Islamic law are ordinarily solved either through analogy from case to case, or by deduction through the subsumption of a case under a general

---

[41] ABU ḤUSAYN AL-BAṢRI, *supra* note 39, at 1031-32; SAYF AL-DĪN AL-AMIDI, *supra* note 14, at 3.

[42] ABU ḤUSAYN AL-BAṢRI, *supra* note 39, at 1036.

[43] Guest, *supra* note 4, at 188-90; ABU-ḤĀMID AL-GHAZĀLI, *supra* note 37, at 62-63. Notably, Muslim legal theoreticians do not always agree with regard to the types of arguments subsumed under *qiyās*. Only in a few works, such as those of Abu Naṣr al-Fārābi, Abu Ḥāmid al-Ghazāli, and Taqi al-Dīn Ibn Taymiyya is one presented with more or less a full account of these arguments. However, a close examination of the definitions of *qiyās* in the jurists' writings reveals that these definitions are left broad enough to allow the inclusion of many types of arguments. Some of the common definitions of *qiyās* are the following: (1) "predicating a known thing to another (known thing) on grounds of a common matter [i.e. cause] in order to establish, or negate, a rule for both of them" (*ḥamlu maᶜlūmin ᶜalā maᶜlūmin fī ithbāti hukmin lahumā aw nafyihi ᶜanhumā bi'amrin jāmiᶜin baynahumā min ḥukmin aw ṣifa*); (2) "applying the rule of the precedent to the new case on grounds of a similarity between the two cases" (*taḥṣīlu hukmi al-aṣli fī al-farᶜi li'shtibāhihimā fī ᶜillati al-ḥukmi*); (3) "the subsumption of a particular under a general" (*idrāju khuṣūṣin fī ᶜumūm*). MUḤAMMAD B. ᶜALI AL-SHAWKĀNI, supra note 14, at 198. *See also* ABU AL-WALĪD AL-BĀJI, AL-ḤUDŪD FI AL-UṢŪL 69-70 (N. Ḥammād ed. 1973). For other, but similar, definitions, see F. KHOLEIF, A STUDY ON FAKHR AL-DIN AL-RAZI 151-52 (1966) .

Such definitions are indicative of the inclusiveness of *qiyās*. In his chapter on legal reasoning, ᶜAbd al-Jabbār notes that the form of judicial *qiyās* does not differ from that of non-juridical *qiyās* (*wa-ṭarīqatu al-qiyāsi al-sharᶜiyi lā tukhālifu ṣūratuhā ṣūrata al-qiyāsi al-ᶜaqli*). Ghazāli held the same view and added that the difference between the two is only in the premises. "The premises which are good for rational *qiyās* are good for juridical *qiyās*, but not all the premises which are good for juridical *qiyās* are good for rational *qiyās*" (*lā mukhālafata baynahumā fī ṣūrati al-qiyāsi wa'innama yatakhālafāni fī al-mādati, bal mā yaṣluḥu an yakūna muqaddimatan fī al-ᶜaqliyyāti yaṣluḥu lil-fiqhiyyāti, walākin qad yaṣluḥ u lil-fiqhiyyāti ma la yaṣluḥu lil-ᶜaqliyyāti*). ᶜABD AL-JABBĀR AL-ASADABĀDI, XVII AL-MUGHNI FI ABWĀB AL-TAWḤĪD WAL-ᶜADL 280 (Cairo 1963). *See* ABU ḤĀMID AL-GHAZĀLI, *supra* note 8, at 154. *See also* author's article *Non-Analogical Arguments*, in SUNNI JURIDICAL QIYAS (forthcoming).

principle. In induction, the common rule for a number of cases is extended to another case because this case is similar or identical in relevant aspects. Induction is then possible only when a number of identical cases exist. The form of the argument is: *A*, *B*, *C*, *D* . . . are cases which have the common characteristic *X* and the rule *J*; all cases which have the characteristic *X* must have the rule *J*; *S* has the characteristic *X*; therefore, *S* has (or must have) the rule *J*. A concrete example of induction from Islamic substantive law is the case of interest (*ribā*). The Prophet was said to have prohibited the exchange of gold for gold, silver for silver, date for date, wheat for wheat, and barley for barley unless they were equal in quantities and delivered immediately. The *ᶜilla* for this prohibition was determined (e.g., in the Ḥanafi School) to be their nature as fungible commodities sold by weight and measure. For this reason, exchange by unequal amounts was prohibited.[44] In accordance with this line of reasoning, all goods possessing this *ᶜilla*, such as raisins, must be subject to prohibition if exchanged under the aforementioned conditions.

The question then becomes: What differentiates induction from analogy in legal reasoning? The legitimacy of this question derives from the fact that the relevant similarity between the new case and the already solved cases is the same. This being so, an analogy between the new case and a single precedent would suffice. However, the common law lawyers would object that the extention of the rule by induction leads to a degree of certainty which is higher than that attained in analogy. The multiplicity of cases (instances) gives inductive support to the rule of the new case which analogical inference fails to provide. Thus, as in scientific induction, legal induction in common law belongs to a class of arguments superior to that of analogy; it stands in the middle position between analogical and deductive arguments.

In Islamic law, induction ranks even higher on the scale of certainty. It can be complete (perfect), leading to the same degree of certainty yielded by deduction. The entire corpus of common law is, as a practical matter, unlimited, making complete induction infeasible. In Islam, however, the sources of the law are defined and exhaustible. A complete enumeration of the instances supporting or negating a point of law yields the highest degree of certain knowledge about that point, provided counter-evidence does not exist. In the context of religion where a single explicit statement in the sources has a force of finality, it may be argued that multiple propositions should lead to a degree of certainty at least tantamount to that yielded by deduction. Such an inductive process would simply constitute a multi-deductive argument. For this reason a number of Muslim jurists hold complete legal induction to have a force equal to deductive arguments. However, even when incomplete, induction derives its force

[44] ᶜABD ALLĀH B. MAUDŪD AL-MUSILI, II AL-IKHTIYĀR LI-TAᶜLIL AL-MUKHTĀR 30-33 (Cairo 1951).

from the relative number of instances which can be observed with regard to a particular case. "The larger the number of pieces of textual evidence is, the stronger our knowledge becomes."[45]

In addition to its function as a method of reasoning, induction in Islamic law plays the significant role of reinforcing uncertain or weak premises. The equivalent of such a role is not to be found in common law. In the Islamic legal system, uncertain propositions from the Sunna (which alone constitutes the greatest bulk of the legal sources) may gain an added aggregate support by use of the inductive method, transforming them into certain premises.

How does this process work? To answer this question, it must first be observed that the dicta of sunna are divided into two basic categories: the *mutawātir* and the *aḥādi*. The *mutawātir* traditions are transmitted by countless persons who hear or see the Prophet say or do a certain thing. The large number of transmitters makes it inconceivable that the witnesses or the transmitters could have agreed on falsifying the report. Due to the authenticity of such a report and the certitude surrounding its transmission, the *mutawātir* traditions are said to lead to certain knowledge of what they contain. Traditions transmitted by fewer people than those who have witnessed and transmitted the *mutawātir* traditions are called *aḥādi*. The latter, when taken individually, do not lead to certain knowledge of the information they convey. Accordingly, when used individually as premises in an argument, a *mutawātir* tradition with an explicit meaning leads to certainty while an *aḥādi* tradition with the same clarity of meaning leads only to probable knowledge. Thus, rules based on individual *aḥādi* traditions are only tentative and experimental. Many Muslim jurists, however, argue that *aḥādi* traditions can lead to certain knowledge if they are supported by other pieces of circumstantial evidence (*qarā'in*) which may include other traditions of the same type and indecisive or ambiguous Quranic verses.[46] These textual pieces of evidence must, when interpreted, have the same meaning as the tradition which they purport to support. Another precondition for reaching certainty in such an arrangement is the number of supporting traditions and verses: They must be altogether as numerous as those in the *mutawātir* category. But unlike the latter which cannot, whether individually or collectively, be dubious, an *aḥādi* tradition can only be probable insofar as its authenticity is concerned. The aggregate of *aḥādis*, however, cannot be

---

[45] *See* ABU HĀMID AL-GHAZĀLI, *supra* note 8, at 120.

[46] Indicisive or ambiguous (*mutashabihāt*) verses are capable of more than one interpretation. If an indecisive verse can be interpreted in such a way as to support the meaning of an *aḥādi* tradition, this verse is said to be a *qarīna*, a supporting piece of evidence. An unambiguous Quranic verse cannot be used as a *qarīna* to support an *aḥādi* tradition, because, by itself, it constitutes indisputable evidence which need not be supported by any *qarā'in* (plural of *qarīna*). However, a deductive or analogical argument based on an unambiguous verse can always become inductive if other ambiguous verses conveying the same meaning are available.

dubious because Muslim jurists reason that a multitude of reports transmitted through so many channels and by so many transmitters who could not have known each other cannot possibly constitute a lie or a conspiracy in fabricating the report. In their multiplicity, the *aḥādi* traditions gain a strength tantamount to that of the *mutawātir*.[47]

The doctrine of inductive support is undoubtedly the product of a compromising approach to blend the elements of form and material substance in legal argument. Unlike the Aristotelian logicians who were primarily concerned with form, Muslim jurists paid equal attention to the material substance of the premises in relation to the degree of certainty to which they can lead. The emphasis that Islamic law places on the premises as the determinant of the degree of certainty of the conclusion may be illustrated by discussing the views of the influential Ibn Taymiyya on this subject.

Ibn Taymiyya's argument must be seen as a response to the traditional view which holds syllogistics superior to analogy. Against this view, he argues that syllogism and analogy are equivalent because any analogical argument can be converted to first figure syllogism.[48] Writing in the Islamic tradition, Ibn Taymiyya sees the analogical argument as consisting of four terms: (1) the *aṣl*, the precedent which is extracted from the scripture; (2) the *farᶜ*, the new case requiring a solution; (3) the *ᶜilla*, the similarity common to the *aṣl* and the *farᶜ*; and (4) the *ḥukm*, the rule which is transferred from the former to the latter. The weakness of analogy does not lie in its form since it can be converted to syllogism. Rather, the weakness lies in the material substance of the premises and, more particularly, in the *ᶜilla*. "If the subject matter (of the premises) is certain, whether the form of the argument is analogy or syllogism, then (the conclusion) is certain."[49] For instance, should the jurist conclusively establish that the consumption of wine was forbidden in the Quran because it is an intoxicant, he would be able to convert this possible analogy to a syllogism in which the major premise is "All intoxicants are forbidden;" the minor premise is "Vodka is an intoxicant;" the conclusion is "Vodka is forbidden;" with the middle term being the property of intoxication.[50]

---

[47] ABU BAKR AL-SARAKHSI, I UṢŪL 292 (Abu al-Wafa al-Afghāni ed. Cairo 1372 H.); BAYḌĀWI, II MINHĀJ AL-WUṢŪL 197-205, with Sh. Ismāᶜīl's II TAHDHĪB SHARḤ AL-ISNAWI (especially last paragraph of p. 205) (Cairo 1976). In fact, Shāṭibi went so far as to say that induction is the only method by which certainty can be reached in law. *See* SHĀṬIBI, I MUWĀFAQĀT 10-15 (1969).

[48] TAQI AL-DĪN IBN TAYMIYYA, JAHD AL-QARIḤA FI TAJRID AL-NAṢIḤA (an abridgement by JALĀL AL-DĪN AL-SUYŪṬI OF NAṢĪḤAT AHL AL-IMĀN FI AL-RADD ᶜALĀ MANTIQ AL-YŪNĀN 289, 299-300, 328, 331 (Cairo 1947). *See also* N. HEER, IBN TAYMIYAH'S EMPIRICISM (unpublished).

[49] TAQI AL-DĪN IBN TAYMIYYA, *supra* note 48, at 289.

[50] On the classes of textual premises, see ABU ḤĀMID AL-GHAZĀLI, *supra* note 8, at 155-56. Examples cited are not those of Taqi al-Dīn Ibn Taymiyya but correspond perfectly to his arguments.

Here, the conclusion is formally and materially valid. Thus, whatever form of argument is used, a *certain* middle term will surely lead to a *certain* conclusion. In answer to the question of how one can know for certain whether or not a universal proposition is true, Ibn Taymiyya argues that statements derived from an infallible source (e.g., the Quran) are always certain.

The fundamental idea underlying Ibn Taymiyya's theory of logic in general, and legal logic in particular, is that the knowledge of the external world results from the observation of particular things.[51] Universal propositions are inferred by analogy and induction from particular propositions. If it is true that analogy and induction yield probable knowledge, our knowledge of the external world can only be probable. The only exception, however, is scriptural knowledge, which by virtue of being decreed by God, can only be certain.[52]

IV. Conclusion

This brief analysis of the logic of legal reasoning in Islamic law and common law has shown that the ultimate causes for difference between the two systems stem from the obvious fact that Islamic law is steeped in religion, whereas common law is a product of an essentially secular culture. The effect of this fundamental difference manifests itself in two main areas, the first of which is deductive and analogical reasoning. Law in the common legal tradition is conceived as a man-made instrument of social control which is in need of constant modification in line with social change. Accordingly, judges in common law have persistently endeavored to reason in keeping with the primal need of adapting law to current reality. Deductive logic, as one method of reasoning, is viewed as sufficiently stringent to disallow a gradual change in legal formulations. This is why deduction is often rejected and referred to as "dry logic." The ramifications of this attitude are even more evident in analogical reasoning. The similarity between two cases can justify an analogy on the basis of a *ratio* which the new case dictates, rather than on the basis of a *ratio* which the judge in the earlier case determined. Therefore, the similarity between the two cases becomes that similarity which the current policy of "ethics" and "justice" require. A change of this policy will most likely call for a change in the similarity which will result in a different rule.

Islamic law can be said to be more consistent in the application of logical principles, mainly because of the marginal importance of the element of change in Islamic law. Being strictly religious, law is bound by the letter and spirit of the fixed sources from which it is derived. In the

---

[51] Taqi al-Dīn Ibn Taymiyya can be said to have anticipated the theory of J. S. Mill. *See* E. Nagel, *supra* note 34, at 120-35.

[52] Taqi al-Dīn Ibn Taymiyya, *supra* note 48, at 319, 341; N. Heer, *supra* note 48.

process of formulating the law, the Muslim jurist has no choice but to abide by the prescription of these sources. In accordance with this conception, the current needs of society have no particular importance in determining the similarity between the two cases. The material similarity is that which is dictated by the sources; any analogy to be drawn subsequently (which has been determined by scholars to be valid) must be based on the already established similarity. Thus, logical consistency takes priority over other considerations, including change.

Induction is the second area in which the difference between Islamic law as a religious system and common law as a secular system manifests itself. While induction serves as a method of legal reasoning in common law, Islamic law takes induction beyond this limited scope to employ it for the reinforcement of uncertain legal propositions. As demonstrated, induction can bring greater certainty into law because the bulk of the legal sources in Islam is defined and exhaustible.

All in all, Islamic law can be described as more "logical" than common law. This is clearly the result of the absence of the consideration for change in Islamic law. This seemingly positive characteristic of "logicism" has cost Islamic law a high price, manifesting itself in drastic reforms in the modern era, including the wholesale borrowings of European codes to replace the inoperative traditional laws. Common law, on the other hand, proved flexible enough to forestall the need for such radical reforms.

[20]

EQUITY AND DISCRETION IN A MODERN ISLAMIC LEGAL SYSTEM

LAWRENCE ROSEN*

Kadijustiz is a concept well known from the work of Max Weber. Its essential element, the means by which judicial discretion and equitable assessments are actually made, is, however, less clearly documented. Drawing on a detailed study of a *qadi*'s court in contemporary Morocco, the present article shows how cultural assumptions give shape to the judge's modes of reasoning, factual assessments, and choice of remedies. The study suggests that if careful attention is given to the broader cultural precepts within which judicial discretion is located, *Kadijustiz*, whether represented by an Islamic court official or a Western justice of the peace, will be seen to possess definite regularities.

In *Terminiello* v. *Chicago* (1949), Mr. Justice Frankfurter, commenting on his own court, said: "This is a court of review, not a tribunal unbounded by rules. We do not sit like a kadi under a tree dispensing justice according to considerations of individual expediency." For Justice Frankfurter, as for many others, the image of the Islamic law judge, the *qadi*, is often that of a man sitting barefoot and turbaned under a tree or in the corner of a mosque dispensing justice off the top of his head. Even Max Weber (1967: 351), who appreciated that actual Islamic adjudication was neither capricious nor unrestrained, chose the term *Kadijustiz* to refer to a type of legal system in which judges have recourse to a general set of ethical precepts unevenly employed on a case-by-case basis rather than to a series of rules abstractly formulated and uniformly applied (see generally Turner, 1974: 107-121). Although the traditional role of the *qadi* has been greatly altered by the introduction of western codes and the development of bureaucratic structures, the quest in many Moslem countries for an authentically Islamic way of life has given renewed emphasis to classic

* The research on which this study is based was carried out during three field trips: January, 1967-August, 1968; summer, 1969; and June-October, 1978. Support was provided by the National Institutes of Health, the University of Illinois, and the American Council of Learned Societies. Arabic terms are transcribed in the text without the use of diacritical marks.

precepts of Islamic jurisprudence. It is important, therefore, to appreciate that, far from being arbitrary or unsystematic, *qadi* justice partakes of regularities which reveal not only Islamic legal history but also the interplay between Islamic law and the society in which it is rooted.

Justice Frankfurter's statement, however, points up more than the limitations in our understanding of contemporary Islamic adjudication: it also raises fundamental questions about the nature of discretion and equity within a given legal tradition. Notwithstanding the existence of a body of legal rules or acceptable judicial procedures, the *qadi*, like his colleagues elsewhere, is often called upon to give substantive content to principles that cannot simply be mechanically implemented. How, under such circumstances, is he to define what shall for purposes of adjudication be regarded as a fact? By what means is he to choose among competing solutions? In what way is he to render a decision when the proper justification for his action is not immediately apparent from prior cases or guidelines? And where shall he turn for help when confronted with a situation in which rules, principles, or doctrines of law, if strictly applied, would lead to a result which seems contrary to his own comprehension of what is fair or just for all concerned?

Faced with these problems of equity and discretion, the Islamic judge finds considerable guidance in the precepts, procedures, and forms of judicial reasoning that have shaped the tradition within which he works. But this tradition, from its most settled rules to its most idiosyncratic decisions, is deeply suffused by a set of assumptions and concepts that have currency and implications in the wider cultural context. Thus, in his assumptions about human nature and social relationships, in his comprehension of the role of language and social discourse, and in his perception of recognizable modes of rational decision making, the *qadi* is affected not only by substantive and procedural elements distinctive to Islamic legal thought but also by a set of cultural propositions that render his actions comprehensible, if not universally acceptable, to the society he serves.

Admittedly, within the expansive realm of Islamic law, no single court or local tradition can fully represent all instances. In order to show how the justice of the *qadi* may be at once institutionally distinctive and culturally characteristic—how, in short, law is suffused by culture and culture is integral to law—the close analysis of a particular jurisdiction may prove most illuminating. The present study will, therefore, focus on the *qadi*'s court in the Moroccan city of Sefrou and its surrounding countryside. In this ancient city of 50,000 people lying just south of Fez, and in the hinterland of the Middle Atlas Mountains with a population of 200,000 that it serves, one can see themes with analogues throughout the Islamic world while gaining an appreciation of the way *qadi* justice is embedded in local society and culture.

Factual Determinations and Legal Reasoning: The Nexus of Law and Culture

"It is a feature of the human predicament," says H.L.A. Hart (1961: 125), "that we labour under two connected handicaps whenever we seek to regulate, unambiguously and in advance, some sphere of conduct by means of general standards. . . . The first handicap is our relative ignorance of fact; the second is our relative indeterminacy of aim." For the *qadi*, no less than for judges elsewhere, the dual predicament of factual assessment and purposeful adjudication turns, initially, on the way in which an issue is framed for judicial consideration, the procedures available for assessing proffered facts, and the acceptable style of judicial reasoning and justification.

Pleading and Proof: The Social Construction of a Legal Case

In Morocco, the litigants and lower court personnel are primarily responsible for framing an issue for decision. The petitioner's complaint, whether made out by the court clerk, a public scribe, or the plaintiff, must set forth the nature of the case, the identity of the defendant, and the precise remedy sought. If the complaint lies within the subject matter jurisdiction of the *qadi*—presently limited to those matters covered by the 1958 Code of Personal Status[1] (marriage, divorce, filiation, inheritance, child custody), civil suits for which the amount in controversy does not exceed the statutory limit, or issues involving documents signed by the court notaries—the case will be listed on the court docket. The central concern for court and litigant alike will, however, be the construction of appropriate evidence. Here, the nature of

[1] The Arabic text of the Code (*Mudawwana*), together with an occasionally misleading French version, is most readily available in Colomer (1963, 1967). Portions of the Code also appear in English in Mahmood (1972: 121-128). For analyses of the Code, see Anderson (1958), Borrmans (1977), Lapanne-Joinville (1959), and Gallagher (1959).

persuasive evidence, the role of the court notaries, and the cultural creation of binding assertions become vital.

In a sense, all evidence that comes before the court is conceived of as oral in nature. From the point of view of classical Islamic legal theory, documents are regarded simply as written reminders of individual witnesses' statements, reminders that will serve to recall their testimony in any future dispute (Schacht, 1964: 193; see also Brunschvig, 1960; Linant de Bellefonds, 1965: 130). In actual practice this theory has long since given way to the use of documents as sufficient in themselves for purposes of evidentiary presentation (cf. Wakin 1972). Nevertheless, the *qadi*'s courts in Morocco still tend to scrutinize documents for probative value in terms of the courts' perception of the nature of oral assertions and to consider documents, regardless of the literacy of those involved, as embodying and supplementing that which has been uttered before appropriate court personnel.

The most impressive evidence a litigant may produce on trial is a document signed by two notaries which supports the litigant's factual claim. However, such a document is regarded as simply the reduction to writing of oral evidence presented to the notaries. Thus, in a marriage contract or a deed—the two kinds of documents that appear most frequently in litigation—the notaries merely inscribe the terms that have been orally presented to them by the parties involved. While the notaries may refuse to certify a relationship which is contrary to law—a marriage contract lacking some transfer of wealth from the groom to the bride or her marital guardian, a business agreement for an illicit purpose—it is less in their control over the content of such documents than in the form of validation supplied by such a document that the importance of the notarization process lies.[2] To appreciate this point one must understand the nature of binding obligations in the structure of Moroccan social life.[3]

To many westerners, Moroccan society appears reassuringly exotic and disconcertingly familiar. That women should appear veiled in public, that an ancient walled city should enclose a featureless maze of byways and blind alleys, that the marketplace should be a cacophony of hawking and

[2] By telling potential litigants that their case is of dubious merit, notaries may significantly affect the kinds of cases that come before the court. For an example of a notary discouraging litigation, see Wigmore (1936: 587).

[3] The following analysis of Moroccan society is developed more fully in Geertz, Geertz, and Rosen (1978); and Rosen (1968, 1970, 1972a, 1972b, 1973, 1978).

haggling is somehow more easily comprehended simply for being so different. More troubling, because superficially more recognizable, is the schema of social relationships. Notwithstanding references to tribe or urban quarter, genealogy or religious brotherhood, Moroccan society is not built up of a series of corporate groups for which membership alone might define one's place in society or one's expectable behavior. Quite the contrary, Moroccan society evokes a sense of the familiar by being constructed of a series of interpersonal ties, freely negotiated and highly expedient, which center on each individual. Associations of residence or kinship, identities of interest and occupation, affiliations of friendship and common experience constitute not a binding set of relationships but a repertoire of relational possibilities to be drawn upon in the formation of a personal network of relations. But where the individualism and instrumentalism of this social organization strike a recognizable chord for many Westerners, the nature and implications of the ways in which such ties are conceptualized and formed makes easy identity more elusive. For at the heart of Moroccan personal ties are a series of unapparent assumptions about the order and meaning of social life, assumptions that deeply affect the course and content of judicial decision making.

For Moroccans, every relationship implies an obligation. To be related in a particular degree of kinship, to be another's neighbor, to be the client of a merchant in the bazaar carries with it certain idealized expectations of mutual aid and potential recompense. Of crucial importance, however, is the fact that the specific content, the meaning, of each of these relationships is highly negotiable. Even within a family, for example, one can choose to have closer economic and political ties with some individuals than with others, or with outsiders than with family members. It is, however, clearly understood that every action one takes creates an obligation in the other, and the key to the formation of a network of personal ties, as well as to a sense of how others are most likely to act toward oneself, is to organize and learn about such obligations in the most effective way possible. This sense of mutual ingratiation and indebtedness is broadly subsumed by Moroccans under the central Arabic concept of *haqq*.

The term *haqq* has a variety of interconnected meanings (see Macdonald, 1961: 126). It means "right," "duty," "truth," "reality," and "obligation." In one context it can mean "you are right"; in another, "you are wrong." *Al-Haqq* is one of the ninety-nine names of Allah known to man. (The hundredth, it is said, is known but to the camel; hence his enigmatic smile!) To speak of *haqq* is, in short, to convey that sense of mutual obligations which bind men to men, and man to God. What is "true" or "real" is the web of indebtedness which links sentient beings to one another in a chain of obligations. But since each obligation, of kinship or contract, residence or political aim, is itself subject to negotiation, and since each obligation formed may be fulfilled in a variety of reciprocating forms, each Moroccan must try to get his or her definition of a situation—as implying some specific form of obligation—to prevail. In this highly flexible and manipulable system, this running imbalance of one-upsmanship and ingratiation, one tries to add a degree of certainty by employing some of the recognized social conventions through which particular ties may be given more concrete definition and networks of affiliation an air of predictability.

Thus, one might make a form of ritual sacrifice at the doorway of a particular individual or at the threshold of a saintly shrine, a form of ingratiation which implies that failure to fulfill the request may call forth supernatural sanction. Or one may seek out an intermediary who, because of his own network of ties, can act as an agent for one's present request. One can bargain over the applicable term to characterize a given bond—as a tie among close kinsmen, or as a pact between neighboring tribes—in an attempt to make the broader ideals of these affiliations govern the relationship and its forms of reciprocation. Whether it is in the request for a woman in marriage to a dependent or for help in contacting a government official, the governing factors are the terms by which action will proceed, the knowledge that an obligation formed for one purpose can be called up for quite another, and the recognition that all men are bound up in such personal and ephemeral webs of indebtedness.

But if such obligations are indeed so flexible and changing, how are people to gain a sense of order in their relationships and how is a court of law to recognize a binding tie of a particular sort to which judicial sanction may be applied? The answer, of course, lies in the conventions by which particular obligations are given a degree of fixity in ordinary social life and by a series of mechanisms, consonant with social practice, by which the courts can give concrete meaning to such a bond. If two litigants disagree over their perception of the sort of tie they have indeed negotiated, the court, like the participants, will look to the social conventions characterizing their relation and to the means by which their bond may be said to have taken on concrete obligations. In doing so the court will be mindful of the central importance of language in defining relationships in Morocco.

For Moroccans, no utterance can by itself create a binding obligation. Indeed, because individuals constantly try to get a relationship defined in a personally convenient way, it is well understood that where relationships of obligation are being formed, mere utterances imply nothing about the truth of the thing asserted.[4] For one man to say that his bond to another incorporates a mutual right and duty does not of itself convey any implication of its truth. What is crucial is that his assertion be validated. Here certain social conventions come into play. An assertion may be validated by formal agreement in front of others, by virtue of specific actions by both parties to demonstrate the particular meaning of their statements, or by means of one or both taking an oath. In a sense, therefore, mutual expressions mean nothing until something more has happened—until the *haqq*, in the sense of "obligation," has been sufficiently validated to render it capable of being assessed as "true" or "real."

One of the primary mechanisms for validating assertions is having some individual who is in a position to do so verify such utterances. In ordinary social relations this may, for example, involve the use of a go-between who, because of his dominance in the network of obligations he possesses to both parties, will be regarded by them and others as a guarantor of the facts asserted. In other domains, this role is more formalized. Thus, in the marketplace most occupational groupings choose one individual, called the *amin*, who because of his knowledge and the respect of his colleagues, acts as the articulator of acceptable standards and the verifier of commercial relationships. Overseeing the market as a whole stands another official (the *muhtasib*) who, like the *amin*, acts both as a regulator of market practice and a person who may be called upon to give acknowledged credence to what he has heard or seen.

It is in the broader context of seeking individuals who may validate actions and statements that the role of the notaries and other court officials is to be understood. The Arabic term

[4] I am indebted to Clifford Geertz for calling my attention to this issue. For data supporting this assertion see Bourgeoise (1959-60, fascicule no. 3: 80), and the discussion of truth in Crapanzano (1980: 80-81).

for notaries, *ᶜadul*, from a root meaning "just" or "equitable," has been wisely translated by Tyan (1960: 239) as "reliable witness."[5] For when a document has been signed by the requisite pair of notaries, they are really doing in the realm of the law what is sought, though not always with such formality, in other relationships: they are adding their stature, their word, as reliable witnesses to a bond that only takes on implications of truth, of interrelationship, by virtue of having received some form of validation. Along with court-appointed experts, who possess special knowledge on such diverse topics as construction, boundaries, or pregnancy, the notaries perform an indispensable function for the *qadi*: they "create" things as "facts" in order that they may be judicially recognized as facts.

There is, however, quite a range of documents a litigant may obtain from the notaries in order to make the oral testimony embodied by these documents more persuasive. Consonant with the emphasis on face-to-face evaluations of testimony, a litigant will often try to support his claim by having three, or preferably twelve, eligible witnesses come before two notaries and give testimony in support of the litigant's claims. The resultant document (called a *teleqiya*, if at least three witnesses testify; a *lafif*, if twelve or more do so) may be given still greater force by having each witness appear before two separate pairs of notaries. If the testimony of all witnesses remains consistent, the notaries will certify this in a document called a *stifsar*. This distinctively Moroccan practice may be derived from the custom of co-swearing among the Berbers in which a man chosen by the plaintiff swears to the truthfulness of the defendant's assertions, and an additional ten men add their voices in support of the reliability of the lead oath-taker (see Brunschvig, 1963: 180; Milliot, 1953: 737). To paraphrase Aeschylus, perhaps it is not the oath that makes the man believable, but the man the oath. The use of group witnessing in the *qadi*'s court, however, is directed toward the question of actual occurrences rather than character, and the court will subject even the testimony sworn separately before two sets of notaries to rational scrutiny. The unreported case of *Hussaini* v. *Alahami* (1965), involving the presentation of documents by both sides, will help illustrate this point.[6]

---

[5] On the notarization process generally, see Tyan (1945). On the related role of experts, see, e.g., Dwyer (1977).

[6] Sefrou *Qadi*'s Court, No. 1965/65. Cases from the *qadi*'s court in Sefrou are not published. With the aid of an assistant who orally translated each dossier from classical to colloquial Arabic with the author, over 400 cases were collected from the court records. The citation system is that used by the

(3/4/65: Complaint) The plaintiff claims that his wife, the defendant, left their home five months ago and that although he has sent members of their tribe to request her return she has refused to come back. He wants the court to make her return.
(7/13/65) The defendant's father, appearing as his daughter's legal representative, says that the plaintiff divorced his wife seven months ago, and he presents a document in which fifty people testify to this effect. The document was not made out before notaries. The plaintiff denies having divorced his wife and says the defendant's witnesses are ineligible because they are all her close relatives. The *qadi* says that if the plaintiff wishes to contest the testimony of the witnesses he may request that they submit to a *stifsar* examination.
(10/26/65) The *qadi* states that a valid divorce must be conducted before notaries. Article 48 of the 1958 Code says that if there are witnesses to a divorce that is said to have occurred in the absence of notaries this testimony must itself be notarized. Since the defendant has not produced a *stifsar*, judgment must be entered for the plaintiff. Pending the introduction of any new evidence on appeal, the defendant must return to her husband.
(7/19/66: Before the Appellate Court) Two documents are presented. The defendant presents a notarized document in which twelve witnesses state that they know the couple was married for a little over one year, after which the husband repudiated his wife. The second document, presented by the plaintiff, contains the notarized testimony of twelve witnesses who state that the couple has been married for four years, that a brideprice of 750 dirhams was paid at the time of the marriage, and that all of the witnesses were present at the wedding and took part in the festivities. They further assert that at no time has the plaintiff divorced his wife.

The appellate court, reviewing the documents, rules that whereas all of the plaintiff's witnesses come from the

court: the year litigation began is indicated to the left of the stroke, the docket number to the right. As presented here, the cases are summaries rather than direct translations of the records. Occasionally, cases from different levels of the judicial hierarchy appear in the *Revue Algerienne, Tunisienne, et Marocaine de Legislation et de Jurisprudence*, the *Revue Marocaine de Droit*, and the *Revue Juridique, Politique et Economique du Maroc*. A major collection of cases from the Protectorate period will be found in Milliot (1920; 1924) and Milliot and Lapanne-Joinville (1952). For a full translation of a case drawn from the Milliot collection, see Wigmore (1936: 593-614). Examples of various notarized documents can also be found in Zeys and Said (1946).

settlement in which he and his wife lived, while those of the defendant live some distance away, and whereas it is more likely that those living in the same village would know if a divorce had been uttered, the ruling of the *qadi* is upheld. The woman must return to her husband's home, be a good wife, and pay court costs.

Confronted with two sets of witnesses, the court chose to assume that those living in the same settlement as the couple were more likely than those living at some distance to know the actual state of their relationship. But this was not the only assumption at work. Officials in the *qadi*'s court told me that in a case like this the burden of proof is largely placed on the wife. Obviously, they argued, the husband is eager to live with his wife or he would exercise his legally recognized right to divorce her unilaterally. And since no charges of mistreatment were made, the *qadi* might well suspect that the wife's family had played a significant role in creating the dispute. Moreover, they said, it was unlikely that the husband was holding out for a settlement in which he would receive some consideration for divorcing his wife, since he was willing to expend a good deal of time and money litigating his claim. Whatever the merits of these arguments, they demonstrate the kinds of cultural assumptions and legal presumptions that shape the *qadi*'s discretionary powers.

The testimony of the litigants and their witnesses, as well as the notarized documents they introduce, may be totally contradictory. Or there may simply be no evidence on either side to support the parties' assertions. In such a situation the court has the power to require that one or both of the litigants support his or her claims with a holy oath. The oath itself has no set form and may be taken anywhere, although most commonly it is taken in the presence of two notaries at a mosque, a saintly shrine, or in the lodge of a religious brotherhood.[7]

The most interesting feature of these oaths, however, is the apportionment of the burden of swearing and the legal presumptions that accompany its use.[8] The burden of oath-taking is not consistently placed on either the plaintiff or the

---

7 See generally Westermarck (1926: 493-505, 564-569) where it is noted that both oaths and solemn promises usually begin with the word *haqq*.

8 On the importance of oaths in Islamic society, see Mottahedeh (1980: 42-52). On the order of oathtaking in various Islamic jurisdictions and periods, see Berque (1944: 24), Brunschvig (1963: 177-180), Jennings (1979), Kellal (1958), Liebesny (1975: 243-254), Tribunal d'Appel du Chraa (1956), and Westermarck (1926: 510).

defendant in the case, and indeed the burden may shift within any one proceeding, depending on the subject matter involved in the oath. The standard procedure is for the plaintiff or the court to demand that the defendant take the oath, swearing, for example, that he did not take any of his wife's belongings with him upon their divorce. If the defendant takes the oath, he or she will be presumed innocent. If, however, the defendant refuses to swear, the plaintiff must take the oath; and if the latter does so, the case will be awarded to him or her. Should both parties take oaths—and only one such case has been found in the records of the Sefrou court—the *qadi* will dismiss the suit outright. The roles of plaintiff and defendant in this sequence may, however, be reversed when the matter involves an object of knowledge that the court regards as more likely to lie within the competence or control of only one of the parties involved. Thus, if a wife claims that her husband took something that would normally belong to a woman and it is she who is the plaintiff in the case, the burden of oath-taking will fall first to her and to her husband only if she refuses.

The importance of all this is related to the power that the oaths themselves are believed to contain. For the overwhelming majority of people in the Sefrou region whom I have interviewed, there is a real fear that a false oath will result in harsh supernatural punishment; and it is not at all unusual for an individual to maintain a particular testimony right up to the moment of oath-taking and then to stop, refuse the oath, and surrender the case. Even the fear of mistakenly swearing what the person thinks is true but about which he possesses some slight doubt may prevent an innocent party from taking the oath. Thus the presumptions and the order of oathtaking may, in certain circumstances, be the deciding factor in the case.

For present purposes, however, the point that bears stressing is simply that while the *qadi* may exercise some discretion in the matter, oath-taking itself places a significant limitation on the extent to which the *qadi* will have to rely on his personal judgment in deciding cases where no clear line of evidence has been established. Custom—and in a few instances the 1958 Code (e.g., Article 39)—will indicate the order of swearing and the nature of the presumptions involved. But as a release from the burden of adjudication and as a limitation on fact-finding procedures, the oath is a vital factor in confining and structuring the procedural and evidentiary discretion of the Moroccan religious law court judge.

Inquiry and Procedure: The Case in Court

Once a complaint has been filed and any pretrial documents acquired, the case is brought before the *qadi*. The following description, derived from notes taken during an early visit to the *qadi*'s court in Sefrou, will give some flavor of the proceeding.

> The *qadi*'s court meets in a long narrow room at the side of the city hall. The *qadi*, a clerk by his side, sits behind an expansive desk at one end of the room while litigants mill about in a courtyard just beyond the door at the other end. A uniformed aide ushers parties in as their case is called. This aide serves as a translator for Berbers who cannot understand the *qadi*'s Arabic and as a monitor of courtroom order, although his embellishment of the court's inquiries and his patronizing choreography of litigants lends an air of self-aggrandizement to these otherwise modest tasks. The *qadi* first determines who is who and how, if at all, they are related to one another. His first substantive question is usually the signal for the shouting to begin. The parties begin by talking to the *qadi* but often end by addressing the aide, the clerk, others crowded into the courtroom, and even a stray anthropologist. The *qadi* mutters, nods, and questions; the principals sit, stand, shout, and cry; the aide tries to quiet people by pinning down their hands, in the certain knowledge that no Moroccan can speak if his hands are not free; and the clerk rushes to finish writing up the last case and find the correct dossier for the present one. Eventually one person gets to tell a more or less coherent story, and women no less than men speak with great verve and style. Most cases are treated very rapidly. In one case a woman and her son appeared before the *qadi*. The woman, quite old and sick, claimed that her husband—the man's father—left her some land when he died and that she later sold it to her son with the understanding that a share of the income from its use would be given her as support. There were no witnesses or documents to support her claim. The woman kept interrupting her son as he denied that any support agreement was attached to the land sale. The woman kept trying to swear that what she said was true, but the *qadi* cut her off and summarily ordered the man to pay some eight dollars per month in support. Turning to the clerk, the *qadi* said that the father would certainly not have wanted his wife to be dispossessed by the son. The

aide shouted out the *qadi*'s judgment almost before the latter had finished and, with the litigants still shouting, hustled mother and son out of the courtroom in one great sweeping motion.

Almost twenty cases were heard in the two-hour court session—cases of inheritance and divorce predominating—and in each instance the *qadi* seemed most concerned with the relationships of the parties, the documents they presented, and only rarely with a detailed examination of the elaborate arguments each person seemed eager to present. Little deference was shown to the *qadi*, and the style of discourse reminded one of the public marketplace or a neighborhood dispute more than the forum of a high religious and legal official.

Throughout this seemingly chaotic proceeding there runs both method and purpose. *Qadis* in Sefrou, as well as in other parts of the country, are intent on determining certain basic factors about the people who come before them and initially give them wide latitude in arguing their case. Social background is especially important, and its relevance to judicial decision making is not unrelated to its role in general social interaction. The constant focus in Moroccan society is on the individual as the locus of a series of distinctive ties of obligation. Each of the social traits the individual possesses—place of origin, kin connections, residence, and occupation—contributes both to the repertoire he or she may draw upon in establishing a network and to the series of traits which others may use to predict his or her most likely affiliations, customary ways of forming ties to others, and the probable course and consequences of any relationship with the interlocutor. The extent to which any relationship may be governed by the stereotype of a person as Berber or Arab, townsman or countryman, member of a given tribal faction or practitioner of a given trade will vary with the situation and the parties. But this information is invariably regarded as useful to the overall assessment of one individual by another. For the *qadi*, the relevance of this information goes not to the question of any potential tie of his own to the litigant but to two related points. First, such information is taken as an indicator of a person's most likely ways of acting in any situation. To comprehend who someone is, say *qadis*, is to know what he may have done. And second, it is assumed that, within certain broad limits, it is only fair to gauge the standard of conduct to which an individual should be held according to what sort of person he is. To hold an educated man to the same standards as one who is unlettered, or a woman to the same standards as a man, would, most *qadis* insist, be grossly unjust.[9] Just as in ordinary social life the constant focus is on what a person does and the range of relationships it affects, so in the judicial context it is through an assessment of the consequences of one's actions, measured against the traits and ties by which one is identified, that the *qadi* gains insight into the claims and actors before him.

Awareness of a critical feature of personal identity, therefore, leads to a series of cultural implications which, for all their variation within the society and across time, provide a code for the assessment of both character and action (see Dominguez, 1977). It is broadly assumed, for example, that women are more likely to be guided by passion and men by reason, that these motivating forces structure one's knowledge of the world, that knowledge is what sets one person's social stature above that of another, that stature is broadly related to particular types of obligational networks, and that interrelationships of various kinds entail qualities of social responsibility and harm on which the evaluation of social and legal repercussions may be based. The locus of these implications resides in neither a set of roles nor institutions, but in the individual as a concatenation of traits and ties, and hence this implicational code operates as both a cultural guide and a malleable gauge. Faced with the task of interpreting motives and acts, however, the code of cultural entailment becomes a tool of major significance in the *qadi*'s determination of facts and choice of legal remedies.

That there exists, in the *qadi*'s perception and evaluation of others, considerable scope for discrimination and injustice is a point not lost on many Moroccans. Yet the line of inquiry the *qadi* follows is so similar and the data he appears to seek so familiar from everyday life that approbation for his way of proceeding broadly outweighs criticism of particular results. This point is brought home both in the style of discourse between judge and witness and in the characterization of wise adjudication.

We noted earlier the importance of validating assertions in Moroccan life and the institutionalization of this process in the role of the notaries. The style of questioning and the modes of

[9] On the relation between social position and duty, see Yamani (1968: 17). On the role of character evidence in Moroccan criminal proceedings, see Morere (1961).

response often follow a common pattern. After his initial inquiry into social background, the *qadi* will ask the plaintiff to tell his story. Almost invariably, the plaintiff will be interrupted midway by the defendant, and both parties will begin to argue with one another. When asked, most *qadis* say that they want to see the two parties interact and want to gauge the intensity of their attachment to the issue. Moreover, the *qadi* is trying to determine how widely or narrowly to set the bounds of relevance in the case. If, for example, a woman has run away from her husband in part as the culmination of a property dispute between two kin groups, the *qadi* may or may not take this into consideration in his decision. His discretion in this matter is limited by the specific rules of the 1958 Code—e.g., a runaway wife must return to her husband unless severely mistreated and then file a separate suit seeking his proper behavior—but the boundaries he sets may also be influenced by his perception of how people of the sort before him are expected by him to comport themselves. Thus he may simply chide an unlettered country woman for running away but seek out the full nature of an educated urbanite's dispute while reminding him of the example he should set.

Often, too, a litigant will use a style of argument common to the broader social process of validating assertions. To get another to accept one's own definition of a situation, it is common to engage the other in a kind of Socratic dialogue in which a set of questions is posed to which the other is forced to respond on a yes or no basis. In court, litigants will often use this style with the judge. Accused of beating his wife, a man may say to the judge, "Is she not a woman? Doesn't the Quran say a man is the 'governor' of a woman? Is it not shameful for a woman to say these things to a man?" At each point he seeks to get the *qadi* to affirm his statement in the presence of others, just as he might in his ordinary social discourse.

In short, for the *qadi* the "facts" are estimations of character assumed by background and displayed by courtroom encounter as much as they are weightings, based on related considerations, of the notarized documents presented. It is interesting in this regard to note that when stories are told of really clever *qadis* they often involve the *qadi* trapping one of the parties in a display of his true character. Thus, a story may be recounted of how a *qadi* disguised himself and entrapped the person in a relationship similar to the sort he denies ever having formed, or how a *qadi* will have provoked a person in court until the litigant does or says what was earlier denied.

Interestingly, too, no penalties exist for perjury, even if a person has taken an oath, it being assumed that the harm to one's reputation as one who stands by a validated assertion, the loss of the case, or supernatural sanction will suffice as punishment (see Schacht, 1964: 159; Westermarck, 1926: 509).

In his evaluation of conflicting evidence the *qadi* may also have recourse to certain established presumptions. In line with Moroccan legal tradition, he may, for example, presume that testimony asserting a positive fact is more reliable than assertions about a negative—e.g., that a sale took place rather than that it never occurred—since every change of obligation, each shift in the distribution of *haqq*, constitutes an act, and acts have greater consequences than forbearance.[10] Here, as in ordinary social relations, the focus is not on a person's state of mind as such but on those actions which only a sane and competent adult must have intended to have engaged in such an act. And here, too, since consequence is perceived to vary with social characteristics, the *qadi* believes he can gauge his remedy according to the harm done by such a person acting in such a way. As in any judgment his decision embodies elements of the arbitrary, though his discretion is clearly bounded by law and culture alike.

Law and Equity: The Nexus of Reasoning and Justice

The 1958 Code of Personal Status controls a substantial proportion of the cases that come before the *qadi*. For issues not dealt with by the Code, as well as for some aspects of those that are, the *qadi* may utilize concepts and modes of analysis that contribute significantly to the shape of his discretionary and equitable powers. In particular, he may look for substantive guidance in local custom or past decisions and for legal justification in the concepts of analogic reasoning and the public good.

Most of the present-day creative use of custom is associated with the laws of personal status, and it is, therefore, to this domain that the present discussion will be limited. For example, in the formation of any marriage in Morocco the husband must pay to his wife or her marital guardian (*wali*) a sum of money or quantity of goods agreed upon by the parties as a brideprice (*sdaq*). It is usually the wife's father who serves as her marital guardian—generally seeking the mate as

---

[10] For a detailed listing of presumptions in the Malikite school of Islamic law, see Lapanne-Joinville (1957).

well as negotiating the marriage contract—and although local customs vary he will generally add at least an equivalent sum to the brideprice and then use the entire amount to purchase the girl's dowry (*attat l-bit*). This dowry remains the wife's property and will leave the marriage with her in the event of a divorce. The brideprice is always recorded in the marriage contract; but the recordation of the dowry is a matter of local custom, personal preference, and judicial discretion. It is a matter of some importance, too, because in the absence of any record to the contrary, the legal fiction obtains that all the "furnishings of the household" (the literal meaning of the Arabic term for dowry) belong to the wife even though they may have been purchased during the course of the union. And since much of a woman's marital security in this society, which still grants the husband the right of arbitrary divorce, resides in the threat to the husband of the financial loss he stands to suffer in the event of a divorce, the recording of a dowry may play an important role in the stability of the marriage itself (Rosen, 1970).

The *qadi* also possesses the power to order a girl's marital guardian to agree to a given marriage; and if the guardian refuses, the *qadi* may himself give the girl in marriage. The purpose of this provision, coupled with that which grants a woman freedom from arbitrary actions by her own marital guardian, is to insure that girls are not prevented, in effect, from contracting their own marriages if they choose to do so. In Sefrou this provision is employed in those cases in which a girl has been raped and her marital guardian opposes a subsequent marriage or where the girl herself has developed a bad reputation and it is thought best to marry her off so that her husband will keep her respectable. Moreover, Article 13 of the Code says that in such a situation the girl should be married "by means of an equivalent brideprice to a man of equal condition," which "condition," according to Article 14 (b), is to be determined "by reference to local custom (*ᶜurf*)." The determination of "equal condition" is thus left to the *qadi* and his sense of local customs to determine (cf. Ziadeh, 1957). On the few occasions in which Sefrou *qadis* have exercised this power, they have proved to be as sensitive to criteria of ethnicity, skin color, and familial reputation as to the financial status of the principals and their respective families.

One final example also concerns marital relations. The Code provides that when a man divorces his wife he must pay her a sum in compensation. This sum, called the *mutaᶜa*, is left to the *qadi* to set; and in Sefrou, where such payments were often employed before the advent of the Code, the figure has customarily been set at one-third of the brideprice. However, if the marriage occurred long ago or involved a particularly high or low brideprice, the *qadi* will vary the amount due according to his own discretionary judgment.

In sum, the *qadi* possesses some leeway in utilizing local custom in his decisions. His perception of local custom may be highly idiosyncratic or represent the perspective of only one segment of the population. Custom, like prior cases, may serve as persuasive evidence or as the basis for a legal presumption, but even where the present code permits resort to custom, *qadis* appear to avoid controversy by relying on court experts and notaries to indicate the acceptable forms of local customary practice.[11]

In classical Islamic legal theory, a *qadi* was expected to justify his interpretation of novel facts or situations by means of an analogy firmly rooted in Quranic precept, the practices of the Prophet and his companions, or the consensus of scholars or notables. Early Islam permitted the exercise of personal reasoning (*ijtihad*) by those who were so knowledgeable in the sacred sources that they might penetrate to the correct solution of a problem when the answer was not immediately evident by strict analogy. By the tenth century, however, opinion hardened against new interpretations, and distinct schools of legal doctrine crystallized around notable scholars. Since Islamic law has long been an object of ethical contemplation as much as an instrument of adjudication, one or more legal scholars might be asked by a litigant to supply an advisory opinion to the court. Although the opinions of *qadis* were almost never published or cited in subsequent decisions, the views of respected scholars were more frequently collected and distributed.

Contemporary Moroccan jurisprudence is heir to this tradition in several key respects. Like his predecessors, the modern *qadi* may ignore analogic reasoning by basing his decision on an approach known to have been preferred by the consensus of earlier scholars. He may also rely on the principle of public utility (*istislāh*), arguing, for example, that it is better for society to force a man into marriage with a girl he has molested than to impose the penalties and shame of a

[11] The relation of Islamic law to custom and case law is discussed in Coulson (1959) and Ziadeh (1960).

criminal accusation.[12] He may also turn to a body of legal literature unique in Islamic law to Morocco, the *ᶜamal*, which are collections of actual judicial practice which often did not correspond with the preferred opinion of scholars. This latter body of literature has some of the qualities of both case law and substantive law, even though it lacks binding force and internal consistency.[13] Reference to *ᶜamal* decisions serves primarily to support the stature of individual judgments and adds to the flexibility and creativity by which judicial powers may be exercised.

Custom, prior opinions, analogic reasoning, and public interest evaluations all constitute sources of principles used by the *qadi* where code and text may be wanting. Coupled with his use of social perception and the modes of determining facts, they give substantive shape to discretionary power. But what happens when the law on a matter is quite clear, when there is no lacuna that would legitimize recourse to these other mechanisms, but the *qadi* nevertheless feels that justice would be violated by strict application of the law? This may be particularly true when the case involves a wife who possesses insufficient grounds to obtain a judicial remedy to her marital situation but who is clearly suffering some hardship as a result of her husband's actions. A single unreported case, *al-Haji* v. *Hedraz* (1961),[14] will serve to illustrate this point:

> (9/19/61: Complaint) The plaintiff states that her husband, the defendant, has been sent to jail for two years. For three years and two months prior to that he did not support her or their young daughter. She requests that the *qadi* divorce her because she cannot wait until her husband gets out of jail to support her and because a woman needs a husband to support her. Twice, she says, she has filed suits against her husband: the first case was thrown out on a technicality, and in the second the court ruled that the defendant should pay her support for the

---

[12] Obviously, the assessment of what serves the public weal can yield both varied and amusing results. Yamani (1968: 11) cites as "an excellent example of public interest consideration" the following story: "Ibn Al-Kayem related that his teacher Ibn Taimiah passed a group of Tatar drinking wine. His disciples wanted to forbid them from doing so, but Ibn Taimiah did not allow this, his reasoning being that God prohibited wine because it distracts from prayer and devotional rituals, but in the case of the Tatars wine distracts them from murder, loot, and rape." On the principle of *istislah* generally, see Kerr (1968).

[13] On the role of *ᶜamal* as case law or substantive law, compare Berque (1944: 33-42, 119-132; 1960) with Milliot (1953: 167). For an analysis of one of the leading collections of *ᶜamal*, see Toledano (1974).

[14] Sefrou *Qadi*'s Court, No. 1961/262.

period of one year and four months, but he has not paid anything on this judgment. The plaintiff therefore also asks that the earlier judgment be enforced.

(10/16/61) A summons for the defendant has been sent to the jail in which he is incarcerated, but no answer has been received. The plaintiff tells the court that she knows her husband does not have the money with which to pay the support judgment leveled against him.

(2/19/62) Defendant absent. Public prosecutor in Fez claims communication foul-up between his office and the court. Delay ordered.

(3/12/62, 6/21/62, 9/12/62, 9/24/62) Each time the chief of the Fez court district has been asked to send the defendant for trial of the suit, but each time the defendant is absent.

(10/29/62) Again the defendant is absent. The court says it has communicated by letter and phone with the warden of the jail, the prosecutor, and the chief of the Fez court district asking for the man to be presented, and each time they have failed to bring him. As always, the plaintiff is present. She says she mainly wants a divorce. Her husband still has a year to serve.

(1/21/63) The *qadi* notes that the defendant is in jail for theft. He says that the plaintiff is always present, that the court itself is at fault for not presenting the defendant, and that a special effort must be made to help the plaintiff in reaching a decision on her petition. The *qadi* notes the defendant's admission in the earlier case that he did not support his wife and that he has since failed to obey the judgment entered against him. It is not right, says the *qadi*, for a woman to be alone while her husband is in jail: Allah considers marriage to be of great importance and wants the children of a marriage to be raised properly. Divorce is preferable to the continuation of the sort of situation with which we are presented here. The defendant has failed to support his family and has twice failed to obey the court order to do so. The defendant is therefore acting against the defining principles of a marriage and the laws of support. The law gives the *qadi* the right to divorce a couple if the husband cannot or will not support his wife. (A quotation from the Quran is cited here.) The *qadi* says that he knows the plaintiff's condition and that she has lived as a good woman throughout this period. Moreover, the defendant is a convicted thief. One school of law, says the *qadi*, says that a woman cannot request a divorce until she has lived one year without her husband ever being present, while another school sets the minimum period at three years. Both schools would be satisfied by the circumstances of the present case. Finally, says the *qadi*, a judicial divorce in this kind of case would be irrevocable (*b*^{c}*ain*). A revocable kind of judicial divorce (*rja*^{c}*i*) would be less preferable anyway because the husband might take the plaintiff back as his wife again before the divorce became final thus granting him the opportunity to bring further hardships on his wife. There are, says the *qadi*, so many reasons to favor such a divorce that even if the defendant should appear in court it would not alter his decision. Therefore, the *qadi* pronounces an irrevocable judicial divorce. This judgment may, he concludes, be appealed.

(8/14/63: Before the appellate court) The court notes that the defendant has not paid the proper costs necessary to appeal the case within the allotted time. The defendant says he does not know the law. The appellate court dismisses the appeal.

It is important in analyzing the above case to understand that in Morocco there are two different kinds of divorces, revocable and irrevocable. Briefly, a man may repudiate the same woman three different times. After the first repudiation he may take her back as his wife within three months whether or not she wishes to return to him. After the second repudiation she must consent to being reunited within the three-month period. And after the third repudiation no direct reunion is permissible. Thus, only if the three-month separation period has elapsed and the man has twice previously repudiated the wife, a consideration is paid the husband to obtain the divorce, or the *qadi* grants the woman a judicial divorce for cause is an irrevocable divorce recorded. Absence of more than a year is sufficient grounds for an irrevocable divorce. Imprisonment of the husband does not constitute grounds for any kind of judicial divorce. Thus, as a matter of strict law the *qadi* could only grant the plaintiff a revocable form of divorce, one which would leave her husband free to reclaim her as his lawful wife any time within the following three months. The *qadi*, however, clearly felt that it would be unfair to the plaintiff to subject her to this possibility.

Two questions of central importance to our study of Islamic law must therefore be considered. First, on the basis of what information and through the medium of what processes did the *qadi* decide that in this case it would be more equitable to violate the strict letter of the law than to obey it? And second, in terms of what principles did he construct the justification for his result? In order to answer the first of these questions we must have recourse to certain additional information; in order to answer the second we must relate this particular situation to those fundamental legal concepts mentioned earlier in our study.

To the extent that it is possible to reconstruct the history of this judicial decision and others like it, it is necessary to take into account the social positions of the participants and the process of decision making in which the *qadi* himself engaged. In his opinion the *qadi* points not only to the husband's bad record but also to the fact that he has acquainted himself with the circumstances in which the plaintiff lives and knows that she has constantly displayed the characteristics of a respectable woman. In cases of this sort the *qadi* obtains such information through two major sources. First, he may inquire, directly or through others, into the plaintiff's habits and condition from the head of the urban quarter (*muqqadem al-huma*) or *sheikh* of the rural settlement in which the plaintiff resides. These government-appointed officials have no formal ties with the judicial system, but may be relied on by the court to inform it on matters of this sort. In this particular case, the *qadi* learned that the plaintiff was from a good family of the city, that the husband had proved to be a scoundrel of uncertain background, and that the plaintiff's neighbors regarded her as circumspect, well-behaved, and long-suffering.

In addition to inquiry through the local officials, the *qadi* relied for information and general advice on several other persons in the community. In Morocco, as throughout the Arab world, people will often refer to certain individuals as "the notables of the area" (*a^{c}yan al-bilād*). These community leaders possess no formal organization or recognition: they are merely those persons who, by general reputation, familial background, or position, are generally regarded as the standard-bearers of the distinctive customs and highest values of their region. They are at once the unofficial arbiters of local propriety and the embodiment—at least ideally—of the distinctive characteristics of the community as a whole. Many of these "notables" come into regular contact with the *qadi* or his closest associates and may be officials in the local court system itself. Indeed, since they form no corporate group or institutionalized entity, the determination of who is a "notable of the area" is neither regular in its process nor subject to precise and uniform interpretation. The fact remains, nevertheless, that in some situations the *qadi* will consult informally with some of these persons in an attempt to determine certain facts about the litigants and—more importantly—what local practice, as articulated by these community leaders, is and should be in a given case. This is, then, a kind of informal consultation rather than a formal concilium, by means of which the *qadi* can determine the practice and sentiments of the community as articulated by some of its more notable citizens and diminish the exercise of his individual discretion through a process of consultation with important community leaders.[15]

In the present case the *qadi* did indeed consult with such notables about the disposition of the matter. He was apparently convinced that the equity of the woman's case was very substantial and that a decision granting her an irrevocable divorce would be regarded favorably by all knowledgeable persons. There remained only the determination of a proper rationale for such a decision.

Earlier in our discussion, reference was made to the concept of *istislah*, the implementation for reasons of public utility of a judicial approach which, though not based on strict analogies with formal legal sources, is adopted as the preferred approach to a given problem. The *qadi* in the present case clearly relied on this traditional form of Moroccan legal reasoning in reaching his decision. He refers in his opinion to the reasons why an irrevocable divorce should be granted the plaintiff and why it is better for her, her family, and society as a whole to dissolve her union irrevocably. The *qadi* was doubtless aware that the present Code allows reference to such sources and reasoning in the absence of an applicable statutory provision, but he was apparently willing to argue its importance even when there is an appropriate provision if the equities of the case appear overwhelming. The fact that the appellate court, which rarely enforces the technicalities of filing dates, did not choose to overrule his decision indicates that the *qadi*'s argument was convincingly presented. Although no formal confrontation of the rule of law and the role of equity was joined in this case, it appears that by using his powers of consultation and utilitarian reasoning, the present-day *qadi*

[15] On the concept of concilium in Islamic law, see Tyan (1955: 245-247).

may indeed be able to render an essentially lawless decision justified in terms of countervailing equities.

The Nature of Qadi Justice

In his critique of Weber's concept of *Kadijustiz*, Max Rheinstein wrote:

> Case law may tend toward irrationality, but even in that most extreme form in which it appears, that is, the practice of the khadi, it does not lack all rationality. Neither the Mohammedan khadi nor his counterpart, the English (or American) justice of the peace, is expected to administer justice according to his own arbitrary whim or momentary fancy. The "good" khadi is the one whose decision is in accordance with popular conviction, that is, with the religious or ethical value system prevailing at the time and place. In primitive or archaic circumstances this value system may be more felt than consciously known, but it exists wherever there exists a society and it is the very art of the khadi to articulate it as it applies to a concrete case. He is the one who is able to express in words, although of concrete application, what the common man but vaguely feels but cannot so easily apply and even less put into words. Only where he has succeeded in articulating in his decision the "sound feeling of the people" will the khadi's decision meet with that approval without which he cannot permanently maintain his authority. This practice will often contain a good measure of irrationality, but basically his thought is of the pattern of the substantively rational, although largely inarticulate, kind (1967: xlvii).

In fact, the equitable and discretionary powers of the contemporary Moroccan *qadi* are shaped as much by the sources of his legitimacy and the similarity of legal and cultural reasoning as by the articulation and enactment of assumptions that are characteristic of his society. Traditionally, the power of the *qadi* to interpose his own judgment was legitimized by the belief that adjudication in conformity with divine law is one of those duties which some individual must perform on behalf of all if the society is to remain a proper community of believers in the eyes of Allah (see Juynboll, 1961; Schacht, 1964: 206; Tyan, 1955: 243). In the past men have been known to refuse judicial appointment for fear that they might inadvertently mislead their fellow believers or be corrupted by deriving their powers from necessarily tainted secular officials.[16] For those who did serve, however, the burden of spiritual guardianship legitimized the search for morally

[16] So onerous is the responsibility of *qadi* said to be that even pious men might refuse to accept the post. "The *qāḍī* of Spain, Muhājir b. Naufal, who . . . is supposed to have spoken from his grave of the evil outcome of the office of *qāḍī*, used to weep and lament for his soul when he recalled the 'reckoning which awaits the *qāḍī* in the world to come for the discretionary choice and the *ijtihād* (personal interpretations) he is forced to employ'" (Coulson 1956: 219). More indicative of the potential entanglement with civil authorities may be the story of the man who was dissuaded from accepting a post as *qadi* when his traveling companion said: "Are you not then aware that when Allāh has no more use for a creature He casts him into the circle of officials?" (Coulson 1956: 212).

correct decisions. Although classical Islamic ethical thought turned, in part, on the categorization of all acts as obligatory, recommended, permissible, blameworthy, or forbidden, Moroccan juridical thought eschewed the elaboration of abstract concepts of right action in favor of more pragmatic evaluations of human relationships and the common weal. As Schacht (1974: 397) noted generally for Islamic law, "considerations of good faith, fairness, justice, truth, and so on play only quite a subordinate part in the system." Rather, it has been in the assessment of the features characterizing those who come before them and in the role of procedural constancy that one finds the distinctive qualities of *qadi* justice.

Moroccan jurisprudence, like Moroccan society, focuses on a series of human characteristics as they cohere in particular individuals. Notwithstanding the provisions of the 1958 Code, the *qadi*, once he has determined to keep the bounds of relevance widely set, probes for the background and relationships that bear on the network of obligations between or among the parties. Although *qadis* undoubtedly vary in their assessment of these factors and weigh them differently in setting the boundaries of the case or their depth of inquiry, each of the factors involved entails certain consequences. It is interesting to note in this regard that the term *asl*—which refers to one's origins, background, set of presumed associations and customs—also refers to that form of legal reasoning by entailment which a judge may rely upon in the implementation of legal presumptions. Thus, as we have seen, the *qadi* may legally presume who is most likely to possess certain knowledge in assigning the order of oath-taking. Or he may invoke a form of that implicational code which suggests that gender implies motivation; motivation, knowledge; knowledge, social position; position, network; and network, repercussions. Here, too, one may be able to discern significant shifts in the code of cultural entailment over time. It may be said of Moroccans, as of Saudi Arabians, that theirs is a world "in which people define tasks, roles, and institutions, not the other way around" (Iseman 1978: 50). What may be changing is not the overall tendency toward personalism but the fact that in the past a man's occupation, residence, kin group, and religious brotherhood ties cumulated such that knowledge of any one feature implied a series of others, whereas now the set of implications may be less tightly integrated or the need to consider it rendered less pressing because of the 1958 Code. Stereotypes, loosed from their cultural context, may now come to serve judicial efficiency more than the articulation of community norms.

Indeed, it may be argued that Islamic law is, to borrow John Dewey's (1924) distinction, based on a logic of consequence rather than a logic of antecedent. Instead of considering prior cases or similar examples, the *qadi* focuses on the consequence of actions as the index of validated assertions and as the criterion for judging social implications. It is in the harm done or the alteration in relationships that the critical point lies. Thus, as in everyday social perceptions, the court ignores intent as an independent factor and concentrates instead on occurrences. The more serious the impact on society, the more serious are the legal implications. The requirement, for example, of four eyewitnesses to an act of fornication is not solely an evidentiary burden of extraordinary weight: it is also an assertion that if, contrary to the tradition (*hadith*) that "God loves those who hide their sins," one commits an act in so blatant a fashion that four people may have seen it, the harm to society must be serious indeed.[17] Similarly, the use of numerous witnesses to a man's mistreatment of his wife is a statement about social consequence converted into a legally recognizable infraction.

Justice, then, lies not in the simple invocation of rights and duties but in their contextual assessment and the mode of analysis. Procedure and reasoning are central. Asked how similar cases which result in divergent judgments can be justified, *qadis* invariably offer two answers: first, that no two individuals are identical and hence no two cases are the same. But more important, they insist that the same reasoning process—of drawing analogies, of weighing moral implications, of adducing evidence, of assessing entailments, of gauging the social interest—may reasonably lead to different conclusions, but that if the procedures are the same, the most important criterion for treating similar cases similarly will have been met.[18]

The emphasis on the form of procedure as opposed to its momentary result and the concern with individual assessment over routinized processing is closely related to the second handicap noted by Hart for the establishment of general rules: namely, the relative indeterminacy of aim. In the *qadi*'s court,

---

[17] This interpretation is taken from Yamani (1968: 34). The internal reference to the tradition of the Prophet is elaborated in Juynboll (1961).

[18] Berque (1944: 21) places particular emphasis on contradictory judicial results being understood as linked by common procedures.

the aim is neither the strict enforcement of rights nor the reconciliation of the parties, however much each of these elements may play a role in some cases. Rather, the aim is to give at least momentary order to shifting relationships and to validate their present status long enough to avoid violence and to set people back on a social course of negotiating their own ties peaceably. It is more than mere cynicism, therefore, that leads many Moroccans, when discussing the nature of *qadi* justice, to refer to the popular saying: "when the times are just, one day is for me and one day is against me."

Qadi justice in Morocco gives the appearance ultimately of an entity constructed around an elaborate exoskeleton. Rather than being built up from within by a series of rules and regulations, the system is bounded by a structure of assumptions and conventions by which the nonlegal world is set apart from the legal but within which both that outside world and the peculiar institutions of the law itself have merged to form an entity of enormous cohesion and resilience. The presence of statutes and appellate courts may contribute to greater rigidity or, as the authors of the 1958 Code hoped, to a new body of flexible judicial practice (*ᶜamal*). Whatever its particular course, it is clear that legal precepts and procedures will continue to be influenced by changing cultural and moral ideas. Just as in American law where, for example, a witness may testify that someone was "drunk" but may not conclude that a person was "in love," so, too, in Moroccan law evidentiary standards and modes of legal reasoning partake of everyday assumptions about human conduct and fairness. For the student of law, a close analysis of *qadi* justice may demonstrate that the goal need not be that posed by the legal realists—the prediction of what judges will do—nor that suggested by the legal positivists—the enumeration of specific rules. Rather, one can show that discretionary judgments and equitable assessments are suffused by principles and standards which are as incomprehensible without an understanding of how cultural precepts shape them as would the study of social relations be incomplete without an understanding of their judicial articulation.

REFERENCES

ANDERSON, J.N.D. (1958) "Reforms in Family Law in Morocco," 2 *Journal of African Law* 146.

BERQUE, Jacques (1944) *Essai sur la Méthode Juridique Maghrébine*. Rabat.

——— (1960) "ᶜAmal," 1 *The Encyclopaedia of Islam, New Edition* 427.

BORRMANS, Maurice (1977) *Statut Personnel et Famille au Maghreb: de 1940 à nos Jours*. Paris: Mouton.

BOURGEOISE, Paul (1959-60) *L'Univers de l'Ecolier Marocain, fascicules no. 1-5*. Rabat: Faculté des Lettres et des Sciences Sociales.

BRUNSCHVIG, Robert (1960) "Bayyina," 1 *Encyclopaedia of Islam, New Edition* 1150.

——— (1963) "Le Systeme de la Preuve en Droit Musulman," 18 *Recueil de la Société Jean Bodin pour l'Histoire Comparative des Institutions* 169.

COLOMER, André (1963) *Droit Musulman, Tome Premier, Les Personnes—La Famille*. Rabat: E'ditions La Porte.

——— (1967) *Droit Musulman, Tome Deuxième, Statut Successoral*. Rabat: Editions La Porte.

COULSON, Noel (1956) "Doctrine and Practice in Islamic Law," 18 *Bulletin of the School of Oriental and African Studies* 211.

——— (1959) "Muslim Custom and Case-Law," 6 *Die Welt des Islams* 13.

CRAPANZANO, Vincent (1980) *Tuhami: Portrait of a Moroccan*. Chicago: University of Chicago Press.

DEWEY, John (1924) "Logical Method and Law," 10 *Cornell Law Quarterly* 17.

DOMINGUEZ, Virginia R. (1977) "Social Classification in Creole Louisiana," 4 *American Ethnologist* 589.

DWYER, Daisy Hilse (1977) "Bridging the Gap between the Sexes in Moroccan Legal Practice," in Alice Schlegel (ed.), *Sexual Stratification: A Cross-Cultural View*. New York: Columbia University Press.

GALLAGHER, Charles (1959) "New Laws for Old: The Moroccan Code of Personal Status," 5 *American Universities Field Staff Reports, North Africa Series* 1. Hanover, N.H.: American Universities Field Staff.

GEERTZ, Clifford, Hildred GEERTZ and Lawrence ROSEN (1979) *Meaning and Order in Moroccan Society: Three Essays in Cultural Analysis*. Cambridge: Cambridge University Press.

HART, H.L.A. (1961) *The Concept of Law*. Oxford: Oxford University Press.

ISEMAN, Peter A. (1978) "The Arabian Ethos," 256 *Harper's* 37 (February).

JENNINGS, Ronald C. (1979) "Limitations of the Judicial Powers of the Kadi in 17th C. Ottoman Kayseri," 50 *Studia Islamica* 151.

JUYNBOLL, Th.W. (1961) "ᶜAdhāb," in H.A.R. Gibb and J.H. Kramers (eds.), *Shorter Encyclopaedia of Islam*. Leiden: E.J. Brill.

KELLAL, Almenouar (1958) "Le Serment en Droit Musulman, Ecole Malékite," 74 *Revue Algerienne, Tunisienne et Marocaine de Legislation et de Jurisprudence* 18.

KERR, Malcolm H. (1968) "Moral and Legal Judgment Independent of Revelation," 18 *Philosophy East and West* 277.

LAPANNE-JOINVILLE, J. (1957) "Etudes de Droit Musulman Malékite: Les Présomptions," 73 *Revue Algerienne, Tunisienne et Marocaine de Législation et de Jurisprudence* 99.

——— (1959) "Le Code Marocain du Statut Personnel," 1959 *Revue Marocaine de Droit* 97.

LIEBESNY, Herbert J. (1975) *The Law of the Near and Middle East: Readings, Cases, and Materials*. Albany: State University of New York Press.

LINANT DE BELLEFONDS, Yvon (1965) *Traité de Droit Musulman Compareé, Tome I: Théorie Générale de l-Acte Juridique*. Paris: Mouton.

MACDONALD, D.B. (1961) "Hakk," in H.A.R. Gibb and J.H. Kramers (eds.), *Shorter Encyclopaedia of Islam*. Leiden: E.J. Brill.

MAHMOOD, Tabir (1972) *Family Law Reform in the Muslim World*. Bombay: N.M. Tripathi Pvt. Ltd.

MILLIOT, Louis (1920) *Recueil de Jurisprudence Chérifienne*, Tomes I, II. Paris: Editions E. Leroux.

——— (1924) *Recueil de Jurisprudence Chérifienne*, Tome III Paris: Editions E. Leroux.

——— (1953) *Introduction à l-E'tude du Droit Musulman*. Paris: Recueil Sirey.

——— and J. Lapanne-Joinville (1952) *Recueil de Jurisprudence Chérifienne*, Tome IV. Paris: Librairie du Recueil Sirey.

MORERE, Maurice (1961) "Le Procès Criminel: L'Enquête sur 'la personnalité des Inculpes' au Maroc," 1961 *Revue Marocaine de Droit* 433.

MOTTAHEDEH, Roy P. (1980) *Loyalty and Leadership in an Early Islamic Society*. Princeton: Princeton University Press.

RHEINSTEIN, Max (1967) "Introduction," to *Max Weber, On Law in Economy and Society*. New York: Simon and Schuster.

ROSEN, Lawrence (1968) "A Moroccan Jewish Community During the Middle Eastern Crisis," 37 *The American Scholar* 435.

——— (1970) " 'I Divorce Thee,' " 7(8) *Transaction* 34.

——— (1972a) "Muslim-Jewish Relations in a Moroccan City," 3 *International Journal of Middle East Studies* 435.

——— (1972b) "Rural Political Process and National Political Structure in Morocco," in Richard Antoun and Iliya Harik (eds.), *Rural Politics and Social Change in the Middle East*. Bloomington: Indiana University Press.

——— (1973) "The Social and Conceptual framework of Arab-Berber Relations in Central Morocco," in Ernest Gellner and Charles Micaud (eds.), *Arabs and Berbers: From Tribe to Nation in North Africa*. London: Duckworth.

——— (1978) "The Negotiation of Reality: Male-Female Relations in Sefrou, Morocco," in Lois Beck and Nikki Keddie (eds.), *Women in the Muslim World*. Cambridge: Harvard University Press.

SCHACHT, Joseph (1964) *An Introduction to Islamic Law*. Oxford: Clarendon Press.

——— (1974) "Islamic Religious Law," in Joseph Schacht and C.E. Bosworth (eds.), *The Legacy of Islam*, 2nd edn. Oxford: Clarendon Press.

TOLEDANO, Henry (1974) "Sijilmāsī's Manual of Maghribī ᶜAmal, al-ᶜAmal al-Mutlaq: A Preliminary Study," 5 *International Journal of Middle East Studies* 484.

TRIBUNAL D'APPEL DU CHRAA (1956) "Audience du 12 avril 1955," 1956 *Revue Marocaine de Droit* 468.

TURNER, Bryan S. (1974) *Weber and Islam: A Critical Study*. London: Routledge and Kegan Paul.

TYAN, Emile (1945) *Le Notariat et le Régime de la Preuve par E'crit dans la Pratique du Droit Musulman*. Beirut: Université de Lyon, Annales de l'E'cole Française de Droit de Beyrouth.

——— (1955) "Judicial Organisation," in Majid Khadduri and Herbert J. Liebesny (eds.), *Law in the Middle East*, Vol. I. Washington: The Middle East Institute.

——— (1960) *Histoire de l'Organisation Judiciaire en Pays d'Islam*, 2nd edn. Leiden: E.J. Brill.

WAKIN, Jeanette A. (1972) *The Function of Documents in Islamic Law*. Albany: State University of New York Press.

WEBER, Max (1967) *Max Weber on Law in Economy and Society*. New York: Simon and Schuster.

WESTERMARCK, Edward (1926) *Ritual and Belief in Morocco*, Vol. I. London: Macmillan.

WIGMORE, John Henry (1936) *A Panorama of the World's Legal Systems*. Washington: Washington Law Book Co.

YAMANI, Ahmad Zaki (1968) *Islamic Law and Contemporary Issues*. Jidda: The Saudi Publishing House.

ZEYS, E. and Mohammed Ould Sidi SAID (1946) *Recueil d'Actes et de Jugements Arabes*. Algiers: Editions Jules Carbonel.

ZIADEH, Farhat (1957) "Equality (Kafa'ah) in the Muslim Law of Marriage," 6 *Journal of American Comparative Law* 503.

——— (1960) "ᶜ*Urf* and Law in Islam," in James Kritzeck and R. Bayly Winder (eds.), *The World of Islam: Studies in Honor of Philip Hitti*. London: Macmillan.

CASES CITED

Terminiello v. *Chicago*, 337 U.S. 1, 11, 1949.

Part V
Legal Cultures in Co-existence and Conflict

[21]

LEGAL PLURALISM IN ROMAN LAW

G. C. J. J. VAN DEN BERGH*

Legal pluralism means that within a single society different legal systems are in force at the same time (1). Pluralism is not just another word for conflict of laws; this is the dogmatic problem faced by lawyers who, when confronted with conflicting provisions, try to find an answer to the question as to which of them is to prevail. Pluralism is a word borrowed from social sciences and so the attitude it represents is quite different. The question is not, what is the law when different provisions apply, but how can different legal systems exist side by side, how do they interact, influence each other, assimilate to each other or not, as the case may be.

Pluralism as a concept has only recently been introduced to legal studies. This is no wonder, and it is not only because jurists as a rule take little interest in sociology. Our concept of law has been for ages and still is predominantly monistic. We all believe that law is one, at least in principle. Although there are different compartments, such as private law, criminal law, public law or international law, these are only parts of one all-embracing system, ruled by the same fundamental principles and the same logic. In my my view there are two main reasons why we believe this, a philosophical one and a political one (2).

We mostly define law in terms of justice and the essence of justice is that it rules blindfolded, without respect of persons. Since justice demands that identical cases be treated in the same way, law should extend its scope as far as it can go in time and place. That, as Pascal said, something which is lawful on one side of the mountain may be unlawful on the other side, is nothing to be proud of.

(1) Literature on legal pluralism is sparse: H. Lévy-Bruhl, "Note sur les contacts entre les systèmes juridiques", *Symb. Taubenschlag* (1956) I, 27-33; Gurvitch, Théorie pluraliste des sources du droit positif. *Ann. Inst. Philos. du droit et sociol. jur.* (1934) 114; id., *Traité de Sociologie* II; E. A. Hoebel, "*The law of Primitive Man*" (Atheneum 116) New York 1968, 50; Pospisil, *The Kapauku Papuans and their law* (Yale University, Publ. in Anthrop. 54) Yale U.P. 1958, 274; M. A. Jaspan, "In quest of new law: the perplexity of legal syncretism in Indonesia", *Comp. Studies in Society and History* 7 (1964-1965) 252-266. A symposium on "pluralisme juridique" planned for May, 1968, in Brussels by Professor John Gillissen could not take place as a result of the occupation of the university buildings. The papers of the symposium will be published. Valuable observations are found in the handbooks on Roman legal history and private law of Kunkel and Kaser, e.g. on such topics as "Reichsrecht und Volksrecht" or "law and custom".

(2) Naturally these are not the only reasons which can be mentioned. For systematic jurisprudence, as it was developed in Europe on the basis of Roman law, unity is a logical postulate. See e.g. E. Kussbach, "Recht und Kultur; der Rechtsbegriff bei Huizinga", *ARSP* 54 (1968) 179-216: "Die Rechtsordnung ist materiell und formal gegliedert und stellt eine Einheit dar, einen logischen Bau, innerhalb dessen es keine Widersprüche geben kann".

Secondly, the unity of law was a major issue in the age-long struggle to establish the modern, national, constitutional state. As administration and justice were the two functions of medieval government, the drive for a national unified state implied unification of law. On the continent the setting up of national courts of appeal was a standard policy ever since the later middle ages. The development that began here, which I cannot follow now in detail, found its consummation in the great codifications of the nineteenth century which—in spite of all the bad things that can be said about them—meant real progress in terms of freedom, equality and legal security. That is why unification and codification appeal to so many new states in Africa and Asia that are now, in their turn, struggling to make a collection of tribes into a national state.

In the meantime, in highly developed states the heyday of monism seems long past, although much lip-service is still rendered to it. As a matter of fact, unity, as far as it went in codified legal systems, never was complete. The law always had to leave many things to local or commercial custom and there have always been conflicts between legal systems and sub-systems, or between the rule of law and the rule of certain professions such as physicians and priests. But to nineteenth-century jurists this did not seem to infringe legal unity. Any liberty, any privilege, any disciplinary law such as military law, any local or commercial custom was said to be valid only on account of its acknowledgement by the law. By that it became as it were incorporated in the one big body of law.

But this idea has become less and less convincing. No codification ever succeeded in ruling out the spontaneous growth of living law, whether on a local or a national basis. In all modern industrial states extensive and more or less independent systems of disciplinary law, commercial law and industrial law have been developed and are still growing. Standard conditions, collective contracts and forms of arbitration are used to such an extent that it seems that most conflicts, that may be termed legal, never reach the courts any more.

A topical example is provided by the discussion about the right to strike in the Netherlands. Strikes to many lawyers are a form of collective self-help for which theoretically there can be no place in the constitutional state. Nor does there seem to be a place for them in the system of codified private law, since most lawyers hardly get beyond the definition of a strike as an individual non-fulfilment of a labour contract. Nevertheless no one dares to deny the existence of the right to strike; so that apparently there are conflicting legal convictions at work here.

The principle of unified law within the constitutional state is particularly entrenched in the field of criminal law, where unhappy memories of darker ages are still alive. The maxim *nulla poena sine lege* derives directly from our principles of freedom and equality (3). Nobody can be allowed to take the law into his own hands. Yet it may be asked whether we do not deceive ourselves when, for the sake of the principle, we refuse to look for differences between principle and reality. It is not only gangsters and *mafiosi* that can punish people and get away with it. There are also forms of popular justice like boycott or charivari against which regular legal process is as a rule ineffective. We say that nobody should be forced to indulge in some medieval ritual in the village he happens to live in, but we seldom can do much to prevent it. Besides, our point of view is profoundly individualistic. When you believe that being part of a community is not just an accident, you will see things quite differently. So here too there are different legal systems, or at least different systems of social control.

This brings me back to the problem of customary law. As I said before, in the heyday of monism it was held that custom was only valid to the extent that it was acknowledged by the law. We do not hold this any longer. Just as monism appeals to legal principles, pluralism can do the same. Since the nineteenth century customary law has been much discussed and plays an important part in legal thinking at large. Now traditional definitions of customary law include two elements: long-established practice, *longaevus usus,* and the conviction that this practice is law, *opinio necessitatis.* When these elements go into your definition of law, the implication is, that if you find some people living according to different rules, and if you cannot deny that their practice is rooted in deep convictions, you have to acknowledge their custom as such as law. Otherwise you would subvert your own legal principles. It was exactly in this way that a western jurist like Van Vollenhoven came to plead for the recognition of *adat* law in Indonesia. And although, for him, the ultimate aim of his studies may have been an independent systematic *adat* law codification, later students of primitive law simply had to recognize the fact of legal pluralism (4).

The first attempts to give customary law its place in the legal system were dualistic. Nineteenth century Romantics set off the poetry of primitive and early law against the cold rationality of modern law, or living law against ossified law. Others, in the Greek philosophical tradition, spoke of written and unwritten law. In legal history, too, we find only dualistic concepts: state law versus local law, *Reichsrecht* versus *Volksrecht* (5), classical law versus vulgar law,

(3) It is interesting to note, however, that from the point of view of international penal law the validity of even this "absolute" principle seems to need restriction. See Van Agt, *Naar een extravert strafrecht* (inaugural lecture, Nijmegen, 1969) p. 11.
(4) Cf. Jaspan, *o.c.*
(5) Reference is made to the epoch-making book of L. Mitteis, *Reichsrecht und Volksrecht in den östlichen Provinzen des römischen Kaiserreichs,* Leipzig 1891.

jurists' law versus popular law. But all these dualistic concepts, useful as they may have been, have the same disadvantage: the second term is defined as the negation of the first and so can never be adequate to describe a complex reality.

We should, therefore, do away with dualistic concepts and accept the concept of pluralism just as the social sciences have long since done. We can even learn a lot from them, from their achievements as well as their failures. I am fully aware that it is dangerous to use in historical investigations some concept that is profoundly anachronistic as far as the period I am studying is concerned; but it cannot be avoided. There are only differences in degree of anachronism regarding the concepts historians use.

There is one disadvantage in the concept of pluralism that has been emphasised in social sciences recently: that is, that it tends to become a static concept (6). We miss an essential aspect of reality when we stop at a description of the different legal systems and subsystems that exist concurrently. Pluralism is not a situation but a process that develops in time, a complex pattern of continuous interaction. It may even appear that pluralism is just one word for many different processes. Legal historians, especially, have something to learn here. They often speak courageously of influences, receptions, and the like, without realizing that their concepts are much too simple. For the rest we cannot blame legal historians too much when we find here a field that is hardly studied at all, even by legal sociologists and anthropologists, namely the acculturation of legal sytems (7).

Naturally we should not suppose pluralism behind every inconsistency we find in a given legal system. Any legal system has its inconsistencies, even systems as highly sophisticated as our own. No doubt they can be found in Roman law too. One of them seems to be the problem of tombs (8). These, as *res religiosae,* were *extra commercium,* and yet many inscriptions prove that places in tombs were hired and sold as if they were not. Another striking inconsistency, observed already by Cicero, was that in Rome the *artes liberales* as a social, political and cultural pursuit were highly esteemed, while professors of the arts had a very low social status and legal position (9). For this there are historical reasons that have nothing to do with legal pluralism.

The question whether you can speak of legal pluralism is a little

(6) See e.g. A. J. Köbben on the concept of plural society, *Mens en Maatschappij,* 1967, 47-48.
(7) As Paul Bohannan says, anthropologists have been lax here. See: "The differing realms of the law", in: *Law and Warfare,* New York 1967, p. 56.
(8) See F. de Vischer, *Le droit des tombeaux romains,* Milano 1963.
(9) See D. Nörr, "Zur sozialen und rechtlichen Bewertung der freien Arbeit in Rom", *ZSS* 82 (1965) 74.

more complex with regard to so-called vulgar law *(10)*. The concept of vulgar law was derived from that of vulgar Latin. Now vulgar Latin is defined as the living speech of all strata of the population in all periods of *latinitas;* postclassical Latin is only a manifestation of this. In exactly the same manner Ernst Levy postulated that vulgar law existed in all periods of Roman law, but this has been little more than an assertion thus far. Practically speaking, vulgar law is the Roman law of postclassical times, mainly in the Western part of the Empire, from about 400 to 800 A.D.

As a matter of fact, Levy tried to prove that vulgar law in itself was a legal system. Most Romanists have not accepted this thesis. Yet when Wieacker objects that the concept of vulgar law as a legal system would imply the existence of a "Rechtsgemeinschaft" of vulgarians in the Roman empire *(11)*, this objection may also be questioned. Much depends on how you define "legal system". From a sociologist's point of view any complex of rules and institutions that is actually in force within some group or population may be termed a legal system if it has the formal characteristics of a legal system. That vulgar law is essentially the same Roman law as that elaborated by the jurisprudents only on a lower, unscientific level, is of no concern to the sociologist, if he finds that they were actually competing with one another.

In speaking of pluralism in Roman law, it seems appropriate to start with the observation that pluralism lay at the very root of Roman law, at least if the recent thesis of my compatriot van den Brink *(12)* deserves credit. He has brought to the field of legal history a thesis that has been hotly discussed by classical scholars for some fifty years, namely that the foundations of Rome resulted from the fusion of at least two distinctive ethnic groups, which for convenience may be called Sabines and Latins, each with their own social structure, religion, culture and legal system. What he tries to prove is that all legal institutions of early Roman law reveal traces of this fusion. I cannot follow this argument in detail here; I am afraid we will never get beyond pure speculation in this field. According to the now prevalent opinion among specialists, for one thing, both Sabines and Latins were, even before the fusion, a mixed stock of Mediterranean and Indo-Germanic elements. So it seems a hopeless enterprise to try to discern Latin and Sabine elements in early Roman law.

When we look for instances of legal pluralism in the sources of

(10) In the discussions about this concept, which was strongly promoted by Ernst Levy, nearly all Romanists have taken part. Very important contributions to the discussion were made by F. Wieacker. A recent survey of the discussion is given by Gudrun Stühff, *Vulgarrecht im Kaiserrecht* (Forsch. z. Röm. Recht 21) Böhlau 1968, 1.

(11) *Vom röm. Recht*, p. 225.

(12) *Ius fasque, opmerkingen over de dualiteit van het archaisch-Romeins recht*, Amsterdam, 1968.

Roman law we can find hardly any, especially as far as the Republic and the early principate are concerned. One instance may be the existence of "plebeian law" alongside civil law before the *lex Hortensia* of about 286 B.C., which provided that the decrees of the plebeian assemblies would be binding on the whole people (Gai. 1.3). But how things actually worked before the *lex Hortensia*, we do not know (*13*).

The Romans of republican times tried hard to avoid double citizenship; they had no concept of customary law; and the social organisations they knew, had no legislative power for their group or trade. On each of these subjects I can now only make a few remarks.

First, the much discussed topic of double citizenship (*14*). Being a citizen, that is, belonging to a city-state, was for the ancients quite different from being a national of a modern state. Socially and religiously the city was the cosmos of man's life, the place where he was to fulfil his destiny. Being a citizen was a way of life, and obeying the cities' laws was only an aspect of that. This can hardly be expressed by saying that in ancient law the principle of personality was predominant. Only gradually did another concept of citizenship develop; and the original one was never given up altogether.

Although Greek cities already used to grant honorary citizenship to foreigners as a political expedient, republican Romans like Cicero found it improper to be a citizen of another city besides Rome. And when the Romans, from Caesar's time onwards, began to grant citizenship on a considerable scale, they did not find the legal implications a difficulty.

The Romans used the granting of citizenship, apart from rewarding veterans, first and foremost as a means of political pacification. By granting Roman citizenship to members of the ruling classes of captured cities and countries they managed to make them allies in the ruling of the expanding empire. Thus Roman citizenship became a matter of high social status, to which certain privileges and immunities attached.

In principle, the Romans did not interfere with local communities if they could avoid it; everybody was left to live in his own traditional way and by his own law. Apparently it was understood, though not expressed until much later, that the new Romans also continued to live by local law as far as the local community was concerned. In other words, the principle of personality was nothing like a hard and fast rule. This is no wonder. Truly, as Holmes said in his famous dictum, law is what the courts will do.

(*13*) The thesis of Van den Brink, that patricians and plebeins were ethnic groups, is interesting, but offers no clue to the question either.

(*14*) The literature about this topic is immense. See Taubenschlag, *The Law of Greco-Roman Egypt*, 586, note 24 and D. Nörr, "Origo, Studien zur Orts-Stadt-und Reichszugehörigkeit," *TRG* 31 (1963), who gives more literature in note 150 on p. 556. I can make only a few superficial remarks on this complicated subject.

Now, obviously, courts as a rule only know their own law well enough to pass judgment with the assurance that is essential for any judgment to be accepted by the parties concerned. Even nowadays, while the availability of information about foreign legal systems is excellent, courts only reluctantly apply foreign law. Thus the fresh Roman citizen somewhere in the provinces could in practice only get his case tried according to Roman law if he could manage to get it before the court of the Roman *praeses provinciae*. When he resorted to local courts he would be well aware that local law would apply to his case. So practically speaking there can have been few probems, and Roman jurists never raised theoretical problems when there was no reason to do so.

Only when Roman citizenship during the principate was granted on an ever increasing scale, and finally, by the *Constitutio Antoniniana* of 212, was given to nearly all inhabitants of the empire, did things become different. Not that people in every corner of the empire suddenly stopped living by the law they were used to; in Egyptian sources, for instance, we can observe in detail that the *Constitutio Antoniniana* as a matter of fact made no difference at all in the process of interaction between Egyptian, Greek and Roman law that went on there for ages and resulted in the romanization of Greek and Egyptian law and the hellenization of Roman law, as Taubenschlag puts it (*15*).

But in the expansion of Roman citizenship that was completed in the *Constitutio Antoniniana*, a profound transformation of the concept of citizenship manifests itself, which affects legal history and practice as well. Citizenship is by then no longer a way of life. This idea was already weakening when the Romans used citizenship as a political expedient and so made it a mark of social status. The more it was expanded, the more it naturally lost this value, and became in the end something like membership of a territorial state. It was then no longer impracticable or unseemly for a Roman citizen before a Roman court to appeal to some rule of local customary law; and if Roman courts did apply such rules, customary law should certainly have its place among the sources of law.

Although the Romans held that many of their legal institutions derived from ancient *mores*, the extant catalogues of sources of law of classical times do not mention custom at all (*16*). One of the main

(*15*) *The Law of Greco-Roman Egypt*, 21-51. See also H. J. Wolff, "Faktoren der Rechtsbildung im hellenistisch-römischen Aegypten," *ZSS* 70 (1953) 20-57.

(*16*) The literature about custom in Roman law is hardly less immense than that on double citizenship. I mention only J. A. C. Thomas, "Custom and Roman Law," *TRG* 31 (1963) 39-53 and B. Schmiedel, *Consuetudo im klassischen und nachklassischen Römischen Recht* (Forsch. z. Röm. Recht 22) Böhlau 1966, where further literature is mentioned. See also Gaudemet, "L'autorité de la loi et de la coutume dans l'antiquité," *VI. Cong. int. de droit comp., Hamburg 1962, Rapports généraux*, Bruxelles, 1964, g-36. The catalogues referred to are Gai I.2 and Pap. D.1.1.7.

reasons for this seems to me to be, that for the Romans, who managed to separate law from religion quite early, law as an autonomous system was based on tradition and authority. Or, to put it more precisely, extending an idea of Wieacker (*17*), the core of the law for them was the public acts—present and past—of bodies and persons vested with authority on account of tradition. This is true for all periods of Roman law and for all of its acknowledged sources, whether the king, the pontiffs and the *comitia*, the republican magistrates, the *concilium plebis*, the senate and the jurists, or the emperors and provincial governors. Even so, when *mores* were accounted for as a source of legal institutions, this meant that the *maiores* from immemorial times had acted in that way, so here again authority and tradition were the basis of law. Besides, as Professor Thomas has observed (*18*), civil law, whether based on legislation or *mores*, depended from early times for its application on *interpretatio*, that is, on the authoritative word of a legal specialist: pontiff first, jurisprudent later on.

Now from this point of view it is quite understandable that a classical Roman jurist, when confronted with custom, never considered it as a matter of law but just as a matter of fact (*19*). It was becoming and wise to take such facts into account, but no legal principle required him to do so. Romans saw foreign legal systems, about which they knew very little indeed, in the same way. Foreign legal practice confronted them as a matter of colonial administration and they treated it as such in their usual manner, that is, purely pragmatically and extremely liberally, so long as no threat to their political power was involved.

It seems that only in early post-classical times was a theory of customary law developed. The implications of that theory were treated only in a casual way. It was neither recognition of the normative force of facts, nor consideration for legal convictions different from their own, that brought the Romans to the concept of customary law. They developed their theory, as a matter of fact, within the framework of their traditional legal thought, where authority was the basis of law. As we know, the early Principate for political reasons set much value on keeping up a façade of republican institutions. One of these was that authority, *imperium*, was vested in the chosen magistrates—and the Principate actually was a bundle of magistracies—by a formal law, the *lex de imperio* (*20*). This

(*17*) *ZSS* 70 (1953) 101: "Fast alle nicht-didaktische römische Rechtsliteratur wurzelt in der Grundform der Aufzeichnung des Rechtskenners über geschehenes öffentliches Handeln, mag es sich in Gesetzesgestalt oder prätorischer Institution, in *responsum* oder *cautio*, oder in kaiserlicher Rechtsprechung darstellen". On the ideas of authority and tradition in Roman Law see especially F. Schulz, *Prinzipien des röm. Rechts*.

(*18*) *Custom and Roman Law*, 43.

(*19*) Cf. v. Lübtow, *Das römische Volk*, 514; Schmiedel, *op. cit.* pp. 247-367.

(*20*) Part of the *lex de imperio Vespasiani* of c. 70 A.D. is preserved on a bronze tablet found in Rome (*FIRA* I, 15).

institution was used skilfully, in about the same way as the notorious "Ermächtigungsgesetz" that formally legitimated Hitler's tyranny (21), to give the *princeps* as lawmaker a place outside and above the closed circle of traditional legal authorities. It was held that the legislative power of the *princeps* ultimately derived from this law, and the more absolute the power of emperors became, the more stress was laid on the *lex de imperio*, which Justinian called *lex regia*, as an ideological justification of imperial power. In this way also the *fact* of imperial power could be reconciled with the *theory* that the law was a convention of the whole nation, a theory predominant in rhetoric, which through the law schools penetrated later classical legal thinking (poleós synthéké koiné, Dem.; cfr. D.1.3.1, (Pap.), 2 (Marc.); Gell. XI.18.4: XII, 13.5: XX.10.9; Plin. n.h. VII.210). This construction of the *lex de imperio* is found among other places in D.1.4.1.pr. (Ulp.) (22).

There is an allusion to it, as it seems to me, in the famous passage about customary law in D.1.3.32.1, a passage that stands in the name of Julian, but must in fact be of postclassical origin:

> *Leges nulla alia ex causa nos teneant, quam quod iudicio populi receptae sunt* . . .

Now the argument that follows in this text is clear, though somewhat academic: when the authority of a law rests on popular consent, then also the will of the people, as it is expressed without words or writing, *rebus ipsis et factis*, should be valid. Here again we have public acts of a body vested with authority—the people itself—and consequently here we have law. So the concept of *tacitus consensus populi*, which soon became a stereotyped phrase (23), was in itself no breach of the principle that law rests on authority and tradition.

Once customary law is accepted, naturally the possibility of conflicts between law and custom arises. The Roman jurists with their usual casuistic approach never produced general solutions for these conflicts. As a matter of fact, the Justinianic compilation reflects different attitudes towards customary law, and so the question whether custom was valid *contra legem* became one of the most famous antinomies of the Digest, over which, as Gothofredus says, the glossators quarreled loud and long (24), using all the instruments of their craft to find solutions.

The recognition of custom as a source of law threw up yet another problem that the Romans also knew of, but as usual treated only

(21) See Ilse Staff (Ed.), *Justiz im dritten Reich*, Fischer Bücherei 1964, 50.
(22) Cfr. Gai I.5; D.1.2.11 (Pomp.); *Const. deo auctore* 7; 1.2.6. That there had once been doubts about the legal force of imperial interpretation is expressly stated by Justinian in C.1 14, 12.1, Cfr. Savigny, *System* I, 301.
(23) Cfr. D.1.3.32 (Iul.) D.1.3.35 (Hermog); *Ulp. reg.* 4; *Inst.* 1.2.11.
(24) The antinomy is caused especially by D.1.3.32, *in fine* (glo *abrogentur*) as against C.8.53.2 (glo. *aut ratione*). To the last text Gothofredus notes: " . . . qua de re tamen multa et longa rixa hic refertur inter glossographos".

casually. That is, whether we can acknowledge customs of subjected people that are repugnant to our religious, moral or social convictions. This problem has confronted colonial powers from the beginning, and it still has to be solved by a lot of new countries that have to deal within their territory with tribal custom (25).

It may be typical of the way the Romans administered their colonial empire that we only find a few texts about it. Naturally there was no question that a custom could stand when disapproved of by the Roman rulers, but they did not interfere if they could avoid doing so. The emperor did not approve of marriage between brother and sister, nor of bigamy, and that is nearly all there is. Only once in a much discussed constitution of Constantine (C.8.52 (53), 2), which in part must have been worked over by the compilators, do we find an abstract announcement (26). Custom has no mean value, but it may not oppose *ratio* or *lex*. Now it has been much discussed whether "*ratio*" here means something like natural reason or rather "*raison d'état*", so this does not bring us much further (27). Only when the glossators are discussing the topic of law and custom do we find, among the *distinctiones* they use, that between good and bad custom. This distinction is stressed even more in canon law (*Extra* 1.4.11) and that is no wonder. Already in Roman sources the extant condemnations of bad custom mainly date from the Christian era. Christians believe that they have, in natural law, an absolute moral measure to judge custom by. In some form or other the same distinction is found all along the line in the history of private law. Nineteenth century Pandectists as well as most modern lawyers hold that custom is valid only when it is a "löbliche Gewohnheit" (28), when it does not oppose natural law or (to put it in secularized form) public order, public morals or progress.

If you ask why the Romans made so little fuss about all this, the answer may be that the Romans, imperialistic as they were, never were imperialistic in the field of ideas, never pursued a "culture policy" (29). Else they would never have succeeded in keeping up their empire for some six centuries. Besides the Romans had no idea of progress whatsoever. Their outlook, as that of most ancient people,

(25) See e.g. Jaspan, *op. cit.* and F. D. Holleman, "The recognition of Bantu customary law in South Africa", in: *The Future of Customary Law in Africa*. 1955, 232-256.

(26) Cfr. *Nov.* 134.1: "male enim adinventa nec ex longa consuetudine confirmantur", a text which also has provoked a lot of learned comment.

(27) See von Lübtow, *Das römische Volk*, 519, where literature is given.

(28) See Dernburg, *Pand.* I, 60 and Windscheid, *Pand.* I, 42.

(29) See F. Vittinghoff, *Römische Kolonisation und Bürgerrechtspolitik unter unter Caesar und Augustus.* Wiesbaden 1952, 1225 and the review of this book by Kunkel, *ZSS* 70 (1953) 446. A typical example, stressed recently by P. Pestman (*Over vrouwen en voogden in het oude Egypte*, Leiden, Brill, 1969, p. 20) is that the Romans in Egypt did not interfere with the existing custom of marriage between brother and sister. As it seems, this practice was even expanding during the first two centuries of Roman rule. Prohibitions come only much later.

was rather pessimistic, if that isn't an anachronistic expression in itself. Cosmic order was unchanging. Time was a circular movement, an ever recurring circle of life and death that generates new life.

Progress, and the feeling of being ahead of other people can develop only on the basis of a linear concept of time such as the Christians took over from the Jews and such as we all still have, whether we are Christian or Marxist. This is what makes our view of the world so much different from that of the Romans. Everything we do has to fit into a divine plan—however secularized that may be—that unfolds in time. Besides, Christians tend to think antithetically, so that imperialism somehow meant spreading the Kingdom of God, the advancement of civilisation. Any native legal system could hardly be recognized as valid, because naturally it would be full of sin. This position was held in its most extreme form in *Calvin's* case in 1608 (30), in which it was said that:

> "if a Christian King should conquer the Kingdom of an infidel . . . the laws of that infidel are abrogated . . . and in that case, until certain laws be established, the King by himself, and such judges as he shall appoint, shall judge them and their cases according to natural justice."

Although this decision was overruled soon, and colonial powers for practical reasons accepted the Roman policy of not interfering with local custom, the predominant opinion to this day is still that custom cannot be valid if it is contrary to public morality, natural law, progress or whatever you like (31). It is still much the same position as Raffles held in 1814 in Java, ordering that "a judge shall be guided in his decisions by existing native laws and ancient customs of the Islands, provided the same be not decidedly at variance with the universal and acknowledged principles of natural justice" (32). It may be time we got beyond this position at last, but this is a problem that it is not for the legal historian to solve.

There is another source of legal pluralism in medieval and modern society that the Romans of classical times hardly knew, that is, professional organisations (33). There were, as a matter of fact, in Rome *collegia* of all sorts, for instance of carpenters, blacksmiths, silversmiths, shipbuilders, bakers and tax-collectors. They were entitled to hold meetings, to make rules for domestic matters and to have property. They even played a part in local politics, as inscriptions from Pompeii prove, and this may have been a reason why regulations

(30) 7 *Rep.* 17 Lord Coke. Cited after F. D. Holleman, *op. cit.* p. 233 note I.

(31) On the other hand, in the same order of ideas the main motive to let indigenous people live by their own law becomes the supposition that they are not yet advanced enough in civilization to live by the "ordinary laws". See e.g. R. Verloren van Thermaat, "Regsopleiding van die Bantoe", *Tydskr.* 31 (1968) 40-57; Holleman, *op. cit* p. 238.

(32) Cited after Jaspan, *op cit.* p. 255.

(33) See W. Liebenam, *Zur Geschichte und Organisation des Römischen Vereinswesens*, Leipzig 1890; Kornemann, *RE* 4, 415.

on *collegia* were very strict indeed. But *collegia* and *sodalitates* had no public function or legislative power. They did not set rules for their trade, fix tariffs, quality standards or contractual conditions, and they had neither privileges nor jurisdiction. So their position differs greatly from that of medieval guilds or many modern industrial organisations. Only in the totalitarian state of the Dominate, when *collegia* became compulsory organisations that held a monopoly of their trade, did they begin to make price-regulations in return.

Recently Professor Hans Julius Wolff (34) has asked why, in the ancient world, we nowhere find organisations like medieval guilds, although with regard to commercial and industrial development ancient cities cannot have differed much from medieval ones. Part of the answer may be found indeed, as he suggests, in social and religious concepts. The predominant structure of ancient society was that of organic wholes centred around a cult: the city, the *gentes*, the family. Besides, in medieval society public authority is a private matter that was bought and sold and could be in the hands of anybody that proved his title to it, whereas in Rome only bodies vested with authority had what might be called legislative power. Therefore Roman *collegia*, vested with no authority, could have no legal power.

But that may be only part of the answer. Another reason is that in the ancient world in general the social and concurrently the legal position of handworkers and tradesmen were very low (35). In Rome manual labour was little appreciated, at least in ruling senatorial circles, especially when it was performed in subordination and for money. Commerce was even forbidden to senators by law. Now we should never forget that Rome in all the periods of its existence was an aristocratic society in its social structure as well as in its law. Social and industrial organisations lacked power on account of the social status of their members, and that is part of a system. The low status of people who had to work for a living was paralleled by the weak legal position of people—mostly the same group—who had to rent a house, to give only one example. In this respect things have changed a lot, though perhaps not enough. Nowadays it is economic and concurring political power that enable industries to dictate standard conditions—not to speak of investment regulations—and trade unions to bargain on collective contracts or influence housing policy and legislation. And it is this power that may bring new legal systems and sub-systems into existence.

These are no more than hints of the complex social, religious, economic and political factors that can be at the root of legal pluralism.

(34) A summary of the paper he had planned to present to the Congress of SIDA in Fribourg, 1968, is among the papers of that Congress. As far as I know it is not yet published elsewhere.

(35) See D. Nörr, "Zur sozialen und rechtlichen Bewertung der freien Arbeit in Rom", *ZSS* 82 (1965) 67-105.

I have hardly said anything about the one group of sources that seems most important for the study of legal pluralism in antiquity, namely the collections of papyri from Egypt. Above all, these give us an insight into legal practice; it is in them that the interaction of Egyptian, Greek and Roman law can be studied in great detail.

If one asks what lessons can be derived from history in this field, the answer is, that it mainly depends on what lessons one is ready to accept. The main point may be, that law never was one and that, however sublime justice may be, law is a complex of systems of social control among other complexes of systems of social control. All should work for a better society, but in the process of change, why start from irrational monistic beliefs?

As far as underdeveloped countries are concerned, for some purposes tribal jurisdiction indeed may be best. It is quick, free, and simple, and it restores moral and religious solidarity in the group. And that is something that the state jurisdiction can never do. On the other hand, tribal jurisdiction may favour traditionally privileged and exploiting groups, or may hamper industrial and commercial development. So why strive for uniform solutions that may have as many bad effects as good ones? Man has enough imagination to do better than that, and he may yet learn something from the Romans (36).

(36) This is the text, with a few changes and additions, of a lecture delivered at University College, London, on 29 April, 1969.

[22]

PEOPLE'S LAW, DEVELOPMENT, JUSTICE

By Upendra Baxi

I INTRODUCTION: LAW AND "DEVELOPMENT"

1. Conceptions of "Development"

The law is resorted to almost talismanically for initiating and implementing social change decisions by the elite of the "developing" (or more accurately impoverishing) societies. In this sense, the law (as a body of rules and precepts, as a group of social institutions making, applying and enforcing rules and precepts, and as a carrier of ideologies, values) is an important resource for, and adjunct to, development or directed social transformation. Notoriously, most change-oriented laws designed to further social and economic transformation turn out to have rather limited efficacy, at least in the not too short run. They do not bring about optimum behavioural compliance, much less changes in attitudes and values. This, in turn, affects the symbolism of the law and its processes generally; and threatens to erode, in the long run, the legitimacy not merely of the law but of its makers and upholders as well. A related aspect, well worth recalling, is that the attempt to use the law to initiate and accomplish planned change is, in basic respect, a "bootstrap operation" for the "developing" societies. Glib talks of law's potential for development simply overlook that substantial economic and social costs have to be borne in order to make the law an effective instrument of social change. Resources have to be constantly and consciously allocated to the making of law (which is not just a matter of copycat drafting but of relating change aspirations to obdurate social realities by a painstaking grasp), its dissemination, creation of supportive structures (mobilization through public opinion), favoured interpretation systems (courts, tribunals), adequate implementation/enforcement systems, continuing social audit of the law's operations and ongoing repair and reform jobs. All this requires a rather substantial investment of manpower and money. Typically, however, the net outlays of national budgets for administration of justice, legal enforcement, supportive structures is low and even miniscule. Very often, political elites want just this: a veneer of change over the substance of status quo. Most changes sought to be ushered in by the law are such that they only nominally, if at all, affect the dominant patterns of distribution, and management of distribution, of power in society. But even for elites, who somehow manage to transcend their class base, and for whom recourse to law for social change may not be chicanery and ritualism, the problem of the use of law for developmental purposes may well be an aspect of underdevelopment itself. In other words, even where the fundamental drive of developmental effort may be to reduce poverty, such effort itself continues to be affected by the very context of poverty and scarcity at every level (Baxi, 1976_a: 38 – 94). We thus have to ask in contexts like India not merely whether the law can affect changes in the lives of the poor but also how far poverty itself affects initiation and accomplishment of ameliorative legal changes.

In order to understand the relevance of law to development, we need at the outset a clear understanding of both the notions. What is "development"? The many conceptions of "development" floating around in the massive literature are, I suspect, by themselves a means of exploitation. But this is a subject by itself. Let me point out one or two ambiguities and then move on. It is said that "development" may be looked upon as the process of planned or directed social change. But the real questions are: Development for whom? development of what? development through what? development from whom? These are very crude questions: so crude that very few social scientists pause to ask these. For me in my relative lack of scientism these are the questions which matter. Undoubtedly, in most countries the Gross National Product has increased. But Gross National Poverty (the other GNP) has also simultaneously increased. That is why I am more comfortable with the expression "impoverishing" societies than "developing" societies. From the notorious, and somewhat nefarious, scholarly concern with "development" in the fifties and sixties we have arrived, in the seventies, with a more engaging and promising concern with "another development". One might say, with some risk of overgeneralization, that the literature of the sixties revealed, in essence, a hegemonial, unilinear, eurocentric model of "development"; it was, notably, the work of Western scholars. Concurrent with the model of development were certain preferred strategies for it, which were either emulated by or imposed upon the elites of the developing societies (Inaytullah, 1975). The quest for "Another Development" in the seventies has arisen out of the realization that development is a multilinear, history and culture specific process and is conditioned by the nature of international political and economic orders.

It is now accepted that development is all about distribution. The technocratic approach to development emphasises "technological modernization, managerial efficiency and growth in GNP". Underlying this approach is the assumption that "the system could be made to work if equitable distribution is built into an essentially growth model" (Haque et al., 1977· 12). This has been the prevalent approach so far in India. The results are not all that impressive. This approach in any case relies on the "classical" conditions of capitalistic accumulation such as frugality, innovativeness, access to home market, and the political and military power to create international markets conducive to industrial growth at home" (Haque et. al., 1977: 13). The realities do not support these assumptions.

The other way of looking at development seeks to redefine the processes and objectives of development "into the direction of rapid social change and redistribution of political power". On this approach, development is not just to be measured in terms of technoeconomic variables but rather as development of "the collective personality of the society". The processes of development are, on this view, designed to foster a "collective" sprit ("a sense of belonging to a society, pride in national achievement, fulfillment in helping one's distressed neighbours"), creation of "aspiration frontiers" (dissemination of appropriate values), generation of self-reliance and "participatory democracy". The latter is one way of eliminating "consciousness gap" between leaders and masses (Haque et. al. 1977: 12, 15 – 19). Ultimately, these processes should lead to de-alienation.

From this standpoint, the "development" resulting from growthmodel (stressing centralized planning, expansion of modernized industrial sector and assistance from developed countries) is really "anti-development". The second model of development judges developmental process by what it does to man; de-alienation, self- reliance and participation are the three crucial components here. Clearly, this is, for India, (as indeed for most "developing" societies) only a statement of preferred future; but it may provide critical bases for devaluation and even delegitimation of the existing liberal-capitalistic growth model.

2. Law, Legitimation and Development

Where and how do we place law on the debate concerning development? The current development literature is devoid of any critical thought on law's relation to social organization and change. Nor are the mainstream social scientists much bothered to understand the nature and function of modern law. This was not of course the manner in which the founders of modern social theory regarded law. Durkheim, Marx and Weber gave sustained attention to law as a social form and process in arriving at the understanding of social development. The recent serious attempts made by lawmen (ILC, 1974; Trubek, 1972; Unger, 1976; Trubek & Galanter, 1974; Trubek, 1977; Balbus, 1977; Hurst, 1950, 1964) to provide some theoretical basis for relation of law to development have still to be related to the current debate on alternative conceptions of development.

The simplest way in which law is often approached in the context of development is through an emphasis on its instrumental and technocratic dimension. Law is regarded as a technique for ordering of social relations. It is also seen as a conversion technique, i.e. public and positive law norms convert social, political and economic choices into a system of binding rules and precepts. Law is also regarded, in this view, as facilitating organization of choice and enterprise. In this sense, law is no more than a manual of instructions for people who want certain things done. The instrumentalist notion of law also included a concern with forms of conflict resolution provided under the auspices of the legal system. In this conception, law is merely seen performing certain jobs felt necessary from time to time to keep society as a "going concern". Karl Lewellyn called these the "bare bones" law jobs, whose task is to make group living possible (1940, 1368 – 70). On such a conception, law may not appear to be of any fundamental significance in understanding of social change, and even planning of it. The entire social technology that is law is here reduced merely to a kind of toolkit.

A wider conception of law, both as an aspect of social consciousness and of social organisation, gets us closer to understanding its linkages with social change. Law is not just social technology; it is an aspect of culture (or ideology, if you please). Law as a system, reflects, reinforces and often mutates and innovates values and ideals: whether these be of the dominant groups in society or ascribed to people at large. Law is also to be viewed as a social system – a system of social relations, roles/statuses and institutions. Interaction, through a network of institutions of law having their own "subcultures", between and among the makers, interpreters, enforcers, compliers, breakers, and beneficiaries of law constitutes law as a social system. Law, thus conceived, performs important legitimation functions in a society. A prime function of law is to establish, maintain and justify distinctions between permissible and proscribed uses of force in social relations. Legal systems, more or less, appropriate unto themselves the domain of legitimate force in society. This appropriation function is among the key functions of law in society. But because law appropriates force, it also accustoms us to its exercise according to legally ordained procedures. We think of and feel the legal application of force in purely normative rather than existential terms. Above all, and here lies the danger, the institutionalization and routinization of use of force continually reinforces the authority of law, indeed to a point where the mere existence of a rule prescribing behaviour becomes self-justifying. The intervention of law inhibits the fundamental question: what are the good reasons for the state's continuing appropriation of force? Thus, it contributes to the legitimation of law and the power of its makers.

Normative and social systems of law tend to "institutionalize class conflict" (Dahrendorf, 1957) by providing certain adjustments of conflicting interests and a vast repertoire of conflict-resolution techniques and institutions. Law functions in this manner to sustain existing patterns of distribution and management of distribution of power in society. This too is among the principal legitimation functions of law.

Finally (without being exhaustive) there is the notion of the "rule of law", a heavily overworked notion which performs certain legitimation functions for those who hold power in any society. In one sense, it simply means conformity with the lawyers' law, that is due observance of the procedures prescribed. This is not the most significant aspect of the notion as such conformity is consistent with the grossest inequity. The other and the more important aspect of the notion "imports both a minimal justness of rules and a dynamic responsiveness of substantive law to the needs of social and economic development" (Stone, 1966: 621). In this sense, the rule of law signifies a complex of standards of redistribution and justice; and in this sense it is a highly variable achievement. Such, however, is the symbolic appeal of the notion "rule of law" that it prevents fundamental questions concerning justice from arising at all: For whom, and for what purposes, and to what extent does the "rule of law" (conceived primarily as an attainment of a modicum of justice through legal processes) exist? Can it be claimed with integrity that it exists for most, let alone, all people in society? Indeed, by solely addressing its constraints to the exercise of public power, the rule of law notion diverts attention from the very real violations of minimal justice in social relations by those who wield extensive "private" power. (The problem in India is precisely of this nature: the state is not the most significant holder of power). Moreover, is the "critical premise" of the doctrine of rule of law that rules can make power impersonal and impartial "not" fictitious? (Unger, 1976: 180). Indeed, as Unger points out, "the very assumptions of the rule of law ideal appear to be falsified by the reality of life in liberal society. But, curiously, the reasons for the failure of this attempt to ensure the impersonality of power are the same that inspired the effort in the first place: the existence of a relatively open, partial rank order, and the accompanying disintegration of a self-legitimating consensus. The factors that make the search necessary also make its success impossible. The state, a supposedly neutral overseer of social conflict, is forever caught up in the antagonism of private interests and made the tool of one faction or another. Thus, in seeking to discipline and justify the exercise of power, men are condemned to pursue an objective they are forbidden to reach. And the repeated disappointment accentuates still further the gap between the vision of the ideal and the experience of reality" (Unger, 1976: 181). And yet this experience of "gap", which is a structural property of legal system, does not serve to delegitimate power. Balbus has recently argued that "the legitimation of the legal order is not primarily a function of its ability to live up to its claims" but "rather of the fact that its claims . . . are valued in the first place". Thus, for example, the notion of the formal equality of men before the law has been so firmly entrenched as to make unproblematic the substantive equal treatment of unequals. The law of theft and the punishment for theft is the same, for example, for the rich and the poor; and in fact the punishment actually awarded may be much less stringent for the former rather than the latter. The equality before the law argument does not countenance the claim that the rich, who should have no reason to commit the crime, should be more severely punished as compared with the poor. To allow such questions would be to initiate delegitimation of the legal order, a "fundamental break with the values and (formal) mode of rationality of the legal form itself". Balbus urges that an adequate theory of "legitimation and/or delegitimation would have to explain why the logic. of the legal order . . . is ordinarily accepted as unproblematical, and is not called into question in the name of a radically different logic" (Balbus, 1977: 581–582).

In outlining the wider notion of law, we have already seen how law is itself a form of social consciousness, in which are embedded certain ideals of justice, equality, authority. A mere technocratic/instrumental view of law would not have taken us this far. We may briefly turn to the understanding of law as social structure to complete the picture. Max Weber, in his rich and seminal analysis of the organization of authority in society, was the first to insist on the relative autonomy of the legal order. He was concerned to show that while the development of law was intimately related to certain socio-economic formations, law as such cannot be reduced to be a mere reflection of relations between classes. Thus, he recognizes that "the alliance of monarchical and bourgeois interests was one of the major factors which led toward formal legal rationalization", and gave rise to a calculable and predictable system of rules based on the principles of formal legal equality. The specific forms of rationalization in law cannot be explained wholly by taking capitalism as a "decisive factor" in the process (Weber, 1954) Weber clearly saw that law was autonomous at four distinct levels, now sharply formulated by Roberto Unger (1976: 52–54). Law is substantively, institutionally, methodologically and occupationally autonomous. Law is substantively autonomous when its norms "cannot be persuasively analyzed merely as statement of any identifiable" set of economic, political or religious beliefs. Law is institutionally autonomous "to the extent that its rules are applied by specialized institutions whose main task is adjudication". Methodological autonomy of law can be seen by special types of reasoning and justification adopted by legal institutions as compared with other social institutions. Finally, a legal order is occupationally autonomous when a specialized group of people (legal notables to use Weber's expression) – legal profession – "defined by its prerogatives, and training manipulates the rules, staffs the legal institutions, and engages in the practice of legal arguments" (Unger, 1976: 53).

Weber pointed out that a legal order, thus seen, differed from politics and administration by its objectives of generality and uniformity of application: there is a belief that the law "consists essentially in a consistent system of abstract rules" uniformly applied in "particular cases". Obedience is accorded to rules and to legal authority and not to persons occupying office as they too do so, and act, on the basis of obedience to rules in the first place (Weber, 1964: 330). The abstract character of law was favoured by all those interest-groups "to whom the stability and predictibility of legal procedure was of very great importance". It was equally important to those "who on ideological grounds attempt to break down authoritarian controls" (Weber, 1954: 229). Clearly, an autonomous legal order in this sense was a crucial component in the development of liberal capitalist societies in the West (Trubek, 1972). Indeed, it has been argued that while the legal order may be autonomous in the sense that it is "autonomous from the preferences of actors outside this order", it would be wrong to say therefore that it is "autonomous from the capitalist system" (Balbus, 1977: 272). In this brilliant analysis Balbus goes further to show that there is an essential identity between the "legal form and the very 'cell' of capitalist society, the commodity form").

A tolerably clear corelation between legalism and state authority structure thus emerges from the work of, and since, Weber. Weber stressed that "legalism, while seeming to constraint the state really strengthened class domination" (Trubek, 1972: 53). The system of formal justice, Weber maintained, "legalizes" unequal distributions of economic and political power by "guaranteeing maximum freedom for the interested parties to represent their formal legal interests" (Weber, 1968: 812) Whether or not growth model of development is viable, or constitutes "anti-development", legalism is a very crucial aspect of that model and no understanding of it can be complete without some grasp of the nature and relationship of law to social formations.

The same is indeed true when we move away from the technocratic growth model of development to the broadly humanistic model articulated earlier in this part. How would legal systems be related to the essential tasks of fostering "collective spirit", creating new "aspiration frontiers", and a movement towards new forms of social order enhancing participation, self-reliance and de-alienation? Would not all this require major transformations in law as social consciousness and social organization? Given the existing forms of law and social orderings, and the nature of their relations, would it be at all possible to meaningfully decentralize power, escalate participation and restore human autonomy and dignity for the masses? These indeed are no strange questions for the Indian mind. Gandhi raised them eloquently on the eve of constitution making (Baxi, 1967). Jayprakash Narayan raised them again, not just at the level of ideology but of political action, in the mid-seventies. The contemporary increasingly feeble "dialogue" between the neo-Nehruites and neo-Gandhians is an aspect of the same quest.

II PEOPLE'S LAW, DEVELOPMENT, JUSTICE

1. People's Law: Problems of conceptualization:

One way in which we can begin towards a new consciousness of law (especially in a country like India) is to relate "people's law" to "state" law. One factor contributing to the vicissitudes of the law as an instrument of directed social change is simply that most ex-colonial societies of the Third World were (and remain) multilegal, possessing more than one legal system and legal "culture". The imported western legal systems interacted in different ways with indigenous systems of administration of justice. Initially, the imported/inherited western based legal systems were alien both historically and existentially to the people at large. This alienness may still persist after most of these countries have become independent and yet have continued to operate with the received systems of law and justice whether as a matter of deliberate choice (in terms of the maxim "what is good for the elite is good for the masses") or as historical hangover. There are close parallels here between the European "reception" of the Roman law (Stone, 1966) and the ongoing crisis of legality in the newly independent societies which have twice received the European law.

Of course, it is now being discovered all over again (there is no commandment in social sciences forbidding the reinvention of the wheel!) that all societies including those which are highly developed are multilegal, an insight unforgettably proffered sometime ago by Otto von Gierke, Eugen Ehrlich, Max Weber and others. The sociological literature of the sixties and seventies celebrates the return to this theme. It not merely stresses the inadequacies and inhumanities of the state law's "assembly line" justice but also highlights the comparatively superior qualities of non-state, informal, people's law. All this indeed has come to a point that one hears of the "peaceful uses of anthropology" (Lowy, 1973: 205) and creation of African type moots in the suburbs of San Francisco (Danzing and Lowy; 1975: 685)! Interesting too is the semantic distinction (manipulation?). The Asian/African societies have "tradition" and "custom". The same phenomenon is described for the developed societies differently as: "private government", private sectors of law and justice, "informal law", "living law", "people's law".

To return to the main point: the theme of plurality and multiplicity of legal systems is now well worn, although it is differentially assimilated by sociologists and jurists. But the central perplexities remain. Can we describe group ordering of social relations, and group handing of social conflicts, outside the dominating frameworks of state authority and power as law? Too much intellectual energy has been dissipated over this question; but not over the counterquestion: why not? One suspects all this is highly ideological. The liberal democrats who have all along urged political pluralism as their fighting faith have forgotten their own message when they come to the law. The state (behaviourally, the bureaucracy and army) is only one of the many social groupings, howsoever imperious and dominating it may be. If the state, for its operations, needs a technique of social ordering, social control and institutionalization of conflict – namely, the law – so do the other non-state groups. I do not deny (who can?) the increasing power of state over all other groupings. But the latter exist; nay, sometimes they are even resilient. To refuse to conceptualize their regulatory systems as law (in any significant usage of that term) is to commit a kind of genocide by definition. If not that, at least, it is a goodbye to pluralism.

That hurdle over, arise the more vexing ones of further conceptualization. Thought has moved here in dichotomous pairs: we hear of "state law" and "people's law", "official law" and "living law", "formal law" and "informal law", "private" and "public" legal systems, "national" and "local" law ways, and finally "high culture" and "low culture" law. Bases for classification here vary: in terms of origin (state/people), qualities (formal/informal), scope (national/local), social acceptance (living/enforced) and cultural foundations (high culture/low culture). One clear basis of differentiation is the presence of state power and authority (which is not omnipresent, witness for example the vicissitudes of the "state action" doctrine in the American Constitutional law). This gives us two main types of legal systems in any society: those organized under the auspices of the state and those organized under the auspices of social groups other than the state. The state legal system (hereafter SLS) – itself a large bundle of hundreds of state legal systems – simplified and abstracted, provides a kind of reference group for the conceptualization of non-state legal systems (NSLS). The NSLS in any society would have higher demographic presence than SLS. Anyway, pending this kind of census enterprise, it is possible at least to say that NSLS display substantial variations in origins, development, structure, process, efficiency and viability and values (Pospisil, 1979: 97–126). Inter se relations, and comparisons between (and among) NSLS still represent an uncharted arena of investigation, both theoretically and empirically. When such investigations develop, a search for conceptual tools and organizing principles other than those furnished by the presence or absence of state power and authority may well become imperative.

2. Perspectives für The Study of Interaction between SLS & NSLS

The study of interaction between NSLS and SLS is of prime importance at least, for sociologists of law in the "developing" countries. But it is equally important to prevent such study from becoming dogenerate factology. Perhaps, an identification of perspectives may be useful. May we not study this interaction from social system, social actor, and social development perspectives? Each needs some explaining.

On the social system perspective, the configuration call "law" will now look different. Our universe becomes overpopulated, even congested. We would need to bring some order: identify the main "types" of NSLS; their relation to social structures (roles, statuses, role-sets, status-sets, "culture"). Having done that, we would need to re-explore the SLS in the same manner. Then only we may begin the task of correlating preferred SLS types with NSLS types. And this will need typification of interaction patterns. Jargonistic, all this; but necessary. SLS/NSLS may be symbiotically co-existent; this is conceivable, though not likely. Or they may be related in terms of collaboration, reciprocity or the relation may be of antagonism. A relation of complementarity would exist when NSLS performing the very same law-jobs (which Karl Lewellyn so seminally identified) which the SLS strive to perform. (See Baxi, 1976b: 93–95). On the other hand, the NSLS may be in active antagonism with the SLS. The antagonism or conflict may be at the level of values as well as of interests. Conflict may be so acute as to generate hegemonial drives - NSLS may seek to eclipse or oust SLS or vice versa. There may be loot and plunder – also disaster, as when state laws coopts the features, even institutions of non-state law through statutory adoption in an effort at hegemony (the state attempts to statutorize community dispute institutions through Nyaya Panchayats in India afford one striking example of this: See Baxi, 1976a: 411-30, Baxi & Galanter, 1979: 341). Alternatively, there may be a "mix" of complementarity and conflict in the relations between NSLS and SLS. This mix may well be a kind of division of social labor between state and people. In a given law-region, the NSLS may do all social control jobs save those of dealing with major crimes (e.g., murder), though theoretically there is no inherent reason for this division. What is all this, one may ask, but a saga of social change?

The social actor perspective wants, rightly, us to look at human beings not just as systems. Curiously, or perhaps not so, man disappears almost altogether in social system/structure analysis; the actor, it is said, becomes the receptacle. He is at the "receiving end of the system", never at the giving end (Dawe, 1970: 207). Even if that be not so, it is true that social systems interact only in the dark night of social scientist's soul; in real world, only people, human beings, interact. Berger and Luckmann have reminded us (1966: 72): "The institutions, with its assemblage of 'preprogrammed' action, is like the unwritten libretto of drama. The realization of the drama depends upon the reiterated performance of its prescribed role by living actors." Take the man into account and the picture begins to look different. Now we find human beings in time and place using the norms, processes, institutions of SLS and NSLS for their choicemaking and social action. The actor's values and interests (not these of the institution's or system's) guide our understanding here. Just one example should do here. Recourse to the court-system of SLS by Indians, villagers particularly, does not necessarily imply any acceptance of the values of SLS or signify any bankruptcy of the resources and values of NSLS (say, Panchayats). Court recourse may merely be a strategy for conflict-handling (an input for more favourable outcome in extra-judicial handling of conflict). It may also be motivated by the desire to correct status-asymmetries in village society (Epstein, 1962: 123–24): or to wage status competition, not quite permissible within the NSLS networks (Rudolph and Rudolph; 1967: 36–66). The results of such recourse may not signify any fundamental departure from the hierarchical, sacral value system of the Hindu society or any confirmity with the "modernistic", secular-rational goals of the constitutionally desired social order. This must remain an open question. What is not open to question, however, is the observation: that from the actor's perspective, adjudication may be "just one of the many contingencies in what is essentially a process of negotiation in a changing social environment" (Kidder, 1973: 137).

We identify the third perspective as developmental. We may proceed here both from the standpoint of the top-down technocractic model of development and from that of the humanistic development model. From the former standpoint, we identify the development inspiration in terms of the constitutionally stated values and aspirations, relation of these with the political elites policies and programmes and the translation of these bureaucratic formulations and implementation. Identification of the normative conceptions of elite espoused notions of development and of development achievement (which may involve, in the stream of time, dialectically, reformulation not merely of the strategies but goals as well) will then provide the foci of the study of development. If the blood group of aspiration and achievement compare well, we have development. If not, we have problems: what went wrong? unintended effects? lack of legitimacy? lack of political will? lack of social learning? (Development is indeed, identifiable, with a process of social learning in the direction of espoused values). If we want to look at development from this standpoint, the study of NSLS in interaction with SLS, or indeed by themselves, would be of considerable help. The NSLS may reflect the tenacity of social formations and values, these in turn displaying the "folk" notions of development, as distinct (and even opposed to) the elite notions. Where these notions coincide, we may discover different institutional pathways for the attainment of the same set of goals and values. Either way, we would be reaching a reappraisal of both types of legal systems (SLS and NSLS) in their development profiles.

On the other hand, we may wish to study the NSLS in terms of the values of the humanistic or "Another Development" approaches. To what extent the NSLS reflect or preserve a movement towards forms of social order enhancing participation, self-reliance and community? To what extent the NSLS foster dealienation? What are the fundamental presuppositions involved in the structure and functioning of the NSLS concerning the nature of man, state and conflict? Do these presuppositions diverge substantially or radically from the values of the SLS? In other words, what is the delegitimation potential of NSLS for the SLS? What, on the other hand, is the scope and impact of the spread of the culture of SLS in the NSLS and vice versa?

3. Village Law and Justice in India

Let me plunge now into specifics of the Indian situation. Insofar as the study of village law and justice is concerned, we have in India instead of cross-fertilization across disciplines the situation of cross-sterilization. Juristic preoccupation with the SLS has generally led to the belief that NSLS are wayside relics, of marginal importance and destined to disappear in the great March to Progress. Indeed, the general tendency has been to subsume studies of NSLS (dispute institutions) under the rubric "cultural" or "legal" anthropology, an exotic field for a few specialists which a busy judge, lawyer, or legislator finds of little immediate relevance. On the other hand, even legal anthropology has yet to win recognition in India as an integrated discipline. Social anthropologists have studied "village" life; but in the proliferating studies the facus is on kinship, caste, and now-a-days "class". It is incomprehensible but true that very little attention is paid to social conflicts and their management outside (or indeed even within) the main frames of caste and class. Law as a category of structural analysis is virtually absent. The state of art qualifies what follows by way of an overview of literature.

There seem to be three main types of NSLS in rural India. Very generally, these are caste-based NSLS; community-based NSLS; innovative, reformist NSLS. The distinction between caste and community NSLS is (as we will shortly see) relative. It is based on the view that "most individuals in rural India have two sets of predominate social relations, one that ties them to a village community which may be viewed as a vertical set of ties and one that connects them horizontally to their biradari and jati (subcaste)". Each set of social relations has "norms that can be considered legal and 'individuals and groups possessing the socially recognized' authority to apply physical force to enforce them within the local communities" (Cohn, 1965:82). The community NSLS extend beyond the caste to the village unit itself, though patterns of caste dominance – or of power distribution – here intrude, sometimes to a point that a village panchayat becomes the very extension of dominant group government. The innovative/reformist NSLS are dispute institutions like the "People's Court" (Lok Adalat) at Rangpur which are sponsored by acculturating agents or agencies, with the ideologies which centre upon the principle of generation of Lokshakti or people's power for social transformation, and which deny, or circumscribe, the state power (Baxi: 1976b).

The dominant form of the organisation in each case is a set of dispute institutions (cf. Abel, 1973: 217) called panchayats. Panchayats normally are a group of five people who hear and decide disputes mostly when they are summoned to do so but frequently on their own. However, in each type of NSLS, the subject matters vary. Very generally, caste (jati) panchayats deal with conflicts of interests and values within jati-groups, including factional alliances within those groups. Village or territorial panchayats deal with conflicts of interest cutting across caste factors, though those very factors may play often a crucial role in the "resolution" of a particular conflict.

Jati panchayats vary enormously in structure and scope. Bernard Cohn has insightfully grouped the structure and scope of jati panchayats in terms of territorial units as well as patterns of caste dispersal and domination. His classification yields three types of jati NSLS:

(a) villages with a small population of a single caste;

(b) multi-caste villages with single head (authority figure);

and

(c) multi-caste village with a dominant caste (Cohn, 1965: 83–98; see also Srinivas, 1962: 118–9).

It is clear that jati NSLS may have wide territorial reach in terms of aggregation of jati circles, so that it is not unusual to find as many as fifty villages falling within the scope of jati NSLS. The limits of the territorial reach are conditioned only by "the means and the speed of transportation" and "by the kinship radius of the convenors" (Mandelbaum, 1966; 281). There is equally clearly a federal component in jati NSLS and different levels of hierarchy e.g., Cohn, 1959). The nature of the conflict or its importance to jati solidarity patterns may, however, involve the use of the highest collectivity of jati NSLS (panchayats comprised by as many as 20–25 villages). Jati panchayats also show interesting variations in organization of power and authority. While these remain to be systematically studied, a mix of any of the following variables offers some clue to authority and sources of legitimation. The close correlation between age and wisdom provides one mix – the panchayats are often led, even composed, by such men. Esteem, reputation, integrity, and charisma provide another mix. Economic base, as related to social status (Weber's analysis of status-groups as distinct from class is still, despite its seminality, largely ignored in Indian studies) also invests power and authority in certain men. So does the status of being a faction leader. Although not so prevalent now, we cannot altogether ignore the hereditary or royal allocations of role and authority (Cf Cohn, 1965: 85–90).

Jati NSLS primarily involve disputes and conflicts which are related to the maintenance of jati ranking (in terms of ritual axis and of pollution and purity) and solidarity. Ritual lapses, marital relations, commission of polluting acts, sexual deviance, inter se land disputes, credit transactions, patron-client (jajmani) relations – all these fall typically within the range of jati NSLS. As in SLS, the jati NSLS involve application of pre-existing norms (See Srinivas 1962: 118–19. Contra: Cohn, who says "there is, apparently, little question of what 'the law' is in panchayat proceedings" 1965: 91) as well as instant norm creation and norm innovation. (The distinction between norm-creation and norm-interpretation is, in most decisional processes, never so sharp as some wish it to be.) The breach of pre-existing "customary" law is always a major gradient in the convening of jati panchayats: indeed, jati NSLS sometime make law prior to occasions of adjudication. For example, it has been frequently noted that untouchable jati groups, in their desperate bid for social uplift, have adopted regulations "for whole sections of a caste forbidding practices believed to be responsible for their low status . . . Chamars are prohibited from removing dead cattle" (Cohn, 1965: 108 and the literature there cited).

There is general agreement that the processes of dispute handling, howsoever complex, in jati and village panchayats share common features of informality, flexibility, democraticity, and decision-making (at least always in style if not in substance) by consensus. The state law strives to attain justice inter partes through "impartial" judges and elaborate procedures for ascertaining "truth". Indigenous dispute institutions promote justice with notorious informality through village notables who know disputants personally. The adversary systems (broadly speaking) of state law seek to individualize justice: village law and justice seek collectivized justice. Village law and justice seek social, group harmony through consensus, where both sides engage in give and take: whereas state law, followed to its end, rests on "winner-take-it-all" principle. The flexibility of jati and village panchayats consists in a wider sense of relevance, not the straitjacket notion of relevance. The village elders, it is often observed, assembled to hear one dispute will "discuss another which lies behind it" (Cohn, 1959: Rudolph and Rudolph: 1966). This is partly a function of democraticity – that is free-wheeling public participation in the hearing process – of the proceedings – indeed an element fast disappearing in state law systems. Indeed, the democraticity has not been confined to random public "say" but it has a distinctly egalitarian character. Mandelbaum observes, at least in relation to jati panchayats: "The egalitarian aspect of the traditional panchayat seems to pose a paradox. The need for unanimous consent and the right of every man to be heard appear dissonant to the leitmotif of hierarchy . . . The answer seems to be that most define a jati council as a council of peers . . . even a poor man will speak if he feels moved to do so (1966: 291)." While the substance of this account is correct, it remains ideal typical. The prevalence of the so-called tradition of consensus in India needs very critical examination. On most vital issues, the appearance of consensus may well be a mask for domination. They style of consensual decision-making, cleverly manipulated, may legitimate a decision which, in substance, only serves dominant interests. One may assume that in most situations consensus would be "prefabricated", "contrived" or "manipulated". Yet, all in all, in most of the foregoing respects, the ideology of the professional justice, its structure and process are thus at fundamental variance with those of the lay justice.

The jati and village panchayats have a repertoire of sanctionswhich include fine, public censure, civil boycott, ostracism, and varied public opinion pressures by village notables and sometime by predominant groups in the area. The jati panchayats, additionally, have the very potent sanction of "outcasting" and "excommunication". Andre Beteille in his study of cheri panchayat (village panchayat) in Tanjore district village describes the range of sanctions thus: "Fines are levied for a wide variety of offences. For petty thefts, cash fines of small amounts are levied. Higher fines are levied for adultery and other sexual offences. Rape is regarded as a very serious offence and a special punishment is imposed in addition to fines. The culprit has his face smeared with soot, a bucket containing mud is placed on his head, and he is made to go around the cheri (area) in this guise, while a drum is beaten along the route. This is considered the most degrading form of punishment (Beteille, 1969: 63–64)." Primitive? Strange? May be. But social stigmatising is the essence of all sanctions: here it takes a culturally specific form, which is also highly functional. (Similar adaptations of social censure as sanction are to be found in the Russian law – e.g., the famous "windows of satire".) Apart from stigma, public expression of penitence, self-correction assurances also serve as sanctions.

One striking example of a new kind of sanction is provided by the Lok Adalat at Rangpur. When disputants are sent an "invitation" to join the meeting of the Adalat, the last paragraph of the notice reads: "You surely know (appreciate) that expensive and frequent visits to law courts are not in the interests of us poor farmers". One may conceptualize this kind of admonition as a sanctioning device itself. Indeed, in the inter-subjectivities of the villagers, such a statement might imply that if a party does not even appear before the Lok Adalat, the

Adalat itself may encourage court action or, at any rate, it may not discourage such action. Conceptually, then, the threat of recourse to the instrumentality of the state legal system is itself stressed and apperceived as a sanction, whose very probability generates compliance. This is a rather unique phenomenon wherein the non-state legal system appropriates the intimidating paraphernalia of the state legal system to sustain and enhance its continual efficacy, viability, legitimacy and even hegemony. Of course, parallel processes may be perceived in conflict resolution through out-of-court settlement, private arbitration and other forms of mediation. But the striking peculiarity of the Lok Adalat summoning procedure is that it directly employs the threat of formal litigation as a self-conscious sanctioning process to an extent that the range of choices for alternate means of resolution is endeavoured to be effectively eliminated or at least minimized. This indeed is the very definition of "force". To the extent the threat to recourse to litigation actually operates to reduce parties' choice of action, we have surely an operation of sanction (Baxi, 1976b: 83–86).

The effectivity of sanctions is an empirical question, which has not been closely examined in relation to NSLS. Recalcitrance is both conceivable and likely: its incidence is however unknown. Isolated examples also suggest that the dominant group members or resourceful persons can by acts of defiance occasion changes or bypassing or even momentary collapse of sanctioning processes. But overall, the strength of collective conscience or sentiment in the village (and caste) contexts cannot be gainsaid.

4. Conflicts of values and interests

The NSLS (especially the jati and village systems) no doubt reflect distinctive patterns of social organization and consciousness. The constitutionally desired (proclaimed) social order seeks to foster (in part) through the operation of the legal system the value of equality: whereas the Hindu caste system is based on the principles of hierarchy, religiously and "culturally" sanctified and legitimated. The Hindu society, in Andre Beteille's evocative words, is a harmonic system where inequality exists and is perceived to be legitimate whereas the constitution ushers in a disharmonic system: inequalities exist but they are no longer legitimate (1974: 196) Bernard Cohn has maintained this sort of contrast insistently: "The adversary system has developed to equalize persons in court. To an Indian peasant, this is an impossible situation to understand. The chamar knows that he is not equal to Thakur . . . the Thakur cannot be convinced in any way that the chamar is equal, but the court acts as if the parties to the dispute were equal" (Cohn, 1959).

It would be too much to say that equality is a new concept for Indian culture, as the foregoing sets of contrast do ultimately suggest. What is distinctive about the constitutional vision of equality is in fact a total assault on the pervasive principle of social stratification based on status (and, therefore, mobility) ascribed at birth in a particular jati. The constitution abolishes untouchability, makes discrimination based on untouchability an offence: it forbids sex, caste, religion based discrimination and assures equality of opportunity in public employment. All this is done by way of assurance in the nature of justiciable fundamental rights. Opposed to all this, of course, are the myths and philosophies of an old social order which (not unnaturally) continue to persist. As has been often observed, neither the untouchable in the village nor his high-caste Hindu master can really understand how they can be equal with each other. Discrimination, ex-communication and outcasting continue. Women continue to be treated as being of inferior status to men, markedly in the rural areas, although there are laws guaranteeing more or less equal succession rights for Hindu women, or prohibiting bigamy, or proscribing dowry. Wage-discrimination based on sex is notorious. The values of a resilient "culture" are in constant struggle for hegemony over those of the constitution.

But conflicts of value go even deeper than those contrasts between state and non-state law indicate. Professor R. S. Freed has presented one aspect of such conflicts in his study of village life in North India through the case of Maya. Maya, a married but illicitly pregnant girl, was killed by her father because he believed that his Dharma qua father obligated him to do so for the spiritual well-being of her soul. The sooner her sinful phase in the cycle of births and deaths was terminated, the better would her prospects be in the endless cycle of birth and rebirth. He reasoned also that Maya, if allowed to live, will be ex-communicated from the village society and end up as a cheap urban prostitute, a life full of unmitigated misery. Everybody in both her in-laws' and his village agreed – so much so that two of the kinsmen of Maya's father who were police constables did not do anything to activate legal process. The police visited the village twice but did nothing. Village law was here in sharp antithesis to state law: and the latter, more or less yields to the former (1972: 423–435). Dharma thus conceived, is the legitimating principle of this NSLS which diverges sharply from the democratic belief system sustaining the SLS.

Not all experiments in local law and justice raise perplexing philosophical conflicts as the case of Maya. Some illustrate merely unredressed forms of lynch-justice as the well documented case of the cowherd illustrates. The cowherd committed two "sins": one of covertly cohabiting with a Brahmin's young third wife and his compounding this offence by leaving Brahmin's house by the front door (instead of the back door, as befitted his status). He was first castrated and then killed for this "sinful" behaviour; no official action followed (Gough, 1955; 40; Cohn, 1965: 90). Examples of lynch-justice abound. These indicate the countervailing power of caste and local notables over the state legal system.

On the other hand, well-organized local legal systems may often almost altogether "oust" the state legal system and provide an almost idyllic alternative as is shown by Lok Adalat (People's Court) in Rangpur, North Gujarat – a tribal belt of about 10,000 villages mostly irradiated by the Sarvodaya (Lit. uplift of all) ideology of bhoodan and gramdan (Voluntary gifts of lands and villages for redistribution of common use). Almost all disputes in the region are referred to the Lok Adalat. In the last 25 years, it has settled more than 25,000 disputes. The very fact that the case is brought before it is often enough a valid ground for adjourning proceedings in official courts. Adjudication is done with substantial public participation: each session is attended by 300–400 villagers. The Court's decisions are rarely disobeyed. This is because of their intrinsic fairness and community involvement. In some ways, this Court achieves a quality of justice still sought for by the state legal system: for example, it more effectively protects women's equal rights of inheritance, matrimonial property, etc. The Court's criminal justice system already provides for effective compensation for the victims of crime which is still on the legislative anvil. Its rehabilitative techniques are much more advanced in some respects: a murderer is "punished" to look after the widow and minor children of the victim for a term of years under close supervision of the local community whereas his imprisonment in the official legal system would have rendered both families destitute. The Lok Adalat experiment also illustrates other dimensions of relationship between the state and non-state legal systems. Often, dispute institutions generale and sustain broad based leadership patterns which promote developmental activities – both economic and social. It was through his role as a mediator in village disputes that the leader of the Lok Adalat, Shri H. Parikh (an eminent Sarvodaya worker) attained legitimacy, and a degree of charisma. In turn, he used Lok Adalat to translate his vision of socio-economic reform by making it a vehicle of reform-oriented adult education. He made the adjudicatory occasions into educational ones, both through actual decisions and plain preaching on many themes – family planning, ill-effects of overconsumption of alcoholic drinks, honesty in credit transactions, civil liberties, irrationality of belief in witchcraft, equality of women, agricultural innovation, etc. Today, the area of about 1000 villages has witnessed remarkable socio-economic changes partly forstored and sustained by this kind of didactic adjudication. In this sense, perhaps more has been achieved by mobilization of lay justice for development than by insistence on adoption of professional justice, as is illustrated by the state's abortive attempts at formalizing village justice through the statutory nyaya panchayats (See Baxi, 1976a). The Lok Adalat is not an isolated phenomenon, although it may be in several respects, unique. On a lesser scale, quite a few such experiments exist. Moreover, not too dissimilar functions (of promoting welfare, development, status mobility) have been and are being performed by jati panchayats (caste dispute institutions) as noted by several sociologists and anthropologists. When they perform such functions, as they increasingly do, both in adjudicatory and other contexts, the jati panchayats supplement the role of state in bringing about social change, although they do so on the basis of caste loyalty and patronage.

It would be misleading to assume the conflicts between state and local legal orders are merely conflict of values; there are also conflicts of interests. Adoption of constitutional values naturally calls for sacrifice of personal or group interests, which are clearly not acceptable to those in positions of higher class, status or power. Some would even say that what are spoken of as values are nothing more than rationalizations of interests of vested interest groups. Cohn's approach – or generally the cultural approach – is ultimately an aspect of social system perspective towards the NSLS. The actor approach, stressing interests rather than values, is steadfastly pursued in the Indian context by Robert Kidder. Of course, his universe of study is not comparable to Cohn's (Cohn studied villagers in North India; Kidder's focus is on "outlying districts" of Banglore in South India). But the overall contrast holds. Kidder is certainly correct to the question Cohn's assertion that Indians recourse to the court system of SLS demonstrates "manipulation", use of courts not "to settle disputes but to further them" (Cohn, 1959: 155). Such a view, according to Kidder (and I agree) misjudges "the importance of constructive force in social interaction". It also ignores "the opportunity structure which is created by systems of formal adjudication" (Kidder, 1973). This opportunity structure arises from "the failure of adjudicative ideal". The administration of justice in India is shot through with delays (Kidder notices average delay in civil suits in Banglore Courts in 1967–67 to be slightly over 17 years). Paradoxically, this delay, and frustrations attendant upon it, are utilized by the adversaries to wage a war of attrition in which the idea is not so much to win the case but to maximize the opportunities for a substantially favourable compromise outcome, outside the SLS, and perhaps mostly through NSLS. Manipulation of delay is being regarded by those affected as being the "intentional product of a shrowd adversary". To the extent this aspect becomes the folklore of state law systems, the NSLS may well persist as alternate opportunity structures. But the capital point here is that the cultural approach helps us overlook mobilization of state law in the pursuit of material interests and of dominance. (For the recurrence of this theme in a related context of legal anthropology, see Sally Falk Moore, 1966: 615–24.)

Be that as it may, we must also note that the limits of state power, authority and law are not set just by values and interests but also (and perhaps no less decisively) by the level or organization of efforts. Most "developing" countries are poor (appallingly so, as in the case of India, where a large number of people do not have means of bare subsistence) we immediately perceive that the level of poverty affects adversely the reach of state law and the quality of its justice. Investment in administration of law and justice is not (and probably cannot be) a high priority item in national budgets of poor societies at the very time when they have to resort to the machinery of law to initiate the foster social change. This is one among the many paradoxes of social change in developing societies. All this means, of course, that there are not enough courts, constables and lawyers – carriers of official law – in poor societies. Thus, for example, in India (according to one estimate) there are only 183 lawyers per one million of the population as against 507 lawyers in the United Kingdom, 1595 in the U.S.A. 947 in New Zealand, 638 in Australia and 769 in Canada. Indeed, some areas in India have no lawyers at all; and inter se distribution of lawyers within India reveals even striking disparities (Galanter, 1968–69: 201). As regards police, in 1971, according to the official estimates, there was one policeman for every 800 persons in India; but the distribution is uneven between the rural and urban centres. The average jurisdiction of a police station is about 200 square miles covering 100 villages and a population of approximately 75,000 persons. It was estimated in 1950s that police stations were, on the average, about 8 miles from any village (Bayley, 1969: 79–80). The state legal system, pervasive in urban areas, is only slenderly present in rural areas. The low visibility of state legal system, and its slender presence, renders official law (its values and processes) inaccessible and even irrelevant for people. Other factors (such as the language of the law, which is alien to about 95 % of the people) compound the distance between the state's law and people.

5. Evaluation of NSLS

Ideological compulsions – leaping before looking – have often led to evaluations which characterize most NSLS as problematic in terms of their justicity (that is, values of due process, reasoned elaboration and substantive justice values). Lack of hard data in relation to the NSLS may be irrelevant to cafeteria or armchair evaluations but it is an obstacle to informed and thoughtful judgment. The latter kind of judgment was arrived at by Professor D. F. Honderson after a close study of the institution of Choetei and general conciliation processes in Japan: "... the excessive use of conciliation stunts the growth and refinements of the body of rules necessary to sustain complex community life; it dulls the citizens' sense of right, essential to the vindication of law. It may also allow old rules and social prejudices which new legislation has sought to abolish, to influence the outcome of disputes; or it may allow a new regime to ignore the law in favour of its policy ... In other words, conciliation is neither conservative nor progressive in principle; it is simply unprincipled. It may favour the powerful over the weak, in the name of bargaining; it ordinarily forces the plaintiffs to discount their claims; it may operate to compromise large scale group interests which might be better handled by forthright reform legislation. In short, conciliation is only an adjunct to, not a substitute for, legal order; and if relied upon excessively, it is not merely nonlegal – it has antilegal results ... It takes a legal framework to protect the voluntary character of conciliation and if it is not voluntary, conciliation will likely become in practice simply a standardless use of force" (Henderson, 1965: 241).

The foregoing sort of appraisal is common enough in discussions of most NSLS. The basic ideal-typical contrasts between most NSLS and the SLS are that the non-state law and dispute institutions may allow room for "prejudiced" rather than "principled" decisions; the NSLS may be swayed by power differential between parties; that in some ways NSLS are "antilegal". At this level, the case for cribling and even annihilating (if that were ever possible) most "dysfunctional" NSLS becomes impressive, if not compelling.

But such a comparison needs to be made at the same level. What usually happens is that the normative models of SLS are compared with the operative models of NSLS; this "dacoit track" no doubt yields preferred conclusions. But suppose we check this conclusion with accentuation of different aspects (behavior rather than value, reality rather than myth) of SLS. At the behavioral level, the picture begins to look more or less the same. Are the judicial (and legislative) decisions preeminently grounded in "principles" rather than "prejudice"? (Withess the inconclusive controversy over "reasoned elaboration" and "neutral principles" in relation to American judicial process). Are the SLS "law-ways" substantially free from "old prejudices" cancelling the objectives of social change through law? Do no power differentials between parties affect legal initiations and outcomes? Does not the volume of out-of-court settlements in civil cases, and of plea-bargaining in criminal matters, contrast sharply with the adjudicative adversary ideal? Does not the actually operative Crime Contral Model (as against the normative Due Process Model) involve fairly high incidence of "standardless use of force"? These are, no doubt, big questions; but the outlines of answers, in the available sociological literature, having already begun to point out the great gap between rhetoric and reality, between the proclaimed objectives and dysfunctional results. The lesson to draw from these ongoing explorations is not that there are no significant differences between NSLS and SLS but that these differences are of degree rather than of kind.

In conclusion, one must reiterate that the interaction between SLS and NSLS, and the context for it, is thus complex and many sided. Insofar as the NSLS derive their legitimation from belief systems sharply incongruent from those investing SLS with legitimacy, the multiplicity of NSLS may well pose limits to the legitimation of state power and authority. The resilient people's law may divert and even frustrate the goals of planned development articulated and pursued through the law. On the other hand, nation-building elites and "promoters" of "development" in the Third World need a sophisticated awareness of the undoubted potential of NSLS in achieving social transformation.

REFERENCES

Abel, R. L. — "A Comparative Theory of Dispute Institutions" 8 Law & Soc. Rev. 375 (1973)

Balbus, I. D. — "Commodity Form and Legal Form: An Essay on the Relative Autonomy of the Law" 11 Law & Soc. Rev. 571 (1977)

Baxi, U. — "Access, Development and Distributive Justice: Access Problems of the 'Rural' Population" 18 J. Ind. Law Inst. 375 (1976): this paper is also referred to as "Baxi, 1976a"

Baxi, U. — "From Takrar to Karar: The Lok Adalat at Rangpur – A Preliminary Study" X J. of Const. & Parliamentary Studies 53 (1976): this paper is also referred to in the text as "Baxi, 1976b"

Baxi, U. A.
Galanter, M. — "Panchayat Justice: An Indian Experiment in Legal Access" III Access to Justice 341 (1979)

Bayley, D. — Police and Political Development in India (1969)

Berger, P. S. & Luckmann, T. — The Social Construction of Reality (1966)

Beteille, A. — Class, Status and Power (1965)

Beteille, A. — Studies in Agrarian Social Structure (1974)

Cohn, B. S. — "Some Notes on Law and Social Change in North India" 8 Eco. Development & Soc. Change 79 (1959)

Cohn, B. S. — "Anthropological Notes on Disputes and Law in India" American Anthropologist (Special Number: Ethnography of Law) 82 (1965)

Dahrendorf, R. — Class and Class Conflict in Industrial Society (1959)

Danzig, R. & Lowy, M. J. — "Everyday Disputes and Mediation in the United States: A Reply to Professor Felsteiner" 9 Law & Soc. Rev. 675 (1975)

Dawe, A. — "The Two Sociologies" 21 British J. Sociology 207 (1970)

Freed, R. S. — "The Legal Process in a Village in North India: The Case of Maya" 33 Trans. New York Academy of Sciences 423 (2nd ser. 1972)

Gough, K. — "The Social Structure a Tanjore Village" in Village India (M. Marriott ed.) (1955)

Haque W. et al: — "Towards a Theory of Rural Development" 2 Development Dialogue (1977)

Henderson, D. F. — Conciliation in Japanese Law: Tokugawa and Modern (1965)

Hurst, J. W. — The Growth of American Law (1950)

Hurst, J. W. — Law and Economic Growth: The Legal History of the Lumber Industry in Wisconsin (1969)

I. L. C. (International Legal Centre) — Law and Development (1974)

Inayatullah — Transfer of Western Development Model for Asia and its Impact (1975: ACDA publication)

Kidder, R. — "Courts and Conflict in An Indian City, A Study in Legal Impact" J. of Commonwealth Studies 121 (1973)

Lowy, M. J.	"Modernizing the American Legal System; An Example of the Peaceful usage of Anthropology" 32 Human Organization (1973)
Mandelbaum, M.	Society in India (1966)
Moore, S. F.	"A Social Structural Approach to Legal Reasoning" 39 Southern Calif. L. Rev. 616 (1959)
Pospisil, L.	Anthropology of Law: A Comparative Theory (1971)
Rudolph, L. H. & Rudolph, S. H.	The Modernity of Tradition (1967)
Srinivas, M. N.	Caste in India (1962)
Stone, J.	Social Dimensions of Law & Justice (1966)
Trubek, D.	"Max Weber on Law and the Rise of Capitalism" (1972) Wisconsin L. Rev. 303
Trubek, D.	"Complexity and Contradiction in the Legal Order; Balbus and the Challenge of Critical Social Thought About Law" 11 Law & Soc. Rev. 529 (1977)
Unger, R. M.	Law in Modern Society (1976)
Weber, M.	The Theory of Social and Economic Organization (ed. T. Parsons, 1964)
Weber, M.	Economy and Society (3 vols, G. Roth & C. Wittich ed., 1968)
Weber, M.	Max Weber on Law in Economy and Society (1954; Rheinstein ed.)

[23]

MENS REA AND THE REASONABLE AFRICAN: THE PRE-SCIENTIFIC WORLD-VIEW AND MISTAKE OF FACT †

By

ROBERT B. SEIDMAN *

ANGLOPHONIC Africa, whether independent, self-governing, or still under white settler overrule,[1] is ordered by a penal régime modelled mainly upon the common law of crimes.[2] The penal law is codified in all except the High Commission Territories of Swaziland, Bechuanaland and Basutoland, Southern Rhodesia and South Africa, and Sierra Leone.[3] In every case, the pattern of English criminal law was imposed upon the indigenous society by the imperial master during the long colonial night. Even in the eleven States which have now burst forth into the daylight of self-government or independence, the Penal Codes remain as they were during the latter days of the colonial era. They remain the basic norms of public order for at least one hundred million people.

The common law of crimes traditionally synthesises a number of

† [This article was prepared in November 1965 and does not take account of changes since that date. EDITOR.]

* Presidential Professor of Law, University of Ghana, Legon.

1 Southern Rhodesia and South Africa, at this writing, are the only two States in this category. The Gambia, Sierra Leone, Ghana, Nigeria, Uganda, Kenya, Tanzania, Malawi and Zambia are either independent or self-governing with independence promised by Great Britain. The size of the African population in these countries is largely unknown. The range of possible error in the estimates is demonstrated by the Nigerian experience, where an estimated population of 30,000,000 was shown on enumeration to amount in fact to about 55,000,000. The population of the countries here discussed undoubtedly exceeds 100,000,000 people.

2 The régime in Rhodesia, the High Commission Territories of Swaziland, Basutoland and Bechuanaland, and South Africa is Roman-Dutch law, modified by common law concepts. In the main, the actual position of the criminal law particularly is that the law which is in force is almost entirely the common law, with a few exotic importations from the Roman-Dutch law. See generally, Lansdown, *Outlines of South African Criminal Law and Procedure* (2nd ed., 1960) 4–6.

3 The Penal Code of Nigeria is modelled on the Queensland Code. The Penal Codes of The Gambia, Uganda, Kenya, Tanzania, Malawi (formerly Nyasaland) and Zambia (formerly Northern Rhodesia) are substantially identical; they all have a Penal Code imposed by the Colonial Office in 1950. The Ghana Criminal Code is unique in Africa, finding its origins in the St. Lucia Criminal Code. The Penal Codes of Northern Nigeria and the Sudan are based on the Indian Penal Code (in the case of Northern Nigeria, with some importations from the Moslem Malaki law). Sierra Leone relies on the common law of crimes, uncodified. All the Codes find their source either in Sir James Stephen's Draft Code of 1870, or the Indian Penal Code. See, generally, Read, "Criminal Law in the Africa of Today and Tomorrow" (1963) 7 *Journal of African Law* 5, *passim.*

diverse and indeed frequently contradictory objectives. There is a mystical end of retribution; a utilitarian one of deterrence; and humanitarian or ethical objectives of reformation and rehabilitation, frequently in combination with the objective of restraint during the period of rehabilitation. Practically all modern theoretical analyses of the criminal law as it is applied in England or the United States accept these multiple objectives of the criminal law as their starting point, and vary mainly in the emphasis which they place upon the one objective or the other.

What objectives does the common law of crimes, as embodied in the several Codes, in fact reach in Anglophonic Africa? This issue might be approached in a variety of ways. A criminologist no doubt would want to examine the work of the various trial courts, and examine sentencing policy and practice; a very wide and fruitful research is indicated. An anthropologist might well examine the effect of the Codes upon the thinking and customs of the subjects of the Codes, to discover to what extent the common law of crimes has affected indigenous morality and thought; this, too, remains a large and almost completely unexplored area. A political scientist might discover interesting institutional developments arising from the impact of an imported criminal code.

The approach to be adopted here, however, is perhaps rather more traditional for lawyers and judges. The exercise is to analyse the sufficiency of the doctrines embodied in the Codes and the case law to meet the various problems presented by the world-view of the tribalised African, and to examine possible solutions to the problems posed.

I

As Professor Schiller has pointed out, Africa is a continent in which two cultures today live side by side, each affecting the other, shaping it and forming it in novel ways. Embedded in the common law of crimes and in the Codes lies a system of beliefs drawn largely from the industrial society which was the matrix in which they were formed. The beliefs of what may loosely be described as the westernised segment of African society—which now includes not only the tiny and relatively unimportant European minority, but a substantial and ever-growing population of educated, urbanised Africans—we may assume match those of the Codes as closely as in England or the United States.[4] The governing groups of all the newly independent African States now belong primarily to this culture. The rulers of the New Africa therefore find the world of

[4] But see Hodgkin, *Nationalism in Colonial Africa* (1957) 81.

the Codes congenial—or at least as congenial as do their counterparts in the industrialised common law jurisdictions.

There are, however, vast numbers of Africans who today live in the traditional African culture, for whom modern education has just begun to be a reality, whose economy is one of subsistence agriculture, dominated by starvation, disease and ancient forms of social organisation. For these Africans, the penal régime under which they live is an exotic import.

Africans living in such a society usually have a world-view which can only be characterised as pre-scientific. Not infrequently they commit acts which are logical within the framework of their understanding of natural processes, but which the Criminal Codes, embodying as they do a totally different sort of understanding, characterise as criminal. The problems that arise as a result in such cases cluster around the issues of mistake of fact, negligence, insanity and absolute liability.

Mistake of fact. All of the Codes contain provisions concerning mistake of fact.[5] All of them in essence restate the common law maxim *ignoranti facti excusat*. In many cases, there is no difficulty in its application. In *Nyanya s/o Kweyu*[6] there was a beer party. A quarrel started between Maluba and the defendant, and Maluba hit defendant over the head with a stick. Defendant ran to get his spear, returned and by mistake he speared and killed Matias, who was not involved in the quarrel. On appeal from conviction for murder, the East African Court of Appeal substituted a judgment of manslaughter, on the ground of provocation.[7]

A host of cases, however, have arisen where the African's *Weltanschauung* is pre-scientific. Witchcraft and magic are tenable hypotheses to explain an adverse and sometimes terrifying environment in the light of limited and ill-organised factual knowledge. As a result, practically all indigenous African beliefs, as everywhere

[5] *e.g.*, Penal Code, Tanganyika, s. 11:

> " A person who does or omits to do an act under an honest and reasonable, but mistaken, belief in the existence of any state of things is not criminally responsible for the act or omission to any greater extent than if the real state of things had been such as he believed to exist."

The identical proviso appears in all the East African Codes, and in the Nigerian Criminal Code (s. 25). The Ghana Criminal Code is substantially the same (s. 29: " (1). A person shall not be punished for any act which, by reason of ignorance or mistake of fact in good faith, he believes to be lawful "). See also Penal Code, The Sudan, s. 44.

[6] (1956) 23 E.A.C.A. 593 (Kenya).

[7] Accord: *Mgaru s/o Kampore* (1951) 24 K.L.R. 2, 123 (accused speared a cow in the bush, thinking it a wild pig); *Waera s/o Madoya* [1962] E.A.C.A. 783 (Supreme Court, Kenya) (policemen not in uniform assaulted in belief that they were thieves); *Kakyebuka s/o Nyagara* (1945) 12 E.A.C.A. 77 (Uganda) (accused, provoked by his wife, speared at her through the reed wall of a hut and killed his wife's sister instead; held, manslaughter).

before the advent of the scientific era, find supernatural explanations for the events of their world.[8]

In many of these cases, the defendant kills in supposed self-defence against witchcraft.[9] Every conceivable defence has been raised in these cases; practically every one of them has been struck down. In *Kumakawa Malumbi & 69 Ors.*,[10] the accused genuinely believed that the victim was a witch who had by her dark powers made the wife of the first accused ill and unable to speak. The victim was seized and brought to the ill wife's hut, and ordered to remove the spell; she removed half of it during the night. In the early morning she was detected trying to escape; all the accused pursued her and beat her to death with thin sticks. The defences of native custom and of self-defence [11] were dismissed; all (except ten juveniles) were sentenced to death. In *Muswi s/o Musele* [12] the accused killed his first wife because he believed her to be a witch who was bewitching him. A psychiatrist testified that he was in a state of mild depression, with a background of family insanity and a history of episodes when his head was " not right "; that he was capable of distinguishing between right and wrong, " but his belief as to what was right or wrong was coloured by his belief that his wife was practising witchcraft on him "; and that what he did was not contrary to tribal law. A defence of insanity was dismissed.

Provocation, too, except in one narrowly defined circumstance, has been denied as a partial defence. In *Akope s/o Karuon* [13] the accused, two cousins, believed that their father and uncle was being

8 See generally, Parrinder, *Witchcraft: European and African* (1958). Practically all of the many anthropological studies of African tribes include some information about witchcraft. For Ghana, see Field, *Search for Security* (1960), *passim*, and Debrunner, *Witchcraft in Ghana* (1959). For Nigeria, see Bohannan, African Homicide and Suicide (1960), 42–58 (the Tiv Tribe); Meek, *Law and Authority in a Nigerian Tribe* (1935) 79–84 (Ibo, of Eastern Nigeria). For East Africa, see Middleton and Winter (eds.), *Witchcraft and Sorcery in East Africa* (1963). For Basutoland, see Ashton, *The Basuto* (1952), *passim*.

9 " Witches were or still are ' fair game ' in many African societies, and killing a witch was sometimes considered not only non-culpable but justifiable. . . . Usually the witch is killed because he or she was bewitching the killer's kinsman. Among the Uyoro (Uganda) particularly, the witch is likely to be female. The Tiv (Nigeria) situation of witch killing is more equivocal. Killing a witch may be a jural act. Much more common, however, is killing a person thought to be killing one (usually by witchcraft) for ritual purposes. Instead of a jural or ritual act, this is an example of self-defence when the legal or ritual force of the community is directed against one. By their act of choosing a victim, the rationale goes, the community has placed him outside the pale of the law—he may fight with any weapons available to him." Bohannan, *op. cit. supra*, note 8, at 233–234. I have elsewhere examined the witchcraft cases in detail: (1965) 28 Mod.L.Rev. 46.

10 14 K.L.R. 137 (1932).

11 Accord: *Galikuwa* (1951) 18 E.A.C.A. 175; *Kasalo* [1944–46] R.L.R. 110; *Kajuma s/o Mbake* (1945) 12 E.A.C.A. 104 (Tanganyika).

12 (1956) 23 E.A.C.A. 622 (Kenya). See further *infra*, p. 1150.

13 (1947) 14 E.A.C.A. 105 (Kenya); see also *Kelementi Magnga s/o Ochiang* (1942) 10 E.A.C.A. 49 (Uganda).

slain by the deceased; the sick man had so claimed six days before his death. They killed the supposed witch after the victim died. A claim of provocation was denied, on the ground that sufficient time had elapsed for a reasonable man to gain control of his emotion. And the defence of mistake of fact [14] has received equally short shrift.

An analogous case arises where tribalised Africans kill under sway of a powerful superstition, from their point of view in self-defence. *Dominiko Omenyi s/o Obuka* [15] was such a case. There, eleven appellants were convicted of the murder of a European member of the Uganda Medical Service. The accused were all members of the Acholi tribe, and killed because they adhered to an Acholi belief that Europeans kidnapped and ate Africans.[16] They were, of course, all found guilty of murder and sentenced to death.[17]

In all these cases the defendant has acted under ignorance or mistake of fact. His whole approach to the physical world is, as we have suggested, sharply at variance with that of the average Englishman. The difference is not simply a relativistic matter. One cannot assert dogmatically about custom that it is wrong. One can assert dogmatically that witchcraft is factually erroneous.[18]

In the usual case, the sensory impression received is interpreted in accordance with a world-view which is held in common by both Africans and Englishmen. Africans and Englishmen can agree that a wild pig is a wild pig, and a cow is a cow, and that under certain circumstances the sense impressions received from observations of a

[14] *Mbombela* [1933] A.D. 269 (South Africa); *Akope s/o Karuon* (1947) 14 E.A.C.A.; *Gadam* (1954) 14 W.A.C.A. 442 (Nigeria).

[15] (1943) 10 E.A.C.A. 81 (Uganda).

[16] It is probable that this belief arose upon appeal by some hospitals for blood for a blood-bank; that Europeans would be viewed as vampires seems a reasonable result. See Apter, *The Political Kingdom in Uganda* (1961) 226.

[17] The defence of mistake was not even urged on appeal.

[18] In *Otchere* (November 9, 1963, SCD 2/1963, High Court, Special Criminal Division (Ghana), cyclostyle), a treason trial, a portion of the evidence led by the prosecution tended to show that one of the accused, then a Minister, had defrauded the Bank of Ghana of £25,000, whose expenditure did not appear on accused's records. The inference sought to be drawn was that it was used to finance treasonable activities. The accused, by training a lawyer, testified that he took the money to a field in the bush, and there recited certain magic words (including Psalm 25). A spirit, Zebus, then appeared, and took the money, promising to return it redoubled. Zebus did not again reappear. The Chief Justice formally announced from the bench that the court took judicial notice that Zebus did not in fact exist. See the cyclostyled opinion at 80–81.

Money-doubling is a relatively frequent swindle in Africa. It has been held to be theft by false pretences, on the ground that the owner's intention is only to part with possession, not the property. In the allied fraud of money-changing, in which paper money is to be magically changed to coin (in times of shortage of metal coinage), the offence is larceny by trick, for in such a case the victim intends to part with both ownership and possession. *Mustafa Adegboyega* (1937) 3 W.A.C.A. 199 (Nigeria).

cow will be similar to those received from observations of a pig. Hence mistake of fact is a tenable defence.[19]

But in the cases here under consideration, the sensory impressions received by the African defendant are interpreted in the half-light of witchcraft and magic. What result ought to obtain under such circumstances?

The common law in England and the United States has answered this question in the main by insisting that "ignorance of ordinary factual knowledge, possessed by every 'normal' adult in the community except such eccentrics as these defendants, is no defence." [20] This rule has been applied in cases where the defendant failed to provide medical care for those under his control because he was ignorant of the need for medical care or because of eccentric religious beliefs.[21]

This "solution," even in England and the United States, raises as many questions as it solves. Hall, speaking of the rule, says that "Such decisions raise difficult questions regarding the application of objective *mens rea* and the quality of legal justice." [22] The difficulties arise because the ethical quality of the criminal law is a function of *mens rea* of the defendant. If the defendant is not aware even of the factual basis for the criminality of his act—let alone its actual criminality—the law in punishing him cannot even take refuge in the rubric that he might have done otherwise.[23] But the problem is not serious in England and America, where widespread education has largely eradicated such ideas as witchcraft, and a wise exercise of the prosecutor's discretion, the judge's power over sentence, and the use of executive clemency probably provide sufficient escape valves.

In Africa, however, where such beliefs are widespread in the bush, a different situation obtains. What rule ought to obtain there?

With rare exceptions, the courts have taken the position that since the Code which they must interpret finds its origins in the English common law, the standard against which the individual African must be measured is that of the reasonable Englishman. *Attorney-General of Nyasaland* v. *Jackson* [24] is the leading case. In that case, the accused had killed his oldest relative. There had been a quarrel over her responsibility for brewing ritual beer to commemorate the death of the accused's older brother, and in the course

19 *Mgaru s/o Kargore*, *supra*, note 7.
20 Hall, *General Principles of Criminal Law* (2nd ed., 1960) 375.
21 *Senior* [1899] 1 Q.B. 283.
22 Hall, *op. cit. supra*, note 20, at 375–376.
23 Michael and Wechsler, "A Rationale of the Law of Homicide" (1937) 37 Col.L.R. 701, 754.
24 [1957] R. & N.L.R. 443.

of this the deceased had said that the accused " would not see the sun today." This was apparently a threat of death by witchcraft; two of the assessors [25] went so far as to say that the mere pronouncing of these words would be thought sufficient to cause the accused's death. After brooding for an hour or more, accused took his bow and arrow and shot his aged relative, and then surrendered himself to the police.

The trial judge found him not guilty.[26] Reasoning from the general concept that self-defence justifies homicide, the judge concluded that he must decide the case on the basis of the facts as they appeared to the accused.[27] He thus reached the question whether the mistake was both genuine and reasonable; following the assessors' opinions, he held that it was.

> . . . If the accused believes in the necessity, then even if such necessity does not in fact exist, there is a mistake of fact and not of law. . . . In the circumstances in which the accused was placed, and believing what he in fact believed, nothing short of the actual killing of the perpetrator of the spell could avail him, so that the excuse, once admitted must extend even to the killing of the deceased.[28]

The attorney-general appealed to the Supreme Court of the Federation, on the principal ground that the trial judge erred in holding that the mistake was " reasonable " within the meaning of the Code.[29] The court reversed, and upheld the appeal.

> The test of reasonableness in itself implies an objective standard. . . . The test of reasonableness is one that is constantly invoked in English law. In applying it, the standard is what would appear reasonable to the ordinary man in the street in England. . . . Each case must be referred to one norm, and this must be so or otherwise the test becomes meaningless. . . .
>
> On this basis, and bearing in mind that the law of England is still the law of England even when it is extended to Nyasaland, I do not see how any court, applying the proper test, could hold that a belief in witchcraft was reasonable. . . .[30]

Jackson is in accord with all the cases which have considered the

[25] In most parts of Anglophonic Africa, trials upon serious criminal charges are typically held by a judge sitting with three assessors. The assessors are African, usually of the same language and area of the accused. Their advice is sought in matters of native custom and the like. The judge sums up to them as to a jury, and records their verdict. That verdict is, however, not binding, the final decision being the judge's alone.

[26] *Sub nom. R.* v. *Jackson* [1956] R. & N.L.R. 666.

[27] *Rose* (1884) 15 Cox 540.

[28] *Jackson*, *supra*, note 26, at 671.

[29] Penal Code, Nyasaland, s. 10, is identical with s. 11 of the Tanganyikan Penal Code, *supra*, note 5.

[30] *Att.-Gen. of Nyasaland* v. *Jackson* [1957] R. & N.L.R. 443, 448.

matter in Anglophonic Africa.[31] The central concept has been repeatedly restated: The threat must be physical, not metaphysical.[32] The threat must be the sort that a reasonable Englishman would recognise, not the sort which would seem frightening only to an African steeped in the culture of the bush.

This distinction between "physical" and "metaphysical" threats is based upon an understanding of the aetiology of physical sickness which Western science comprehends, but which no pre-scientific culture has attained; after all, it is in large part in the understanding of cause and effect that scientific knowledge is distinguished from non-scientific knowledge. Witchcraft is a plausible hypothesis to explain the frightening and unbelievable, just as, in early Biblical times, there was assumed to be a causal relationship between what appears to the scientific mind to be wholly accidental factors and the favourable outcome of prayer.[32a] The Codes, based as they are upon a system of thought quite different from that obtaining in the bush, reaches absurd results in many cases.

The difficulty is demonstrated plainly in *Musomi s/o Rutengoru*.[33] There the accused was charged with murder. A witness testified that accused said that he killed the victim because he had "bewitched" his child. The Kikerewe word for "to bewitch" is the same word as "to poison"—the Kikerewe obviously do not make the distinction between "physical" and "metaphysical" threats that Western science recognises. The court acquitted, since the context of the word was as consistent with the one use as the other. But one may question whether the distinction is relevant to the question of guilt.

The refusal of the judges construing the Codes to adjust to the reality of the world-view of the Africans in the subsistence economy defeats the purposes of the Codes most frequently by convicting persons without moral fault; but occasionally, by freeing persons

31 There are a few cases from non-African jurisdictions. With apparently only one aberrent American decision, they have reached the same conclusion. See Williams, "*Homicide and The Supernatural*" 65 L.Q.R. 491, 497.

32 *Kajuma*, 12 E.A.C.A. 104; *Akope*, 14 E.A.C.A. 105; *Galikuwà* (1951) 18 E.A.C.A. 175 (Uganda).

32a Thus part of the cleansing ceremony for a leper in Biblical times was that "The priest shall take some of the blood of the guilt offering [a male lamb], and the priest shall put it on the tip of the right ear of him who is to be cleansed, and on the thumb of his right hand, and on the great toe of his right foot. Then the priest shall take some of the log of oil, and pour it into the palm of his own left hand, and dip his right finger in the oil that is in his left hand, and sprinkle some oil with his finger seven times before the LORD. And some of the oil that remains in his hand the priest shall put on the tip of the right ear of him who is to be cleansed, and on the thumb of his right hand, and on the great toe of his right foot, upon the blood of the guilt offering. . . ." Lev. 14: 14–18. See Hamilton, *The Prophets of Israel* (1936) 25–39.

33 2 E.A.C.A. 91 (Tanganyika).

plainly dangerous to society. In *Palamba s/o Fundikila*,[33a] for example, the defendant saw his eleven children die from inexplicable causes. He therefore forced his two wives, his mother and his daughter to a trial by ordeal to see if they had killed the children. He forced them to take a medicine called Mwavi, which the defendant believed was regurgitated by the innocent, but was deadly to a witch. One wife and his mother died. His conviction for murder was reversed. In local lore, Mwavi is not believed to be in itself a poison:

> It requires, in order to be fatal, an additional element, namely, the guilt of the person taking it, that is to say, guilty of witchcraft. This court cannot possibly proceed on any other basis than that Wamlunda was innocent of witchcraft, which so far as this court is concerned does not exist. On the basis that Wamlunda was innocent of witchcraft, where is the malice aforethought in the first appellant, who, *ex hypothesi*, believed that the administration of Mwavi to a person innocent of witchcraft would not cause death?

The defendant's conviction for murder was quashed, and he was freed, presumably to administer Mwavi under similar circumstances again.[33b] Again, in *Agumagu Nwaoke* [33c] the accused demanded the return of £1 10s. he had paid as " head money " for his wife, Noacha, when she refused to continue to live with him. She did not repay it. Accused brought a *juju*, pointed it at Noacha, and said that " since you refuse to pay me my money this *juju* will kill you." Noacha became depressed, and six days after the bringing of the *juju* she hung herself. The court reversed a conviction for manslaughter, on the ground that the death was not the immediate consequence of the accused's invocation of the *juju*; the act of the woman in hanging herself was held to be an independent intervening cause.

The most frequent cases, however, are those, like *Jackson*, in which a prisoner is found guilty although he plainly acted as his belief compelled him to act. *Jackson* rested upon the holding that a belief in " metaphysical " threats is " unreasonable," using an English model to determine what might be unreasonable. *Wilson v. Inyang* [34] furnishes an instructive contrast. There the accused

33a (1947) 14 E.A.C.A. 96 (Tanganyika).

33b Many jurisdictions have statutes making the administration of trial by ordeal a crime. See, *e.g.*, Criminal Code, 1960 (Ghana), s. 315 (" The trial by ordeal of sasswood, esere-bean, or other poison, boiling oil, fire immersion in water, or exposure to the attacks of crocodiles or other wild animals, or by any ordeal which is likely to result in the death or a bodily injury to any party to the proceeding is unlawful ").

33c (1939) 5 W.A.C.A. 120 (Nigeria).

34 [1951] 2 All E. R. 237 (Div.Ct.).

was an African who had lived in England for only two years. He had received a diploma from a school of natureopathy, and conceived that he was entitled to use the title " doctor," which he was not. The magistrate held that such a belief would be unreasonable in a person brought up in England, but was not unreasonable in the defendant, and therefore he was acting honestly. The decision was sustained on appeal.

At first blush it seems difficult to understand why an African in England seemingly is judged on the basis of the reasonable African, but the African in Africa is measured by the standard of the reasonable Englishman. On analysis, however, the cases are not at war. The concept of error, as Hall has pointed out, implies:

1. That facts exist;
2. That sense *impressions* of fact, " sensa," are different from the facts;
3. That the sensa fit (correspond to, are congruent with) or do not fit the facts;
4. That erroneous sensa (those that do not fit the facts) are for a time accepted as true, *i.e.*, they are believed to be congruent with the facts; and
5. That this is later recognised as erroneous, *i.e.*, certain opinions become error when they are subjected to broader experience, especially when relative adequate conditions of correct perception obtain.[35]

Implicit in Hall's analysis is the notion that the defendant and the judge interpret their perceptions through the same lenses. If both defendant and judge agree about what is a wild pig and what is a cow, then there is no difficulty. The defendant, on the basis of inadequate sensa, interprets them to imply a wild pig; when the judge, assisted by more complete and accurate sensa, learns that it in fact was a cow, he can understand how the mistake arose.

Thus in *Wilson* v. *Inyang* defendant and the judge could in fact agree that there was a difference between a medical doctor and a natureopathic doctor. But in *Jackson*, the defendant made no error in sensa. The judge had no more factual information about the matter in hand than did the defendant. The inferences the defendant drew from the sensa were *toto coelo* different from that drawn by the judge, because they saw the facts through totally different lenses. That may have been mistake, but it was " unreasonable."

On a verbal level, it may be doubted that *Jackson* was required by the language of the Code. The well-spring of the decision lies in the court's interpretation not of the word " reasonable " but rather

[35] Hall, *op. cit.*, *supra*, note 20, at 362.

of section 18 of the Penal Code, which requires that " criminal responsibility for the use of force in the defence of person or property shall be determined according to the principles of English law." The court might also have referred to section 4, which requires that the Code be interpreted " in accordance with the principles of legal interpretation obtaining in England," and that expressions used in it shall be presumed to be used " with the meaning attaching to them in English criminal law. . . ." [36] There is no similar provision in the penal codes of Ghana, Nigeria, Northern Nigeria or the Sudan, but considering the origins of these Codes any court in interpreting them would probably feel bound to follow the same standards.[37]

Despite the origins of the Codes and even their explicit language, however, so narrow an interpretation does not seem required. As a recent Nigerian writer has said of the provisions of the several Interpretation Acts of Nigeria [38]:

> It is wrong to suggest that our courts are absolutely bound by the specifically English text or version of the common law. Though its basis is admittedly the " system and habits of legal thought " of Englishmen, the common law can no longer be regarded as an exclusively English heritage. Having adopted the English habits of legal thought, we are to apply and develop them according to our own lights and circumstances, and not to regard ourselves as absolutely bound by their particular elaborations in the English courts.[39]

The Privy Council in other contexts has sometimes felt free to adopt this rather more liberal approach. In *Laila Jhina Maeji* [40] a husband and wife, both Ismaili Khojas, were convicted of conspiracy under Tanganyikan law. That statute made no explicit exception

[36] Similar clauses appear in all the East African Codes and that of the Gambia.

[37] In *Wallace-Johnson* [1940] A.C. 231, the defendant was convicted of sedition under a Gold Coast statute. There was no evidence of *mens rea—i.e.*, that he intended the statement to be seditious. The Gold Coast statute did not require such intent; the British common law cases did. The Privy Council affirmed, on the ground that where a colonial statute is complete and self-contained, it must be read free of glosses derived from English or Scottish cases. That case does not contradict the position taken in the text. To interpret terms of a statute in accordance with the presumed intent of the legislature is not to write a gloss on them. There can be small doubt that the colonial administrators and legislatures used the expressions of the Codes in their traditional English way.

[38] Interpretation Act, s. 45 (1) (" . . . The common law of England and the doctrines of equity . . . shall be in force in Lagos and, in so far as they relate to any matter within the exclusive competence of the Federal legislatures, shall be in force elsewhere in the Federation "). See also: High Court Law, No. 27 of 1955 (Eastern Region, Nigeria); High Court Law, No. 8 of 1955 (Northern Nigeria) (referring only to " the common law " and " the doctrines of equity," without specific reference to England); Law of England (Application) Law, Cap. 60.

[39] Nwabueze, *The Machinery of Justice in Nigeria* (1963) 21.

[40] 2 Tang.L.R. 371; (1956) 23 E.A.C.A. 609 (P.C.).

for husband and wife as co-conspirators, as does the common law. On appeal, the Privy Council interpreted the word "conspiracy" to exclude a concert between husband and wife, following English common law. It then went on to consider whether a husband and wife by a potentially bigamous marriage were within the phrase "husband and wife" as used in English law. But for this purpose the Privy Council held that Tanganyikan law would apply; and since defendants were husband and wife in Tanganyikan law, they were not guilty of conspiracy under the Code.[41]

A similarly flexible approach was taken by the magistrate in *Jackson*. Just as the Privy Council in *Laila Jhina Maeji* interpreted the words "husband and wife" in the light of Tanganyika conditions, so did he interpret the word "reasonable" in the light of Nyasaland conditions. Why did the Federal Supreme Court reject that approach?

The reason is probably spelled out in numerous decisions in other jurisdictions, in which the policy position has been stated explicitly. The court in *Gadam*[42] approved this passage from the judgment appealed against:

> I have no doubt that a belief in witchcraft such as the accused obviously has is shared by the ordinary members of his community. It would, however, in my opinion be a dangerous precedent to recognise that because of a superstition, which may lead to such a terrible result as is disclosed by the facts of this case, is generally prevalent among a community, it is therefore reasonable. The courts must, I think, regard the holding of such beliefs as unreasonable and leave it to those who exercise the Royal Prerogative of mercy to say whether the sentence prescribed by law should be mitigated.[43]

Another, but only verbal, defence might have been found in the notion of intent. In *Abdullah Mukhtar Nur*[44] the defendant, while walking home to his village at night, met a figure walking towards him dressed in black and carrying a stick. He spoke to the figure, which refused to answer. He became frightened, took the accused for a ghost and started beating it with a stick until it fell to the ground. He then ran to his village to tell his fellow-villagers. When

41 Compare Criminal Code, Nigeria, s. 34: "A husband and wife of a Christian marriage are not criminally responsible for a conspiracy between themselves alone." *Contra*, apparently, if married by customary or Muslim rites.

42 (1954) 14 W.A.C.A. 442, 444 (Nigeria).

43 Ghana, whose Code contains a mistake of fact clause without explicit requirement of reasonableness, has taken the same position. *Konkomba* (1952) 14 W.A.C.A. 236 (Gold Coast) ("In murder cases a defence founded on witchcraft has always been rejected except in cases where the accused himself has been put in such fear of immediate danger to his own life that the defence of grave provocation has been held proved").

44 [1959] S.L.J.R. 1 (Major Court, Sudan).

they came to the scene they discovered that the "ghost" was an old woman, now quite dead. One prosecution witness stated that he had seen a ghost himself. Another prosecution witness, the President of the Native Court, stated that belief in ghosts was common, and that he himself had seen moving fires in the valleys. The court found the defendant not guilty, on the ground that his intent was to slay a ghost, not to kill a human being.[45] This is the solution advocated by Glanville Williams, who urges that the inquiry should seek to ascertain whether the defendant believed that what he killed was a supernatural being in the form of a human being, or a human being with magical powers.[46] Whether the defendant be guilty of murder depends upon what he intended to kill.

This is only a resurrection, in exotic guise, of the mistake in fact-mistake in law dilemma. If two men go hunting on a Sunday, when hunting is illegal, he is exonerated who mistakenly believes the day to be Monday, but he is guilty who mistakenly believes that it is legal to hunt on Sunday. So here, if the defendant believe that he is killing a ghost, it is a mistake in fact, and he is found not guilty; but if he believes he is killing a human being with all the dread powers of a ghost, whom he has a right to kill, it is a mistake of law, and hence he is guilty. The difference is verbal, and bears little relationship to the objectives of the criminal law.

Cases of ritual murder raise problems not dissimilar in principle to those thus far discussed. The Basuto, for example, believe that every physical substance has its own specific characteristic given it by God. Some of these, such as the use of a particular sort of bark for a purgative, are plainly based upon some chemical characteristic of the substance. Others, such as the belief that a stick of a certain sort will ward off hail, are perhaps less clearly so. In the Basuto view, animal substances are viewed as more powerful than vegetable, as animal life is a higher form of being; and human life being a higher form than animal, so human flesh is a more powerful medicine than animal flesh; and the living being more powerful than the dead, living flesh is more powerful than dead flesh.[47] In cases of extreme urgency, when the Basuto is menaced by the many uncertainties of his uncertain world,[48] some Basuto will mutilate a living

45 In *Machekequonabe*, 28 Ont.Rep. 309, a tribe of Indians believed in the existence of a Wendigo, an evil spirit clothed in human flesh, who ate people. Defendant saw what he imagined was a Wendigo, hailed it, and on receiving no answer, shot it. The Wendigo turned out to be his own foster father, who died from the wounds. He was convicted of manslaughter, apparently for negligence in ascertaining whether the figure was a Wendigo or a human being.

46 *Loc. cit. supra*, note 31.

47 Ashton, *The Basuto* (1952) 307–316.

48 It is said that the Basuto medicine-horn murders have become more frequent in recent years in response to the dislocations caused by the racial policies of South Africa, where most Basutomen go to work. *Ibid.* at 316.

victim until he dies, in order to obtain living flesh for their medicine horns.[49]

On a conceptual level, a distinction can be drawn between these cases and the cases of presumed self-defence against witchcraft. If there is a defence in the ritual murders, it must be comprehended under the heading of necessity. There would appear to be two bases for rejecting the claim in these cases. In the first place, following *Jackson*, the mistake would necessarily be viewed as unreasonable. In the second place, in assessing the defence of necessity, the common law probably requires the defendant to make a value-judgment, that he may not kill an innocent even to save his own life.[50] The Gambia, whose Code alone in Africa has a statutory provision admitting the defence of necessity, excludes it in cases of homicide.[51] The justice of requiring the Basuto to adopt the value-standards of the common law at their peril may perhaps introduce an element irrelevant to the present discussion; but it would seem plain that the defence of mistake, which would precede any claim of necessity in such cases, would not lie. In the event, the issue never seems to have been discussed in the reported cases.

The problems raised by the issue of the defence of mistake of fact must be sharply distinguished from cases in which the question is whether the superstitious world-view is honestly held. This issue arises principally in two situations, on a claimed defence of provocation, and in cases of larceny by trick.

The witchcraft cases have reached the conclusion that in one narrow circumstance, a belief that the deceased is trying to bewitch the defendant will be provocation. If the defendant actually sees the deceased engaged in an act of witchcraft against him, and loses his self-control in a fit of passion, then the defence will lie.[52] In *Fabiano* [53] the defendants believed that deceased was a wizard who had killed members of their families. They discovered the supposed wizard crawling about the compound at night, naked. They believed that the deceased was then and there practising witchcraft against them, and so they killed him by stuffing green plantains up his anus.[54] The defence of provocation was sustained.

All the African Codes [55] have been construed to require that the

[49] See, *e.g.*, *Jobere Motsie* [1959] H.C.T.L.R. 3 (Basutoland High Court); *Mokhuele Leuta* [1959] H.C.T.L.R. 3 (Basutoland High Court).

[50] *Dudley and Stephens* (1884) 14 Q.B.D. 273.

[51] Criminal Code, s. 15.

[52] *Fabiano* (1941) 8 E.A.C.A. 96 (Uganda); *Galikuwa* (1951) 18 E.A.C.A. 175 (Uganda); *Konkomba*, *supra*, note 43.

[53] *Supra*, note 52.

[54] This was a method of killing wizards traditionally used in Uganda. Haydon, *Law and Justice in Buganda* (1960) p. 283.

[55] See, *e.g.*, *Criminal Code* (Nigeria) ss. 283, 318; Criminal Code, 1960 (Ghana) s. 53; Penal Code, Nyasaland, s. 313.

provocation be " reasonable," [56] following the lead of the Privy Council.[57] At first blush it would seem contradictory to deny that witchcraft is a reasonable belief, and still admit it, even in narrowly confined situations, as a " reasonable " provocation. The similarity is, however, superficial. The reasonableness of mistake tends to be tested against the standard of the reasonable Englishman, as we have seen. The reasonableness of provocation is measured against the judge's estimate of the average person of the community from which the defendant comes.[58]

The difference arises from the function of the notion of " reasonableness " in the two situations. Provocation, as has been frequently said, is at best a concession to the frailty of the common herd.[59] Thus the function of the requirement of reasonableness in provocation is to exculpate the defendant when he suffers from the same weakness as his fellow-men.[60] The requirement of reasonableness with respect to mistake, on the other hand, is to ensure that he is held to a standard of conduct which the judges deem to be proper in the premises. The measure in the one case is the judges' notion of the average man; the measure in the other is a normative one, expressing not an average but a standard of conduct.

A second group of cases has arisen where persons professing to have supernatural powers have been charged with false pretences or larceny by trick. It is generally a defence to such a charge that the accused believed that what he represented to be true was in fact true.[61] One of the tests of whether the defendant in fact believed what he said is whether or not it was " reasonable."

In England it was said long ago in such a case that

> It is absurd to suggest that this man could have believed in his ability to predict the fortunes of another by knowing the hour and place of his birth and the aspect of the stars at such

[56] See, *e.g.*, *Atta* [1959] G.L.R. 337 (Court of Appeal) (*Semble*; the Ghana Criminal Code, s. 53 (*a*), limits provocation in the case of assault and battery to circumstances " as to be likely to deprive a person, being of ordinary character, and being in the circumstances in which the accused person was, of the power of self-control "); *El Baleita Balla Baleila* [1958] S.L.J.R. 12 (Court of Criminal Appeal); *Raji Afonja* (1956) 15 W.A.C.A. 26 (Nigeria); *Fabiano*, *supra*, note 51.

[57] *Kwaku Mensah* (1945) 11 W.A.C.A. 2 (P.C.); see *Lee Chun Chuen* [1962] 3 W.L.R. 1461 (P.C.).

[58] *Lee Chun Chuen*, *supra*, note 57.

[59] Holmes, *The Common Law* (1881) pp. 61–62, Macauley, *A Penal Code Prepared by the Indian Law Commissioners* (1838) Note N, pp. 107–108; Williams, " Provocation and the Reasonable Man " [1954] Crim.L.Rev. 740, 741–742. But see Michael and Wechsler, " A Rationale of the Law of Homicide " (1937) 37 Col.L.Rev. 1261, 1281–1282.

[60] The reason for denying the defence in most witchcraft cases is that in all except the *Fabiano* situation there is presumably time for the passions of a reasonable man to cool.

[61] Kenny, *Outlines of Criminal Law* (17th ed., Turner, 1958) 334; Criminal Code, 1960 (Ghana), s. 133 (1); Penal Code, Uganda, s. 288.

> times. We do not live in times when any sane man believes in such power.[62]

But in Africa judges have many times conceded that however "unreasonable" the belief may be for purposes of mistake, there can be no doubt that many perfectly sane Africans believe in witchcraft.[63] In *Nqweshiza* [64] the defendant was charged with falsely pretending that "she could tell who was the mtakati [wizard] by holding a lot of thin sticks attached to a piece of string." The court held that in the absence of affirmative proof to the contrary, it could not be presumed that the defendant did not believe in her own power:

> Although such a representation might appear to this court to be palpably false, there is no doubt that many natives do not think so. . . . The court will, in determining whether pretences stated to be false were false to the knowledge of the accused, be guided by the knowledge it possesses and by the present state of enlightenment, as well as by common sense and experience . . . but . . . there must be evidence from which an inference of knowledge can be drawn.[65]

The distinction between these cases and the mistake of fact cases seems obvious. In the one case the reasonableness of the belief is used as a test of the honesty with which the belief is held.[66] In the other, as we have seen, the requirement serves a normative function.[67] The norm to which the African is held is not that of the average African, but that appropriate to a civilisation thousands of miles distant, and, with respect to the tribalised, bush Africans who are the defendants in these cases, centuries away.

Negligence. Another group of cases have arisen out of crude notions of medicine. For most bush Africans, there is a sheer continuum of inherent powers of various substances, although few carry it so far as do the Basuto. In most of the cases which have arisen, the actor was honestly trying to help the victim. In *Zanhibe*,[68] the

[62] *Penny* v. *Hanson* (1887) 18 Q.B.D. 478, 480.
[63] *Muswi s/o Musele* (1955) 23 E.A.C.A. 622 (Kenya).
[64] 1948 (1) S.A. 106.
[65] At 108. In most cases, however, that the accused was not aware of the falsity of the pretence has not been urged by the defence. *Saida s/o Ngoja* (1955) 2 Tang.L.R. 130 (accused represented that he had the power to resurrect a dead grandchild); *Ceesay and Gomez* (1956) 2 W.A.L.R. 87 (The Gambia) (money doubling); *Mubwana* [1958] R. & N.L.R. 890 (High Court, Northern Rhodesia) (changing leaves into money).
[66] See *Wilson* v. *Inyang*, *supra*, note 34.
[67] It may be argued that in the provocation and in the fraud cases, the use of reasonableness as a test, even for the limited function of testing honesty, actually serves as a norm. No doubt it does. In these cases, however, the judges purport to inquire only if the superstition is in fact generally held. In the mistake cases they consciously create a norm.
[68] 1954 (3) S.A. 597 (Transvaal Provincial Division).

accused, a native doctor, received £1 10s. to cure the deceased, who was showing signs of mental derangement. A bath of hot water was prepared over a brazier, and some medicine placed in it. To exorcise the evil spirits who had seized her, the deceased was held down over this steaming bath by some relatives, under a blanket. After a while she ceased screaming and struggling, since she had been steamed to death. The treatment was a common one in the vicinity. The accused was, of course, convicted of culpable homicide.

Yaro Paki [69] poses a more difficult problem. There, a barber on the Jos Plateau in Nigeria was prosecuted for having negligently carried out a tonsillectomy. He had performed the operation more than 2,000 times, all successfully; his father and grandfather had performed the same operation before him. The patient died of sepsis following the operation. " What would one think," asked the court, " of a surgeon who operated without first sterilising his instruments and making sure that they were as clean as possible? The defendant has never, I am sure, heard of Lord Lister or has the slightest idea about the need for care to avoid infection." Presumably because he had never heard of Lord Lister, he was found guilty of negligent homicide.

In all these cases the defendant is held to a wholly objective standard of due care. His subjective appreciation of the risk is irrelevant. Moreover, the standard of care to which he is held is not one appropriate to his training, background and experience, but one appropriate to European physicians. In *Gija Dhlamini*,[70] for example, the accused was a practising herbalist. The deceased asked him for some medicine to cleanse his body so that he might have more children. Accused gave him a deadly poison, cantharidin, made from crushed bodies of a kind of beetle, apparently a powerful aphrodisiac. The dose prescribed was greatly in excess of a lethal one, and the patient died of the cure. The accused was held guilty of negligent manslaughter. The court said:

> Mistake of fact, in order to be a defence in criminal law, must not only be a bona fide belief but must also be a reasonable belief.[71] The standard to be adopted in deciding whether mistake of fact is reasonable is the standard of the reasonable man, and the race and the idiosyncrasies or superstitions or the intelligence of the person accused do not enter into the question.[72]

69 21 N.L.R. 63 (Supreme Court, Nigeria, 1955).
70 [1926–53] H.C.T.L.R. 33 (Swaziland High Court, 1940).
71 Swaziland, like all the High Commission territories, is governed by the Roman-Dutch law of South Africa. That country has, however, adopted the English rule requiring the mistake to be " reasonable," despite the expressed dissatisfaction of the judges. *Griffin*, 1962 (4) S.A. 495 (Eastern Cape Division).
72 At 34, quoting from *Mbombela* (1933) A.D. 269.

As in the cases of mistake of fact, the negligence cases deny the world-view of the ordinary African, and hold him rigidly to a foreign standard. In the case of native doctors, apparently they are to be held not only to the standard of the reasonable Englishman, but to that of the reasonably trained English medical practitioner.

Insanity. In England today, a man who claimed that he had killed to defend himself against witchcraft would in all probability be committed for insanity, not tried for murder. The host of cases in which Africans have been sentenced to death for killing under the sway of the same delusion testifies that a different rule seemingly obtains in Africa.

The Codes,[73] like the common law,[74] distinguish between sane and insane delusions. In *Hotema* v. *U.S.*,[75] the Supreme Court of the United States held that a delusion that the victim was a witch will only exculpate if it was the product of an insane mind, but not if it were the product of a sane one. The rule comports to the general notion that only physical incapacity of the mind will serve to bring the defendant under the umbrella of insanity; mere brutishness acquired through a perverse upbringing will not.[76]

Insane delusion suffices in itself to excuse the commission of a harm otherwise criminal only in those who, suffering from a delusion, believe that the facts are such that their acts would be lawful. The justification for the rule is that such persons.

> . . . must be unaware of the applicability of the legal threat; and the very conception of an *idée fixe* implies that the men

[73] All the codes appear to make some changes in the M'Naghten rules. As to the Ghana Code [Criminal Code, 1960, s. 27], see Seidman, " Insanity as a Defence under the Criminal Code, 1960 (Ghana) " (1964) 1 University of Ghana L.J. 42. The East African Codes exculpate if defendant was " through any disease affecting his mind incapable of understanding what he was doing, or of knowing that he ought not to do the act or make the omission." See, *e.g.*, Penal Code, Uganda, s. 12. They omit the insane delusion provision. Nevertheless, they have been interpreted as though they restate the M'Naghten rules. *Nyinge s/o Suwatre* [1959] E.A.C.A. 974. The rules in East Africa have been interpreted to exclude uncontrollable impulse, although the language of the Codes [that defendant was prevented from " knowing that he ought not to do the act "] might readily have been otherwise construed. *Ebrahim Neraga s/o Wamala*, 10 E.A.C.A. 48 (Uganda); *Shekanga alias Roman s/o Ndeka*, 15 E.A.C.A. 158 (Tanganyika). The Nigerian Criminal Code admits of partial delusions not necessarily arising out of disease of the mind. Criminal Code, s. 28 (" A person whose mind . . . is affected by delusions on some specific matter or matters . . ."); nevertheless, the clause has not been invoked in the witchcraft cases.

[74] *M'Naghten's Case* (1843) 10 Clark & F. 200.

[75] (1901) 186 U.S. 413, S.Ct. 895, 46 L.ed. 1225.

[76] *Kemp* [1956] 3 W.L.R. 724, 731 (" The rule [of *M'Naghten's Case*] was not intended to apply to defects of reason caused simply by brutish stupidity without rational power. It was not intended that the defence should plead: ' although with a healthy mind he nevertheless had been brought up in such a way, that he never learned to exercise his reason, and therefore he is suffering from a defect of reason.' ").

> who suffer from them have not the capacity to take a reasonable view of the facts. They differ, therefore, from sane men who make unreasonable mistakes of fact precisely in this—that sane men can be stimulated to appraise the facts more carefully, whereas deluded men cannot be threatened away from their delusion.[77]

Delusion is also important in the law as indicia of insanity.[78] The practical administration of the M'Naghten rules

> affords a wider immunity than their language would seem to recognise. For many forms of insanity, which do not in themselves constitute those particular defects of reason which the judges recognised as conferring exemption from responsibility, have often been treated as sufficient evidence to show that one or other of these exemptive defects was also actually present.[79]

But it is evidence of insanity only because the delusion is so aberrant that in ordinary experience it can only arise from a diseased mind. In Africa, where most of the tribalised defendants' peers have the same delusions about witchcraft as the defendant, his belief is not extraordinary.

This rule is applied even in the cases in which the accused believes herself to be a witch. In *Alice Eriyamremu* [79a] the prisoner was charged with the murder of her three-year-old granddaughter. She testified in part:

> Apart from making *gari* I used to serve *juju* also. . . . Between the night of Tuesday and Wednesday my mates in witchcraft came to my house and instructed me to kill my granddaughter Oyinbo and I killed her that very night with a stick . . . and before this done I held her legs swinged her round my head and knocked her on the floor three times. . . . After the death I used a matchet to cut her two legs and I threw the matchet into a brook. . . .

But the court denied a defence of insanity.

> Having regard to the prisoner's reference to her worship of *juju* and to witchcraft and to the clear manner in which she gave her evidence I am of the opinion that, even if it is arguable that at the time she killed the girl she was afflicted with mental infirmity which deprived her of capacity to know that she ought

77 Michael and Wechsler, " A Rationale of the Law of Homicide," 37 Col.L.R. 701, 754.

78 The literature is voluminous. See, *e.g.*, Glueck, *Mental Disorder and the Criminal Law* (1925) 304–312, 329 *et seq*; Z. Iboorg, " Misconceptions of Legal Insanity," 9 Am.J. Orthopsychiatry 540, 552; *Durham* v. *United States* (1954) 214 F. 2nd 862, 45 A.L.R. 1430 (App.D.C.).

79 Michael and Wechsler, *loc. cit.*, *supra*, note 77, at 752, note 180.

79a (1959) W.N.L.R. 270 (High Court, Western Region, Nigeria).

> not to kill the girl, on the balance of probabilities the infirmity was not natural and that it was induced by the prisoner's worship of *juju* and/or witchcraft. . . . Mental infirmity which is self-induced and is not a defence. . . .

The African who commits a crime because of his pre-scientific world-view, then, falls between the two stools of mistake and insanity. On the one hand, his mistake is measured by the standard of reasonableness appropriate to Englishmen. On the other hand, his sanity is measured by a standard appropriate to Africans. An Englishman who killed another because he believed that the victim, like all Europeans, were vampires, would no doubt find a safe refuge in insanity [80]; the eleven Acholi who did the same thing were sentenced to death. As the East African Court of Appeals has said, "Perfectly sane Africans believe in witchcraft." [81]

Nor can it fairly be said that because it is a sane, but unreasonable, delusion, the African who holds a pre-scientific world-view can be "stimulated" by threat of punishment to appraise facts more carefully. As Meek has forcefully put it:

> Witches and witchcraft do not, of course, exist; but the belief in their existence is one of the most potent in the lives of most African [tribalised] people. And it is a belief which cannot easily be exercised, for it is not an isolated factor, but an integral part of the whole psychological and magico-religious system.[82]

One can only appraise facts in terms of his whole understanding of the world. To expect an African to be "stimulated" by fear of penal sanction to abandon his whole ethical, factual, religious and psychological world is to adhere to a delusion no less superstitious than those to which the tribalised Africans themselves adhere.

Absolute liability: the anti-witchcraft legislation: All of the Anglophonic States have adopted some sort of anti-witchcraft legislation.[83] They vary in content, and there is constant confusion over the sorts of conduct forbidden. The central concept of the statutes seems to be to forbid two areas of activity in general: The practice of "pointing out" a witch, and the receiving of money for the pretended exercise of magical powers.

These statutes have been interpreted to prohibit the forbidden practices without regard to the subjective beliefs of the actor.

80 Kenny, *Outlines of Criminal Law* (18th ed., Turner, 1962) 54.

81 *Supra*, note 63.

82 Meek, *Law and Authority in a Nigerian Tribe* (1935) p. 79.

83 See, *e.g.*, Laws, 1951 (Uganda), Chap. 23; Laws, 1948 (Kenya), Chap. 25; Criminal Code, The Gambia (Laws, 1951, Cap. 21), s. 294; Criminal Code, Nigeria.

Musanki and Namusaka [84] is the leading case. There it was held that " a bona fide belief in the efficacy of witchcraft or non-natural powers," such as would negative any intent to deceive, was not a defence under the statute. The court conceded that " some such defence is at the back of the mind of both accused and witnesses in many, perhaps in most, cases brought under [the witchcraft statute]." The argument was that the statute makes the gist of the offence " pretending " to exercise powers of witchcraft; and one cannot " pretend " if one honestly believes that he has the claimed powers. Following Shearman J.'s judgment in *Stonehouse* v. *Mason*,[85] the court held that the offence prohibited does not require any *mens rea* other than an intention to commit the offence outlawed by the statute.

Now there are many crimes in which a person is commanded not to do what he desires to do; rape, seduction, theft, and many other crimes arise because of a conflict between desire and the norm. But for most bush Africans, witchcraft is not a matter in which they can choose to participate or not; they are impelled to it. In Akan belief, for example, it is believed that an *obayi* or spirit seizes the personality of the witch willy-nilly; one is a witch not because she desires to be a witch, but because she is compelled to be one.[85a] Similarly, it will not suffice to tell persons who believe they have power to detect witches not to use their powers to save their kinsmen; that imposes an impossible standard of conduct upon the subjects of the legislation. Because the offender is impelled to act by processes and forces beyond his conscious control, the anti-witchcraft legislation imposes a liability analogous to the absolute liability imposed by certain public-welfare offences. In neither the witchcraft cases, nor in the public welfare cases, can the accused consciously avoid doing the act outlawed by the statute, in one case because of the iron frame of his ideology, in the other by reason of ignorance of fact.

The principal justification for statutes imposing absolute liability has always taken into account not only the desirability of punishing the prohibited acts, but also the relative slightness of the penalties usually involved.[86] But the penalties for witchcraft are heavy: two

84 (1924) 4 L.R.N.R. 193; *accord*: *Wirumayi* [1955] S.R. 240.

85 91 L.J.K.B. 93.

85a Field, *op. cit. supra*, note 18, *passim*.

86 *Hobbs* v. *Winchester Corporation* [1910] 2 K.B. 471 (" Then it is said that this is a criminal offence and that we ought not to construe this section [as creating an absolute offence] because a criminal offence is committed which may involve imprisonment. The answer to that contention is that reliance may be placed upon the justices not to send a man to prison in a case where he did not know the meat was unsound."); *Morisette* v. *United States* (1952) 342 U.S. 246, 72 S.Ct. 240, 96 L.ed. 288; *Tolson* (1889) 23 Q.B.D. 168, 177; *cf.* Williams, *Criminal Law: The General Part* (2nd ed., 1961) 255; Howard, *Strict Responsibility* (1963), *passim* (criticising the rationale).

years' imprisonment in Zambia,[87] ten years in Kenya.[88] The alternative of fine is illusory in a subsistence economy, where cash income is negligible.

Not only do the Codes impose a quasi absolute liability for practising witchcraft, but they try to distinguish between witchcraft and medicine in a way that may seem sensible to reasonable Englishmen, but plainly wars with indigenous beliefs. In *Swaine*,[89] the defendant was charged in five counts with taking money by false pretences, in that the payments were received for the pretended exercise of the use of charms. A statute [90] made it a conclusive presumption that such payments were obtained by fraud, thus barring a defence that the accused believed that his representations were true. As to some of the counts, the accused had plainly invoked magic, by giving charms which were supposed to tell the recipient what the future would hold. But on Count 4, the customer had asked for a medicine to prevent a further pregnancy of his wife until she had ceased nursing the present baby. The defendant gave him two roots which his wife was to wear tied around her waist at all times; this, he said, would prevent pregnancy. The court held that he was wrongly convicted on this count: " It may be assumed that the roots had, in fact, no medicinal or contraceptive value; but there is nothing to show that the accused did not believe that they had such effect without resort to magic." [91]

The court's opinion assumes that there is a distinction between magic and medicine. That there is no such distinction in most indigenous systems of belief seems apparent. In the very case at issue, there were a number of other counts against the accused. In each count, the diagnostic method was to " throw the bones." After diagnosis, the defendant prescribed " medicine ": in some cases, charms; in others what the court chose to call non-magical medicine (like the roots tied about the waist to prevent pregnancy). Patently, the subjects of the law do not make the same distinctions that the law does.

II

Thus with respect of a wide spectrum of situations, the common law and the statutes imposed by the central government assume a system of beliefs which is at war with that of the indigenous population. The impact is obvious: In all these cases the defendants are convicted without any subjective appreciation that what they have done was wrong, let alone criminal.

87 Laws, 1953, Cap. 30, ss. 4, 5.
88 Laws, 1948, Chap. 25, s. 3.
89 [1957] R. & N.L.R. 897.
90 Witchcraft Suppression Act, s. 9.
91 [1957] R. & N.L.R. 897, 900–901.

Hall points out the relevant ethical principle: ". . . moral obligation is determined not by the actual facts, but by the actor's opinion regarding them."[92] It can hardly be gainsaid that in all these cases the criminal law is punishing people who believed, in most cases, that what they were doing was completely moral, because of their opinion concerning the facts.

The common law of crimes has always trodden a knife edge between the objectives of general and special deterrence. General deterrence operates to prevent others from acting as did this defendant; it purports to use the convict as an example, by means of which to intimidate other potential criminals. Special deterrence operates to prevent this criminal from acting again as he did in this case. General deterrence can be operative whether or not this particular criminal could have been deterred from doing the crime with which he stands charged. After all, the argument goes, if the public learns from the hanging of this murderer that murder will be punished by death, then potential murderers will be intimidated. Special deterrence, on the other hand, would not punish this criminal unless in the circumstances of the crime which he did commit he might have been deterred, considering his own idiosyncratic circumstances at the time of the crime.

The common law has resolved the inherent dilemma in the ambiguity of the objective of deterrence by the externalisation of *mens rea*. The test of criminal guilt under the common law has come to be not whether this accused was aware of the criminality of his act, but whether he acted intentionally or negligently.[93]

The Codes of Anglophonic Africa have given this doctrine a statutory dimension. The East African Codes,[94] that of the Gambia[95] and of Southern Nigeria[96] contain a clause drawn verbatim from that of the Queensland Code:

> Subject to the express provisions of this Code relating to negligent acts and omissions, a person is not criminally responsible for an act or omission, which occurs independently of the exercise of his will, or for an event which occurs by accident.
>
> Unless the intention to cause a particular result is expressly declared to be an element of the offence constituted, in whole or in part, by an act or omission, the result intended to be caused by an act or omission is immaterial.

[92] *Op. cit. supra*, note 20, at 363.

[93] *See* Shearman J. in *Wheat and Stocks* (1921) 15 C.A.R. 134, 135; Stallybrass, "The Mental Element in Crimes at Common Law," in Radzinowicz and Turner (eds.), *The Modern Approach to Criminal Law* (1945) 198–199, 205.

[94] See, *e.g.*, Penal Code, Tanganyika, s. 10.

[95] s. 7.

[96] s. 24. The Criminal Code, Ghana, contains analogous provisions, s. 13.

> Unless otherwise expressly declared, the motive by which a person is induced to do or omits to do an act, or to form an intention, is immaterial so far as regards criminal responsibility.

Of this clause, the draftsman, Sir Samuel Griffiths, said:

> Under the criminal law of Queensland, as defined by the Criminal Code, it is never necessary to have recourse to the old doctrine of *mens rea*. . . . The test now to be applied is whether the prohibited act was or was not done accidentally or independently of the exercise of the will of the accused person.[97]

Despite this dictum, however, the courts of Anglophonic Africa have persisted in solving specific cases by recourse to English cases on *mens rea*.[98] In the result, they have in fact applied a doctrine which is not different from that of the English courts, and probably one which is not too far distant from that set out in the Codes.

To the extent that the *Weltanschauung*—the whole system of beliefs, mores, and ideologies—of its subjects matches that imminent in the criminal law, no doubt objective *mens rea* reaches a defensible, ethical result in most cases, for in most cases the subjective appreciation of his criminality by the accused will be the same as that of the reasonable man in his society. In such a case, to punish will achieve the objective of general deterrence, and at the same time it is relevant to the objective of special deterrence. Where the particular individual varies too radically from the norm, mitigation of punishment and executive clemency are available to prevent too gross a violation of ethical notions.

The use in Africa of standards drawn from another society, however, in many cases involving the tribalised Africans' world-view, results in the imposition of strict liability under the guise of adherence to common law doctrines which traditionally abhor strict liability. Serious crimes, which have always found their ethical justification in the insistence upon *mens rea*, are treated as though they were petty public welfare offences for which no *mens rea* is required—except, of course, that instead of trivial penalties these defendants are sentenced to imprisonment or even death.

The boast of the common law of crimes has always been its ethical content. Lord Goddard has said:

97 *Widgee Shire Council* v. *Bonney* (1907) 4 C.L.R. 977.

98 This has been strikingly apparent in the African courts' examination of statutory liability without fault. See, *e.g.*, *Att.-Gen.* v. *Nagaru s/o Kanyere* (1951) 24 K.L.R. 123; *Clegg* v. *C.O.P.* (1949) 12 W.A.C.A. 479 (Nigeria); *Copperfield Cold Storage Co. Ltd.* (1953) 5 L.R.N.R. 248, *appeal dismissed* (1953) 5 L.R.N.R. 564; *Dewji Prahji Mehti* (1945) 13 E.A.C.A. 80 (Tanganyika). The Queensland courts have held that the section of the Code quoted in the text bars any crime of absolute liability in the absence of express exclusion. *Anderson* v. *Nystrom* [1941] St.R.Qd. 56; *Brimblecombe* v. *Duncan* [1958] Qd.R. 8; *Hunt* v. *Maloney* [1959] Qd.R. 164.

> The general rule applicable to criminal cases is *actus non facit reum nisi sit mens rea*. . . . It is of the utmost importance for the protection of the liberty of the subject that a court should always bear in mind that, unless a statute, either clearly or by necessary implication, rules out *mens rea* as a constituent part of a crime, the court should not find a man guilty of an offence against the criminal law unless he has a guilty mind.[99]

The tap-root for Lord Goddard's dictum lies in the value-judgment which, however imperfectly, furnishes the secret juices which nourish the common law of crimes: The humanist belief in the value and dignity of human personality. That humanist principle has been expressly adopted by the new régimes in Anglophonic Africa; ex-President Nkrumah of Ghana, for example, asserted that it was the central ethical postulate of his philosophy that no man should be treated as a means, but only as an end.[100]

Where the world-view of the criminal law matches the world-view of its subjects tolerably well, the secret juices of humanism vivify—but only moderately well—the common law of crimes. Where, however, as we have seen, there is no such fit, the criminal law flourishes without benefit of the humanist sap. In Africa, in the sorts of cases here discussed, it would seem plain that the fragile plant of the criminal law produces but withered ethical flowers.

Several solutions suggest themselves. The rules themselves might be manipulated in such a way as to produce perhaps more defensible results; the difficulties arising might be dealt with in terms of mitigation of punishment; or an entirely new approach might be forged.

The possibility of manipulation of the rules is of course the first solution to suggest itself to the common law trained lawyer. The requirement of reasonableness as a condition for successful assertion of mistake of fact as a defence might be abandoned[101]; indeed, there is serious doubt that it is anything more than an unauthoritative accretion to the case law,[102] now enshrined in the African Codes. The test of negligence might be narrowed to comprehend only those cases in which the accused subjectively appreciated the risk; again, there is no dearth of eminent authorities who so urge in any case.[103] Finally, as Kenny suggested, delusions so bizarre—to a person not

99 *Harding* v. *Price* [1948] 1 K.B. 695, 700.

100 Nkrumah, *Consciencism* (1964) p. 95.

101 Eminent scholars have so advocated. Hall, *op. cit. supra*, note 20, at 366–368; Williams, *op. cit. supra*, note 87 at 201–205.

102 *Ibid.*

103 Williams, *Criminal Law: The General Part* (1953) 99–100; but see Holmes, *The Common Law* (1881) 53–56.

steeped in the culture of the African outlands—might be treated as a form of insanity which would exculpate from crime.[104]

The real difficulty in all these suggestions is that they go too far. Persons who kill presumed witches—usually the weakest members of the community—ought not to be allowed at large until something has been done to train them into more wholesome modes of conduct. The ethical problem that arises in these cases does not arise on the question of guilt or innocence; it arises because we have strong ethical reservations about the infliction of exemplary punishment upon a person who did not have subjective awareness of his guilt. To manipulate the rules in any of the ways suggested resolves the ethical problem by removing the finding of guilt; but it leaves the social problem, for society remains unprotected. What is required is some solution which will keep the accused under some sort of control until he can safely be released into society, but which will meet the ethical objection raised when a person without moral guilt is used as an example to others.

One possible solution might be in terms of mitigation of punishment by the sentencing judges. The difficulty is that judges are themselves notoriously ambivalent with respect to the objectives of punishment. In *Petero Mukasa*,[105] for example, the two appellants set upon some herdsmen in the honest, though possibly mistaken, belief that the herdsmen were stealing bananas; one of the herdsmen died from the beating received. They appealed from a sentence of ten and seven years, respectively, in hard labour. The court reduced the sentences sharply, stating:

> In determining sentence it has to be borne in mind that the theft of food crops by night is in native eyes very rightly regarded as a very serious offence. The appellants are natives of Buganda and . . . prior to the advent of British rule the killing of persons caught stealing foodstuffs was held by the Buganda to be justifiable homicide.

A precisely contrary position, however, has been taken in closely analogous cases. In *Zanhibe*,[106] for example, leave was refused to appeal against a sentence of twelve months' imprisonment. The court spelled out an opinion wholly at variance from that expressed in *Petero Mukasa*:

> " The end of punishment . . . is no other than to prevent the criminal from doing further injury to society, and to prevent others from committing the like offence. Such punishments, therefore, and such mode of inflicting them, ought to be chosen

104 Kenny, *Outlines of Criminal Law* (17th ed., Turner, 1958) 54.
105 (1944) 11 E.A.C.A. 114 (Uganda).
106 *Supra*, note 68.

> as will make the strongest and most lasting impressions on the minds of others, with the least torment to the body of the criminal. . . ." It seems to me thus, particularly where one is endeavouring to protect a somewhat primitive community, that it is clear . . . that almost paramount consideration must be given to the possible deterrent effect to others of the punishment, without at the same time overlooking the punishment the accused himself merits. . . . It . . . seems to me that even where moral guilt may be found to be absent a court may, in a proper case, where a very large section of the community, especially an unenlightened one, requires to be protected against dangerous practices, disregard the existence of that form of mitigation.

One may indeed question whether exemplary punishment has in fact any deterrent effect upon a population which views the act for which the convict is being punished as proper; but until judges have empirical data upon which to base their opinions, the evisceral judicial response no doubt will remain, in Africa as elsewhere, largely in favour of general deterrence.

A second possible approach lies through institutionalisation of executive clemency. The judges in cases involving the sharp cultural conflicts suggested here have more frequently than not, after a careful opinion identifying the reasons why the accused must be found guilty, with obvious relief called the executive's attention to the merits of the cause. In *Kajuna s/o Mbake*,[107] for example, the court even went so far as to state that the element of witchcraft in the case is an element always taken into account as a mitigating factor by the Governor General-in-Council.

The institutionalisation of executive clemency in this regard is perhaps further advanced in Northern Nigeria than any place else on the continent. There the Criminal Procedure Code [108] requires that a native court may not execute its sentence of death in a capital case until the sentence has been confirmed by the Minister for Internal Affairs, who has the responsibility for matters arising concerning the exercise of the prerogative of mercy. The Ministry requires the Native Court to furnish the Ministry with particulars in each capital case, which include, *inter alia*:

(a) an indication of the state of culture of the deceased;
(b) if considered relevant, an assessment of the influence of the accused's environment on his behaviour;
(c) a statement whether the murder is in any way connected with witchcraft, *juju*, etc., and, if so, to what extent this should be regarded as extenuating circumstances;

107 (1945) 12 E.A.C.A. 104 (Tanganyika).

108 s. 394.

(d) the connection, if any, with local custom, belief, or superstition.[109]

The overlay of executive clemency upon the criminal law is a useful safety-valve for the aberrant " hard " case. When it becomes institutionalised, however, it would seem apparent that somewhere there lies a deep fallacy in the law itself. In cases of the sort here described, the courts are majestically demonstrating the guilt of the accused, whilst nevertheless aware that the whole procedure is sham. Moreover, the exercise of executive clemency is rarely surrounded with sufficient firm rules of procedure or of substance to provide the fairness and assurance of equality of treatment which is the essence of true legality.

The South African courts, in an intriguing development which seems far more sensitive to the problems of the African population than one might expect in the country of apartheid, have developed a partial solution for the problem with respect at least to murder cases arising out of witchcraft. They have held that a killing done under the sway of belief in witchcraft is a sufficiently exculpating circumstance to warrant the reduction of a charge of murder to one of culpable homicide.

In *Fundakubi* [110] the issue was whether the fact that the accused killed a person whom he honestly believed to be a witch who had killed numerous members of his family was an extenuating circumstance within the meaning of a statute [111] which gave the jury the power to decide whether such circumstances existed. The court held that it was, quoting approvingly from an earlier case:

> In our view an extenuating circumstance . . . is a fact associated with the crime which serves in the mind of reasonable men to diminish morally, albeit not legally, the degree of the prisoner's guilt. . . . A mind (which) though not diseased so as to provide evidence of insanity in the legal sense, may be subject to a delusion, or to some erroneous belief or some defect, in circumstances which would make a crime committed under its influence less reprehensible or diabolical than it would be in the case of a mind in normal [*sic*] condition. . . . When we find a case like this, where there is a profound belief in witchcraft, and that the victim practised it in great harm, and when we find that this has been the motive of the criminal conduct under consideration, we feel bound to regard the accused as a person labouring under a delusion which, though impotent in

109 Ministry of Internal Affairs Circular No. 28/1960, dated December 17, 1960; discussed in Richardson and Williams, *The Criminal Procedure Code of Northern Nigeria* (1963) 234–235.

110 1948 (3) S.A. 810 (A.D.).

111 s. 206 (2) of Act 31 of 1917.

> any way to alter their guilt legally, does in some measure palliate the horror of the crime and thus provides an extenuating circumstance.

The court then went on to display the usual ambivalence; for having suggested that the absence of moral guilt properly should reduce the quantum of punishment, it promptly urged that the basic consideration to be taken into account should be exemplary deterrence:

> But it is of importance to emphasise that the prevalent belief in witchcraft is a very great blight upon the native peoples of the Union, which the existing penal legislation has failed to eradicate. . . . Excessive leniency in dealing with cases where such a belief has led to the commission of cruel crimes, often against the weakest members of the community, may conceivably help to delay the disappearance of such belief. Not that great reliance can be placed on the severity of punishment alone to get rid of the evil. . . .

Despite the remarkable confusion of penological theories which this opinion displays, oscillating as it does between notions of retribution based upon the degree of "moral guilt," general deterrence, special deterrence, and even of reformation, the South African position may point to a partial solution of the problem.

Capital punishment can have no other justifications than retribution, or exemplary deterrence. Since, under our modern dispensation, retribution is no longer a wholly respectable objective of the criminal law, capital punishment is justified in the literature mainly on the basis of exemplary deterrence. The reduction of the crime to culpable homicide, thus removing the possibility of a death sentence, makes it possible for a humane judge to give fair weight to the claims of special deterrence and reformation in passing sentence.

It would appear to be possible to apply this principle to a wider spectrum of crimes than merely that of murder. A new, partial defence might be created, perhaps to be called the Defence of Outmoded Custom or Belief. Upon pleading and proving that the act, otherwise criminal, was done by the accused under the sway of superstition, pre-scientific belief, indigenous custom, or the like, the accused would then be found guilty not of the crime charged, but of the offence of Primitive Custom or Belief. In determining sentence for that crime, a judge would be plainly enjoined to consider only the question of the re-education of the accused, to the end that he will not commit a similar crime in the future. The mode of re-education lies in the area of penology rather than that discussed in this paper.

Yet this solution is ameliorative rather than structural. These cases suggest that in Africa, at least, there is a wide divergence between the ethic of the Codes and that of much of the population. If in so many cases this contradiction is so strikingly displayed, there must be a host of circumstances in which the contradiction is present but not so obvious. The difficulty arises because there is in Africa—and, it may be tentatively suggested, elsewhere—no such thing as a community morality which is common to all but an insignificant fragment of the population. Morality and ethic derive from the total economic and societal matrix. Where, as in Africa, this matrix is unbelievably parti-coloured, no Code painted in a monochrome can possibly match the morality of more than a minority of the subjects of the Code.

But, as Hall has demonstrated,[112] the final ethical justification of a soundly-based criminal law based on general deterrence lies in its correspondence to the morality of the community. It would seem impossible, in the present African circumstance, to find any criminal Code based on general deterrence as its primary objective which meets Hall's criteria; which is to say, that it is impossible—at least in Africa—to formulate an ethical Code based on general deterrence.

It is, of course, difficult to find a wholly satisfactory answer. One avenue that seems perhaps hopeful of fruitful results would be to explore the possibility of a Code which abandons general deterrence as its objective. It would then be possible to abandon the notion of responsibility expressed in *mens rea* as a requirement—a requirement which is at best an effort to justify general deterrence by invoking ethical notions drawn from vague religious race-memories. Such criminal Codes have from time to time been suggested for the more developed countries in the common law world. There, a façade of uniformity has tended to obscure wide differences of morality arising by reason of class or other group differentiation. In Africa, however, that façade is absent; the dichotomy of the culture is writ plain. If the African States are to meet the humanist imperatives of their expressed ideologies, basic reform of the Penal Codes would seem desirable.

112 Hall, *op. cit. supra*, note 20, at 163–170; ("Especially in the light of the fallibility of any individual's judgment, *mens rea* must be given objective meaning—no man's or group's conscience can supersede the conscience of the community as that is expressed in its penal law").

Part VI
Degeneration of Legal Cultures

[24]

LENIN AND REVOLUTIONARY LAW-MAKING (*)

Csaba Varga

Senior Research Associate at the Institute of Political and Legal Sciences of the Hungarian Academy of Sciences

Revolution and revolutionary law

A social revolution in the course of which a new class seizes power with the desire to make radical changes overnight in the socio-economic order can achieve its objectives only in the teeth of a great many factors making for uncertainty as to its success. It is not enough to make the theoretical and practical preparations for the revolution by drawing up an outline revolutionary programme and making the plans for the take-over; the orientation of the revolutionary action, the concrete form it assumes and the details of its conduct vary from case to case and are influenced by numerous unforeseeable factors, first and foremost among which are the degree of resistance put up by the classes whose power has been overthrown, the attitude of the political allies, and the change, should one occur, in foreign relations.

The final choice from among the various tactical alternatives which may be adopted within the framework of the revolutionary strategy and the detailed decisions once this choice has been determined can be made only in the actual course of the revolutionary action. Further uncertainty derives from the impossibility of foreseeing whether, in the course of revolutionary change, that choice will remain valid or will require modifying. And there is also the risk of subjective errors due to the difficulties encountered by the class in power, obliged to govern under new conditions and by new methods (1).

(*) Cf. *Review of Contemporary Law* N° 1, 1970, S.N. Bratus, "Lenin's Ideas on Socialist Law and Socialist Legality".

In view of these factors, and of the impossibility, for a revolution, of achieving all of its objectives at once without creative participation on the part of the revolutionary masses and occasional and temporary concessions to other social strata, and without trial and error and momentary setbacks, revolutionary legislation must necessarily bear a special character distinct from that of the subsequent legislation of the more stable period after the final achievement of power, which will have the advantage of permanent structures, traditions of its own and a certain amount of practical experience. The difference is particularly real in the case of revolutions of a socialist character, since the aim of these is the creation of a socio-economic order which is qualitatively new. It is visible above all on the formal level, in the actual technique of revolutionary law-making.

The main features typical of revolutionary legislation are its very general nature, the fact that the laws and statutory instruments frequently take the form of an appeal or a proclamation of a declaratory character or a statement of principle, the wording of the clauses, which is clear, fluid and direct, and the often almost total liberty of structure, to be noted in particular in the lack of separation between the "whereas" clauses and the legal provisions. In general, such legislation has the character of an instrument of revolutionary propaganda designed to stimulate and educate, partly because of the language and structure adopted for the norms; in other words — to quote an expression of Lenin's — it suffers from the "formal imperfections" which characterize the sort of norms which scarcely meet the requirements of professional jurists.

This is not, of course, to say that such features are typical of *all* revolutionary legislation, or are the general or inevitable features of revolutionary legislation alone. It is, I believe, merely a difference of degree, and some, most, or all of these features are to be found in a more distinct form and with greater frequency than elsewhere as the outward symptoms peculiar to revolutionary legislation — the reflection of the dialectics of the revolutionary change in the course of which a major struggle has abolished the system formerly in force and set up in its stead institutions which are qualitatively new.

1. The need to remain on the level of generalities

We have just said that the opening stage in the development of Soviet socialist law was primarily characterized by the fact that laws and other instruments often took the form of declaratory statements of principle by reason of the essentially genera nature of the norms they contained. Lenin was not merely passively aware of this fact : as is clear from the attitude he adopted on a variety of occasions, he was personally taking steps to see that the legal provisions adopted by the new Soviet régime did not go into questions of detail or stipulate the precise form and manner of their practical enforcement.

On the very first day of the Revolution, when, at the Second Congress of Workers' and Soldiers' Deputies, Lenin presented the draft of the first revolutionary instrument — the decree on the ownership of land, worded by himself — he made the following emphatic statement :

"We thus express our opposition to any amendment to this draft; we do not wish to enter into all the details, for what we are drafting is a decree and not a programme of action. Russia is a big country and local conditions vary; we would like to think that the peasantry itself will be better able than ourselves to solve the problem correctly" (2).

A bare ten days later, during the discussion, at the meeting of the Central Executive Committee, on the question of proclaiming a monopoly affecting private press organs, he was to declare :

"There are naturally flaws in our Bill. But the Soviets will everywhere put it into practice as local conditions demand. We are not bureaucratic and do not wish to enforce it universally to the letter, as the old ministries were in the habit of doing" (3).

For Lenin, the general character of the laws and regulations was not an *ad hoc* necessity but derived from a conscious revolutionary programme adapted to suit the peculiarities of Russia, and this he explained at the same meeting as follows :

"The local Soviets can, as time and place demand, extend and supplement the basic principles established by the government" (4).

The requirement that laws should be general in character naturally meant that any person called on to enforce a norm must do so in a *creative* manner, in the strictest sense of the term, with due allowance for local peculiarities, thus contributing, with the aid of the manifold tests offered by practical experience, to the finding of the most suitable ways of implementing it and to the crystallization of concrete solutions to the problems involved.

The basis — and the prerequisite — of the maintenance of a general character only for the fundamental provisions of the law is confidence in the masses and in the power of original creation of the revolutionary vanguard. Lenin relied on that power; as early as the tenth day of the Revolution he declared : "Socialism is not the outcome of decrees handed down from above... Live, creative socialism is the work of the popular masses themselves" (7).

He was aware at the same time of the fact that the giving of a purely practical nature to legal norms could also lead to the emergence of numerous undesirable features, not to say abuses, and that there would be a legal pretext for such abuses in the form of the purported requirements of law enforcement which might become particularly detrimental to revolutionary change (8).

In reality, in the case of the majority of basic laws there was no choice, since the specific conditions obtaining — the enormous size of the territory, and the absence of any uniformity in local conditions, of programmes prepared in detail or of time to spare — in themselves prevented the turning of abstract provisions into decentralized, concrete and direct instructions to fit practical circumstances. This situation was to continue for several years after the seizure of power. For example, in December 1919, in connection with the law on assistance to the peasantry, Lenin was obliged to observe :

"In a law we could not express ourselves otherwise, or provide concrete instructions; we were obliged to institute general rules, relying for their scrupulous local enforcement on understanding comrades capable of finding a thousand different ways of carrying them out under the practical economic conditions of each place" (9).

Thus Lenin's initial conception with regard to the level on which legal norms were to be formulated was the outcome of an analysis of the circumstances and conditions of the revolutionary change and of the need to find the optimum level and optimum method. He looked at these questions as a politician. He did not intend his conception of them to have an absolute validity or to apply to the subsequent stages in the development of Soviet law or to socialist law in general.

But despite the relatively special scope of its validity, it is not in the least unreasonable to draw from this conception conclusions of a more general character.

The most elementary of these could be that the principle — generally accepted in socialist countries — that any given legal norm should cover a given specific area cannot unconditionally be treated as a universally valid principle or requirement; its admissibility implies an accumulation of previous experience of law-making and distinctly more stable socio-economic relations.

To a greater or lesser extent, each innovation in law carries with it an element of uncertainty. Newly created law cannot prove to be totally successful, and applicable within the context of the realities of society, except insofar as its theoretical basis is sound, or in other words reflects the true trends in the development of those realities, and insofar as the legal text suitably expresses the purpose of its underlying principle, or in other words gives it proper legal expression and adopts the appropriate procedure for its enforcement. Ample allowance for these two factors is visible in Lenin's writings; for example, he himself asks whether "the *legislative* activity of the Soviet Republic... has been based on just principles and has been enforced in a rational manner" (10).

This at the same time gives us a more direct answer to the question of the reason why Lenin's tendency to remain on the level of generalities and basic principles was justified, and was indeed the only course to be followed. Under the momentary conditions created by the Revolution, in the total absence either of any stability in social relations or of previous experience of partial practical solutions, it was clear that the optimum course, affording the smallest likelihood of error, lay in legislation in the form of general principles rather than specific rules. There were the many variations in the state of the class struggle from one point in the huge territory of Soviet Russia to another, and the *temporary* character of the new legislation as a result both of the fluid nature of the revolutionary change-over and the constantly changing conditions of the practical development of the struggle; or in other words of the need for systematic changes in tactics (11) and the growing need for experimental legislation in the various areas. This meant that the laws must not lay down the specific procedure required, in the sense of the form and manner in which they were to be enforced in practice to suit a given purpose, but must leave such decisions to those directly in charge of their enforcement, namely, the revolutionary forces, with their conscience, experience and aspirations to guide them.

The provision of no more than guidelines of a general character was thus prompted by the desire to allow for the multiplicity of cases to be dealt with, the necessary variations in the manner of dealing with them, and the gradual progress in practical experience of their enforcement; it was sought to prepare the ground for a subsequent general choice of method based on assessments of results and so lay the foundations for legislation which would no longer be temporary and would contain standardized provisions on matters of detail.

Consequently, Lenin's theory of the need for legislation to be general in character was intended to be applicable only during a transition stage, and carried with it the requirement that the subsequent legislation, based on an appraisal of past experience and making provision for specific matters, should be more directly dependent on the practical results achieved and on the political, social and technical experience acquired in the course of the enforcement of existent laws in a creative manner.

2. The question of form

The other main feature typifying Soviet revolutionary legislation lies in what, in the strictest sense of the term, may be called its form, and is a matter of language and structure. The relative simplicity of the language used for the laws or decrees, the looser and less conventional nature of their structure, and their adoption of a wording enabling them to serve an educative purpose and be an incitement to action, are organically bound up with the fact that their content is of a general nature. All these features derive from the conditions and requirements of the revolutionary struggle.

We must draw attention here to a further circumstance which likewise had a degree of influence. During the initial period, legislation was one of the foremost implements of political propaganda (12) — a propaganda consisting of "ordinary truths" (13). Revolutionary legislation was designed to convince the revolutionary classes and was intended for the masses; its fundamental purpose at the outset was less the making of laws in the strict sense than an appeal for creative revolutionary action. It was this peculiarity of function which gave it its peculiar formal nature; the educative role of law and its role as a stimulus to action, which the requirements of revolutionary change demanded, assumed extreme prominence, and this meant the finding of appropriate solutions of a specifically legal nature.

Whereas the essentially general nature of the revolutionary legislation was partly the outcome of purely Russian factors — such as the size of the territory affected by the Revolution and the variations in local conditions — the greater simplicity of language and looseness of structure deriving from this need to educate and stimulate to action could well be typical in general of revolutionary legislation in any society.

What are called for among other things on the formal level are non-ambiguity, simplicity and clarity of legal language, and a comprehensible, straightforward and sincere statement of purpose, or in other words simultaneous intelligibility of motive, purpose and provisions; frequently, as a result, one finds positive-law provisions mingled with the political explanation serving as a preamble.

Lenin's practical activity was marked by an extraordinary awareness of these requirements. He vigorously stressed the need for simplicity and clarity of language in any political or legal instrument of importance (14). His draft of the decree dissolving the Constituent Assembly begins with a concisely-worded statement of fact, preceding an eighty-line explanation of the political reasons for which "the Central Executive Committee decrees that the Constituent Assembly is dissolved" (15); in numerous cases, in the course of the discussion on the drafts of various pieces of legislation, he himself asked, or ordered, "that the decree be preceded by... an explanation intelligible to all" (16), or else that "the fundamental idea" providing the basis for the provisions be "more strongly emphasized" (17).

The Revolution necessarily had to rely on the conscientiousness and enthusiasm of the revolutionary forces, as a vital condition of the maintenance of the revolutionary impetus and hence of its own success, which required sincerity in the relations between government and governed. Lenin emphasized this idea on the very day following the Revolution (18) and it consistently recurs in his observations with regard to legislation (19).

However the development of law also presupposes the development of a legislative technique. In the course of the technical process of establishing a legal system, specifically legal notions crystallize out, and, for purposes of coherence and non-ambiguity, and avoidance of contradictions between the various provisions forming the basis of the system, a legal language develops which, though closely related to everyday speech and not to be isolated from it, is not actually identical with it and has more or less the character of a professional language.

When drafting laws the legislator comes up against two mutually conflicting requirements : the need for the language to be at once understandable and perfectly logical. The two represent opposite extremes, and in any legal text they can be satisfied only by means of a compromise, the nature and degree of which will vary in accordance with social conditions. During a revolution, the need for intelligibility — or, to be more exact, for a popular style of wording which is a stimulus to action — make for a bolder form of expression, even at the cost of a temporary sacrifice of some of the technical exactitude. This does not in itself lessen the reliability of law; it is merely a phenomenon occurring when one type of law is replaced by another, concomitant with the momentary "destruction" necessarily inherent in this process, or in other words with the search for a reliability having its basis in law of a new kind.

Such was the situation in which Lenin, for the sake of intelligibility and a clear popular form of expression, considered it necessary, and held it to be a wise course, to assign less importance for the time being to technical perfection. He pointed out on numerous occasions and in connection with a number of laws that the latter "contained flaws of a formal nature" (21), were "very imperfect from the technical and perhaps also from the juridical point of view" (22), and could not, by a long way, be considered as "models of perfection" (23). Of one law he remarked : "We know it was not invented by some commission or other, or worded by lawyers" (24). As a politician he had, in effect, realized that the decisive aspect of the Revolution was the conquest, preservation and consolidation of power — including legislative power — and that revolutionary transformation called for the speedy enactment of legislation which would stabilize relations within society on as broad a scale as possible and intensification of the social effects of such legislation, and not for laws or decrees worded with minute technical accuracy by professional lawyers. Ten days after the Revolution Lenin himself declared that he considered the fundamental question to be the retention of power and the enactment of laws laying the foundations of the new order, "leaving aside all difficulties with regard to form". "It is perfectly probable", he remarked, "that such laws, for bourgeois society, contain flaws in wording. But the power, let us not forget, is in the hands of the Soviets, which can make the necessary corrections" (25).

3. The consolidation of society and the question of technically correct drafting

Naturally, the requirement that the new laws must have a popular form is far from meaning that they should be inaccurate or that negligent wording should be tolerated. Even during the initial phase Lenin several times spoke of the need for accuracy (26), while at the same time he was perfectly aware that with the conclusion of the transitional phase — i.e. the stabilization of the social relations of the new order — proper professional drafting of legislation would inevitably become necessary and indeed assume primary importance, which meant that a fresh compromise would be necessary between the need for the language to be popular and the need for expert drafting. In Lenin's view of things this did not mean a *total* shift in emphasis, but rather implied that, once stabilized, society should, in legislation now technically of a high standard, continue to use a popular and comprehensible style while abandoning the methods used during the transition, or, to be more exact, while adapting such methods to suit a higher technical level corresponding to the creation of a coherent legal system free from illogicalities.

This requirement began to emerge in the early twenties and became absolute in 1922. By this time Lenin was raising with growing urgency the question of the plethora of legislation enacted by the Soviet government and the lack of stability and unity in the legal system, and hence the need to recapitulate and systematize (27). At the same time he was placing increased emphasis on the need for an appraisal of the experience so far accumulated, for a legal system fully mature down to its lesser details, and for unification of the legal order — or in short on the practical workability of the new legislation (28).

This was also the period when Lenin was formulating his opinion that even in a stabilized socialist society law must at once be worded in a direct and popular style and be flexible enough for adaptation to all local conditions; the idea of unification must, however, be doubly emphasized during the phase of stable development, through more highly centralized law-making and through unified central control of law enforcement from the point of view of legality (29).

It is true that Lenin had already previously given much attention to preparations for the new legislation. In several instances he requested several different bodies to draft given legal provisions, in order to be able to choose "the best programme" or "the most practical programme" (30) from among several alternatives. But the shift in emphasis is plain; by now Lenin was looking at legislation not only from the point of view of political tactics but also from that of correct legal wording. It was at this point that he spoke of the need to convene the Central Executive Committee for "longer sessions than usual for the purpose of discussing the main questions of legislation" (31). He was also, at this stage, to ask the members of the Central Executive Committee to discuss drafts of laws more thoroughly. "It is better", he remarked, "to postpone things till later and leave our local authorities time to examine things attentively; we must be more demanding of our legislators than we are at present" (32). He was even anxious that, during the drafting of the Civil Code, the literature and experience of the West European countries should be studied in order that everything serving for the protection of the working people might be used (33).

Revolutionary law and socialist legislation : a conclusion

We have now examined the formal peculiarities of the revolutionary phase of Soviet law, which forms an essential part of Lenin's achievement, and have in particular noted the general character of the laws enacted, the direct form of linguistic expression adopted and the consequent temporary assigning of less importance to technically expert drafting. We have attempted to show that this general character, which Lenin demanded, was a necessity born of the conditions of the revolutionary struggle and, more particularly, of the specific conditions of the October Revolution. The highly complex conditions of the class struggle at the time, and of the civil war, provided a further reason for the deliberate neglect of technically perfect drafting in the new Soviet law.

In Hungary the features which characterized the October Revolution were at least partially absent when the Republic of Councils was set up, with the result that these various trends were less marked in our country.

The foundations of the new Soviet law as laid in the course of the struggle and the major principles as established could not in themselves be considered as representing the creation of a complete legal system. Lenin himself was fully conscious of the fact and, once the time had come for socialism to be "placed in the compartments provided by articles and paragraphs", was to a large extent personally instrumental in the forging of a coherent unified system with a relative degree of stability, devoid of contradictions or ambiguities and capable of providing for specific cases, where there had formerly been only a mass of general rules, frequently of ephemeral importance and technically of a low standard.

It is thus clear that the institution of a coherent legal system is not an automatic necessity valid whatever the circumstances. The need for it will depend on conditions which are independent of the will of the legislator and presupposes a relative stability in social relations and relatively conclusive experience of previous law-making.

Further, socialist legislation, with its improved structure and more direct and intelligible wording, should in itself be an aid to abolition, so far as this is possible, of undue compartmentalization of legal texts. Despite the fact that the institution of a formal system of law and the drafting of laws by professionals may tend in the direction of maintenance or even aggravation of the habit of dividing into paragraphs and sub-paragraphs, the trend may be to a large extent neutralized by such simplification of structure and more direct and comprehensible wording, which need not prevent substantial satisfaction of the various specific technical requirements.

The need for optimum satisfaction of the two frequently conflicting demands was stressed again by Lenin at a later stage. At the time of the stabilization of the régime and the change-over to the institution of a complete legal system it was he who produced the examples which have had a major and lasting influence on socialist legislation. This influence is to be seen in the preambles to the laws — which are a feature now more or less generally adopted by socialist legislation — and in the almost systematic publication of explanatory statements by the ministries concerned in the official gazettes, as well as in the adoption of constantly improved methods of drafting, and determined efforts on the part of the legislator to state legal norms in a manner which is simple and intelligible. In short, it is reflected in the constant search for improved methods and procedures for achieving a formulation suited to the new socialist type of law.

1. Lenin had foreseen these factors of uncertainty, which he held to be explicable on historical grounds and in fact unavoidable. Shortly after the beginning of the Revolution he made the following statement: "The emergence of a new class on the scene of history as head and leader of society never occurs without a period of violent unrest, tremors, struggles and storms, and also a period of trial and error, experiments, waverings and hesitations in the choice of new processes suited to the needs of an objectively new situation" (Quoted from Vol. 27 of the French language edition of Lenin's *Collected Works*, Moscow, Foreign Languages Publishing House and Paris, Editions Sociales, 1961, p. 271).

2. Lenin, *Collected Works*, French language edition, Vol. 26, 1975, p. 269.

3. Ibid., p. 298.

4. Ibid., p. 300.

5. In March 1918 Lenin declared: "Each factory, each village, is a commune of production and consumption which has the right and duty to enforce in its own way the general legal provisions laid down by the Soviets ('in its own way' not in the sense of violating them but in that of choosing out of the many forms in which they may be put into force), and to solve in its own way the problem of evaluating the volume of goods produced and distributing them fairly" (*Collected Works*, Vol. 27 of the French language edition, p. 270).

6. "Our decrees on peasant farms", Lenin observed in 1919, "... are just as indications of the general path to be followed and as appeals for practical action. When we say: 'Encourage association' what we are giving are instructions which must be tried out again and again before the final form in which to execute them is found". (Lenin, *Selected Works in Three Volumes*, French language edition, Moscow, Progress Publishers, 1968, p. 204).

7. Lenin, *Collected Works*, French language edition, Vol. 26, p. 300.

8. "And if the assistance given to the peasants by the communes of production is merely given in order to comply strictly with the law, such assistance, far from being useful, may even simply cause harm" (*Selected Works*, Vol. 3 of the French language edition, p. 311). "But naturally one can get round any law, even while pretending to enforce it. And the law on assistance to the peasants, if enforced in an insufficiently conscientious manner, can transform itself into a perfectly futile trick and bring about diametrically opposite results" (Ibid., p. 314).

9. Ibid., pp. 313-314 and p. 201, sqq. We should note that in Lenin's proposal to introduce the principle of analogy into the Criminal Code of 1922 the need for the law to retain a general character is still invoked. The story told by Endre Sik in his *Memoirs* may perhaps be no more than an anecdote, but it is certainly not uninstructive. It tells how the President of the Revolutionary Court of Chita in Siberia remarked, of the relative degree of generalization made permissible by the use of analogy, "The bourgeois judge, if he was to present the interests of bourgeois exploitation as objectively valid, had need of voluminous codes and collections of laws. Soviet justice, which serves the interests of the revolutionary proletariat, has a far simpler and easier task. If you look at the Criminal Code, which runs only to 28 pages, the general and the specialized section together comprise 227 articles. Of these 56 compose the general section and the other 171 the specialized section. In reality there are only two of all these which are of importance for us here: Article 6, which defines what is to be considered as a breach of law, and Article 10 which deals with the use of analogy. If something is to be considered as a breach of law in the light of Article 6, it is immaterial that it should also be covered by a separate article in the specialized section... These two articles tell us everything we need to know. The rest was not intended for us. The other articles are intended for the world at large, for those who consider that what matters are the articles, as such, not the essentials". (Endre Sik, *Probaévek* ("Years of Trial and Error"), Budapest, Ztinyi, 1967, p. 752).

10. *Collected Works*, French language edition, Vol. 28, 1961, p. 315. The italics are the author's.

11. "During an age of transition, laws have a temporary value. And if a law obstructs the progress of the revolution it is abolished or amended" (*Collected Works*, French language edition, Vol. 27, p. 551).

12. Such use of law was also prompted and justified by the requirements of revolutionary change. "They laughed at us", Lenin recalled, "they said : 'The Bolsheviks fail to see that their decrees are not being obeyed...' But such a phase was legitimate when the Bolsheviks had just seized power and told the ordinary peasant or worker : 'This is how we would like the State to be governed; here is a decree, try it out.' To the ordinary worker or peasant we presented our political conceptions straight away, in the form of decrees. Result : we gained the enormous degree of confidence on the part of the masses we have so far enjoyed and are continuing to enjoy". (*Selected Works*, French language edition, Vol. 3, p. 716).

13. Ibid., p. 201.

14. "The people must be addressed without using Latin terms, simply and intelligibly" (*Collected Works*, French language edition, Vol. 36, 1959, p. 450.

15. *Collected Works*, French language edition, Vol. 26, p. 453.

16. *Collected Works*, French language edition, Vol. 28, p. 41.

17. Ibid., Vol. 27, p. 372.

18. "For us, a state is strong by virtue of the awareness of the masses. It is strong when the masses know everything, when they can judge everything and go into action consciously. We must not be afraid of telling the truth..." (*Collected Works*, French language edition, Vol. 26, p. 263).

19. Thus he wrote : "In our Constitution there are no fine words" (*Collected Works*, English language edition, Moscow, Progress Publishers, Vol. 30, 1965, p. 242). This same idea is reflected in his letter to Kursky on the Criminal Code, in which he stresses that it would be "deception or self-deception" to camouflage the temporary maintenance of the use of terror and states that the main idea will be "to put forward publicly a thesis that is correct in principle and politically (not only strictly juridical), which explains the *substance* of terror, its necessity and limits..." (Ibid. Vol. 33, 1973, p. 358).

20. *Collected Works*, French language edition, Vol. 27, p. 529.

21. Ibid., Vol. 26, p. 299.

22. *Collected Works*, English language edition, Vol. 33, p. 392.

23. Ibid., Vol. 30, p. 240.

24. Ibid., French language edition, Vol. 28, pp. 145-147.

25. Ibid., Vol. 26, p. 299.

26. As early as 17 November 1917 Lenin had expressed concern at the fact that a decree "by its wording... could lead to regrettable misunderstandings" (Ibid., p. 301). Later he drew attention to the need for the drafts of the decrees to have "a more precise juridical formulation" (Ibid., Vol. 27, p. 372) and for the need for the regulations and laws defining certain punishments to be "formulated with greater exactitude" (Ibid., Vol. 28, p. 41).

27. *Collected Works*, English language edition, Vol. 30, pp. 468-469; Vol. 33, pp. 83 and 224-225, etc.

28. "At one time we needed declarations, statements, manifestos and decrees. We have had enough of them. At one time we needed them to show the people how and what we wanted to build, what new and hitherto unseen things we were striving for. But can we go on showing the people what we want to build ?... Gone is the time when it was necessary to draw political pictures of great tasks; today these tasks must be carried out in practice" (Ibid., Vol. 33, p. 73). "The practical fulfilment of decrees — of which we have more than enough, and which we bake as fast as Mayakovsky describes — is never checked" (Ibid., p. 224). "In my opinion, what matters is to shift the centre of gravity of our work of wording decrees and orders (and in this connection our stupidity verges on idiocy) to *the way the men are chosen* and *the checking of the way they are carried out*. That is the crux of the problem" (Ibid., Vol. 36, p. 578). "The crux of the problem lies not in the institutions, nor in reorganization, nor in new decrees, but in the choice of *the men* and the monitoring of the way decrees are carried out" (Ibid., p. 586).

29. Ibid., English language edition, Vol. 33, pp. 363-367.

30. Ibid., French language edition, Vol. 28, p. 465, and, similarly, English language ed., Vol. 30, p. 307. On criticism of legislation see Vol. 27 (French language ed.), p. 324 sqq.

31. Ibid., English language ed., Vol. 33, p. 253.

32. *Selected Works*, French language ed., Vol. 3, p. 720.

33. *Collected Works*, English language ed., Vol. 33, p. 203.

[25]

THE RUSSIAN JUDICIARY ACT OF 1922 AND SOME COMMENTS ON THE ADMINISTRATION OF JUSTICE IN THE SOVIET UNION

W. J. WAGNER†

During his recent research in the National Archives in Washington, Professor Boleslaw Szczesniak, of the University of Notre Dame, found two interesting texts which appear in their entirety following this article.[1] Attached to Dispatch No. 632 from the American Representative in Riga (1923) were: a summary in English of a report of the Acting Commissar of Justice of the Russian Republic, Krylenko,[2] on a bill concerning the organization of courts in the Republic, and the English translation of the final version of the act, as adopted on October 31, 1922.[3] The act has never been published in English until now. This Judiciary Act set the foundation for the organization of courts in the Russian Republic, which —with some changes—is still valid today. The Russian pattern, of course, influenced, or was copied by, the other Soviet Republics.

That the abuses, arbitrariness, and corruption of the Tsarist administration incurred the wrath of the liberal as well as of the left wing of Russian public opinion needs no elaboration. However, the administration of justice in pre-revolutionary Russia, particularly after the reform of 1864, was quite liberal and satisfactory.[4] The participation of assessors and justices of the peace who were elected added a democratic flavor to the system.

After a revolution, coup d' état or some other upheaval in the governmental system, the victorious new regime may select one of two ways to implement its political theories: either by a gradual replacement of the old law and institutions by new enactments and reorganization procedures, or by abolishing all that existed until then, creating a vacuum, and beginning to build a new order from scratch. Post-World-War II

---

† Professor of Law, Indiana University.

1. The texts were transcribed by Mr. Stefan Maczynski, at that time Prof. Szczesniak's assistant, and at present, Professor of Political Science at St. John Fisher College.

2. Krylenko became the Union's Commissar of Justice after this post was established in 1936, and then was purged and executed as a traitor.

3. The act was adopted in 1922; however, some authors state that the date is 1923. See, *e.g.*, GSOVSKI, I SOVIET CIVIL LAW, 233 n.1 (1948). It seems that the confusion is due to the fact that in the official publication of the act, RUSSIAN SOCIALIST FEDERATED SOVIET REPUBLIC LAWS at p. 902 (1923), the year has been erroneously given as 1923.

4. For details, see GSOVSKI & GRZYBOWSKI, I GOVERNMENT, LAW AND COURTS IN THE SOVIET UNION AND EASTERN EUROPE 511-13 (1959).

Poland may serve as an example of the first approach.[5] An example of the second approach would be Communist China which declared the old legal order as extinct *in toto,* with the result that for a period of time the country did not live under any legal rules.[6] In the field of the administration of justice, one possibility is to retain the old courts (with a gradual introduction of changes) and staff them as quickly as possible with new members, and the other—to abolish the old judicial system altogether. The triumphant bolsheviks, desirous of severing all connections with the "bourgeois" past, decided to take the latter step. The first case in a new court was heard on December 16, 1917.[7]

The vacuum created by the abolishment of the old machinery for the administration of justice was not filled overnight.[8] The new regime had more urgent problems to take care of. The very question of its survival was at stake for quite a long time. Resistance on the part of "White" Russians and the moderates, internal struggles in the ranks of the communists, sporadic threats from some other groups such as the anarchists, independence claims of large minorities such as the Ukrainians, the war with Poland, which—initially successful—soon turned into a disaster, all those tribulations and uncertainties made the continued existence of the first communist state in the world subject to much doubt. *Silent leges inter arma.* In the general state of lawlessness, justice (or injustice) was administered by the strong, usually by the red army and the revolutionary police. Even after the first decrees on the establishment of the new courts were enacted, nobody hurried to have those de-

5. The pre-war Polish legal system was not abolished in a sweeping manner by the new communist government. Some laws and decrees abrogated old provisions which could seem at variance with the new political reality in the country. The government enacted some general principles and rules which lent themselves to various interpretations. Former Polish judicial decisions were declared by a plenary session of the Supreme Court, in 1948, as good law if not "repugnant to the present system of government and the statutes which are in force." Wagner, *The Interplay of Planned Economy and Traditional Contract Rules in Poland,* 11 AM. J. COMP. L. 348, 364 (1962).

6. McAleary, *The People's Courts in Communist China,* 11 AM. J. COMP. L. 52 (1962). A somehow intermediate approach was taken by Yugoslavia. "All the Yugoslav laws enacted before the second world war were declared null and void by a law enacted in 1945. This law also prescribed that provisions of the former laws could be applied as 'legal rules' provided that they were not contrary to the new social system and that there were no new prescriptions regulating the matter in question." KAPOR, INTRODUCTION TO THE GENERAL USAGES OF TRADE 4 (1964). (Published in the English translation by the Institute of Comparative Law in Belgrade.)

7. HAZARD, SETTLING DISPUTES IN SOVIET SOCIETY 1 (1960).

8. This state of affairs resulted in a deplorable atmosphere of lawlessness, in which the breaching of an obligation or the commission of an offense was indulged in by some persons taking advantage of their impunity. Even after the new tribunals were established, they lacked prestige and had a hard time in convincing the parties that their decisions should be respected. HAZARD, VIII LE DROIT SOVIETIQUE ET LE DÉPERISSEMENT DE L' ETAT 32 (1960). (In Univ. Libre de Bruxelles, Facultē de Droit, Travaux et Conferences.)

crees implemented. Besides, the decrees were sketchy and fragmentary. For example, initially there were no provisions for any appellate and supreme court jurisdiction.

For the English-speaking reader, there are some excellent publications describing the development of the judicial organization in the Soviet Union,[9] and it seems unnecessary to repeat here the information, comments and analysis given by some outstanding scholars in the field of Soviet law. All that should be done in presenting the Judiciary Act of 1922 is to place it in its proper setting.

The first observation which comes to the mind of a student of the Soviet system in its historical development is the necessity of approaching the problem of the administration of justice by the courts in conjunction with the power of non-judicial bodies to impose penalties, the omnipotence of the communist party, and the discrepancy between the printed word and actual practice. The political reality in the Soviet Union is stronger than any theoretical considerations or nicely formulated rules on human rights, due process, rule of law, fair procedure, etc. All those terms may be used in the Western as well as in the Soviet legal systems, but their meaning and application may be completely different. It would be grossly misleading to rely only on the text of the statutes dealing with the administration of justice and draw far-reaching conclusions as to the situation in the Soviet Union. For example, the very concept of "democracy" and "democratic elections" conveys quite different connotations in the West and East. Therefore, the reading of some official Soviet publications[10] without proper preparation and ability to take a comparative approach does not enable one to draw useful conclusions. And a disservice is rendered by Western commentators who despite frequent warnings by realistically minded comparatists[11] seemingly do not realize that statute books cannot be analyzed *in abstracto,* in detachment from the society in which they are being applied.[12]

To some extent, this discrepancy exists in every legal system. It would be an error, for instance, in studying the organization of American courts, to assume that all disputes are settled by the system of regular courts, ignoring administrative quasi-judicial procedures, frequent resort to arbitration in some types of controversies, and factors which prompt

9. And particularly, BERMAN, JUSTICE IN THE U.S.S.R. (1963). GSOVSKI & GRZYBOWSKI, *op. cit. supra* note 4, at 511-87; GSOVSKI, *op. cit. supra* note 3, at 233-56, 836-46; HAZARD, *op. cit. supra* note 7.

10. Such as ROMASHKIN, FUNDAMENTALS OF SOVIET LAW (1962); or DENISOV & KIRICHENKO, SOVIET STATE LAW (1960).

11. See, *e.g.*, SCHLESINGER, COMPARATIVE LAW 491-97 (2d ed. 1959).

12. Such is apparently the case of DEKKERS, PRINCIPES NOUVEAUX DE DROIT SOVIETIQUE 11-16 (1962).

extra-judicial settlement, particularly in personal injury cases. In Soviet Russia extra-judicial considerations were, and to a large extent continue to be, determinative of the outcome of problems generated by human behavior on a scale hardly known in any other system.

On its face the Judiciary Act of 1922 and other Soviet enactments in this field may seem to have many democratic features in the Western meaning of the word, apt to mislead superficial observers. Thus (irrespective of whether popular participation in the government is advisable only in the legislative and executive branch or also in the judicial), it could appear that the democratization of the administration of justice was certainly brought about by such institutions as lay assessors in the courts, elected judges, and their responsibility with the possibility of their recall.

Upon a closer investigation, the advantages of such a "democratic" character of Soviet justice fade away for three reasons: first, resort to methods of administering justice outside of the regular system of courts; second, the way the courts were staffed and the way they functioned; and third, the role attributed to the law and the legal profession in the communist ideology.

Soon after the outbreak of the October Revolution, special Revolutionary Tribunals were established[13] to crush the counter-revolutionaries, help the new regime to rid itself of the opposition and enable it to become more deeply entrenched. Indeed, they were unusually harsh whenever the defendants appeared to be enemies of the new order. Summary judgments and executions became routine.

Those special tribunals (abolished and replaced by military courts in 1922), with all their excesses and abuses, still had some features of judicial bodies and (at least in theory) were subjected to some rules of procedure. The contrary was true as to some other devices set up by the regime with the view of eliminating the "enemies of the people" from public life by the usual method of taking away their life or at least deporting them to faraway places, concentration or hard labor camps, where they had hardly any chance to survive due to overwork, starvation, lack of elementary medical care, and most primitive living conditions coupled with harsh treatment on the part of the guards and rough climate.

The most effective method to achieve this goal was an extraordinary committee known as the "Chrexvychaika" or Cheka which was granted unlimited powers to investigate any possible threat to the new regime or conspiracy against the government and to take any action however radical

13. Decree of Nov. 24, 1917, providing for the People's Tribunals as well as Revolutionary Tribunals.

that was deemed proper to eradicate the danger. Soon the Cheka became the master of life and death of millions of citizens. It was not subject to any control by the commissar (later: minister) of justice or courts. It was independent from any interference on the part of other organs of government and there were no appeals from its decisions. The lash of the Cheka reached into the ranks of the communist party itself, and its abuses became so flagrant that it was abolished after about four years of wild activity.

However, the situation hardly improved as the job done by the Cheka was continued by its successors. The next was the feared G.P.U. and, after the establishment of the Union in 1923, the O.G.P.U. The story repeated itself. Very soon this administrative organ became the most powerful, lawless, and hated organ in the country. The same may be said about the N.K.V.D., and later, the M.V.D., which took over the problem of "state security" after the abolition of the G.P.U.[14]

The notion of the "enemy of the people" became a catch-all term applicable to any one whose existence displeased the government or, sometimes, some influential governmental official. The best denunciation of the sad state of affairs occasioned by those abuses was made by Khrushchev himself who accused Stalin of inventing this concept, adding: "This term made possible the usage of the most cruel repression . . . against anyone who in any way disagreed with Stalin, against those who were only suspected of hostile intent, against those who had bad reputations."[15]

In order that proper authorities might learn about the "enemies of the people" and all instances of disloyalty or even criticism of the government, the institution of the informer became deeply entrenched in the Soviet system. Citizens were encouraged and even required in the name of higher interests of the state and the party to spy on others and report what they learned to the officials. This duty was imposed on everyone. Pupils were to inform on their teachers, wives on their husbands, and children on their parents. Those who complied were recognized as model citizens of the Soviet Union, sometimes as real heroes. But they incurred the wrath of the community in which they lived resulting in some instances in physical reaction and violence which in turn brought about bloody repressions. In a somewhat different context, the obligation of the citizens to contribute to the preservation of the existing order has been expressed in the statute on the Increase of the Role of the Society

14. It was followed by the M.G.B. and the K.G.B. See, Gsovski & Grzybowski, *op. cit. supra* note 4, at 564.

15. Gsovski & Grzybowski, *op. cit. supra* note 4, at 881.

in the Protection of the Social Order.[16]

The whole atmosphere in the Soviet Union, at least during the long Stalinist period, was one of terror.[17] Not only was this fact clear to everyone, but it was even recognized by the government. One of the decrees, of September 5, 1918, was officially termed: "On the Red Terror."[18]

In the light of the extra-judicial methods of dealing with a person suspected of an unfriendly attitude towards the Soviet reality (and in general, "suspicion was tantamount to guilt"),[19] it would seem that a defendant accused of a political crime would be happy to be brought before a regular court. In fact, he had little reason to rejoice. The odds against him were still tremendous, and in the great majority of cases his fate was sealed in advance of the trial. This was due to the second factor to be considered in examining the administration of justice in the Soviet Union: the method of staffing the courts, the way they were functioning, and the procedures which were applied in order to bring about a desired result of the case.

The quality, integrity and independence of the judges determines, according to the traditional approach, the level of the administration of justice in a given society. It has been rightfully observed that good judges may efficiently function in a poorly organized judicial system "just as a good mechanic can sometimes do excellent work with a poor machine."[20]

In the Soviet Union, particularly in the early years, qualities of competence, integrity, and independence in judges were discouraged by the method of their selection. Being well versed in the law was not required. Political reliability was the test for eligibility. By virtue of art. 11 of the Judiciary Act of 1922, in order to become a People's Judge, one had to have the right "to vote, and to be elected to Soviets," and a two year record of "responsible political work" or three years experience working in "organs of Soviet justice" at a stated level. Thus, uncertain elements were eliminated.

Whether the judges were elected by the Soviets[21] or the general elec-

16. Art. 1 of the statute states that "each Soviet citizen shall not only follow the rules of law, but shall act as a law enforcement officer and demand that others conform to the rules of socialist legal order." See GRZYBOWSKI, SOVIET LEGAL INSTITUTIONS 260-61 (1962).

17. For elaboration of this statement, see *e.g.*, HAZARD, THE SOVIET SYSTEM OF GOVERNMENT 66-80 (4th ed., 1964).

18. GSOVSKI & GRZYBOWSKI, *op. cit. supra* note 4, at 565-66.

19. *Id.* at 880.

20. Hallows & De Witt, *The Need for Court Organization*, 1954 WIS. L. REV. 376.

21. This was the general pattern until 1949. The communist party assured for itself the selection of the members of the Soviets, who in turn elected the judges.

torate, or appointed, the decisive factor was always the wish of the communist party,[22] and the position of a judge was usually held by party members. It has been reported that by 1935 the percentage of communists in the judiciary reached 95.5 in the lower courts and 99.6 in the higher courts, while in 1947 only 14.6% of judges and other high officials connected with the administration of justice had legal education at the university level, and 21.8% had received some legal training at the secondary level.[23]

The traditional requirement that the judges should be independent in the performance of their functions was ridiculed for a long time and particularly by Vyshinsky who stated that such an approach "acquires, under the conditions of proletarian dictatorship, a counter-revolutionary character."[24] After the enactment of the Constitution of 1936, its art. 112 which provided that "Judges shall be independent and subject only to the law" was understood by Vyshinsky as referring to independence from personal and local influences only.[25] Some other commentators, like Karev,[26] agree that there is no question of independence of judges from the policy of the party and the government. A typical statement was laid down by Vyshinsky:

> A court of whatever sort is an organ of the authority of the class dominant in a given state, defending and guarding its interests. . . . Bourgeois theorists strive to depict the court as an organ above classes and apart from politics, acting, supposedly, in the interests of all society and guided by commands of law and justice common to all mankind, instead of by the interests of the dominant class. Such a conception of the court's essence and tasks is, of course, radically false. It has always been an instrument in the hands of the dominant class, assuring the strengthening of its dominance and the protection of its interests.[27]

However, other communist commentators claim that Soviet judges are independent in the true sense of the word. Curiously enough, after undermining the very possibility of an independent judiciary, Vyshinsky stated that "Soviet judges are independent, . . . being subordinated only to the law, which sets forth the will of the entire people, is independent

22. The 1936 constitutional provision that lower judges would be elected directly by the voters was not implemented until 1949.
23. Citing Soviet sources, GSOVSKI & GRZYBOWSKI, *op. cit. supra* note 4, at 517.
24. *Id.* at 520.
25. *Ibid.*
26. GSOVSKI & GRZYBOWSKI, *op. cit. supra* note 4, at 521.
27. VYSHINSKY, THE LAW OF THE SOVIET STATE 500 (1948).

of all influence and inducements whatsoever in deciding specific court matters."[28]

Even if a Soviet judge should have decided to be truly independent, he would not be permitted to exercise his independence for long. If he dared to displease the government, several ways were available to eliminate him. First, there was always the possibility of resorting to repressive measures imposed by the security agencies of the state. Second, the judge could be recalled in the same manner in which he had been appointed or elected (see, for example, articles 13, 42, 57, of the Judiciary Act of 1922), with approval, in proper cases, of the commissar of justice. Third, far from the idea of irremovability of judges denounced by Lenin himself,[29] the term of office of Soviet judges is unusually short, and after its expiration the incumbent bears the risk of losing his job. By virtue of the Judiciary Act of 1922, the judges of the People's Courts and of the Provincial Courts were to be elected for only one year. In 1938, the term was raised to three years for lower judges, and to five for higher judges, and in 1958 the uniform term for all judges was set at five years.[30] Besides the possibility of recall, there were provisions about dismissal from office for cause (by a court's decision or as an outcome of disciplinary proceedings; articles 13, 42, 69, 84 of the Judiciary Act of 1922).

Again, there is no division of powers in the Soviet Union in the traditional sense, and the functioning of the courts and the decision-making is supervised by other branches of the government. Thus, for example art. 112 of the Constitution of 1936 provided that the Supreme Court of the Union "is accountable to the Supreme Soviet . . . and, in the intervals between its sessions, to the Presidium of the Supreme Soviet. . . ."[31] Indeed, the courts' power is delegated to them by the Supreme Soviet (and the lower soviets) to which they are responsible. Should it be deemed proper, the Supreme Soviet has the final authority to reverse a judicial decision.[32] And a control of the activities of the courts is exercised by the ministries of justice.[33]

The institution of lay assessors (or "People's Jurors") could bring about an element of popular participation in the Soviet administration of

28. *Id.*, at 514. The principle of the independence of the judges and assessors is also expressed in art. 9 of the GENERAL PRINCIPLES OF THE ORGANIZATION OF COURTS of 1958 and in art. 7 of the RUSSIAN JUDICIARY ACT OF 1960, invoking art. 116 of the CONSTITUTION OF THE RUSSIAN REPUBLIC.

29. VYSHINSKY, *op. cit. supra* note 27, at 512.

30. GENERAL PRINCIPLES OF THE ORGANIZATION OF COURTS, arts. 19, 20, 22, 24, 26.

31. The same provision is repeated in art. 2 of the STATUTE OF THE SUPREME COURT OF THE U.S.S.R., adopted by the Supreme Soviet of the U.S.S.R. on February 12, 1957. For English text, see DENISOV & KIRICHENKO, *op. cit. supra* note 10, at 438.

32. HAZARD, *op. cit. supra* note 17, at 171.

33. For details, see *e.g.*, KULSKI, THE SOVIET REGIME 291 (1956).

justice.[34] The assessors are not comparable to jurors in the common law world. They exercise the regular functions of a judge, deciding with the professional member of the courts questions of law and fact.[35] However, because of the general atmosphere prevailing in the Soviet courts, the assessors hardly ever dared to contradict their professional colleagues. It seems that only one case was reported in which they outvoted a judge.[36] Besides, the selection of the assessors is such that it assures that they be politically reliable. As Krylenko pointed out in his report (see below), his system rejected "the principle of democratic elections from below, which in political life always leads to a casual comer being elected," and was founded on the principle "of singling out the staunchest representatives of the proletariat."[37] And art. 21 of the Judiciary Act of 1922 required consideration in their selection, "the level of their political development."

The seemingly "democratic" character of the Soviet courts was further undermined by many different devices which deprived the accused of the chance to defend himself effectively. It would require a long discussion to describe in full all the institutional and procedural rules which made it often impossible for the defendant to exonerate himself from the guilt attributed to him by the prosecutor with the judge often appearing to act as a second prosecutor.[38] Although some Soviet theorists asserted that the centuries old presumption of innocence existed in their legal system actual practice denied it repeatedly.[39] One of the critics of the Stalinist era of lawlessness was Khrushchev who confirmed in his denunciation of the older regime many facts branded by foreign observers long ago as the very negation of justice: forced confessions obtained by refined tortures, fabricated testimony, instructions given by the government to the prosecutor to bring about the conviction of given persons by any possible means.

The requirements of a fair trial and the rule *"nulla poena sine lege"* meant little. Frequently, defendants were tried secretly, *in absentia,* or without the benefit of a defense counsel. In some cases, during the period from 1934 to 1956, trials in the absence of the accused were mandatory.

34. There were no assessors in Revolutionary Courts, but there are assessors in other courts, including the Supreme Court of the Union.

35. The same is true in other European countries.

36. HAZARD, *op. cit. supra* note 17, at 177.

37. It will be noticed that Krylenko suggested that 50 per cent of the assessors be drawn from among the labor classes, and 25 per cent from among the Red Army and the peasants. In the final statute, the participation of the peasants was increased to 35 per cent at the expense of the military units.

38. HAZARD, *op. cit. supra* note 17, at 181.

39. *Id.* at 180; GSOVSKI & GRZYBOWSKI, *op. cit. supra* note 4, at 904.

Death sentences could not be appealed and were immediately executory.[40] And penalties could be imposed even before the law which provided for them became effective, or by the application of "crime by analogy." The famous art. 16 of the Russian Criminal Code of 1926 (no longer in force) read as follows: "Where a socially dangerous act has not been expressly dealt with in the present code, the basis and limits of responsibility in respect thereof shall be determined in conformity with those articles of the code which deal with the crimes most closely resembling it."

An interesting instance of sentencing a defendant to death without the background of statutory authority in force at the time of the commission of the crime was recently analyzed by Professor Berman who spent the academic year 1961-1962 in Moscow. A decree of July 1, 1961, provided for the possibility of imposing the penalty of death for "black market" transactions in foreign currency. Applying the law retroactively, the Supreme Court of the Russian Republic sentenced two speculators to death. The rationalization of this result, given by some Soviet lawyers, was that "it was an exceptional case and that the public—which means, of course, the Party—had demanded it,"[41] and that the Presidium of the Supreme Soviet, by an edict which was never published, authorized the Court to apply the law retroactively.

Soon after, the author and another American law professor had the opportunity to meet a distinguished legal scholar from the Soviet Union. During the conversation, the Russian jurist undertook to defend the outcome of the above speculators' case. To the remark that the imposition of a penalty which is not provided for in a law officially announced to the general public before the time the crime is committed violates the principles of legality, he answered that such a stand was too formalistic and technical.

Certainly the approach to legal rules may be either flexible or not, with a range of intermediate possible positions. It is also true that the common law tends to protect rigidly the rights of the accused, and recent developments in the United States have tended to make conviction extremely difficult if not impossible in many cases. Added to the old evidentiary obstacles which prevent finding a defendant guilty who undoubtedly committed the crime, such as the hearsay rule or the inadmissibility of unlawfully obtained evidence, are new ones. The Supreme Court has excluded the use of a voluntary confession and required that at every stage of the proceedings the defendant should have the advantage

40. Gsovski & Grzybowski, *op. cit. supra* note 4, at 883.

41. Berman, *The Role of Soviet Jurists in the Struggle to Prevent a Return to Stalinist Terror,* 14 Harv. L. S. Bull., No. 3, at 3, 4 (Dec. 1962).

of counsel even if his crime is not a felony. Those rules, coupled with the impossibility of the prosecution to appeal based on an excessively broad interpretation of the protection against double jeopardy, make the United States a country in which it is difficult to fight the criminal. In their technical abidance by the defendant's constitutional rights in their broadest possible construction, the courts neglect the rights of the general public to protection against crime. The situation has deteriorated so much that in an address delivered in January, 1965, the President of the American Bar Association Lewis F. Powell asserted that there are good reasons for criminals to think that crime does pay, that "slow and fumbling justice can be evaded," and that "there is growing belief that recent Supreme Court decisions have tipped the scales of justice too far in favor of a criminal and subordinated the rights of law-abiding citizens."[42]

This is one dangerous extreme for which the United States Supreme Court is hardly to be felicitated. Another one is the Soviet approach applied in the speculators' case. The crime that they committed was not a *malum per se,* and their conduct would not be objectionable in many legal systems. Yet, without a law providing for a capital punishment at the time of the offense they were sentenced to death. To some representatives of the communist world the shock of a traditionalist may seem puzzling. What is the life of one person worth compared to the overall goals of "progressive" social movements? Any objections may be branded as obsolete sentimentalism or unreasonable formalism and technicality. After all, in this case the defendants *were* clearly guilty. And the interests of the society may require that even those who are not guilty be subjected to punishment—either for the purpose of terror, or as victims of collective responsibility, or else as a method of deterring some conduct and serving as an example—such as provided for by a statute imposing a penalty of exile on the members of a family of an escapee from the armed forces to a foreign country even if they were unaware of his intention to run away.[43]

Many of the differences between the administration of justice in the traditional and communist systems are due to fundamentally opposite

42. U.P.I. release, January 29, 1965. Recently, Judge Desmond, Chief Judge of the New York Court of Appeals, stated that the effect of the new Supreme Court decisions is to deprive "the public, not just the prosecutors and the police, of reliable, convincing, real evidence." Referring to the case of Mapp v. Ohio, the Judge asserted that its rule does not protect the average citizen "who never needs it," and continued: "What the rule does is to insure and safeguard the professional criminal . . ." New York Times of April 30, 1966.

43. HAZARD, LAW AND SOCIAL CHANGE IN THE U.S.S.R. 108 (1953).

views as to the very concept of the law and the role it should fulfill in the society.

According to Marxist-Leninist ideas, economic relations are the basis of every society, and all the rest, including the law, are only a superstructure, conditioned on the basis. All organs of a communist state, whether falling into the category of essentially executive, legislative or judicial, have one predominant duty: to advance the interests of the state in accordance with communist ideas. A striking example is a provision of the General Principles of the Organization of Courts of 1958 which, repeating previous enactments to the same effect, requires the courts to "educate the citizens of the U.S.S.R. in the spirit of devotion to the country and the cause of communism." This is hardly an education in the traditional meaning of the word. And yet, taking some Soviet texts and institutions on their face value, reinforced by comments received from some communist jurists, some Western commentators seem to view their legal system in the light of traditional ideas, seemingly misled by words and appearances. Thus, a Belgian writer, after a superficial venture into the problem and a short visit to the communist countries committed in his comments the gravest mistake of a comparatist by taking the printed word for granted without investigating the conditions in which it is to be given effect.[44]

According to the communist doctrines, there is no such thing as objective justice. One of the recent treatises on "The Soviet Legal System"[45] opens with the quotation of a statement by Lenin: "A law is a political measure, it is politics." And as in a communist system the policy is formulated by the party, it is inconceivable that a court might thwart whatever decisions could be taken by the party. As the division of powers is not a necessary attribute of the communist organization of the society, the courts might as well not be established at all. It was decided to set them up for some important reasons,[46] but avowedly they were to maintain their political character. Said Krylenko: "Our judge is above all a politician, a worker in the political field . . . and therefore he must

44. DEKKERS, *op. cit. supra* note 12. The author's fallacies have been pointed out by HALL, COMPARATIVE LAW AND SOCIAL THEORY 102 (1963). Mr. Dekkers admits in the foreword to his booklet, that he "would never dare to publish those pages" without the benefit of his conversations with jurists from Moscow, Leningrad, Tbilisi, Warsaw, Prague and Bratislava, whose "expertise is equal to their devotion." It would be advisable to juxtapose Mr. Dekkers' work with studies going deeper into the problems, such as *e.g.*, HAZARD, *op. cit. supra* note 17, and in particular, with chapters: 4 on Controlled Mass Participation; 5 on Terror and its Rationalization; 9 on State Intervention in Private Affairs; and 13 on The Peril-Points.

45. By HAZARD & SHAPIRO (1962).

46. Those reasons are discussed in HAZARD, *op. cit. supra* note 17, at 169-71.

know what the government wants and guide his work accordingly. . . ."[47]

Thus, the law is the dictate of the ruling class—it is an instrument of class struggle, and it should be administered accordingly. Other standards were applied by the courts to an accused from the workers' and peasants' class, and others to someone from former upper classes.[48] The social origin of the defendant, his past and economic situation could well be the determinative factor in sentencing him.[49] To what Vyshinsky had to say in connection with the independence of the judges, may be added his statement that "the courts represent various forms of the class struggle of the proletarian dictatorship,"[50] and Krylenko's remark that "the court is, in the first place, an agency for the protection of the interests of the ruling class and of a given social order."[51]

After what was said about the role of the courts and the judges in the Soviet system, it is hardly necessary to add that the prosecutor is a very powerful and feared person. That he has the right to appeal is not a unique feature of the Soviet system[52] (incidentally, he can appeal both when he would like the penalty imposed by the court to be more severe or less severe); but as Krylenko pointed out in his report (see below), the prosecutor general was granted the power to "suspend" the decisions of the Supreme Court and submit them for final determination to the Presidium of the Central Executive Committee.[53]

Even since recent reforms, the role of the procurator in the U.S.S.R. is strikingly more significant than in the traditional legeal systems;[54] thus art. 14 of the General Principles of the Organization of Courts of 1958 provides that he "exercises control over the legality and the validity of judicial decisions, criminal or civil . . .,"[55] which in other systems would amount to usurping the function of the judiciary. And the procurator general exercises "supreme supervisory power to ensure the strict

47. Gsovski & Grzybowski, *op. cit. supra* note 4, at 516.

48. Hazard, *op. cit. supra* note 17, at 66.

49. Gsovski & Grzybowski, *op. cit. supra* note 4, at 880; Hazard, *op. cit. supra* note 43, at 98.

50. Gsovski & Grzybowski, *op. cit. supra* note 4, at 520.

51. *Id.* at 516.

52. However, in the Soviet system his right to appeal is broader than that of private individuals who are permitted to appeal only once, to the immediately higher court, while the right of the prosecutor is not so limited.

53. The powers of the procurator were settled in the statute of May 22, 1922, five months before the adoption of the Judiciary Act.

54. An unorthodox observation is that the important role of the prosecutor is obvious, for a keen person, from the very arrangement of his seat in the court room, which indicates that this position is not inferior to that of the judges. Hazard, *Furniture Arrangement as a Symbol of Judicial Roles,* 19 Etc., No. 2, p. 181 (July, 1962).

55. A similar provision is found in art. 22 of the Ordinance on the Supervisory Powers of the Procurator's Office in the U.S.S.R., May 24, 1955.

observance of the law by all ministries and institutions subordinated to them, as well as by officials and citizens. . . ."[56]

As to attorneys-at-law, their position can hardly be compared to that in traditional legal systems. After an early attempt to eliminate the legal profession altogether, it was decided to retain it on reorganized foundations. Collegia or teams of lawyers were established in which they have to practice collectively. The role of the attorney is relevant to the problem of the organization of courts inasmuch as they are also considered as an element in the administration of justice. In exercising his duties in the Soviet Union, a defense attorney in a criminal case had to proceed with great caution. Traditionally, as Vyshinsky stated, their functions were merely "tolerated," and anyhow, they were required to have high political qualifications and to keep in mind primarily "the interests of the building up of socialism" rather than those of their clients.[57] Therefore, having a defense attorney was sometimes of questionable value for a defendant, the more so that a significant exception to the lawyer's duty to keep in confidence information that he received from his client was his obligation to decline the defense, and to report to proper authorities, in case he learned about the preparation or commitment of a counter-revolutionary crime.[58] After the reforms of 1958-1960, the position of defense attorneys became stronger. They are no longer treated by the courts and the prosecutors, "with contempt and disfavor,"[59] but all that they can do for the defendant is to "point out the unfortunate set of unfavorable circumstances which, by a haphazard interplay, pushed the culprit towards the commission of the crime."[60] The position of the Soviet attorney "will undoubtedly never equal that of a lawyer in Western Europe or of a lawyer in pre-revolutionary Russia."[61]

The foregoing observations should necessarily be kept in mind in order to understand the conditions and atmosphere in which the judicial system, laid down by the Judiciary Act of 1922, was to function for many years.[62] A few other remarks are in order. First, most of what was said

---

56. *Id.* at art. 1, modeled after art. 113 of the Constitution. For a detailed analysis of the prosecutor's role, see MORGAN, SOVIET ADMINISTRATIVE LEGALITY (1962).

57. GSOVSKI & GRZYBOWSKI, *op. cit. supra* note 4, at 561.

58. Strogovich, cited by KULSKI, THE SOVIET REGIME 301 (1956). Besides, "[t]he procedure of admission and threat of expulsion from the Bar association give a guarantee to the Government that Soviet attorney will function in utter loyalty to the Party." *Ibid.*

59. Fridieff, *L'Organisation Judiciaire Sovietique,* 14 REV. INT. DR. COMP. 725, 141 (1962).

60. *Ibid.*

61. *Ibid.*

62. The immediate background and analysis of the act has been given in detail by HAZARD, SETTLING DISPUTES IN SOVIET SOCIETY 176 (1960).

refers, quite naturally, to cases with a political or class flavor. In disputes between private individuals of the same social origin and standing, in which the party was absolutely not interested, there would be hardly any reason to resort to any kind of pressures or unorthodox settlement of the difficulty. Second, the act was enacted in the Russian Republic before the Soviet Union as a kind of a federation was called into being. The establishment of the Union and the drafting of its Constitution dates back to 1923; and its final ratification took place on January 31, 1924. A federal Judiciary Act was enacted in the same year. The Judiciary Act of 1922 established the bases of the Soviet court structure for a long period to follow. The next important federal statute on the court organization was enacted on August 16, 1938, after the 1936 Constitution went into effect. The present Russian Judiciary Act was enacted on October 27, 1960, after the federal General Principles of the Organization of Courts were adopted in 1958.

The judicial and extra-judicial ways of imposing penalties, as mentioned above, including the regular and long application of terror, seem to be so revolting that the natural question arises: how is it possible that such a situation could be tolerated for such a long period of time? There is no single reason for it. One reason among many others is the innane passiveness of the Russian people whose history accustomed them to suffer under a yoke, be it that of a totalitarian Czarist regime or of a Stalinist oppression.[63] Another is the method by which the communist minority imposed and maintained its grasp on the country, where the slightest opposition resulted in deportation, tortures, or death. Even so, individual or mass resistance was often heavy, and resulted in a variety of desperate acts including assassinations of some hated state officials or party agitators and refusal to carry out the laws or regulations. Naturally, savage reprisals followed, whole villages were exiled into Siberia and in order to crush the anti-governmental opposition in the Ukraine, literally millions of people were permitted to starve to death in the thirties. A reflection of the desire to live without terror was manifested in a spectacular way during the first weeks of the Soviet-German War in 1941, when large formations of the Red Army were surrendering to the Germans often without fighting, the inhabitants of the towns and vil-

63. A typical example of this attitude was demonstrated by an inmate at the Lubianka prison, who was confined because of a mere suspicion, without any evidence of his counter-revolutionary activities or feelings. After being submitted to tortures and initial despondency and bitterness, he found the measures against him as reasonable and justified them on the ground that the authorities can take no risk: maybe, it is better to punish many innocent people than to let one dangerous person pursue his activities.

lages were greeting the invaders with flowers, and the original advances of the German army were spectacular. It is an easy guess to assert that if the Nazis had been better politicians, and had known how to promote friendly feelings towards themselves, the Soviet Union would have collapsed. But for the victorious German forces, moderation and psychological strategy seemed unnecessary. Hatred was the *spiritus movens* of their actions, and a show of force seemed the most persuasive weapon in all circumstances. This resulted in a haphazard display of atrocities on the conquered territories and inhuman treatment of prisoners of war, including starvation and gas chambers. The news spread quickly and cemented resistance which contributed to the final collapse of the Reich. It may be recalled, again, that Soviet citizens who were found by the Allies on the German territories, either as prisoners of war or forced laborers, were reluctant to return to their country; as a matter of fact, thousands of them refused to go. But the Allies forced them to go back. Suicides among the repatriated were not uncommon.

And yet, one of the keen observers of the Soviet system, Professor Hazard, states that the Soviet people appear "in the main to have accepted terror during Stalin's time as a necessary evil."[64] That it was an evil can hardly be controverted. But it does not seem that the author was able to prove that it was necessary. The introductory statement to Professor Berman's comments on his stay in Russia appears to be more realistic: "In the Soviet Union today people in all walks of life welcome their Government's condemnation of the terror of the Stalin era."[65]

The Russian Judiciary Act of 1922 was in force during the Stalin era, which began not long after the death of Lenin in January of 1924. After a short struggle for power following Stalin's death, Khrushchev emerged as the strongman and founder of a new era, which unexpectedly ended with his deposition in 1964. His criticism of Stalinist atrocities brought about some theoretical as well as practical changes in the Soviet system of government, in the direction of eliminating the most objectionable practices amounting to the travesty of justice. It remains to be seen whether Kosygin and Breshnev will establish an era of their own, and what developments await the administration of justice in the Soviet Union under their leadership.

Two features of the recent reforms should be mentioned. First, article 5 of the Federal General Principles of 1958 and of the Russian Act of 1960 proclaim the principle of equality of the citizens before the law and before the courts. A commentator observed that this provision

64. HAZARD, *op. cit. supra* note 62, at 71.
65. Berman, *supra* note 41, at 2.

can possibly be understood by some students of the Soviet system as evidence that the old class of "profiteers" disappeared from the Soviet economy.[66] Irrespective of factual considerations, the above provision marks an important theoretical change in the approach of the Soviet legislators to the administration of justice. The old dogma of class justice seems not to obtain any longer.

However, the seeds which were being sown for a long time continue to grow in various places. A good example is a recent study by a foremost Czech jurist who emphasizes the significance of the use of cybernetics in the realm of human behavior, and associates his attempt to make use of quantitative methods in the field of law with the provision of art. 18, sec. 2, of the Czechoslovak Constitution which provides for the application, "in the Society of toilers," of the "results of science relating to the direction of society and the planning of its future development."[67]

The author discusses the possibility of using cybernetic machines for the purpose of arriving at judicial decisions. He distinguishes between simple and complex cases. In certain simple cases, after furnishing to the machine all relevant facts, the machine will provide the proper decision to the judge. Complex cases are those, in particular, in which there are alleviating and aggravating circumstances to be taken into consideration in the meting out of the penalty. In such a situation, the results arrived at by the machine (possibly, presented in a form of some alternatives), will be only guides or suggestions for a decision ultimately made by men.

In pointing out circumstances bearing on the severity of the punishment, the author lingers on "the problem of the class consideration (class consciousness) which, as is well known, is of great significance in law."[68] He proposes to feed the machine with the information as to the class identity of, for example, the perpetrator of a crime, such as: worker; privately operating farmer; farmer-member of a cooperative; official; former capitalist, etc. The machine should be so arranged that, after having received and digested the basic information, it would take into account also the class status of the accused. While the author points out that the use of the machine in such a situation should not be mechanical, as the machine cannot become "dialectical," he attaches importance to the class background of the defendant as an element bearing on the penalty

66. Ancel, *Introduction* to *Centre Francais de Droit Compare*, LA REFORME PENALE SOVIETIQUE, p. L n. 1 (1962). The author mixed up the federal law of 1958 and the Judiciary Act of the Russian Republic of 1960.

67. My attention to this book was drawn by Professor Benes, of Indiana University, who translated the relevant passages into English.

68. KNAPP, O MOZNOSTI POUZITI KYBERNETICKYCH METOD V PRAVU 111 (1963).

to be imposed.[69]

Another feature of the recent reforms is that apparently all justice should be administered by a unified set of regular courts. Art. 7 of the Federal General Principles of Criminal Law of Dec. 25, 1958, provided as follows: "(A)dministration of justice in criminal matters belongs exclusively to the court. Nobody may be declared guilty of committing a crime and be subjected to penalty except by court sentence." However, at least three exceptions have to be noted.

First, the Military Tribunals were retained. Their obligation is "to combat any criminal encroachments on the security of the Soviet state, the fighting capacity of the Armed Forces, military discipline and rules of military service. . . ."[70]

Second, for minor acts of misbehavior, lack of discipline at work and petty offenses, comradely courts may be established in the various units of the Soviet life. They were first provided for in a decree of 1928 and subsequently came into near-oblivion before they were resurrected as a consequence of Khrushchev's appeal for greater popular participation in the administration of justice at the XXI Congress of 1959.[71] The present regulations of the comradely courts were enacted by a decree of the Presidium of the Supreme Soviet on July 3, 1961. Art. 1 of the law indicated that their duties consist of "educating Soviet citizens in the spirit of communist attitude to work, . . . observance of the rules of socialist coexistence, promoting with the Soviet people the spirit of collectivism. . . ."[72]

The most important exception to the rule that a penalty may be imposed only by judicial organs is provided for, in some Republics, by "parasite" statutes. This time, the Russian Republic did not set the pattern, but followed it, after some hesitation. The Russian statute[73] deplores the fact that some persons "refuse to work honestly, . . . live from income which does not come from work, . . . exercise prohibited professions, engage in activities of free enterprise, in speculation, in begging, employ salaried manpower, derive income from . . . exploiting personal automo-

69. Simultaneously with the publication of the book, the same author published an article: Knapp, *On the Application of Cybernetics of Law*, 9 Rev. Contemp. L. 15 (1963). There is no discussion of the class background of the accused in the article.

70. Denisov & Kirichenko, Soviet State Law 307 (1960). For a short description of Military Tribunals see, *e.g.*, Fridieff, *supra* note 59, at 735-38.

71. Ancel, *supra* note 66, at LV; Grzybowski, Soviet Legal Institutions 255 (1962).

72. Grzybowski, *op. cit. supra* note 71, at 256. For recent examples of cases decided by the comradely court of Moscow University Law School, see Sharlet, *Russia's Courts of Public Pressure*, 200 The Nation, January 18, 1965, No. 3, p. 55. See also, Morgan, Law in Eastern Europe (1963), chapter 7 on the Comrades' Courts.

73. Decree of the Supreme Soviet of the Russian Republic of May 4, 1961.

biles or building grounds . . . and commit other anti-social acts."[74] The statute declares a severe fight against those "parasites," who are subjected to an exile of two to five years with the obligation to work in places especially established for that purpose, and a forfeiture of their assets acquired not by working. The penalties are imposed either by the People's Tribunals, or by "social decisions reached by collectivities of toilers of enterprises, workshops, administrations, organizations, kolkhozes. . . ." Such a decision can be taken after a warning to the "parasite" has been left unheeded; it should be approved by the Executive Committee of the local soviet, and cannot be appealed.

Such procedures like those envisaged by the rules on comradely courts and parasite statutes, together with provisions on assessors and lack of requirement that judges should have legal training, result in the de-emphasizing of the importance of the law and the legal profession. They may be a step in the direction of a classless society, foreseen by Marx and Engels, "in which disputes would be settled by the spontaneous, unofficial social pressure of the whole community, by the group sense of right and wrong or at least of expediency."[75] The "withering away" of the state and the law, predicted by the founders of communism, advanced by Soviet jurists purged in the thirties and then postponed for an indefinite period of time (until capitalism will disappear everywhere, and communism reaches its final stage) may develop little by little, even though abidance by "socialist legality" should be an important feature of the society in the long period of transition. However, to every Marxist, law is only a by-product of the economic foundations of the society, overshadowed by communist ideology, politics, etc. Therefore, the author was not surprised when upon asking a prominent jurist from one of the communist countries whether his son would study law, he received the following answer: "Oh no! of course, he will do something more reasonable!"

In this connection, it is interesting to note the striking decrease in the number of students at many law schools in the Soviet Union (and particularly, in other republics than Russia). In 1963, there were less than 50% of law students as compared with 1956. There is an especially low enrollment in law schools in the Asiatic part of the Soviet Union, and in large cities like Kiev, Kishinev, Voronezh, Tashkent, Tbilisi, only 25

74. Listening to foreign broadcasts may also be treated as such an "anti-social act." HAZARD, *op. cit. supra* note 62, at 79.

75. BERMAN, JUSTICE IN THE U.S.S.R. 280 (1963).

new law students are being admitted per year.[76] If there are few candidates, the conclusion may be that there is just lack of interest, and "more reasonable" fields are being selected; if admissions are limited by the authorities, maybe the government prefers that there should not be many trained lawyers, at least in non-Russian Republics.[77]

Enclosure 2 in Despatch No. 632

REPORT OF THE ACTING COMMISSAR OF JUSTICE, COMRADE KRYLENKO, ON THE LEGISLATIVE BILL CONCERNING THE ORGANIZATION OF SOVIET LAW COURTS.

At the Night Session of the IV Session of the Central Executive Committee on October 23, 1922. (Summary from the Shorthand Account reproduced in the Official Publication ACT ORGANIZING LAW COURTS OF THE R.S.F.S.R., Moscow Edition of the People's Commissariat of Justice, 1922.)

Krylenko first characterizes the old system, which contained two principles, as it were: on the one hand there were the People's Courts, Soviets of People's Judges, and the Commissariat of Justice, while on the other hand there were tribunals: military, transport, provincial, and supreme. The new law was to do away with this dualism and give a unified system of law courts. The makers of the new law were confronted with certain questions of greatest practical and political importance: first, who was eligible for People's Judge; secondly, how are People's Judges to be appointed; thirdly, how are People's Judges to be recalled from their posts: fourthly, to whom are they subordinated; and fifthly, how are People's Jurors to be selected and appointed.

As regards the first question, who is eligible for People's Judge, they must abandon the idea that everybody is eligible. The Legislative Bill under discussion provides that for this post is eligible only he who has active and passive suffrage, who has a previous two-years' record in responsible proletarian, public, trade-union or party work, or, as an alternative, who has been three years a People's Judge under the old system. Concerning the second question: how are People's Judges appointed, the Bill provides that candidates are to be proposed by the Provincial Court, and appointed for one year by the Provincial Executive Committee, with the right to recall any Judge from his post by resolution of the said Executive Committee, in which case the Commissariat of Justice must be apprised of the motives underlying such recall. The third question is: to whom are the People's Judges subordinated. The Bill subordinates them to the next higher court, the Provincial Court. This creates in the province a "strong fist," a legal center. And then the last question: how is the personnel of the People's Jurors to be made up. In this respect the Bill professes deliberately its class character, in that it provides that 50 percent of the jurors must be drawn from the labor classes, 25 percent from the Red Army, and 25 percent from "representatives of settlements, volosts, etc." In each uyezd (county) a special "Distribution Commission" is to be formed, which is to compile jurors' lists. The number of jurors required per uyezd (county) will vary between 800 and 1,000. This system deliberately breaks with "the principle of democratic elections from below, which in political life always leads to a casual comer being elected, while our system is based on the openly avowed electric principle of singling out the staunchest representatives of the proletariat." In this fashion the primary court is formed, that court which deals with 92 percent of all legal cases of the R.S.F.S.R., the People's Court with two jurors.

Now the next higher court. First of all, as regards the name it is to be given, the Bill proposes to call it the Provincial Tribunal (this name was eventually, after the debates, changed to "Provincial Court."—Note by translator). This Provincial Tribunal has three principal functions: first, it deals with cases of counter-revolution, banditism, murders, etc.; generally speaking, with such transgressions of the law which entail

76. Izvestia, August 4, 1964: cited by *Recht, Rechtswissenschaft und Justizausbildung,* OST & WEST, November 15, 1964, v. 8, No. 6, p. 240. (Brought to my attention by Dr. Fedynskyj, of Indiana University Law School.)

77. From among the five cities mentioned, only Voronezh is in the Russian Republic.

severer punishment; the second function is that the Tribunal acts as court of appeal in respect to lower court; and the third, that it is an organ of supervision. How are the Provincial Tribunals to be constructed, with or without jurors? With a view to observing uniformity of structure, the compilers of the Bill eventually decided to retain for this court too the institute of jurors. But "political expediency" required that even still greater vigor be exercised in the selection of jurors for the Provincial Tribunal. The Bill provides that in each province a Commission of seven members shall be formed, which will compile the list of jurors for the Provincial Tribunal. The jurors must have a two-years' record of work in public organizations. There will be about 100 to 200 jurors per province, and each of them will have to sit on the jury about six days in the year. Besides a Collegium of Appeals, the Provincial Tribunal is also to have a Disciplinary Collegium, the task of which is to supervise the People's Judges and People's Examining Magistrates. These Disciplinary Sections will deal only with two kinds of offences: first, "conduct incompatible with the dignity of a legal worker," and secondly, "the pronouncing by the judge of a number of verdicts, subsequently rescinded by the higher courts, 'contradictory to the spirit of our Soviet laws'." "This latter handle for the institution of disciplinary proceedings is given to the Provincial Tribunals in order to maintain in legal practice a line of conduct which corresponds to the principles of the central Soviet Power." The Provincial Tribunal is to consist of 15 members, and in its Presidium, that is in the President and the two Vice-Presidents, special administrative and technical functions are to be vested. The Plenary Session has the right to raise questions of "interpretation of laws in connection with a concrete case."

As regards the Supreme Court of the R.S.F.S.R., it combines the functions of the old Supreme Tribunal with all its Collegiums (Sections): Military, Transport, Legal, and of Appeals, creating anew the Section for Civil Appeals, and taking over from the Commissariat of Justice all functions of supreme control of jurisdiction. As regards functions of administration and organization, this sphere of activity belongs, according to the Bill, entirely to the Commissariat of Justice. Thus, the just and expedient distribution of functions is one of the most signal achievements of the Bill. Transport Tribunals are left only in eight large towns. Speaking of Courts-Martial, Krylenko says that "their time was not come yet," they must still continue in existence, but they are a branch of the general system of courts, and they are subordinated to the Military Collegium (Section) of the Supreme Court.

The Plenary Session of the Supreme Court has the right to interpret the "Material" laws and the laws of legal procedure. "But by no means all laws of the R.S.F.S.R. We do not want to construct a new Senate." With a view to establishing closer contact between the Supreme Court and the Commissariat of Justice, the Public Prosecutor-General of the Republic is to be present at the sessions of the Supreme Court; he also has the right to suspend verdicts of that Court, and to submit them for settlement to the Presidium of the Central Executive Committee. The members of the Supreme Court are appointed and approved by the Presidium of the Central Executive Committee, the candidates to be nominated by the Commissar of Justice, and for military and transport courts by the respective Commissars.

Turning once more to the military and transport courts, Krylenko admits that they constitute a "gross drawback," that they "violate the whole system," but he contends that at the present moment they cannot be done without. Incidentally it transpires that these tribunals are without jurors. "There is one more drawback: that new system is not as simple as our present system: The People's Judge with two jurors, and then the same judge with six jurors. This simplicity had to be sacrificed to another aim, the aim of establishing a uniform line of conduct in Soviet criminal law. I feel constrained to point out that in our time, since we are resolved to have the New Economic Policy 'in earnest and for a long time' (Words said by Lenin—Note by Translator), it is necessary that we, the labor classes, have also law-courts of our own and keep them well in our hands, in order to maintain our dictatorship as a means of protecting the interests of the labor classes. This principal task has been clearly expressed in Article I of the Bill, with the reading of which I am going to conclude my report. That Article I reads as follows: "For the purpose of protecting the achievements of the proletarian revolution, safeguarding the interests of the State, the rights of the toilers and their associates, the following uniform system of courts of justice shall function on the territory of the R.S.F.S.R." Should a bourgeois lawyer read this article, he would say: "From this article it follows that your courts function, in the first place, for the purpose of protecting the achievements of the proletarian revolution, and in the second place for safeguarding the rights of the toilers and their associations," in other words, they do not exist for the protection of rights of non-toilers and their associations; and from the point of view of formal logic such a formulation of the question would not be unfounded. To him we would reply: "Yes, you are perfectly right, the interests of the toilers are that principal aim for which our courts exist. To that aim we make subservient our entire system of administration of justice, that is to say the formal weapon of class self-defense in the hands of the labor masses. If for these aims, or on the road to the achievement of such aims, we have had, or in future shall have, to trample underfoot the rights of non-toilers or their organizations, our courts will not hesitate in doing so. . . ."

After this report was heard, a Commission was appointed to scrutinize the Bill. At the session on October 31, 1922, the revised Bill was submitted to the Executive Committee once more, and, after some minor amendments had been proposed and accepted, it eventually passed "unanimously." One of these amendments was that the middle court was called not the "Provincial Tribunal," but "Provincial Court."

Enclosure No. 3 in Despatch No. 632

Act Organizing the System of Law Courts of the R.S.F.S.R.

Resolution of the Central Executive Committee Concerning the Introduction of the above Organizing Act, passed at the Fourth Session on October 31, 1922.

(Translation from the Official Publication of the Commissariat of Justice, Moscow, 1922.) Sjorslin v. I p. 233. The R.S.F.S.R. Judiciary Act of Oct. 31, 1922 (R.S.F.S.R. Laws 1922, text 902).

The Fourth Session of the Central Executive Committee, having heard on October 31, 1922, the report of the Commissariat of Justice concerning the legislative Bill on the organization of the law courts, as well as the amendments proposed by the Commission, has resolved on the following:

1. To accept the Bill as introduced by the Soviet of Commissars, together with the amendments to it, and to let it become law throughout the territory of the R.S.F.S.R. commencing January 1, 1923.

The Session of the Central Executive Committee invites the Executive Committees of all allied republics to introduce this law as passed by the Session also on the territories of their respective republics.

2. To make it incumbent upon the Central Executive Committte and the Commissariat of Justice to revise by that time, also the Code of Laws of Legal Procedure, making it conform to the new law passed.

3. Being desirous, at the same time, of raising the personnel of the court workers to a due level, the Session of the Central Executive Committee has resolved:

(a) To make it incumbent upon the Soviet of Commissars to improve the material conditions of the legal workers carried on the State Supply Roll in a measure which would correspond to the importance of the tasks entrusted to them; while the Provincial Executive Committees should in a similar fashion attend to the needs of the legal workers of these institutions which are maintained and supported on local resources;

(b) To make it incumbent upon the Commissariat of Justice and the Head-Committee of Trade and Technical Instruction to elaborate with the least possible delay, and to submit to the Soviet of Commissars a Bill concerning the opening, in the course of the year 1923, of no fewer than 10 law schools in various localities, and of one supreme law school in Moscow for the purpose of preparing a body of experienced legal workers.

Signed: President of the Central Executive Committee: M. Kaliuim.
Commissar of Justice: Kursky.
Secretary to the Central Executive Committee: A. Enukidze.
November 11, 1922.

Act Organizing the System of Law Courts of the R.S.F.S.R.

Part I.

Chapter I.

Fundamental Provisions.

Article 1. For the purpose of protecting the achievements of the proletarian revolution, safeguarding the interests of the State, the rights of the toilers and their associations, the following uniform system of courts of justice shall function on the territory of the R.S.F.S.R.

1. The People's Court consisting of one permanent People's Judge.
2. The People's Court composed of the same permanent People's Judge and two People's Jurors.
3. The Provincial Court.
4. The Supreme Court of the R.S.F.S.R. and its Collegiums (Sections).

Article 2. For the examination of special cases which are more complicated, to deal with which special knowledge and certain practice is required, and in view of the particular danger inherent in criminal offenses of a certain kind to the military power of the Republic, or to its economic welfare, the following special courts shall function temporarily, parallel to the uniform system of People's Courts of the R.S.F.S.R.: (a) for offenses endangering the firmness and the power of the Red Army, Military Tribunals; (b) for more important offenses threatening the transport service, Military Transport Tribunals; (c) for infractions of the Labor Laws, 4 Special Labor Sessions of the People's Courts; (d) for cases in connection with land affairs, Land Commissions; and (e) for disputes concerning proprietary rights between State organs, Central and Local Arbitration Commissions formed at the Soviet of Labor and Defense and at the Provincial Economic Conferences. The principles of organization and the functions of such courts are stipulated in Part IV, Chapter XII, of the present Act.

Article 3. The People's Judge, acting by himself or conjointly with two People's Jurors, attends to his duties within his fixed district in the uyezd (county) or in the town. For such activity within his district he shall be responsible only to a court, or the next higher legal institution in the fashion set forth below.

Article 4. The Provincial Court carries on its functions in the territory of that province or oblast in which it is formed, and, apart from dealing with cases coming within its competency, it exercizes supervision over all courts in the territory of the province or oblast, except only the Travelling Sessions of the Supreme Court and the Military and Military-Transport Tribunals.

Article 5. The competency of the Supreme Court of the R.S.F.S.R. includes: legal control of all courts of justice of the R.S.F.S.R. without exception, examination of appeals against decisions of the Provincial Courts; examination, by way of control, of any case on which a verdict has been pronounced by any court of justice of the Republic; and trial of cases of particular importance to the State which in accordance with law come within the competency of the Supreme Court of the R.S.F.S.R.

Article 6. General supervision over the observance of laws, control over the conduct of preliminary examinations, and public prosecution in courts of law come within the competency of the State Public Prosecution.

Article 7. For preliminary examination of offenses indictable before courts of justice, People's Examining Magistrates are appointed who perform their duties within fixed divisions and who are attached to certain courts of law, under the supervision and control of the Public Prosecutors and the Provincial Courts.

Article 8. With a view to rendering the toilers legal assistance in civil cases, as well as in criminal cases before Provincial Courts, Collegiate bodies of "legal defenders" (counsel, solicitors?) are to be established under the control of the Provincial Courts.

Article 9. For the purpose of carrying out verdicts of court, the office of Bailiff is to be created in connection with Provincial Courts and People's Courts; and the office of Notary Public for the performance of acts required by the law.

Article 10. The competency, functions, and responsibilities of all above mentioned institutions and offices are fixed in corresponding chapters and articles of the present Act.

Chapter II

Appointment and Recall of People's Judges, and People's Courts Divisions.

Article 11. For the office of People's Judge is eligible every male and female citizen of the R.S.F.S.R. who is not disfranchised by verdict of court, and who complies with the following conditions:

(a) has the right to vote, and to be elected to Soviets,

(b) has not less than a two-years record of responsible political work in labor-peasant public, trade-union, or party labor organization, or a three-years record of practical work in organs of Soviet justice in capacities not below the office of People's Examining Magistrate.

Note: Persons expelled from public organization for disgraceful conduct are not eligible for the office of People's Judges.

Article 12. People's Judges are elected by the Provincial Executive Committees after nomination by the Provincial Court or the Commissariat of Justice, according to the number of People's Courts Divisions or Districts in the given province.

Article 13. People's Judges are elected for the period of one year, and may be re-elected. People's Judges may be re-called prior to the expiration of their term of office, or transferred to other courts within the province, solely by resolution of the Provincial Executive Committee which has appointed them, at the initiative of the Commissar of Justice or the said Executive Committee itself. In the latter event, however, the reasons for such a recall must be communicated in detail to the Commissar of Justice. Dismissal from the office of People's Judge may take place solely by verdict of court, or in accordance with the provisions contained in Articles 69 to 84 of the present Act.

Article 14. The number of People's Courts Divisions in each province, and the boundaries of such divisions, are to be fixed each time by resolution of the Provincial Court, and approved by the Provincial Executive Committee and the Commissariat of Justice. In the event the Commissariat of Justice does not agree with the fixing of divisions, it is entitled to demand the establishment of a certain minimum of People's Courts Division in the given province.

Chapter III

People's Jurors, and Impanelling of Jurors.

Article 15. For People's Juror are eligible all toiling citizens of the R.S.F.S.R. of both sexes, who have the right to vote and to be elected to local Soviets.

Article 16. For the office of People's Juror are not eligible persons disfranchised by verdict of court, or persons expelled from public and trade-union organizations for disgraceful acts and conduct.

Article 17. Each People's Juror shall participate in court proceedings no longer than six days in the year, and his participation is to continue uninterrupted the whole term fixed.

Note: Exceptions from this rule are mentioned in the Code of Criminal Procedure.

Article 18. The lists of People's Jurors for each People's Courts Division are compiled on the basis of three jurors per week, that is to say two jurors impanelled and one in reserve, which makes a total (52 x 3) of 156; adding 25 percent -39- for cases of nonappearance, and rounding the figure off, the total of jurors is fixed at two hundred to each people's court per year.

Article 19. The lists of People's Jurors are to be compiled once a year, by December 1. One month prior to that date a special Commission formed in each uyezd (division) center assigns a corresponding number of candidates to be elected—according to the number of People's Courts Divisions—to the industrial establishments, volosts and military units situated in the territory of the uyezd.

Article 20. The Special Commission for the Nomination of Jurors is to be presided over by a number of the local Uyezd Executive Committee, its members being the local assistant of the Provincial Public Prosecutor and one of the People's Judges of the uyezd. The candidates to be elected are to be assigned approximately as follows: 50 per cent of the jurors are to be drawn from the labor classes, 35 per cent from the settlements and volosts, and 15 per cent from military units. The lists of assigned vacancies are to be sent to the respective Divisional People's Judges, works and factory committees, political commissars of military units, and volost executive committees.

Article 21. On receipt of the respective notice the works and factory committees, as well as the other institutions mentioned in the previous article, "attend to the election of candidates, taking into consideration the level of their political development"; the lists of candidates are exhibited for public notice at the works, on the premises of the volost executive committees, labor clubs, etc., and in the course of one week every toiler has the right to challenge any of the candidates, lodging his protest with the institution which has compiled the list, and stating the motives of his protest. After the protests have been scrutinized, the lists are sent by the respective institutions to the People's Judge.

Article 22. The challenged candidates have the right to lodge their protests against such challenges with the next higher analogous institution, the competent trade-union, the Uyezd Executive Committee, or the Political Section of the next higher military unit, etc., within one week, and these institutions are bound to consider and examine such protest within a similar period of time.

Article 23. On receipt of the lists, the People's Judge forwards a copy of them for confirmation to the President of the Uyezd Commission, and not waiting for their definite confirmation, proceeds to impanel the juries, selecting the jurors by alphabet.

Article 24. On receipt of the lists from all People's Judges of the uyezd, the Uyezd Commission (Article 20) compiles a general list from which it is entitled to exclude any such persons that for some reason or another do not come up to the standard required for a People's Juror, and of these included in the lists it compiles a special list of People's Jurors for participation in the Travelling Sessions of the Provincial Court.

Article 25. Persons excluded by the Uyezd Commission from the list of jurors shall be entitled to lodge a protest against such exclusion with the local executive committee the decision of which in this matter shall be regarded as final.

Article 26. On the arrival of the People's Jurors at the People's Court, the People's Judge shall be bound to explain to them their rights and functions, to make each of them sign a document to the effect that such explanation has been made to them, and to receive from them the solemn promise to perform their duties in accordance with their consciences.

Article 27. During the time the jurors are sitting on the jury they are to continue to draw their wages at the places of their respective employment, including also the time spent in travelling there and back. Persons drawing their means of subsistence from agricultural labor or domestic handicraft shall receive an extra allowance per diem fixed in accordance with the minimum wage in the given locality; such allowance to be paid by the Uyezd Executive Committee to the order of the People's Judge.

Article 28. In the event of sickness or other lawful causes for non-appearance of a juror to serve on the jury when his turn has arrived, his name shall automatically be transferred to the end of the list, of which fact he shall be apprised by the People's Judge.

Chapter IV

Location of People's Courts and the Judge's Offices. Accounts of the People's Judges.

Article 29. The address of the People's Court is to be brought to public notice. The expenditure in connection with the maintenance of the People's Judge's office is to be fixed by the People's Commissariat of Justice. The maintenance of the office shall be charged to the local Provincial Executive Committees, the necessary funds to be paid through the Provincial Court in accordance with Estimates.

Article 30. Each Divisional People's Court shall have a Secretary (Clerk of the Court) who shall be confirmed in his office by the Provincial Court on the representation of the People's Judge. Persons disqualified by verdicts of court or excluded from public organizations for disgraceful acts and conduct, shall not be eligible to the office of Secretary of People's Court.

Article 31. Direct control over the People's Judge's activity, including also the technical arrangements incumbent upon him, shall be exercised by the Provincial Court, to which the People's Judge shall also be subordinated in a disciplinary sense. Shape and form of accounts, to be rendered by the People's Judge, financial or of any other description, and everything appertaining to them, shall be fixed by instructions of the Commissariat of Justice, and by orders and explanation of the Provincial Court.

Chapter V

People's Examining Magistrates.

Article 32. The office of People's Examining Magistrates is established at:

(a) corresponding Magistrates Divisions,
(b) at the Criminal Section of the Provincial Court,
(c) at the Supreme Court of the R.S.F.S.R.,
(d) at the Public Prosecution Department of the Commissariat of Justice, for the purpose of carrying on urgent examinations in important cases.

Article 33. The examining magistrates of the Division are named "People's Examining Magistrates," these at the Provincial Courts are called "Senior Examining Magistrates," and these at the Supreme Court or at the Public Prosecution Department of the Commissariat, "Examining Magistrates for important affairs."

Article 34. To the office of Examining Magistrate are not eligible:

(a) persons disqualified by verdicts of court, or excluded from public organizations for disgraceful acts and conduct;
(b) persons who have not at least a two-years record of Soviet legal work in a capacity not lower than that of Secretary of a People's Court, or who have not passed a corresponding examination at the Provincial Court;
(c) persons who are not entitled to the vote at local Soviet elections;
(d) persons who during the civil war have been disloyal to the Soviet regime, or have belonged to anti-Soviet political parties.

Article 35. The precincts of the Magisterial Divisions shall be fixed, and People's Examining Magistrates appointed, by resolutions of the Provincial Court which shall require the sanction of the Provincial Executive committee and the Commissars of Justice. People's Examining Magistrates may be removed from their offices by a mere resolution of the court at its own initiative, or at the representation of the Provincial Executive Committee or the Commissariat of Justice.

Article 36. Senior Examining Magistrates and Magistrates for Important Affairs shall be appointed, transferred, and recalled by resolutions of the respective institutions to which they are attached. All these examining magistrates exercize their functions throughout the territories within the scope of the respective institution to which they are attached.

Article 37. The Divisional People's Examining Magistrate employs the services of a secretary and a messenger. Funds for the maintenance of people's examining magistrates are assigned by the Provincial Court, the same as for the maintenance of People's Courts, in accordance with the estimates, from local resources. All the other examining magistrates are paid from the general State funds.

Article 38. In their relations with courts, the Public Prosecution Department, organs of investigation, and any other official authority, the examining magistrates shall be guided by the relevant provisions of the Code of Criminal Procedure, as well as by instructions and explanations emanating from the Commissariat of Justice and the Provincial Courts.

Part II

Chapter VI

The Provincial Court.

Article 39. The Provincial Court functions:

(a) as the center of administration of justice in the province, and as the organ for direct supervision of the subordinated People's Courts;

(b) as the organ for examining appeals lodged against the findings of the subordinate people's courts, and private complaints filed against their decisions of the mentioned courts;

(c) as lower court in cases specified by the law.

Article 40. In accordance with the above the Provincial Court is composed of a President and two Vice-presidents, one of them for the Civil Section and the other for the Criminal Section; twelve Permanent Members of the Provincial Court, and Provincial People's Jurors who are called up for services on the jury in accordance with rules set forth below; further of a sufficient number of Provincial Court Secretaries and other officials required by the Provincial Court and the Institutions attached to it, in accordance with approved estimates.

Article 41. The president and the vice-presidents must have a record of not less than three years practical legal work, in the capacity of people's judge or members of the revolutionary tribunal, in addition to answering the requirements established for filling the office of People's judges (see Article 11 of this Act). As Members of the Provincial Court are eligible only persons who have worked not less than two years in the above mentioned capacities.

Note: Deviations from this rule are admissible only with the consent of the Commissariat of Justice.

Article 42. The president, vice-president and members of the Provincial Courts are elected by the Provincial Executive Committee for one year, subject to the sanction of the Commissar of Justice who in his turn has the right to nominate also his own candidates for president, vice-president, and members of the Provincial Court. On expiration of their term these persons may be reelected. The recall, however, or the dismissal of a president (or vice-president) of the Provincial Court prior to the expiration of his term by a mere resolution of the Provincial Executive Committee, without the sanction of the Commissar of Justice, is absolutely inadmissible, unless it is done in execution of a verdict of court, or ordered as a disciplinery measure by the competent section of the Supreme Court. The same rules apply also to members of the Provincial Court.

Article 43. In the event of the Commissar of Justice withholding his confirmation of the elected president (and vice-president) of the Provincial Court, and the inability of the Provincial Executive Committee to nominate other candidates, the Commissars of Justice may appoint the said officials at his own discretion.

Article 44. People's Jurors for participation in the sessions of the Provincial Court are called up in accordance with a special list of citizens who have a record of not less than two years' work in public and trade-union organizations. Such lists shall be compiled at the initiative of the Provincial Court by a special commission which is to be presided over by a member of the Provincial Executive Committee specially appointed by that Committee, two members of the Provincial Court as appointed by the President of such Court, the Provincial Public Prosecutor, and three members of the Provincial Trade Unions Soviet as appointed by the latter. The lists are subject to sanction by the Provincial Executive Committee which has the right to challenge candidates, its findings in this respect to be considered as final.

Article 45. The provincial People's jurors are elected to the number of no fewer than 200 persons, of whom no fewer than 25 must be people's judges who are by preference to participate in the sessions of the Civil Section of the Provincial Court. The requirements stipulated in Articles 15, 16, 17, 24, 25, 27 and 28 of this Act, and referring to the jurors of people's courts, apply also to the jurors of the Provincial Courts.

Article 46. As secretaries of sections of the Provincial Court shall be eligible only persons who answer the conditions established for candidates for posts not lower than People's Examining Magistrates.

One of the secretaries is to be named Senior Secretary of the Provincial Court.

Article 47. The remaining institutions and officials attached to the Provincial Court shall function in accordance with rules specially to be established.

DOCUMENT 447

Chapter VII

Functions of the Provincial Court.

Article 48. The President and the two Vice-presidents are wholly responsible for the correct and lawful carrying on of work in the Provincial Court, and for correct and lawful compliance with all existing rules and regulations, by the Court itself, as well as all subordinate institutions.

Article 49. In accordance with the above, the competency of the President shall be as follows:

(a) To distribute and appoint the duties of the members of the Provincial Court of the various sections; to make representations to the Provincial Executive Committee for confirmation of People's Judges and People's Examining Magistrates; to ensure correct compilation, and in due time, of the lists of People's Jurors; to ensure the issue of funds to the People's Courts and the People's Examining Magistrates in due time; and to see that their accounts are properly rendered; to compile and submit accounts and reports concerning the Provincial Court and the People's Courts to the Provincial Executive Committee and to the Commissariat of Justice; to control the clerical work, as well as the financial, material, and other accounts of the Provincial Court, and all correspondence of the Court with the Commissariat of Justice and other departments of State; to control the activity of notaries public and the body of legal defense, (attorneys-at-law—Note by Translator.)

(b) To appoint plenary sessions of the Provincial Court, to preside over the same, to examine all matters submitted, and to submit at his own initiative to the plenary sessions of the Provincial Court matter within the competency of that Court, including: preparation of material bearing upon disciplinary responsibility of People's Examining Magistrates, People's Judges, members of the body of legal defense, and other officials; and imposition of disciplinary punishment upon People's Judges, People's Examining Magistrates, and other officials, as far as such power is vested in the President.

Article 50. The Plenary Session of the Provincial Court is composed of all members of the Court available at that moment, but of not less than half of their total number, the participation of the Provincial Public Prosecutor or his Assistant being obligatory. The competency of the Plenary Sessions of the Court is as follows:

(a) To deal with all questions concerning the fixing of the numbers and extent of People's Courts Divisions; the transfer of People's Judges within the jurisdiction of the Provincial Court; the fixing of the numbers and extent of Examining Magistrate's Divisions; the appointment and transfer of such magistrates; the examination of accounts of people's judges and of relevant reports of members of the Provincial Court oppointed for this purpose by the President; the appointment of scrutiny commissions to investigate the activity of people's judges and people's examining magistrates; and the examination of reports in connection with such scrutinies; the elaboration of instructions and regulations relating to the conduct of business of the Provincial Court.

(b) To examine all questions connected with the institution of disciplinary proceedings against people's judges and people's examining magistrates, as well as other officials subordinate to the Provincial Court, including members of the Provincial Court itself; to pass resolutions concerning the temporary suspension from office of people's judges and people's examining magistrates, pending final settlement of their cases; and to arrange the appointment of the Disciplinary Collegium of the Provincial Court.

(c) To examine questions submitted by the president of the Provincial Court, or by any separate session of the ordinary or the Appeals Section, or by the Provincial Public Prosecutor, resulting from insufficient clearness or incompleteness of the existing laws; but solely, each time, in connection with some concrete case or decision, and submitting at the same time all considerations in connection with such questions to the Supreme Court.

Article 51. If the person presiding over the session agrees with the finding of the plenary session—with the exception of cases mentioned in clause "c" of the previous Article—such decision shall immediately be carried into effect; but if there is discrepancy of opinion, the entire material shall be submitted to the Commissariat of Justice or the Supreme Court, or the Provincial Executive Committee concerned, for decision. If the Provincial Public Prosecutor objects to the finding of the plenary session of the Provincial Court, such objection cannot delay the execution of such decision of the Provincial Court.

Article 52. The Criminal Section of the Provincial Court consists of 7 permanent members of the Provincial Court, including the Chief of the Section who is to be one of the Vice-Presidents, and comprises the Criminal Sub-section, as well as the Sub-section of Criminal Appeals. The sessions of the Sub-section of Appeals are composed of three Permanent Members, and the sessions of the Criminal Sub-section of one Permanent Member of the Provincial Court and two Provincial People's Jurors who are called up from service by resolution of a special organizing session of the Criminal Sub-section, according to the list of jurors in the possession of the Provincial Court. The appointment of members of the Criminal Section to the Criminal and Appeals sessions, as well as the appointment of presidents of travelling sessions of the Criminal Sub-section, comes within the competency of the Vice-President presiding over the Section, and requires the sanction of the President of the Provincial Court. The President of the Provincial Court is free to preside, at his own discretion, at the hearing of any case dealt with by the Appeals Sub-section of the Criminal section of the Provincial Court.

Article 53. The Civil Section of the Provincial Court is to consist also of seven members, including the Chief of the Section who is to be one of the Vice-Presidents, and comprises the Civil Sub-section and the Sub-section of Civil Appeals. The latter is to be composed of three Permanent Members of the Provincial Court, including the Chief of the Section—one of the Vice-Presidents—and the former of one Permanent Member who acts as president, and two People's Jurors drawn for perference from the number of People's Judges enrolled as people's jurors (Article 45 of the Act). The appointment of members of the Civil Section of the ordinary civil or appeals sessions, as well as the appointment of presidents for the travelling sessions, rests with the Chief of the Section and requires the sanction of the Presdient of the Provincial Court. The People's Jurors are called up by a special organizing session of the Section, at which session, however, participate only Permanent Members of the Provincial Court. The President of the Provincial Court is free to preside, at his own discretion, at the hearing of any appeal case by the Civil Section of the Provincial Court.

Note: The re-arrangement of the members of the Provincial courts in sub-sections, the forming of special bodies of members not belonging to one or the other sub-section for the hearing of special cases, likewise the application to the Commissariat of Justice for an increase of the number of the members of the Provincial Court to meet contingencies, shall, consequent upon the increase in the volume of work, come within the competency of, and be attended to by, the President of the Provincial Court, with the concurrence of both Vice-Presidents.

Article 54. The Disciplinary Collegium of the Privincial Court is to consist of three persons, including the President or one of the Vice-Presidents of the Provincial Court, all of whom are to be elected by the Plenary Session of the Provincial Court.

Part III

Chapter VIII

The Supreme Court of the R.S.F.S.R.

Article 55. The Supreme Court of the R.S.F.S.R. (Article 5 of the Act) is to comprise the following:

(a) The Presidium of the Supreme Court;
(b) The Plenary Session of the Supreme Court;
(c) The Criminal and Civil Appeals Sections of the Supreme Court;
(d) The Legal Collegium, the Military and the Military-Transport Collegium of the Supreme Court;
(e) The Disciplinary Collegium of the Supreme Court.

Article 56. The (appointment of) the President and the members of the Supreme Court requires the sanction of the Presidium of the Central Executive Committee. The President of the Supreme Court, the Vice-President, and the Chiefs (presidents) of the Legal, the Military, and the Military-Transport Collegium are appointed direct by the Presidium of the Central Executive Committee, while the remaining members of the Supreme Court are appointed on the representation of the Commissar of Justice. The members of the Military and of the Military-Transport Collegium are appointed by the Presidium of the Central Executive Committee on the representation of the Revolutionary Military Soviet of the Republic and the Commissariat of Roads of Communication, with the recommendation of the Commissar of Justice.

Article 57. The President and the Members of the Supreme Court cannot be recalled or removed from their offices except by resolution of the Presidium of the Central Executive Committee.

Note: All other officials attached to the Supreme Court and its component sections and parts, public prosecutors, secretaries to legal collegiums, and examining magistrates for important cases, are appointed and recalled in accordance with rules and regulations existing in respect to such offices.

Article 58. In autonomous republics and territorial unions there may be established Territorial Branches of the Supreme Court by special resolutions of the All-Russian Central Executive Committee; the Members of such Branch Courts are appointed by the Central Executive Committees of the respective republics or by a special Organizing Act which is to be sanctioned by the President of the All-Russian Central Executive Committee; the President and the Vice-President of such Branches must, however, at any rate be approved by the Presidium of the All-Russian Central Executive Committee.

Chapter IX

Limits of Competency of the Presidium and of the Plenary Sessions of the Supreme Court.

Article 59. The President of the Supreme Court, the Vice-President, the Chiefs of the Appeals Collegiums, the Chief of the Legal Collegium, and the Chiefs of the Military-Transport Collegiums constitute the Presidium of the Supreme Court, the competency of which is as follows:

1. Concerning the management and the administration of the Supreme Court and its subordinate institutions and officials:
   (a) The assigning of their duties to the various members of the Supreme Court;
   (b) The examination and confirmation of accounts and reports of the separate Collegiums and sections, and the compilation of accounts and reports embracing the entire Supreme Court.
2. In respect of control of legal institutions:
   (a) The appointment of special inquiries into, and investigation of, the activity of provincial courts and other courts of equal status, at the initiative of the Public Prosecutor of the Republic, and hearing the results of such inquiries;
   (b) The institution of disciplinary proceedings against the members of the Supreme Court, the presidents of provincial courts and of other courts of equal status, as well as against vicepresidents, either in consequence of inquiries held, or upon individual information received from the

Public Prosecutor of the Republic, and the imposition of disciplinary punishment upon the officials mentioned within the limits of the power vested in the Presidium.

(c) The convoking of plenary sessions of the Supreme Court.
Note: At the sessions of the Presidium the Assistant Public Prosecutor of the Republic (Public Prosecutor of the Supreme Court) shall be bound to participate with an advisory vote.

Article 60. The plenary sessions of the Supreme Court are to consist of all available members of the Supreme Court, but of no fewer than one half of their number, and shall be presided over by the President or the Vice-President; the Public Prosecutor of the Republic or his Senior Assistant are bound to be present at such sessions; the competency of the Sessions is as follows:

1. The correct interpretation of the laws concerning questions of "legal practice," on the initiative of the various Collegiums or special sessions of one or another Collegium, or on the representation of the Presidium of the Supreme Court, the Public Prosecutor of the Republic, or his Assistant attached to the Supreme Court.
2. The investigation, alteration and revision of judgements of ordinary or appeals collegiums of the Supreme Court and of any other court in the Republic, on the representation of the Presidium of the Central Executive Committee, the Public Prosecutor of the Republic, the Presidium of the Supreme Court, and in consequence of protests lodged by the presidents of the sessions of such collegiums or by the public prosecutors attached to them.
3. The election of the Disciplinary Collegium of the Supreme Court.
4. The examination of all other questions submitted to the Plenary Session of the Supreme Court.

Chapter X

Personnel of the Appeals and Ordinary Collegiums (Sections) of the Supreme Court.

Article 61. The Appeals Sections function under the personal supervision and management of the President of the Supreme Court. His direct assistants in the Appeals Section are the president's of the Criminal and Civil Appeals Sub-sections of the Supreme Court. The President has the right to preside over the examination of any case dealt with by the appeals sub-sections.

Article 62. The ordinary session of an appeals collegium (sub-section) is to be composed of three persons: the chairman, and two members out of the eight permanent members of the appeals sub-sections (four per each sub-section).

To the Criminal and Civil Appeals sub-sections are attached two Assistant-Public Prosecutors of the Supreme Court to each.

Article 63. The Vice-President of the Supreme Court has within his competency all matters dealt with by the Supreme Court without previous examination by any lower court; his direct assistants are the chairman of the judicial (ordinary) collegium (section), and the chairman of the military and the military transport sections of the Supreme Court.

Article 64. The Judicial (ordinary) Section consists of the Chairman (president) of the Section, and four members. A session of the section is to be made up of three participants, including the chairman. As chairman of the Judicial Section may act also the Vice-President of the Supreme Court.

Two Assistant-Public Prosecutors of the Supreme Court are attached to the Judicial Session.

Article 65. The Military and the Military-Transport Sections consist each of a president, vice-president, and four members of the Supreme Court.

A session of each section is also to be composed of three participants, including the chairman, and two members who are to be told off for duty by a mode to be fixed by the president of each section.

To the military and the military-transport sections two assistant-public prosecutors of the Supreme Court are attached, one to each.

Article 66. For the judicial sections of the Supreme Tribunal a uniform preliminary investigation department is to be established to be made up of examining magistrates for important affairs; further a uniform record system for the registration of cases under examination, which is to be under the supervision of the Public Prosecutor of the Supreme Court and the Vice-President who has the entire judicial part of the Supreme Court under him.

Article 67. The mode of appointing and approving members of sessions, of rendering accounts and reports, and of supervision of local military and military-transport legal institutions subordinate to the military and military-transport sections is dealt with by special rules set forth below (Chapter XII).

Article 68. The Disciplinary Section of the Supreme Court is composed of three persons from the number of the Members of the Supreme Court, including the "presiding member" of the Presidium, all of whom are elected by the Plenary Session of the Supreme Court.

Chapter XI

Disciplinary Liability of Legal Workers.

Article 69. The Public Prosecutor of the Republic has the right to institute disciplinary proceedings against all persons, without exception, working in legal institutions of the R.S.F.S.R.

Article 70. The President of the Supreme Court and the Assistant-Public Prosecutor of the Republic attached to the Supreme Court have the right to institute disciplinary proceedings in respect to all legal workers employed in institutions subordinate to the Supreme Court, that is to say, presidents of sections and members of sections of the Supreme Court, presidents and vice-presidents of Provincial Courts and courts of equal status, Provincial Public Prosecutors and the Assistants (deputies), and all officials attached to the Provincial Court.

Article 71. The presidents of the Provincial Courts and Provincial Public Prosecutors have the right to institute disciplinary proceedings against all persons employed in institutions subordinate to the Provincial Courts.

Article 72. The president and the Public Prosecutors of the Military and the Military-Transport Sections of the Supreme Court have the right to institute disciplinary proceedings against all persons employed in subordinate institutions.

Article 73. As reasons for instituting disciplinary proceedings the following shall be regarded:

(a) Offences committed by, and conduct or actions of, legal workers, which, although not constituting criminal offences, are yet incompatible with the dignity of legal workers, irrespective of whether such conduct or actions have taken place while in an official capacity or not.

(b) Revision, by the Supreme Court, of a number of judgements and findings pronounced by legal workers, which are not in keeping with the general spirit of the laws of the R.S.F.S.R. and the interests of the masses of the toilers.

Articles 74. The following disciplinary punishments may be imposed:

(a) Reprimand;
(b) Severe reprimand;
(c) Transfer and reduction to a lower grade of office;
(d) Dismissal from service and withdrawal of the right to work in legal capacities for a fixed period.

Article 75. Disciplinary proceedings may be instituted not later than one year after the incriminated offence has been committed.

Article 76. Disciplinary proceedings instituted in consequence of a complaint lodged by a private person cannot be dropped at the request of the complainant.

Article 77. Prior to the trial of the case by the Disciplinary Section the latter is to collect the necessary evidence, to hear the explanations of the accused, and may instruct a member of the Section, or a member of the Provincial Court, or a People's Judge, as the case may be, to conduct personal investigation.

Article 78. The Disciplinary Section shall inform the accused of the date when the case is to be examined, and the accused may be present at the session to give personal explanations.

Article 79. If required the Disciplinary Section may summon the accused to appear at the trial, in which case it shall be compulsory for the accused to put in an appearance.

Article 80. The Disciplinary Section is not bound to any formalities; the mode of conducting the case is entirely left to the discretion of the Section, on the condition, however, that if the Section resolves to hear the Public Prosecutor on the subject, it shall also after him hear the accused.

Article 81. Members of the Section may be challenged in the ordinary way.

Article 82. The decisions of the Disciplinary Section are called "resolutions," the records of the sessions are to be kept in the form of records of the organizing sessions of the court, stating the names of the persons present at the session.

Article 83. Appeals against resolutions of disciplinary sections of Provincial Courts may be lodged with the Supreme Court within seven days. Resolutions of the Disciplinary Section of the Supreme Court cannot be appealed against.

Article 84. If, in the case dealt with, the Disciplinary Section perceives characteristics of an indictable criminal offence, the Section shall be held to suspend proceedings and to hand over the case to the competent criminal investigation authorities.

Part IV

Chapter XII

Special Judicial Institutions (Courts) for Special Offenses.

Article 85. The military and military-transport legal institutions of the R.S.F.S.R. and of all allied and autonomous Republics function under the general control and supervision of the Commissariat of Justice and the Supreme Court of the R.S.F.S.R. The organization and the immediate supervision over the activity of the military and military-transport legal institutions are incumbent upon the Military and the Military-Transport Sections of the Supreme Court.

Article 86. The following are military legal institutions:

(a) Military District or Front Tribunals—attached to the Revolutionary Military Soviets of Military Districts or Fronts;
(b) Military Corps Tribunals—attached to Army Corps;
(c) Divisional Sections of District Tribunals—attached to divisions;

In times of war or at the theater of war Military Army Tribunals or Military territorial Tribunals may be organized in addition to the above; also branches of Military Corps Tribunals may be attached to divisions on active service in the field. The number of Military Tribunals in action, in times or war as well as of peace, shall be fixed each time by resolution of the Presidium of the Supreme Court, on the representation of the Military Section of the Supreme Court.

Article 87. Transport Tribunals are established:

In Moscow, Petrograd, Kharkov, Rostov-on-Don, Omsk, Tashkent, and Smolensk.

The liquidation of existing transport tribunals, and the foundation of new ones, are to take place by resolution, each time, of the Presidium of the Supreme Court, on the representation of the Military-Transport Section of the Supreme Court.

Article 88. The Military Tribunal of the District of the Front is to consist of its President, Vice-President, and four members elected by the Military Section from the number of candidates nominated by the Revolutionary Military Soviet of the District or the Front, or by the commander of the forces, and approved by the Military Collegium, with the concurrence of the Revolutionary Military Soviet of the Republic.

The Military Corps Tribunal consists of a President and four members selected by the Military Section of the Supreme Court from the number of candidates nominated by the Revolutionary Military Soviet of the District or the Front.

The Military Tribunal of the Division consists of President, Vice-President, and four members approved by the Military Tribunal of the District or the Front.

Article 89. The Transport Tribunals consist of a President, a Vice-President, and four Members, nominated by the District Plenipotentiary of the Commissariat of Roads of Communication and approved by the Military-Transport Section of the Supreme Court, with the concurrence of the Commissariat of Ways of Communication.

Note: According to the volume of business to be dealt with, the number of members may in the separate Transport Tribunals be increased to seven, by resolution of the Presidium of the Supreme Court.

Article 90. The Military and Military-Transport Sections have the right to transfer and remove at any time the presidents and the members of Military and Transport Tribunals, giving notice of it at the same time to the Revolutionary Military Soviets concerned, or to the Commissar of Ways of Communication.

Article 91. In all disciplinary matters the Military Tribunals attached to the districts corps and armies, and the Transport District Tribunals, are subordinate to the Disciplinary Section of the Supreme Court; and the Military Tribunals at the divisions—to the disciplinary sections of the Military District and Corps Tribunals.

Article 92. Labor Sessions of People's Courts are to be formed at each Provincial Court, and are to consist of one permanent people's judge, and two permanent members of court: one appointed by the local Provincial Trade Union Soviet, and the other by the local Provincial Labor Section; and shall function in the same fashion, and according to the same rules as the People's Courts.

Article 93. Appeals against decisions of the Labor Session are to be lodged in the usual fashion with the Provincial Court which is charged with immediate supervision and control of the Labor Sessions of the People's Court (Article 4 of the Act.) Conditions of eligibility to the post of people's judge presiding over labor session, and the mode of his appointment and recall, are the same as in the case of all other People's Courts of the province.

Article 94. The Land and Arbitration Commissions formed for the settlement of land and property disputes between State organs (decree of May 24, 1922, Collection of Laws, 1922, No. 428; and decree of September 21, 1922, Collection of Laws, 1922, No. 769) function in accordance with their respective promulgated organization acts, and are subordinate to the Commissariat of Justice and its organs; in the province—to the plenary sessions of the Provincial Courts and the Public Prosecutor's Department, and in the center—to the Supreme Court and the Public Proscutor of the Republic (Articles 4, 5 and cause 2 of Article 60 of the Act).

SOME ASPECTS OF THE GERMAN LEGAL SYSTEM UNDER NATIONAL SOCIALISM.

THE legal system of a country may be perverted in two different ways. On the one hand, what Professor Campbell has called 'the spirit of legality'[1] may be openly denied; law is then regarded merely as the instrument whereby the arbitrary will of the ruler is put into effect. It is Professor Campbell's contention that in National Socialist Germany this was the dominant conception of law. On the other hand, it is possible to pay lip-service to the spirit of legality, but at the same time to deny it in practice by evasion of the legal process and by permitting or encouraging corruption and by covert interference in its functioning. Perversion of justice of the latter type is not peculiar to totalitarian countries. Its remedy is not mysterious; it is a question of a sound administrative framework and the right personnel. The first type of perversion, however, does not respond so readily to these well-tried remedies. The more honest the judge, who conceives as law the will of the Fuehrer, the more completely will he suppress in his decisions that judicial independence which is one of the most important characteristics of the spirit of legality. It is this difficulty which leads Professor Campbell to describe the problem of Germany's future treatment as a question not of teaching a wrongdoer a lesson, but of curing a madman.[2] It is submitted, however, that Professor Campbell, in making a contrast between Fascist Italy and National Socialist Germany, underestimates the role which straightforward—if the word is permissible—deception, corruption and political pressure played in the perversion of German justice. This is not to say that National Socialist legal theorists like Professor Höhn, whom Professor Campbell cites, did not enjoy great influence in Germany, particularly with lawyers trained after 1933. Nor does it minimize the extent to which German justice was perverted under the National Socialist regime. But it is doubtful whether the subservience of the law to the executive would have been so complete in Germany, unless there had been something more substantial than a theory of law to secure it. Having had some special facilities for studying the working of the German legal system before and during the war, the present writer is impressed by the extent to which, in the later years of the Nazi regime, it became necessary to employ an increasing measure of political and financial pressure on judges and lawyers to make this subservience effective. It may therefore be of interest to give some details of the less mystical aspects of law under National Socialism before they are forgotten; the importance of theoretical writings is sometimes overestimated by historians because they are more easily accessible than the actual practice, and future historians of the German legal system may find themselves in difficulties if they have to explain the

---

[1] 62 L. Q. R., p. 141.
[2] *Ibid.* p. 151.

prostitution of a once respected legal system[3] solely as the result of general belief in a theory of law, which a practising lawyer in any country may think hard to swallow.

I. Evasion of the Legal Process.

National Socialism had its own theory of law, but it never had complete confidence that the theory had been accepted by the legal profession. It sought, therefore, to discourage recourse to the professional legal adviser and to stifle litigation by the exercise of various forms of pressure on the interested parties.

(a) *Criminal Cases.*

The power of the Gestapo to arrest without warrant, to imprison without judicial sentence and to re-arrest after judicial acquittal are well known; in such cases it was not merely the judge but, as a general rule, the lawyer also who was deprived of his function; only where a lawyer had some personal 'pull'—as, for example, where he could find among the Gestapo officials a former fellow-member of some student organization—was it possible for him to achieve anything on behalf of a client who had fallen foul of the Gestapo. The encroachment of the Gestapo on the criminal jurisdiction of the Courts had some formal legal basis, as far as protective custody was concerned, in decrees of February 28, 1933, and March 8, 1934, while within the confines of Prussia a decision of the Prussian Administrative Court, confirmed by a Prussian law of February 10, 1936, laid down that the activities of the Gestapo were not subject to judicial review.[4] But the real power of the Gestapo to ignore the Courts was based on their influence with the Public Prosecutor's Office (Staatsanwaltschaft). They could, through the Staatsanwaltschaft, suppress proceedings in the ordinary Courts, if they wished to deal with the offender themselves, or if the proceedings might throw unwelcome light on their activities. The control of the Gestapo over the Staatsanwaltschaft was no doubt made easier by the appointment of Staatsanwälte who shared with Gestapo officials the conception of law as a mere instrument of the executive. But, in fact, the existence of the Gestapo with its own intelligence service (Sicherheitsdienst) meant that many cases never came to the ears of the Staatsanwaltschaft at all, whereas before 1933 the Staatsanwaltschaft and police worked in the closest collaboration. After 1933 the police, and particularly the Criminal Police, came more and more under the central authority of the Secret Police, instead of under the local Staatsanwaltschaft. Indeed, the complete abolition of the Staatsanwaltschaft was mooted, but here, as in other spheres, Nazi policy seemed to have been to preserve existing legal institutions, while undermining their importance by little publicized but fundamental changes in administrative practice.

The Gestapo was not the only organization that filched business from the Courts. Submission to penalties imposed by officials in respect of offences against certain revenue laws existed before 1933, but such sub-

[3] See, *e.g.*, Ensor, Courts and Judges, O. U. P. 1933, p. 52. The author, writing at the beginning of 1933, considered that the German judicial system had high claims to be regarded as the best in Europe.

[4] On the legal basis of the Gestapo, see O. C. Giles, The Gestapo, Oxford Pamphlets on World Affairs, No. 36, pp. 10–15.

mission was voluntary. After 1938 this procedure (Unterwerfungsverfahren) became much more frequent in all matters concerning taxes, price control and foreign exchange; the offender still had the nominal choice of submission to the decision of the official or of a formal trial, but in practice he was subject to very strong pressure, as he knew that the official concerned could at any stage put his case in the hands of the Gestapo. Legal control of the official, theoretically ensured by administrative Courts, was actually ineffective. The administrative Courts, although never abolished, lost their importance owing to a severe curtailment of remedies; during the war they had little or no business, and new judicial appointments were frequently not made when vacancies occurred.

As between its members the Party asserted the right to hear all cases of defamation before any proceedings were brought in the ordinary Courts. There was no formal law to justify this encroachment of the Party Courts of Honour on the jurisdiction of the ordinary Courts, but the Party obtained knowledge through the Staatsanwaltschaft of all cases of defamation pending in the ordinary Courts and could apply appropriate pressure to the prosecutor. It should be explained that in German law a private prosecution is practically the only remedy open to a person who considers himself libelled or slandered; further, that the extent of the Party's encroachment on the Courts was in practice much greater than might at first sight appear, because the conception of defamation was widely interpreted; the Party authorities could, for example, include within it a simple case of breach of contract merely by regarding the allegation of the breach as an attack on a person's reputation.

(*b*) *Civil Cases.*

Direct interference by the Party authorities in civil cases was much less frequent than in criminal cases. But one reason was that the Party ensured that comparatively few civil cases in which it was interested ever came before the Courts. The local Party leaders, Ortsgruppenleiter, Kreisleiter, or in important cases Gauleiter, generally encouraged persons in their area to bring their difficulties to them rather than to professional lawyers; assisted by advisers with some elementary legal training, they would attempt to effect a settlement on a non-legal basis, naturally with an eye to Party interests. The other person in the dispute who had not appealed to the Party leader could still proceed with the case at law, but disregard of the Party's efforts at reconciliation was dangerous.

Apart from the quasi-judicial role assumed by Party leaders, various Party organizations maintained departments, which offered the public free legal advice and discouraged recourse to the ordinary legal process. Even the organization of the lawyers themselves, the Nationalsozialistischer Rechtswahrerbund (N.S.R.B.), organized legal advice bureaux (Rechtsbetreuungsstellen) at the Courts. But it is significant that for the most part these bureaux were manned by civil servants in the executive grade. The work was nominally voluntary and unpaid; the Party could therefore be reasonably certain that the sort of advice given would generally be in accordance with National Socialist principles. The Deutsche Arbeitsfront (D.A.F) also had its own Rechtsbetreuungsstellen, nominally to advise employers and employees on labour problems; in fact, the D.A.F. interfered in many matters only very indirectly concerned with employment, such as defamation between employer and employee, landlord and tenant questions and even disputes relating to mortgages. Similarly, the Nationalsozialistische Volkswohlfahrt (N.S.V.) claimed to offer legal advice and effect reconciliation in any matter connected with social welfare. For example, they often ran a Mietschlichtungsstelle or office for settling disputes between landlord and tenant; if, in spite of their efforts, a case reached the Courts they might send a representative who would sit by the party they favoured and possibly attempt to address the judge; a judge so placed had to be very firm and tactful if he was to succeed on the one hand in maintaining his judicial independence, and on the other, in keeping out of the black books of the Party. The quasi-judicial functions of the organizations mentioned above had no specific legal authority, but the commissions set up by every Chamber of Commerce (Industrie- und Handelskammer), in order to attempt a reconciliation in cases concerned with unfair competition, were provided for in an amendment to the law dealing with the topic. The Nazi policy in this respect is perhaps characteristic of their general attitude towards law. On the one hand, the jurisdiction of the ordinary Courts to try cases of unfair competition was not denied; the amendment merely ordered the Courts to stay proceedings until an attempt at reconciliation had been made by a committee of local business men. Failing reconciliation, the committee would express an opinion on the merits of the case which, although it had no binding force, might be cited as persuasive authority in any subsequent proceedings before the ordinary Courts. This was, on its face, a not unreasonable scheme, calculated to appeal to the business man with a healthy dislike of litigation. On the other hand, it was highly improbable in reality that a case which had come before the committee would ever be brought before the Courts; a tradesman who challenged its decision would hardly find it possible to continue business. Further, National Socialism could be fairly sure of the 'reliability' of the committee, which was appointed by the President of the Industrie- und Handelskammer, almost invariably a confirmed Party man.

Another way in which the Courts were deprived of civil business was by increasing recourse to what was in effect compulsory arbitration. The various Trade Groups (Wirtschaftsgruppen), in which every aspect of industry and business were organized, would insist on an arbitration clause in all contracts made between their members; the arbitrator—who might or might not be a lawyer, and, if he was a lawyer, was probably a briefless Party man—was appointed by the organization concerned. In such arbitration proceedings representation by lawyers, although not forbidden, was discouraged, by disallowing a lawyer's fees in the costs, which lay in the discretion of the arbitrator.

II. Legal Personnel.

German legal training is prolonged. Before the war it involved a minimum period of study of three years at a University, culminating in an examination for the grade of Referendar. This was followed by a further three years' practical training at various Courts, public prosecutors' officers and administrative departments of the judicial service.[5] After a further examination the Referendar became an Assessor and had a further three years of training before he was appointed Gerichtsassessor, if he intended to be a judge, or a Staatsanwaltsassessor if he had chosen the public prosecutor's office. If he wanted to set up in practice on his own account he had first to serve what was in effect three years' articles with an approved lawyer. After 1939 some shortening of these periods took place, but in the twelve years of National Socialist rule, during six of which a large proportion of possible candidates were at the front, it was clearly impossible to produce any considerable number of lawyers who were the complete products of National Socialist legal teaching. It is true that great efforts were made to indoctrinate all persons concerned in the administration of law with National Socialist legal conceptions. To this end special courses were run by the N.S.R.B. and were attended under varying degrees of compulsion by judges, public prosecutors, practising lawyers and Court officials. These Schulungskurse continued even during the later years of the war. The instruction was given by local lawyers with reliable Party connexions and the subjects discussed were of a politico-legal significance, such as the interpretation of the law relating to hereditary farmsteads (Erbhofgesetz). Nevertheless, it does not appear that the legal profession as a whole ever swallowed the National Socialist concept of law, although doubtless, if the regime had continued for another ten or twenty years, it would have succeeded in producing sufficient selected recruits to the profession to ensure a generally accepted viewpoint. This is not to say that the legal profession proved a serious obstacle to National Socialist plans, but the reasons for its ineffectiveness were not wholly ideological; it was also the result of clever National Socialist exploitation of weaknesses in the organization of the German legal profession and of the ordinary human frailty of lawyers.

National Socialism had not complete faith in its power to indoctrinate the legal profession with a new conception of law. This is shown by the attention which was given not merely to what was taught but to whom it was taught. At various stages in the course of his education the law student had to satisfy the authorities of his 'political reliability', a test which was easy to impose in view of the direct responsibility of the State in Germany—even before 1933—for legal education. Thus, the law student, apart from passing an examination, had to submit proof of his 'political reliability' before he was admitted as Referendar, the authority competent to issue certificates of such reliability being the Gauleitung of the Party. At a later stage in his career the student, who, as Assessor, applied for employment in the judicial service or in the Staatsanwaltschaft, had to produce a political testimonial (politisches Führungszeugnis) from the Kreisleitung of the Party. And no promotions in the judicial service or in the Staatsanwaltschaft could take place with-

[5] The National Socialists opened in 1933 the Hans Kerrl Gemeinschaftslager, a camp for the political and physical training of Referendare, who had to attend for a two months' course. Until 1937 great emphasis was laid on physical training, which was carried out by S.A. and S.S. leaders. This seems to have met with a good deal of resistance from the Referendare, most of whom had already done their military service. After 1937 the course mainly consisted of lectures and discussions on the Nazi conception of law, the interpretation of specific laws and political indoctrination. The camp was disbanded shortly after the outbreak of war.

out a similar Führungszeugnis. The National Socialist plan was to avoid a wholesale purge of the judiciary or Staatsanwaltschaft but to appoint long-standing Party members to key positions, such as that of Oberlandesgerichtspräsident or Generalstaatsanwalt, who then gradually effected new appointments and promotions in accordance with Party views.

Control of the practising lawyer presented a somewhat different problem, but it was facilitated by the fact that there was in Germany, even before 1933, no single body with comparable powers and prestige to that enjoyed by the General Council of the Bar and the Inns of Court or by the Law Society. Local Chambers of Lawyers (Anwaltskammern), elected by all the lawyers practising in the district, were, before 1933, responsible for admissions to, and disciplinary supervision of, the profession. The Anwaltskammer continued to exist after 1933, but lost its independence. The President of the Anwaltskammer became the appointee of the President of the Reichsrechtsanwaltskammer after consultation with the leader of the N.S.R.B. in the Gau and with the Gestapo authorities. The President of the Anwaltskammer in his turn appointed the other members of the Anwaltskammer. Thus professional solidarity against the attacks of the State was made impossible, while the outward appearance of a separate professional organization was maintained. The independence of the profession was further undermined by the organization of practically all persons engaged in the administration of law in a specifically Party organization, the N.S.R.B. Membership was not compulsory, but non-membership involved many serious disadvantages. For example, the lucrative post of Notar was reserved in practice for members of the N.S.R.B., who also were the sole recipients of poor persons' cases, which in Germany provide most practising lawyers with a substantial part of their income; similarly, a lawyer who was not a member of the N.S.R.B., was excluded from the use of their law libraries and from the special insurance scheme against sickness and death which was run by the N.S.R.B. The fact that virtually all lawyers were members of the N.S.R.B. did not of itself ensure that they would carry out their functions in accordance with National Socialist policy, but it gave the National Socialist legal theorists the formal right to speak in the name of the legal profession as a whole, and emphasized the isolation of the lawyer out of sympathy with the regime.

Where it was impossible to secure the co-operation of all lawyers, National Socialism was not above the well-tried device of offering material advantages to Party lawyers. For example, the Courts were instructed when appointing trustees in bankruptcy, judicial liquidators, etc., to give preference to old Party lawyers. It has already been mentioned that no lawyer other than a member of the N.S.R.B. could become a Notar, but even amongst members of the N.S.R.B. it was the old Party members who received preferential treatment. Similarly, when the Party leaders failed to settle disputes which had come to their notice it was naturally to the Party lawyers that they gave the opportunity of any legal 'pickings'.

III. THE COURTS.

(a) Special Courts.

In spite of the wide powers given to judges to create new offences by analogy,[6] National Socialism had not full confidence that they would exercise their authority in accordance with Party policy. As in civil cases, the attempt was to take business out of the hands of the Courts altogether, so in criminal cases an increasing number of cases were exclusively dealt with by the Gestapo. But it is characteristic of the whole National Socialist policy towards the law that the functions of the criminal Courts were never entirely superseded by the Gestapo; it was judged more expedient to set up special Courts, nominally within the framework of the judicial system, but in fact subject to close State control. These Sondergerichte were created in March, 1933, with the ostensible purpose of expediting the administration of criminal justice, and before the war they dealt mainly with infringement of the Law relating to Malicious Attacks upon State and Party and the Protection of Party Uniform, 1934 (Heimtückegesetz). After the outbreak of war the jurisdiction of the Sondergerichte was extended to cover offences against the Broadcasting Decrees (Rundfunkverordnungen), offences against the Decree for the Protection of the German War Effort (Verordnung zum Schutze der Wehrkraft des deutschen Volkes),[7] offences against the War Economy Decree (Kriegswirtschaftsverordnung), rationing offences (under the Verbrauchsregelungsstrafverordnung) and offences against the Decree against Crimes of Violence (Gewaltverbrecherverordnung). Furthermore, the Sondergericht could try any criminal case which the Public Prosecutor thought fit to bring before it. By the end of the war the Sondergerichte dealt in practice with all serious crimes which did not go to another National Socialist judicial creation, the Volksgerichtshof in Berlin, or which were kept exclusively in the hands of the Gestapo.

The Sondergerichte were more satisfactory from the National Socialist point of view than the ordinary criminal Courts. In the first place, there was no possibility of appeal. Indeed, the scales were weighted against the accused in that the Public Prosecutor had the right to lodge a 'complaint of nullity' (Nichtigkeitsbeschwerde) with the Reichsgericht where he wished to set aside an acquittal or to increase a sentence; in theory, he could equally apply to have a conviction quashed or a sentence reduced, but here again we have a good example of National Socialist tenderness with the forms of law once they were sure of the reliability of the men who would put the theory into practice. In the second place, the judges of the Sondergericht were carefully chosen by the President of the Oberlandesgericht of the district to which the particular Sondergericht belonged. The Oberlandesgerichtspräsidenten, or, at any rate, their personnel advisers, were almost always reliable Party men, and they took particular care to obtain co-operative presiding judges in the Sondergerichte. The latter were in several cases drawn not from the judiciary but from the Staatsanwaltschaft; the junior judges were often quite young men, who had undergone at least a part of their training

[6] Cf. the law, dated June 28, 1935, quoted by Professor Campbell, at p. 149.

[7] Offences against this Decree committed by 'undermining the will of the German people to defend itself by warlike means' were later transferred to the People's Court (Volksgerichtshof) at Berlin.

since legal education had come under National Socialist influence, and who, in any event, were anxious not to jeopardize their careers by a show of scruples.

(b) *Methods of Controlling the Judges.*

Constitutional lawyers in considering the machinery whereby the independence of the judiciary may be ensured generally lay the main emphasis on the irremovability of the judges, as guaranteed by such enactments as the Bill of Rights or Article 104 of the Weimar Constitution. But although the National Socialists certainly undermined the independence of the judiciary it is a remarkable fact that they did not find it necessary to remove any high proportion of the judges, apart from those of Jewish race. Nor, on the other hand, did they secure general acceptance of their peculiar theories of law. The explanation of German judicial subservience to the State—in as far as the ordinary judges were allowed to decide important issues—is mainly to be found in the special forms of pressure which the State could bring to bear on the individual judge. Less obvious, but more effective than the crude threat of the Gestapo, was the power to block the promotion of the comparatively ill-paid junior judge. There are many cases of Amtsrichter whose career of compromise with National Socialism began with some minor act of compliance—acquitting a local Party leader of some motor offence, for example—which was induced by the lively fear of remaining an Amtsrichter all their lives; and there are some cases in which Amtsrichter who had faithfully carried out the law were relegated to an obscure country town for the rest of the regime. The disadvantages of the system, whereby the judicial and legal profession are separated from the outset, which Mr. Ensor pointed out in 1933,[8] have been amply demonstrated in Germany under National Socialist rule.

Having carefully chosen the judges on the Sondergerichte, it might have been expected that National Socialism would have had sufficient confidence in their understanding of the National Socialist theory of law to allow them a comparatively free hand. It is therefore instructive to examine the process whereby the judges in the Sondergerichte arrived at their decisions, because such examination reveals behind the façade of judicial independence an elaborate system of administrative directions enforced by various forms of pressure. This system was not the product of an uncertain revolutionary phase, to be superseded when the judges had fully assimilated the new theory of law. It was a semi-secret procedure, carried out by persons who, generally speaking, were fully conscious of its illegality, and it was intensified rather than relaxed in the last years of the regime. Indeed, the system was not fully developed until after the death of the Minister of Justice, Gürtner, in 1942. His death was followed by a struggle between two notorious Nazis, Frank and Freisler, for the post; in the result a third person, Thierack, was appointed, to the dissatisfaction of Party circles. By way of compensation, they secured the appointment of Rothenberger, an ambitious and unscrupulous judge from Hamburg, to the post of Secretary of State in the Ministry of Justice, a position which he held until 1944. During his

[8] *Op. cit.* at p. 80.

tenure of office the main features of the system described below were developed.

A comparatively mild form of direction was contained in the 'Judges' Notes' (Richterbriefe), issued once a month by the Ministry of Justice to all judges and public prosecutors in Germany. These notes summarized and commented on recent decisions, both criminal and civil. The novelty lay in the fact that the comment was official. As far as criminal cases were concerned, the comments were mainly directed to adequacy of punishment. More specific direction was given to the presiding judges and sometimes to all the judges of the Sondergerichte, who were periodically summoned to a conference at the Oberlandesgericht of their district. At such conferences the Generalstaatsanwalt might add his comments to those of the Oberlandesgerichtspräsident on general policy governing verdict and sentences. Criticism of past judgments in Richterbriefe and at conferences in the Oberlandesgericht, however, did not achieve the results desired by the political authorities. Judges were therefore given a hint before the trial of official expectations in regard to individual cases. Every week the presiding judge had to send a short summary of all cases to be heard in the following week to the Oberlandesgerichtspräsident of the district. This summary was called the 'preview' (Vorschau). Before the trial the Oberlandesgerichtspräsident informed the Landesgerichtspräsident what punishments were expected in higher circles to be inflicted in the forthcoming cases; the Landesgerichtspräsident duly informed the presiding judges of the Sondergerichte in order that official circles might not be disappointed. However, it seems that they sometimes were, because it was found necessary to introduce a 'review' (Nachschau) as well as a Vorschau. This was a summary of all judgments delivered by the Sondergericht during the previous week, and was presumably used to check the extent to which earlier instructions had been obeyed.

A study of German law, as it actually worked under National Socialism rather than as it was professed by academic writers, invites both discouraging and hopeful conclusions. On the one hand, it becomes clear that many members of the legal profession participated under varying pressure in a system which violated their own conceptions of law. On the other hand, we are not, as Professor Campbell suggests, forced to conclude that the more familiar methods of dealing with a corrupted legal system can have little application to Germany. A careful examination of National Socialist legal appointments, the re-establishment of the independence and quasi-judicial function of the Staatsanwaltschaft and of the professional solidarity of the legal profession, the freeing of judges (possibly by a new policy of appointments from the Bar in middle life) from the dangerous quest for promotion, and above all the suppression of authorities usurping the judicial function—these are measures which may go a long way towards the restoration of the German legal system to its former respected place. May this article conclude with the hope that before long a member of the Legal Division of the Control Commission for Germany will give some account to his fellow-lawyers of the work which is being done towards this end.

NORMAN S. MARSH.

[27]

KEITH S. ROSENN

The Jeito

Brazil's Institutional Bypass of the Formal Legal System and its Developmental Implications

I. INTRODUCTION

A perceptive satirical study of the Brazilian way of life relates a European immigrant's first contact with Brazilian administrative practice.[1] During his visa appointment with the Brazilian consul in Paris, the would-be immigrant was asked his profession. He replied that he had recently graduated from medical school. The consul responded, "Then in place of doctor, let's put down agronomist. In that way I can issue you a visa immediately. You know how these things are? Professional quotas, confidential instructions from the department of immigration. Nonsense! . . . In any event, this way will make it perfectly legal."

At first the European protested, thinking the consul was trying to trap him into making a false declaration. But the consul persisted, explaining putting down agronomist instead of physician would create no problem. Indeed, what he was doing was resorting to the *jeito* (an untranslatable term that corresponds roughly to a "knack," "twist," "way," or "fix"), which is in the finest Brazilian tradition. But it was only after living some time in Brazil that this "medical-agronomist" grasped what the consul had been trying to explain. It was then he realized that he had immigrated to a country "whose governmental regulations and instructions are decreed with prior calculations about the percentage that will be obeyed, whose people constitute a large legal filter, and whose civil servants, be they small or powerful, create their own law. And though this law does not happen to correspond with the original law, it meets with general approbation, pro-

---

KEITH S. ROSENN is Professor of Law, Ohio State University and Member of the Board of Editors. He wishes to thank the Social Science Research Council for financial support that enabled him to return to Brazil to complete research on this article, and to thank the Centro de Estudos e Pesquisas do Direito (CEPED) for generously extending research facilities to him. A number of colleagues offered helpful criticisms of an earlier draft, especially Professor Henry Steiner of the Harvard Law School, Professor Howard Wiarda of the Department of Political Science of the University of Massachusetts, and Eric Seiff, Esq., Legal Advisor to the AID Mission in Rio de Janeiro. He is grateful for their assistance and comments, but is solely responsible for opinions and any errors.

1. P. Kelleman, *Brasil para Principiantes* (8th ed. 1964).

vided that it is dictated by common sense."[2]

There is obviously some hyperbole in this description, but it contains a kernel of truth. Brazilian laws and regulations are regularly twisted to the demands of expediency by government officials and private citizens alike. Plainly Brazil is not unique in this respect; bending of legal norms to expediency occurs in all countries, be they developed or developing.[3] It is especially common in Latin America, where the gap between the law on the books and actual practice is notoriously large. Thus much of what is said here in the context of Brazil has more universal application. But what is striking about Brazil is that the practice of bending legal norms to expediency has been elevated into a highly prized paralegal institution called *jeito*. The *jeito* is an integral part of Brazil's legal culture, and in many areas of the law it is employed normally rather than exceptionally.

Jeito is easier to describe than to define, for the Brazilians use the term and its diminutive, *jeitinho*, in many different senses. A visiting French social scientist, unable to find any equivalent in French, simply characterized the *jeito* as "an ingenious maneuver that renders the impossible, possible; the unjust, just; and the illegal, legal."[3] A Brazilian sociologist has characterized the *jeito* as "a genuinely Brazilian process for resolving difficulties despite the content of [legal] norms, codes, and laws."[5] The difficulty with this definition (indeed with the *jeito* itself) is that it is a catchall encompassing several distinct modes of behavior that have very different implications for a society's functioning. Whether the Brazilian consul classified the European doctor as an agronomist because of sympathy, a bribe, or a sincere belief that the country needed doctors just as urgently as agronomists, Brazilians would refer to the act as a *jeito*. For analytic purposes the *jeito* can be broken down into at least five different kinds of behavior frequently observed in Brazil:

(1) When a public servant deviates from his legal obligations because of private pecuniary or status (friends, family, or clique) gains. *E.g.*, a government contract is awarded to the highest briber.

(2) When private citizens employ subterfuges to circumvent legal obligations which are sensible and just (in an objective sense). *E.g.*, a few essential parts are removed from an illegally imported car,

---

2. Id. at 11-12.

3. The functional equivalent of the *jeito* is well known in the United States, as any lawyer who has handled an uncontested divorce, invented the minutes of fictitous meetings of shareholders in small corporations, or engaged in plea bargaining in criminal cases will attest. Indeed, the keystone of American constitutional law, *Marbury v. Madison*, is a classic example of the utility of bending legal norms to expediency.

4. C. Morazé, *Les Trois Âges du Brésil* 195 (1954).

5. A. Guerreiro Ramos, *Administração e Estratégia do Desenvolvimento* 380 (1966).

which is reported to the authorities as contraband; when the car is sold at public auction, as required by law, the smuggler, who is the only one with the missing parts, is the only bidder, thus enabling him to sell the car with a clear legal title.

(3) When the speed with which a public servant performs his legal obligations depends upon private pecuniary or status gains. *E.g.*, a passport application remains unprocessed for months unless the applicant knows or tips someone in the passport office.

(4) When private citizens employ subterfuges to circumvent legal obligations which are unrealistic, unjust, or wasteful (in an objective sense). *E.g.*, real property is transferred by an agreement of sale rather than by deed to avoid capital gains taxation on nominal profits rendered largely illusory by severe inflation.

(5) When a public servant deviates from his legal obligations because of his conviction that the formal norms are unrealistic, unjust, or wasteful. *E.g.*, a labor inspector condones the failure of a marginal firm in an area of high unemployment to pay the official minimum wage on the theory that strict enforcement would likely throw many employees out of work and perhaps shut down the plant altogether.

The first two elements constitute the dishonest behavior benefitting an individual at the expense of the state—the conventional conception of corruption. The third element may also be labelled corruption by conventional standards, though most people, particularly in Brazil, would consider this kind of behavior less morally offensive than the first two forms of corruption. It is the fourth and fifth components, which illustrate behavior in which public purposes are served by evading legal norms, that bear no stigma and have made the *jeito* into such a highly prized national institution.

Obviously these categories are not mutually exclusive. Some civil servants become aware of a law's uneconomic or unjust aspects only after their palm has been greased. Occasionally, public officials cooperate with private citizens in legitimizing or facilitating vitiation of legal norms by subterfuge, such as occurred with Brazil's rent control. Residential rents remained frozen during a seventeen year period in which the cost of living rose at an annual average of more than 22 percent. The statutes prohibited the landlord from raising the rent or evicting the tenant, but permitted the landlord to retake the premises for his own use or that of his family. Many landlords simulated a personal need for the leasehold in order to secure an under-the-table rent increase or evict an undesired tenant. Recognizing the injustice created by the statute, the courts facilitated this simulation by placing the burden of proving the insincerity of the request upon the tenant, *a priori* an almost impossible task.[6] This type of *jeito*

6. Rosenn, "Controlled Rents and Uncontrolled Inflation: the Brazilian Dilemma," 17 *Am. J. Comp. L.* 239 (1969).

incorporates both the fourth and fifth elements of the above schemework.

Curiously, the *jeito* has not been considered a topic worthy of serious scholarly inquiry. As with the related institution of corruption, research on the *jeito* has been taboo for lawyers and social scientists. Part of the explanation lies in the basis of the Brazilian law schools (which until fairly recently included the social sciences) against empirical research and in favor of classical exegesis of the legal texts. Perhaps even more important is the difficulty in carrying out such research. Since the *jeito* is an extralegal transaction, people are less than candid in describing what has transpired. And the written record, at least on its face, usually appears entirely legal. In addition, there is the problem of what Gunnar Myrdal has characterized as "diplomacy in research." The *jeito* is so entwined with problems of corruption that it may be far more politic to pretend that legal rules correspond to what is done than run the risk of embarrassing friends by calling attention to the disparities.

Yet those concerned about the relationship between law and development cannot afford to neglect this aspect of the legal process, for in the long run, attitudes towards law reflected in an institution like the *jeito* or its counterparts in other societies are likely to be at least as important to the developmental process as institutions enshrined in the formal legal structure. Unfortunately, far too little is known about the frequency and the contexts in which the formal legal system is bypassed in developed or developing nations, nor has there been much analysis of the socio-economic implications of such bypassing. Considerable empirical research remains to be done. Hopefully, this preliminary attempt to outline the origins and contours of the *jeito* and to indicate some of its costs and benefits will serve to stimulate serious inquiry, particularly of an empirical bent, into the legal cultures of developing nations. If I have inadvertently offended Brazilian sensibilities in the process, I apologize.

II. The Colonial Background of the Jeito

The development of the *jeito* cannot really be understood without a brief historical background. The roots of the *jeito* run deep into the Portuguese past, which still conditions Brazilian attitudes towards governmental functioning. Portuguese colonial rule, like that of the Spanish, was the product of an absolute monarchy, with "the King as its head, chief, father, representative of God on earth, supreme dispenser of all favors, and rightful regulator of all activities, even to all the personal and individual expressions of his subjects and vassals."[7]

7. C. Prado Junior, *Formação do Brasil Contemporâneo* 297 (1942).

A. *The Legacy of Administrative Chaos*

Portuguese rule was essentially authoritarian, paternalistic, particularistic and *ad hoc*. Scanning the confused and contradictory mass of statutes, orders, opinions, regulations, *alvaras*, decrees, *cartas-de-lei*, edicts, and instructions appropriately termed the *legislação extravagante* (literally, extravagant legislation) through which the sovereign's will was transmitted to the Brazilian colony, one is amazed that the administrative machinery functioned at all.[8] Equally astonishing is extra-ordinary preoccupation with trivia. The Overseas Council (Conselho Ultramarino), the Lisbon-based administrative organ that superintended the Portuguese colonies from 1642 to 1808, directly concerned itself with even the pettiest details of Brazilian life, such as the quality of wood used for crating sugar and sex life of slaves. As one of the most astute students of Brazilian colonial life put it:

> Lisbon wanted to know about everything, and the Council was interested in everything, at least theoretically, for in practice, the

8. The Portuguese legal labyrinth was similar to that which prevailed in the Spanish colonies, though somewhat more confusing. After 1680 the Spanish colonies at least had the benefit of the *Recopilación de Leyes de los Reynos de Indias*, an official compilation of more than 6,300 laws and regulations affecting colonial life. Brazil lacked even this crude sort of official compilation.

Probably the best summary of the nature of Portuguese colonial rule is the description of two Belgian scholars:

> The institutions in the Portuguese colonies were mostly copied from those of the metropolis, without being, however, adapted to their new destination. Administrative organization never proceeded according to a uniform plan: it was determined by the march of events. The duties of many officials, their hierarchy and relations of service, were not stipulated by laws or general rules, but by a mass of special decrees, some appointing functionaries for the places, others dealing with the solution of a transitory difficulty or the supression of some abuse. Often the administrative machinery worked of itself, as a result of habit or routine, sometimes in accordance with the designs of the central government, other times against them.
>
> If the Portuguese kings since the reign of John II (1481-95) had their lawyers who gave the laws of the kingdom the interpretation most suitable to the interest of the Crown, the colonial governors also had their own legal authorities, who furnished the texts with the meaning most favorable to the power of the chiefs who respectively employed them. It is certainly not an easy task to describe this administrative machinery, even when one knows the text of the laws and decrees which have organized it, which is not always the case; but it is still more difficult to explain their real working. It is frequently impossible to distinguish with certainty the laws that were applied from those which were not applied, or which were not applied as they ought to have been, and it is not without difficulty that we are enabled to define with precision the duties of the several authorities.

C. Lannoy and H. Van Der Linden, *Histoire de l'expansion coloniale des Peuples Européens* 87-88 (1907), cited in M. Oliveira Lima, *The Evolution of Brazil compared with that of Spanish and Anglo-Saxon America* 57-58 (1914).

physical impossibility of attending to such an accumulation of paper work not only delayed dispatches, sometimes for decades, but also left a great number of cases to repose eternally in the drawers of the archives.[9]

Even the basic code, the *Ordenações Filipinas or Código Filipino*, displayed much of the same confusion, particularization, and *ad hoc* quality that characterized the supplemental *legislação extravagante*. Promulgated in 1603, the code was plainly not designed with colonial conditions in mind. Rather it was a compilation of prior compilations, which in turn had awkwardly amalgamated Roman law, the *foraes* (municipal charters and statutes), customary usage, the Visigothic Code, the *Siete Partidas*, canon law, and the general legislation of Portugal since 1211. Much of its draftsmanship was unclear to begin with, and it soon became such a hodgepodge of overlapping and inconsistent amendments that a divining rod seemed as sure a guide to legal research as any.[10] Nevertheless, the *Ordenações* remained the bulwark of Brazil's civil law until 1917, almost a century after independence and a full fifty years after Portugal itself had abandoned it.

Lei da Boa Razão (Law of Good Sense). The Portuguese did bequeath the Brazilians a canon of statutory interpretation that is but a step removed from the *jeito*. The *Lei da Boa Razão*, enacted on August 18, 1769, under the aegis of the Marquis de Pombal, *inter alia* directed the judiciary to apply Roman law to fill legislative lacunae only when it accorded with "good human sense." "Good human sense" theoretically meant consistent with natural law, defined as "the essential, intrinsic and unalterable truths which Roman ethics had established, and which were given formal recognition by divine and human laws to serve as moral or legal rules of Christianity," but in practice it encouraged judges and lawyers to look to common sense and the spirit of the law as the basis for decision when the *Ordenações* were unclear or omissive, which was often the case. The *Lei da Boa Razão* substantially increased the doctrinal freedom and legal discretion of the Brazilian judiciary and bar at the expense of Roman law and Portuguese decisional law.[11] Orlando Gomes, one of Brazil's leading civil law scholars, has suggested that the secret of the longevity of the *Ordenações* in both Brazil and Portugal can be traced to its wealth of omissions coupled with so flexible a source of subsidiary law as good sense.[12] Thus the Brazilian custom of reinterpreting laws in the light of good sense has enjoyed a respectable and long-standing heritage in Portuguese positive law.

9. Prado Junior, supra note 7, at 303.
10. See Gomes, "Historical and Sociological Roots of the Brazilian Civil Code," *1 Inter-Am. L. Rev.* 331, 334 (1959).
11. See id. at 331, 332-33, fn. 6 (1959).
12. Id. at 333.

B. The Weakness of Portuguese Control

Another source of flexibility in Portuguese rule resulted from its very weakness. With a population estimated at only one million in the 15th century, Portugal lacked sufficient manpower to enforce rigid controls over its widespread empire. Whereas Spanish rule over much of the New World was facilitated by the prior existence of tightly controlled, autocratic Indian civilizations, the Portuguese had no such base upon which to build in Brazil.[13] Moreover, Portugal ceded more extensive jurisdictional powers to Brazil's original colonizers than did other colonial powers and subsequently had great difficulty reestablishing the authority of the Crown over the great landholders.[14] Particularly in the backlands, Portuguese administration was ineffective. Justice (what there was of it) was in practice administered by *coronéis* (colonels), large landowners who controlled the military in their area.[15] Gilberto Freyre summarized the prevailing relationship succinctly: "Over [Brazil's colonial aristocracy] the King of Portugal may be said, practically, to have reigned without ruling."[16]

While the Brazilians do not appear to have elevated the celebrated response of the Hispanic settlers to royal legislation calling for more humane treatment of the Indians into a principle of administrative law ("one obeys but does not comply"), in practice the same principle was widely applied.[17] Additional flexibility and autonomy for colonial administrators resulted from the Iberian practice of encouraging all officials and even the meanest vassal to appeal directly to the King if they disagreed with the order or policy of a superior.

---

13. W. Pierson and F. Gil, *Governments of Latin America* 70 (1957).

14. See E. Lahmeyer Lobo, *Processo Administrativo Ibero-Americano* 454-58 (1962). The text of one of these extensive grants appears in English translation in E. Burns, *A Documentary History of Brazil* 33-50 (1966).

15. When the Crown tried to curb their excesses at the end of the 17th century by enacting legislation appointing resident magistrates every five leagues, as well as restricting the terms of office of local military leaders, the law understandably went unenforced. C. Boxer, *The Golden Age of Brazil* 307 (1964).

16. *The Masters and the Slaves* 27 (1946).

17. See E. Lahmeyer Lobo, supra, note 14, at 434-44; M. Kieman, *The Indian Policy of Portugal in the Amazon Region:* 1614-1693 (1954). Law 24, Book II, title 1 of the *Recopilación* expressly recognized the right of Spanish viceroys and other officials to stay the execution of orders where special circumstances rendered their implementation inopportune. Spanish colonial administrators were thereby enabled to shelve inconvenient or impossible decrees by applying the "One obeys but does not comply" formula. C. Haring, *The Spanish Empire in America* 122-23 (1947).

Writing in 1616, the great Spanish jurist Castillo de Bavadilla explained the reasoning underlying this formula: "By laws of these realms it is provided that the royal provisions and decrees which are issued contrary to justice and in prejudice of suitors are invalid and should be obeyed and not executed . . . and the reason for this is that such provisions and mandates are presumed to be foreign to the intention of the Prince, who as Justinian has

The reputation of the colonial judiciary was one of inefficient venality. Lack of justice was a constant complaint in colonial Brazil even though apparently well-qualified magistrates were dispatched from Portugal to man the benches. Justice was regularly bartered like any other commodity, though delivered more slowly. Judicially collecting a debt was an extremely onerous, time-consuming, and expensive proposition, subject to many exceptions and much paperwork. Supervision over the notaries and judicial clerks was practically nil. Since these offices were frequently leased or subleased, sometimes for more than the position's salary, the investment in the office was commonly recouped through acceptance of bribes. Not even the laws regulating the conduct and qualifications of the magistrates themselves were observed. Although expressly forbidden by law to marry Brazilians, the Portuguese magistrates did so regularly. They also became involved in business ventures with the colonists, permitting some of the magistrates to become quite wealthy. And though the statutes prohibited Brazilians from serving on the high courts and in other judicial capacities, in practice these statutes were continually bent to permit Brazilians to hold these posts.[18] That most colonists preferred the justice of their own (or hired) hands, family, or friends to that of the King's magistrates was hardly surprising.

Several other factors contributed to the disregard for law that prevailed in colonial Brazil. Portugal punished serious crimes with exile to Brazil, making the colony a dumping ground for a sundry collection of social misfits, whose respect for law and order was attenuated prior to arrival. In comparison with the English colonies, relatively few of the colonists who came to Brazil in its early years had any intention of making it their permanent abode. Most came with the intention of reaping riches rapidly and returning posthaste to Portugal. Few brought wives or families; instead they indulged their sexual appetites freely with Indian and Negro concubines in a veritable carnival of licentiousness and immorality that extended even to the clergy.[19]

---

said, cannot be believed to desire by word or decree to subject and destroy the law established and agreed to with great solicitude." Quoted ibid.

Of course, in practice Spanish officials, like the Portuguese, ignored general rules and regulations for routine conduct in their office as well as special decrees. Ibid. There were clearly limits as to how much administrators could get away with under this formula, though a great deal obviously slipped by. See Phelan, "Authority and Flexibility in the Spanish Imperial Bureaucracy," 5 *Administrative Science Quarterly* 47, 59 (1960).

18. Schwartz, "Magistracy and Society in Colonial Brazil," 50 *Hispanic American Historical Rev.* 715, 726-28 (1970).

19. G. Freyre, supra note 16 at 85-86. After 1680 the caliber of colonists improved markedly with some of Portugal's better families fleeing to Brazil in the wake of Spanish subjugation. Manchester, "The Rise of the Brazilian Aristocracy," 11 *Hispanic American Historical Rev.* 145, 147 (1931).

The strict mercantilist policies and heavy taxation imposed by Portugal gave the Brazilians strong economic incentives for devising ingenious techniques to avoid compliance. As in other colonies, smuggling became a way of life. Towards the end of the 18th century, one French consul estimated that at least one tenth of Lisbon's total population made their living from the contraband trade.[20]

Even if Portuguese law had been crystal-clear and appropriately designed for Brazilian conditions, and the powers that were had been inclined to enforce it, a gap between the law on the books and practice would certainly have resulted from the lack of effective communications. One of the most striking features of Brazil is the enormity of its land mass, larger than that of continental United States and twice that of Europe excluding Russia. Littoral areas are cut off from the interior by sheer escarpments. Even today roads are few and far between, and the malfunctioning of the telephone, telegraph, and postal services is notorious. Given the extreme precariousness of communications, decision makers have had to fall back on improvisation.

III. The Legacy of Portuguese Character

The roots of the *jeito* can also be found in several character traits which the Portuguese bequeathed to the Brazilians. These character traits have continued up to the present in Brazil.

A. *Tolerance for Corruption*

One such legacy is a poorly developed expectation of honest, public-serving behavior by government officials. Even by the relaxed standards of the colonial era, the Portuguese enjoyed "an unenviable reputation for corruption."[21] In a dispatch from Lisbon dated February 14, 1738, Lord Tyrawly reported:

> The Portuguese, more than any other people, adhere to that rule of Scripture, that a gift maketh room for a man, and it is incredible how a present smooths the difficulties of a solicitation; nay, they even expect it, and though the presents necessary are not considerable, since a few dozen bottles of foreign wine, or a few yards of fine cloth will suffice, yet this often repeated amounts to money.[22]

Brazilian history abounds with tales (many with a basis in fact) of corruption and dishonesty on the part of colonial administrators, most

20. "Notations générales sur le commerce de Portugal par /consul/ Helfflinger" (1786), cited in D. Alden, *Royal Government in Colonial Brazil* 389 (1968).

21. C. Boxer, supra, note 15, at 209.

22. Tyrawly to Newcastle in Public Record Office London, State Papers/ Portugal 89/40, cited in id. at 209.

of whom viewed their office as a franchise for private gain, a common practice in Western Europe and colonial America during the period.[23] One has only to recall the successful campaign slogan circulated about the late Adhemar de Barros when running for the governorship of São Paulo—*Rouba mas faz*! (He steals but gets something done!)—to realize the persistency of this negative expectancy of public morality.

1. Lack of Civic Responsibility

The Portuguese also bequeathed the Brazilians a weak sense of loyalty and obligation towards the body politic, and a strong sense of loyalty and obligation towards family and friends. In comparing the Portuguese character with the Spanish, Marcus Cheke noted:

> . . . [A] trait that is common to both peoples is their lack of what may be termed "civic sense". Even more than the Spaniard, the Portuguese is kind and charitable to five categories of persons: to his family, to his friends, to the friends of his family, to the friends of his friends, and lastly, to the beggar in his path. But to other fellow citizens he acknowledges little obligation.[24]

The proposition that the law should be applied even-handedly and impersonally to all citizens conflicts with this Iberian heritage. The dominant attitude is reflected in the familiar Brazilian maxim: *Para os amigos tudo, para os indiferentes nada, e para os inimigos a lei.* (For friends, everything; for strangers, nothing; and for enemies, the law.) As José Honório Rodrigues, a leading student of Brazilian history and national character, explained, ". . . [T]he basic Brazilian personality . . . stresses direct personal relations, based upon liking rather than unconditioned, impersonal, practical relations. Personal liking is above the law."[25]

2. Sentimentalism

A corollary of this stressing of direct personal relations might be termed the *coitado* complex, the compassion and sympathy which Luso-Brazilians so readily extend to those in unfortunate circumstances. If forced to opt between helping someone whom he pities and respecting a legal norm, the Luso-Brazilian frequently chooses the former. Emílio Willems, an anthropologist with extensive field work in Brazil, has observed:

> Portuguese and Brazilians live in a world which is essentially

23. See D. Alden, supra note 20, at 389.

24. "The Portuguese Character," in H. Livermore (ed.), *Portugal and Brazil* 42, 45 (1953).

25. J. Rodrigues, *The Brazilians: Their Character and Aspirations* 57 (1967).

> human. Human frailties are to be tolerated and sympathetically accepted as unavoidable. The tolerant attitude of Brazilians towards delinquents and criminals has often been discussed. With regard to Portugal a revealing remark was made by Link and Hoffmansegg. After discussing the frequency of murder, usually caused by vengeance or jealousy, the authors comment on the attitude of the people: "The evildoer almost always escapes, and moved by a strange compassion, everybody facilitates his flight. *Coitadinho* [the diminutive of *coitado*] says the Portuguese, and they do everything to save him." Although this reaction was observed at the end of the eighteenth century, it still applies to contemporary Brazil.[26]

The *coitado* is someone to be befriended, and once befriended, that direct, personal obligation rises above the impersonal, abstract legal norm. This national sentimentalism tends to soften the law's rigors and multiply instances of the *jeito.*

B. *Feudalism*

Though feudalism was dying out on the Iberian peninsula at the time Brazil was being settled, the captaincy system, through which enormous areas of land and effective sovereignty over it were conveyed in perpetuity to a dozen nobles, transplanted an analogous institution. The feudal-like control over the lives of the masses of rural laborers has been continued in the social system of the *fazendas*, the large agrarian estates that still dominate much of the Brazilian countryside. "Feudalism is a system of profound juridical disequality, in which the law's rigor is only applicable to the serfs and vassals, but it is extremely flexible for the baron or sovereign. The latter govern themselves through voluntary relations; the former through imposed formulas."[27] Despite the rhetoric of democracy, quasi-feudal notions have persisted in Brazil, as in other nations of Latin America, up to the present day. In dealings with the bureaucracy, and particularly with the police, norms applied to the upper classes are generally different from those applied to the lower classes. There are still vestiges of this class discrimination in the formal legal structure, such as the requirement that educated persons be detained in special jails.[28]

C. *The Influence of Catholicism*

Another important Iberian attitudinal legacy has been Catholic-

26. "Portuguese Culture in Brazil," *Proceedings of the International History of Latin American Civilization Colloquium on Luso-Brazilian Studies* (1953), reprinted in L. Hanke (ed), I *History of Latin American Civilization* 51, 57 (1967).
27. "A Sociologia do jeito," in *A Técnia e o Riso* XI, XV (2nd ed. 1967).
28. Code of Criminal Procedure, Article 295.

ism. Law and religion, the fundamental instruments of the Spanish and Portuguese conquests, were inseparable. With its rigid dogmas, moral intolerance, great formalism, and slowness to change, Catholicism has stimulated considerable *jeito*-like behavior. More than 90 percent of Brazil's population is Catholic, but the great bulk are Catholic in name only, paying lipservice to the precepts of the Church in much the same fashion as they pay lipservice to much of the laws. For example, in deference to the Church, Brazil is one of the few countries which does not permit divorce under any circumstances. Nevertheless, Brazilians, especially in the large cities, treat the legal separation (*desquite*) as though it were a divorce *a vinculo matrimonii.* Though the formal legal system refuses to recognize the validity of divorces contracted abroad by Brazilians and denies legally separated persons the right to remarry, divorce and remarriage abroad, often by proxy, or an informal union are common and have met with a large degree of social acceptance in urbanized areas.[29] Moreover, legislation has steadily expanded the legal rights of concubines and the children of these unions, permitting the concubine under certain circumstances to receive accidental death benefits and government pensions to the detriment of the legal wife, and according the children the full status of legitimacy.[30]

D. *The Art of Compromise*

Gilberto Freyre writes that: "The secret of Brazil's success in building a humane, Christian, and modern civilization in tropical America has been her genius for compromise."[31] Though this is obviously an overstatement, there is little doubt that the ability to conciliate and compromise has been developed into an art and a tradition by the Brazilians. This may have resulted from the natural obstacles encountered in colonizing such a vast territory with so few people and so little might.[32] The history of Brazil is replete with examples of crises surmounted by resort to good sense and compromise instead of abstract philosophic doctrine. To be sure, Brazilian history is not without its episodes of violence; however, the country has been spared the splintering and bloody revolutions that have characterized the historical process in much of Spanish America.[33] The

29. See De Azevedo, *Social Change in Brazil* 26-31 (1963); "El Divorcio en America Latina," *Visión,* Vol. 37, No. 11, Nov. 21, 1969,p.50.

30. See W. Barros Monteiro, *Curso de Direito Civil, Direito da Família* 15-22 (8th ed. 1968).

31. *New World in e Tropics* 7 (1st Vintage Ed. 1963).

32. Vianna Moog has suggested that the true origin of the *jeito* lies in the Brazilian's need to conquer the overwhelming natural obstacles by subtlety and indirection. *Bandeirantes e Pioneiros* 258-59 (8th ed. 1966).

33. See generally, J. Rodrigues, *Conciliação e Reforma no Brasil* (1965).

jeito is simply one manifestation of this proclivity, inherited from the Portuguese, for finding pragmatic ways out of impasses.

IV. The Legal Culture: Paternalistic, Legalistic, and Formalistic

A. *Paternalism*

The paternalism which stemmed from the Portuguese monarchy, the Catholic Church, and the extended patriarchal family still permeates Brazilian society. It is commonly expressed in the *patrão* (patron) complex of traditional Brazil. In return for fealty and service the *patrão,* a member of the local elite, customarily looks after the interests of his employees, tenants, or debtors. The *patrão* plays the role of protector, interceding with the authorities when any of his flock is in trouble.[34] This aspect of the *patrão* system serves to personalize and particularize legal relations for the lower class.

The ultimate *patrão* is the state, from which the Brazilians seem to expect just about everything. "From jobs, stable prices, credit, high wages, security, and transportation, to subsidies for carnival masquerades, there is hardly anything for which the government is not expected to provide."[35]

Authority is tightly concentrated in Brazil, and there is great reluctance to delegate it. As in a great many developing countries, almost all decisions, even in the most petty matters, must come from the top. In a recent interview, the present Minister of Education, Jarbas Passarinho, complained that no sooner had he taken office than his subordinates began appearing with "urgent" documents that required his signature—permission to unload 156 pieces of paper and a lease of a home for an inspector of secondary education in the Northeast.[36] Hélio Beltrão, Planning Minister in the Costa e Silva regime and a leading advocate of administrative reform, recently observed:

> The concentration of the power of decision at the highest levels was, and still is, the most serious ill of the country's administrative organism. This repugnancy for delegation has been responsible for the incredible delay in solving the most routine matters, . . . for the interminable routing of processes for "higher consideration", and, in the final analysis, for the demoralization of those governing, who see themselves separated from the governed by a veritable bulwark of paper.[37]

Cf. Keith, "The Nonviolent Tradition in Brazilian History: A Myth in Need of Explosion", and Love, "Commentary," in H. Keith and S. Edwards (eds.), *Conflict and Continuity in Brazilian Society* 231 (1969).

34. See C. Wagley, *An Introduction to Brazil* 106-11 (1963).
35. Willems, "Brazil," in A. Rose (ed.), *The Institutions of Advanced Societies* 525, (1958).
36. Reported in *Realidade* of March 1970 at p. 36.
37. *O Globo,* Aug. 24, 1970, p. 23.

The long waiting period during which documents wend their way to the top creates a strong temptation to resort to the *jeito*.

Historically, elites have paternalistically bestowed constitutions and laws upon the Brazilian populace with little regard or awareness of the desires and capabilities of those governed.[38] Instead of being the product of popular pressures, an objective fact-finding study, or a crystalization of custom, legislation has tended to be the product of what a small group imagines would be ideal for the people. Thus, the labor legislation which the Vargas regime enacted in the late 1930's and early 1940's paternalistically granted many benefits and protections to the worker that have been the object of extensive struggles by labor movements in other parts of the world. Paid vacations, maternity benefits, job security, minimum wages, special treatment for women and children, health and sanitary conditions on the job, were all regulated in the Consolidated Labor Laws to protect the employee. But instead of creating a strong, independent labor movement, this legislation turned the labor movement into a ward of the state. To this day labor has remained dependent on the Ministry of Labor and the labor courts to secure wage increases, better working conditions, and enforcement of the labor laws, many of which have been more breached than honored.[39] Similarly, the Code of Civil Procedure provides for indemnification of tort victims for loss of future earnings by pensions instead of lump sums to prevent possible squandering of the money.[40] But until recently, these pensions had to be funded with government bonds paying a flat five percent per annum interest (which was not always paid), and were not adjustable for inflation. Since the system seriously prejudiced plaintiffs and defendants alike, the great majority of cases were resolved out of court on another basis.

---

38. O. Viana, *I Instituições Políticas Brasileiras* 30, 149 (2nd ed. 1955). The same point has been made with respect to Latin America generally. Busey, "Observations on Latin American Constitutionalism," 24 *The Americas* 46 (1967).

39. Perhaps the most circumvented provisions have been the tenure and minimum wage provisions. Since a worker could not be fired after ten years of service except for grave fault, duly proven before the labor courts, employers routinely discharged workers just before completing the tenth year of service. When the labor courts began to treat nine and a half years as equivalent to ten to prevent the practice, employers simply discharged employees sooner. Exposition of Motives of the Law of the Fund of Guaranty of Service, Law 5107 of September 13, 1966; R. Alexander, *Labor Relations in Argentina, Brazil, and Chile* 121-22 (1962). As in many countries, even today minimum wage legislation has been impossible to enforce in Brazil, particularly in the interior. Employees are frequently obliged to sign a paper indicating that they have been receiving the legal minimum to satisfy the regional labor inspector, but it is an open secret that many workers receive less. Even the present government, in employing refugees from the draught in the Northeast on the Transamazonic Highway, has been paying only two cruzeiros a day, far less than the minimum wage.

40. Code of Civil Procedure, Articles 911 and 912.

Because the government's view of what is best for the people does not always correspond with what the people view as best for themselves, Brazilians have been prone to act according to an old adage—*manda quem pode, obedece quem quer* (he who can, gives orders; he who wants to, obeys.)

B. Legalism

The Brazilian legal culture is highly legalistic; that is, the society places great emphasis upon seeing that all social relations are regulated by comprehensive legislation. There is a strong feeling that new institutions or practices ought not be adopted without a prior law authorizing them. As has been said with reference to German legalism, there is a "horror of a legal vacuum."[41] Brazil has reams of laws and decrees regulating with great specificity seemingly every aspect of Brazilian life, as well as some aspects of life not found in Brazil. It often appears that if something is not prohibited by law, it must be obligatory.

Lawmakers are generally not content to set out desired conduct in general terms. In many areas they seem constrained to try to preregulate all possible future occurrences with detailed, comprehensive, and occasionally incomprehensible legislation. Situations that would typically be left to judges or administrators in other countries to work out on a case basis under the rubric of "reasonableness" are preordained by statute in Brazil.

For example, the Law of Directives and Bases of National Education (Law No. 4,024 of December 20, 1961) is a lengthy statute which attempts to spell out the nature and structure of primary, secondary, and university education in all of Brazil. The statute attempts to establish uniform curricula, schedules, and programs for the entire country. Article 92 states: "The Union shall apply annually for the maintenance and development [of education] 12% of its tax receipts, and the States, Federal District and the Counties a minimum of 20%." As might be expected, provisions of this type have not always been honored. The legislative style reflects a deep-seated mistrust of those administering and interpreting the laws, as well as the entire legalistic and codifying tradition of the civil law, which exalts certainty as a supreme value.[42]

Another facet of this legalistic mentality is the tendency to regard as done that which is enacted into law. The faith that almost any social or economic ill can be cured by legal prescription appears

41. H. Spiro, *Government by Constitution* 184 (1959).

42. J. Merryman, *The Civil Law Tradition* 50-51 (1969). See generally H. Spiro, supra, note 41, at 211-36.

boundless.[43] Whether the society is willing and able to shoulder the costs of enforcement is seldom a suitable topic for discussion.

Evidence of legalism can be found everywhere. Little stands or street corners sell copies of the latest laws. By far the most popular profession has been law; even today almost 30 percent of all professionals are lawyers.[44] Questions such as whether a particular student was properly failed or which professor won a competition to be a chair professor are regularly litigated, even carried to the nation's highest court.[45] A separate court system has even been set up to resolve disputes growing out of sporting events, particularly soccer matches, and learned treatises are written on the Law of Sports. Even when behaving arbitrarily and unconstitutionally, Brazilian governments often feel compelled to go through a legalistic charade.[46]

Legalism has contributed to the *jeito's* popularity in two basic ways. It has led to a superabundance of regulatory legislation and a failure to build sufficient flexibility into that regulation. The *jeito* can be viewed as a legalistic response to both problems.

C. *Formalism*

Closely related to legalism is the exaggerated concern with legal formalities. Every nation has some formalistic behavior, but Brazilian

43. Roberto de Oliveira Campos, former planning minister and chief architect of Castelo Branco's economic program, recently satirized the country's legalistic mentality by suggesting the following bill to reduce the nation's high interest rates despite the acute inflation and great shortage of credit:

> Decree Law No 001—Regulates the Law of Supply and Demand and prohibits the scarcity of money or merchandise.
> Article 1.—The Law of Supply is maintained.
> Article 2.—The Law of Demand is repealed.
> Article 3.—The natural or artificial scarcity of money or any other merchandise is permanently prohibited.
> Article 4.—The just profit shall be equal to 10 percent per annum, because we are all born with ten fingers on our hands.

"Os Pseudojuristas," in *Ensaios contra a Maré* 47, 50 (1969).

44. A study undertaken by the Getulio Vargas Foundation and coordinated by Professor Rubens Porto reported that there were 65,731 lawyers presently in Brazil, making up 28.6 percent of the country's professional population. *Jornal do Brasil*, August 8, 1970, p. 14, 1st *Caderno*.

45. *E.g.*, União Federal v. Camin, RE 56.595, 33 *Rev. Trim. Juris.* 738 (S.T.F. 1965); União Federal v. Rocha Castro, RE 59.496, 40 *Rev. Trim. Juris.* 492 (S.T.F. 1966).

46. Thus, when the Vargas regime confiscated the estate of Paul deLeuze, a wealthy French newspaper owner, whose sole heir was a nephew, the government did not simply appropriate the estate; the wealth transfer was "legalized" by enactment of a statute retroactively disinheriting any nephew claiming as an heir, thereby producing an escheat. See K. Loewenstein, *Brazil under Vargas* 46-49 (1942). Similarly, when Costa e Silva suffered an incapacitating stroke in 1969, the reins of government were lifted by a junta of the heads of the armed forces, despite the constitutional provision for succession by the vice president (in this case a civilian). The official explanation given was that there had been no "succession" in the constitutional

concern with authenticity and verification is both impressive and oppressive. Legally permitting a friend to drive one's car requires written, notarized authorization. In many situations the signature of the notary must itself be verified. Foreigners may be validly divorced abroad, but before Brazilian officials will accord the foreign decree any validity, the document must be translated by the Foreign Office and homologated by the Supreme Federal Tribunal. Cashing a traveler's check at a government bank requires presentation of one's passport or identity card, supplying a local address and telephone number, signing eight copies of a form, which is then typed up, stamped, and initialed by a plethora of bank clerks. Exportation of a single shipment of coffee requires filling out 38 different forms, each with multiple copies.

The presumption appears to be that every citizen is lying unless he produces written, documentary proof that he is telling the truth. The formal legal system, whether ascertaining criminal guilt or issuing employment benefits, displays a decided tendency to believe only documents and not people. Hélio Beltrão's personal experience as Planning Minister bears this out well:

> . . . Brazil was born under the sign of the notary's office, the act, the registry, and the certificate. From this stems a certain inclination to believe that something really happened only after it is transformed into a written document: the undeniable presence of the deceased proves much less than the sacrosanct death certificate. . . . Undoubtedly, the curious decree which I had the occasion to submit to the President of the Republic during the Week of Administrative Reform in October of 1968 was . . . scandalizing. This decree abolished the requirement of a "life certificate" *(atestado de vida)* in cases in which the beneficiary personally appears at the window of the government department to receive his retirement benefit or pension. It appears incredible that a decree was necessary to permit the functionary making the payments to believe that the person before him was alive.[47]

Another facet of formalism is the obvious discrepancy between concrete conduct and the legal norms designed to regulate such conduct. Brazilians commonly refer to laws in much the same manner as one refers to vaccinations. There are those which take, and those which do not.[48] It was only partly in jest that Capistrano de Abreu,

---

sense. The junta was merely acting as attorneys of the stricken president. This extra-legal takeover was then "legalized" by an "institutional act," the 12th of a series of 17 such measures promulgated by fiat of a military group that has assumed the duties of a continuous constitutional convention in the name of the revolution.

47. *O Globo*, August 24, 1970, p. 23.

48. Francisco Campos, Vargas' durable Minister of Justice, was reported to have responded to the criticism that a new law was identical to one that

one of the nation's most distinguished historians, proposed, as a panacea for Brazil's ills, passage of the following law:

Article 1. The law shall be obeyed.

Article 2. All dispositions to the contrary shall be revoked.[49]

Many factors explain the prevalence of formalism in Brazil, and indeed for much of Latin America as well. Independence brought little relief from legislation ill-suited to the demands of Brazilian society. In general, Brazilian laws have not been autochthonous; most have been imported wholesale from Europe or the United States with little, if any, consideration given to their suitability for implantation in Brazilian soil. This in turn is largely attributable to the way in which the legislative process functions. Most Brazilian legislation has been drafted by distinguished jurists or law professors in an atmosphere far removed from the clamor of special interest groups. The draftsmen have typically consulted the various solutions to the problem that have been enacted abroad and tried to select one,that as an abstract proposition, appears best, rather than seek a rule which crystallizes custom or practice. Seldom has there been a fact finding inquiry about the peculiarly Brazilian nature of the economic, social, political, or administrative problems involved. There are frequently disputes among jurists and professors about the rule being adopted, but these are typically disputes of a technical, doctrinal nature. The end product of this process has been the legislation of idealized standards of behavior, continuing a tradition that harks back to Roman law.

1. *The Heritage of Roman Law*

Iberian legal culture has been heavily influenced by Rome, which dominated the peninsula for more than six hundred years prior to the fifth century. Fundamental to the Roman concept of law was the effort to set out ethical standards of behavior to which society ought to aspire. Roman lawyers and jurists continually searched for universal, rational principles inherent in nature. By elevating moral principles determined from natural equity and universal reason over custom and tradition as a source of law, the Romans, particularly in the late Empire, produced an impressive body of abstract, idealized legal rules that were frequently honored in the breach. This legislative style was passed on virtually intact from Portugal and Spain to their colonies.[50]

Campos himself had written only a year earlier, by saying: "There is no harm done, my son. We are going to publish this one now because the other did not catch on. *Correio da Manhã*, December 11, 1966, p. 3, 4th *Caderno*.

49. *Jornal do Brasil*, October 18, 1967, p. 6, 1st Caderno.

50. F. Moreno, *Legitimacy and Stability in Latin America: A Study of Chilean Political Culture* 3-17 (1969); Davidson, "The Brazilian Inheritance of Roman Law," in *Brazil: Papers Presented in the Institute for Brazilian Studies Vanderbilt University* 59 (1953).

This view of the legislative process is also a natural outgrowth of legal science, which has heavily influenced many, though by no means all of Brazil's lawyers. Generations of Brazilian law students have been taught that law is a science, and that the task of the legal scientist is to analyze and elaborate principles which can be derived from a careful study of positive legislation into a harmonious systematic structure. The components of this system are believed to be purely legal, a set of ultimate truths related by rigorous deductive logic. Hence, the legal scientist's inquiry is almost exclusively directed towards the legal norm. Though lip service may be paid towards the relevance or utility of facts derived from nonlegal disciplines such as anthropology, sociology, political science, or economics, it is hard for the legal scientist to escape the feeling that consideration of nonlegal facts detracts from his search for absolute principles and the true nature of legal institutions.

Brazilian legal education has been overwhelmingly formalistic. Almost exclusive emphasis is placed upon classical exegesis of the formal legal text. Little effort is devoted to examination of how a particular norm functions in practice. The prevailing attitude appears plainly in a classic introductory text to the study of law by Hermes Lima, a former minister of the Supreme Federal Tribunal:

> Obedience to the juridical order is not conditioned on the opinion or the acquiescence of the subject: *lex iubet, aut vetat.* The relation between norm and conduct is subordination, not causality. The juridical imperative is, as defined by B. Somló, "the expression of will which is directed to the behavior of a third party, without worrying about whether this third party is disposed to abide by it."[51]

Viewing law as a science and legal education as a means of imparting the true meaning of legal norms leads to a divorce between the formal legal system and actual conduct. One of Brazil's leading jurists, Santiago Dantas, perceived the problem clearly in a seminal address calling for a reform in legal education:

> In the study of abstract legal rules presented as a system one can easily lose the sense of the social, economic, or political relationships the law is intended to control. The legal system has a logical and rational value, autonomous, so to speak. The study we make of this system, with strictly deductive and *a priori* methods, leads to a condition of self-sufficiency which enables the jurist to

51. *Introdução à Ciência do Direito* 35 (15th ed. 1966). See generally Steiner, "Legal Education and Socio-Economic change: Brazilian Perspectives, 19 *Am. J. Comp. L.* 39 (1971); Rosenn, "The Reform of Legal Education in Brazil," 21 *J. Legal Education* 251 (1969).

turn his back on the society and lose interest in the matter regulated as well as in the practical significance of the legal solution.[52]

2. *Strategies for Promoting or Avoiding Social Change*

But there is much more to formalism than legal science and the superimposition of imported forms ill-suited to Brazilian needs. In certain instances formalism may well be a conscious strategy for promoting social change. This thesis has been elaborated by Guerreiro Ramos, who argues that in the Brazilian historical context, formalism has been an important strategy adopted by the elite in order to forge a nation.[53] In his viewpoint, "formalism is not a bizarre characteristic, a sign of social pathology . . ., but a normal and regular fact which reflects a global strategy of [transitional] societies by which they attempt to move beyond their current phase."[54] Given the rudimentary state of Brazilian society in the 19th century, any institutional framework that the architects of the legal system wished to adopt was necessarily formalistic.

Thus viewed, many of the legal institutions which the elite imported have an essentially hortatory and aspirational function. Though Brazil may have lacked the social and political infrastructure for the constitutional system imported from the United States to function in 1891, the hope was that the Brazilian society would evolve sufficiently to convert the constitutional theory into practice. Though plausible, Guerreiro Ramos' theory is unsupported by historical evidence. Whether supportive evidence will ever be adduced is uncertain.[55]

On the other hand, one can argue that there are cases when formalism has been adopted as a conscious strategy for averting social change. In Brazil, as in a great many developing nations, it is frequently easier and less socially divisive for opponents of legislation aimed at effecting fundamental changes in the society to prevent implementation rather than enactment. Proponents of basic reforms are accorded a symbolic victory, but in practice nothing changes because supporters of the *status quo* have sufficient political and economic power to nullify the reform at the administrative level. For example, in 1964 the Brazilian Congress passed an elaborate and largely unintelligible land reform statute,[56] similar in many respects to the bill which it had rejected a year earlier when Goulart was still in power.

52. "A Educação Jurídica e a Crise Brasileira," 13-14 *Revista Jurídica* 7, 18 (1955).
53. Supra, note 5 at 387-93 (1966).
54. Id. at 365.
55. The same difficulty surrounds this theory as advanced for other Latin American countries. See Busey, supra, note 38.
56. Law No. 4.504 of November 30, 1964.

The bill's passage was assured by confidence that the new military government would leave land reform at the formalistic level, a confidence that thus far has not been misplaced. The six years that have passed since enactment have witnessed much study, a constitutional amendment and more legislation, creation and abolition of administrative agencies to deal with the problem, but virtually no land reform.[57]

V. The Bureaucratic Imbroglio

Intertwined with the problem of formalism and essential to a comprehension of the persistence of the *jeito* is the nature of the Brazilian bureaucracy. Historically, the bureaucracy has served as a means of employing educated persons whom the private sector could not absorb. This practice has imparted a "make work" character that has continued to the present day. Since the late 1930's, when the first Vargas regime began to intervene earnestly in the operation of the economy, the proliferation of New Deal-like governmental agencies has greatly swollen bureaucratic ranks. Occasionally, it seems that the most favored solution to any given problem is the creation of a new agency to deal with it. As in most developing nations, there are critical shortages of well-trained personnel and equally critical surplusages of unemployed or under-employed persons. Voters are readily attracted by the promise of governmental jobs, and the Brazilians have humanely refrained from dismissing civil servants when regimes change. Despite longstanding civil service legislation providing for selection on the basis of competitive examinations, positions have historically been filled by the *pistolão* (literally, the big gun; hence anyone who uses his power and influence on behalf of others.) A recent article estimates that a maximum of 89,000 out of the approximately 500,000 in the federal service, or about 17.8 percent, have entered by merit examinations,[58] a sad indication that the civil service law (Law No. 284 of October 28, 1936), is simply another of the many statutes which have not taken.

57. The 1964 revolution abolished Goulart's SUPRA (Superintendency for Agrarian Reform) and created two new organs, INDA (National Institute of Agrarian Development) and IBRA (Brazilian Institute of Agrarian Reform). The Costa e Silva regime created another organ, GERA (Executive Group for Agrarian Reform). In July of 1970 the Medeci regime decided to consolidate INDA, IBRA, and GERA into a single new agency, INCRA (National Institute of Colonization and Agrarian Reform). Though some 9,000 bureaucrats have been employed in the three consolidated agencies, as one of Rio's newspapers caustically observed: " . . . [T]he system has not had any real change, for the law did not take; that is to say, in practice nothing has resulted." *O Globo*, July 13, 1970, p. 1.

58. Lambert, "Trends in Administrative Reform in Brazil," 1 *J. Lat. Amer. Studies* 167, 181 (Part II, Nov. 1969). Circumvention of civil service requirements was particularly blatant when Kubitschek and Goulart were in power; attempts were then made to bestow permanent status on thousands of temporary employees. See Siegel, "The Strategy of Public Ad-

Political clientage, whose roots go back to the *patrão* system of traditional rural Brazil, still dominates the bureaucratic structure.[59] One who owes his job to political clientage is less likely to be averse to doing favors for family or friends. Moreover, the influx of large numbers of untrained and unqualified personnel has itself generated more red tape, partially to give superfluous employees something to do, and partially to diffuse responsibility so that fixing blame for incompetence becomes more difficult. Attraction and retention of top flight talent has been seriously hampered by the low level of governmental salaries, which have not kept pace with the breathtaking inflation and the increasing competition from the private sector.[60] Large numbers of civil servants have at least one other daytime job; substantial numbers show up only to collect their paychecks.

Bureaucratic practices could hardly be designed more appropriately to promote administrative inefficiency. Many departments are open but a few hours a day. A plethora of documents are required for any claim. Official documents usually require stamps, which must be purchased elsewhere than the agency processing the documents. Governmental forms must be purchased separately from commercial stationers; until recently, even income tax returns had to be purchased. Payments of processing fees generally must be made at commercial banks and the receipts presented to the processing agency. As a general rule, a person is compelled to run from place to place and endure the customary slow-moving lines many times before he has arranged all the necessary pieces of paper. Then he may be forced to wait weeks, months, or years while the process is sent up for "higher consideration."[61]

In this setting it is relatively simple for civil servants to rationalize levying direct taxes upon those members of the public requiring their services. Brazilians complain, not without justification, that "*êles criam dificuldades para vender facilidades*" (they create difficulties in order to sell facilities).

---

ministration Reform: The Case of Brazil," 26 *Pub. Admin. Rev.* 45, 52-53 (1966).

59. See Pease, "Some Characteristics of Urbanization in the City of Rio de Janeiro," in P. Hauser (ed.), *Urbanization in Latin America* 191, 202 (1961).

60. For statistical data with respect to the progressive deterioration in real terms of governmental salaries at the upper levels, see Guerreiro Ramos, supra, note 5, at 378-79.

61. Peter Bell relates the experience of a professor from Minas Gerais who waited ten years for a tax refund and then made the magnanimous gesture of donating the sum, whose real value had been whittled away by inflation to a pittance, to the government. The startled tax official pleaded earnestly with the professor to forego his civic gesture, for the procedure to enable the treasury to accept the gift was equally lengthy and involved. "Brazil," in J. Honey, *Towards Strategies for Public Administration in Latin America* 89, 92 (1968).

A. *The Despachante*

The jeito normally operates palm in glove with another Brazilian institution, the *despachante* (roughly, an expediter), who has counterparts in many nations. The ubiquitous *despachante* lubricates Brazil's sticky administrative process and has become a thriving, specialized professional, replete with his own union and competitive examinations. Some *despachantes* handle only customs matters; others specialize in police work, naturalizations, auto licenses, marriages, or "legalization of real estate." The yellow pages of Rio's phone book, which is but a partial listing, contain more than 300 separate listings for *despachantes.* Each *despachante* typically has several employees working for him, and almost all sizeable businesses maintain their own *despachantes.* The *despachante* is an intermediary who, in return for a commission or fee, purchases and fills out the multiplicity of legal forms, delivers them to the proper persons, and extracts the needed permission or document. *Despachantes* who arrange for the importation and exportation of goods have long enjoyed a legal monopoly. Only those authorized by presidential decree and their assistants may process papers before the customs officials. Until recently, not even the owner could go through the laborious process of extracting his goods from customs without an authorized *despachante.*[62] Even when a *despachante* is not legally required, it may be practically impossible to secure anything quickly from the bureaucracy without one. Securing necessary documents can be so difficult that it is not unheard of for one governmental agency to employ a *despachante* to extract something from another. The simplest transactions, such as obtaining a marriage license or identity card, may take ages or days or hours, depending on whether one has used a *despachante* and how much he has been paid.

The pace of bureaucratic sloth is illustrated by the government's experience with Decree-Law No. 499 of March 17, 1969, which required every resident alien to exchange his old-fashioned identity card for a stream-lined plastic model within a year. This period has had to be extended through July of 1972, for as Rio's leading newspaper reported in October of 1970—one who fills out the form to exchange his identity card today cannot expect to receive the new card for at least nineteen months.[63] But a good *despachante* can shorten that wait by at least eighteen and a half months.

62. Decree-Law No. 4.014 of Jan. 13, 1942, Art. 1. Customs *despachantes* received governmental authorization to ply their trade only after passing an examination on their knowledge of customs practice and serving of a two year apprenticeship. Id. at Art. 14. This system has been modified by Decree-Law No. 366 of Dec. 19, 1968.

63. *Jornal do Brasil,* Oct. 9, 1970, 1st *Caderno.*

The *despachante* functions effectively because he knows how to fill out the bewildering variety of forms, to whom the copies should be delivered, and what documentation will be required. He attends to several matters at the same time, and is adept at breaking in ahead of the long lines waiting to handle their own affairs.[64] Most importantly, he operates expeditiously because he has cultivated friends in the bureaucracy. This cultivation is frequently fertilized by the turnover of a portion of his fee or by appropriate Christmas or birthday presents. Of course, if one is fortunate enough to have a friend, or a friend of a friend, in the right governmental office, the services of the *despachante* can be foregone. But it ofttimes appears that were it not for the *jeito* and the *despachante*, the entire administrative apparatus of Brazil would grind to a halt.

B. *Administrative Reform*

For the past thirty years a series of fruitless efforts have been made to reform Brazil's ungainly, bloated, inefficient public administration. These efforts have been directed primarily through an elite centralized agency, the Administrative Department of Public Service (DASP), and substantial inputs of foreign technical assistance. The reasons for this failure have been spelled out elsewhere.[65] Suffice it to say that the underlying political structure has not been conducive to implementation of a merit system.

Operating on the theory that modernization and development require impersonal, predictable, and efficient administrative behavior, the military regimes ruling the country since the 1964 seizure of power have given administrative reform high priority. A series of measures, clustering around Decree-Law No. 200 of February 25, 1967, have been introduced to diffuse decision making and reduce red tape. Between March of 1967 and the end of 1969, some 347 governmental departments have been reorganized and nearly two-thirds of the steps in their processing documents eliminated. The result has been the reduction of the number of documents passed up to the ministries for further consideration by more than ten million during this period.[66] The military has also sought to reduce the large numbers of super-

64. One practical reason for permitting the *despachante* to avoid the long lines of people handling their own affairs is that the *despachante's* papers are normally in order, while the bulk of people trying to cope with the bureaucracy on their own are ill-informed and lack the necessary documentation, at least on the first few visits. Dealing directly with the *despachantes* makes the public servant appear more efficient. I am indebted to Prof. Roberto Sfoggia, of the Law School of the Federal University of Rio Grande do Sul, for this observation.

65. See, e.g., L. Graham, *Civil Service Reform in Brazil: Principles Versus Practice*, Chap. X (1968)

66. *Visão*, Jan. 17, 1970, p. 23.

fluous civil servants by pensioning them off. In addition, sizeable numbers have been dismissed or retried for corruption or political reasons, while many others have voluntarily left federal service rather than transfer to the new capital at Brasilia. Implementation of such measures has become possible because of the abrupt changes in the rules of the political game. Though it still leaves much to be desired, administrative efficiency has been increasing somewhat in the past few years.

VI. Penetration of the Formal Legal System

Brazil's formal legal system, as developed in the latter half of the Empire and the early years of the Republic, revolved around the constitution and comprehensive basic codes of civil, criminal, and commercial law, as well as criminal and civil procedure. The constitution was modeled after that of the United States, while the basic codes were largely drawn from European models. Disputes within the formal legal system have been resolved by a hierarchical arrangement of courts on the basis of the wording and legislative history of the statutory norms, scholarly doctrine, opinions of distinguished jurists, and prior court decisions. This part of the legal system has been administered by a specially trained highly influential group of law professionals—lawyers, judges, and notaries.

This formal legal system has had all the earmarks of a modern, developed institutional structure. Official determinations of rights and obligations have been based upon application of impersonal, universalistic principles by professionals trained in the system. However, this formal system failed to penetrate very far into Brazilian society. With the exception of the elite and the small, emerging middle class, the great bulk of the population has remained largely unaffected by the formal legal structure. Their disputes have been resolved by the *patrão*, *paterfamilias* or local custom.

Even today penetration of the formal legal system is quite limited. Improvements in modern communications and transportation have done surprisingly little to reduce Brazil's vastness and enormous regional disparities. Approximately half this huge country still lies in remote and inaccessible areas, for all practical purposes outside the market economy. Much of the rural interior still is only nominally under the control of the formal authorities. Though the situation is slowly changing, especially since the military takeover, what Jacques Lambert wrote in the mid-1950's is essentially valid today:

> But when one leaves the "new country" in which the Government's action is exercised directly, federal and even state legislation is weakened by intervention of local authorities, whose command is more respected than that of the distant Government. The man of the interior is accustomed to go to the local authorities to

seek protection against laws which he does not know and fears, instead of going to functionaries of the Central Government to ask them to apply the law. In spite of centralizing institutions, the old Brazil effectively continues decentralized, because the uniform . . . law is not respected or even known.[67]

The system has been built upon compromise, with the local bosses delivering the rural vote to federal and state authorities in exchange for ample extra-legal autonomy.[68] Though the municipalities have lacked legal autonomy, as a practical matter incumbent heads of municipalities have been free to "render justice to one's friends and to apply the law to one's adversaries."[69]

Not only in rural regions has the penetration of the formal legal system been limited. Millions of urban Brazilians live in *favelas*, squatter settlements that ring all major cities. Penetration of formal legal structure in the *favela* is fragmentary and precarious, for the *favela's* very existence is of doubtful legality. Instead, the *favela* is governed by a mixture of the formal legal system and an informal, customary system, as well as a curious set of laws and regulations designed to permit the formal authorities to deal with the *favelados* without having to acknowledge the lawfulness of the *favela's* existence.[70]

A. *Caligula Revisited—Finding the Governing Law*

Penetration of the formal system into even the modern, urban sectors is greatly hampered by difficulties in ascertaining its provisions. Caligula was reputed to have had his laws and decrees posted high off the ground where none of the populace could read them. The Brazilian method is not so obvious, but it is nearly as effective. Discovering the governing law in Brazil is still as perplexing and difficult a task today as in colonial times. The myriad forms of the federal government's positive law—the Constitution, amendments, institutional acts, complementary laws, decree-laws, laws, decrees, regulations, resolutions, ordinances, *portarias*, circulars, instructions, etc.—are published in the *Diário Oficial*, an official gazette. (There are corresponding publications at the state level.) However, the federal *Diário Oficial* is unindexed, undigested, and occasionally unreadable. Only recently has a decent unofficial index for legislation been published. While there is a semi-official collection of laws and decrees, the *Coleção das Leis do Brasil*, the precarious indexing is on a volume

67. J. Lambert, *Os Dois Brasis* 238 (2nd ed. 1967).
68. V. Nunes Leal, *Coronelismo, Enxada e Voto* 8, 31 (1948).
69. Id. at 158.
70. See generally, S. Conn, *The Squatter's Rights of Favelados* (CIDOC *Cuaderno* No. 32, 1969).

by volume basis. Whether one finds a particular law or decree frequently depends upon luck and the caption's phraseology. Even at the federal level, there is no official codification integrating the multiplicity of legislative pronouncements on any given subject. While an attempt is made from time to time to bring the plethora of income tax statutes together into an official compilation, it is incomplete, some times incorrect, and quickly obsolete.

Instead of amending basic code provisions, Brazilian practice has been to adopt supplemental legislation, which, in turn, is amended and reamended. Generally one is forced to read a host of separate statutes and decrees regulating a given subject (and many others as well) and then undertake the jigsaw job of piecing together the provisions still in force to arrive at the governing law.[71] For example, so many different rent control laws were enacted between 1942 and 1964 that no fewer than 18 different regimes regulating rentals were simultaneously in force.[72]

Laws are frequently drafted with such haste that clarifying legislation follows hard on the heels of the original statute, producing generalized confusion. Thus Decree-Law No. 62 of November 21, 1966, a carefully and intelligently conceived statute, authorized firms to effect monetary correction of their balance sheets starting with fiscal year 1968. But the law was not self-executing. It depended upon issuance of regulations by the Treasury, and the regulations were never issued. Just before 1968 expired, a hastily concocted and poorly conceived statute, Decree-Law No. 401, was promulgated as a substitute for Decree-Law No. 62. In less than six months, Decree-Law No. 401 was amended and clarified by no fewer than five decree-laws and one *portaria*.[73]

Many decisions of important tribunals, including the nation's highest court, remain unpublished. Since there is no doctrine of *stare decisis* (though the introduction of the *Súmula* in 1964 was a step in

71. For an interesting tour of the technical aspects of elaborating Brazilian laws, as well as collection of horrors of past efforts, see H. Fernandes Pinheiro, *Técnica Legislativa* (2nd ed. 1962). While private compilations, such as the *Vademecum Forense* and the *Carteira da Revista Forense*, collect most of the basic statutes and some of the decrees, they are far from complete. Though there are occasional footnotes for cross reference and some integration of successive legislative pronouncements on the same subject, the reader is not spared the bulk of the task of integrating the jumble of conflicting and complementary laws.

72. Statement of Motives, Law No. 4.494 of Nov. 25, 1964, Sec. XI.

73. Decree-Law No. 427 of Jan. 22, 1969; Decree-Law No. 433 of Jan. 23, 1969; Decree-Law No. 519 of Apr. 7, 1969; Decree-Law No. 545 of Apr. 18, 1969; Decree-Law No. 614 of June 6, 1969; *Portaria* No. GB-31 of Jan. 31, 1969. Theoretically, a *portaria*, an administrative pronouncement, cannot modify the terms of a law. However, since this one modifies the law intelligently, no one complains. It is simply another example of the ubiquitous *jeito*.

that direction[74]), it is common to find numerous decisions on both sides of a given question. Indexing of reported cases depends on the terminology employed in the headnote; it is unreliable and sketchy at best. One looks in vain for comprehensive digests, Shepard's, a key number system, CCH or PH type services, or an index to legal periodicals. To be sure, cases are not as important in civil law jurisdictions, and Brazil is far ahead of most of her neighbors in indexing and reporting cases. Nevertheless, the system falls far short of what is available in the neighboring civil law jurisdiction of Argentina.

Hence it is quite common to discover that the authorities charged with administering a particular body of law are unaware of significant changes in the statutory or case law. Inertia, ignorance, and inability to keep abreast of rapid-fire legal change frequently combine to produce substantial differences between the formal norm and the law actually being applied.

B. *The Delays of Court*

The malfunctioning of the court system has also been responsible for the limited penetration of the formal legal system. In general, the Brazilian courts, particularly in the urban centers, have enjoyed a reputation for honesty and integrity in discharging their official functions. However, the rapid growth of the population and the economy has heavily overcrowded court dockets. In some courts delays are so long that the often heard lament—"What enters, never leaves!"—appears justified. The Federal Tribunal of Appeals (*Tribunal Federal de Recursos*) only recently decided a case begun in 1892. Brazil's civil procedure offers seemingly endless opportunities for delay. Loopholes and possibilities for filing additional appeals abound.

Those with good tort or contract claims have been reluctant to enter the courts to enforce them. Brazil has been characterized as a "defendant's jurisdiction, that is, one in which being sued is generally not cause for major concern, in view of the historic tendency of Brazilian judges to award small amounts to those bringing suit."[75] Inflation has reduced the real value of court awards sharply. Only recently have the courts been adjusting contract and tort claims for in-

74. The *Súmula* is a collection of rules of law which have become firmly settled in the decisions of the Supreme Federal Tribunal. Its provisions are summarily cited to dispose of those issues in future litigation. The *Súmula* can be and is modified, but on constitutional isues the votes of at least three ministers are required to reopen the issue.

75. P. Garland, *A Businessman's Introduction to Brazilian Law and Practice* 21 (1966). Reportedly the highest tort verdict ever awarded in Brazil is only Cr. $350.000 (about US$70,000), granted in September of 1970 by the Tribunal of Justice of São Paulo to the widow of a judge murdered in 1961 at the order of a dissatisfied litigant. *Jornal do Brasil*, Sept. 22, 1970, p. 24, 1st *Cad.* The verdict is far out of line with typical wrongful death awards.

flation.[76] The legal interest rate has remained six percent per year, while commercial interest rates in the past decade have varied between two and five percent per month, giving the tortfeasor or debtor an enormous incentive to stall.

Litigation is also expensive. Almost all testimony is reduced to writing prior to trial. Since the facts are normally tried by a judge upon the written record, appellate courts have felt free to make *de novo* findings of fact, thereby contributing to delays in the judicial process.[77]

The lengthy delays, coupled with the expense and the unlikelihood of receiving anywhere close to a complete indemnification, have made many Brazilians reluctant to enforce their rights in court. Because the judicial process has become dysfunctional, many are inclined to seek alternative methods of protecting themselves.[78]

C. *After Goulart, the Deluge*

The acceleration of modernization, which in the past three decades has so strikingly transformed much of Brazil from a traditional, semifeudal, agrarian society into an urban, industrialized nation, has rendered much of the basic law hopelessly obsolete. Moreover, the acceleration of the modernization process has been accompanied by an acceleration of the inflationary process, itself an important cause of legal obsolescence.[79] A number of projects have been commenced to reform outmoded codes, but with few exceptions, they have dragged on without producing any changes.

In an effort to bring the legal system to grips with many of the nation's most pressing economic and social problems, the military regimes since 1964 have unleashed a legislative deluge. Just between April of 1964 and November of 1966 more than 7300 new laws, decrees, and regulations were promulgated.[80] Though much of this legislation has been directed towards solving urgent socio-economic problems, a good deal of it is incredibly complicated and difficult to administer. This is partially due to so much of it being drafted by economists and engineers. It is also due to enactment of so much of it by executive decree, eliminating the opportunity for Congressional debate that might have eliminated some of the ambiguities and complexity. Even-

76. See, e.g., Pardi v. Gruninger, No. 157.122, 222 *Revista Forense* 149 (5th Cam. Civ. Trib. Just. S.P. 1966).

77. P. Garland, supra, note 75, at 22.

78. Cf. B. Kozolchyk, *Law and the Credit Structure in Latin America* 26-30 (Rand Monograph 4918-RC, Mar. 1966).

79. See Rosenn, "Adaptations of the Brazilian Income Tax to Inflation," 21 *Stan. L. Rev.* 58 (1968); Lefcoe, "Monetary Correction and Mortgage Lending in Brazil: Observations for the United States," 21 *Stan. L. Rev.* 106 (1968).

80. Estado de São Paulo, Jan. 5, 1967, p. 11.

tually, this phase of constant experimentation with new legislation will draw to a close, and the new legal framework will have a chance to be absorbed by the groups whose conduct is being regulated. Until then, there is always the *jeito.*

VII. Developmental Costs and Benefits of the Jeito

The nature of the relationship between law and development in legal cultures in which there is a fairly high correspondence between the laws on the books and actual practice is far from clear. In legal cultures which function largely on the basis of an institution like the *jeito* the nature of that relationship is much more murky. Cranking aspects of the formal legal structure into economic growth models is a formidable task; trying to crank individualistic, *ad hoc* arrangements like the *jeito* into a growth model is likely to send economists twitching back to *ceteris paribus.* But perhaps one may profitably begin by suggesting tentatively some of the ways in which the *jeito* appears to have hindered and helped Brazilian development.

A. *Costs of the Jeito*

Several hindrances of the corrupt components of the *jeito* are patent. Resources are frequently misallocated when the criterion of the private gain of the allocator is employed. Procurement or construction contracts become more costly, either through the total price paid or the inferior quality of the performance received. Much social injustice and unrest stems from permitting certain firms and individuals to avoid compliance with the law through payment of bribes or utilization of family connections.

The government's power to redistribute income, stimulate desirable conduct, or discourage undesirable conduct through taxation or regulatory legislation is sharply limited by the loopholes carved through corruptive practices. As Gunnar Myrdal has observed in the South Asian context, "Corruption introduces an element of irrationality in plan fulfillment by influencing the actual course of development in a way that is contrary to the plan or, if such influence is foreseen, by limiting the horizon of the plan."[81] Governmental power to promote development is also weakened to the extent that tolerance of corruption saps popular support and respect for the government.

It is expensive and time-consuming to have to resort to *despachantes* every time licenses or permissions are needed. Particularly among the lower classes, many cannot afford this expense and are forced to forego economic opportunities. The cycle can be vicious indeed. A person whose papers are not in order has great difficulty securing em-

81. 2 *Asian Drama* 952 (1968).

ployment, but he may not be able to secure the necessary documents without the aid of a *despachante*, whose services he cannot afford. The small entrepreneur may be thwarted from opening his own business because he has insufficient capital to pay for the expenses of legalizing the business. The system heavily discriminates against the poor, who are forced to wait patiently in the long lines in front of the windows of governmental departments. Millions of potentially productive man-hours are lost waiting in these lines.

The corrupt aspects of the *jeito* retard administrative efficiency. People are reluctant to assume personal responsibility for decision making, preferring to pass documents up for higher consideration. Civil servants do nothing without written authorization, and fear of an investigation leads to much collegiate decision-making to spread the responsibility. The practice of exacting "speed money" or "delay money" also slows down administrative efficiency. While speed money may accelerate the administrative process in individual cases, studies in other countries have concluded that the practice actually aggravates delays in the administrative apparatus as a whole.[82] *A fortiori*, payment of "delay money", a common practice for defendants unanxious to see their cases speedily determined or a competitor licensed, bogs down the system.

The non-corrupt, public service aspects of the *jeito* also entail serious costs. It is expensive to have to resort to legal subterfuges, such as the separate credit and finance companies that banks were forced to set up to escape the unrealistic usury statute.[83] Credit transactions are more expensive than they would be if creditors were assured of prompt court enforcement of their rights. Imports and exports are seriously burdened by unnecessary delays and *despachantes'* fees. These expenses are added on to the price of most transactions, exacerbating an already bloated price structure.

The *jeito* is essentially an *ad hoc* institution, and its uncertainty and unpredictability discourages some potential investors. Lack of a universalistic operational legal structure makes business planning difficult. Transactions cloaked in the dubious legality of the *jeito* may wear well today but come apart at the seams tomorrow.

There is a significant moral cost as well, for frequent resort to the bypass of the *jeito* contributes to the general disrespect for the rule of law and orderly processes, a very serious problem in present day Brazil. The fact that competitors resort to the *jeito* with im-

82. This was the finding of the Indian Committee on Prevention of Corruption (Santhanam Committee 1964), cited in id. at 953.

83. See Simonsen, "Brazilian Inflation: Postwar Experience and Outcome of the 1964 Reforms," in *Economic Development Issues: Latin America* 261, 301-04 (Comm. for Econ. Develop. Supp. Paper No. 21, 1967).

punity forces the businessman who may wish to respect the law to circumvent it in order to compete. Just as widespread tax evasion is a logical product of the corrupt side of the *jeito*, the blatant activities of the *Esquadrões da Morte* (execution squads of police and vigilantes which have been systematically liquidating common criminals with whom, in the opinion of certain squad members, the criminal courts have dealt too leniently or to dilatorily)[84], the systematic torture of political prisoners, and the refusal of certain authorities to honor habeas corpus orders are all logical outgrowths of the public service type *jeito*. Once the principle that officials and private citizens may reinterpret or ignore laws they deem overly restrictive or unwise is condoned, its limitation is extremely difficult. Unjust, discriminatory law enforcement and the breakdown of legitimacy may well be the result.

Finally, by acting as a safety valve, the *jeito* tends to prevent the building up of sufficient pressure for sorely needed legal and administrative reform. Legal structures which have long since broken down are enabled to continue functioning with the patchwork of the *jeito*. All too frequently the patch works poorly, producing serious misallocations of resources.

Consider the case of regulation of the electric power industry. Legislation adopted in 1934 limited the return on a power company's investment to 10 percent of its historic or original cost, less depreciation.[85] However, the government either could not or would not determine these rate bases, despite Decree-Law 3,128 of March 19, 1941, which required the government to inventory the assets of the electric companies.[86]

Though it may have been appropriate for a stable economy, this regulatory scheme was most inappropriate for Brazil, where inflation has been chronically severe. But since the chief power companies were foreign owned, there was widespread nationalistic opposition to changing the law in order to benefit the power companies.[87] Brazil's impressively rapid economic growth in the post World War II decades re-

84. Approximately 250 persons have been killed in Rio and Saõ Paulo alone in the past two years by the *Esquadrões da Morte*. Just as disturbing is the popular support for their activities. A recent survey found that 60 percent of those interviewed in São Paulo and 37 percent of those in Rio approved of the *Esquadrões*. *Veja*, July 29, 1970, p. 24.

85. The Water Code, Decree No. 24.643 of July 10, 1934, art. 180, cf. Decree-Law No. 3.128 of Mar. 19, 1941, articles 2 and 9.

86. Parecer do Ministro Orosimbo Nonato, in *A Verdade Sôbre as Concessões de Eletricidade no Brasil* 15, 16 (1962).

87. J. Tendler, *Electric Power in Brazil: Enterpreneurship in the Public Sector* 55-59 (1968). There was also widespread political opposition to recognizing in any law the general principle of inflation adjustments on the theory that this would be tantamount to a public concession of the government's inability to control inflation. Id. at 57.

quired large increases in electric power, and the power companies were understandably reluctant to increase their investments without being assured an adequate return. Characteristically, the impasse was resolved by retaining the basic regulatory statute but bending it to expediency via special temporary decrees and the *jeito*. Instead of modifying the basic rate structure, the government permitted the power companies to increase their total revenues through "additionals" or surcharges, preferential exchange subsidies, generous financing, toleration of dubious accounting procedures, and forcing consumers to finance connections to the net. The power companies were also permitted to increase their revenues by overextending their distribution systems. In addition, the government itself assumed major responsibility for generating electric power, leaving the private companies with the distributing phase of the operations.[88]

In this case the *jeito* enabled Brazil to muddle through some twenty years of serious inflation without modifying a totally obsolete regulatory structure. But the accommodation of the *jeito* was far from ideal. The uncertainty and instability of the extralegal negotiations and special arrangements by which the power companies were regulated discouraged much-needed investment and long range planning for the power industry. Existing equipment was seriously overloaded and allowed to run down, producing chronic blackouts. This in turn impeded industrial production and commerce, as did the substantial delays in connecting new service applicants. In addition, factories and businesses had to incur the additional expenses of installing their own generating equipment for the frequent emergencies and to bear the costs of interpreted service.

B. *Benefits of the Jeito*

When the formal legal structure contains serious impediments to development, the *jeito* may play a positive role in the development process by permitting avoidance of legal and administrative hangups at relatively little cost. When stymied by restrictive legislation, the innovator is able to resort to the *jeito* to introduce new approaches without governmental interference, just as the sufficiently capitalized enterpreneur is able to utilize the *jeito* quickly to legalize a new venture.

When the government short-sightedly adopts policies inimical to development, the *jeito* can be an important factor in minimizing the damage. For example, both Chile and Brazil tried to fight inflation by freezing food prices. Chilean bureaucrats struggled valiantly to enforce these price controls, thereby stagnating the food supply and

88. Id. at 44-79.

increasing inflationary pressures. On the other hand, Brazilian bureaucrats characteristically permitted the *jeito* to operate. Consequently, agricultural prices were allowed to rise enough to stimulate an increase in the production of foodstuffs, helping relieve some of the inflationary pressure.[89] Of course, to the extent a governmental policy is designed to promote development, the *jeito*, particularly the corrupt type, may have precisely the opposite effect. This was the case with Brazilian exchange controls, which were subverted by a number of devices such as underinvoicing exports or overinvoicing imports.[90] But the net effect of the *jeito* in practice is frequently to push the government into assuming a more *laissez faire* position than it is ideologically disposed to assume. Like many developing nations, Brazil has much comprehensive regulatory legislation designed to curb economic abuses and cater to nationalistic sentiment, *i.e.* antitrust and remittance of profits laws. If rigorously enforced, such legislation might well nip economic growth in the bud. Permitting their circumvention, as the Brazilians have done, enables the government to cater to popular pressures for restraining certain kinds of economic activity that is quite likely conducive to economic growth without actually preventing such activity.

In a world in which laws and regulations are constantly changing, the *jeito* serves as an important source of stability and predictability. Industrial and commercial activity is much less precarious when businessmen and industrialists have a sense that no matter what changes tomorrow may bring in the law, the *jeito*, be it corrupt or public serving, will insure business as usual.

It can be argued that the corrupt type *jeito* will in the long run promote economic efficiency, since the most efficient firms will be able to offer the largest bribes and eliminate their more inefficient competitors.[91] But to the extent that the *jeito* functions equally well on kinship or friendship ties, inefficient firms will still be able to compete.

One can also argue that the *jeito*, particularly in its speed money form, operates as a direct tax on those best able to pay, and is thus one of the few progressive features in Brazil's regressive tax system. There is little leakage in the system since the sums paid go directly to poorly paid public servants as salary supplements. But this analysis ignores the very real economic burden placed on the poor who need the governmental service but cannot pay the tax. The poor ultimately

89. See Leff, "Economic Development Through Bureaucratic Corruption," 8 *Amer. Behavioral Scientist*, No. 3, pp. 11-12 (Nov. 1964).

90. Kafka, "The Brazilian Exchange Auction System," 38 *Review of Economics & Statistics* 308, 315 (1956).

91. Leff, supra note 89 at 11.

pay an even heavier tax in the form of man-hours lost from work and the time spent without the governmental document or license.

The chief benefit of an institution like the *jeito* to the development process is that it permits a society to buy time to work out serious institutional tensions without violently rupturing the social fabric. Major overhauls in a nation's legal and administrative structure produce severe strains and stresses. Frequently, there is little political consensus about whether and how basic institutions should be modernized. The *jeito* may be considered a way of temporizing to avert, or at least postpone, civil strife. By preserving the façade of legitimacy in the face of rapid social and economic change, the *jeito* has been invaluable in enabling the Brazilian system to operate without violent conflict.

Conclusion

It is difficult to separate the costs of the *jeito* from the costs of having an obsolete or unsuitable legal system, for the two plainly overlap. If the choice were between continuing to operate with an obsolete or unsuitable legal structure and operating with the *jeito*, there is little doubt that in the great majority of cases the latter will produce a net benefit, especially where employed in a public service sense. At least the *jeito* enables a society to continue to function despite the inappropriateness of its formal legal system. But the choice is more apparent than real. Brazil could not have tolerated the closing down of its power companies because of inadequate returns. If the *jeito* had not been employed, the country would have had to modify its regulatory legislation or nationalize the foreign power companies. Either of these avenues entailed serious political and economic costs, which must be subtracted from the costs of resorting to the *jeito*.

Although the *jeito* results in a number of important developmental benefits, they are primarily short run benefits. In the long run the *jeito*, and the style of operations which it permits to continue, constitute serious obstacles to development. Development requires a high degree of social integration and community cooperation, as well as departure from traditional, personalistic, authoritarian patterns of behavior. It also requires greater productivity and fairer redistribution of income. The formal legal system can be one of the modern state's most effective instruments for promotion of social interdependence and more equitable distribution of wealth. But the existence of an institution such as the *jeito* enables a society to continue individualistic, traditional patterns of behavior despite the state's attempt to substitute more progressive, achivement-oriented patterns of behavior via the formal legal structure.

Ultimately, development should imply far more than increases in per capita income, investment, or productivity. Development ought also imply the existence of an institutional structure which will permit meaningful equality before the law. Conditions precedent to such equality are a formal legal structure reasonably attuned to the times and culture, a high degree of obedience to the rule of law, and impersonal, efficient administration of the laws. There should be comparatively little room for the operation of an institution like the *jeito* in a modern, developed society. But in a society undergoing rapid transitions on the road to development, there would appear to be room aplenty.

Name Index

Abel, R.L. 473
Abreu, Capistrano de 589
Accursius 47, 48
Acton, Lord 92
Aeschylus 426
Aethelbert, King 71
Aethelred, King 71, 72
Aethelstan, King 71
Agricola, Rudolf 49
Akiba, Rabbi 364, 365
Alciato, Andrea 51
Alfenus Varus 358
Apel, Johann 50
Aristotle 27, 39, 40, 48, 50, 95, 104–6, 107, 108, 116, 120, 123, 126, 155, 343, 353
Arnaud, A.-J. 60
Ash Shafi'i 305, 306, 308, 310
Ashurst 382
Atkin, Lord 382, 390
Aubry, Dean 368
Augustus, Emperor 74
Austin, John 83, 341, 350–1, 371
Ayrault, Pierre 55
Azo 28

Babco 146
Bacon, Lord 123
Balbus, I.D. 467, 468, 469
Baldus 47–8, 53
Ballot-Beaupré 369
Baron, Eguinaire 51, 52, 58
Barr, Mr and Mrs 384–5
Barros, Adhemar de 582
Barrot, Odilon 381
Bartolus 48, 53
Baxi, U. 465, 470, 471, 472, 473, 476, 478
Bayley 479
Becket, Thomas 27
Bellapertica, Petrus de 47
Beltrao, Hélio 585, 589
Benedict 279
Bentham, Jeremy 3, 101, 102, 123, 198, 341, 350, 351, 371
Berman 538, 544
Beseler, Gerhard von 107, 358
Beteille, A. 475, 476
Bicchieri, Guala 27
Black 85
Blackburn 382, 390
Blackstone 370
Bodin, Jean 54, 55, 58, 60, 75
Bohannan, Paul 8, 17, 190–1, 193–4, 196, 197, 198
Bosman, W. 210, 212
Bourjon 77
Boutaric, François de 60
Bracton 27, 28, 30–2, 75, 84, 86, 124
Brandeis 372
Breitel, Charles D. 373
Breshnev 544
Brunner 122
Brunschvig 422, 426
Buchanan 146, 148
Buckland 102, 131
Buddha 230–1, 233–4, 235, 236–7, 238, 239, 242
Bulgarus 117, 118, 119, 120
Bülow, Oscar von 153
Burke, Edmund 84
Burton, Richard 209, 214

Cairns 106
Caligula 206
Campbell 563, 571
Camus, Albert 206
Canute, King 71, 72
Capito, Ateius 342
Cardozo, Justice 85, 183, 335, 351, 405
Celsus 120, 131, 357
Cetschwayo 174
Ch'i, Marquis of 228
Chafee, L., Jr 370, 371
Charlemagne 76
Charles I (England) 78
Cheke, Marcus 582
Chrystostom, Dio 57
Cicero 40, 42, 108, 353, 354, 360, 454, 456
Claudius Cantiuncula 49
Cohn, Bernard S. 473, 474, 475, 476, 477, 478
Coing 106
Coke, Sir Edward 28, 32, 79, 86, 157
Collinet 15
Columela 108

Condillac, Abbé de 167
Confucius 228, 244, 246, 249, 272
Connan, François 51, 52, 53
Conquest, Robert 94
Conring, Hermann 61
Constantine 113, 114, 116, 120, 127, 460
Cooper, Lord 158
Coras, Jean 50
Cross, Sir Rupert 405
Cujas, Jacques 55, 59, 60, 63

Daguesseau, Henri 60
Dahrendorf 467
Dalzel 214, 221
Dantas, Santiago 591
Danzing 470
Daries, Joachim 60
David, René 77, 297
Davis, Lord Edmund 146, 148, 149, 154
Dawe 472
Dawson, John P. 102, 163, 165, 334
Dehen, Madame 387
Democritus 44
Denning, Lord 145–51, 154, 155, 157, 159, 167, 382, 384, 386
Descartes 56, 60, 61
Devos 279
Dewey, John 444
Diamond 15
Diocletian 119
Diplock, Lord 382
Doi 279
Domat, Jean 58, 59, 63
Dominguez 432
Doneau, Hugues 51, 53, 54, 60, 64, 66
Draco 104
Dumoulin, Charles 60
Durkheim 467

Eadric 70, 71
Eckhoff, Torstein 378, 388
Edgar, King 71, 72
Edward I 28, 29
Edward II 28, 77
Edward, King (c.900) 71
Edward the Confessor 72
Ehem, Christopher 50
Ehlermann, Dr C.D. 145, 157
Ehrlich, Eugen 226, 227, 228, 470
Eichhorn, Johann 67
Einstein 24–5
Eliezer, Rabbi 365
Engels, Friedrich 94, 193, 204, 218, 219, 547
Ensor 570
Epstein 472
Escarra 226, 243
Esdras 364
Esser 356
Euclid 56
Evans-Pritchard 185

Farabi 412
Flavius Josephus 364
Fleming, Sir Alexander 95
France, Anatole 333
Franciscus Accursii 27
Frank, Judge 85, 570
Frankfurter, Justice 419, 420
Franklin, Henry 78
Freed, R.S. 477
Freisler 570
Freud 219
Frey, Johann 50
Freyre, Gilberto 579, 584
Froissart 75

Gaius 39, 40, 41–5, 46–9, 51, 52, 56, 57, 60, 64, 65, 66, 68, 74, 87, 130
Galanter, M. 467, 472, 479
Galenza 92
Galileo 56, 61
Gallo 76
Gammaro, Pietro 50
Gandhi 470
Gascar, Pierre 94
Gény, François 155, 156
Germain, St 123
Gershom, Rabbi 367
Gerson 123
Gibbon, Edward 59–60, 61, 63, 67
Gierke, Otto 56, 135
Gilmore, Grant 335, 336
Glanvill 75, 123
Glanville 84
Gluckman, Max 8–9, 208
Gnaeus Flavius 87
Goddard, Lord 506–7
Godefroy, Jacques 61
Gomes, Orlando 578
Goodhart 408, 409
Gothofredus 459
Gough, K. 477
Goulart 592
Gravina, Giovanni 61
Gray, John Chipman 371–2
Gray, Mr and Mrs James 384–5
Grégoire, Pierre 54, 55
Griffiths, Sir Samuel 506

Grimm 73
Grotius, Hugo 57, 58, 59, 60, 61, 62, 63, 132, 152
Guarnerius 116
Gürtner 570
Güterbock 28

Halifax 79
Hall 488, 492, 512
Halsbury, Lord 181
Hamburger 105
Han Fei-tze 244
Hanbal, Ahman ibn 305, 306
Hanbury 126
Hanifa, Abu 305, 306
Hart, H.L.A. 35, 73, 360, 421, 444
Hattori, Shiro 294
Hayek, Friedrich 168
Hazard 544
Heck, Philip 156
Hedemann, Justus 164
Heffernan, Detective Sergeant John 193
Hegel 45, 83, 94
Heidegger, Martin 169
Heineccius, Johann Gottleib 59, 61, 63
Henderson, D.F. 479
Henry I 72
Henry VIII 29
Henry of Susa 27
Hilary, Judge 77
Hillel 365, 366
Hitler 164, 168, 197, 459
Hlothhere 70, 71
Hobbes, Thomas 59, 60, 219
Hoebel, A.E. 5
Höhn 563
Hölderlin 169
Holdsworth 124, 125
Holfeld, Wesley Newcomb 83
Holmes, Oliver Wendell 9, 85, 160, 335, 337, 351, 372, 403, 409, 456
Homer 103, 348
Horak 353, 354, 358, 359
Hotman, François 60
Hsiao Ho, Prime Minister 227
Hsien-feng, Emperor 230
Hsüang, Duke of 228
Huber, Eugen 161
Hugo, Gustav 63, 64, 65
Hui-yuän 238, 240
Hume, David 83
Hurst 467

Ibn Taymiyya 416–17
Ine 70, 71
Ioffe 96
Irnerius 115
Iseman 443
Isidore, St 74
Iulianus 118

James I 29
James, William 95
Jerome, Saint 39
Jesus Christ 231, 233
Jhering, Rudolph von 65, 67, 153, 155, 203, 221, 337
John, King 79
Jones 104
Jones, J.W. 15
Joshua, Rabbi 365
Julian 350, 357, 362, 459
Justinian 27, 39, 40, 42, 45–7, 49, 50, 52, 53, 54, 59, 74, 87, 89, 113, 114, 115, 117, 127, 130, 135, 338, 342, 459
Juynboll 442

Kant 63, 108
Karev 535
Kawashima 294
Kelsen, Hans 83
Kenny 507
Khruschchev 537, 544, 546
Kidder, Robert 472, 478
Keobler, Gerhard 72
Koebler, Gerhard 72
Koestler, Arthur 94
Komsky 92
Köschaker, Paul 85
Kosygin 544
Kowlaski, Stanley 375
Krylenko 537, 540, 541

Labeo 343–51
Lactantius 54
Lagus, Conrad 51, 61
Lambert, Jacques 597
Lanfranc 27
Lang, Master 241
Lange 116, 117, 119, 120
Lasswell 36, 37
Lawson 4, 21, 375–6
Le Douaren, François 51, 52–3, 58, 59, 60, 61, 64
Leibnitz, Gottfried Wilhelm 56, 57, 61, 64
Lenhoff, Arthur 151, 153, 155, 156, 162
Lenin 92, 94, 516–24, 536, 540, 544
Lévi-Strauss 222

Levy, Ernst 131, 455
Li Hung-chang 229
Lima, Hermes 591
Linant de Bellefonds 422
Lister, Lord 499
Littleton, Sir Thomas 13, 32
Livy 109
Llewellyn, Karl 166, 369, 467, 471
Locke, John 85, 95
Loisel, Antoine 40, 54, 60, 88
Louis the Pious (France) 75
Lowie, Robert H. 5
Lowy, M.J. 470

Macdonald 423
Machiavelli 55, 216
MacKinnon 381
Mahalihali 178
Mahalihali the Second 178–9
Maine, Sir Henry 28, 83, 198, 199, 201, 202–3, 213, 344
Mair 202
Maitland 9, 27, 28, 30, 122, 143, 210
Malik 305, 306, 308
Malinowski 16
Maluba 485
Mandelbaum 474
Mansfield, Lord 80
Mao 244
Marcianus 358
Marcus Aurelius 356
Margenau 35
Markby, Sir William 209
Marshall 85
Martin 386
Martinus 117, 118, 119, 120
Maruyama 279
Marx, Karl 45, 63, 64, 67, 68, 83, 94, 96, 216–17, 218, 467, 547
Matias 485
Maya 477
Mayda, Jaro 155, 161, 162
McDougal 36, 37
Meek 502
Megarry 386
Meijers 116, 117, 118, 120
Melinkoff, David 70
Mencius 229
Milliot 426
Modestinus 85, 358
Mohammed 303, 304, 307, 318
Mommsen, Theodor 65
Montague 77
Montaigne 208, 217, 219
Montesquieu 58, 59, 60, 61, 63, 67, 160, 166, 367, 379
Moore, Sally Falk 478
Morris, Charles 37
Moses 363, 364, 367
Mourlon 368
Mpande, King 174
Muratori, Ludovico 61
Mwavi 491
Myrdal, Gunnar 576, 602

Nadel 204, 220
Nakamura 279, 280
Napoleon 130, 135
Narayan, Jayprakash 470
Neratius Priscus 118
Niebuhr, Barthold Georg 39, 61, 67
Nietszche 168
Nkrumah, President 507
Noacha 491
Noda 276, 282, 290, 297
Norris 212
Northrop, F.S.C. 6, 10, 22, 23, 25, 34, 35, 286

Oldendorp, Johann 50, 51, 59
Orwell, George 94

Papinian 85, 118
Parikh, Shri H. 477
Pascal, Blaise 58, 451
Pasquier, Étienne Pasquier 54
Passrinho, Jarbas 585
Paulus 113, 118, 119, 121
Pepin 75
Perham, Margery 214
Peristiany, J.G. 184–5, 195, 207, 214
Perizonius 61
Petri, Olaus 73
Planiol, Marcel 138
Plato 27, 83, 94, 104, 105, 197, 216, 217, 218, 219
Plucknett 124–5
Pollock, Sir Frederick 27, 30, 372
Pomponius 39, 42, 119, 342, 362
Popper, Karl 95
Portalis 155, 158, 376
Pospisil, L. 5, 471
Pothier, Robert 58, 60, 64
Pound, Roscoe 201, 373
Powell, Lewis F. 539
Pringsheim 21, 106, 110, 111
Proculus 342, 357, 362
Proust, Marcel 97

Pufendorf, Samuel von 60, 152

Quénum, N. 211–12, 221
Quintilian 54

Radbruch 73
Radin, Paul 194, 213
Raffles 461
Ramos, Guerreiro 592
Ramus, Petrus 49, 50, 54, 56
Ranke, Leopold von 67
Rattray 202, 204, 208, 210, 213, 214
Redfield, Robert 196
Renan, Ernest 87
Renner, Karl 94
Reusner, Nicolas 51
Rheinstein, Max 442
Riccobono, Salvatore 107
Richards, A.I. 202
Richardus Anglicus 27
Robespierre 94
Rodrigues, José Honório 582
Rogerius 117
Romano, Damiano 60
Rosate, Alberigo de 48
Rosen 435
Rousseau, Jacques 94, 97, 219, 222, 367
Rudolph, L.H. 472, 475
Rudolph, S.H. 472, 475
Russell 6, 34

Sabinus 342, 344, 346–51
Sachs 380
Sagnac 168
Salmond, Sir John 70, 208
Samuel, Rabbi 365
Sandrock 386
Sapir, Edward 6
Sartre, Jean-Paul 94
Savigny, Friedrich Karl von 21, 39, 45, 49, 53, 60, 61, 64–8, 115, 152
Sawer 8
Scaevola, Cervidius 358, 362
Scaevola, Quintus Mucius 23, 42, 54, 110
Schacht 422, 434, 442, 443
Schiller 108, 484
Schultz, Fritz 21, 42, 358, 359
Schulz 110, 112
Seagle, William 9, 15, 17, 196, 207, 211
Seius 27
Selden, John 61, 101
Severus 356
Shaka 174, 175
Shargorodskii 96
Shearman 503
Sherman, Charles Phineas 28, 29, 333
Shotoku, Prince 289, 291
Shu Sun Tung 227
Simonds, Lord 150
Simpson 20
Skertchly 212
Skinner, Lord Chief Baron 80
Socrates 405
Solon 104
Somló, B. 591
Sophocles 193
Speiser-Sarasin, Paul 107
Spelman, Henry 61
Srinivas 474
St Germain, Christopher 80, 84
Stalin 533, 544
Stein, Peter 333–5, 336, 356, 361
Stintzing, R. 53
Stone, Julius 83, 201, 409, 468, 470
Stonore, Judge 77
Story 85, 123
Stroux, Johannes 107, 108, 110
Sykes, M.L. 333
Syng Man Rhee, President 250
Szczesniak, Boleslaw 529

Taubenschlag 457
Terence 108
Terrasson, Antoine 60–1
Theobald, Archbishop 27
Thibaut, A.F.L. 65, 67
Thoël 152
Thomas 458
Thomasius, Christian 60
Thorne 151
Titius 27, 346
Toulouse, Grégoire de 60
Trebatius Testa, C. 354
Tribonian 45
Trubek, D. 467, 469
Tulane, Paul 134
Turner 419
Tyan 426, 442
Tylor, E.B. 216, 217, 218
Tyrawly, Lord 581

Uchendu, Victor 215
Ulpian 39, 46, 61, 63, 116, 118, 358, 362
Unger, Roberto 467, 468, 469

Vacarius 27, 28
van den Brink 455
Van Vollenhoven 453

Vargus 593
Veidt 386
Vergil 67
Vico, Giambattista 57, 61, 62, 63, 67
Viehweg 353, 354
Vigelius, Nicolaus 50
Vinogradoff, Sir Paul 84, 107, 123, 199, 218
von Gierke, Otto 470
von Lubtow 353
von Mehren 296
Vyshinski 92, 96, 535, 541, 542

Wakin 422
Wamlunda 491
Warren 85
Weber, Max 67, 83, 217, 419, 442, 467, 468–9, 470
Wetsermarck 434
Whitehead 6
Whitelock 72
Wieacker 109, 458
Wihtred 71
Wilberforce, Lord 146, 148
Willems, Emilio 582
Willes 382
William of Drogheda 27
William the Conqueror 27, 72
Williams, Glanville 495
Wittgenstein 6
Wolf, Erik 60, 103
Wolff, Hans Julius 21, 462
Wolsey 125
Wu, Emperor 242
Wulfstan 72

Ziadeh 435

www.ingramcontent.com/pod-product-compliance
Lightning Source LLC
LaVergne TN
LVHW102107300926
849161LV00014B/3070